The Rural Sociology of
the Advanced Societies

The Rural Sociology of the Advanced Societies:

CRITICAL PERSPECTIVES

edited by FREDERICK H. BUTTEL
and HOWARD NEWBY

ALLANHELD, OSMUN   Montclair
CROOM HELM   London

Published in the United States of America in 1980
by Allanheld, Osmun & Co. Publishers, Inc.
19 Brunswick Road, Montclair, N.J. 07042

Published in Great Britain in 1980 by
Croom Helm Ltd., 2-10 St. John's Road
London SW 11
ISBN 0-7099-0408-8

Library of Congress Cataloging in Publication Data

The Rural sociology of the advanced societies.

    Includes index.
    1. Sociology, Rural--Addresses, essays, lectures.
2. Agriculture--Economic aspects--Addresses, essays,
lectures. 3. Agriculture and state--Addresses, essays,
lectures. I. Buttel, Frederick H. II. Newby, Howard.
HT421.R85   301.35   79-5177
ISBN 0-916672-30-1
ISBN 0-916672-34-4 pbk.

Grateful acknowledgment is made to the following for
permission to reprint previously published material:

Routledge & Keegan Paul: "A Summary of Selected Parts of
    Kautsky's The Agrarian Question," by Jarius Banaji,
    Economy and Society, Vol 5., No. 1 (February 1976),
    pp. 2-49. Copyright   1976 by Routledge & Keegan Paul.

British Sociological Association: "The Highlands of
    Scotland as an Underdeveloped Region," by Ian Carter,
    in Emanuel de Kadt and Gavin Williams, eds., Sociology
    and Development (London: Tavistock, 1974), pp. 279-311.
    Copyright   1974 by the British Sociological Association.

Printed in the United States of America

Contents

Preface

This volume was conceived in the course of correspondence between the two co-editors during 1977 and 1978. We discovered that we shared two important assumptions that underlie this reader. Firstly, we felt that prevailing theoretical paradigms and methodological postures in rural sociology in North America and Western Europe were limited in terms of both understanding the structural changes occurring in our respective societies and providing practical or applied leverage on how rural social problems can be solved. Secondly, however, we rejected a supposition--currently a fashionable one in many quarters--that rural sociology will continue to be a moribund subdiscipline with little chance for scholarly redirection. We offer the present volume as evidence that we are witnessing a modest, but still substantial, nurturing of alternative theoretical perspectives in rural sociology.

As we point out in our introductory essay to this volume, rural sociology has had more than its share of agonized introspection about the theoretical and methodological adequacy and practical relevance of the subdiscipline. Since our own arguments about these issues are laid out in our introductory essay below, we will not repeat them here. However, there is one observation we would like to make about contemporary rural sociology that is not fully fleshed out in our essay but which is quite central to the design of this reader. In our view, one of the problems plaguing rural sociology is its parochialism, deriving in large part in the U.S. from the tendency for most rural sociologists to be located at land grant universities and state agricultural experiment stations. The fact that each land grant university and state agricultural experiment station receives a substantial share of its funding from its state legislature presents a strong "localizing" or "parochializing" influence on the rural sociologist because of the land grant university's strong identification with its own state and the perceived need to place highest priority on problems specific to that state. The structure of the land grant college system thus tends to steer rural sociologists toward studies

conducted principally within their own state. This localizing tendency
serves to mitigate against societal analysis, and virtually precludes
comparative research.

This volume seeks to be comparative in two separate, although related,
ways. Firstly, we have sought out contributions from authors from a number
of countries in North America and Western Europe. The authors represented
below are from the U.S., Canada, England, Scotland, and Italy. In addition,
another contributor was born and educated in France and brings a number of
insights from that nation to his work. Secondly, several articles are
explicitly comparative in focus. A further purpose of this volume in
addition to exploring the prospects for redirection of rural sociology thus
has been to stimulate more attention to the analytical leverage that compara
tive methods can bring to rural sociology.

In keeping with our intention of introducing a comparative dimension
to rural sociology, we have included excerpts of the seminal work of Karl
Kautsky on the development of agriculture that have been translated by
Jarius Banaji and published in the English journal Economy and Society.
However, a more basic rationale for including Kautsky's work in this book
is to make his writing more broadly accessible to English-speaking rural
sociologists, particularly those from North America. Kautsky's The Agrarian
Question certainly remains one of the most bold and provocative statements
of a general theory of agricultural development under capitalism, but unfortunately there has yet to appear a complete English translation of Kautsky's
book. Banaji's translation of the excerpts that follow, however, largely fi
that void.

We were assisted by a number of individuals and organizations in the
preparation of this book. Buttel and Newby received travel fellowships to
attend the X World Congress for Rural Sociology in Cordoba, Spain, during
April 1979, from, respectively, the College of Agriculture and Life Sciences
of Cornell University and the Fuller Bequest to the University of Essex.
The Cordoba meeting proved to be quite valuable in allowing us to contact
potential contributors. We are extremely grateful to Professor Douglas
Ashford, Director of the Western Societies Program of the Cornell University
Center for International Studies, for the Program's financial support of
the translation of the paper by Mottura and Pugliese. Eleanor Bertacchi
performed this translation with both skill and speed.

The bulk of the typing for the book was done by Beverly Hastings and
Mark Spiro. Brenda Creeley and Linda George, our secretaries at the western
and eastern shores of the Atlantic, respectively, were also of great assistance. Michael R. Hattery, doctoral candidate in rural sociology at Cornell,
did yeoman work in proofreading the manuscripts. We also wish to thank the
British Sociological Association and Routledge & Keegan Paul for permission
to reprint papers in this book. Finally, Matthew Held of Allanheld, Osmun
& Co. was a cooperative and patient publisher.

In addition to these mutual debts, Howard Newby wishes to call attention to the helpful discussions he has had with a number of North American rural sociologists. In particular, a clearer need for this book emerged at the inaugural meeting of the Sociology of Agriculture Research Group of the Rural Sociological Society at Davis, California, August 1978. Visits, brief or extended, to the departments of rural sociology at the University of Wisconsin-Madison, Cornell University, and Pennsylvania State University have also been influential in shaping Newby's ideas concerning fruitful directions for rural sociological research in the coming decades.

Frederick H. Buttel
Ithaca, New York

Howard Newby
Colchester, Essex

INTRODUCTION

1. Toward a Critical Rural Sociology

HOWARD NEWBY and FREDERICK H. BUTTEL

INTRODUCTION

During the 1970s, rural sociology has given every appearance of having lost its way. New problems, both social and sociological, have emerged and have left rural sociologists with the uneasy feeling that they are ill-equipped to cope with them. The result has been a profound lack of self-confidence, particularly in the United States where rural sociology first emerged as a sub-discipline and where it remains most securely institutionalized. Thus in his presidential address to the Rural Sociological Society in 1972, James Copp declared that:

> Many of us think that we know what rural sociology is, but I am not sure that we do... In my opinion we know less about contemporary rural sociology in 1972 than we knew about the contemporary rural sociology in the 1940s... If most of the research which rural sociologists were doing in 1969 and 1970 were to have somehow disappeared the world would have noticed very little loss... I came to the conclusion that rural sociologists really were not the masters of the phenomena of rural society. We toyed with it, but I did not perceive a great depth of understanding. The world was changing faster than the discipline was growing in its knowledge of the phenomena occurring in rural areas (1972: 515, 516, 521).

Copp was not, however, alone in his verdict. Subsequent addresses by Warner (1974) and Lowry (1977) returned to this theme. Lowry, for example, identified problems of subject matter, theoretical relevance, public accountability, and even research competence.

1

It was as though, in the words of an earlier European observer, "the basic insufficiency of the sociological concepts with which rural phenomena have been apprehended has finally caught up with their users" (Galjart, 1971: 254). These do indeed seem to be "hard times" for rural sociology (Hightower, 1973; Nolan and Galliher, 1973).

Agonized introspection is not something new in rural sociology-- indeed reflexive "state of the art" papers have proved to be a thriving sociological pastime in the discipline (see Newby, 1980). The purpose of this book is not, therefore, to add to the fasionable dissection of the "crisis" in American rural sociology. While we shall be mindful and respectful of the history of rural sociology's current malaise, our intention is to offer a more positive, useful, and essentially forward-looking collection of papers which, we hope, will stimulate and provoke the reader rather than offering a comprehensive review of the field or an anodyne summary of existing findings. For this reason we have inserted the word "critical" into our title. It is our strongly-held view that rural sociologists need to develop a more independent and skeptical attitude towards the rural phenomena which enter into their purview than has been apparent in the recent past. All too often the rural sociologist has been lulled into the condition which anthropologists refer to as "capture"--adopting a wholly uncritical stance towards the structure and institutions of rural society and thus rarely going "beyond the cliched and subjective experiences of the people he is studying" (Olson, 1965: 350).

We have therefore selected the contributions to this volume with this prescription in mind. Many of the essays which follow offer an historically informed critique of the status quo--both in rural sociology and in rural society. We have, however, attempted to be reasonably catholic in our choice: the analyses are by no means coincidental nor even compatible. Moreover we have edited (we hope our contributors will agree) with a light hand. Given the preliminary nature of much of the work that is presented here we have looked for stimulating questions rather than glib answers. Our intention has been to redirect the focus of inquiry in rural sociology towards hitherto under-examined issues and to stimulate discussion, analysis, and even speculation in these areas, in the hope that this will set much-needed research in motion. We have concentrated, as will be apparent, on the rural sociology of advanced capitalist societies. This represents to a considerable degree a purely expedient and arbitrary decision not to become deeply enmeshed in the sociology of development (though the reader will find frequent references to this literature in many of the papers which follow). However, it is also a recognition of the need to develop a more comparative rural sociology of advanced capitalism--and, indeed, all advanced industrial societies--whereas hitherto this has been virtually absent. For this reason we have invited contributions from Western Europe as well as North America, although the emphasis remains on the latter. In

addition we have not been concerned exclusively with the work of
sociologists, for we have been more than happy to poach contributions
from other relevant disciplines which we consider relevant to the
analysis of sociological problems in rural society. We can all gain
from a multi-disciplinary approach.

Problems and Prospects in Rural Sociology

In this Introduction we wish merely to indicate in a general
way our views on the causes of rural sociology's current problems,
thereby setting the scene for the readings which follow. This should
also help to locate our concerns and our anxieties in some sort of
historical and conceptual context. In our view the causes of the
"sleeping crisis" (Lowry, 1977) in rural sociology are more profound
than is sometimes credited, involving not only a lack of perception
of the subject-matter (both theoretical and empirical) of rural
sociology, but also in its institutionalization. The lack of confidence which has afflicted rural sociology over the last decade therefore runs to quite basic issues of organization and intellectual
endeavor. In this respect it does indeed resemble a Kuhnian "crisis,"
something which is manifested in the persistence of a very basic
problem indeed: the definition of what constitutes rural sociology
in the first place.

A common means of sidestepping this problem is to define "rural
sociology" in terms of what self-proclaimed "rural sociologists" do.
Although Copp rightly terms this definition "facile" (1972: 515), it
does point to one very important aspect of rural sociology: its
institutional structure. Rural sociology in this arbitrary--and in
many ways mischievous--sense tends to be separated from two other
subject areas which are equally rural and equally sociological--the
sociology of development and peasant studies. In terms of textbooks,
journals, research activity, and even teaching, rural sociology has
been, for the most part, institutionally divided from them, an un-
fortunate separation which has tended to deny rural sociology both a
historical perspective and a holistic approach from which it would
otherwise benefit. This institutionalization of rural sociology also
lends itself to a second kind of definition, for rural sociology has
also been defined by a particular style of research. The label which
is usually applied to this research style is "scientific," which turns
out on close inspection to mean: positivist, inductive, quantitative
and "applied." These characteristics legitimate and certify "scientific" research in rural sociology no less than its subject matter.
Hence rural sociology is only recognized as such if it corresponds
to the correct research style: the style in itself defines the substance.

As we shall see, there has been a constant elision of style and substance in rural sociology, a merging of theory, methods, and findings that at times makes it difficult to perceive which is which. Attempts have been made to solve substantive problems by conceptual re-definition and to solve theoretical problems by methodological fine-tuning. Consequently some of the more fundamental conceptual problems have remained. For, as Copp has pointed out:

> There is no rural society and there is no rural
> economy. It is merely our analytic distinction,
> our rhetorical device. Unfortunately we tend to
> be the victims of our own terminological dupli-
> city. We tend to ignore the import of what hap-
> pens in the total economy and society as it affects
> the rural sector. We tend to think of the rural
> sector as a separate entity which can be developed
> while the non-rural sector is held constant. Our
> thinking is ensnared by our own words (1972: 519).

The history of rural sociology has been dogged by this problem. There has been an ultimate futile search for a sociological definition of "rural," a reluctance to recognize that the term "rural" is an empirical category rather than a sociological one, that it is merely a "geographical expression." As such it can be used as a convenient short-hand label, but in itself it has no sociological meaning (see Wakeley, 1967). Thus although the most common definition of rural sociology is "the scientific study of rural society," this merely begs the most crucial question--whether "rural sociology" can be sociologically defined. The result, as Kaufman (1963) has pointed out, has been superficiality and a lack of focus in the field.

If no sociological definition of "rural" is acceptable, then it is only what Wakeley calls an "empirical referent." Two consequences follow from this. First there can be no theory of rural society without a theory of society tout court. Although this has often been recognized by rural sociologists they have tended to pay only lip service to the fact that rural society can only be studied as part of the larger society. Instead rural sociology has been characterized by its atheoretical, even anti-theoretical, nature (a common observation) or has attempted to develop a specifically rural sociological theory inductively without reference to "general" sociological theories. In some respects, however, this theoretical reticence is understandable. Rural sociology has been very badly served by the classical writers in the history of sociological thought who, in their endeavor to create theories of urban-industrial society have all too often misunderstood or even ignored the nature of rural society. The rural has frequently been regarded as residual and therefore given very little attention in general sociological theory, a lack of interest from which rural sociology has undoubtedly suffered. Secondly, it is not only apparent that rural sociology cannot operate without an acceptable theory of society, but that it also requires a theory of the spatial allocation of the population (since "rural" is a spatial, geographical category) which is also sociologically relevant. In other words, rural sociology demands a theory which links the spatial with the social. Moreover, in order to be a sociological theory, the social must be given primacy. This requirement has only been infrequently perceived by rural sociologists who have, if anything, preferred to emphasize the spatial at the expense of the social (through such notions as the "rural-urban continuum").

At the present time, however, such a theory is conspicuous by its absence in rural sociology, although there are, perhaps, some interesting lessons to be learned from urban sociology which is afflicted by the same theoretical problem viewed from the obverse side (see Newby, 1980). Indeed traditionally, rural sociologists have been uninterested in macro-sociological theories which would explain the emergence of particular "rural" spatial and social forms. Hence the nature of rural sociology's current crisis: the decline of the rural-urban continuum has left the subject matter of rural sociology bereft of a theory while the continuing "eclipse" (Stein, 1964) of the rural world has threatened to deprive it of its subject matter, too. If the processes which are shaping contemporary rural society cannot be reduced to, or explained in terms of, the category "rural," where does this leave rural sociology? This is the unanswered, and even unacknowledged, question which has hung like a pall over rural sociology for the last decade or more. It accounts for the fact that, despite the "aversion to theory" (Sewell, 1950) which is prevalent in rural sociology, there has been no lack of theoretical reflection and anxious re-conceptualizing. Sewell (1965: fn 3) lists 21 reflexive papers in the 15 years between 1950 and 1965, Stokes and Miller (1975) found that in the subsequent decade more papers in Rural Sociology were actually concerned with the self-evaluation of the discipline than with policy and welfare issues. In the light of these figures it is possible to understand Bealer's comment that "the field might not be as bad off when it comes to 'theory' as some might think" (1975: 472). But this slightly misses the point. While rural sociologists individually have not been unaware of these issues, the outcome has been disappointing, to say the least. Rural sociology remains in a state of considerable theoretical disarray.

Theoretical Considerations

As we already observed, the classic nineteenth-century European writers in sociological theory devoted comparatively little attention to agriculture and rural life, concentrating their efforts instead upon explanations of the emerging urban-industrial sector. Their general approach comprised a brisk dismissal of the significance of rural society as archaic and backward, while economic and social innovation would emanate from the towns and from industry. Although rural life would in turn be transformed by these material and cultural innovations, it was cast in the role of the passive receiver of these processes to be subsequently molded and adapted by them. However, rural sociology in the United States departed in certain important respects from this model. It certainly did not share the idea that rural life was marginal or backward. On the contrary, much rural sociology was devoted to upholding the integrity of what were believed to be the distinctive qualities of rural life. In addition the diligently empiricist research style which characterized rural sociological research was a form of practice which impressed upon its practitioners the intractability of many rural social phenomena to easy generalization. It was Sorokin and Zimmerman who first sought to integrate the European tradition of theorizing with this detailed empirical observation in their textbook, Principles of Rural-Urban Sociology (1929), thereby inaugurating that which, until the mid-1960s, formed the major theoretical framework for rural sociological research: the rural-urban continuum.

In many respects the rural-urban continuum was a thinly-veiled expression of very common nineteenth-century perspectives on rural life in academic sociological theory. By this means a range of literacy and artistic conventions taken from the pastoral form became almost unproblematic assumptions about rural society, partly because they fitted in so well with the prevailing cultural perspective. Ruth Glass has, with some justification, referred to this as

> a lengthy, thorough course of indoctrination, to which all of us everywhere, have at some time or other been subjected... Especially in the Anglo-Saxon world we are still conditioned to think in terms of a sharp distinction between rural and urban places and 'ways of life.' And to many of us the adjective 'rural' has pleasant, reassuring connotations--beauty, order, simplicity, rest, grass-roots democracy, peacefulness, gemeinschaft. 'Urban' spells the opposite--ugliness, disorder, confusion, fatigue, compulsion, strife, gesellschaft (1966: 142).

Once the broad characteristics of rural social traits had been derived it merely remained for the myriad American locality studies from Galpin onwards to gauge the "health" of the individual communities concerned by matching them against such criteria. Very few, however, were used to examine the theoretical presuppositions themselves (cf. Olson, 1965).

Hence Tönnies's original typology of gemeinschaft and gesellschaft--originally used to represent forms of human association without any particular geographical referrent--became reified into a

rural-urban continuum in the hands of Sorokin and Zimmerman and later
the folk-urban continuum of Redfield (1947). Sorokin and Zimmerman's
aim was to establish the "differential characteristics of the urban
and rural community whose totality gives the type of each of these
social aggregates" (1929: 15). They did so by listing the differences
between rural and urban society on a number of dimensions--occupation,
environment, size, density, etc. Despite (or perhaps because of) their
highly sentimental vision of rural life (see, for example, pp. 466-
467 and p. 509) their text, together with its companion sourcebook
(Sorokin et al., 1930), fixed the theoretical framework of rural sociology for a generation. As late as 1957, Smith, in his trend report for
Current Sociology, commended Sorokin and Zimmerman's book as "the
finest synthesis of the field of rural sociology achieved to date"
(1957: 12). As McGee was to point out in retrospect:

> The main problem is that once the model of the rural-
> urban continuum, with its fallacious assumptions of
> the nature of rural and urban society, is created, it
> becomes rather like an institution--self-perpetuating
> (1971: 43).

At times it therefore seems to matter very little that the characteristics of rural society which were offered were a skillful blend of
normative prescription and wishful thinking rather than empirical description. However, this problem was compounded by the fact that the
rural-urban continuum was not simply intended to be a set of empirical
generalizations, but an explanation of the nature of social organization by reference to settlement patterns. Hence, as Duncan was later
to observe,

> ... there was an effort to develop a peculiar kind of
> sociology for rural people, under the illusion that
> they are a law unto themselves and cannot be accounted
> for as are other social groups. It took a long time
> to discover that rural sociology is nothing but socio-
> logy employing data about rural people and their social
> behavior (1954: 8).

This "discovery" was based upon detailed empirical investigation
at both the rural and urban "ends" of the continuum. From Lewis's re-
study of Tepoztlan (Lewis, 1949) down to Gans' clinical demolition of
Wirth (Gans, 1962), a series of community studies questioned the
validity of the rural-urban continuum as an explanatory scheme (see
Bell and Newby, 1971: Ch. 2). It remained for Pahl to finally dismiss the utility of the rural-urban continuum in his important
critical article which appeared in 1966. In effect, Pahl considered
the concepts of "rural" and "urban" to be neither explanatory variables
nor sociological categories. He adduced evidence from community
studies in both the United States and Europe to show that far from

there being an exclusive continuum from gemeinschaft to gesellschaft, relationships of both types could be found in the same localities. Therefore, he argued,

> Any attempt to tie patterns of social relationships
> to specific geographical milieux is a singularly
> fruitless exercise (Pahl, 1966: 293).

Instead Pahl believed that sociological analysis in rural areas should concentrate on the confrontation between the local and the national and that between the small-scale and the large-scale:

> It is the basic situation of conflict or stress that
> can be observed from the most highly urbanized metro-
> politan region to the most remote and isolated peasant
> village (Ibid., p. 286).

The implications of Pahl's arguments for the continuation of rural socio-logy in its traditional form were profound. At a stroke he had demol-ished the conceptual scheme upon which rural sociology had been based since Sorokin and Zimmerman, while demonstrating that the rural sector could no longer be considered in isolation from the rest of society. Yet there have hitherto been few signs of a theoretical scheme which could fill the gap which the demise of the rural-urban continuum left behind it.

Unfortunately the almost institutional character of the rural-urban continuum to which McGee draws attention has resulted in an abundance of attempts to resurrect it as a viable explanatory scheme (e.g., Frankenberg, 1966; Hillery, 1969; Jones, 1973; Lowe and Peck, 1974; Lupri, 1966; McGee, 1971; Poplin, 1972; Schnore, 1966). Most of these efforts consist of cataloguing various demographic, economic, and social differences between rural and urban inhabitants. Obviously such differences continue to abound and can be quite easily demon-strated, and a great deal of American rural sociology, at least, con-tinues to consist of a codification of these differences. Bealer (1975: 465) calls this "the single most dominant 'general orientation' with a substantive referent." It forms a "shared tradition" or "rally point" (ibid., p. 466) for the field. The issue at stake, however, is not the lack of any rural-urban differences in behavior, but the necessity of demonstrating any causal link between the concept of "rural" and particular kinds of social action. In the absence of such a link the concept of "rural" becomes sociologically uninterest-ing, if not spurious. The inductivism which characterizes rural sociology has compounded this problem by taking the differences which have duly been discovered between rural and urban behavior as though they in themselves provide a justification for establishing a rural sociology. As an essentially empirical, descriptive term, however, the notion of "rural" is simply incapable of bearing any explanatory significance in this way.

The fact that "rural" is not a sociologically defined category has also been responsible for the problems of definition in rural sociology. In the past this problem was disguised by the coincidence in most rural areas in advanced industrial societies of residential and occupational locations. Rural sociology could plausibly be defined as the study of those living in a rural locale and who were engaged in, or closely allied to, the production of food. What has sapped the confidence of those rural sociologists actively engaged in cataloguing rural-urban differences has been the disappearance of this demonstrably appropriate object of study (see Warner, 1974; Lowry, 1977). As the occupational basis of the rural population becomes less homogeneous in all advanced industrial societies, so rural sociologists have become less clear over what, precisely, constitutes "rural." Only in the limiting case of where the geographical milieu defines patterns of social relationships through the constraints which they apply to the local social structure, can this appropriateness be retained. That is to say, if social institutions are locality-based and if they are inter-related then there might be a "local social system" (Stacey, 1969) worthy of sociological attention--which we may, for the sake of convenience only, call "rural." But this is conditional on a number of empirically-determined properties (which seem to be present in, say, many peasant societies), and that any causal connection between the nature of this local social system and its "rurality" is purely spurious--it merely stems from the inability of the inhabitants to transcend the spatial constraints imposed upon them, this incapacity being linked to inequalities rooted in the wider system of social stratification rather than in a rural milieu per se. Thus, to paraphrase Pahl, there is no rural population as such; rather there are specific populations which for various, but identifiable, reasons find themselves in rural areas.

In recent years these problems have been aired on a number of occasions in rural sociological journals (e.g., Benvenuti et al., 1975; Galjart, 1973; Lowry, 1977; Munters, 1972; Redclift, 1974; Warner, 1974). The deepening social crisis in rural America has also prompted some re-thinking (Hightower, 1973, 1975; Merrill, 1976; Perelman, 1977). No single systematic body of theory has, however, emerged in rural sociology which has taken account of these problems. Instead increasing attention is being paid to theories which have been developed elsewhere, principally in the sociology of development. A range of influences are discernible in such approaches as dependency theory, center-periphery theory, and internal colonialism which at present perhaps constitute no more than potentially interesting lines of inquiry. Many of the papers which follow in this book use one or another of these approaches, and it should be emphasized that they very much signify "theoretical work in progress" and by no means reconcile all the various difficulties between and among them. These papers do, however, represent a start on the difficult task of replacing the now discredited rural-urban continuum with a new conceptual apparatus or set of theoretical problems which would provide rural sociology with a new research agenda and a new impetus.

The Institutional Framework

The current malaise of rural sociology is not simply a function of theoretical disarray, however. As we have already noted, many of the shortcomings alluded to in the previous section are widely acknowledged and have been stated on numerous occasions since Sewell's famous charge of "aversion to theory." Sewell, it will be recalled, directed his criticisms towards

> the pervasive aversion of rural sociology generally
> to theoretical work coupled with its traditional
> insistence of keeping everything on the "practical"
> level. This is further borne out by insistence on
> a definition of needed research in terms of what
> agricultural leaders, administrators and congress-
> men think rural sociology should be doing, by the
> domination... of the problems emphasis [and] by
> schemes for the evaluation of the field...(1950:
> 121).

In other words, the institutional framework within which rural sociologists operated also represented a danger to the pursuit of fundamental research. Thus Sewell warned that

> ... our preoccupation with the immediately practical
> has forced us to fit into large economic, education-
> al and political programs in minor administrative or
> advisory roles where there was little or no oppor-
> tunity to do any research which would test our know-
> ledge beyond the common-sense level, much less allow
> us to test crucial hypotheses under circumstances
> approximating conditions of control (ibid., pp. 121-
> 122).

Under these conditions, Sewell argued, rural sociologists would never be anything but "handmaidens to professional educators, economists, agricultural program administrators and social actionists of all kinds." Elsewhere Gross (1952: 84) noted that many of the research projects in rural sociology were "at best indirectly related to the discipline of sociology." In part Gross identified this ad hoc problem-solving role with the pressure exerted upon rural sociologists by "agricultural leaders and administrators" while Sletto, in his discussion of Sewell's paper, pointed to the control dilemma confronting American rural sociologists in the immediate post-war era:

The rural sociologist's dilemma is that he is called upon to function as a scientist in doing research into practical problems of rural welfare, but is allowed too little opportunity to do the research needed to scientific proficiency. What rural sociologists seem to need most is not more money for research but the drafting of an effective plan for gaining more freedom to do significant research within their present social settings (Sletto, 1950: 128).

Viewed from this perspective the trend in rural sociological research in the 1950s was not very encouraging. Smith commented in 1957 upon the major shift in research support which had occurred, resulting in an even more marked concentration of activities at the agricultural experiment stations (Smith, 1957: 17). When Sewell returned to survey the field again in 1965, he noted that the old problems remained:

One quite definite impression is that rural sociological research tends to be decidedly parochial not only in its focus on local people and problems, but also in its intellectual orientations.... Attention to local populations and local situations tends to restrict the sociological imagination and the inventiveness of the rural sociologist and to prompt him to give undue attention to problems and findings which may have local significance but may be trivial in the larger context (Sewell, 1965: 446, 447).

Similarly Stokes and Miller in their methodological review 10 years later noted a further advance in data-collection and data-analysis techniques, but as they rightly pointed out, the increased use of more sophisticated and powerful statistical tools does not always mean an improvement in the knowledge produced (1975: 432). In this area they note that:

The major areas of interest to rural sociologists have remained fairly stable over the past two decades. Studies in the areas of social organization and social psychology continue to dominate the field (ibid., p. 431).

This line of criticism has been given added stimulus by the publication of Hard Tomatoes, Hard Times, Jim Hightower's strident and partisan attack on the American "land grant college complex" for being the quiescent clients of corporate agribusiness:

In their efforts with food gadgetry, in their work for the in-put and out-put industries and in their

> mechanization research, land grant colleges and
> state agricultural experiment stations exist pri-
> marily as tax-paid clinics for agribusiness. Land
> grant college research is directed towards those
> private interests that least need assistance,
> while it ignores or works against the interest of
> those who desperately need help. The advantage is
> all on one side--agribusiness, millions; folks, zero.
> It is an outrageous allocation of public resources
> (Hightower, 1973: 50-51).

The main force of Hightower's attack is against agricultural economics
(see Hathaway et al., 1974; and Farrell, 1976, for discussions of agricultural economics' "own Watergate"). Rural sociology is depicted
as being of only secondary importance to the land grant complex--"the
stepchildren of the system" (Hightower, 1973: 51)--but Hightower does
not spare it his vitriol; "sociological bullshit," in his view, constitutes "the bulk of rural sociological research" (ibid., p. 56).
After listing some of the more arcane samples of recent research effort he concludes:

> Land grant college research for rural people and
> places is a sham. Despite occasional expressions of
> concern from land grant spokesmen, a look at the bud-
> gets and research reports makes clear that there is
> no intention of doing anything about the ravages of
> the agricultural revolution. The focus will continue
> to be on corporate efficiency and technological gad-
> getry, while the vast majority of rural Americans--
> independent family farmers, farm workers, small town
> businessmen and other rural residents--will be left
> to get along as best they can, even if it means
> getting along to the city. If they stay in rural
> America, a rural sociologist will come around every
> now and then to poke at them with a survey (ibid.,
> p. 57).

Whatever the validity of Hightower's assertions, they were presented
with a force which could hardly be ignored. Rural sociologists, who
had long prided themselves on their ability to research into the problems of rural people, now found that what had customarily been regarded
as their greatest strength was being dismissed out of hand and that
even their motives were being impugned.

To hard-pressed rural sociologists it seemed impossible to win.
For over 20 years they had been assailed by criticisms that they
were too concerned with applied research rather than with sociological problems. Now they were being accused of failing to render a
public service and indulging in research which was increasingly

irrelevant to the needs of the rural population. Perhaps Sewell's prescriptions had been taken too much to heart, for Stokes and Miller noted in their review that

> ... a dedication to policy relevant, applied research
> may well have characterized rural sociology during
> the 1930s and 1940s. It is difficult to make the
> same assertion today. Since 1965, less than one article
> in every ten dealt with social welfare and policy (1975:
> 416).

However, the true situation was more complicated than this, for Stokes and Miller found little overall change in the characteristics of the discipline, while many of Hightower's complaints were directed not towards any concentration on abstract theorizing, but to the triviality of much of the empirical work--an entirely familiar accusation. The issues raised by Hightower could not, therefore, be fitted into the "applied" versus "basic" categories used by Sewell, for criteria of public accountability and social relevances were also invoked. In the light of Hightower's comments the lesson to be learned from the previous 20 years' experience was that notions of "basic" and "applied" research represented a false antithesis, that indeed the major fallacy was to regard them as opposites or even as alternatives. The real weakness was one of problem definition: to much research was unimportant, inappropriate, or inconsequential for both a sociological and a public audience (see Copp, 1972; Ford, 1973).

The dependence on funding from the land grant complex has certainly abetted the continuation of inconsequential research in rural sociology, but, somewhat in reaction to this, rural sociologists have also sought an ultimately self-defeating escape route by introducing a more "scientific" research style in a misconceived attempt to compensate for the acknowledged inadequacies in the discipline. As Nolan and Hagan have observed:

> The point here is that by adopting criteria such as
> those outlined by Sewell, rural sociologists appear
> to have been drawn into defining problems and gather-
> ing data in such a way that the probabilities of being
> "scientific" are maximized but relevance for policy
> is minimized. We wish to stress that we see no neces-
> sary correspondence between one's research problems
> and one's method of analysis but there may be strong
> proclivities which flow from a decision to "scientific-
> ally upgrade" by using such analytical tools as multi-
> variate analysis. In short, as long as rural sociolo-
> gists allow a methodological tail to wag their research
> dog (as it seems is currently the case) they will never
> have very much to offer in the way of social policy
> recommendations (1975: 444).

Moreover the pressures to appear "scientific" by the use of quantitative techniques whatever the problem (see Stokes and Miller, 1975)
is in turn a product of the institutional context of rural sociology.
As Nolan and Galliher (1973) indicate, only "hard" data are usually
considered acceptable in the research ambience of the land grant
college complex, whatever the vagaries of sampling and validity or
considerations of relevance.

The application of a "scientific" methodological rigor has therefore proved to be a false solution, on its own,[1] to rural sociology's
fundamental weakness in specifying research problems considered relevant both to a wider sociological audience and to rural inhabitants
themselves. The false antithesis between a "scientific" emphasis and
a concern with rural problems, policies and programs has contributed
to this crisis. Indeed a return to "applied" research in its old
form would only serve to renew the jibes about "privy counters" and
"dust-bowl empiricism" and grant a license for doing shoddy research.
Rural sociology by the mid-1970s, therefore seemed to have reached
an impasse caused by "trained incapacity" (Nolan and Galliher, 1973:
496). However, the purpose of this book is not to encourage continuing pessimism, but to demonstrate that innovative and important work
is possible. The funding agencies are not monolithic: work of the
kind presented in this volume is funded by them. Intellectual timid-
ity and self-censorship are equally part of the problem. At least
there is now some hope that after the last 20 years, the drip, drip
of criticism may be producing some discernible shifts of emphasis.

ISSUES IN CRITICAL RURAL SOCIOLOGY

Research Issues

The emergence of a critical perspective in an area such as rural
sociology is of course not an unusual circumstance among the sociological subfields. Virtually all specialty areas in sociology have been
experiencing the same ferment in North America and Western Europe.
Even the most innocuous or tradition-bound fields such as the family,
crime and delinquency, and social psychology currently have visible
proponents of neo-Marxist or related perspectives who are sharply
critical of prevailing theoretical models. Given the "crisis of
Western sociology" (Gouldner, 1970) as a whole, the nurturing of a
critical rural sociology was hardly unexpected.

In contrast to much of the critical evaluation that characterized
the other major subfields of sociology, this new perspective in rural
sociology was rather quick to set forth and act upon a specific research agenda. One need only remember the sterility of years of un-
ending criticism of pluralist perspectives in political sociology to

realize how important it is for persons representing a new theoretical posture to move from the critique of orthodoxy to the establishment of a distinctive research tradition. Many of the papers assembled in this book are indeed representative of concrete empirical research and accordingly devote little attention to mere disputation with prevailing views.

One of the distinctive characteristics of the appearance of neo-Marxist and kindred perspectives in rural sociology is the emphasis on a somewhat different set of issues than had occupied the subdiscipline prior to 1970. In addition to the high level of attention accorded to sociological studies of rural-urban differences and disparities, as noted earlier, mainstream rural sociology was primarily preoccupied with matters such as the adoption and diffusion of agricultural technology, quality of life and social indicators, community development, demography, and the educational and occupational achievement process among rural youth. While most rural sociologists of this new genre would not deny the legitimacy of exploring such issues, they have tended to stake out decidedly different empirical terrain. The principal research foci of this "new rural sociology" include the structure of agriculture in advanced capitalism, state agricultural policy, agricultural labor, regional inequality, and agricultural ecology.

For those who have attended recent meetings of the Rural Sociological Society (in North America) or the European Society for Rural Sociology, many would agree that the most dramatic change in program content over the last decade has been the increased attention paid to the structure of agriculture under advanced capitalism. It is clearly not the case that most rural sociologists now engaged in studies of structural change in Western agriculture work from the theoretical perspectives represented in this volume. However, it is fair to say that the "rediscovery" of agriculture as a legitimate focus of rural sociology inquiry was largely inaugurated by representatives of this new theoretical tradition in rural sociology. Curiously, rural sociologists in the 1930s and 1940s devoted considerable attention to the structure of agriculture in the U.S., with much of this attention being generated by the severe "tenancy problem" that emerged during the Great Depression. But as levels of tenancy declined following World War II, most rural sociologists complacently accepted the apparent vitality of the "family farm" in the advanced societies. The rapid decline in the number of family farms during the post-War period along with the emergence of a significant trend toward corporate farming in the 1960s and 1970s were largely responsible for this increased attention to agricultural structure in the present decade.

The sociology of state agricultural policy had never been a major issue of concern to rural sociologists until the 1970s. As

much as the pioneers of North American rural sociology prided themselves on producing applied, practical knowledge that could be of
use to policy-makers, rural sociologists historically were almost
completely unaware of the major social and economic forces that
shaped government agricultural policy. The increased attention paid
to state agricultural policy has a number of origins. The first is
the realization that state policy had been at least partially responsible for the dramatic structural changes witnessed in Western
agricultures during this century. Secondly, Hightower's (1973)
scathing attack on the public higher education portion of state
agricultural policy--particularly corporate involvement in setting
research priorities in the agricultural experiment stations--began
to generate inquiry into other ways in which state policy tended
to benefit a relatively small, privileged stratum of large farmers
and agribusiness corporations. Finally, the massive attack on
pluralism--the prevailing model in political sociology--invited
attention to how agricultural policy departed from the pluralist
assumptions of bargaining and compromise among a diversity of social
groups with relatively equal amounts of actual or potential political
power (see, e.g., Chasin and Chasin, 1974; Miliband, 1969; Parenti,
1978). These new emphases on how agricultural policies are shaped
and on how these policies both arise from and generate new contradictions in the political economy forcefully demonstrate that a
"policy-relevant" rural sociology is a two-edged sword. By providing policy-makers with accurate information about the full range
of policies open to them and their possible socioeconomic effects,
the rural sociologist may become an unwitting servant of power.
Rural sociological research, then, should not only be designed so
that it illuminates the options open to policy-makers. Rural
sociologists must also understand the nature of policy-determination
in order to recognize that social policies are not arrived at in a
vacuum, but rather an interplay--usually on unequal terms--of
concrete sociopolitical interests.

     Similar to the structure of agriculture, agricultural labor is
hardly a new area of inquiry by rural sociologists. For example,
rural sociologists were prominent among members of the (U.S. President's Advisory Commission on Rural Poverty (1967) that strongly
argued for programs to assist migratory farm workers. For decades
rural sociologists have conducted countless descriptive studies of
the socioeconomic conditions of migrant workers, and most were
acutely aware of the deprivations experienced by these workers.
Recently, however, the focus in agricultural labor research has
shifted away from documenting how and explaining why migrant agricultural workers receive low wages and suffer from substandard
working and living conditions. One new concern is with the nature
of the "labor process" (Braverman, 1974) and how this labor process
shapes technological change in agriculture. For example, Friedland
et al. (1978) have been concerned with how class conflict between

capitalist farmers and migrant farmworkers has led to the rapid adoption of mechanical technologies in California. Another recent area
of research is on full-time--usually resident--farm workers. Virtually all of this work has been conducted in England (see, for example,
Newby, 1977; Newby et al., 1978), however, and the full-time hired
farm labor force in U.S. agriculture remains virtually unexplored.

A further important area of inquiry in the movement toward a
more critical rural sociology is regional inequality. It has been
widely recognized that all of the advanced societies display marked
regional polarization and inequality (see, for example, Holland,
1976; Review of Radical Political Economics, 1978), and much attention has been focused on how uneven spatial development is intrinsic
in the capitalistic mode of production. The analysis of the causes
and consequences of regional inequality is of course the logical
arena for rural sociologists to more fully explore the interrelations of social structure and space. Using the conventional definition of "rural" areas as those territories characterized by
primary production and small population concentrations, it is
apparent that most rural regions are underdeveloped, stagnant,
economic backwaters. However, it is not the case that the regional
polarization process is a simple rural-urban polarization process.
The "urban" is not synonymous with "developed," nor is "rural"
equivalent to "underdevelopment." Rather large cities may exist
in regions with generally low per capita incomes and low levels of
living, while the rural hinterland of dynamic metropolitan regions
typically is economically privileged as well. Nevertheless, analysts
of regional economic disparities have provided a provocative assessment of the tendency toward rural underdevelopment by focusing on
how the decapitalization of primary producers and the transfer of
this economic surplus to the metropole are integral elements in
the development of Western economies.

A final research issue of major concern to representatives of
this critical rural sociology is rural ecology--particularly the
environmental problems of agriculture. Much of this attention to
the agricultural environment was stimulated by a series of studies
which detailed the massive energy subsidies required by U.S. agriculture (see, for example, Pimentel et al., 1973, Steinhart and
Steinhart, 1974; Stockdale, 1976). Other analysts have also stressed
the tendency for Western--especially U.S.--agriculture to result in
severe environmental degradation, especially soil erosion and chemical contamination of agroecosystems (Perelman, 1977). While not
all persons examining the rural ecology issue are critical rural
sociologists, there has been a discernible trend toward linking
rural environmental problems to the exigencies of capitalist development in agriculture. Several studies have emphasized that
the dynamics of agriculture under capitalism--especially the
secular trend toward concentration and centralization of capital

which yields increasing farm sizes--can in large part be seen to account for the emergence of rural environmental degradation (Buttel, 1979; Buttel and Larson, 1979; Perelman, 1977).

While these five principal research foci by no means exhaust all available research possibilities, we see these new research areas as the central empirical terrain of a more critical approach to rural sociology. To repeat an observation made previously, this "new rural sociology" can be largely characterized in terms of its "rediscovery" of agriculture as a focus for inquiry in the advanced societies. However, as rural sociology has come to reacquaint itself with agriculture, this is being done on decidedly different terms than in the past. For example, the earlier emphasis on conducting studies which will facilitate more rapid diffusion of agricultural technologies has yielded to research into topics such as the socioeconomic consequences of technological change in agriculture.

Theoretical Issues

As we noted previously, the work included in this volume represents considerable diversity in theoretical and methodological postures. We thus resist the suggestion--or perhaps on the part of some, the accusation--that a critical rural sociology must rest on a single (presumably Marxist) theoretical stand. While much of the scholarship represented herein does draw from the Marxist heritage, it will become quite obvious that there is simply no such thing as a Marxist perspective in rural sociology. In addition, many of our authors primarily draw from classical or contemporary theorists other than Marx. While we make no pretention that this volume incorporates all possible theoretical postures within this broad critical tradition, we trust that the fundamental diversity of this work will speak for itself.

In this portion of the paper we attempt to provide an overview of some of the major theoretical issues represented in the articles that follow. Before proceeding, it should be noted that these theoretical issues are largely those internal to the cadre of critical rural sociologists in North America and Western Europe. The theoretical differences between critical and traditional rural sociology have been explored above and will not be repeated here. We would also like to preface these comments with the observations that while these issues are internal to critical rural sociology, they do not represent mere quibbling about trivial details. Each of these issues is of great importance in a scholarly, as well as in an applied or practical, sense.

It will become obvious that an overarching issue in research into the structure of agriculture is the nature of the "family"-- or in some cases, "peasant"--farm in advanced capitalism. One broad body of thought can be characterized by its argument that the family farm is inexorably destined to annihilation or extinction. It is postulated that the family farm under capitalism is subject to the overwhelming forces of concentration and centralization of capital and that the class of petty bourgeois farmers continues to undergo a progressive differentiation process. A small group of family or "peasant" farmers continues to accumulate capital and means of production, while the remainder is continually marginalized and eventually proletarianized. The end point of these processes is a sharp class division between the dominant group of capitalist farmers and absentee landlords, on one hand, and an impoverished group of tenants and rural proletarians, on the other. This general point of view is most clearly expressed by de Janvry below and by Kautsky (1976).

A decidedly different perspective on the family farm stresses that there are substantial barriers to capitalist development (i.e., differentiation) within agricultural production and that the family farm is likely to continue to be (at least) numerically predominant in advanced agricultures. The basis for this notion, however, is not a presumption of the social and economic vitality of the family farm; available data on the miserable condition of large minorities of family farmers in the U.S. and elsewhere clearly are not in record with a notion of the vitality of the family farm (see, for example, Perelman, 1977). Rather, the theoretical argument surrounding the work of Mann and Dickinson (1978), and Davis and Mottura and Pugliese (below), is that the family farm may be functional for the maintenance of capitalist production relations in the dominant metropolitan sectors of the economy (at least at certain junctures of development).

Mann and Dickinson have argued that the general conditions of production in agriculture--especially the excess of production time over labor time--limit the potential for profitable capital accumulation in agriculture. Their argument is that because of the necessary tie of agricultural production to the seasons, production time (the time in which capital is tied up in commodity production) will be greatly in excess of labor time (the portion of the production period in which labor is allocated to creating value). This gap is seen to reduce the potential for profitable levels of capital accumulation in agriculture, thereby discouraging capital from investing in agricultural production. Davis also makes the argument below that if we view the family farmer as "propertied labor" (as opposed to an "independent" petty bourgeois entrepreneur), exploitation of propertied labor through unfavorable terms of trade allows the preservation of the family farm (albeit in ways markedly different from

previous periods) to serve the interests of capital. Mottura and
Pugliese, drawing on the Italian experience, further suggest that
in addition to agriculture's obvious "production" function, agriculture may at certain junctures of capitalist development come to
serve an "industrial reserve" function as well, i.e., absorbing
masses of redundant labor releases from capitalist agriculture or
industry.

The practical consequences of this debate over the nature of
the family farm are obviously profound. If the family farm is
destined to disappear through a progressive differentiation process,
the major emerging force in the agricultural sector will be the
agricultural proletariat; the eventual decomposition of the family
farmer into a rural bourgeoisie and rural proletariat would make
efforts to "save" the family farm increasingly utopian. On the
other hand, if petty commodity production is likely to persist in
the indefinite future, efforts to improve the terms of trade for
and otherwise assist the petty commodity producer (e.g., through
agricultural cooperatives and restructuring of marketing channels)
can be expected to bear some fruit.

Exploration of state agricultural policy has also come to be
characterized by two competing theoretical and methodological
postures--essentially two competing theories of the state under advanced capitalism. One of these perspectives, the instrumentalist
theory of the state, basically sees the state as an "instrument" of
the dominant class. This perspective combines certain elements of
Weber's work on the state with a quite literal interpretation of
Marx's notion that the bourgeoisie tends to "capture" or "conquer"
the state and use the state to advance its own interests. For
example, Sweezy (1942: 243) argues that "state power must be
monopolized by the class or classes which are the chief beneficiaries" and the state should be viewed as "an instrument in the
hands of the ruling classes for enforcing or guaranteeing the
stability of the class structure itself." The principal methodological premise of the instrumentalist perspective on the state is
that the composition of state policy can be largely inferred from
the composition of the state elite. The recruitment of the principal members of state elite has been demonstrated in numerous
studies (e.g., Mills, 1956; Domhoff, 1971) to be primarily from
the dominant class of corporate capitalists or from upper-middle
class families who largely share the aims and goals of this dominant class. The implication of this approach is that to effectively rule, members of the dominant class or their upper-middle
class functionaries must occupy important positions of state
power and directly shape state policy in the interest of capital.

An alternative perspective on the state which can be termed a
"structuralist" one suggests that there are systematic structural

constraints on the state apparatus that tend to yield policies
favorable to capital, regardless of the class composition of the
state elite. The underlying notion is that managers of the state
are dependent on some reasonable level of economic activity in
order to: (1) adequately finance state operations through tax
revenue, and (2) maintain public support. Actions of the state
that would reduce "business confidence" and stifle investment would
threaten to both decrease tax revenues (thereby crippling state
operations) and arouse public discontent (if the lack of investment
would lead to unemployment and declining real wages). Since the
level of economic activity in a capitalist economy is viewed to be
largely determined by the level of private investment, the state
elite faces a structural imperative to enhance investment and thereby benefit capital, even if the state elite is ideologically pre-
disposed to do quite the opposite (see especially Block, 1979).

Although we have not included a representative of the instrumentalist approach to state agricultural policy in the present
volume, a rather visible example of the point of view is readily
at hand. Hightower (1973), although not a self-declared sociologist,
clearly employs an instrumentalist approach when examining the agricultural research portion of state agricultural policy in the U.S.
Hightower carefully documents how representatives of corporate agribusiness and large capitalist farms occupy private and public
decision-making roles in agricultural research. Hightower essentially views the formation of agricultural policy as "agribusiness,
agrigovernment" (Hightower, 1975). Groups who have direct interests
at stake in research policy determination have been able to penetrate
the state decision-making structures--often through a revolving door
of agribusiness executives moving into major government positions
and then back to their corporate origins--and directly shape state
policy to their benefit. Hightower thus suggests that the capture
of the agricultural policy-making apparatus and the social policies
resulting from this penetration have been largely responsible for
the decline of family farming, the rise of corporate agriculture,
and the excessive control agribusiness firms have over the food
system.

The papers by Sinclair and by Mann and Dickinson in this volume
are broadly representative of the structuralist orientation toward
state agricultural policy. While the two papers have quite different
foci (Sinclair is primarily concerned with comparative aspects of
agricultural policy in several advanced capitalist societies, while
Mann and Dickinson focus on historical aspects of agricultural policy
in the U.S.), both tend to see the formation of agricultural policy
in terms of the structural constraints faced by various state elites.
For example, Sinclair suggests that one can view state agricultural
policy in terms of the "accumulation" and "legitimization" roles of
the state as elaborated by O'Connor (1973). He therefore sees

agricultural policy being shaped more by the nature of the political-economic roles that the state in advanced capitalism must perform than by the tendency for representatives of agribusiness to become state elites or have close access to them.

The theoretical issues developed in critical research on regional inequality do not lend themselves to nearly as tidy a summary as do the structure of agriculture and the determination of agricultural policy. In part, this is because the analysis of regional polarization and inequality is still in something of a state of disarray. To be sure there are readily identifiable "schools of thought" in regional socioeconomic analysis. These schools of thought, however, have advanced very little beyond argument over which analogy or metaphor--internal colonialism, dependency, center-periphery relations, or uneven development--is most applicable for accounting for historic patterns of regional socioeconomic disparities in the advanced societies (see, for example, Newby, 1980). Accordingly, one can best get a handle on the intellectual "sorting out" process in this area by reviewing, more or less chronologically, the evolution of critical thought on issues of regional development and underdevelopment.

It is relevant to note before proceeding with this evolutionary glimpse at regional/spatial research that despite the marked regional inequalities that have characterized all developed capitalist societies, relatively little attention was paid to this phenomenon (other than by neoclassical regional economists) until the late 1960s. In fact, it is fair to say that analysts of regional inequality first began to look at these problems in a critical way by borrowing perspectives--essentially analogies--from research on neocolonialism and imperialism in the Third World. A significant portion of the internal theoretical ferment that continues is the realization that theories developed in the context of Third World nations or theories most suitable for the analysis of economic asymmetries in the world-system may not be fully appropriate for examining social relationships within a particular advanced social formation.

Internal colonialism was the first such theoretical device lifted from the Third World context and applied to spatial aspects of development and underdevelopment in the advanced societies. Internal colonialism essentially involves an analogy of the underdeveloped region with a colonially-subjected Third World country, on one hand, and the developed region with a colonial nation-state, on the other (see Gonzalez-Casanova, 1965; and Stavenhagen, 1975, for illustrative applications of internal colonialism in the Latin American context). Applications of the internal colonialist perspective became especially popular in accounting for Appalachian underdevelopment (see, for example, Lewis, 1971; Tudiver, 1973), while Hechter's (1975) work on the relationships between the English

"core" and the Celtic fringe of Wales, Scotland, and Ireland has
become the most visible application of this "theory" to regional
polarization in the advanced societies. The major bases of regional
polarization in internal colonial terms are: (1) "colonial" political administration, and (2) absentee ownership of productive
property in the peripheral or hinterland. On one hand, the periphery
is seen to be politically dominated by core elites who seek to perpetuate the periphery's economic subjugation. On the other hand,
internal colonialism analysts have given great emphasis to absentee
core ownership of the resources and industries located in the
periphery (e.g., the coal mines and oil wells of Appalachia and
Scotland, respectively) as a mechanism by which the periphery loses
control over its resources and surrenders its economic surplus to
the core.[2]

Dependency, another perspective on international development
and underdevelopment more recently brought to bear on issues of
regional inequality, largely emerged in regional inequality research
as a critique of the internal colonialism model. Following Frank
(1967) and Wallerstein (1974), the dependency model of regional
underdevelopment emphasizes the space economy as a mechanism of
surplus extraction. In other words, it is suggested that an integral part of the process of capital accumulation and capitalist
development in the advanced societies is the extraction of surplus
from periphery to center; the "development" of the center is thus
premised on the "underdevelopment" of peripheral areas. The dependency perspective thus sees that the subordination of the internal
periphery to the metropole is more systematic--that is, inherent in
the process of capitalist development--than it would appear to be
through the lens of internal colonialism. While accepting the
applicability of notions such as political domination of internal
peripheries and the pervasiveness of absentee ownership of productive property in the periphery, dependency theorists suggest
that reduction in center hegemony and absentee ownership would do
little to attenuate regional disparities. The mechanisms of
internal colonization are seen as being only historic features of
center-periphery (or "metropole-satellite;" Frank, 1967) relations
and not the ultimate causal forces that generate and reproduce
regional disparities.

What, then, are the major causal mechanisms behind the internal
dependista assertion that regional differentiation and inequality
are inherent in capitalist development? Essentially three factors
can be identified. The first is the mobility of capital--that, is
the freedom of capital to invest in places where the highest profits
can be obtained. Given the presence of pre-capitalist or emergent
capitalist cities, firms typically prefer to locate in already developed areas (since economies of agglomeration and service provision
in such places reduce the costs of production). The concentration of

investment in already developed places leads to further spatial differentiation. Secondly, since capital tends to be more mobile than
labor (Holland, 1976), the penetration of capitalist production
relations into the periphery and the labor displacement this results in
(e.g., from agriculture) yield a "labor reserve" in the periphery.
This labor reserve is suggested to depress the price of labor throughout the economy, enhancing the overall profitability of investments.
Finally, dependency analysts suggest that the essence of exchange in
capitalism is the transfer of value--part of which takes on a regional complexion. Mandel (1976: 43), for example, notes that

> the entire process of capitalist industrialization
> is based on series of exchanges which imply the
> transfer of value: exchange between industry and
> agriculture, exchange with foreign underdeveloped
> nations, etc. Without these unequal exchanges, the
> accumulation of capital would rapidly slow down, or
> would disappear.... The unequal development between
> regions and nations is the very essence of capital-
> ism, on the same level as the exploitation of labour
> by capital. If the rate of profit were always the
> same in all regions of a nation and in all the
> branches of industry, then there would be no more
> accumulation of capital other than that made neces-
> sary by demographic movement. And this itself
> would be modified in its own way by the impact of
> the severe economic stagnation that would ensue.

While dependency theory was at one point the cutting edge of work
on international underdevelopment, it has come in for some rather
strident criticism in recent years (see especially Brenner, 1977).[3]
Likewise theories of domestic dependency in the context of the advanced societies have come under attack, although for somewhat different reasons. The principal objection raised concerning internal
dependency concerns this theory's assumption that capitalist development inherently is spatially uneven. While not denying that capitalist
development in the advanced societies does tend to exhibit regional
unevenness, recent research has been critical of the assumption that
regional imbalances are generic to capitalist development itself.
Fox (1978), for example, has pointed out that there has been a discernible process of regional convergence in the U.S. since the turn
of the century (following a protracted era of regional economic
polarization in the 19th century). He suggests that the transition
from competitive to monopoly capitalism has resulted in a shift in
spatial unevenness of development from within the U.S. to uneven
development on a world-scale. Accordingly, Markhusen (1979: 5-6)
argues that

> it is not capitalism per se, but the environment
> which capitalism encounters on its expansion path
> which renders the process of expansion "uneven."
> Particular capitalists and corporations may be
> able to exploit conditions existing in any one
> region at a particular point in the process, but
> the system as a whole has no stake in ensuring
> uneven development. This interpretation of uneven
> development also permits convergence and reversals
> in the positions of different regions.

Markhusen especially emphasizes the fact that particular regions may decidedly reverse their positions of dominance and subordination as capitalist development proceeds. The economic decline of the once ascendent Northeast and the boom of the sunbelt in the past decade are dramatic examples of this process of reversal--these changes being at least partially at odds with the mechanistic and economistic image that dependency theory typically conjures up.

The perspective that is emerging in the wake of critiques of domestic dependency theory does not carry any convenient label. Perhaps it can be most aptly characterized as a multicausal, dialectical, historical model. While the critics of dependency theory do acknowledge a tendency for the progressive economic specialization under capitalism to have a spatial character--leading to spatial specialization and regional unevenness--there is an increasing recognition that there is a variety of interacting sources of prevailing patterns of regional polarization that overshadow the specialization process alone. Markhusen, for example, argues that many aspects of regional inequality can be traced to the role of the State and to political conflict (see also Markhusen's and Moore's papers in this volume). Fox (1978) accordingly notes that the rise of the economic fortunes of the sunbelt can be largely attributed to class conflict in the frostbelt which presents increasing pressures for higher wages. Capital in turn has migrated toward cheap sunbelt labor. Simon (1978) similarly argues that elements of precapitalist production relations in the Appalachian coalfields have historically resulted in a lack of stimulus for technological advance on the part of coal firms, in part leading Appalachia to be a technologically-stagnant economic backwater.

The final theoretical issue we wish to explore pertains to the analysis of rural and other ecological issues. This issue essentially concerns whether environmental concern--at least in the forms in which it is presently expressed--is a progressive social force. Shortly after the emergence of the environmental movement in the U.S. and other advanced societies there was a flood of criticism of the social class composition, ideologies, and impacts of environmentalism (see especially Sills, 1975). Environmentalists were argued to be upper-middle class or otherwise privileged persons whose ideologies were insensitive to the needs of the poor and often a thinly-veiled guise for the maintenance of privilege (see, for example, Horowitz, 1972). More importantly, evidence of the inegalitarian effects of environmental policies (Schnaiberg, 1975) ushered in even harsher criticism of the progressivity of environmentalism. Lowe and Worboys in this volume accordingly view ecology as "a deeply conservative response to a perceived crisis of authority in Western society."

While there has been broad acknowledgement of the elitism--in ideological if not distributional terms--of the dominant thrust of environmentalism during the late 1960s and 1970s, there is increasing recognition that this need not be the deeply conservative response that Lowe and Worboys detect. It is clearly the case that the rural and urban producing classes suffer the most from degradation of work and residential environments (Morrison, 1979) and have much to gain from environmental improvement. There is also evidence that conventional environmentalism has reached an impasse in the aftermath of the most recent energy shortage. This shortage has prompted the state to place major emphasis on nuclear power and liquefaction of coal--two energy sources that involve unknown risks and massive environmental degradation, respectively. This has forced environmental groups to look toward conservation and renewable energy resources as twin agendas to circumvent the dismantling of environmental laws that expanded nuclear and coal production would dictate. Environmentalists therefore have moved increasingly toward the left-leaning "soft technology" movement for allies and direction (Morrison, 1979). An interesting manifestation of this trend is the attempted formation by Barry Commoner--probably the most well-known American environmentalist--of the leftist "People's Party" organized around advocacy of renewable energy resources and dismantling of corporate power. Thus the tendency for capitalist development to be accompanied by environmental degradation may be seen as not only contributing to political-economic contradictions that threaten to undermine capitalism, but also the development of a meaningful environmental critique of the political economy.

Aspects of these controversies surface in the papers by Geisler and Buttel below. Geisler's examination of one aspect of environmental policy--the "quiet revolution in land use control," or the increasing socialization of private property rights of small-holders of property in the periphery--leads to a conclusion that this "quiet revolution" is actually a counterrevolution that rationalizes resource structures in the periphery to the benefit of monopoly capital. Geisler sees the socialization of control over peripheral property to lead to the disappearance of the small capitalists and independent producers in the face of monopoly capitalism. Buttel's paper, while critical of the naive neopopulism that has accompanied efforts to enhance the quality of the agricultural environment, sees a potentially larger role for the independent producer or small capitalist in these efforts. Although recognizing the tendency for petty commodity producers to be politically drawn toward a hopeless return to competitive, small-holder capitalism, Buttel suggests that the realistic and intensely felt dissatisfactions of petty commodity producers with the present political economy of agriculture may be shaped in progressive directions.

It should be emphasized once more that these issues in critical rural sociology should be viewed as little more than a sampling of the important issues being generated in this field. It is our feeling, further, that the issues we have identified in this paper are illustrative of the immense potential that further work in this area can yield. Rather than being trivial debates over dogma, each issue explored here has the most profound implications for social policy and political strategy.

CONCLUDING REMARKS

We noted at the outset that rural sociology has seemingly lost its way at the very time that it should be maturing into a routinized area of inquiry. We would like to think, however, that the papers represented in this volume are evidence of rural sociology in the advanced societies of having stumbled onto fruitful--if contested-- theoretical and empirical terrain. While the approaches we have sampled are unlikely to become an orthodoxy in their own right, the tendency for younger rural sociologists and contemporary graduate students to be comfortable with and curious about these perspectives is unmistakable. We therefore fully expect that this critical rural sociology will not merely be a trendy, faddish remnant of the 1960s but rather will increasingly become a permanent, although clearly a minority, aspect of the subdiscipline.

We trust that the present volume and rapidly accumulating literature that it parallels will not bring an end to the anguished introspection of rural sociologists concerned about the course their subdiscipline is taking. And it is possible that the type of work we have assembled herein will be reacted against in no less anguished tones. Nevertheless, we feel that this diverse collection of theory and research is a creative, positive response to the widely felt crisis of Western rural sociology.

FOOTNOTES

[1]However, we would just as quickly disassociate ourselves from the view that quantitative methodology is the problem in rural sociology,

or even a major one. Quantitative methodology is clearly a useful
tool in rural sociological analysis, and we see no merit to the
notion that familiarity with or use of quantitative methods leads to
irrelevant research.

[2]Theories of internal colonialism also typically involve cultural
explanations of regional dominance and subordination. Hechter (1975),
in fact, views internal colonialism and regional inequality to be
a "cultural division of labor." The subordination of peripheral
regions to the core is thus seen to involve aspects of "racism" or
cultural domination. At the same time, Hechter and others view a
structure of internal colonialism to generate peripheral resistance
that is frequently expressed in cultural or ethnic terms. However,
Walls (1976) has persuasively argued that the cultural component of
internal colonialism theory clearly breaks down in the Appalachian
case (and presumably most other instances of regional underdevelopment as well). He notes that while there may be some level of pre-
judice against "hillbillies," this is more a bias against the society's
lower class than it is against all people in the region.

[3]The major criticism leveled against dependency as a theory of international development is its tendency to focus only on the sphere of
exchange, rather than the sphere of production. The notion that
economic surplus is extracted from peripheral to core nations assumes
that the major locus of exploitation is in the unequal exchanges that
take place on the world market. Brenner (1977) and others have
persuasively argued that the underlying dynamics of development are
to be found in the sphere of production (i.e., the dynamics of class
structure) rather than in the sphere of commodity exchange.

REFERENCES

Bealer, Robert C.
     1975 "Theory and rural sociology." Rural Sociology 40: 455-477.

Bell, Colin, and Howard Newby
     1971 Community Studies. London: Allen and Unwin.

Benvenuti, Bruno, Benno Galjart, and Howard Newby
     1975 "The current status of rural sociology." Sociologia Ruralis
     14: 3-21.

Block, Fred
     1979 "The ruling class does not rule." In R. Quinney (ed.),
     Capitalist Society. Homewood, Illinois: Dorsey.

Braverman, Harvey
    1974 Labor and Monopoly Capital. New York: Monthly Review Press.

Brenner, Robert
    1977 "The origins of capitalist development: A critique of neo-
    Smithian Marxism." New Left Review 104: 25-92.

Buttel, Frederick H.
    1979 "Agricultural structure and energy intensity: A comparative
    analysis of the developed capitalist societies." Comparative
    Rural and Regional Studies 1: forthcoming.

Buttel, Frederick H. and Oscar W. Larson III
    1979 "Farm size, structure, and energy intensity: An ecological
    analysis of U.S. agriculture." Rural Sociology 44: forthcoming.

Chasin, Barbara, and Gerald Chasin
    1974 Power and Ideology. Cambridge, Massachusetts: Schenkman.

Copp, James H.
    1972 "Rural sociology and rural development." Rural Sociology
    37: 515-533.

Domhoff, G. William
    1971 The Higher Circles. New York: Vintage.

Duncan, Otis Durant
    1954 "Rural sociology coming of age." Rural Sociology 19: 1-12.

Farrell, Kenneth R.
    1976 "Public policy, the public interest, and agricultural
    economics." American Journal of Agricultural Economics 58:
    785-794.

Ford, Thomas R.
    1973 "Towards meeting the social responsibilities of rural
    sociology." Rural Sociology 38: 372-390.

Fox, Kenneth
    1978 "Uneven regional development in the United States."
    Review of Radical Political Economics 10: 68-86.

Frank, Andre Gunder
    1967 Capitalism and Underdevelopment in Latin America. New York:
    Monthly Review Press.

Frankenberg, Ronald
    1966 Communities in Britain. Harmondsworth, England: Penguin.

Friedland, William H., Amy E. Barton, and Robert J. Thomas
    1978 Manufacturing Green Gold: The Conditions and Social Con-
    sequences of Lettuce Harvest Mechanization. Davis, California:
    California Agricultural Policy Seminar, University of California,
    Davis.

Galjart, Benno
    1971 "Rural development and sociological concepts: A critique."
    Rural Sociology 36: 31-40.

    1973 "The future of rural sociology." Sociologia Ruralis 13:
    254-263.

Gans, Herbert J.
    1962 The Urban Villagers. Glencoe, Illinois: Free Press.

Glass, Ruth
    1966 "Conflict in cities." In CIVA Symposium, Conflict in
    Society. London: Churchill Press.

Gonzales-Casanova, Pablo
    1965 "Internal colonialism and national development." Studies
    in Comparative International Development 1: 27-37.

Gouldner, Alvin W.
    1970 The Coming Crisis of Western Sociology. New York: Avon.

Gross, Neal
    1952 "Review of current research on the sociology of rural life."
    American Sociological Review 17: 83-90.

Hathaway, Dale E. et al.
    1974 "Public sector research and education and the agribusiness
    complex: Unholy alliance or socially beneficial partnership?"
    American Journal of Agricultural Economics 56: 993-1002.

Hechter, Michael
    1975 Internal Colonialism. Berkeley: University of California
    Press.

Hightower, Jim
    1973 Hard Tomatoes, Hard Times. Cambridge, Massachusetts:
    Schenkman.

    1975 Eat Your Heart Out. New York: Crown.

Hillery, George A.
    1969 Communal Organizations. Chicago: University of Chicago Press.

Holland, Stuart
1976 Capital Against the Regions. New York: St. Martin's Press.

Horowitz, Irving Louis
1972 "The environmental cleavage: social ecology versus political economy." Social Theory and Practice 2: 125-134.

Jones, Gwyn
1973 Rural Life. London: Longman.

Kaufman, Harold F.
1963 "A perspective for rural sociology." Rural Sociology 28: 1-17.

Kautsky, Karl
1976 "A summary of selected parts of Kautsky's The Agrarian Question." Economy and Society 5: 1-49 (Jarius Banaji, trans.).

Lewis, Helen
1971 "Fatalism or the coal industry." Mountain Life and Work 46: 4-15.

Lewis, Oscar
1949 Life in a Mexican Village. Urbana: University of Illinois Press.

Lowe, George D., and Charles W. Peck
1974 "Location and lifestyle: the comparative explanatory ability of urbanism and rurality." Rural Sociology 39: 392-420.

Lowry, Sheldon
1977 "Rural sociology at the crossroads." Rural Sociology 42: 461-475.

Lupri, Eugen
1966 "The rural-urban variable reconsidered: the cross-cultural perspective." Sociologia Ruralis 7: 1-20.

Mandel, Ernest
1976 "Capitalism and regional disparities." Southwest Economy and Society 1: 41-47.

Mann, Susan A., and James M. Dickinson
1978 "Obstacles to the development of a capitalist agriculture." The Journal of Peasant Studies 5: 466-481.

Markhusen, Ann R.
1979 "Regionalism and the capitalist state: the case of the United States." Kapitalistate 7: forthcoming.

McGee, T.G.
    1971 The Urbanization Process in the Third World. London: G.
    Bell and Sons.

Merrill, Richard (ed.)
    1976 Radical Agriculture. New York: Harper Torchbooks.

Miliband, Ralph
    1969 The State in Capitalist Society. New York: Basic Books.

Mills, C. Wright
    1956 The Power Elite. New York: Oxford University Press.

Morrison, Denton E.
    1979 "The softening of environmentalism: why and how appropriate
    technology is changing the movement." Unpublished manuscript,
    Department of Sociology, Michigan State University.

Munters, Q.J.
    1972 "Sociologia Ruralis on the Balance." Sociologia Ruralis 12:
    No. 2.

Newby, Howard
    1977 The Deferential Worker. London: Allen Lane.

    1980 "Rural sociology: a trend report." Current Sociology,
    forthcoming.

Newby, Howard, Colin Bell, David Rose, and Peter Saunders
    1978 Property, Paternalism and Power. London: Hutchinson.

Nolan, Michael F., and John F. Galliher
    1973 "Rural sociological research and social policy: hard data,
    hard times." Rural Sociology 38: 491-499.

Nolan, Michael R., and Robert A. Hagan
    1975 "Rural sociological research, 1966-1974: implications for
    social policy." Rural Sociology 40: 435-454.

O'Connor, James
    1973 The Fiscal Crisis of the State. New York: St. Martin's
    Press.

Olson, Phillip
    1965 "Rural American community studies: the survival of public
    ideology." Human Organization 10: 342-350.

Pahl, R.E.
    1966 "The rural-urban continuum." Sociologia Ruralis 6: 299-327.

Parenti, Michael
1978 Power and the Powerless. New York: St. Martin's Press.

Perelman, Michael
1977 Farming for Profit in a Hungry World. Montclair, New
Jersey: Allenheld, Osmun and Co.

Pimentel, David et al.
1973 "Food production and the energy crisis." Science 182:
443-449.

Poplin, Dennis E.
1972 Communities. New York: Macmillan.

President's Advisory Commission on Rural Poverty
1967 The People Left Behind. Washington, D.C.: U.S. Government
Printing Office.

Redclift, Michael
1974 "Interpretive research and structural change in rural sociology." Sociologia Ruralis 14: 22-32.

Review of Radical Political Economics
1978 "Special issue on uneven regional development." Vol. 10,
No. 3.

Schnaiberg, Allan
1975 "Social syntheses of the societal-environmental dialectic:
the role of distributional impacts." Social Science Quarterly
55: 5-20.

Schnore, Leo F.
1966 "The rural-urban variable." Rural Sociology 37, No. 1.

Sewell, William H.
1950 "Needed research in rural sociology." Rural Sociology 15:
115-130.

1965 "Rural sociological research, 1936-1965." Rural Sociology
30: 428-451.

Sills, David L.
1975 "The environmental movement and its critics." Human Ecology
3: 1-41.

Simon, Rick
1978 "The labor process and uneven development in the Appalachian
coalfields." Unpublished paper, Morgantown, West Virginia.

Smith, T. Lynn
    1957 "Rural sociology in the United States and Canada: a trend
    report." Current Sociology, Vol. 6, No. 1.

Sorokin, Pitirim, and Carle C. Zimmerman
    1929 Principles of Rural-Urban Sociology. New York: Henry Holt.

Sorokin, Pitirim, Carle C. Zimmerman, and Charles J. Galpin
    1930 A Systematic Source Book in Rural Sociology. Minneapolis:
    University of Minnesota Press.

Stacey, M.
    1969 "The myth of community studies." British Journal of
    Sociology 20: 134-147.

Stavenhagen, Rodolfo
    1975 Social Classes in Agrarian Societies. Garden City, New
    York: Anchor Doubleday.

Stein, Maurice
    1964 The Eclipse of Community. New York: Harper & Row.

Steinhart, John S., and Carol E. Steinhart
    1974 "Energy use in the U.S. food system." Science 184:
    307-316.

Stockdale, Jerry D.
    1976 "Technology and change in U.S. agriculture: model or warn-
    ing?" Sociologia Ruralis 17: 43-58.

Stokes, C. Shannon, and Michael K. Miller
    1975 "A methodological review of research since 1965." Rural
    Sociology 40: 411-434.

Sweezy, Paul
    1942 The Theory of Capitalist Development. New York: Monthly
    Review Press.

Tudiver, Neil
    1973 Why Aid Doesn't Help: Organizing for Community Economic
    Development in Central Appalachia. Unpublished Ph.D. Disser-
    tation, University of Michigan.

Wakeley, Ray E.
    1967 "Definitions and relationships of rural sociology." Rural
    Sociology 32: 195-198.

Wallerstein, Emmanuel
    1974 The Modern World-System. New York: Academic Press.

Walls, David S.
    1976 "Central Appalachia: a peripheral region in an advanced
    capitalist society." Journal of Sociology and Social Welfare
    4: 232-247.

Warner, W. Keith
    1974 "Rural society in a post-industrial age." Rural Sociology
    39: 306-317.

Part I
THEORETICAL PERSPECTIVES

2. Summary of Selected Parts of Kautsky's *The Agrarian Question*

JARIUS BANAJI

As soon as social-democracy extends its work to the countryside, it becomes clear to it that the small holding is not in a process of rapid disintegration, that big holdings are only gaining ground slowly, in places even retreating. The whole economic theory on which social-democracy is founded thus appears false as soon as its application to the domain of agriculture is attempted. As Sombard remarked, the essence of the agrarian question as the social-democrats understand it, boils down to the dilemma--what happens if in the economic sphere there are sectors which do not conform to the laws of socialization, e.g., if the small holding is more productive than the big? "As far as I know," Sombart writes, "up to now no one has established with any certainty the tendencies of development of agriculture, or the type of holding which could be characterised as 'most advanced,' or even whether such a type exists in the field of agricultural production. As far as I can see, this is where the limits of Marx's system lie; Marx's conclusions cannot be transposed in simple form to the domain of agriculture. His theory of development, which predicts the expansion of the big holding, proletarianisation of the masses and the necessity of socialism, holds true in this clear form only for industry." For over a century economists have concerned themselves with the question of which is best--the big or the small holding? The evolution which agriculture underwent in this period cannot, however, be understood by focussing solely on the struggle of big and small holdings, or by studying agriculture in isolation, independently of the whole mechanism of social production.

Of course, agriculture does not develop according to the same process as industry; it follows laws of its own. But this does not imply that the development of agriculture and that of industry are somehow in opposition or incompatible with one another. On the contrary, we believe that both are developing in the same direction, but to show this we have to regard them as elements of a single process. Moreover, the Marxist theory of capitalism production does not reduce the development of capitalist production to the simple formula: "disappearance of the small holding before the big," as if such a formula were a key to the understanding of modern economy. To study

39

the agrarian question according to Marx's method, we should not confine
ourselves to the question of the future of small scale farming; on the
contrary, we should look for all the changes which agriculture experiences under the domination of capitalist production. We should ask:
is capital, and in what ways is capital, taking hold of agriculture,
revolutionizing it, smashing the old forms of production and of poverty
and establishing the new forms which must succeed. Only when this question has been answered, can we decide whether Marx's theory is applicable
to agriculture or not. Our task is thus defined.

THE PEASANT AND INDUSTRY

If we make exception of some of the colonies, capitalist production generally develops first in the towns, in industry. Though it
escapes for a while, sooner or later the character of agricultural
production is modified by the development of industry.

The peasant family of the medieval period composed an economic
society that was entirely, or almost entirely, self-sufficient, a
society that produced not only its own food, but built its own home,
furniture and utensils, forged its own implements of production, etc.
Naturally the peasant went to the market, but he sold only his surplus
produce, and bought only trivialities, except for iron, which he used
only sparsely. This self-sufficient society was indestructible. The
worst that could happen was a bad harvest, a fire, an invasion of enemy
troops. But even these misfortunes were only of passing significance.
Reserves built up from the past offered security against bad harvests;
from the forest the peasant could extract wood to rebuild his house
after a fire.

In our own century it was the conservative economist Sismondi who
described with such clarity the comfortable position of these independent peasants whose condition he regarded as ideal. "The peasant
who works his own inheritance with the help of his children, who pays
rent to no one, nor employs any one, who subordinates production to
his own consumption, who consumes his own corn, drinks his own wine,
makes his own clothing, is hardly concerned about market prices; he
has little to buy or sell, and he is not affected by the disruptions
of commerce..." Sismondi was thinking mainly of Switzerland and parts
of Northern Italy. Although the picture he drew was not true of all
peasants, it was drawn from real life.

But if we now compare it with the present state of the peasantry
in Europe--not excepting Switzerland--we cannot fail to acknowledge
that a powerful economic revolution has occurred over these sixty
years. The starting point of this revolution was the dissolution of
small peasant industry brought about by urban industry and trade.

This process of dissolution began in the Middle Ages, when small industries first appeared in the towns. But the products of this industry
penetrated the countryside only slowly. It required the action of
capitalist industry to bring about a rapid destruction of the peasant's
domestic industry, and it required the growth of a communications system
peculiar to capitalism to break down the insularity of the countryside.
In dissolving the peasant's small industry, capitalism increases his
need for cash; the peasant requires cash, in these new conditions, to
purchase not only his luxuries but even those goods which are essential
to his consumption. Parallel to this, the cash requirements of the
peasant's overlords also increased, and led to the substitution of payment in kind by payment in cash and to a general rise in the level of
payments (thus increasing the peasant's own requirements of cash even
further). The only means available to the peasant of earning this cash
was the sale of his products, not, of course, those which he produced
in his backward home-based industry, but those which the industry of
the towns did not itself produce. In this way the peasant was finally
forced to become what we today understand by "peasant"--a pure agriculturist. The further he was forced into this specialization, the
wider became the gulf separating industry and agriculture.

Against this new dependence on the market, the peasant had no
"reserves" to fall back on. He had no means of preventing a fall in
prices, or of selling grain for which there was no demand. In former
times, good harvests were a blessing; now they became a scourge. This
became especially clear early in the 19th century; by this time commodity production was the prevalent form of agricultural production in
western Europe, but communication was still difficult and not sufficiently developed to establish an equilibrium between the overproduction of one district and the scarcity of another. Just as bad harvests
pushed prices up, good ones forced them down.

The more agriculture developed a commodity character, the greater
became the distance separating him from his market, the more dependent
the peasant became on an intermediary. The merchant found a place
between the producer and consumer. Side by side with the merchant came
the usurer; in bad years the peasant's cash receipts were not sufficient
to cover his requirements of cash; he was therefore compelled to borrow.
Exploitation by usurer capital was established on this basis; what even
the worst harvest or epidemic had failed to achieve in the past--the
peasant's alienation from his land, his conversion   into a proletarian
--became possible now whenever the markets for grain and beef entered a
crisis.

The emerging shortage of land to meet his family's consumption
(in the given conditions of production) coupled with the appearance of
seasonal unemployment following the dissolution of domestic industry
compelled the peasant to reduce the size of his family to a minimum
(disposing of them as farmhands, soldiers, factory workers, etc.).

The employment of thrashing machines to perform a task which had formerly absorbed a substantial amount of labour in the winter months reinforced this tendency. But those who remained on the farm could not compensate for this withdrawal of labour, when labour was required in large quantities in the summer months--however hard they worked. Thus they were compelled to employ seasonal workers, who were themselves drawn from the peasantry and consisted of peasants seeking additional income or of the redundant sons and daughters of the peasant.

The same development which on the one hand creates a demand for wage labourers, creates, on the other hand, these wage labourers themselves. It proletarianises masses of peasants, cuts down the size of the peasant family and throws the redundant members on the labour market. Finally, this process enhances the peasants dependence on subsidiary sources of income: as they find it impossible to earn an income from the sale of agricultural produce, they sell their labour power. Up until the 17th century we only rarely encounter day workers or farm hands. Their employment becomes widespread around this time. As wage labourers come to replace the family members who have left, the condition of the others, who stay behind, deteriorates to the level of wage labour, subordinated to the head of the family. The old society centred on the self-sufficient peasant family is thus replaced by troops of hired labour engaged on the big peasant holdings. This process began, as we said, already in the middle ages, but it became dominant only under capitalism. It continues today, invating new regions, converting subsistence production into commodity production, enhancing the peasant's cash requirements in the most diverse ways and replacing family labour by hired labour. Thus the growth of capitalism in the towns is by itself sufficient to transform completely the peasantry's established way of life, even before capital has itself entered agricultural production and independently of the antagonism between big and small holdings. But capital does not confine itself to industry. When it is strong enough, it invades agriculture.

AGRICULTURE UNDER FEUDALISM

To each mode of production corresponds a maximum level of population which can be fed within a definite territory. It is possible that at the time of their migrations the Germans had reached this limit and that the pressure of overpopulation pushed them into the Roman Empire; but this is a point open to discussion. What is certain, however, is that due to the transition to the higher mode of production which their contact with the Romans produced, the food resources at the disposal of the German peoples increased considerably in the period following the migrations. Once peace was restored, the population grew rapidly, and new lands were continually brought into cultivation. The collapse of German power in Poland in the 15th century marked the end of the process of German

colonisation in the east. About this time the population of the
middle reaches of Europe had expanded considerably, if not actually
reached the limits within the given mode of production. Land became
scarce. This process induced the most bitter and violent conflicts
between the peasantry and feudal nobility, from which the latter
emerged, almost everywhere, the victor. The triumphant nobility
took up commodity production in a unique combination of feudalism
and capitalism. On its huge estates it began to produce surplus value,
but on the basis of feudally-subjugated forced labour. Forestry lent
itself best to feudal-capitalist exploitation[1] to the bulk production
of commodities. As soon as urban expansion increased the demand for
wood, the lords made a drive to acquire the forests, either by dis-
possessing the land-communities or by restricting the peasant's rights
of usage.

If in areas where a market for wood existed, it was not difficult
to convert forests into private property, administered on capitalist
lines, but still under feudal forms, it was no less easy, where the
market for pastoral products (specially wool) expanded and where natural
conditions were favourable, to pass over to livestock production on a
capitalist basis; like forestry, livestock production is neither labour
--nor capital--intensive, and involves few complications. This form of
extensive production requires only private ownership of large pastoral
tracts, which the lords made every effort to acquire in the course of
the 15th and 16th centuries in England and Spain, later in northern
Germany.

The trend of growing production for the market compelled the feudal
lords to expand their own estates at the expense of peasant land, either
by circumscribing more narrowly than before the limits of the common
lands, or directly by expelling peasants; and, on the other hand, to
exact more from the peasantry in the way of dues. Thus even before
population pressure really built up beyond a critical point, the resources available to the peasantry in the form of arable and pasture
land were progressively shrinking. The profound changes which this
introduced into the peasant's way of life were already clear in the
matter of his diet. The level of meat consumption in the earlier
period is indicated by Kloeden's calculation that at Frankfurt-on-
Oder annual per capita meat consumption was 250 lbs c. 1308 for Breslau
in the 1880s the corresponding figure is only 86 lbs. In the course of
the 16th century the German peasant became progressively impoverished
and eventually ceased to consume meat. Both the intensified exploitation of the peasantry due to heavier dues and the decline in stock-
raising had adverse effects on the peasant holding--either because of
a smaller supply of manure at a time when intensive cultivation was
becoming more necessary than ever as agriculture was being forced to
increase its own supplies to the towns, or because the enhancement
of labour-rent (cervees) diverted the peasant's labour time and draught

resources from his own holding. The progressive soil exhaustion which
this produced meant that the peasant could just survive in good years,
and was now bound to be ruined in bad ones. Bad years in fact became
more frequent: for example, between 1698 and 1715 the population of
France declined from 19 to 16 millions due to repeated crises. The
persistence of heavy feudal levies led to a flight of the peasantry
into wage labour or beggary. By 1750, as Quennay observed, a quarter
of the arable land was uncultivated; immediately before the French
Revolution, according to Arthur Young, the uncultivated portion reached
one-third.

The growing pressure of population had already led to a more
intensive mode of cultivation in England. Side by side with this process, the abandonment of the traditional mode of exploitation was accelerated by the appearance of a big peasantry with marketable surpluses. For this stratum the reservation of land for common pasturage
appeared as a criminal waste. To effect the transition from this system it became necessary to break up the medieval compromise between
communal and private property, to establish the dominance of private
property, divide up common pasture, surpress communal rights of usage
and consolidate holdings into continuous stretches of land under the
landowner's complete control. Yet the rural population itself produced
no class which could carry through this revolution in the conditions
of rural property.

In modern social conditions, the development of agriculture loses
its former independence and becomes bound up with social development
as a whole. The revolutionary impetus which agriculture itself failed
to produce was thus provided by the towns. The economic evolution of
the town had totally transformed the economic situation of the countryside and prepared the ground for a transformation in the conditions of
rural property. In the course of this evolution the towns saw the birth
of new classes which set themselves in revolutionary opposition to
feudal power and carried through a political and juridicial revolution
in the countryside, sometimes despite the peasantry. In France this
transformation bore the character of an illegal and violent act which
in one blow both abolished the feudal charges on the peasantry and
distributed land formerly included in the domains of the clergy and
(now emigre) nobility. In Prussia, as in Germany in general, the
change occurred in a peaceful and legal fashion, through the agency of
a hesitant bureaucracy which proceeded slowly and ensured that the
peasants paid dearly, to state and nobility, for the abolition of the
dues imposed on them (on one estimate, payments may have totalled 3
billion marks). The modernisation of agriculture followed a similar
course in Russia after the Crimean War. The peasants were relieved
both of serfdom and of the better part of their land. But regardless
of the pacific and legal character which it assumed in these cases,
the revolution in property resulted in establishing the dominance of
private ownership of the land. That is, the way was now open for the
rise in agricultural capitalism.

MODERN AGRICULTURE

In the course of the 19th century, technical improvements in the raising of livestock--a sector which expanded rapidly in the early part of the century, favoured by the expanding urban market for meat and by low transport costs--coupled with the adoption of improved methods of farming expanded acreage under cereals, and made higher yields possible (due to the increased supply of manure and draught animals)--in France, for example, the average yield of wheat per hectare rose from 10.2 hectolitres in 1816-20 to 15.8 hectolitres by 1891-95. The trend of rising productivity was reinforced by the shift to more rational cropping patterns (based on an infinite number of combinations, such as cereals-tobacco, cereals-rapeseed) and paralleled by the increasing specialization of agricultural production within its different branches and between them. Where conditions were ripe, this growing division of labour led back to the production of lifestock, but now on a higher, more intensive basis, and in a capitalist form (cf. the south of England). Superimposed on this growing overall specialization of agricultural production was the intensified specialization of prevailing within the enterprise itself. In feudal agriculture, big holdings had been no different from small ones in this respect. The lords derived the greater part of their labour and equipment from the enserfed peasantry; the difference consisted, not in the serfs' greater specialization, but in the fact that the serfs showed far less enthusiasm in the execution of their tasks on the demesene than they did in the operation of their own farms. Big holdings could develop a division of labour qualitatively superior to that prevailing on peasant farms only in modern conditions, where on big holdings as on small, production is carried on with the proprietor's own implements, draught animals, workers, etc.

The growing specialization of agricultural production enchances the peasant's dependence on the market. He is now compelled to buy on the market not only his means of production, but even a part of his subsistence. In particular where increasing specialization displaces the production of cereals to second place, he is forced to buy grain or flour on the market. Growing specialization increases the volume of market transactions in seed and draught animals. Finally, the revolution in means of transport increases this dependence on the market and produces incessant changes in the market conditions which peasants face. As an inter-regional transport network develops on top of the sporadic rail connections linking this or that isolated region to the world market, the relative profitability of one branch of production, e.g., cereals, collapses, while that of another, e.g., dairy products, increases. The revolution in transport introduces new seed varieties from other countries, and widens the boundaries of the trade in horses, cows, etc. But the modernization of agriculture reaches its high point only when the latest achievements of engineering, chemistry and biology are introduced into the countryside from the towns.

First in importance is the production of machinery for employment
in agriculture. Despite the obstacles which it encounters in agriculture (the high technical base which it presupposes, low utilisation rates, low agricultural wage rates, its greater requirements of
skill), the employment of machinery has expanded rapidly on the continent and in Britain, where it started and the USA. However, the
situation in Germany is less favourable than in either of these countries.
In the west and south the land is too fragmented; in the east, where big
holdings predominate, the standard of living and level of education
of the agricultural labourers is quite low and the enterprises producing machinery dispersed over large distances. The most favourable
situation prevails in Saxony, where big holdings are combined with an
intelligent working population and numerous machine shops.

Machinery has several advantages, apart from the obvious one that
it saves labour. Machines like threshers and reapers save time as
well, and in a context of expanding commodity production economy of
time is of considerable importance. Savings in labour and time also
increase the independence of the producer vis-a-vis his workers, who
generally advance their highest wage claims during the harvest, when
they are least dispensiable. It is, for example, not uncommon even
for farms which use wage labour for reaping to be equipped with reapers solely as a precaution against strikes. In his book on the Silesian
and Polish workers who search for employment in Saxony, Karger reports
that all the big sugar estates of this province are equipped with reapers,
chiefly as a means of preventing workers from going on strike. Further,
machinery can execute tasks which are either difficult to perform, or
are generally not performed, manually, e.g., deep ploughing
which has become more common now due to steam ploughs, the use of which,
according to Perels, raises crop yields and ensures speed of operation.
Steam ploughs are wide-spread on the big holdings of the province of
Saxony, and are becoming more widespread on the big estates in Austria
and Hungary. In Prussia there has been a prodigious growth in the
employment of steam-driven machinery of various categories. More
spectacular are the achievements in the field of electrical machinery,
which in practice has meant mainly the electrical plough.

In the space of a few years, due to the increasing employment of
machinery, the expansion of electricity in the countryside, the development of a railway network for the long-distance transportation of goods
of a low specific value (straw, fertiliser, etc.), improvements in irrigation, drainage and fertiliser technology agriculture has become one of
the most revolutionary, if not the most revolutionary of all modern forms
of production. A final symptom of the increasingly scientific character
of modern agriculture is the expansion of various institutes specializing
in agronomy, the growing complexity of the courses taught in them, and
the penetration of agronomy, as a specific branch of science, into the

established universities in Germany, Austria, France, Italy, etc. The
teaching of agriculture in the cities is the most striking illustration
of its complete dependence on the town and of the seminal role of the
town in stimulating the progress of agriculture. The tight alliance of
science and business which characterizes the whole modern system of production is nowhere expressed more sharply than in agriculture.

THE CAPITALIST CHARACTER OF MODERN AGRICULTURE
VALUE, SURPLUS VALUE, PROFIT:

In modern conditions agricultural production is impossible without
money, or, what amounts to the same thing, without capital; in the
modern organization of production, any sum of money which is not used
for personal consumption, can become, and generally does become, capital,
or value which produces surplus value.

Modern agricultural production is capitalist production. In it
occur the specific features of the capitalist mode of production, but
under special forms. To understand these forms, we shall make a slight
digression at this point into the realm of economic abstractions, so
that our own theoretical position, based on Marx's theories of value,
surplus value, profit and ground rent, may be clarified.

When we look at modern agriculture, two basic characteristics immediately strike us: individual ownership of land, and the commodity
character of its products. Here we are concerned only with the second.
A commodity is a product of human labour that has been produced not for
the consumption of the producer himself or of his retinue, the producer
having no need of it, but for the process of exchange. In a system of
developed commodity production, each commodity possesses a fixed exchange
value. The particular sum of money, or cash, which exchanges for a given
commodity, is called the price of that commodity.

The value of a commodity expresses itself only as a tendency or a
law which tends to govern the phenomenon of exchange or sale. The result of this phenomenon (sic) is the real exchange relationship at any
particular moment, i.e., the real price. The labour theory of value,
according to which the value of a commodity depends on the amount of
labour that is socially necessary for its production, is fiercely resisted in modern university courses. But if we examine the question
more closely, it should become clear that all the various objections
spring from a confusion of commodity values on the one hand with use
value, on the other hand with price. The established university theories
of value end up by conceiving the utility of a product and the demand
for it as constituents of its value, and both are thus juxtaposed with
the labour embodied in it. But use value is a precondition of commodity
value, not the factor which determines the amount of this value. The
condition of each act of exchange is that any two commodities should be

different in nature: unless this holds true, there would be no basis for exchange. But between the use values of any two commodities different in nature there cannot obtain a quantifiable relationship. When I say, a yard of cloth has a value ten times that of one pound of iron, it would be absurd to think that this means that it is ten times more useful, or satisfies ten times as many wants.

What holds true for utility of a greater or lesser order holds true, equally, for wants of a greater or lesser order. Variations of supply and demand can, of course, explain why the price--note that I do not say "value"--of a given commodity can rise or fall from one day to the next: but they cannot themselves explain why there should be a constant relation between the prices of two sorts of commodities, why, for example, for several centuries, and despite numerous oscillations, a pound of gold possessed an average value thirteen times greater than a pound of silver. The only explanation is that for several centuries the conditions of production of these two metals remained more or less constant. It would be ridiculous to argue that the demand for gold was always thirteen times greater than the demand for silver.[2]

Simple commodity production is the primitive type of this form of production. It is characterized by the fact that under its regime the producers are not only free and equal vis-a-vis one another, but owners of the means of production which they operate. But simple commodity production has never prevailed in its pure form, no more than any of the other epochs of economic development: it has always mixed with other economic forms, such as natural economy (where the goal of production is the producer's immediate consumption), feudal economy, the economy of trade guilds. Likewise, the law of value was not always fully effective: it became effective precisely to the degree that, within the given limits, there developed a regular production for the market on the basis of free competition. At a certain stage of development, capitalist commodity production replaces simple commodity production, that is, the worker ceases to be the owner of his means of production. The capitalist stands opposed to the worker, who has lost his property; the worker can no longer work directly for the consumer; he has to work for the capitalist employer, owner of the means of production, to whom he sells his labour power; he becomes a hired worker.

Only when production is organised on this basis does commodity production become the dominant form of production: the natural economy disintegrates rapidly, exploitation on a feudal or guild basis is no longer possible, producers are free and equal. But precisely this organisation of production, which creates the conditions for the unfettered operation of the law of value, produces, between value and market price, an intermediary which masks the law of value and modifies its effects, namely, the costs of production, or money expenditure necessary for the production of a commodity. Under simple commodity production it would make no sense to have commodity prices determined as a function of costs of production. Take a rural weaver who produces his own raw material and manufactures his own loom. In his case no expenditure is involved; his product costs him only his labour. Fixing prices according to costs of production does not seem so absurd in the case where, as a consequence of the division of labour, the producer purchases his means of production. As with the weaver in our first example, when weaving is carried on on a professional basis the value of the cloth is likewise determined by the socially necessary labour time involved in its production; but this is no longer so apparent. The professional weaver produces neither the thread nor the loom; he buys them. Their value constitutes his costs of production, and these enter into the value of the final product, the whole of the value of the thread and part of the value of the loom. But these costs of production do not compose the total value of the cloth; to obtain its total value, we have to add to production costs the value created by the weaver's labour. The matter is entirely different under capitalist commodity production. The owner of the means of production and the worker are two distinct persons. The capitalist who wishes to start production must buy not only the raw materials, and instruments of labour, as with the weaver in our second example, but the worker's labour power as well. Of course, for the capitalist all the elements of production resolve themselves into money expenses, or costs, but this is true only of the capitalist. The production of commodities does not cost him labour, but money; for him it is the costs of production, the money he has spent, which determine the price, not the labour expended. Now the real costs of production do not exhaust the costs of production which the capitalist takes into account when calculating his prices. If the price of his commodity were equal to the sum of money which he advances by way of expenditure on production, he would gain nothing from its sale. Profit is the goal of capitalist production. If an investment yields no profit, it would be better for the capitalist to spend the same amount on his personal consumption. It is precisely the profit which makes a certain sum of money capital. Capital may be defined as any sum of money advanced to yield a profit. The capitalist therefore adds to his total costs of production a certain increment. What he means by "costs of production" are his outlay on production plus the average profit; he calculates the price of his commodity according to costs defined in this way. Adam Smith had already made the distinction between labour value which regulates the fluctuations of market prices under simple commodity production, and the modification of value, under capitalism, by the costs of production or natural price (not value, as Brentano imagines), i.e. what Marx calls the price of production. The progress that political economy has made in the modern universities over the "outdated" economists like Smith is evident in the fact that after confusing simple commodity production and capitalist commodity production, it goes on to confuse value, natural price and market price, and asserts that the classical theory of value must be abandoned because "natural value" does not explain price movements.

In Ch. 7 of Book One (Wealth of Nations) Smith states that in any given country there is an average rate of wages, profit and rent; he calls these average rates, natural rates. Like value, the "natural" rate of profit only exists as a tendency; just as prices gravitate towards value, profits gravitate toward the natural or average profit. But what determines the sum of this "natural" profit? Here neither Smith nor Ricardo nor any of the bourgeois economists tell us anything; they resort to factors like the degree of risk, the level of wage rate, and so on, but these factors only explain the margin separating actual profits and average profits, just as supply and demand only explain the margin separating market price and value or price of production; they do not explain the average rate of profit at any given moment; they provide an explanation as to why the rate of profit is 19 percent here or 21 percent there, and not the average rate of 20 percent, but what they do not explain is why the average rate is 20 percent and not 200 percent or 2000 percent for example. Marx was the first to provide an explanation with his theory of surplus value. Of course, Marx was not the first to discover the fact of surplus value (you can find it in Ch. 6, Book One, of the Wealth of Nations). But he was the first to show in a detailed and systematic way how surplus value is generated and how it functions, and all the discoveries of Menger and his colleagues put together will not change that.

Surplus value arises from the fact that at a certain stage of development of technique man's labour power can produce a sum of products greater than that necessary for his own preservation and re-production. Under simple commodity production this net product takes the form of commodities, but we could not call it surplus value as yet, because at this stage the human labour power which generates values does not itself possess a value, as it is not yet a commodity. In this case the surplus product accrues to the worker, and he can use it to augment the well-being of his family, to build up reserves, and so on. A part of the net product is alienated by way of payment of dues and interest charges. Under simple commodity production merchant's profit results from the sale of commodities above their value and from the fact that they are bought below their value. As competition intensifies and the situation of the producer becomes more vulnerable, this source of profit becomes more widespread. We are already on the threshold of capitalist production when we reach this stage. It is not difficult to see that instead of extorting products from the producer below their value, the merchant may prefer to exploit the worker's precarious situation to convert him into a hired labourer, i.e., one who produces commodities no longer on his own account, but for the capitalist and one who earns his living not from the sale of his produce, but from the sale of his labour power. Labour power becomes a commodity and acquires a value equal to the value of the subsistence necessary for its repro-duction. The surplus of value which the worker produces over and above the value of his own labour power is thus surplus value. The whole of this surplus value accrues to the capitalist when the price of labour power, the wage, is fixed according to its value.

    In industry the entire product generated by hired labour accrues
to the capitalist. The value of this product is equal to the value of
the means of production employed plus the value of the worker's labour
power (in common language, his wage) plus surplus value. It is this
last component which constitutes profit. But the transformation of
surplus value into profit is an even less simple operation than the
transformation of value into price. What the capitalist advances in
production is not labour, but capital. To him profit appears not as
the product of the surplus labour of his workers, but as the product
of his capital. He calculates the rate of his profit not according to
the quantity of labour employed, but according to the sum of capital
advanced. It follows that at a given and uniform rate of surplus
value, different capitalists will realise different rates of profit
according to the different sums of capital advanced. Suppose there are
3 enterprises with a uniform rate of surplus value, a uniform period of
circulation of capital and identical quantities of variable capital;
suppose that they are distinguished only by the amount of constant
capital they employ. The first has an exceptionally low constant
capital, the second an exceptionally high constant capital (e.g., a
chemical factory which employs relatively few workers) and the third
an average constant capital. We make one final assumption, namely,
that the entire amount of the constant capital is consumed in the
course of a year and reappears in the value of the final product.
Then assuming that each enterprise employs 100 workers at a wage of
1000 francs, that the rate of surplus value is uniform at 100 per cent,
but that the constant capital becomes progressively larger as we go
from the first enterprise (say a timber yard) to the one with average
constant capital (e.g., a factory producing furniture) and from there
to the third enterprise (a chemical factory); by the amounts shown
below:

Enterprise	Capital			Surplus Value	Surplus value to total capital
	Variable	Constant	Total		
A	100000	100000	200000	100000	1/2
B	100000	300000	400000	100000	1/4
C	100000	500000	600000	100000	1/6

    If commodities sold at their value, A would realise a profit of
50 percent, B a profit of 25 percent, and C a profit of 16.6 percent.
The supreme law of the system of capitalist production, namely, the
equality, not of men, but of profits, would be violated here in the
most blatant manner. Capital would avoid branch C like the plague,
and rush headlong into branch A. In branch C supply would fall and
prices would consequently surpass value; the reverse would take place
in branch A, and finally prices in A and C would attain a level at
which they would yield the rate of profit in B. This rate of profit
is the average rate which determines the price of production. Then

we shall have:

Enter-prise	Total capital	Surplus value	Total value of the produce	Rate of profit (& profit)	Total price of production of the product
A	200000	100000	300000	25% (5000)	250000
B	400000	100000	500000	25%(100000)	500000
C	600000	100000	700000	25%(150000)	750000
	1200000	300000	15000000	25%(300000)	1500000

A certain margin thus separates prices of production as determined by "costs of production" from the value of the product, but this margin does not abolish the law of value, it merely modifies it. This law remains the regulator operating behind prices of production, and it remains completely valid for the total mass of commodities and the total mass of surplus value. It constitutes the solid foundation both of prices and production and of the rate of profit, without which neither of these would be founded on anything.

DIFFERENTIAL RENT, ABSOLUTE RENT

Besides the "normal" profit, capitalists can realise surplus profits, e.g. when thanks to exceptionally efficient machinery (which only they possess) they produce below the prices dictated by the normal conditions of production. Suppose there are two capitalists, whom we can call Muller and Schulze respectively. Muller produces, with the average sort of machinery, 40,000 pairs of shoes each year on a capital of 320,000 frs. At an average rate of profit of 25 percent Muller would have to fix the price of his shoes so as to obtain a profit of 80,000 frs., otherwise he will regard the business as a loss. His total price of production would thus be 400,000 frs., each pair of shoes selling at 10 frs. On the other hand, thanks to his excellent machinery, Schulze produces 45,000 pairs for an identical investment. For him the unit price of production is not 10 frs., but 8.00 frs. But he is free to sell his shoes at the normal production price, like his competitor, i.e., 10 frs. So he receives 450,000 frs., that is, apart from his usual profit of 80,000 frs., he receives the tidy sum of 50,000 frs. by way of "surplus profit."

Now we can transpose this to agriculture. Instead of two factories we can imagine there are two fields (each of 20 hectares for example) of unequal fertility, both exploited on a capitalist basis. Both comprise an identical investment, 3200 frs., but one produces 400 quintals of wheat, the other 450. Then assuming an average rate of profit of 25 percent, the first capitalist would have to raise the unit price of his wheat by 2 frs. (to make 10 frs. per quintal) if he is to realise a normal profit. His price of production will be 10 frs. and his profit 800 frs. The second capitalist also sells his wheat at 10 frs. per quintal, for which he receives a total of 4500 frs., and realises, as a result, apart from his average profit, a surplus profit of 500 frs.

On the surface the two cases seem identical, but there is a basic difference. In agriculture this type of profit is subject to very special laws, and constitutes a specific category of political economy--ground rent.

The land, in which we include the productive forces that are indissolubly tied to it, is in fact a means of production of a very special type. Its quantity cannot be increased at will, and its quality varies from one instance to the next; furthermore, the particular qualities of a given piece of land are specific to it and cannot be transferred at will. In each of these respects land and machinery are quite different therefore. Due to the mobility of capital, in industry a surplus profit is an exceptional and transitory phenomenon. The situation is different in agriculture where surplus profit flows from the different fertility of different pieces of land. This inequality is determined by natural conditions and, given the level of technique, is a fixed quantity. Even supposing all other conditions of production were identical, there would still remain this difference in the quality of the soil. Ground rent is for this reason not, as in industry, a transitory phenomenon, but one which persists. In the second place, in industry price of production is determined, as we saw, by the normal profit plus the average costs of production. Enterprises which produce at below average costs realise a super profit. In agriculture, on the other hand, cost price is not determined by necessary costs of production on an average land. The capitalist seeks, apart from his cost price, an average profit. He will not therefore cultivate land of less good quality except under certain conditions, i.e., when the volume of supply is such that the price of food is sufficiently high to promise an adequate return even when land of less good quality is cultivated. In other words, in agriculture the price of production is determined not by the necessary costs of production on an average land, but by those prevailing on land of the worst quality.

From these two differences there springs a third one. As industry expands, population and thus the demand for foodstuffs also expand. New land has to be brought under cultivation. From this it follows that in the normal course of economic development differences in fertility between different pieces of land under cultivation will tend to increase, and, as a result, so will ground rent.

We can show this with a few numerical examples. Suppose cultivation extends from land of bad quality which yields, for an investment of 3200 frs., 400 qs of wheat, to land of even worse quality, which for the same investment (and on the same area) yields only 320 qs.

We can see that as a result of the extension of the boundaries of cultivation, A's ground rent rises by an additional 500 frs. to 1650 frs. B, which formerly (table one) yielded no ground rent, now has a ground rent of 1000 frs.

TABLE ONE

Type of Land	Wheat produced (qs)	Capital advanced (frs)	Rate of profit	Price of production total	Price of production unit	Overall price of prod. total	Overall price of prod. unit	Ground rent
A...	450	3200	25%	4000	8,88	4500	10	500
B...	400	3200	25%	4000	10,00	4000	10	0

TABLE TWO

A...	450	3200	25%	4000	8,88	5650	12,50	1650
B...	400	3200	25%	4000	10,00	5000	12,50	1000
C...	320	3200	25%	4000	12,50	4000	12,50	0

In the course of capitalist development the rate of profit tends to fall. On the other hand, ground rent has a tendency to rise. Suppose, however, that land of a better quality is brought into cultivation after land of poor quality: in that case we would have,

TABLE THREE

X...	500	3200	25%	4000	8,00	5000	10	1000
A...	450	3200	25%	4000	8,88	4500	10	500
B...	400	3200	25%	4000	10,00	4000	10	0

In this case, A's ground rent remains constant (cf. table one), but land X, which formerly yielded no rent, now yields 1000 frs. The mass of ground rent accruing to the owners is of a greater value, both absolutely and relative to the capital advance, than in table one.

It is also possible that new land brought into cultivation is of such quality and extent that the price of foodstuffs falls, with the result that poor land no longer yields a rent and has to be abandoned. In this case, the ground rent of certain specific lands will fall, and yet, even here, the total mass of ground rent can rise both absolutely and relatively, as shown below:

TABLE FOUR

Y...	600	3200	25%	4000	6,00	5328	8,88	1328
X...	500	3200	25%	4000	8,00	4440	8,88	440
A...	450	3200	25%	4000	8,88	4000	8,88	0

In this case land B goes out of cultivation, while A no longer yields a rent, and the rent of X falls from 1000 frs. (table 3) to 440 frs. And yet the total mass of ground rent increases from 1500 frs. (table 3) to 1768 frs.

Differences in the fertility of the soil are not the only component of ground rent; others include locational differences or distance from markets. As demand rises in any given centre, the distances over which foodstuffs are now sought increase. But the lands located furthest away are only cleared for commodity production when the price of foodstuffs is sufficiently high to cover transport costs, in addition to production costs, and yield an average profit. Lands located nearest to the market thus obtain a ground rent. In the following example, lands situated at unequal distances from the market are assumed to have the same degree of fertility; transport costs for wheat are assumed to be 1 centime per quintal per kilometre:

Land	Distance from market (km)	Wheat produced	Price of production	Transport costs	Market price of 400 qs wheat	Ground rent
A...	5	400	4000	20	4400	380
B...	50	400	4000	200	4400	200
C...	100	400	4000	400	4400	0

This type of ground rent also has a tendency to rise in proportion to the growth of population. But improvements in transport which reduce transport costs counteract this tendency.

Finally, a third type of ground rent is possible, which is particularly important in countries of long-established cultivation. The production of foodstuffs may be increased not only by clearing new, formerly uncultivated land, but also by improving land already under cultivation, employing more labour on it, investing more capital in it and so on. If this additional capital invested in land of a better quality realises a profit which exceeds any profit accruing from land of poorer quality which would in the absence of such investments, have to be cleared and brought into cultivation, the additional profit constitutes a new surplus profit or rent. Let us go back for a moment to table 1. Let us assume that land B in that table is part of the worst land and that its price of production (10 frs per qu of wheat) is the current market price. Now if an additional sum of capital is invested in A, say its total capital doubles, and this new investment, while not as productive as the original investment, is nevertheless more productive than any investment would be on the worst land, we would have,

TABLE FIVE

Invest-ment	Wheat	Level of investment	Rate of profit	Production costs	Market price per q.	Market price total	Ground rent
A1...	450	3200	25%	4000	10	4500	500
A2...	420	3200	25%	4000	10	4200	200
A1+2...	870	6400	25%	8000	10	8700	700
B...	400	3200	25%	4000	10	4000	0

The total value of A's rent increases due to the additional investment.

Now all these various types of ground rent have one common character-istic: they all derive from differences in fertility or location, i.e., they are differential rents. Where the agricultural capitalist and the landowner are two distinct persons, the surplus profit accrues to the latter. But normally the landowner will not receive any more than this (assuming that the tenant cultivates according to capitalist norms), for unless the tenant expects to retrieve an average profit, he will not continue business and the landowner will have no tenants left. On the other hand, where the landlord's rent-charge is less than the ground rent, a part of the surplus profit will stay with the tenant and he will thus have realised a profit higher than the average.

In industry the persistence of a surplus profit depends on a capital-ist being able, due to some exceptional circumstances, to limit compe-tition to some extent. Such is the case with landed property. The latter constitutes a monopoly, and land can be withdrawn from cultivation if it yields no rent. Even the owner of the worst piece of land, one which yields no differential rent, has an interest in obtaining ground rent all the same. He could, for example, clear the land when market prices are sufficiently high to yield a surplus profit, but this condition is not necessary to the existence of such a profit. It was Marx who first studied the laws of the particular form of rent called absolute ground rent. Like every monopoly price, the price of foodstuffs and provisions generally, determined by the monopoly constituted by landed property, can rise above the value of those commodities, though there are limits to which the landowners can push up the level, of absolute rent.[3] To summarise, differential rent results from the capitalist character of production, not from the private ownership of land. Absolute rent results from private ownership of land and from the opposition of interests that obtains between the landowner and the society as a whole. Secondly, differential rents do not, like absolute rent, enter into the determination of the prices of agricultural produce. The former derive from prices of production, the latter from the margin between market prices and prices of production. While the former consists in a surplus profit, the latter can only be a charge, levied by the landowner, on the existing mass of values, a charge on the mass of surplus value, hence a cut in profits or wages. When a rise in the price of foodstuffs is accompanied by a rise in wages, profits shrink. When the rise in food prices exceeds that in wages, it is the workers who stand to lose. Finally it is also possible, and is generally the case, that both workers and capitalists share the loss to the benefit of the landowner.

Fortunately there are limits to the extent to which absolute rent can be pushed up. Due to the competition of overseas products, absolute rent has fallen to the gain of the working classes. If the condition of the latter has improved since 1870, particularly in England, this is due in large part to the fall in absolute rent.[4]

LARGE HOLDINGS AND SMALL HOLDINGS

The further capitalism penetrates agriculture, the deeper becomes the technical gulf separating the large holding from the small. The former is favoured by the operation of scale economies (in land, labour, means of production) at the level of the household, in the particular mode of circumscription) of the farm, and in the actual process of production. To begin with, fifty small peasant holdings require fifty ploughs, fifty harrows, fifty carts, etc., where perhaps one tenth this quantity would suffice on a large property (covering the same area). Thus the large holding realises considerable economies in draught animals and implements of production, even assuming that its process of cultivation is the same. Statistics pertaining to agricultural machinery show this. Among the few machines which can be employed on small as well as large holdings is the thresher. In 1883, to give one example, to every 1000 hectares of cultivated land, there were 2.84 steam-driven threshing machines on holdings in size classes ranging from 2 to 100 hectares, as against 1.08 on holdings above 100 hectares, and 12.44 threshing machines of other sorts, as against 1.93. No one would argue that this is because small holdings tend to use more steam-driven threshers than large ones. In spite of this economy in the use of machinery, it is possible that large holdings employ a larger number of implements, absolutely and relatively, because the character of cultivation on them is not the same. There is of course a whole series of implements, particularly machines, which cannot profitably be used on holdings below a certain level. According to Krafft, the minimum cultivated acreage necessary for the profitable use of certain implements is as follows:

		Hectares
for a plough with a team of	--	30
for seed-lips, reapers	--	70
for steam-threshers	--	250
for steam-plough	--	1000

Again, only the large holdings offer scope for the profitable use of electricity in cultivation.

We should recall that in the German Empire in 1895 of a total of 5.55 million agricultural holdings there were only 306,828 which exceeded 20 hectares, and only 25,061 which exceeded 100 hectares. The enormous majority of holdings are too small even for the profitable employment of a yoked plough, let alone any machinery. For every hundred holdings in different size classes, the number of farms employing various implements was as follows:

Size of holding (hectares)	Machines in general	Steam ploughs	Seed lips	Reapers	Steam threshers	Other threshers
less than 2	2.03	0.00	0.46	0.01	1.08	0.49
2-5	13.81	0.00	1.29	0.06	5.20	6.56
5-100	45.80	0.01	4.88	0.68	10.95	31.89
20-100	78.79	0.10	17.69	6.93	16.60	64.09
over 100	94.16	5.29	57.32	31.75	61.22	60.53

In each category it is the large holding that employs the most machinery. Leaving aside the thresher, machinery is scarcely used at all on the small holding.

The same principles hold in the employment of labour, human and animal. The small holdings spends proportionately more labour to obtain the same result, and however high its productivity, it cannot use labour with the same efficiency as the large holding. According to Reuning, there were 3.3 horses to every hundred acres of small peasant property in Saxony around 1860, against 1.5 to every hundred acres on the estates of the nobility. On the small holdings cows are used both to produce milk and other cows as draught animals. The large number of cows on small holdings is also, to some extent due to the fact that on such holdings the raising of cattle tends to be more important than the production of cereals as compared to the larger holdings.

Economies in the use of implements, draught animals and labour saving machinery implies, finally, an economy in the use of labour power itself. But if the stock of implements and draught animals is proportionately lower on the larger holdings, per unit of land area, and their use of labour power proportionately less, it is equally clear that they employ a greater absolute quantity of these factors than the small holdings. This only shows that the former are able to profit more from the division of labour than the latter. The large holding alone allows the degree of specialization and adaptation of the tools and implements to specific tasks that is the basis of the superiority of modern production over precapitalist production. The big landowner distributes

the various functions into two categories, those which require a particular aptitude or skill and those which demand a mere deployment of
effort. Functions of the first type are reserved for those of his workers who have shown a particular skill or diligence, and whose aptitude
and experience are likely to increase as a function of their specialization in a specific task. Workers work longer at a given job and
change jobs less frequently, with the result that big holdings eliminate
the loss of time and effort that characterizes frequent shifting of
labour from one task or place of work to another. Finally, the large
holding can benefit from the advantages of a planned and systematic
cooperation of a large number of workers to a specific end.

   The most important advantage accruing to the large holding from
its greater deployment of labour consists in the specialization of
tasks into purely manual ones and purely intellectual ones. We saw
earlier how important scientific management has become for agriculture.
Only the large holding can ensure the production on a scale sufficient
to require the services of the agronomist in the directtion and surveil-
lance of the different tasks. This scale varies with the type of cultivation: with cultivation of a highly intensive character, e.g., viti-
culture, it may be only 3 hectares; with more extensive modes of cultivation, e.g. livestock production, it could be 500 hectares. On an
average we can say that in central Europe a holding of 80-100 hectares
exploited extensively, requires enough management to occupy one
specialist whole time. But in Germany there were barely 26,000 holdings
of over 100 hectares in 1895, which explains why there is so little
trace of any rational agriculture in the country. Goltz argues that the
average yields are very low when compared to those which could be obtained, and are obtained, even on land of inferior quality through the
adoption of better methods of cultivation. With improved methods
Germany could produce an additional 100m quintals of grains without
any further expansion of acreage.

   The resistance that the peasant farm puts up before the large
holding is based not on its higher productivity[5] but on its lesser
needs. The large holding has to produce more than the small one to obtain the same net income, for its expenditure comprises the maintenance
costs of urban bourgeois workers. From this point of view, the medium
holdings are the worst sufferers, because of their proportionately
higher costs of management. The bigger the holding, the faster these
costs fall. Management of a farm of 100 hectares requires an agronomist; for a holding of 400 one functionary is the most you need: other
things being equal, the product is four times larger, while management
costs are only one and a half times a s great. Within the peasantry,
all other things being equal, the larger the holding the better it is;
the same holds for the class of big landowners. On the other hand,
at the limit dividing the peasant farm from the large holding, it is
possible that the peasant farm is superior, if not technically then at
least economically, to a bigger holding administered by an agronomist.

For the small estate owner the costs of management often exceed the value of its services.

To these and other advantages in the sphere of production, we should add those which accrue to the larger holdings in the sphere of credit and commerce. Of all the buyers and sellers engaged in the market, the peasant is undoubtedly in the worst situation. He is the worst off as far as his knowledge of the market goes, and the least able to make rapid gains from changes in the market or to forestall a slump. The more diversified character of his production entails buying and selling in various disparate markets. Apart from his implements the peasant has to buy draught animals, seed, fodder, fertilizer; he sells draught animals, grain, milk, butter, eggs, and so on. His dependence on the merchant is thus extreme. Both the intensity of this dependence and its effects are worst where the merchant is at the same time a usurer, that is, where the peasant's requirement of cash for the payments of taxes and interest forces him to part with his product at any price or even to sell it in advance.

We saw earlier that modern agriculture cannot do without capital. We also saw that outside of areas where renting is the dominant system, mortgages are the principal means of procuring money (apart from personal loans, which tend to be used as circulating capital, as against mortgages which are used to purchase fixed capital). In the acquisition of credit the large holding is again favoured by definite advantages. It costs no more, in labour or money, to register a mortgage of 200,000 frs. compared, say to one of 20,000 frs. Moreover, there is a definite economy of scale in the procuring of loans on mortgage (e.g. as Lafargue shows in his excellent article on "small landed property in France," a relatively small loan of 300 frs. entails a cost, by way of interest charges and ordinary expenses, of 48 1/2 frs). The fact that in Prussia big landed property is more heavily mortgaged than small property indicates not that the former is in a deeper crisis but only that peasants find it more difficult to procure loans on mortgage. Peasants are thus generally forced to resort to personal loans, which are far worse than mortgages. The big agriculturist sells his produce directly on the big market, he is in constant touch with it and consequently finds it easy to obtain as much credit as the merchant or industrialist in the economic centres which are the base of big capital. The isolated peasant who has only a small quantity of produce to sell, stays away from the big markets. He restricts his transactions to the merchant who resides in the neighbouring small town or who visits him. His commercial trans- actions have nothing to do with big urban capital. When the peasant needs cash, he borrows locally, often from a merchant, owner of the village or big peasant, all of whom know how to make as much profit from these small loans as the conditions of the rural capital market, the peasant's desperation and their own dominance permit. While capital- ism generates indebtedness in big property and small holdings alike, the character of small scale production binds it to medieval forms of debt incompatible with the requirements of capitalist production.

The advantages of large holdings thus include--a bigger proportion of cultivated acreage, economies in the consumption of labour power, draught animals, and implements of labour, efficient utilisation of all resources, the possibility of using machinery, division of labour, specialist management, a superiority in the market, easier access to credit. What for its part does the small holding show against these advantages? One of the most passionate advocates of small cultivation, John Stuart Mill defines as its most important characteristic the untiring labour of its workers. The peasant condemns himself and his family to forced labour. In agriculture the household and the holding are closely connected; it follows that child labour is at the disposal of the farm. In small scale cultivation, as in domestic industry, the use of child labour for family exploitation is even more pernicious than the hiring out of child labour for wages. The insanity of peasant labour was not, however, always inherent in the condition of the peasantry. Roshcer cites the example of Lower Bavaria where in the medieval period some 204 days of the year were holidays. The sort of overwork which prevails today only really begins when the produce of labour is sold on the market; it is the effect of sharpening competition. Under the pressure of competition, the intensity of labour must be increased in proportion to the technical backwardness of the farm. This process has a reverse side however. A holding which cannot compete on a technically superior basis is forced to exact the maximum effort from its workers. On the other hand, a holding where the workers can be driven to any limits does not require the latest technical equipment, as do holdings where the workers impose limits on the intensity of their labour. The possibility of increasing the labour time of a given workforce is a serious obstacle to technical progress. The intensification of labour on the peasant holding independently of any moral or other constraint cannot pass for an advantage of small scale production, even from the purely economic point of view.

The same holds for the peasant's modest needs. The self-restraint which compels the peasant to drive himself harder than the landless wage labourer compels him, to the same degree, to reduce his requirements to a minimum. Some examples will show how under the pressure of competition the condition of the small peasant can degenerate below that of the wage labourer. Around 1880 an Englishman observed that one could not imagine anything more wretched than the condition of certain French peasants. This is his description of one of their homes: "No windows, two panes which you cannot open, no air, no light, even with the door open. No shelves, tables or cupboards; on the floor, onions, dirty clothes, bread, plough-shares and a foul-smelling heap of rubbish...Every night, the men, women, children and animals sleep together in one mass..." Their greed is sordid, writes the author in another passage, regarding their obsession for saving the last penny. "It is impossible to imagine a life as backward or destitute of any sort of enjoyment..." But the situation is no better on the small holdings in England, going by the most recent report of the

parliamentary commission on agriculture (1897). In this report a small
peasant is quoted as saying, "We work harder than the day workers, like
slaves. Our only advantage is that we are free." Mr. Read described
the condition of the small farmer in the following terms: "Their only
means of survival is to work as hard as two day workers and consume no
more than one. Their children are much worse off and more badly looked
after than those of the day labourers." Of Germany, Hesse writes, "the
small peasant leads the most wretched existence you could imagine: the
day labourers are far better off. With their wages they are not exposed
to the whims of time, except in the bad years when their diet is not as
good." Their staple food is potatoes. A. Buchenberger provides another
example from Germany, from the commune of Bischoffingen. He compares a
medium holding of 11 hectares with a smaller one of 5 1/2. Due to
exceptional circumstances the medium holding was cultivated exclusively
by wage labour--a bad situation because the land was too small to compensate for the drawbacks of wage labour with the advantages of size; the
other holding was cultivated entirely by the owner and his family (his
wife and six elder children). The bigger holding ended with a deficit
of 933 marks, the smaller with a profit of 191 marks. The difference
consisted in this, that on the holding run on wage labour the diet was
fairly good, the equivalent of almost 1 mark per person per day, while
on the smaller farm where the family was fortunate enough to be working
for itself, the cost of consumption amounted to only 48 pfennings per
person per day, not even half as much-as on the other farm. If the
peasant proprietor's family had been as well fed as the wage labourers
of the bigger farm, instead of a profit of 191 marks, he would have
shown a loss of 1256 marks. The profit did not mean that his barns
were full; it meant that their stomachs were empty. A report from Weimar
district completes the picture: "If, in spite of so much poverty, land
sales are not more frequent, this is because our peasant, in order to
preserve his independence, knows how to endure an incredible amount of
suffering. As long as the smallholders do not plough their own fields
but work instead as day labourers, they are relatively well off." A
final example: Aughan compared two holdings, one of 4.6 hectares the
other of 26.5 hectares, taking into account their net income, not their
relative labour productivity. He found that the small holding yielded
a larger net income. How? The small peasant made his children work,
even the youngest aged seven. On their schooling he spent 4 marks per
year. The big peasant sent his children to school and his son aged
fourteen to a gymnasium at a cost of 700 marks per year--more than the
total household expenses of the small peasant.

For us the subhuman consumption of the small holding does not constitute any more of an advantage than the superhuman labour that it exacts.
Both facts show that the small farm is an economic phenomenon of the past,
and both are an obstacle to future progress. Thanks to them, small scale
exploitation produces a class of barbarians, almost outside society,
which combines in itself all the crudeness of primitive social forms
with the wretchedness and misfortunes of the civilised countries. That

conservative politicians should seek by any and every means to preserve this barbarism, the last bulwark of bourgeois civilisation, is not difficult to understand! Of course, there is no doubt that peasants show an enormous amount of diligence, and that diligence has an important role in production, both in agriculture and in industry. But we should not exaggerate this point. In fact, all the other advantages of the small holding--its excessive work, underconsumption, general ignorance-- reduces its effectiveness. The longer the peasant works, the less he consumes, the less time and money he has for his own development--the less diligence he can show. And what use is this diligence if he has no time to take proper care of his livestock and stables, overworks them and nourishes them as poorly as himself.

The peasant holding is worst where it fails to produce an adequate subsistence and the peasant has to resort to supplementary work. According to the 1895 census, of the total number of 5,600,000 owner cultivators only 37 percent are independent farmers without any subsidiary occuparion; of the 3,236,000 holdings under two hectares, only 13 percent-- 147,000 holdings in this latter category belong to independent cultivators with a subsidiary occupation, 690,000 to agricultural labourers, 743,000 to factory workers and 534,000 to independent artisans.[6]

THE LIMITS OF AGRICULTURAL CAPITALISM

Despite the evident superiority of large holdings in all the important branches of agriculture, a number of economists maintain that the two are in some sense equal and, further, that the large holding is disappearing. Now it is perfectly true that the most recent census data do not corroborate the view that small holdings have vanished before the expansion of the larger ones. In Britain and Germany, for example, taking the period 1885-95, we find that it is the medium holdings that have expanded most--in Germany mainly holdings from 5 to 20 hectares, in Britain holdings from 40 to 120 hectares. In America the declining average size of holding is to be attributed mainly to the disintegration of the big plantations of the south and the shrinkage of the uncultivated portion of land in the old north Atlantic zone (by contrast, in the states of the centre-north the average size has increased over the 1880s). Even so, it would be premature to conclude from these figures that the general direction of development in agriculture is quite different from that in industry. But "figures show...". This is true, but we have to ask, what do the figures show? To take an example, does the rise in the number of deposits on savings bank accounts show an increase in the welfare of the masses under capitalism? Take another example: suppose a small peasant in the past earned an income of 500 frs, but paid no rent and produced most of his subsistence on the farm; this peasant then encountered some mishap, was forced to move to the town and take up employment in a factory, for

1000 frs, double his previous income. The situation of such a peasant could only be worse now than it was formerly, because now he has to pay rent, spend money travelling to work, buy food which he previously produced hims elf, clothe his children, and spend more on doctors. To the statistician, however, it is beyond any doubt that his welfare has increased. In the same way, we should be careful not to draw any conclusions about the development of capitalism in agriculture from figures which show that far from decreasing, small holdings are on the increase. Such figures only provide guidelines for further research. What they do show, in the first instance, is that capitalism does not develop in agriculture in the s imple way we thought, and that its development is probably more complicated in this sector of the economy than in industry.

   In the march of modern industry the most different tendencies interact in opposing directions, and often it is difficult to determine those which are dominant in all this chaos. Large scale production does not implant itself in all branches of industry at once. It conquers them in succession. Where it establishes its dominance, the small enterprises disintegrate, which does not mean, however, that all the small enterpreneurs become workers of the large enterprise. They go over to other professions and encumber those. In this way capitalist competition succeeds in ruining even those branches of industry where large scale production is only weakly developed. Nor does this process express itself in a general decline of small enterprises; here and there they may actually increase, which could give the impression that they are therefore thriving. The branches of industry where small enterprises predominate numerically are domestic industries exploited by modern capitalism. The proliferation of enterprises in these sectors does not indicate a triumphant struggle against big capital. But even in the branches where machine production predominates, the progress of big industry does not necessarily entail the disappearance of small units. It ruins them, renders them superfluous from an economic point of view, but these units have enormous reserves of resistance. Hunger and overwork prolong their death-agony to extreme limits. The wretchedness of the Silesian weavers had become proverbial in our century, but for all that they still exist. Other factors perpetuate small scale production. Among these is the conscious political support of the State, which attempts to retard the disintegration of the middle strata. The development of capitalism itself induces a rebirth of feudal forms which for a long time were economically obsolete, for capitalism entails an increase in the mass surplus value, an increase not only in the mass of accumulated capital but also in the incomes of the capitalist class, and thus a growth in their wasteful expenditure. The growth of such expenditure leads to the renewed expansion of forest land required for the hunting sports, to the expansion of domestic service, to the rebirth of handicrafts whose products now pass for luxuries. But this process is sporadic, it operates only for some regions and some industries. In its decay small scale production follows a complicated and contradictory line of evolution, the general tendency of which is, however, firm.

The currents and tendencies which thwart the process of concentration in industry are active in agriculture as well. But in agriculture other tendencies operate, which do not appear in industry, and the question is thus much more complicated. To begin with, industrial means of production can be multiplied, whereas in agriculture land is, within the given conditions, a fixed resource. Under capitalism we can distinguish two broad movements--accumulation and centralisation. The centralisation of capital signifies, by contrast, a reunion of the different scattered capitals into one capital. In agriculture the big landowner cannot generally increase his wealth except through centralisation, reuniting several holdings into one. In industry accumulation proceeds independently of centralisation: a big capital can form without suppressing the automony of the lesser enterprises. When this suppression occurs, it is the effect of the formation of big industrial capital. Accumulation is here the starting point. On the contrary, where the land is fragmented into different properties and where small ownership prevails, large holdings can only acquire land by centralising several smaller ones. The disappearance of the smaller holdings is thus the precondition for the formation of a large enterprise. But this is not enough; it is also necessary that the holdings that are expropriated should form a continuous surface. Thus the mortgage banks which in any given year acquire hundreds of small properties cannot, for all that, concentrate them into one big one; they are scattered and dispersed in the most different localities. When the landowning class was dominant, it was easy for it to acquire land for the creation of big estates. They simply expelled the peasantry, through naked force or by some other means. But bourgeois property recognises only one basis for expropriation--default. As long as the peasant repays the capitalist and the state, his property is sacrosanct. This poses a serious obstacle to the growth of big landed properties. The process is most difficult where small property predominates exclusively. But even where the two co-exist, big property cannot always advance so easily, for the small holdings which come on the market are not always those which are required by the landowner for his expansion. An agriculturist who finds his existing property too small and wants to expand generally prefers to sell that property and acquire a new and better one rather than wait indefinitely for the chance to buy up the neighbouring land. This is one of the factors at the root of the great mobility of property in land, the numerous transactions in land which characterise the bourgeois epoch.

Secondly, in industry large units of production are always superior to small ones. In agriculture this is true only up to a point. The expansion of an industrial enterprise signifies a growing concentration of productive forces with all the concomitant economies--of time, costs, material, management, and so on. In agriculture, on the other hand, the expansion of a given enterprise on the same technical basis amounts to a mere extension of the area under cultivation, and thus entails a greater

loss of material, a greater deployment of effort, resources, time, for
the transport of material and men. These losses increase in proportion
to the degree of expansion. This might imply that profits are highest
where the property is small. This is not so, of course. The advantages
of the big holding more than compensate for the diseconomies of distance.
But this is true only within certain limits. Beyond these limits the
diseconomies of distance grow at a faster rate than the economies of
size. Beyond this point every further extension of the area of the
property diminishes its income. Naturally it is impossible to determine where these limits lie with any accuracy. Generally they differ
according to the nature of the soil and mode of cultivation. Certain
innovations tend to push the limits upwards, while other factors--an
increase in the labour force or stock of animals--has the reverse effect.
In general one might surmise that the limits beyond which marginal
revenue begins to decline are narrowest for forms based on intensive
cultivation and heavy concentrated doses of capital investment.

Following the same line of thought, the smaller a given holding,
the easier it is to exploit it intensively for a given amount of capital.
A small holding cultivated on an intensive basis can constitute a larger
enterprise than a bigger farm that is exploited extensively. The figures
which refer only to the size of a holding do not enable us to decide
whether a declining average size of holding reflects a real shrinkage
or cultivation at a higher level of intensity. Exploitation of forest
resources and pasture land generally takes place over large surfaces.
As production for the market developed, these forms of exploitation
were the earliest instances of capitalist production in agriculture.
They required neither machinery, nor specialists nor large sums of
capital. They require only the power to be able to dispossess the
peasantry and assert exclusive control over forests and pasture. Similarly, in the colonies where land is abundant and labour scarce, exploitation of forests and production of livestock were the earliest base of
large scale agricultural enterprise, e.g., in the USA, Argentina,
Uruguay, Australia. Here some of the pastoral holdings attained the
size of entire German principalities. The surfaces associated with
arable farming are generally smaller, but even here the maximum size
and average area exceed those characteristics of intensive forms
of production. Grain production in North America was based on a
system of clearing virgin land, exploiting it harvest after harvest,
then moving on to another piece of land. This nomadic agriculture
was equipped with the latest implements and excellent machinery, and
as the farmer incurred no cash expenditure in acquiring the land,
he could invest the major part of his cash on purchasing fixed capital.
This type of agriculture required no fertilizer, hardly any draught
animals nor any system of rotation. The whole cycle centred on a single
product, generally wheat, which thus absorbed all the implements,
machinery, and labour employed on the farm. In those conditions the
area of some holdings could become very large indeed. On the other

hand, in England production is of the intensive kind and requires substantial amounts of fertiliser and a system of crop rotation; farms
generally do not exceed 500 hectares; at any rate, 1000 ha. is the limit.
The average size of big capitalist holdings and smaller peasant farms
is generally bigger in America than in Europe. In Germany, for example,
a peasant with 70-100 hectares would normally be regarded as a big
peasant; in 1895 the proportion of such holdings was well below ten
percent. In America, on the other hand, almost half the total number
of holdings were between 40 and 200 hectares. But once private property
in land is firmly established, the foundations of this extensive agriculture crumble. Previously the peasant moved from arable to fallow,
exploiting only the top layer of the soil; as he is progressively confined to a single tract of land, he has to invest in more labour and
circulating capital and increase his stocking density; where either
labour or capital is scarce, the size of holding must be restricted.
Thus the declining average size of holding should not be taken as a
sign of the victory of the small holding over the big, but rather as a
concentration of production over smaller surfaces, which goes hand in
hand with an expansion of the capital employed in production, an increase
in the mass of labour employed and therefore, effectively an increase
in the scale of cultivation. The transition from extensive modes of
production to arable farming tends to diminish the average size of holdings, without diminishing and sometimes even increasing the scale of
production. The same applied when intensive stockbreeding replaces the
production of cereals.

Figures which only cite the surface area of holdings do not mean
much. This is the first conclusion. The second is that the process of
centralisation of the land for the expansion of a given property encounters specific limits for a given type of holding. The continuous
extension of the farm as a means of centralisation characterises only
those regions in which renting predominates. Where the system of owner
cultivation or wage labour exploitation prevails, centralisation expresses itself not through this expansion into contiguous areas but
through the acquisition of new properties (cf. the landowning gentry of
Prussia and Austria). When centralisation occurs on this basis it
implies the growth of a centralised management, that is, it implies the
emergence of a new form of exploitation, the latifundium. Under this
form centralisation can proceed indefinitely. The latifundium clears
the ground for the most advanced form of production known to modern
agriculture, the integration of several holdings under one management
and their progressive fusion into a single organism regulated by a
methodical division of labour and by the cooperation of several units.
But despite the economies which characterise such an enterprise
(economies of scale and of specialization as Krafft shows in his description of the Austrian latifundia), it meets one obstacle which only rarely
affects big industry--the shortage of manpower.

In modern urban industry the household and the unit of production are entirely separate entities. In agriculture this is not so, due to the greater dispersion of the rural population and the economic solidarity of the household and the farm. Survival of proletarianised farm labour thus depends on such labour being maintained by the employer's household (the spectrum of such labour would run from the totally proletarianised "free" labour who form an integral part of their employer's household, through various transitional types such as the Deputanten, Insleute and Keuerlinge, who generally live on the farm but in separate lodgings, to the semi-proletarian day workers who have households of their own). The situation of most categories of farm labour is not conducive to the perpetuation of this class in the countryside. The highest rates of reproduction thus characterise not these segments of proletarianised labour but the small owner cultivators for whom farm and household are one, and it is from their ranks that the large holdings draw their reserves of labour. But the deeper such holdings penetrate into the sector of small property, the lower becomes the rate of reproduction of this labour power. It follows that despite the technical superiority the large holding can never establish an exclusive domination in any country, even in the areas of its predominance. In most cases the shortage of manpower is the basic cause for the retreat of large holdings before smaller ones. This phenomenon takes two forms: either a portion of the large estate is parcellised and sold or leased out to small peasants or the big properties are themselves sold or auctioned and disintegrate into small properties. But like the triumph of the larger holding over the small, its inverse also runs up against definite limits. As the number of small cultivators proliferates on the periphery of the big farms, the pool of available manpower expands, thus reinforcing the vitality and dominance of the large holding. In such areas of recent proliferation the tendency for the large holding to expand is set in motion once again--as long as counteracting influences such as the location of new industries in the countryside do not restrain it. The figures for Germany show, for example, that in areas where big property predominates, the area occupied by it has tended to decline (the mean rate of decline over some thirteen years works out to 1.79 percent), whereas in areas where peasant holdings dominate, big property shows a tendency, however weak, to expand (the mean rate of expansion over the same period = 0.50 percent). The argument that landed property tends to alternate according to this rhythm is not at all incompatible with Marxist ideas, for Marx himself argued in his critique of Girardin's work that under capitalism agriculture is bound to oscillate between concentration and disintegration, though the oscillations are not as abrupt or violent as he imagined. But precisely this tendency shows how absurd it is to suppose that if small holdings continue to survive, then it must be because they are more productive. The real basis of their survival is the fact that they cease to compete with the large capitalist farms which develop by their side. Far from selling the same commodities as the larger farms, these small holdings are often buyers of these commodities. The one commodity which they do possess in abundance, and which the bigger holdings need, is their labour power.

PROLETARIANISATION OF THE PEASANTRY

We said in a preceding section that the ruin of the peasant's home-based industries compels the small peasantry to look for supplementary employment. The small peasant finds the time to do this because the farm does not absorb his efforts except sporadically. He earns cash not by selling his surplus produce, but by selling his surplus time. As a producer of foodstuffs he does not work for the market, but for his own consumption. His role in the market is that of the proletarian. Wage labour generally leads women who are employed in the factory to neglect, rather than completely abandon, the household; the same is true of the small peasant who hires himself out or who works at home for a capitalist. His farming becomes more and more irrational, too much for him, and he finds himself forced to impose limits on it.

A vigorous peasantry stabilises population, and is thus held in high regard by the militarist sections of the ruling class. But when the peasant is reduced to his farming, and deprived of any supplementary source of income, the limits of his property compel him to restrain the size of his family. Where, however, alternative avenues of employment grow up outside the farm, the population grows rapidly and acquires an increasingly proletarian character. The demand for land rises, not for the purposes of farming but as a means of setting up house. Thus the expansion of employment opportunities augments the number of holdings, both because it cuts down the size of existing holdings and because it accelerates the rate of population growth and consequently the demand for such holdings. Here the fragmentation of land predominates over its centralisation.

The price of a piece of land exploited on a capitalist basis is determined by the amount of its ground rent. Its purchase price is equal to its capitalised rent. An entrepreneur would not pay more than this if he is concerned about his rate of profit. But the simple commodity producer peasant does not calculate things in this way. He is a worker, owning no property, living off the produce of his labour, with a life style close to that of a wage labourer. To him land is a means of earning a living, not a source of profit or rent. He can live as long as the price he receives for his produce covers expenses and remunerates his labour. The simple commodity producer peasant can thus pay a higher price for a given piece of land than one who produces on a capitalist basis. But this method of calculation can lead the peasant into serious trouble, if according to the habits of a simple commodity producer he pays an excessive price for land when in his actual situation, if not formally, he has left the stage of

simple commodity production and has become involved in capitalist
production, not, of course, as an entrepreneur, but as a worker exploited by capital. If he has taken the land on mortgage, he has to
extract from it not only the equivalent of his wage, but a ground rent
as well, and an excessive price can be as ruinous to him as to the
entrepreneur. The agriculturist has no interest in high land prices
except when he ceases to be such, i.e., when he sells his holding.
With the small peasant for whom agriculture is wholly or mainly a part
of his household economy, and who earns the greater part of his income
by selling his labour power, things stand differently. Here the relationship between the price of land and the sale of commodities is no
longer relevant, at least as far as the buyer is concerned. For the
seller capitalised ground rent constitutes the minimum price of the
land; the buyer is concerned only with his needs and resources. For
this sort of buyer, who pays an increasingly higher price for land
as the demand for land increases, the labour expended on farming is not
considered a cost, it is taken to cost nothing.

It is a well known fact that small properties are proportionately
more expensive than large ones. Some enthusiasts of small property
have thus tried to argue on this basis that small holdings are superior
to large ones. But the structure of urban rents is analogous. In both
cases it is the desperate situation of the buyers which accounts for
the proportionately higher rents.

The smaller the property, the greater is the peasant's dependence
on supplementary work. The increasing predominance of such work, the
growing shortage of productive means, the increasing subordination of
farming to the needs of the household, the progressively more irrational
character of exploitation in such conditions and its greater affinity
to the proletarian home, where the most miserable results are obtained
at the cost of a tremendous waste of labour and an overworking of the
woman's labour--all this implies that the holding becomes less and less
capable of meeting the needs of the household. In the German Empire in
1895 76.5 percent of all holdings were under 5 hectares (58 percent
under two hectares), i.e. over 3/4 of them are compelled to buy grains
on the market and stand to lose, therefore, from a raising of the tariff.
The vast majority of the rural population no longer figures on the market
as a seller of foodstuffs, but as a seller of labour power and purchaser
of foodstuffs.

The fragmentation of the land along these lines is especially rapid
in areas where employment opportunities exist outside the limits of farming. In Belgium holdings of the smallest size, which expanded fastest
over the latter half of the nineteenth century, have come to account for
almost four fifths of the total number of holdings. Such a process of
fragmentation can lead to a consolidation of big property, as we saw.
Thus both extremes can grow simultaneously. In this case fragmentation
would work itself out chiefly at the cost of medium holdings. This is

the case in France and Prussia. Thus to the alternation of concentration and fragmentation, we must add the combined development of both.

If we leave aside agricultural wage labour, which occupies the time of even those peasants who may have up to six or eight hectares of land, one common subsidiary source of income is domestic industry. The origins of this form go back to the feudal epoch, when the peasant was at once an agriculturist and craftsman. Subsequently the expansion of urban industry forced him to specialise in agriculture, but in spite of this for a long time a number of domestic industries persisted in the peasant household. When agriculture fails to yield a sufficient income such industries tend to revive. But rural industry works not for clients, insofar as it assumes a commodity character, but for capitalists, merchants and brokers, and it tends to be concentrated in branches which require only a minimum of skills and simple equipment. It is located mainly near sources of raw materials (though these are often supplied by the capitalist, for example, yarn where weaving is concerned) or in regions where the soil is poor and the conditions favouring the expansion of big property absent. The limit to the expansion of such industry consists only in the availability of manpower; it is, otherwise, compatible with the smallest holding, the most primitive techniques, requiring no capital or only small doses, and the capitalist himself runs no risk in accelerating its expansion when market conditions favour this. In its periods of boom home-based industry intensifies the irrational character of small scale cultivation, because it absorbs all of the family's productive resources, accelerates the decay of cultivation proper, imposes new cropping patterns that are less labour-intensive and have a lower nutritional content, e.g., cabbages, potatoes--in short, it induces a regression to a form of agriculture inferior even to that which prevailed among the Germans during the great invasions. As the possibilities of technical progress in this branch are limited, the rural workers and capitalists who exploit them sustain competition by increasing the intensity of labour and reducing wages. Home-based industries are characterised by long hours of work, exhausting labour, the worst sort of dwellings, in short, they are characterised by revolting conditions. They form the worst kind of capitalist exploitation and the most degrading form of peasant proletarianisation. Small subsistence plots are the only means of perpetuating the death-agony of this form of industry before the incursions of factory production.

In pushing up the price of land, requiring a constant supply of labour and excluding specific categories of peasant labour from employment, rural-based modern large scale industries disrupt the labour resources at the disposal of the peasant farm, reduce the size of holdings and render cultivation more and more useless. But the conditions of work are better, and the large mass of scattered peasants are brought together in one place of work. Large scale industry augments the ranks of the proletariat without expropriating the small peasants, and even providing some of them with the means to safeguard their property against bankruptcy. Where neither this nor other forms of employment are available in the given surroundings, the peasants engage in long distance seasonal migrations, working on the big estates of Upper Bavaria or Saxony or moving from one country to another. In Ireland the rents of the small peasantry are paid out of the remittance from America. Such migrants, while they constitute a backward element in the towns, often acting as strikebreakers, or impeding unionisation, are tremendous agents of progress in their own villages: they pick up new ideas and needs which play a subversive and revolutionary role in these archaic surroundings. It is often these elements who become agitators and instigators of class discontent and class hatred in their home villages. Thus seasonal migrations play a contradictory role: they consolidate peasant property but at the same time they completely revolutionise the conditions of existence of the small proprietors and feed them with ideas and needs which contradict the conservatism of small property.

THE INCREASING DIFFICULTIES OF COMMERICAL AGRICULTURE

(i) For the industrialist the price of land is a minor part of his total expenses. In agriculture things are different. For example, on owner cultivated holdings of medium size the level of land prices would tend to reduce the portion of capital that is active in production to 1/4. Given the capital at the disposal of such holdings, cultivation assumes a less intensive character than it might have. From this point of view, the system of tenancy is better, for it enables the entrepreneur to devote his capital exclusively to cultivation, so that per unit of capital cultivation takes on a more intensive character. Among the various capitalist modes of production the tenancy system yields the highest net product. But there are drawbacks: the tenant exhausts the soil more quickly, and shows little interest in improving the methods of cultivation. Moreover, as ground rents rise, the duration of tenancy contracts decreases. (ii) Among the effects of the different juridical forms that govern the reproduction of property in land, we can isolate two sorts: (a) those which tend to proletarianise the peasant family, either because they accelerate (not cause) the fragmentation of the soil through the equal division of rural property, or because, in centralising the farm in the hands of one member, they compel the others to migrate; a system of the latter type is the peasant variant of trusteeship which is especially common among the big and medium peasantry of Germany and Austria. (b) those which reinforce the centralisation of land and consolidate the larger properties, e.g., where land becomes the collective property of the family; in this sense the forms of trusteeship that prevail among the gentry facilitate the accumulation of capital and make possible a more intensive and rational type of cultivation (cf. the latifundium). (iii) In various ways the towns continually absorb a portion of the mass of values produced in the countryside: as commodity production expands the demand for capital, an increasing

mass of values flows to the towns by way of interest payments to the
urban banks; with increasing urbanisation and the growing attractions
of the town, absenteeism expands and a larger portion of the rents
generated in the countryside are consumed in the towns; the major share
of the taxes which peasants pay becomes an expenditure on urban services
such as the upkeep of the bureaucracy; the various charges imposed on
the peasantry generate a flow of commodities to the urban sector and
partly because they stimulate new methods of cultivation speed up the
exhaustion of the soil. A separate phenomenon with its own special
importance is the progressive depopulation of the countryside brought
about by the dominance of large properties in some areas, the extreme
fragmentation of the land in others, growing pressure of population,
rising land prices, all of which act as so many fetters on the reproduction of the household in the countryside. The shift to intensive
cultivation creates sharper seasonal fluctuations in the demand for
labour, increases the economic insecurity of life in the villages,
forces labour to migrate; the growing facility of communications between
town and country speeds up the circulation of facts about life in the
towns. As the burdens on the peasantry increase, the soil becomes progressively more exhausted, competition intensifies between large holding
and the peasant plot, hours of work become longer and the mass of the
population sinks voluntarily into barbarism--a powerful current of
migration swells up among the poor peasantry, the relative weight of
the rural population shrinks and its composition deteriorates. The
intellectual abyss separating town and country on which the town founded
its supremacy in education and intellectual development, deepens further.
This movement of depopulation then compels big property to impose
juridical constraints on its workers; small holdings are conceded
against the obligation to furnish a specified amount of labour. A
new feudalism is thus born. But it can not last long. The progressive
march of industry destroys it, except in the most backward areas where
no industries grow up. While the proletarianisation of the peasantry
increases the supply of labour, the incessant flow of workers to the
industrial areas increases the demand for labour. Agriculture becomes
impossible without recourse to imported labour, but these displacements
merely redistribute the shortage of labour, and machinery cannot compensate. A number of machines require a larger number of workers per unit
of area. Finally, even higher wages, which anyway require the organised
pressure of the workers, do not compensate. cf. A. Graham in his book
Rural Exodus, "when wages are low, as in Wiltshire, they migrate; when
wages are high, as in Northumberland, they migrate. They migrate from
Sleaford, where the farms are small, from Norfolk, where the farms are
bigger. It is as if a desperate idea has taken hold of the countryside,
that in the country no happiness is possible..."

Against the growing labour shortage of agriculture no remedy is
possible under capitalism. Like feudal agriculture at the end of the
eighteenth century, capitalist agriculture at the end of the nineteenth
is in an impasse. If the shortage persists, the decay will become

widespread. Worst hit are the small holdings, which can neither import labour over long distances nor rent out land against share contracts. In the sector of commodity production the farms least affected by the desertion of the countryside are those which employ the least wage labour and depend on family labour, generally holdings between 5 and 20 hectares. They gain from the desertion because as labour migrates the rate of fragmentation declines and it is precisely this size of holding that loses in a process of fragmentation. It is not surprising then that these are the only farms that have really expanded in Germany; between 1882 and 1895 they accounted for close to 90 percent of the additional area under holdings. The big peasantry with farms of 20 to 100 hectares have lost the most. But the day agriculture solves the labour question and enters a new period of growth, the tendencies which now favour the expansion of the medium holdings will cease to operate.

Of all the commodity producing strata of the peasantry it is the medium peasantry, however, that suffers most from the burdens imposed on the peasantry. The medium peasant is the worst exploited by the usurer and intermediary, the worst hit by taxes, military service, soil exhaustion, and the first to endure overwork and under-consumption under the pressures of competition. Finally, as the children of the middle peasantry are drawn into the vortex of migration, the labour question will loom as large for them as for the others. Today the middle peasantry has ceased to be satisfied with the way things stand. It wants change, as much as any diehard socialist, but a different sort of change. They are not a revolutionary class, they will not destroy the state, however brutal their condition. But they have ceased to defend the existing order, for the agrarian crisis envelopes all classes of agriculture.

OVERSEAS COMPETITION AND THE INDUSTRIALISATION OF AGRICULTURE

Up until the last quarter of the nineteenth century, terms of trade favoured agriculture. The prices of agricultural produce rose faster than wages, and the workers were hit not only as producers, by the rising rate of surplus value, but as consumers also. The prosperity of agriculture stemmed from the growing impoverishment of the working class. Since 1870, however, the movement of prices has reversed. The reasons for this change must be sought, as with every major change in modern agriculture, in the expansion of industry and its increasing subjugation of the countryside.

The capitalist mode of production revolutionises production continuously through the processes of accumulation, of the expansion of new capitals and of technical change.[7] The mass of commodities increases year by year, and at a faster rate than population. But this growing accumulation poses problems for the capitalist class, for under their mode of production surplus value accrues to the bourgeoisie while production takes on the character of mass production, production for mass consumption. In this lies a basic difference between capitalist and feudal or slave production. The feudal seigneurs and slave owners also appropriated the surplus production of their workers, but they consumed it themselves. But the surplus value appropriated under capitalism must first take the form of commodities for bourgeois consumption. Like the feudal overlord or slaveowner, the capitalist is compelled to restrict the consumption of the masses to augment his own; but unlike those classes, he is compelled also to increase the consumption of the masses constantly. Here lies one of the most characteristic and difficult contradictions of capitalism. Capitalists would welcome a raising of wages in any industry except their own. It is true that the higher the wages of workers area the more the capitalists can sell. But they do not produce to sell, but to make profits. The greater the mass of surplus value, the larger the mass of profits, ceteris parabus, and the lower the wages per unit of labour time, the greater the mass of surplus value. Moreover, capitalists have other methods, they do not regard the working class as their main market, but the non-proletarian strata of the population, especially the rural masses. The destruction of the home-based industries opened a vast outlet for their commodities. But the further capitalism grows and the larger the weight of the working class in the total population, the less this market suffices. The extension of the market beyond the limits of the nation, production for the world market and its continuous development becomes the vital bases of capitalist industry. The world market becomes the deciding factor in the life of business, and the well being of capitalists, workers, traders, artisans and peasants.

The expansion of the railways and reduction of transport costs achieved in the latter part of the nineteenth century expanded the urban market and accelerated the growth of the industrial population which thus called for a larger volume of imports into Europe from the overseas territories. The threat to European agriculture came not from the volume of agricultural imports so much as the conditions under which they had been produced. As they appeared on the market, they made it progressively less possible for European agriculture to shift the burden of its own charges (a rising absolute rent, etc.) back on to consumers by way of price increases.

We can divide the low-cost agricultural producers into two categories: the sectors of oriental despotism, including Russia, and the free colonies.[8] In the first type of country the agriculturists are completely at the mercy of the State and ruling classes. In them capitalism has still not created a national political life; the nation remains, at least in the countryside, a collection of self-sufficient and isolated rural communities incapable of posing any resistance to the central state power. But as long as the system of simple commodity production remains weak, the situation of the peasant in such a state is generally not too bad. His personal contacts with the public authority are at a minimum. It is in the towns that oriental despotism wreaks havoc--vis-a-vis the bureaucracy and rich merchants. When the public authority establishes relations of one sort or another with European capitalism, the situation changes. Militarism, diplomacy and the national debt constitute the major forms of European penetration into these countries, and once this penetration is established, it increases the pressure of the State on the rural communities by boosting its demand for cash. Taxes are paid in cash, or the existing level of money taxes rises sharply. As agriculture constitutes the main branch of production and the peasantry has a low resistance to the State, the pressure of taxation is heaviest on this sector. The mass of produce increases and anything over and above the absolutely necessary minimum consumption flows into the market. But where is the market in a country where practically the whole population consists of peasants who want only to sell their produce? Thus foodstuffs have to be exported, and it becomes necessary to expand the network of railways between port and hinterland.

We can hardly argue that the price of this produce is determined by costs of production. They are not produced on a capitalist basis, and their sale comes about under the pressure of the State and the usurer. High taxes and interest rates compel the peasant to rid himself of his produce at any price; the greater the sum of labour which he expends to repay his debt and the larger the mass of produce which he brings to the market, the lower will be the price he receives for it. The growing burden that taxes and interest payments impose on the peasantry does not raise the price of his produce, on the contrary, it pushes the price down; it pushes the ground rent and wages of the small peasants to their lowest limits, if we can talk of "ground rent" and "wages" in a case like this. In the face of competition of this sort, there can be no prosperity in an agriculture based on capitalist foundations, an agriculture which has to reckon with the given standard of life of the population, the given level of wages and rents based on the prevailing price of land and rate of interest, and for which a certain level of soil fertility and the available resources of manpower constitute a minimum floor.

The competition posed by the free colonies is quite different from that posed by countries like Russia, Turkey and India. There we find a powerful democracy of free peasants weighed down by neither draft nor taxes, with access to huge quantities of fertile land from which the native populations have been eradicated. Several conditions favour this type of agriculture: capital can be devoted exclusively to production itself; as no rotation is required, production centres on a single crop, e.g., wheat, which implies an economy in labour and implements; for the same input of labour, capital and land, the farmer obtains a higher yield, or, extending the area cultivated but keeping capital and labour constant, the same yield as in Europe. But the situation has been changing more recently, for example, in America, where conditions have been drawing closer to those characterising Europe, and thus reducing the competitiveness of its agriculture.

For countries of the former type, integration into the vortex of
world competition can lead finally only to the outbreak of famines,
as the uncultivated portions of land shrink, the cultivated portions
become more sterile, and the peasantry progressively more impoverished.
India with its recurrent famines is currently exporting twenty to thirty
million quintals of rice. The same holds for Russia. Here, according
to the most recent calculation, the peasants produce annually around
1387 m puds of grain (deducting seed). For their own consumption
they require 1286 m puds of rye plus 477 m puts as fodder. This leaves
a deficit of 376 m puts which the peasants would have to buy. Instead,
as we know, they actually sell grain. They have taxes and debts to pay
off, and nothing else to sell. Probably the same factors will compel
the peasantry of China to sell rice, regardless of their own needs.

As international competition in the grain market intensifies,
European landowners are forced to move into other sectors such as milk
and meat where the smaller holdings are better able to defend themselves.
When competition in that market first developed, England was the worst
hit. Realising that tariffs were out, the English landowners faced the
following alternatives--either imminent bankruptcy or changes in productive organisation. They chose the latter course, and the net income
of landed property declined sharply between 1875 and 1894 as rents fell
and their expenditure on the farm increased. Production shifted from
cereals to livestock, the acreage under wheat contracted and the domestic
supply of wheat was halved. But world competition chased them into their
new sectors of production. Some twenty years ago practically the whole
of England's livestock imports came from Europe; today the dominant
suppliers are the U.S. and Canada. As sharpening competition lowered
the price of raw materials and forced ground rent down, landowners tried
to convert these losses into industrial profits by utilising the raw
materials directly in a process of manufacture. Breweries, sugar
factories, starchworks, distilleries began to fill the landscape. Stimulated by the example of the biggest landowners, the peasants came together in cooperative associations for the production of milk, bread,
flour and so on.

But international competition does not spare these new industries.
Take dairy production which has expanded rapidly in the recent period.
The declining profitability of cereals production induces a rapid growth
of dairy production in most of the European countries, particularly Denmark (butter), and outside Europe, e.g. Canada (cheese) or Australia
(butter), (where export subsidies play a supporting role). Danish and
Australian butter have been rapidly displacing German butter from the
English market, but the German dairy producers have been behaving as
if the larger the number of competitors the more lucrative the industry.
Long before the dairy cooperatives can have a substantial impact on the
incomes of the German peasantry, the industry will plunge into a crisis

of overproduction, compelling the members of the cooperative to sell out
to bigger capitalists, and reducing the peasants to wage workers in a
capitalist factory. Such cooperatives revolutionise agriculture, but they
are no solution for the peasantry. Agroindustries are subject to the
laws of concentration and centralisation, to scale economies and the law
on increasing firm size (cf. the example of Nestle), like other industries.
While this industrialisation of agriculture does not entirely eliminate
the smallholder, it binds him to the monopsonist power of the factory
and converts him into a serf of industrial capital, working to its requirements. The domination of agriculture by industry which these
examples signify is carried further, finally, by the more and more efficient utilisation of raw materials, including the recycling of waste
products, and by the production of synthetic substitutes (margarine,
artificial cheese) which compete directly with the natural products
(cf. the fate of the European wine industry before the double assault
of artificial wine and colonial competition).

We cannot say that agriculture has been ruined under these pressures.
But its conservative character has gone forever wherever the modern mode
of production has taken root. The entire economic life of the countryside which revolved eternally in the same orbits has today fallen into a
state of perpetual revolution which is a necessary feature of capitalism.

CONCLUSION

Bourgeois economists are basically concerned about the relations
obtaining between big and small farms from the point of view of their
size. As the relations at this level hardly change at all, they attri-
bute to agriculture a conservative character. On the other side, the
popular socialist conception sees the revolutionary element in usury,
indebtedness, and the peasant's alienation of his property. We hope we
have shown that the former view is inaccurate. Now we want to show
that we cannot accept the latter without qualification.

Peasant indebtedness is not a phenomenon peculiar to capitalism.
It is as old as commodity production and is known from the history of
Greece and Rome. On its own usury capital can only inspire the peasantry with rebelliousness; it cannot become the basis for the transition
to a higher mode of production. Only under capitalism where the possession of large sums of money makes production on a large scale possible
and usury takes the form of credit, does it extend the sphere of action
of capital and hasten economic development. In agriculture, however,
it retains in large degree its precapitalist character: the indebtedness of the peasant, in this sense, is not only not revolutionary, but
it is conservative; it is not a factor which forces the transition from
one mode of production to another, but one which preserves peasant
production in its current state.

In the countryside debt is a conservative factor both vis-a-vis the mode of production and often also vis-a-vis property relations. Of course, where a new mode of production appears which disrupts peasant property, indebtedness can serve to hasten its expropriation. This is exactly what happened in Rome when a sudden increase in the supply of slaves favoured the growth of a plantation system;[9] this is also basically what happened in England during the Reformation when the expansion of trade in wool promoted the development of sheep estates. But in these instances the debt was only a lever of expropriation, not its motor force: for example, in south Germany during the Reformation ownership of land changed hands, but cultivation proceeded on the same basis. Here usury impoverished the peasantry but left its size intact.

In the present conjuncture, with the profitability of agriculture declining as a result of world competition, and the current stagnation and incipient decline of prices and rents, usury capital shows less and less interest in expropriating the indebted peasantry; if the property is auctioned, it stands to lose not only its interest but a part of its capital too. Far from hastening the process, it is therefore attempting to postpone it by granting arrears in payment and even advancing new loans--just as the worst landlords in England are compelled to grant arrears on the payment of rent, to lower rent rates and take on the costs of improvement. In a recent enquiry, the landowner Winkelmann of Wesphalia states: "many usurers in this part of the country are finding it more to their advantage to get the peasant to work for them and to take from him the whole produce of his labour excepting his subsistence, than to auction his property when the gains are uncertain." Thus the indebtedness of the peasantry does not always signify a revolution in the conditions of rural property. Where, then, should we look for the motor force behind the transformation of its mode of production? The answer is implicit in the whole of our analysis above. Industry forms the motor force not only of its own development, but also of the development of agriculture. It was urban industry that smashed the unity of industry and agriculture in the countryside, that converted the peasant into a pure agriculturist, a commodity producer tied to an unknown market, that established the possibility of his proletarianisation. The agriculture of the feudal epoch ended in an impasse, from which it could not escape through its own dynamism. It was urban industry that generated the revolutionary forces that were bound to, and could, break down the feudal regime and open a new path of development for itself and agriculture. It was industry, moreover, that produced the scientific and technical conditions of the new agriculture, that revolutionised it with machinery and chemical fertiliser and established the dominance of large capitalist holdings over the small peasant exploitation. But while it established a qualitative difference between these forms of exploitation, it established another difference too--the difference between holdings producing purely for household subsistence and holdings producing chiefly for the market. Both types were subordinated to industry, but in different ways. It compelled the first type to earn cash by the sale of its labour power and thus reinforced the dependence of the small peasant on industry and brought his situation closer to that of the factory working class. But the commercial farms were like-wise compelled to seek out extra sources of income in industry. Reduction of costs is inherent in the nature of technical progress, but in capitalist agriculture this tendency is more than paralysed by opposing tendencies which impose ever increasing burdens: the expansion of ground rent and tenancy rates or interest rates, the expansion of mortgages, the parcellisation of property through rights of succession, the intensified exploitation of the countryside by the town, devastation of the soil, the recurrence of plant and animal diseases, and finally the increasing absorption of the rural working class into industry--all of which combine to increase costs of production in agriculture. Initially this leads to an inflation of agricultural prices and an intensified antagonism of town and country. But the same line of evolution which engenders this situation transforms it further by its development of international relations and world competition. Either the landowners retreat and the antagonism of town and country abates, or the landowners compel the State to raise tariff walls, and the antagonism intensifies further. To adapt to the new conditions of competition, agriculture adopts the most varied methods of production only to find its most rational goal in its alliance with industry.

In each of these forms--the small peasant's conversion into a factory worker and the big agriculturist's investment in industry-- the modern mode of production thus returns, at the end of its dialectical process, to its original point of departure, to a suppression of the separation of industry and agriculture. But if on the primitive peasant exploitation agriculture was the decisive economic element, now the relation is reversed. Now it is big capitalist industry that predominates, and agriculture that tails behind, adapting to its requirements.

In this society, dominated by capitalism, pure agriculture is no longer a factor of well being. For the peasantry there is no chance of recovering its golden age. It has arrived at an impasse from which it cannot escape through its own reserves. As at the close of the eighteenth century, its emancipation devolves again on the revolutionary masses of the town, who alone can open for it a path for further development. Capitalism concentrates the working masses in the towns, creates the conditions favouring their organisation, their intellectual development, their capacity to struggle as a class. It depopulates the countryside, disperses rural workers over vast distances, isolates them, deprives them of any means of intellectual development and resistance to exploitation. In the towns it concentrates capital in an ever narrowing circle, in agriculture the concentration of holdings remains partial and combined with fragmentation. In its progress the capitalist mode of production converts industry, sooner or later, into an export industry producing for the world market,

6. Kautsky now goes on to deal with "cooperative societies" arguing
(a) that these have been mainly confined to credit and commerce, (b)
they are dominated by landowners and big peasants, (c) that they face
obstacles inherent in the nature of small scale exploitation (e.g.,
marketing cooperatives which have to deal with a large number of small
peasants have almost everywhere failed), (d) that production cooperatives are not liked by peasants because of their "fanaticism for
property" (p. 193) and that only under the guidance of the victorious
working class will cooperation in production have any chance of success:
"the peasant will come to realise that individual ownership of the
means of production is an obstacle to more rational modes of cultivation only when he ceases to regard with fear the prospect of becoming
a proletarian, i.e., once the socialist cooperatives have demonstrated
their vitality and eliminated the risks which today threaten every
economic enterprise. On the other hand, it is utopian to expect the
peasant to pass over to cooperative production under capitalism..."
(p. 195).

7. It should be noted that the whole of the interpretation which
follows in this paragraph belongs to underconsumptionism, vigorously
combated at that time only by Lenin. For a modern critique, c.f. David
Yaffe, "The Marxian theory of crisis, capital and the state,"
Economy and Society, Vol. Two, May 1973, pp. 186f.

8. Again, it should be kept in mind when reading this paragraph how
little the European Marxists of the generation of Engels and Kautsky
actually knew about conditions in the colonies and semi-colonies.
Access to information was limited, which is perhaps the main reason
why neither Marx nor Lenin nor Kautsky ever took up the "colonial
question" on a systematic theoretical basis, and why the "Asiatic mode
of production" remains among the most nebulous and scientifically
weak concepts in Marx. The paragraph which follows is of an entirely
different nature: it contains the insight that competition in the
world market takes place on the basis of an articulation of modes of
production, including simple commodity production subjugated to the
power of capital (under different forms).

9. By "plantation" here Kautsky means not the type of enterprise which
prevailed in the tropics under colonialism, but integrated estates
closer to what he understood by the word latifundium (literally "large
farm").

because the home market has begun to fail it. As this tendency pro-
gresses pure agriculture becomes a form of production of declining
importance even in the home market, whose own weight is progressively
shrinking before the dominance of world economy.

Human society is an organism, different from those of the animal
or the plant, but an organism none the less. It is absurd to think that
in any society one part can develop in one direction, and another in
some other direction. Society can follow only one line of development.
But it does not follow that each part of this organism should contain
within itself the life force of its own growth; it is enough that one
portion of the organism produces the forces necessary to sustain the
whole of it. If large scale industry is progressing towards socialism
and if large scale industry is the dominant power in modern society,
this line of evolution will win for socialism other domains not capable,
on their own, of creating the conditions for this revolution. It must
do so, in its own interests, in the interests of the unity and harmony
of society.

NOTES

*Based on the French translation La Question Agraire, Maspero 1970,
Page references in this summary refer to this edition.

1. We translate "feudal-capitalist," where the French say feodale et
capitaliste, because Kautsky is clearly referring to the specific
transitional system, combining feudal and capitalist relations, which
he has just mentioned in the previous sentence. It is worth considering
the implications of this image of surplus value being produced out of
feudally-subjected labour.

2. Kautsky allows for the suspension of the law of value under conditions of monopoly, citing the example of Johannesburg wine. "The law
of value presupposes free competition" (p. 88).

3. The sections which follow need not be summarised, as Kautsky's argument here, as in the section on differential rent, follows closely on
Marx, Capital, Volume 3, Ch. XLV, which should therefore be read.

4. The rest of the chapter deals with the determination of the price of
land, the differences between land and capital, the role of credit and
the expansion of the mortgage system. It has not been summarised here.

5. Kautsky obviously means "productivity of labour," not productivity
per unit of cultivated land, as that was the accepted meaning in his
time.

3. The Political Economy of Class Structure in U.S. Agriculture: A Theoretical Outline

KEVIN F. GOSS, RICHARD D. RODEFELD, and
FREDERICK H. BUTTEL

INTRODUCTION

Social class and social stratification are two frequently used
concepts in rural sociology, yet there has been a surprisingly small
amount of attention paid to the class structure of agriculture as a
phenomenon in its own right. Put another way, although American rural
sociologists can hardly avoid social class as an idea, direct confrontation with the reality of agricultural class relations has been
rare. Thus, a most well known and extensively cited paper in this
area, Arthur Stinchcombe's (1961), "Agricultural Enterprise and
Rural Class Relations," was written by a non-rural sociologist.

Stinchcombe credits Marx with a "fundamental innovation in
stratification theory" by basing "a theory of formation of classes
and political development on a theory of bourgeois enterprise."
His stated objective was to extend Marx's mode of analyses to agricultural enterprises. However, the result was a basically static,
descriptive treatment of rural strata in several enterprise types.

*An earlier version of this essay was presented at the annual
meeting of the Rural Sociological Society, San Francisco, California,
September 1978. The authors wish to thank Robert C. Bealer, Ada
Cavazzani, Sam Cordes, Richard C. Hill, Alain de Janvry, Mark A.
Lancelle, Susan A. Mann, Howard Newby, Peter Sinclair and Christopher
K. Vanderpool for their helpful suggestions.

Stinchcombe asserts that property rights are more important than occupational position in determining rural stratification. From the various systems of property relations and the political-economic context in which they occur, he was able to differentiate between the "upper and lower classes," along dimensions of legal privileges, style of life, technical expertise, and political participation. Specific levels and combinations of these "characteristics of class structure" were found associated with five types of agricultural enterprise: manorial, family-size tenancy, family small-holding, plantation, and ranch. However, Stinchcombe leaves unexamined the possible explanations of how each type of agricultural enterprise emerges and, most importantly, the "laws of motion" that underlie their change, development, and transformation.

Although Stinchcombe purports to extend Marx's theories to the study of agricultural systems, the results are decidedly at odds with key Marxian methodological principles. Firstly, as noted, Stinchcombe's theory pertains to a description of classes within agricultural enterprises, not within the social formation. Secondly, the presence of the classes is not based on any particular defining properties of any mode of production; the implication is that some or all of the enterprise types could exist in a variety of economic systems (or modes of production).[1] It seems that the quest for a universal stratification scheme for agricultural enterprises on the part of Stinchcombe and others (for example, Smith, 1969, 1973) has resulted in categorizations that are static, ahistorical, and merely descriptive. What is needed is a dynamic, historical analysis which can provide a theoretical grasp of changes in the structure of United States agriculture. This is essentially the difference between stratification analysis and Marxist class analysis.

Class analysts and stratification analysts, in general, confront the same question of social inequality: the distribution (or maldistribution) of limited social rewards among societal members. Stratification analysis typically describes the distribution of those things valued in society and differential access to them, whereas class analysis attempts to explain such distributions and differential access by analyzing the social change processes that account for inequality in the first place (Stolzman and Gamberg, 1973/74). Class analysis, in a strictly Marxian sense, is not concerned with the individual aspects of inequalities. It is rather "an analytical tool for the explanation of structural change in societies characterized by a capitalist mode of production" (Stolzman and Gamberg, 1973/74: 106).

Marx's concept of class is intertwined with his theory of historical change. The function of class analysis is not a more accurate description of the distribution of social rewards (although accuracy is still important), but rather an explanation of the process of macroscopic social change. For Marx, social inequalities are rooted in the

logic of the capitalist mode of production and are exemplified by a
tendency toward dichotomous classification of groups in contrasting
relations to the productive process itself. Capitalists, who control
the means of production, maintain an exploitative relationship with
wage-labor. Subsequent polarization of class interests would lead to
revolutionary conflict and emancipation of the proletariat from the
dominant bourgeoisie. Marxist class analysis does not deny the
existence of strata within the classes, but maintains that the relationship between the two main classes is the proper focus for understanding
the dynamics of capitalist society.

The aim of this essay is to show that application of Marxist
class analysis can provide fresh insights for analyzing the changing
social and economic structure of U.S. agriculture. This is done by
bringing together (1) the Marxist model of capitalist development
with particular reference to agriculture, and (2) our own conception
of the development of U.S. commercial agriculture.

MARXIST THEORY OF CAPITALIST DEVELOPMENT

It is necessary to return to "first principles"--Marx's theory of
historical change. This entails a review of his general mode of
capitalist development which applies to all social formations and
economic sectors in the capitalist mode of production. When it comes
to reviewing the Marxist contributions to capitalist development in
agriculture the situation becomes more complex. Marx illustrated
his method of analysis with observations from Britain up to the nineteenth century. Agriculture was based on a capitalist tenant paying
ground-rent to a landowning class. Land monopoly was an important
feature of the British "path" to capitalist development. In the North
American "path," however, land was generally readily available, absolute
ground-rent was virtually non-existent, and the petty bourgeois "family
farmer" predominated, rather than the landowner-capitalist tenant
system. Marx's dated analysis of the British path and contemporary
analyses of the North American path are reviewed.

The General Model of Karl Marx[2]

Marx's theory of historical change recognizes certain epochs in
history--ancient, feudal, capitalist, socialist and communist. "The
history of all hitherto existing society is the history of class
struggles" (Marx and Engels, 1888: 9), and the outcome of such conflict
is the transcendence of one epoch by the next. The concern here is
with the disintegration of feudalism and the rise of capitalism, and
later, the emergence of contradictions within capitalism. It is the
manifestation of these contradictions that shapes subsequent social
change. What is distinctive about capitalism as an economic system

is that labor-power itself becomes a commodity, to be bought and sold
on the market. For Marx, this is central to the unique structure of
social relationships in capitalist society.

How does Marx arrive at these assertions and what are their implications? His theory starts with the nature of labor itself. Labor is
the foundation of all human societies, and creative labor distinguishes
humanity from other animals. The relationship between the individual
producer and the material environment acted upon to produce such goods
is mediated by the characteristics of society. The specific technical
form of the production process is the means of production.

Marx attributes changes in the means of production--for example,
new technology or specialization of tasks--to a response to forces of
production (which in turn are shaped by existing production relations).
The specific aids used by producers are the instruments of production.
Each productive system involves a set of social relations which support
and coordinate individuals in that system.. Human beings do not produce
in a social vacuum, but rather as members of a definite form of society,
with its relations of production. Classes emerge where the relations
of production involve a division of labor that allows for accumulation
of surplus production by a minority grouping, in an exploitative relationship to the mass of producers. The mode of production comprises
the means and relations of production along with the resultant class
structure, and hence embodies the overall organization of technical,
economic and social relationships in the production system.

For Marx each epoch in civilization has been structured on a
dichotomous division with respect to property relations, and consequently there are two antagonistic classes, one dominant over the other.
In the capitalist mode of production the axis that divides classes is
ownership/non-ownership of private property in the means of production.
The capitalist class or bourgeoisie owns the means of production, and
monopolizes accumulation of capital by extraction of surplus value
from wage-labor. Members of the proletariat only have control over
their own labor-power, which in capitalism is a commodity like any
other factor of production. They sell their labor-power to the
capitalist in return for wages. The capitalist class is dominant,
the working class is subordinate, and the relationship between the
two is one of dependency and conflict.

Marx's fundamental concepts for class structure and class conflict
are surplus value and capital accumulation. In capitalism, the deriva-
tion of surplus value does not come from forced or customary expropriation of produce from wage-labor, but from a concealed distinction
between labor-power and creative labor. All commodities (including
labor-power) have a use-value and an exchange-value. The use-value
of a commodity is realized only in its consumption by others. The
exchange-value of a commodity is reflected by the proportional

quantities in which it exchanges on a market with other commodities.
The regulation of exchange of one commodity for others is found, not
in the natural qualities of that commodity, but in its social function.
Each commodity has a certain amount of social labor bestowed upon it.
For Marx, the "relative (exchange) values of commodities are determined
by the respective quantities or amounts of labor worked up, realised,
fixed in them" (1901, p. 81). Labor-power is a commodity like any
other, and its exchange-value is determined by the quantity of labor
necessary to produce it; that is, the mass of necessaries to feed,
clothe and shelter the supplier of labor-power and the family which
perpetuates the supply of labor, and to acquire necessary skills, etc.
Labor-power is temporarily disposed of to the capitalist at its exchange-
value, in return for wages. However, the conditions of modern industrial
production allow the worker to produce more than is necessary to cover
the cost of necessaries. The exchange-value of labor-power is determined by necessary-labor to reproduce it, but the use-value of labor
to the capitalist is in excess of this. This surplus labor creates
surplus produce which is realized by the owner of the means of production as surplus value, at no extra cost. Surplus value is the source
of profit, interest and rent.

It is the Marxian abstraction that, for the capitalist mode of
production, there are the two classes constituted by their respective
relations to ownership of private property in the means of production,
and extraction of surplus value. The bourgeoisie and proletariat are
inherently in conflict, and within this conflict is the genesis for
further social change. However, while this dichotomy is the main axis
for social structure and the main source for social change, a more
complicated system of relations is likely to exist at any given point
in the history of bourgeois society.

These transitional groupings often represent a set of relations
of production which are either being superseded (i.e., tied to a past
mode of production) or are ascendent (which become the basis for transition to another production mode). For example, landholders and
peasantry are transitional classes lingering from the feudal mode of
production. There are also groupings that falsely identify with the
"wrong" class or who are on the margins of their own class. Petty
commodity production warrants particular mention. Although commodities
are produced for exchange and there is private ownership of the means
of production, the petty bourgeois family provides most of the labor-
power. Without the hiring of wage-labor there cannot be extraction of
surplus value, and hence class formation. It is the presence of wage-
labor that distinguishes full-scale capitalist production from petty
commodity production, and hence completes the separation of labor and
capital (Mann and Dickinson, 1978). The petty bourgeoisie is transitional because as the "normal" development of capitalism proceeds
toward polarization into two classes, these small scale capital owners

will have either expanded their scale of property ownership (i.e.,
become bourgeoisie) or relinquished ownership to larger capitalists
(i.e., are proletarianized). Thus, a description of social structure
at any one point in time will reveal a complexity of classes, transitional classes, subclasses, and marginal classes, but this does not
deter from the underlying dynamic of social change.

According to Marxian theory, the State is not neutral with respect
to the exploitative relationship between bourgeoisie and proletariat;
the State in fact serves a protective function for the propertied
class. Class relationships largely determine political power, because
political agencies are closely tied to the means of production.
Firstly, the State must preserve the integrity of the market, because
commodity exchange, including labor-power, is a necessary condition
for capitalism. Secondly, the State must protect the integrity of
modern private property because it is the very basis of the national
economy. The modern legal system gives ideological support to the
bourgeois State and legitimizes bourgeois domination of the proletariat.

With mature capitalism there arise the contradictions that
threaten to bring about transcendence of the capitalist mode of production. In the abstract, there is a general tendency for the rate of
profit to decline. For Marx, the rate of profit is in inverse relationship to the ratio of constant to variable capital. Variable
capital is wages. Driven by the competitive search for profit,
mechanization and other technological improvements are adopted that
increase this organic composition of capital, and hence lower the
average rate of profit. At the same time, there is no agency to
regulate the market and match production with consumption. Given
dominance of the profit motive and incentives for expansion, overproduction is endemic. Crises of over-production serve to force the
smaller, less efficient enterprises out of production and create a
"reserve army" of underemployed and unemployed that buffer the fluctuations in production, investment and employment. This contributes to
a trend of concentration and centralization of capital, and increased
exploitation of the proletariat. Larger and larger productive units
are facilitated by formation of joint-stock companies and by centralization of money-capital in the credit system. Monopoly control of
sectors of industry is now possible, and new exploitive relationships
arise. This growing disparity in wealth between a minority of capitalists and the mass of wage-labor contributes to disappearance of transitional classes and increasing polarization to the two class system.
Mature capitalism generates contradictions that Marx predicted will
bring about its transcendence.

The concentration and centralization of capital (in other words,
the tendency towards increasing firm size) can be seen as one of the
major "laws" of capitalist development along with uneven development.

Uneven development refers to the inherent tendency of capitalism to produce abundance as well as scarcity, development as well as under-development, wealth as well as poverty, and growth as well as stagnation. Uneven development is expressed spatially (e.g., in disparities between suburb, central city, and depressed rural regions) and industrially (e.g., contrasts between technologically-sophisticated, rapid-growth, high-profit industries and technologically-stagnant, low-growth, low-profit firms). Such patterns of development derive from the tendencies for capital to seek out the most profitable outlets for investment. Regions and industrial sectors unattractive for investment are prone to stagnation. Also, to the extent that investment in a given region or social sector is made by capitalists in another sector (e.g. multinational oil firms investing in Appalachian coal mining), profits (surplus value) will be extracted from the region, further contributing to uneven development.

This general model of capitalist development provides the dynamic for social change that is important to the explanatory and predictive power of class analysis. However, as recognized by Marx, agriculture exhibits some unique characteristics that tend to modify--but not transcend--these general laws of capitalist development.

Agriculture, Land Monopoly and Ground-Rent[3]

Agriculture occupies a rather peculiar position with respect to Marx's theory of capitalist development. Agriculture was at the origin of the capitalist mode of production, yet remained largely outside it (Wallerstein, 1974). Feudal agriculture in fifteenth century Britain consisted of a relatively small class of landed aristocracy and a relatively large peasant class. The power of the lord was dependent on the number of proprietors on the estate. These agriculturalists produced largely for their consumption, but were free to dispose of their produce as they wished. Land and labor were not commodities (Eaton, 1966: 125-126; Mandel, 1968: 217-272; Dowd, 1974: 38-39).

The rise of the capitalist mode of production entailed the ex-propriation of the peasantry from the land, the emergence of land as private property, and the development of the labor market in the towns. Peasants became a propertyless working class by virtue of selling their labor-power and bestowing surplus value on products for capital accumulation by owners of means of production. The breakup of feudal estates and the usurpation of common lands (i.e., the enclosure movement) were the revolution that marked the end of feudalism and the beginnings of capitalism. This change not only paved the way for the capitalist mode of production in manufacture and industry, but also conditions for a capitalist agriculture. The new urban-based economic order could only continue to the extent that agriculture produced a surplus in food and labor, to be exchanged like other commodities. Agriculture had to change from its largely subsistence nature to a more commercial form. Rationalization of agriculture was now possible. Capitalist farmers on amalgamated holdings could pursue privately-appropriated profits through technological improvements, i.e., pursue capital accumulation through extraction of surplus value from farm labor (Eaton, 1966: 138-140; Mandel, 1968: 273-275; Marx, 1972: 794-813, 823-825; Dowd, 1974: 39-40).

However, land was unique among commodities in Marx's British "path" to capitalist development in agriculture. It was a source of ground-rent. In general, ground-rent is surplus-product from agricultural production acquired by the property-holding of land-owning classes. Consider late feudal agriculture where the landlord's estate was contracted out to a large number of free peasants. Each peasant had at least a customary right to a plot of land and thus individual control over means of production. However, in return, the peasant contributed part of labor (labor rent), or produce (natural rent), or of income (money rent) to the lord. This surplus product is ground-rent. The division of the peasants' product into necessary and surplus product is a fixed ratio, and remains outside the market. In the epoch of pre-capitalist rent, the land was not a commodity (Eaton, 1966: 127-128; Mandel, 1968: 272-273; L. Afanasyev et al., 1974: 118-119).

However, capitalist ground-rent is quite different because land is a commodity, and as an instrument of production has become separated from the institution of landed property and the class of landholder. But land has two unique properties that distinguish it from other factors of agricultural production. Firstly, land is in limited quantity and cannot be produced and reproduced within capitalism itself at a variable price. Land constitutes a natural monopoly. Secondly, land in agriculture does not have the mobility of other capital to enter and leave different enterprises of production. Land is controlled by a class of landowners, who prevent its use unless rent is paid. Land is a property monopoly (Mandel, 1968: 274-275; Marx, 1967: 614-618; Afanasyev et al., 1974: 119-120).

The special circumstances of land and ground-rent necessitated that Marx deal with a specific model of class structure and development:

> The prerequisites for the capitalist mode of production (in agriculture) therefore are the following:
> The actual tillers of the soil are wage-laborers
> employed by a capitalist, the capitalist farmer who
> is engaged in agriculture merely as a particular
> field of exploitation for capital, as investment for

> his capital in a particular sphere of production. The
> capitalist farmer pays the landowner, the owner of the
> land exploited by him, a sum of money at definite
> periods fixed by contract....for the right to invest
> his capital in this specific sphere of production.
> This sum of money is called ground rent....It is paid
> for the entire time for which the landowner has
> contracted to rent his land to the capitalist farmer.
> Ground-rent, therefore, is here that form in which
> property in land is realized economically, that is,
> produces value. Here, then, we have all <u>three classes</u>
> <u>- wage-laborers, industrial capitalists, and landowners</u>,
> constituting together, and in their mutual opposition,
> the framework of modern society (Marx, 1967, p. 618).

A third class, owners of modern landed property, now has to be considered. The distinction between capitalist tenants and landowners is important, because it is based on a conflict relationship (Schwartz, 1976), and one which stems from extraction of surplus value. All capitalist ground-rent is surplus value, arising from the general conditions for existence of surplus value. However, surplus value does not specifically explain ground-rent; this notion needs further explanation (Eaton, 1966: 129-130; Marx, 1967: 633-639).

For Marx, capitalist ground-rent has two components: differential ground-rent and absolute ground-rent. For the sake of distinguishing between the two, an assumption is necessary--that agricultural productivity lags behind population increase so that all produce is absorbed by the market. All land and labor is socially necessary. Thus, the selling price is not determined by average conditions but by the production conditions of the least profitable farm. The more productive farms will have a lower cost of production, and hence realize <u>super-profit</u>. <u>Differential ground-rent</u> arises from the difference between the average selling price and the cost of production for the individual farm. It can arise in two ways: (1) differences between farms in natural fertility or geographic locations, and (2) differences from investment of differential amounts of capital. The second type of rent depends on the degree of intensification of agriculture (Eaton, 1966: 136-137; Marx, 1967: 640-648; Mandel, 1968: 276-278; Afanasyev et al., 1974: 120-125).

In the analysis thus far it has been implicit that the least profitable farm sells produce at a price that recovers only cost of production and average profit; that is, payment of rent can only be taken from this profit. However, because of the landed monopoly, agricultural produce does not share in the social equalization of rate of profit. Products do not sell at their social price of production, but at their value, which is higher. Thus, the limiting farm also produces a surplus from which to pay rent. This incremental rent is derived from all farms regardless of fertility and location and is <u>absolute ground-rent</u> (Eaton, 1966: 132-134; Marx, 1967: 748-772; Mandel, 1968: 278-280; Afansyev et al., 1974: 125-128).

In the capitalist mode of production, agricultural land is a commodity, but from Marx's analysis it has no value because no labor was spent in its production. However, private ownership has transformed land into a property monopoly which gives land a price. This price is ground-rent capitalized at the average rate of interest. With the development of capitalism Marx predicts the rate of profit, and hence the rate of interest, to fall. At constant ground-rent this would cause an increase in land price. However, ground-rent grows as long as all agricultural produce is consumed, and thus further increases the price of land. Should overproduction occur and prices fall to a point where profit over and above ground-rent is eliminated, then capitalist tenants cease to cultivate the least profitable farms. This has rarely occurred because of the relative stability of demand for farm produce, and so the prior assumption generally holds (Eaton, 1966: 137-138; Marx, 1967: 622-624; Mandel, 1968: 282-284; Afanasyev et al., 1974: 130-132).

Agriculture and Petty Commodity Production[4]

Marx explained that capitalist development lagged behind industry because of the special importance of land ownership and its share of surplus value. Surplus value extracted from productive labor is the source of profit, ground-rent, and interest. Firstly, ground-rent represents a loss to capital accumulation in agriculture. Ground-rent removes from surplus value a portion that cannot be immediately reinvested, maintaining a lower organic composition of capital. A large portion of that rent can be withdrawn from the agricultural sector entirely by absentee landowners. Secondly, interest accrues to the capitalist in return for improvements in the land. However, the more permanent fixed investments made by the capitalist tenant revert to the landowner when the lease expires. Such improvements become an inseparable feature of land, and the interest is expropriated as increased differential ground-rent. Thus, the price of the land increases and so does the leasehold charge. This becomes a disincentive for investment in agriculture by tenants. It also creates antagonism and conflict between capitalist and landowners. Thus, land monopoly and the capitalist tenant system were a hindrance to capital penetration in British agriculture (Eaton, 1966: 131-132; Marx, 1976: 618-622; Mandel, 1968: 280-282, 286; Afansyev et al., 1974: 133-134).

The situation was quite different in "free bourgeois colonies" such as the United States, Canada, and Australia. In general, the British tripartite system of class structure has not been present (Newby, 1978: 8-9; de Janvry, 1978, pers. comm.). One reason was that land was in plentiful supply and was obtained by subsistence and petty commodity producers at little or no cost from the State (Bernier, 1976: 423-424; Newby, 1978: 11-12). Second, there was not a previously entrenched feudal agrarian society (Moore, 1966: 111). Consequently, the essential condition for absolute ground-rent--land monopolization --was lacking.[5] While capital penetration and accumulation in the agriculture of these former colonies have lagged behind industry, the constraint has not been persistence of ground-rent but, rather, the persistence of "non-capitalist" units (family farms) due to special qualities of agricultural production (Mann and Dickinson, 1978).

The transformation of petty commodity production to full-scale capitalist production requires the transformation of social relations-- specifically, the separation of labor and capital. However, Mann and Dickinson (1978) argue that the nature of agriculture presents ob- stacles to capital penetration, and an explanation can be found in Marxian theory. For much of agricultural production the socially necessary labor time is only a small proportion of the total produc- tion time, because of the dependence on seasonal, natural processes. Yet it is only living labor that creates surplus value. Hence, capital tends to enter agriculture only where production time more closely coincides with labor time, and petty commodity production remains where production time greatly exceeds the creative labor input (e.g. annual crop and livestock production; Mann and Dickinson, 1978: 471- 473).

Moreover, this excess of production time over labor time causes a relatively long capital turnover (through reinvestment) time. The longer the turnover time, the smaller is surplus value as a proportion of total capital value, and hence the lower is the average rate of profit. All this is consistent with Marx's theoretical formulation and explains why capital penetration of agriculture lags behind industry. It also explains why capital and the State have a vested interest in development of agricultural technology which increases productivity (and surplus value) of agricultural labor and reduces production time (Mann and Dickinson, 1978: 472-476).

It is an important theoretical and methodological principle that the nature of agriculture presents the obstacles to capitalist de- velopment--and not petty commodity production per se. The persistence of petty bourgeois producers is a manifestation of the initial land settlement by small free-holders and the lag in capital penetration of agriculture. Consequently, we can hypothesize that Marx's theory of capitalist development does apply to agricultural change in free bourgeois colonies such as the United States. Given the power of class analysis and a comprehensive knowledge of this theory, some fresh insight can now be gained from analyzing the historical change in the social and economic structure of U.S. agriculture.

Economics and Social Structure of U.S. Capitalist Agriculture

The Marxian approach to class analysis and the Marxian treatment of agriculture suggest what changes to look for in the capitalist development of U.S. agriculture. Firstly, we should start with a historical account of the rise of the capitalist mode of production, and in the case of agriculture, constraints on that development. Secondly, we should attempt to measure the rate of capital penetration and accumulation in agriculture. Thirdly, we should observe the changing pattern of ownership of the means of agricultural production. Fourthly, we should observe the changing wage-labor situation. Fifthly, we should merge the ownership and labor observations into a class analysis of agriculture; in this paper we only go so far as to propose a farm typology based on the dynamics of occupational differentiation. Finally, we should consider the role of the State in the development of capitalist agriculture. These are our tasks for the remainder of the paper, starting with some brief observations on the rise of the capitalist mode of production.

Historical Account

The period up to the Civil War saw formation of the necessary institutional structure for a capitalist agriculture. Two essential requisites--private ownership of land, and commercial production-- were diffused from seventeenth and eighteenth century Europe (Moore, 1966: 111; Padfield, 1971: 40-41). It is true that earliest farms in the northeast or west were mainly self-sufficient and non-commercial, but by the early 1800's, land speculation and rise of a domestic food market (particularly in the south) turned farms toward commercial production (Moore, 1966: 127; Padfield, 1971: 41; Dowd, 1974: 152-154; Frundt, 1975: 15-20). Meanwhile, commercial agriculture was in place from the outset in the south, although the nature of the plantation system (slave labor) was pre-capitalist rather than early capitalist (Genovese, 1965: 13-36; Dowd, 1974: 152-154). Despite these rudiments of a capitalist agriculture, it took the Civil War to set into place all the requisites of a capitalist mode of production.

Moore (1966: Ch. 3) argues that the Civil War was a bourgeois revolution that brought together three regional economies--plantation south, yeoman farmer west, and industrial northeast--into full blown capitalist development. It reinforced the notion of private ownership of land and capital. It cemented the growing interdependence between western commercial farms producing a food surplus and the northeast urban, industrial market. It brought to a close a neo-feudal southern social system based on slave labor, and hence established wage-labor as the dominant form of non-family labor.[6]

Over the 120 years since the Civil War, there has been emergence
of an essentially capitalist agriculture. There have been periods
of surplus production and declining profit, technological changes and
the substitution of capital for labor, and the consolidation of capital
into larger enterprises. It has been marked by the rise of nonfarm
agricultural capital in the form of large farm supply corporations,
food processing and marketing corporations, and financial institutions.
Also the state has interceded to play a role in fiscal policy, overseas
markets, production controls and price supports, and technological
research.[7]

However, it is convenient to distinguish between two periods in
this development process--1860 to 1940, and 1940 to 1980. In the
earlier period capital growth in agriculture was significant, but
lagged behind the rapid industrialization of that time. Petty commodity
production in agriculture continued to expand, although there was a
rise in tenancy. The numbers of farms and farm people grew then
stabilized, while wage-labor was a relatively small proportion of total
labor. Since 1940, by contrast, there have been large decreases in the
number of farms and farm people and a rise in importance of wage-labor.
Technological advances have displaced labor at an unprecedented rate.
There has been concentration of capital within farming. Equally
important have been the changing relations with the nonfarm agricultural sector. There has been a shift in entrepreneurial control and
economic power away from the farm. There has arisen an organizational
complex of farming operations and corporations supplying inputs or
marketing products, no longer mediated by a competitive market. The
degree of this development varies by type of production. Nevertheless,
agriculture since 1940 has developed rapidly towards a full blown
capitalist mode of production.

The remainder of this paper will focus on the 1940 to 1978 period
and, in doing so, must again confront the notion of the "family farm."

The Family Farm and Capitalism

The persistence of agricultural petty commodity production and
the unity of labor and capital under capitalism have led to theories
that the family farm is anti-capitalist and to static conceptions of
a family farm type. These argue that the predominance of small-scale
farms--owned, managed and worked by a family--was a result of their
ability to curtail consumption and remain more competitive than large-
scale farming, in the face of declining real prices (see Lenin, 1964:
18; Mann and Dickinson, 1978: 469-470; Barkely, 1976). Non-Marxist
theories also attribute the persistence of petty bourgeois farmers
to mechanization and other labor saving technology which allow family
labor to account for most of agricultural production (see Mann and
Dickinson, 1978: 470; Nikolitch, 1972a, 1972b). The implication of
these agrarian views is that U.S. agriculture will remain a freeholder,

small-scale agriculture and that it will be "immune" or "insulated" from the social forces that seemed to be fostering corporate monopolies. This view may contain certain basic errors. Firstly, economic and political power in agriculture, as early as 1900, was no longer in the hands of farmers, but rather was moving toward the railroads, machinery manufacturers, bankers, and food processors. Put otherwise, farmers have hardly been insulated from the forces which generate large-scale agriculture. Moreover, the position confuses land tenure arrangements with the mode of production. Capitalist agriculture is compatible with a wide variety of land tenure arrangements--the family farm, tenancy, plantation agriculture, and (nonfarm) corporate agricultural production--each with its own constellation of sub-classes and class antagonisms. But, regardless of prevailing land tenure arrangements, the forces affecting agriculture appear quite similar.[8]

The "family farm" as a policy issue has been particularly strong in the U.S. since 1968 with claims being made that nonfarm corporations were entering agriculture at an alarming rate (Ray, 1968). The U.S. Department of Agriculture has maintained the position that the family farm is competitive with the corporation farm (U.S. House of Representatives, 1972: 17-53), despite mounting evidence for the increased presence of corporation farms (Rodefeld, 1973; Raup, 1973). The "family/corporate" farm debate, despite its apparent centrality to the theory of capitalist development, deflects attention away from the fundamental dynamics of class structure in agriculture (Rodefeld, 1974; Goss and Rodefeld, 1978b). The corporate (or large-scale industrial) farm, to be sure, represents two key trends anticipated by Marxist theory--concentration and centralization of capital, and proletarianization of farm personnel. Nevertheless, proponents of the perpetuation of the family farm typically come to assume that the social forces of capitalist production can be reversed or thwarted if they are able to achieve the elimination of nonfarm corporations from agriculture.

Such a view assumes that the major axis of exploitation within the agricultural sector is direct production by corporations which serves to raise the production costs (especially for land) and lower the profits of family farmers, but the reality of the matter needs a different focus, however. The primary locus of exploitation may lie elsewhere! Food raising is only one aspect of agriculture. The presence of nonfarm corporations in food raising is over-shadowed at the present time by the monopoly of agribusiness firms over inputs, processing and marketing--monopolies that will remain even if corporations are in some way forced to divest their landed property and discontinue direct production. Put another way, the family/corporation farm debate has frequently served to confuse the content and form of capitalist production relations. Many ostensibly family farms exhibit firm characteristics--employment of hired management and labor, large-scale production, contractual integration with input providers and output processors--typically attributed to the corporation farm.

These "eternal categories" of family farm and corporation farm are not directly rooted in the historical development of the capitalist mode of production. The fact is that U.S. farms and the historically dominant family farm, however defined, have experienced numerous structural changes which are not necessarily reflected in the changing number of farms (Rodefeld, 1978a). The remainder of this paper will examine these changes--increased farm size (land and nonland resources), increased off-farm ownership of land and other resources, loss of entrepreneurial control, and increased non-family labor--and interpret their significance for a class analysis of U.S. agriculture without engaging the unenlightening conceptual apparatus of the "family farm."

Agriculture and Farming

Agriculture as production of food and fiber in a capitalist society, can be conceptualized as having three basic stages: provision of farm inputs, food and fiber raising (farming), and farm product processing and marketing (Donald and Powell, 1974: 1-3; Frundt, 1975: 4). The involvement of the nonfarm sector in processing and marketing (food processors, transporters, wholesalers, retailers) is of long standing (Dorner, 1977) and has increased to the present. Beginning largely in the 1940's, there has been a substantial expansion in the provision of inputs by nonfarmers--fertilizer, agro-chemicals, machinery, and equipment, petroleum and finance (Donald and Powell, 1975; Frundt, 1975: Ch. 3). These changes reflect the tendency for the progressive extension of capitalist relations from production of consumption activities. The input and product market stages have bid traditional activities away from the farm enterprise as technologies become available to facilitate and attract investment in these stages. The rise of non-farm stages of agricultural production beyond the farm stage thus breaks down the barriers to capital accumulation in agriculture (since capital accumulation in these stages is no longer limited by landed monopoly). By 1973, the net dollar contributions of the input and product market stages were ten times that of farming (see Table 1). The increasing specialization of farmers in food raising (and the corresponding monopoly capitalist penetration of inputs and product marketing) also creates the conditions under which the farmer becomes subject to exploitation and monopoly control by non-farm segments of agriculture. As Frundt (1975: 6) argues:

> The cost of agricultural inputs, the financing available for land rental or purchase, and the value of commodity sales through contracting and market controls are not determined by farmers. Through these means corporations can extract surplus value from the commodities which farmers produce. They do this through

the manipulation of markets and exchange value rather
than through control over the land itself.

Thus the dominant forces of production in agriculture are not restricted
to the farm--or food and fiber raising--sector, but increasingly have
been rooted outside this sector.[9]

TABLE 1. Net Dollar Contributions of Input, Farm and Product Market
Stages to Agricultural Production, United States, 1973
Estimate.

	Net cash income and flow ($ billion)	
Input stage: Farm origin	22.9	
Nonfarm origin	43.0	
Input-farm flow		65.9
Farm Stage	22.7	
Farm-product market flow		88.6
Product market stage	155.0	
Total flow: Domestic consumers		225.6
Foreign markets		18.0
Total[a]	243.6	

Source: Donald and Powell (1975, fig. 1, p. 2)

[a]In 1967 employment in farming was 3.3 million persons (4 percent of
total work force), whereas employment in the remainder of the food and
fiber production system was 14.8 million (19 percent of total work
force). (Donald and Powell, 1975, table 1, p. 1).

The Growth of Capital in Farming

Since 1935 there have been dramatic changes in agricultural production trends. The number of farms has declined by two-thirds, with a
corresponding increase in acreage per farm because total farmland
acreage has remained roughly constant (Flora and Rodefeld, 1978: 43).
Farms have exhibited general increases in their scale of operations and
have become far more specialized in the commodities they produce (Ball
and Heady, 1972; White and Irwin, 1972; Perelman, 1973). There has
been both an increase and a concentration in the value of products
sold per farm and in fixed capital per farm (Ball and Heady, 1972;
Brake, 1972). Increased farm size, whether measured by acreage, value
of products sold or fixed capital, is a core change process in the
U.S. farming (see Table 2). Provision of new farm capital has exceeded

TABLE 2.   Change in Acreage, Value of Products Sold, and Value of Land
and Buildings per Farm, United States, 1910-1974.

Date[a]	Land Area per Farm (Acres)	Market Value of Products Sold per Farm (current $)	Value of Land and Buildings per Farm (current $)
1910	139	--	5,480
1935	155	1,442	4,823
1945	195	2,770	7,918
1954	242	5,156	20,405
1964	352	11,176	50,646
1969	390	16,705	75,725
1974	417	32,829	147,838
Percent change, 1935-1974	-64	+2,177	+2,965

Sources: U.S. Bureau of the Census, Historical Statistics of the United
States (1975, pp. 457, 464) and 1974 Census of Agriculture
(1977, table 1, p. 1). See also Flora and Rodefeld (1978,
p. 43).

[a]The figures are not exactly comparable through time due to change in
definition of "farm" (particularly 1959 and 1974) and inclusion of
Hawaii and Alaska (1964).

the means of many individual farmers and their traditional sources of internal savings and farm equity. There are indications that an increasing
proportion of farm capital has come from off-farm sources (Brake, 1972;
Rodefeld, 1978a, 1979).

Along with the expansion of the nonfarm stages of agricultural
production there has been a transfer of ownership, labor and managerial
functions from the farm to off-farm entities. Transfer mechanisms
include provision of credit, off-farm ownership (of farm business,
land and nonland resources) and leasing by farm operators, custom
operations (work, feeding, growing) vertical integration, partnerships
and incorporation, cooperatives, and government involvement through
regulation and prices supports (Harris, 1974; Rodefeld, 1978a). These
changes have a common effect of eroding the traditionally dispersed and
undifferentiated organizational structure of farm production, and tend
towards a concentrated and differentiated system of agriculture. "A
concentrated organizational system would typically include both farming
operations and firms that formerly supplied inputs or marketed products
in a single management complex" (Breimyer and Barr, 1972: 16).

Concentration of farm and off-farm capital may occur through a vertical structure or a horizontal structure. A vertical structure would likely consist of agribusiness firms, who through production contracts or ownership have integrated production of specific commodities across input, raising, and marketing stages. A horizontal structure would consist of large farms producing one or several commodities, with a separation of ownership, management and wage-labor functions--typically an industrial-type corporation. In sum, we have seen a concentration of capital in the food and fiber raising sector, not only from accumulation within, but also from various mechanisms linking it to off-farm agricultural capital.

Why has there been this recent rapid rate of capitalist development in agriculture? We may pose the further question of why capital growth in farming has proceeded further in the U.S. than in other developed capitalist economies with similar levels of gross national product per capita (Buttel, 1977).

Overproduction, Cost Price Squeeze and Technological Change

The historic seeds of change in the structure of agriculture may be traced to one of the key consequences of capitalist production arrangements--the tendency toward overproduction. Exascerbated by the physical abundance of U.S. landed resources, overproduction has been a constant companion of American agricultural development, even during the latter half of the nineteenth century (Dowd, 1974: 156-158). For the individual farm operator, overproduction has meant depressed prices for products and has dictated certain strategies to cope with this circumstance. Many farmers saw expansion in size of their operations, primarily through increased cultivation and mechanical labor-saving technology, as the best way to increase farm income (Goss, 1976: 81-88). Nonfarm corporations emerged to supply the needed inputs, provide credit, install transportation facilities, and process and market excess production. Increases in total farm production further compounded overproduction problems and heightened the economic crisis for all farmers. As these nonfarm agricultural firms increasingly assumed a monopoly character (through concentration and superior bargaining power with individual farmers), control over the forces of production shifted to the agribusiness sector (Frundt, 1975: Ch. 2).

These pressures were intensified by the Depression. Between 1930 and 1940, the mortgages of more than 25 percent of farmers were foreclosed (Frundt, 1975: 49). Bold new policies were adopted in an attempt to restore farm viability. There was development of both mechanical technology (which permits increased farm size and production from the same labor input) and biological technology (which allowed increased yields and hence production from the same land area). With the subsequent boom price conditions of World War II and a shortage of labor, technological changes pushed farming to new heights of production and

income. After World War II and the Korean War, overproduction once again
became a problem, and necessitated production controls and expansion of
export markets (Rodefeld, 1974; Flora and Rodefeld, 1978). Not only was
this a stimulus to further growth in agricultural input and product
marketing industries, but also resulted in a rapid rise of capital invested in farming (Dowd, 1974: 161-166; Frundt, 1975: Ch. 3).

It was thus the tendency toward overproduction, fostered by changes
in the instruments of production (new technology), that made possible
accelerated capital accumulation in agriculture and farming, and the
altered social relations of agricultural production. Other factors,
although of less overall importance, may be seen as contributing to
this transformation in farming (Rodefeld, 1978a). Farm subsidy programs
have generally favored large operations and also have reduced fluctuations in prices. In addition, production risks have been reduced
through agricultural research. The result has been increasingly
favorable circumstances for entry of nonfarm capital into farming. An
equally important reason for capital penetration has been the liberal
tax concessions in farming. There are a number of tax benefits to
be gained from ownership of farm land and nonland resources for those
with large nonfarm incomes (Carlin and Woods, 1974). Farming has thus
become a tax shelter for nonfarm corporations and wealthy individuals
(Raup, 1973). Lastly, many agribusiness firms have found it advantageous
to vertically integrate into food raising to further increase their
control over production and supply (Kyle et al., 1972).

The Ownership of Farmland and Other Capital

Historically, large proportions of farms, farm land, and other
farm capital have been owned by the individuals or families residing
on farms and managing them on a day-to-day basis (Rodefeld, 1978a,
1979). As long as U.S. agriculture remains dominated by these petty
bourgeois farmers, we can expect its capitalist development to be
constrained. Conversely, a trend away from on-farm, family ownership
would indicate a lessening of these constraints. This could occur as
a result of increased retention by retired farmers and nonfarm heirs
and/or increased purchase by nonfarmers (individuals, partnerships,
corporations, governmental units). Resources owned by nonfarmers
could either be rented to farmers or they could engage in production
by hiring necessary managers and/or laborers.

The issue of farm land ownership is addressed here by examining
changes in aggregate levels of ownership by farmers and nonfarmers.
Changes in the numbers and percentages of total acres in farms classi-
fied by the tenure status of their operator are also reviewed. The
four major types are full-owner operated (all land is owned by the
operator), part-owner (some land is owned, some is rented), tenant
(all land is rented on a cash, crop-share and/or livestock-share basis)
and hired manager (no land owned, salaried). Three rather distinct

periods of change can be identified in aggregate levels of land ownership. From 1880 to 1935, ownership by farmers (operators) declined
substantially. This trend was reversed from 1935 to 1955 and, then
appears to have declined consistently from 1955 to present (Rodefeld,
1978a; Table 3).

The earliest decline consisted largely of reduced acreage in full-
owner farms and increased numbers and acreage in tenant-operated farms
(Faulkner, 1951: 355-358). By the end of the Depression, 43 percent
of all farms containing 32 percent of all farm land were tenant-
operated. An additional 19 percent of the land was either rented by
part owners (13 percent) or was in hired manager farms (six percent).
Thus, 51 percent of all farm land was not owned by farm operators in
1935. While information is limited, it appears increased retention by
retired farmers and/or their heirs and the rental of this land to farmers
were the most immediate and major causes of decreased ownership by
farmers in this period. Increased ownership by nonfarm investors was
also a factor. Foreclosures during the Depression, for instance, increased ownership by financial institutions and other financiers.

Rising tenancy, particularly in the South where crop-share
arrangements were most common and associated social and economic
problems were of great concern of politicians and social scientists
at the time. Legislation was enacted and Federal agencies created
to address these problems (Maris, 1940). Increased tenancy, part-
ownership, and hired management increased the separation between the
occupants of landowner positions and those occupying manager (operational) and laborer positions. This created potential class divisions
and conflict between landowners and the resident, on-farm workforce.
However, petty commodity production still prevailed, and wage labor
remained relatively underdeveloped.

From 1935 to 1955, land ownership by farmers rose from 523 million
acres (49 percent) to 675 million acres (58 percent). This was the
result of modest increases in acres owned by full-owners and more
substantial increases in acres owned by part-owners. Acres owned by
nonfarmers declined by approximately 46 million acres. The decline
in tenant farm acreage (154 million acres), particularly in crop-share
farms, was much greater than this net change since acres rented by
part-owners and operated by hired managers increased in this period
by approximately 108 million acres (Rodefeld, 1978a, 1979). It appears
the prosperity of World War II and Korean War eras provided the financial means for many farmers to purchase land that was previously rented.
At the same time, outmigration of farmers and workers, labor shortages,
labor displacing and/or replacing mechanical technology, and farm consolidation (i.e., expansion) appear the major forces which reduced numbers
of full-owner and tenant-operated units--the latter consisting primarily
of crop-share units in the South (Rodefeld, 1974; 1978a). It is not
clear which types of nonfarmers experienced either reduced or increased
ownership in this period.

TABLE 3. Number of Farms and Land Owned or Rented on These Farms by Tenure of Farm Operator, United States, 1910 to 1970.

					Tenure of Farm Operator							
	Full Owner		Part Owner				Hired Manager		Tenant		Total Farms	
Date	No. (mill.)	Acres (mill.)	No. (mill.)	Acres owned (mill.)	Acres not owned (mill.)	Total acres (mill.)	No. (mill.)	Acres (mill.)	No. (mill.)	Acres (mill.)	No. (mill.)	Acres (mill.)
1910	3.4	465	.59	-	-	134	.058	54	2.4	227	6.4	879
1935	3.2	491	.69	132	134	266	.048	61	2.9	337	6.8	1054
1950	3.1	419	.83	250	173	423	.024	107	1.4	212	5.4	1161
1959	2.1	349	.83	279	219	498	.021	110	.74	167	3.7	1123
1964	1.8	319	.79	284	249	533	.018	113	.54	145	3.2	1110
1969[a]	1.7	375	.67	291	259	550	--	--	.35	138	2.7	1063
1974	1.4	359	.63			535	--	--	.26	122	2.3	1017
Percent of Total												
1910	52.7	52.9	9.3	--	--	15.2	.9	6.1	37.5	25.8		
1935	47.1	37.1	10.1	12.5	12.7	25.2	.7	5.9	42.6	31.8		
1950	57.4	36.2	15.3	21.6	14.9	36.5	.4	9.2	25.9	18.2		
1959	57.1	30.9	22.5	25.4	19.5	44.9	.6	9.8	20.0	14.3		
1964	57.6	28.7	24.8	25.6	22.4	48.0	.6	10.2	16.9	13.1		
1969[a]	62.4	35.3	24.5			51.8	--	--	12.9	12.9		
1974	61.6	35.3	27.2			52.6	--	--	11.3	12.0		

Sources: U.S. Bureau of the Census, 1964 Census of Agriculture (1968, vol. 2, ch. 8, tables 5,6), 1969 Census of Agriculture (1973, vol. 2, ch. 3, table 4) and 1974 Census of Agriculture (1977, table 3, p. 2). See also Moyer et al. (1969, tables A5, A6), Johnson (1974) and Rodefeld (1978a, table 2, p. 166).

[a] The definition of "farm operator" was changed for 1969, eliminating the hired manager category and changing the composition of the full owner and part owner categories (see Rodefeld, 1976). Data for 1969, 1974 are not comparable to pre-1969 figures.

The definition of "farm" was changed in 1959 and 1974.

103

In the more recent period, acres owned by farmers declined from 675 million acres in 1954 (58 percent) to 603 million acres in 1964 (54 percent). This occurred solely as a result of reduced numbers of and acreage in full-owner farms. Acres owned by part-owners increased slightly. While the numbers of and acreage in tenant farms (particularly crop- and livestock-share) continued to decline, total acreage owned by nonfarmers (and small numbers of farmers renting out some of their land) increased. This was the result of even greater increases in nonfarmer-owned acreage which was rented on a cash basis by part-owners and tenants or operated by hired managers (Table 3; Rodefeld, 1978a). While comparable figures are not available since 1964, other, less direct evidence suggests a continuation of the most recent trend.

As shown in Table 3, land ownership by farm business entities [sole proprietorships, partnerships, corporations, other (owned by either farmers or nonfarmers)] declined from 1969 to 1974.[10] The difficulty here is that no determination is possible of which of these businesses are owned by the individuals and families managing farms on a daily basis. Regarding land purchases, nonfarmers accounted for 33 percent of all farm acquisitions from 1959 to 1967. This increased to 38 percent from 1968 to 1970, and 37 to 40 percent from 1970 to 1977. While tenants accounted for 24 percent of the acquisitions in 1955, they accounted for only 11 percent in 1977. Rental payments to nonfarm landlords and mortgaged indebtedness have increased substantially in recent years (Rodefeld, 1979). Farm sizes have also continued to increase. This may indicate reduced ownership by farmers since size is strongly correlated with the likelihood of rental and the percentage of land which is rented (Moyer et al., 1969: 14-17; Johnson, 1974: 3-9, 17-25; Rodefeld, 1978a: 167). Less definitive, but consistent with the preceeding, are the numerous press reports of large-scale land purchases by wealthy individuals, large nonfarm corporations, and non-U.S. citizens (Rodefeld, 1978a: 161, 165).

Even though landownership by nonfarmers appears to have increased consistently since 1954, little is known of their characteristics or motives. Conversely, little is known about the characteristics of farmers experiencing reduced ownership and the reasons for this decline. We do know that about 20 percent of the rented land is owned by other active farmers (Johnson, 1974: 1-4). Little is known of the nonfarmers owning the remaining 80 percent or those employing hired managers. It is likely a high percentage are still retired farmers or their heirs. Ownership by a variety of nonfarm investors appears to be increasing, however.

Changes have also occurred in the importance of farms with high intermediate and low levels of land ownership by their operators. The numbers of and acreage in full-owner and some types of tenant-operated farms (crop-livestock- and cash-share particularly those in the South) have declined substantially. Although full-owner farms accounted for about 57 percent of all farms from 1950 to 1964, their relative share of farmland dropped (36 to 29 percent), and they were disproportionately found among the smaller and noncommercial farm categories. Their operators relied more heavily on off-farm jobs and income (Table 3; Moyer et al., 1969: 13-15, 25-26; Johnson, 1974: 4-9, 25-28).

At the same time, numbers and/or acreages of farms with inter-mediate levels of operator ownership (part) and some types with the lowest level (none, cash rent and hired manager) increased dramatically, particularly part-owner farms. Part-owners range from those renting a "few acres" and owning the rest, to share who rent nearly all the land and own only a few acres. Part-owners have expanded their acreage in recent years largely through cash rental (as opposed to purchase). They are a good deal larger than full-owner and tenant farms in terms of average acreage, value of sales, and fixed capital assets. In 1964, part-owner farms accounted for 25 percent of all farm and 48 percent of all land in farms (Table 3; Rodefeld, 1978a).

Explanations for recent changes in land ownership appear to con-sist of two major parts. Ownership by farmers--particularly small farmers and/or those just beginning--and intergenerational transfer have become more difficult as farm sizes, land values, and capital requirements have increased. At the same time, numerous incentives have existed for the retention of farmland by former farmers and/or their heirs and its purchase by a variety of nonfarmers (Rodefeld, 1978a). While the causal forces and mechanisms are not entirely clear, rather major changes have occurred in farm land ownership and the statuses of farms with high, intermediate and low levels of owner-ship by their operators. An important fact is that ownership is gradually changing form as capitalist social relations penetrate petty commodity production.

Turning to the ownership of nonland farm capital, it appears similar changes have occurred. The empirical evidence is sketchy, however. While data have existed to determine aggregate levels and trends in land ownership by farm operators, this has not been true for the ownership of nonland capital. We know, however, that reduced capital ownership by farm operators can occur through a variety of mechanisms. These include: purchase and ownership by nonfarm business owners employing hired managers, ownership by landlords (particularly those in share-arrangements), renting and leasing from off-farm sources, crop growing and livestock feeding on a custom basis, hiring of machines on a custom or contract basis, and ownership by integrators (i.e. birds, feed, and equipment in broiler operations). High levels of ownership by farmers historically can be inferred since the per-centages of farms reporting such expenditures and/or arrangements have never been high. One exception is share arrangements. These have de-clined dramatically over the last four decades, however.

More recent data indicate that while on-farm, family ownership of nonland capital is still high, it is in relative decline (Rodefeld, 1978a: 168-169; 1978b: 20-21; 1979). Vertical coordination contracts (some of which involve integrator ownership), custom farming, and the rental of equipment, machines and buildings are among those tenure farms experiencing rapid growth (Moyer et al., 1969). Expenditures by operators for machine rental and leasing, custom, and contract work have tripled since 1949. While the percentage of farms reporting these expenditures has declined in recent years, the number and percentage of total farms reporting large expenditures has increased substantially. Custom feeding of beef was found to be high and increasing in the late 1960's and early 1970's. As pointed out in Table 3, acreage in farms employing hired managers increased from 1954 to 1964. Some evidence exists that this trend has continued (Rodefeld, 1978a: 173-174).

The foregoing suggests reduced levels of nonland capital ownership by the operators of farms containing these resources and increased ownership by nonfarmers and/or off-farm sources. Our knowledge is far from complete, however. Little is known about the characteristics of the farms or operators using capital which is not owned or of those who own this capital. Variability is likely in the importance of the various mechanisms for different types of nonland capital and/or different types of production and regions. Little is known on these subjects.

Why has there been this reduction in land and capital ownership by farm operators, which apparently undermines petty commodity production? While the reasons are numerous, the following appear central. Growth in capital requirements for farming have made sole ownership of land, technological requisites, livestock, etc., increasingly difficult for farm operators. At the same time there have been incentives for ownership by nonfarm interests (Rodefeld, 1978b: 13-27). As the value of land has risen, it has become attractive to nonfarm investors for capital appreciation and a hedge against inflation. Special tax provisions for farm enterprises permit income tax savings for high income nonfarm investors. Also, farming is becoming a consumption item for nonfarm people seeking farm-related hobbies or a rural lifestyle. Finally, risks in farming have been reduced over the years due to government price support programs and improved cultural practices. Although, farming in general gives a low return of capital invested, adequate profits can be returned from larger farms producing particular commodities. The profit motive and the opportunity to control food production from inputs to marketing are some of the reasons why nonfarm corporations enter farming.

It seems fairly certain that there is a trend away from on-farm, operator ownership of land and other capital resources. It also appears that ownership of farm businesses (sole proprietorships, partnerships, corporations) by farm operators has declined, while ownership by nonfarmers has increased (Rodefeld, 1978a: 173-174; 1979). Those represent one "break" within the traditional farm structure--that between ownership and daily operation of the farm. In the next section we will suggest another "break"--that between wage-labor and daily operation of the farm. When these two changes in social relations occur together, there is separation of capital, operational-management, and labor and the transformation of petty commodity production into capitalist production.

Wage-Labor and Exploitation

It was stated earlier that "what is distinctive about capitalism as an economic system is that labour power itself becomes a commodity, to be bought and sold on the market." What sets capitalist production apart from earlier forms, including petty commodity production, is the presence of wage-labor (Mann and Dickinson, 1978). It is no wonder that analysts of the farm land tenure system in America have often assumed that a Marxian analysis of agriculture is inappropriate because the farmer/operator typically hires no labor; thus it is suggested that exploitation is impossible because there are no wage laborers to exploit. We propose that Marxian theory is still appropriate. In this regard, Lianos and Paris (1972) in their study of agriculture have suggested that a "labor exploitation" analysis of the family farm with no hired laborers is plausible. Lianos and Paris noted that farm labor has been increasingly exploited during the last 30 years, despite increases in absolute earnings and in earnings relative to urban wages. They computed Marxian estimates of the relative share of the value accruing to capitalists, the relative share to labor, and the rate of exploitation (capitalist share/labor share) for 1949-1968 and reported a tenfold increase in exploitation, both of hired labor and family labor.[11] They point out that much of this exploitation has been "concealed" within the farm family, since until recently three-quarters of the total farm work force consisted of farm operators and unpaid family workers. For Lianos and Paris (1972: p. 575), these considerations:

> introduce the question of whether farmers in a capital-istic system can meaningfully exploit their own labor and that of their families. In the Marxist economic analysis the phenomenon of self-exploitation is explained in terms of the small farmer's desire to maintain his position as a capitalist. Basic to this goal is the necessity of capital accumulation in an environment of fierce competition and technical progress. The ever-increasing land values are an indication of this process of accumulation, and the concommitant increase in ground rent forces the farmer toward more intensive use of the land and additional nonland investment. As indicated by

the rapidly decreasing number of small farmers the attempt to accumulate is not always successful, thus leading toward the farmer's indebtedness and the necessity of accepting a remuneration for his labor which may be inferior to that of an agricultural worker. Often he requires the same sacrifice from family labor whether or not the family shares his goals.

Thus, for Lianos and Paris, the twin processes of expansion of the forces of production and proletarianisation in agriculture are closely linked to the exploitation of family farm labor in a milieu of competition for survival.

While the absolute size of the farm workforce has declined substantially in the last three to four decades, it has been widely assumed there was little or no change in its composition or in the relative importance of its constituent groups. This has been based on observations that farm operators and family and hired workers have declined numerically at similar rates and that hired labor accounted for approximately 25 percent of total farm employment in both the 1930's and the late 1960's (Nikolitch, 1972b: 256-257). It has also been assumed that no change has occurred in the relative importance of farms employing small and large amounts of hired labor. This was based on the observation that farms employing more than 1.5 man years of hired labor accounted for five percent of all farms and 37-38 percent of all farm sales in both 1949 and 1969 (Nikolitch, 1972a: 4). Recent reviews of the evidence, however, suggest these assumptions are incorrect (Rodefeld, 1978a, 1979).

While hired farm workers accounted for 27 percent of the workforce in 1929, they declined to 25 percent in the 1930's, and 20 to 22 percent in the mid-1940's. Since reaching this low point, their percentage of the workforce has slowly turned upward from 23 percent (1948-1952), to 24-27 percent (1953-1973), to 30-31 percent from 1974 to 1977. While the numbers of all groups in the workforce declined from the 1940's (Rowe and Smith, 1976: 9) to 1970, this has not been true since 1970. Farm operators, family workers, and hired workers of short duration (fewer than 75 days worked) have continued to decline. At the same time, the number of total hired workers and those employed for longer durations (75 days or more) have increased (Table 4). Comparable changes have been observed in other data and for all major geographical and/or type of production regions (Rodefeld, 1979). As a result of these recent changes, full-time (150 days or more) hired workers increased their percentages of hired workforce numbers from 20 percent (1968-70) to 23 percent (1974-76). They increased their percentage of total wage work from 66 percent (1968-70) to 68 percent (1975). Numerous reasons exist to predict the preceeding trends will continue in the future (Rodefeld, 1978a, 1979).

TABLE 4. Frequency and Change in the Incidence of Persons (in Thousands) Who Did Any Farm Wagework During the Year, by Duration of Farm Wagework (in Days). United States.

Time period	Total workers	Duration of Farm Wagework in Year (in Days)				
		Less than 75	75-149	150-249	250 or more	
1968-1970	2659	1857 (69%)	286 (11%)	206 (8%)	310 (12%)	
1971-1973	2677	1761 (66%)	308 (12%)	249 (9%)	358 (13%)	
1974-1976	2713	1774 (65%)	325 (12%)	264 (10%)	352 (13%)	
Percent change	2	-4.5	13.6	28.2	13.5	

Sources: McElroy (1974: 10); Smith and Rowe (1978: 15); and Rodefeld (1979).

It also appears that employment of hired workers has become more concentrated on U.S. farms. Even while total and full-time workers numbers have increased over the last decade, the numbers and percentages of farms employing hired workers declined from 1964 to 1974. This was true for both total and "commercial" (sales of $2,500 or more) farms and for the employment of short and long duration workers. The percentage of commercial farms reporting any ($1.00 or more) hired labor expenditures declined from 66 percent in 1964 to 41 percent in 1974. This was the outcome of a substantial decline in the number of farms with small ($1.00 to $5,000) labor expenditures (from 1.1 to 0.545 million) labor expenditures and a large increase in the numbers reporting no expenditures (612,000 to 994,000). Commercial farms reporting larger hired labor expenditures ($5,000 or more), however, increased their numbers from 99,157 in 1964 (5.4 percent of total) to 155,689 in 1974 (9.1 percent). Increases also occurred in the average numbers of short (5.3 to 7.6) and longer (2.6 to 3.2) duration workers on farms reporting such employment. Similar patterns of change and concentration have been observed for contract labor and machine hire and custom work (Rodefeld, 1979).

The increasing number and percentage of farms with high hired labor expenditures and the growing concentration of labor on these farms suggest they are accounting for growing percentages of U.S. farm production and sales. This has been the case. Farms employing more than 1.5 man-year equivalents of hired labor accounted for 4.5 percent of total farm numbers and 30 percent of all sales in 1959. They were estimated to account for 5.6 percent of the farms and 38 percent of the sales in 1969 (Nikolotch, 1969a: 4). From 1959 to 1964, these farms increased their portion of total sales in all geographic regions. Regional variability in importance was considerable. They accounted for 13 percent of all sales in the Corn Belt and 70 percent in the Pacific Region in 1964.

Large scale farms (1,000 or more acres or sales of $100,000 or more) have increased in both absolute and relative terms in recent decades, in all regions. Farms with sales of $100,000 or more increased their numbers from 31,401 in 1964 (1.0 of total) to 152,599 in 1974 (6.6 percent of total). They increased their percentage of total sales from 24 percent to 54 percent in this period. In 1974, 77 percent of these farms reported hired labor expenditures, and they accounted for 72 percent of all hired labor expenditures by commercial farms. While inflation undoubtedly explains some of the increased numbers in this category, inflation free measures yield similar results. The 50,000 largest farms in the U.S. accounted for 23 percent of total sales in 1960 and 36 percent in 1977. In 1974, farms with sales of $200,000 or more numbered 51,400. Approximately 90 percent reported hired labor expenditures, and 80 percent employed full-time workers (Rodefeld, 1979).

Major conclusions here are: 1) since the 1940's, family labor has consistently declined relative to hired labor; 2) since 1970, seasonal or short-term workers have declined relative to full-time hired workers; 3) the number of farms employing large numbers of hired workers and the concentration of workers on these farms has increased since 1964; and 4) the concentration and centralization of both capital (resources and output) and labor on large-scale farms have increased. The specific conditions and forces which have resulted in these changes are numerous and varied. They have been reviewed elsewhere and will not be repeated here (Rodefeld, 1974; 1978a; 1979).

The Marxian theory of historical change postulates that proletarianisation--the separation of persons from their means of production and subsistence--occurs in the wake of capitalist development. In the past, most persons separated from the means of agricultural production left the farming sector to seek employment in the city. However, the evidence presented here indicates that hired, contract, and custom workers are providing an increasing proportion of total farm labor. It is this trend, combined with the decline of on-farm, family ownership of the means of production, and increased concentration on large-scale farms, that leads us to conclude that while petty commodity production has been dominant historically, it is undergoing a transition to full-scale capitalist agriculture. Consistent with this observation has been an increase in the proletarianization of farm people.

Proletarianization of Small and Part-time Farmers

The forces that have fostered increased size of farm operations, concentration, decreased on-farm ownership, and increased wage-labor (that is, separation of capital and labor)--overproduction, low commodity prices, low returns, and others--have also proletarianized a substantial portion of farm personnel on small and part-time farms. It is apparent that small farms are becoming a relatively stable form of U.S. agriculture. One common definition of the small farm is any operation bringing in less than $20,000 per year in gross farm sales. Such farms were 80 percent of all farms in 1969, and 65 percent of all farms in 1974 (Chapman and Goss, 1978: 373-377). Many farm operators, unable to accumulate sufficient capital and faced with the prospect of leaving farming, have utilized nonfarm employment to supplement low farm earnings (Cavazzani, 1977). Since 1934, the percentage of farm operators working off the farm 100 days or more has probably quadrupled (Table 5). There is a high degree of overlap of small farms and part-time farms.

Part-time farming would appear to have several major implications of concern to class analysis and political economy. The first is that part-time farming, while "functional" for the farmer in terms of offering adaptability to fluctuations in farm commodity prices (Barkley, 1976),[12] may increase the level of labor exploitation in agriculture.

TABLE 5.   Percentages of U.S. Farm Operators Working Any Days Off the
Farm, and 100 Days or More Off the Farm, United States, 1934-
1974.

Year[a]	Operators working any days off the farm (percent)	Operators working 100 or more days off the farm (percent)
1934	30.5	11.2
1949	38.9	23.3
1959	44.9	29.9
1964	46.3	32.1
1969	54.2	39.9
1974	54.9	44.2

Source: Cavazzani (1977, table 1, p. 7); U.S. Bureau of the Census,
1974 Census of Agriculture (1977, table 3, p. 2).

[a]The definition of "farm" was changed in 1959 and 1974.

The 1974 figures are corrected for farms "not reporting." Data for
1969 and 1974 are not comparable to pre-1969 figures because the
definition of "farm operator" was changed in 1969.

Low levels of return to family labor resulting from periods of low
commodity prices may result in increased exploitation of labor (since
nonfarm income partially insulates the farm operator from low commodity
prices). Secondly, the part-time farming trend may portend a possible
diminution of the historic antimony between workers and farmers (Wiley,
1970; Steeves, 1972), since the part-time farmer tends to be a member
of both groupings. The part-time farmer and the full-time hired agricultural wage worker might well become a significant social force since
both are removed from the vested interest in maintaining private property
in agriculture that has characterized otherwise radical agriculturalists
in the past. The result may be a tendency toward narrowing the political
differences between farmer and worker and generate a qualitatively different agricultural politics in the years to come.

The separation of farm capital from farm labor and the proletarianization of farm personnel, both in the context of a food and
fiber production system increasingly dominated by monopoly capital,
constitute the dynamics of capitalist development in agriculture and
the basis for class analysis of agriculture.

A Class-based Farm Typology

At the outset of this paper we asserted that Stinchcombe's analysis of rural class relations resulted in a typology that is static, ahistorical and descriptive. Having reviewed Marxian theory and applied it to the changing economic and social structure of U.S. agriculture, we are now in the position to propose a more dynamic, class-analytic typology of farms.

The farm can be conceptualized as a production system with four basic factors of production: land, capital, management and labor. Five basic status-roles are directly associated with these factors of production--land ownership, capital ownership, organizational management, operational management, and labor. The degree to which these status-roles are differentiated between non-related individuals (that is, not in the same family) on any particular farm determines its structural type.[13] Assuming for the time being there is no differentiation between land ownership, capital ownership and organizational management (i.e., they are provided entirely or mostly by the same individual or family) and that the most important divisions in status-roles have occurred between ownership and operational management, and between operational management and labor, four mutually exclusive farm types can be identified (Figure 1).[14]

FIGURE 1.   Farm Types Based on Classification by Their Amount of Land and Capital Ownership and Amount of Labor Performed by the Farm Operational Manager and Family.

Amount of Land and Capital Ownership by Operator	Amount of Labor Provided by Operator	
	Most or All	Least or None
Most or All	Family type	Larger than family type
Least or None	Tenant-type	Industrial-type

Source: Rodefeld (1978a, fig. 1, p. 159).

Historically, U.S. farm numbers have been dominated by relatively small farms with low levels of differentiation between (land and capital) ownership, management and labor. Such farms were managed on a

daily basis by an individual or family (farm operator) who simultaneously: owned all or most of the
acres providing the land base of the farm; owned
all or most of the capital (nonland resources...)
used in the production of agricultural goods; and
provided for all or most of the physical labor expended in the production process (Rodefeld, 1975:
2).

This farm type identifies what is often called the "family farm," and
here is referred to as the "family-type" farm. The larger than family
type farm, historically found in the south and west, is mainly or
wholly owned by the individual or family who manages it on a daily
basis, but the majority of the work is done by hired labor. The tenant-
type farm, prevalent in the 1930's, is mainly or wholly owned (particularly the land) by people other than the individual or family who
manage it on a daily basis and who contributes most or all of the
labor. The industrial-type farm, which is typical of many farms in
the recent "corporate invasion," has a resident manager, but is entirely
or mainly owned by other people and entirely or mainly worked by hired
labor, each of whom have limited involvement in daily management
decisions.

This four-category farm typology is both basic and simplistic.
For instance, differentiation between land ownership and capital (nonland resource) ownership was temporarily bypassed. A good deal of variability is possible on this dimension, however. For example, the typical
tenant farm will have a nonfarm land owner, but the tenant farmer is
likely to own all or most of the nonland capital. The major exception
here is when the tenant farmer is hired. Other mechanisms were identified earlier, which could result in the separation of capital ownership from either land ownership, operational management or both.
With appropriate data, however, the typology can be expanded to a total
of 15 unique farm types along a gradient of structural differentiation.
between land ownership, capital ownership, operational management and
labor.[15] Even in its most basic, simple form, however, the typology
appears useful.

Rodefeld (1978a: 159-160, 174-175) measured changes across farm
types by adaptation of Census of Agriculture data (Table 6). Family-
type farms have traditionally accounted for more than three-quarters
of farm numbers and one-half of farm sales. For the period 1959 to
1964, there was a slight increase in their percentage of farm numbers
and a slight decrease in their percentage of farm sales. Tenant-
type farms experienced the greatest decline in both percentages of
farm numbers and farm sales. Larger than family-type farms grew
slightly in proportion, of both numbers and sales. Industrial-type
farms increased in both categories. Despite the many limitations to

TABLE 6. Change in Farm Numbers and Gross Sales by Farm Type, United States, 1959-1964.

Farm Type[a]	Number of Farms (thous.)		Change (%)	Gross Sales ($ mill.)		Change (%)
	1959	1964		1959	1964	
Family	2808	2475	-11.9	15224	17276	+11.9
Tenant	721	521	-27.7	5912	5372	- 9.1
Larger than family	139	122	-12.2	7202	8915	+23.8
Industrial	26	32	+23.1	2024	3512	+73.5
TOTAL	3695	3150	-14.7	30362	35075	+15.5
	(% farms)			(% sales)		
Family	76.0	78.6		50.1	49.3	
Tenant	19.5	16.5		19.5	15.3	
Larger than family	3.8	3.9		23.7	25.4	
Industrial	.7	1.0		6.7	10.0	
TOTAL	100.0	100.0		100.0	100.0	

Source: Rodefeld (1978a, table 8, p. 174).

[a]These figures are based on Census of Agriculture data which are not directly suited to Rodefeld's farm typology. The procedures for computation of figures were such that relative importance of family-type and larger than family type farms, both in number and sales, have been overestimated. For further details on computation procedures see Rodenfeld (1973, 1974; or 1975, table 9, footnotes).

115

the data in Table 6 (see Rodefeld, 1978a: 175), they still indicate a tendency away from the family-type farm and toward the industrial.

This farm typology is dynamic and is class-based. The distinction between the family and larger than family-type farms, and the tenant and industrial-type farms (and the transition from the former to the latter types), is based on reduced ownership of the means of production by the farm operational manager and the reduced importance of such farms. The distinction between the family and tenant-type farms, and the larger than family and industrial-type farms (and the transition from the former to the latter types), is based on the increased use of wage-labor and the importance of farms employing this labor. The separation of land ownership from the joint provision of other capital ownership and operational management results in a land owner, capitalist-tenant-like relationship. The transition from petty commodity production to capitalist production in farming should be reflected in a transition from the family type farm to the industrial type farm either directly or more likely via either or both intermediate types--the tenant and larger than family-type farms (Rodefeld, 1974, 1978a, 1979). However, this is a farm typology not an agricultural typology. That is, many of the causal forces and manifestations of capitalist agriculture occur off the farm and increasingly so. Nevertheless, the greatest limitation to this class-based typology is paucity of suitable data.

Role of the State

The state has assumed an active role in reproducing the class structure of agriculture. The circumstances noted above concerning the evolution of agribusiness and the farming sector may serve to clarify the state's role in agricultural transformation. Remembering that food raising is only one of three components of an agricultural system, it is apparent that the agricultural inputs and product marketing components have experienced capitalist penetration--on a much larger scale than in the food and fiber raising sector--and have been centralized within the "monopoly sector" (i.e., the large-scale corporate sector; see O'Connor, 1973) of the economy. This transformation has a number of important consequences. Firstly, it coincides with and contributes to the diminution of the role of land monopoly in retarding capital accumulation in agriculture. The extraction of surplus value from agriculture presently is more rooted in profits of agribusiness firms than in rent, interest, and profit accruing to capitalist landowners and tenants. Secondly, the interests of these nonfarm agribusiness firms come to be more consonant with those of other multinational, monopoly sector enterprises (especially in foreign expansion and foreign trade). Insofar as the role of the state tends to be that of advancing the interests of the dominant class as a whole--not any one particular segment such as that of capitalist farmers--state policy toward agriculture has primarily revolved around ensuring the profitability of its inputs, and product marketing components (Frundt, 1975).[16]

Many analysts of state policy toward agriculture have rightly noted that most U.S. Department of Agriculture programs (particularly commodity programs) have benefitted large farmers at the expense of smaller ones (Bonnen, 1968; Schultze, 1971; Ford, 1973; Marshall and Thompson, 1976: Ch. 3), because the former are more politically influential. However, such a view should not obscure other facets. Agriculture involves many functions other than food and fiber raising, and agricultural politics is not confined to the U.S. Department of Agriculture or the Congress. Rather it involves many other sectors of the state apparatus, for example, other Executive Branch agencies that deal with large corporations, such as the Departments of State and Commerce. Again, one should not ignore the role of agribusiness firms in supporting policies that tend to favor large farmers over small farmers. Larger farmers are the best market for agricultural inputs, and are easier to coordinate marketing agreements with (Raup, 1969; Krause and Kyle, 1970; Marshall and Thompson, 1976: Ch. 3). They are most ideologically supportive of agribusiness activities, while small farmers who bear the brunt of exploitation in the agricultural system are most likely to be critical of these institutions (Schwartz, 1976). Thus large farmers are benefitted not so much because of their autonomous political power (which is often quite circumscribed), but rather because of their coincidence of interest with nonfarm elements in the agricultural system.

It should be noted, however, that large farmers are still subject to the same manipulation of the forces and relations of production that small farmers are. They are merely able to gain greater returns than small farmers (Hottel and Reinsel, 1976) under the same market price conditions through external economies of size--purchase discounts, credit availability, marketing advantages (Raup, 1969; Krause and Kyle, 1970; Rodefeld, 1974; Marshall and Thompson, 1976: Ch. 3). All farmers, even large operators, suffer from the understandable inclination of commodity purchasers to pursue state policies that depress farm prices (e.g., the U.S. Department of Agriculture giving grain traders privileged access to information), although the large operator maintains a relatively privileged position in this milieu.

The State and Agrarian Protest

The state has not been neutral with respect to agrarian protest. Quite understandably, the course of agricultural transformation in the U.S. has not always been a consensual process. Periodically, groups of exploited rural strata have formed political movements to alter the distribution of the social product in agriculture. These movements have generally been constituted by the less privileged strata within farming--especially smaller family farmers, tenants, and

agricultural laborers.[17] Notable episodes of agrarian unrest have been
the Populist movement of the turn of the century and the recent United
Farm Workers' movement of migrant Mexican-American laborers. Considering the tendency for the state to assume a protective position vis-a-vis
the dominant propertied class, the state's role has largely been one of
maintaining existing production relations in agriculture. O'Connor
(1973) has noted that the state in capitalist society must assume two
generally contradictory roles: accumulation (making possible the conditions for profitable capital accumulation) and legitimization (maintenance of social harmony). These roles are presumed to be contradictory because "a capitalist state that openly uses its coercive forces
to help one class accumulate capital at the expense of other classes
loses its legitimacy and hence undermines the basis of loyalty and
support" (O'Connor, 1973: 6). The discussion thus far has emphasized
the state's accumulation functions in the agricultural sphere, but the
legitimization role of course assumes particular primacy during periods
of unrest on the part of subordinate rural strata.

O'Connor (1973) has also noted that a given state policy or expenditure may jointly serve both--the accumulation and legitimization--
functions. This has particularly been the case in the realm of agriculture. Many observers of agricultural policy have viewed the two
major thrusts of agricultural policy in this century--encouragement of
"economic efficiency" on the part of farmers through agricultural
research and extension, and commodity price supports--as the outcomes
of class privilege and power on the part of large farmers. Historically,
however, agricultural research and price supports were the strategies
taken by the state in the midst of various episodes of agrarian unrest
(i.e., these policies also pertain to the legitimization function of
the state in agriculture). Farmers were encouraged to solve their problems individually through increased production and efficiency (rather
than by class action). Further, price supports were introduced to head
off agrarian discontent by placing a "floor" under commodity prices.
It is ironic that farmers' protests were often subdued by agricultural
policies that had the effect of further reducing the competitive
position of small farmers and agricultural laborers (see McConnell,
1953).

Observers of agrarian radicalism have often been concerned with the
reasons for its apparent failures. Even when farmers constituted a
numerical majority of the U.S. population, farmers were never able to
articulate a coherent, unified set of demands (Hadwiger, 1976). Most
analyses have emphasized socioeconomic differences among farmers--race
and ethnicity, religion, income, region, and commodity interests--as
contributing to the failure of farmers to sustain a unified political
movement (Wiley, 1970). Although we do not wish to deny the importance
of these potential cleavages in fostering disunity among farmers, we
feel that the matter is better understood via the class structure in
agriculture.

As noted above, the U.S. food and fiber raising sector has historically been one where the family freeholder form of land tenure has predominated. On one hand, farmers have either been property owners or anticipated becoming property owners at a later point. Farmers, on the other hand, have tended to be excluded from the fruits of capitalist development. For example, farm operators and agricultural laborers continue to be the two aggregate occupational groups in U.S. society with the highest incidences of poverty (Bryant, 1969). As a result, agrarian radicals, while often critical of certain aspects of capitalism (e.g., manipulation of bankers and the railroads), have generally continued to accept the legitimacy of private property (i.e., capitalism) in agriculture. The policies they sought (such as regulation of the railroads, expanded food exports, and price supports) have likewise tended to assume a corresponding contradictory character. Agrarian radicals pursued policies that they felt would reverse the emergence of contradictions in capitalist agriculture, but within a framework of production relations that ensured the appearance of further social dislocations in agriculture.

Thus the inability of farmer movements to secure major social change in their benefit may be attributed at least as much to their contradictory class positions--both property owners and subjects of exploitation--as their internal socio-political differences. In part, this may explain why farmers have so readily accepted state policies that would further exasercbate rural poverty and underdevelopment. More substantively, we feel that the contradictory class character of farmers has circumscribed the content of agrarian protest and helped to mold policies that continue to result in social dislocation in agriculture. This contradictory character of farmers' class positions may help to explain why commodity interests, region, and other factors served to undermine the solidarity of farmers from within. Since farmers came to view their interests in terms of protection from unstable market (rather than, for example, elimination of private property in agriculture), agricultural politics became "distributive," rather than "redistributive" (see Lowi, 1964).[18] Since favored status for one particular commodity would tend to come at the expense of another commodity, farmer struggles often became intra-group conflicts. Thus, the class character of farmers under the past system of land tenure has functioned to block collective strategies for change and reduce discontent to fractionalized contests for advantages in the political and market arenas.

DISCUSSION

As noted at the outset, U.S. rural sociologists have been hesitant to develop a political-economic or class analysis of agriculture. In part, we feel this lack of attention to class structure in agriculture is due to the presumption that the so-called family farm has not de-clined in status relative to more differentiated farm types and that, anyhow, it does not "fit" into a Marxian scheme of classes. The latter notion, however, confused land tenure forms with social classes, and as we have attempted to demonstrate, one can formulate a meaningful political economy of the family farm, as well as agriculture as a whole. We also sense that previous attempts to analyze social class in agriculture have been limited by focusing only on stratification within food and fiber raising. It is important to recognize, however, that an agricultural system has other components--inputs, and product marketing, in addition to farming. Viewing the food and fiber raising sector apart from the dynamics of the other aspects of agriculture has probably served as a barrier to a more sophisticated political economy of agriculture.

The class structure of agriculture is a highly complex, ever-changing phenomenon. On one hand, farmers tend to represent a trans-itional social class (petty commodity producers) whose activities are circumscribed by the unique characteristics of agriculture. However, the dominant class in agriculture has emerged in the form of agri-business corporations that provide inputs, and process and market agricultural outputs. This class comes to gain control of the forces of production in order that surplus value can be appropriated from farm commodities. Agribusiness thus comes to have a manipulative and exploitive relationship to farmers (even though both groups nominally are property owners). Augmented by the protective role of the state, the class structure in agriculture tends to become polar-ized into a small group of wealthy agribusiness elites and a growing stratum of agricultural laborers, part-time farmers, and "self-exploiting" family farmers. Rhetorically limited by their tie to private property, while at the same time "squeezed" by the ongoing social forces in agriculture, farmer protest has thus far been dis-unified and, in some respects, complementary to the interests of the dominant agribusiness segment.

It is appropriate to conclude a political-economic analysis of agriculture by noting certain other emerging contradictions. The most general anomaly is the existence, on one hand, of rapidly devel-oping forces of production, and on the other, the persistent poverty and underdevelopment in rural areas. This theme has been implicit throughout our discussion and reflects the uneven course of develop-ment characteristic of agriculture, as well as other social-industrial sectors of society. The historic displacement of farmers from the land and their replacement by machines and inanimate energy resources also raises two separate, but related, ecological questions. "Modern" agriculture is a creature of fossil fuel subsidies, but supplies of these fuels are limited. Secondly, agriculture based on artificial

fertilizers and pesticides is eroding the natural regenerative properties of agro-ecosystems (Perelman, 1977; Stockdale, 1977). It thus
seems that the present trajectory of the forces of agricultural production may reach certain physical and social limits--foreshadowing
perhaps the emergence at some point of new relationships of humans to
the land.

It is hoped that these preliminary notes towards a political
economic theory of agriculture in the advanced societies will become
the starting point for further critical analyses. Rural sociologists
need to reconsider their historic neglect of class analysis of agri-
culture--a perspective we feel can provide rich insight into the social
and material forces shaping agriculture in Western nations.

FOOTNOTES

1. These criticisms will become more explicit in the following discussion of Marxian theory of capitalist development. It may be
   significant that Stinchcombe's only reference to Marx's own writings
   is pp. 488-495 of Talcott Parson's, The Structure of Social Action
   (1968).

2. This section is a synthesis of the writings of Marx in his Economic
   and Philosophical Manuscripts (1963: 68-95), Capital, Volume I
   (1972: 3-18, 169-207), and Values, Price and Profit (1901). We
   also draw on interpretations by Giddens (1971, 1973).

3. Sources are given at the end of paragraphs, except for quotations.

4. We are indebted to Alain de Janvry, Peter Sinclair, Howard Newby,
   and Susan Mann for helping us recognize that the various "paths"
   of capitalist development in agriculture--British, Russian and
   former European colonies--are not inconsistent with Marx's theoretical formulations. Marxist "textbooks" tend to emphasize the
   British path (Eaton, 1966; Mandel, 1968; Afansyev et al., 1974).
   Newby (1978) illustrates agricultural social change in Western
   Europe, the Americas, and Australasia, while Bernier (1976)
   specifically analyzes Quebec.

5. De Janvry (1978, pers. comm.) cites Karl Marx, Capital, Vol. I
   (Moscow, 1971), pp. 722-723 on this point.

6. For similar interpretations of the role of the Civil War, see
   Genovese (1965: 13-39) and Hacket (1970: Ch. 8-9).

7. The observations in this and the following paragraph have been
   greatly abbreviated. More details will be provided for the

post-1940 period later in this paper. Meanwhile, references for
this historical account include Edwards (1940), Shannon (1945),
Faulkner (1951: Ch. 13-14), Soule (1947: Ch. 11), Mitchell (1947:
Ch. 6), Hackler (1970: 225-234), Padfield (1971), Dowd (1974:
150-156), and Frundt (1975: Ch. 1). References specifically for
the 1940 to 1978 period include Kyle et al. (1972), Breimyer and
Barr (1972), Ford (1973), Raup (1973), Frundt (1975: Ch. 2-3),
Rodefeld (1974, 1978), and Goss and Rodefeld (1978a).

8. A precursor to the current line of research was Lenin's reanalysis
of the 1900 and 1910 U.S. Census of Agriculture which showed a
growing concentration in farm acreage and sales, and an increase
in the prevalence of hired labor. However, he recognized that
the food-raising sector had clearly lagged behind industry in
capital accumulation and attributed this to: (1) a large number
of small-scale operations to start with (i.e., a general agricultural labor surplus that provided a disincentive for technological innovation and expansion of the farm enterprise),
(2) a residue of a natural economy producing for home consumption,
and (3) the "monopoly" of land ownership.

9. See Frundt (1975: 46 ff.) for a discussion of how trends in the
evolution of the multinational agribusiness enterprise have paralleled those in other monopoly industries such as petroleum,
automobiles, and steel.

10. It is important to note definitional changes in 1969 mean that there
is no comparability with pre-1969 figures. The term "farm operator"
used in the following discussion means the "person or family
managing farm operations on a daily basis," which is consistent
with the pre-1969 Census of Agriculture definition. For further
implications of this definitional change see Rodefeld (1976).

11. The capitalist share was [(surplus value) $\div$ (variable capital +
surplus value)] and the labor share was [(variable capital) $\div$
(surplus value + variable capital)].

12. Barkley's class analysis of family farming is constrained, we feel,
by reliance on Ricardian political economy. More specifically,
Barkley is unconcerned with the emergence and change in class
formations in agriculture per se. He sees that "exploitation"
of the family farmer is rampant, but suggests that the farmer is
exploited by "society" (i.e., in terms of the farmer's "resilience"
in the face of unstable prices and low returns), not by a dominant
agricultural class. Barkley also neglects to identify the "laws of
motion" of modern agriculture; as a result, his analysis remains
largely static and ahistorical.

3. This typology was formulated by Richard Rodefeld in 1970 and is explained most fully in his Ph.D. dissertation (1974: Ch. 3).

4. This conception requires a distinction between high and low levels of differentiation. The focus here is on the operational manager [i.e., the individual or family making all or most of the farms day to day (operational) decisions]. A low level of differentiation between this status and any other requires that the operational manager occupy the other status(es) and provide all or a majority (51 to 100 percent) of its (their) content. A high level of differentiation requires that the operational manager either not occupy the other status(es) (i.e., provides zero percent of the content) or occupy it (them), but provide a minority (one to 50 percent) of its (their) content. Thus a managing owner/nonmanaging owner=greater than/less than 50 percent of the land and capital are owned by the resident farm manager and family. A managing laborer/ nonmanaging laboror=greater than/less than 50 percent of total labor is performed by the resident farm manager and family. A fifth, though highly atypical, type is also identified. This type has no or little separation between ownership and labor but a different individual or family manages the farm on a daily basis.

5. For some indication of the multitude of status-roles and structural types available, see Rodefeld (1974: charts 1-3, pp. 60-61, 87, 90-92).

6. Frundt (1975) presents the most detailed, historically-informed analysis of state policies toward agriculture that we know of. Frundt's analysis is especially strong in the area of foreign agricultural policy.

7. However, as Hadwiger (1976) points out, relatively privileged farmers have also periodically taken part in agrarian protest because, as we argue below, the same forces of competition and exploitation pertain to the large as well as the small farmer. Of course, the larger farmer is typically better able to adjust to these forces than is the small farmer (owner-operator or tenant), so relatively privileged farmers' expressions of discontent and radicalism have tended to be short-lived.

8. According to Lowi, "distributive" politics occurs in a context in which individuals or corporations seek advantage in the political arena on an individual basis. The political participant typically does not enter into overt conflict with others. Instead the predominant relations among political participants tend to be "logrolling" and mutual noninterference (i.e., "you help me achieve my goal, and I will help you reach yours"). The loci of distributive politics normally are the Congressional committee or the government agency. Redistributive politics, on the other hand, entails

active political conflict between "peak associations" contending for very opposite goals. This type of politics is exemplified by class conflict. There is essentially no room for bargaining, because any particular decision will tend to benefit one group at the expense of the other. A given decision, in other words, will redistribute scarce social resources from one group to the other (see Lowi, 1964).

REFERENCES

Afanasyev, L. et al.
     1974   The Political Economy of Capitalism (Moscow: Progressive Publishers).

Ball, A.G. and E.O. Heady
     1972   "Trends in farm and enterprise size and scale," In: A.G. Ball and E.O. Heady (eds.), Size, Structure and Future of Farms (Ames, Iowa: Iowa State University Press).

Barkley, P.W.
     1976   "A contemporary political economy of family farming," American Journal of Agricultural Economics 58: 812-819.

Bernier, B.
     1976   "The penetration of capitalism in Quebec agriculture," Canadian Review of Sociology and Anthropology 13 (4): 422-434.

Bonnen, J.T.
     1968   "Distribution of benefits from selected farm programs," In: U.S. President's National Advisory Commission on Rural Poverty, Rural Poverty in the United States (Washington, D.C.: U.S. Government Printing Office).

Brake, J.R.
     1972   "Capital and credit," In: A.G. Ball and E.O. Heady (eds.), Size, Structure and Future of Farms (Ames: Iowa State University Press).

Breimyer, H.F. and W. Barr
     1972   "Issues in concentration versus dispersion." In: North Central Public Policy Committee, Who Will Control U.S. Agriculture (Urbana-Champaign: Cooperative Extension Service, University of Illinois).

Bryant, W.K.
     1969   "Rural poverty." In: V.W. Ruttan et al. (eds.), Agricultural Policy in an Affluent Society (New York: W.W. Norton).

Buttel, F.H.
     1977 "Agricultural Structure and Energy Intensity: A Comparative
     Analysis of the Developed Capitalist Societies." Paper presented
     at the annual meeting of the Rural Sociological Society, Madison,
     Wisconsin.

Carlin, T.A. and W.F. Woods
     1974 "Tax Loss Farming." (Washington, D.C.: U.S. Department of
     Agriculture, Economic Research Service), ERS-546.

Cavazzani, A.
     1977 Part-time Farming: A Functional Form of Agricultural Organiza-
     tion in the United States. (Ithaca, New York: Cornell University,
     Department of Rural Sociology), draft manuscript.

Chapman, J. and K.F. Goss
     1978 "Toward a Small Farm Policy for the United States." Hear-
     ings before the Subcommittee on Agricultural Research and General
     Legislation of the Committee on Agriculture, Forestry and Nutrition,
     U.S. Senate, 95th Congress (Washington, D.C.: U.S. Government
     Printing Office).

Donald, J.R. and L.A. Powell
     1975 "The Food and Fiber System: How It Works." (Washington, D.C.:
     U.S. Department of Agriculture, Economic Research Service, National
     Economic Analysis Division), Agriculture Information Bulletin 383.

Dorner, P.
     1977 "Transformation of U.S. Agriculture: The Past Forty Years."
     (Madison: Department of Agricultural Economics, University of
     Wisconsin), Agr. Econ. Staff Paper Series No. 126.

Dowd, D.F.
     1974 The Twisted Dream: Capitalist Development in the United
     States Since 1776 (Cambridge, Massachusetts: Winthrop).

Eaton, J.
     1966 Political Economy: A Marxist Textbook (New York: Inter-
     national Publishers).

Edwards, E.E.
     1940 "American agriculture--the first 300 years." In: Farmers
     in a Changing World, 1940 Yearbook of Agriculture (Washington,
     D.C.: U.S. Department of Agriculture).

Faulkner, H.U.
     1951 The Decline of Laizzes Faire, 1897-1917 (New York: Rinehart
     and Co.).

Flora, J. and R.D. Rodefeld
   1978 "The nature, magnitude, and consequences of changes in
   agricultural technology." In: R.D. Rodefeld et al. (eds.),
   Change in Rural America: Causes, Consequences and Alternatives
   (St. Louis, Missouri: Mosby).

Ford, A.M.
   1973 Political Economics of Rural Poverty in the South (Cambridge,
   Massachusetts: Ballinger).

Frundt, H.J.
   1975 "American Agribusiness and U.S. Foreign Agricultural
   Policy." Unpublished Ph.D. Dissertation, Rutgers University,
   New Brunswick, New Jersey.

Genovese, E.D.
   1965 The Political Economy of Slavery: Studies in the Economy
   and Society of the Slave South (New York: Vintage, Random House).

Giddens, A.
   1971 Capitalism and Modern Social Theory (Cambridge: Cambridge
   University Press).

Giddens, A.
   1973 The Class Structure of the Advanced Societies (New York:
   Barnes and Noble).

Goss, K.F.
   1976 "Consequences of Diffusion of Innovations: The Case of
   Mechanization in U.S. Agriculture." Unpublished Master's Thesis,
   Michigan State University, East Lansing, Michigan.

Goss, K.F. and R.D. Rodefeld
   1978a "Consequences of Mechanization in U.S. Agriculture,"
   (University Park: Department of Agricultural Economics and Rural
   Sociology, Pennsylvania State University), unpublished paper.

Goss, K.F. and R.D. Rodefeld
   1978b "Corporate Farming in the United States: A Guide to Current
   Literature, 1967-1977." (University Park: Department of Agricultural Economics and Rural Sociology, Pennsylvania State University), A.E.R.S. report no. 136.

Hacker, L.M.
   1970 The Course of American Economic Growth and Development (New
   York: John Wiley and Sons).

Hadwiger, D.F.
1976 "Farmers in politics." In: V. Wiser (ed.), Two Centuries of American Agriculture (Goleta, California: Kimberly Press).

Harris, M.
1974 Entrepreneurial Control in Farming (Washington, D.C.: U.S. Department of Agriculture, Economic Research Service) ERS-542.

Hottel, J.B. and R.D. Reinsel
1976 Return to Equity Capital by Economic Class of Farm (Washington, D.C.: U.S. Department of Agriculture, Economic Research Service), Agricultural Economic Report 347.

Krause, K.R. and L.R. Kyle
1970 "Economic factors underlying the incidence of large farming units: The current situation and probable trends." American Journal of Agricultural Economics 52 (5): 748-761.

Kyle, L.R. et al.
1972 "Who controls agriculture now? The trends underway." In: North Central Public Policy Committee, Who Will Control U.S. Agriculture (Urbana-Champaign: Cooperative Extension Service, University of Illinois).

Lenin, V.I.
1964 Capitalism and Agriculture in the United States, in Collected Works (Moscow: Progressive Publishers).

Lianos, T.P. and Q. Paris
1972 "American agriculture and the prophecy of increasing misery." American Journal of Agricultural Economics 54: 570-577.

Lowi, T.J.
1964 "American business, public policy, case studies and political theory." World Politics 16: 677-715.

McConnell, G.
1953 The Decline of Agrarian Democracy (Berkeley, California: University of California Press).

Mandel, E.
1968 Marxist Economic Theory, Vol. 1 (New York: Monthly Review Press).

Mann, S.A. and J.M. Dickinson
1978 "Obstacles to the development of a capitalist agriculture." Journal of Peasant Studies 5: 466-481.

Marshall, R. and A. Thompson
   1976 Status and Prospects of Small Farmers in the South (Atlanta,
   Georgia: Southern Regional Council).

Marx, K.
   1901 Value, Price and Profit (Brooklyn: New York Labor News).

Marx, K.
   1963 "Economic and philosophic manuscripts," In: T.B. Bottomore
   (ed.), Karl Marx: Early Writings (New York: McGraw-Hill).

Marx, K.
   1967 Capital: A Critique of Political Economy, Volume 3 (New York:
   International Publishers).

Marx, K.
   1972 Capital (London: J.M. Dent).

Marx, K. and F. Engels
   1888 Manifesto of the Communist Party, Reprint S-455 (Indianapolis:
   Bobbs-Merrill).

Marx, K.
   1970 The German Ideology (New York: International Publishers).

McElroy, R.C.
   1974 The Hired Farm Working Force of 1973: A Statistical Report
   (Washington, D.C.: U.S. Department of Agricultural, Economic
   Research Services), Agricultural Economic Report No. 265.

Mitchell, B.
   1947 Depression Decade: From New Era Through New Deal, 1929-
   1941 (New York: Rinehart and Co.).

Moore, B.
   1966 Social Origins of Dictatorship and Democracy: Lord and
   Peasant in the Making of the Modern World (Boston: Beacon Press).

Newby, H.
   1978 "The rural sociology of advanced capitalist societies,"
   In: H. Newby (ed.), International Perspectives in Rural Sociology:
   Change and Continuity in the Rural World (New York: John Wiley
   and Sons).

Nikolitch, R.
   1972a Family-Size Farms in U.S. Agriculture (Washington, D.C.:
   U.S. Department of Agriculture, Economic Research Service),
   Agricultural Economic Report No. 499.

Nikolitch, R.
1972b "The individual family farm." In: A.G. Ball and E.L. Heady
(eds.), Size, Structure and Future of Farms (Ames: Iowa State University Press).

O'Connor, J.
1973 The Fiscal Crisis of the State (New York: St. Martin's Press).

Padfield, H.I.
1971 "Agrarian capitalists and Urban Proletariat: The policy of
alienation in American agriculture." In: W.G. McGinnies et al.
(eds.), Food, Fiber and the Arid Lands (Tucson: University of
Arizona Press.

Parsons, T.
1968 The Structure of Social Action (Glencoe, Illinois: Free Press).

Perelman, M.J.
1973 "A minority report on the economics of spatial heterogeneity
in agricultural enterprises." In: U.S. Department of Agriculture,
Monoculture in Agriculture: Extent, Causes, and Problems (Washington,
D.C.: U.S. Department of Agriculture).

Perelman, M.J.
1977 "Farming for profit in a hungry wor ld: The myth of agricultural efficiency." In: L. Junker (ed.), The Political Economy of
Food and Energy (Ann Arbor, Michigan: Graduate School of Business
Administration, University of Michigan).

Raup, P.M.
1969 "Economies and diseconomies of large scale agriculture."
American Journal of Agricultural Economics 51 (5): 1274-1283.

Raup, P.M.
1973 "Corporate farming in the United States." Journal of
Economic History 33: 274-290.

Ray, V.K.
1968 The Corporate Invasion of American Agriculture (Denver,
Colorado: National Farmers Union).

Rodefeld, R.D.
1973 "A reassessment of the status and trends in 'family' and
'corporate' farms in U.S. society." Congressional Record, U.S.
Senate 93rd Congress, Vol. 119, no. 82, May 31.

Rodefeld, R.D.
1974 "The Changing Organizational and Occupational Structure of
Farming and the Implications for Farm Work Force Individuals,

Families and Communities." Unpublished Ph.D. dissertation, University of Wisconsin, Madison, Wisconsin.

Rodefeld, R.D.
    1975 "Evidence, Issues and Conclusions on the Current Status and Trends in U.S. Farm Types." Paper presented at the annual meeting of the Rural Sociological Society, San Francisco, California.

Rodefeld, R.D.
    1976 "The assessment of farm (operation unit) and farm operator characteristics by the U.S. Census of Agriculture: Shortcomings and procedures for their elimination." In: U.S. House of Representatives, Agricultural Census, Hearings before the Subcommittee on Census and Population of the Committee on Post Office and Civil Service, 94th Congress June 1976 (Washington, D.C.: U.S. Government Printing Office), serial no. 94-76.

Rodefeld, R.D.
    1978a "Trends in U.S. farm organizational structure and type." In: R.D. Rodefeld et al. (eds.), Change in Rural America: Causes, Consequences and Alternatives (St. Louis, Missouri: Mosby).

Rodefeld, R.D.
    1978b "The Changing Structure of U.S. Farms: Trends, Causes, Consequences and Research Needs." Prepared for General Accounting Office food policy staff, Washington, D.C., March.

Rodefeld, R.D.
    1979 "The Family-Type Farm and Structural Differentiation: Trends, Causes and Consequences of Change, Research Needs." Revised version of paper presented at NRC - USDA Small Farms Workshop (Phase II), Lincoln, Nebraska, February 1, 1979.

Rowe, G. and L. Whitener Smith
    1976 The Hired Farm Working Force of 1975 (Washington, D.C.: U.S. Department of Agriculture, Economic Research Service), Agricultural Economic Report No. 355.

Schultze, C.L.
    1971 The Distribution of Farm Subsidies: Who Gets the Benefits? (Washington, D.C.: The Brookings Institution).

Schwartz, M.
    1976 Radical Protest and Social Structure: The Southern Farmers' Alliance and Cotton Tenancy, 1880-1890 (New York: Academic Press).

Shannon, F.A.
    1945 The Farmer's Last Frontier: Agriculture, 1860-1897 (New York: Harper and Row).

Smith, L.W. and G. Rowe
1978   The Hired Farm Working Force of 1976 (Washington, D.C.: U.S.
Department of Agriculture, ESCS), Agricultural Economic Report
No. 405.

Smith, T.L.
1969   "A study of social stratification in the agricultural
sections of the United States: Nature, data, procedures, and preliminary results." Rural Sociology 34: 496-509.

Smith, T.L.
1973   "A study of the variations in class structure of farm society
in the United States according to type of farming." International
Review of Sociology 9 (3): 21-41.

Soule, G.
1947   Prosperity Decade: From War to Depression, 1917-1929 (New York:
Rinehart and Co.).

Steeves, A.D.
1972   "Proletarianization and class identification." Rural Sociology 37 (1): 5-26.

Stinchcombe, A.L.
1961   "Agricultural enterprise and rural class relations." American
Journal of Sociology 67: 165-176.

Stockdale, J.D.
1977   "Technology and change in U.S. agriculture: Model or warning?"
Sociologia Ruralis 17: 43-58.

Stoltzman, J. and H. Gamberg
1973-74   "Marxist class analysis versus stratification analysis as
general approaches to social inequality." Berkeley Journal of
Sociology 18: 105-125.

U.S. Bureau of the Census
1968   1964 Census of Agriculture (Washington, D.C.: U.S. Department
of Commerce), vol. 2, ch. 8, table 3, p. 756.

U.S. Bureau of the Census
1973   1969 Census of Agriculture (Washington, D.C.: U.S. Department
of Commerce), vol. 2, ch. 3, table 3, p. 11.

U.S. Bureau of the Census
1975   Historical Statistics of the United States (Washington, D.C.:
U.S. Government Printing Office), part 1.

U.S. Bureau of the Census
1977 1974 Census of Agriculture (Washington, D.C.: U.S. Department
of Commerce), vol. 1, part 51, United States Summary and State Data.

U.S. House of Representatives
1972 Family Farm Act, Hearings before Antitrust Subcommittee of
the Committee on the Judiciary, 92nd Congress, March 1972 (Washington, D.C.: U.S. Government Printing Office), serial no. 28.

Wallerstein, I.
1974 The Modern World-System: Capitalist Agriculture and the
Origins of the European World Economy in the Sixteenth Century
(New York: Academic Press).

White, T.K. and Irwin, G.D.
1972 "Farm size and specialization." In: A.G. Ball and E.O.
Heady (eds.), Size, Structure and Future of Farms (Ames: Iowa
State University Press).

Wiley, N.
1970 "America's unique class politics: The interplay of the
labor, credit, and commodity markets." In: E.O. Laumann et al.
(eds.), The Logic of Social Hierarchies (Chicago: Markham).

4. Capitalist Agricultural Development and the Exploitation of the Propertied Laborer

JOHN EMMEUS DAVIS

INTRODUCTION

An important element of Marx's theory of capitalist development is the destructive, expansive vitality of this modern mode of production. Capitalism arises and develops as the inexorable negation of all pre-existing forms of economic and social organization--penetrating all sectors of the economy, transforming all social relations, and eliminating all "pre-capitalist" forms of production. Sweeping before it the organizational detritus of the past, capitalism prepares the ground for industrial growth and future economic development. Significantly, this is a "universal" phenomenon, occurring on a regional, national, and international scale as capitalism progressively "creates a world in its own image."[1]

Contrary to Marx's theory, however, it would appear that capitalist development has remained incomplete. Many Third World countries, large regions of industrially advanced countries, and important sectors of highly developed capitalist economies continue to be marked by economic underdevelopment and a predominance of pre-capitalist forms of production. Consequently, many writers have chosen to ignore Marx's conception of the universality of capitalism, proposing instead countless explanations for the apparent failure of capitalist relations to penetrate those countries, regions, and economic sectors which, in their view, have been mysteriously by-passed by the advance of capitalism.

In recent years, this view has been vigorously challenged--at least with regard to national and regional underdevelopment. Marxian theorists like Samir Amin and Andre Gunder Frank, for example, have rejected the notion that underdevelopment in the Third World is the result of the incomplete penetration and generalization of capitalist relations. Indeed, they argue that it is precisely because of

capitalist domination that these countries have developed--or failed
to develop--as they have. Thus the forms of social and economic organization that characterize these countries, while not always resembling typical capitalist structures, are not survivals of a pre-
capitalist past; they are not evidence of a lack of capitalist development.[2] They are, instead, an integral part of the world capitalist
system, within which they have been shaped and maintained through decades of dependency and exploitation.[3] A similar argument has been
made with regard to regional underdevelopment. In the United States--
for example, in studies of Appalachia--a new generation of critical
scholars has rejected the view of Appalachia as a "region apart" from
capitalist America. They argue that Appalachian underdevelopment is
explained not by the geographic, cultural, and economic isolation of
the region, but by the very nature of American capitalism, of which
Appalachia is an integral part.[4]

What is evident in these recent theories is a reaffirmation of
Marx's notion of the universality of capitalism. Basic to the viewpoint articulated by Amin and the others is a conception of capitalism
as an expansive world system, reaching into nearly every corner of the
globe. Capitalist relations of production tend everywhere to generalize
and dominate, even where they fail to become exclusive. Thus, while
economic underdevelopment and non-capitalist forms of economic and
social organization do exist, they do so within a hegemonic capitalist
context--and it is only when they are analytically situated within this
context that they can be adequately studied and understood.

Though increasingly used in the study of national and regional
underdevelopment, this Marxian approach has seldom been applied to the
analysis of "underdeveloped" sectors of advanced capitalist economies.[5]
The tendency has been to regard these sectors, distinguished by a predominance of petty commodity production, as pre-capitalist oases
that have remained relatively untouched by capitalist development.
Such has been the traditional view of American agriculture, an economic
sector marked by the continued prevalence of family farming.

The persistence of family farming in the United States presents
studies of agrarian social change with a vexing analytic problem.
Family farming has been usually considered a non-capitalist--or, more
precisely, a pre-capitalist--form of petty commodity production. The
family farmer is a propertied laborer, an independent producer of agricultural commodities who owns both the means of production and the fruits
of his labor. However, according to Marx's theory of capitalist development, all forms of petty commodity production are transitional. The
organizational remnants of an earlier age, they are gradually superseded by capitalist forms of production founded upon the hired labor
of propertyless wage earners. Herein lies the problem: capitalist
development in the United States has not eliminated the family farm.
Despite the dominance of capitalist forms of production in nearly

every sector of the American economy, agricultural production is still largely founded upon the family farm.[7] Consequently, American agriculture has been commonly considered a glaring anomaly, a productive sector that is in capitalist society without being of it--a productive sector that has somehow resisted the intrusion of capitalist relations. The continued presence of family farming has been seen, then, as evidence of a lack of capitalist agricultural development.

This traditional view of American agriculture is challenged in the pages that follow, for the argument is made that this view ignores both the capitalist context of the agricultural sector and the expanding capitalist domination of the family farm. That is to say, it ignores the universality of capitalism in the United States. American agriculture has not been by-passed by capitalist development any more than have Appalachia or the Third World. The family farm, as it exists today, is increasingly integrated into a system of exploitative capitalist relations. It exists within a hegemonic capitalist context, within which it is maintained, dominated--and transformed. Family farming is transformed from a pre-capitalist form of petty commodity production into a capitalist labor process, assuring the transfer of value from the propertied laborer (the family farmer) to the non-farm capitalist firm. The family farm, in turn, is transformed from an institutional barrier to capitalist development into a basis for capitalist development. When situated as elements in a system of capitalist relations, family farms must therefore be understood not as survivals of a pre-capitalist past, but as organizational components of an unfolding capitalist future.

AMERICAN AGRICULTURE AS A NON-CAPITALIST SECTOR: PREVIOUS THEORIES OF THE FAMILY FARM

Previous "theories" of family farming have focused on the anomalous survival of non-capitalist forms of production in the American agricultural sector. That is, they have endeavored to explain the survival of the family farm. These theories may be characterized as each representing either a non-Marxian or a Marxian approach to the problem.

The persistence of the family farm serves, in the first approach, as an "empirical refutation" of Marxist theory. The fact that capitalist development in the United States has failed to eliminate family farming is evidence of either the failure of Marx's analysis of capitalism, or the inapplicability of that analysis to agricultural production and agrarian social change. Those who adopt this perspective, explicitly or implicitly, therefore turn to various "non-Marxian" explanations for the historical viability of the American family farm: the technological efficiency of family farming, the success of government programs in maintaining the family farm, or the willingness of the family farmer to accept returns to capital and labor that are lower than what would be acceptable to competing capitalist firms.[8] In short, various technological, political, and subjective factors--specific to the family farm--have enabled the family farm to survive the rising tide of capitalist development.

In contrast, the second approach attempts to explain family farm- ing in terms of factors specific to capitalism. Implicit in this approach is the assumption that Marx's analysis of capitalism is rele- vant to the study of agrarian society and is not invalidated by the persistence of pre-capitalist forms of agricultural production. Those who adopt this Marxian perspective deal with the problem of the family farm in two ways. First, there are those who predict an imminent end to family farming and see in the changing structure of American agri- culture the confirmation of Marx's theory of capitalist development. Changes such as the steady decrease in the number of family farms, the growing number of corporate farms, and the increasing absentee ownership of farmland are cited as evidence of the transitional nature of petty commodity production in the agricultural sector. Thus, so the argument goes, while it is true that the family farm has survived longer than Marx might have expected, this must be regarded as a temporary phenom- enon. The capitalist annihilation of the family farm has been delayed, not averted.[9] A complementary argument is developed by those who attempt to account for this delay. Using Marxian categories, they seek to discover in the nature of capitalism itself "obstacles to the develop- ment of a capitalist agriculture"--i.e., reasons why the rate of capitalist development is slower in agriculture than in industry.[10] One of the best examples of this particular approach is a recent article by Mann and Dickinson (1978). They argue that the production process for most agricultural commodities is characterized by an excess of pro- duction time, the period in which capital is tied up in the production of a commodity, over labor time, that portion of the production period in which labor is actually applied in creating value. The smaller the gap between production time and labor time, the greater will be the productivity and self-expansion of capital in a given space of time. Since this gap is quite large for most agricultural commodities, where "natural processes" such as ripening may idle labor during much of the production period, most spheres of agricultural production are "un- attractive to capitalist penetration."[11]

What is common to all of these theories, despite their diversity, is a shared assumption that the presence of family farming is indicative of a dearth of capitalist development; that is, the persistence of the family farm is proof that capitalist relations have generally failed to penetrate the agricultural sector.[12] We shall deny that this is so. Using materials drawn from the works of Marx, we shall challenge the assumption that family farming and capitalist development are in- evitably incompatible. Similarly, rather than ask why the family farm has survived, we shall ask how the family farm has become integrated into the capitalist sphere of exploitation and control.

But first, we must deal with the problem of the propertied laborer. Before Marxian categories may be used to examine family farming as a capitalist labor process--and before the family farm may be situated within a system of exploitative capitalist relations--it is necessary to show that Marx did not regard possession of the means of production as absolute protection against capitalist exploitation. We must show that, for Marx, the exploitation of even the propertied laborer is a possibility.

THE CAPITALIST EXPLOITATION OF THE PROPERTIED LABORER

The Capitalist Labor Process

Capitalism, according to Marx, is founded upon a particular set of social relations that constitute and characterize this mode of production, distinguishing it from all other modes of production. The distinctive feature of capitalism is essentially this: surplus value is produced by one class of persons and appropriated by another in a labor process based upon the relation between those who sell their labor power and those who purchase it. Upon this exploitative relation, contractually established between the "free" laborer and the employing capitalist, is founded the entire capitalist system.[13]

It is in the marketplace that capitalist relations are established. However, it is in the workplace that these relations are realized. It is within the labor process that the laborer functions as a laborer, working under the control of the capitalist, expanding his labor-power in the production of commodities which he does not own; and it is within the labor process that the capitalist functions as a capitalist, constantly enlarging his store of capital by extracting value from the labor under his command. The social relations that constitute the structure of capitalist society find their basic expression in the capitalist labor process.

The raison d'etre of this process is the production and appropriation of surplus value. It is thus designed to accomplish two basic tasks. First, because a laborer enters the employ of the capitalist with only the potential for expanding labor power, the labor process must assure that this potential is realized, and that it is realized as completely and intensely as possible. Second, the labor process must assure the appropriation by the capitalist of as much value as possible. It must assure that the laborers' share of the "pool" of value created by labor remains as small as possible, leaving the rest for the capitalist. This, then, is the dual function of the capitalist labor process: control of production in order to maximize productivity, and control of production in order to maximize exploitation.[14]

Capitalist Development and the Annihilation of Individual Private Property

Given the nature of the capitalist labor process, it is necessary to ask why any laborer would knowingly become part of it. Marx's answer is unequivocal: the capitalist labor process is built upon coercion. Only under some form of duress would persons consent to subject themselves to a system of exploitation so clearly contrary to their best interests. How is it, then, that persons are forced to participate in a capitalist labor process? What is the coercive pre-condition for capitalist production? There must exist barriers to autonomous production. Only when it becomes impossible for a laborer to produce by himself/for himself his own livelihood does it become possible to induce him to sell himself to capital.

Historically, autonomous production has had meaning mainly in terms of a laborer's ownership of the means of production. Possession of effective property has usually meant that the owner/laborer is assured of both the means of subsistence and possession of the surplus product of his labor. Marx was therefore led to conclude, as a result of his reading of English history, that laborers become part of a capitalist labor process when they no longer possess the means of production. Laborers participate in capitalist production because the annihilation of individual private property renders autonomous production impossible.

Individual private property, effective property that is based on the labor of its owner,[15] is thus an impediment to capitalist development. The reason is obvious: "So long...as the laborer can accumulate for himself--and this he can do so long as he remains possessor of his means of production--capitalist accumulation and the capitalist mode of production are impossible."[16] Since the laborer may be forced to produce for the capitalist only when he is unable to produce for himself, individual private property must be wrested from the laborer's hands. To that end, capitalism conducts a continuous campaign against "modes of production and appropriation based on the independent labor of the producer," progressively annihilating self-earned, individual private property.[17]

Effective property in the hands of the laborer functions, therefore, as something of a shield against capitalist exploitation, as well as a deterrent to capitalist development. But this is so only to the extent that possession of the means of production assures autonomous production. In other words, individual private property is a barrier to capitalist development only insofar as it supports a mode of production and appropriation that is based on the independent labor of the producer. It is only when the propertied laborer is an independent laborer that the possession of effective property is absolute protection against capitalist exploitation.[18] If the independence of the propertied laborer is eroded, or if autonomous production is rendered impossible even for those who possess the means of production, then the exploitation of the propertied laborer becomes a possibility.

Marx on the Capitalist Exploitation of the Propertied Laborer

Marx clearly considered individual private property to be a hinderance to capitalist exploitation and capitalist development. Yet, on at least two occasions, he describes situations where laborers own the means of production, but are exploited by capital nonetheless. Let us examine these.

The first appears in Marx's analysis of the plight of the French peasantry. The French peasantry of the 19th Century was founded on the small holding, millions of families subsisting on small parcels of land with each family owning--however meager--the means of production. However, despite their "rural self-sufficiency," most peasants existed in a state of "enslavement by capital."

> The small holding of the peasant is now only a pretext
> that allows the capitalist to draw profits, interest
> and rent from the soil, while leaving it to the tiller
> of the soil himself to see how he can extract his wages.[19]

What Marx describes is the paradoxical situation of millions of small property-owners who are, on the one hand, so scattered and self-sufficient that they live "without entering into manifold relations with each other,"[20] yet who are, on the other hand, "enslaved" by their manifold relations with capital. Evidently, the individual private property of the French peasant assures neither independence, nor protection against exploitation.

We must hesitate, however, in calling these "capitalist relations." True, the peasants are exploited; there is an obligatory transfer of value from the propertied peasant to the urban capitalist. There exists a sort of coercive pre-condition for these relations as well, for Marx speaks of State taxes as a "necessary means of compulsion" in breaking down the self-sufficiency of the peasants.[21] Nevertheless, we must hesitate in declaring that the French peasantry is part of a "capitalist labor process." Two essential elements are lacking: a contractual accord between capitalist and laborer, specifying time and terms for the employment of labor-power, and, more importantly, capitalist control of the production process. Thus, while Marx's discussion of the French peasantry shows that the propertied laborer may be exploited by capital, it also reveals that not all exploitative relations are necessarily capitalist relations. Hence a sector may be heavily exploited by absentee capital while remaining itself relatively free of capitalist development.[22]

Marx's analysis of the peasant's situation, then, does not entirely satisfy our desire to prove the possibility that propertied laborers may become involved in capitalist relations. Marx's analysis of piece-wages, however, does. Where production is based on the payment of piece-wages, even laborers who own the means of production become participants in a capitalist labor process and become, thereby, an integral part of capitalist development.

Piece-wages assume many forms. In some cases, piece-wages are paid for work performed within a capitalist's factory. In other cases, piece-wages take the form of various systems of subcontracting or "putting out," where the work is performed outside the factory by laborers who own their means of production.[23] But despite such diversity, all forms of piece-wages share common characteristics and have a common role in the capitalist labor process. Through piece-wages the capitalist attempts to buy labor in the same way in which he buys raw materials--as a specified quantity of work, completed and embodied in the product.[24] However, because the capitalist accepts from the piece-worker a product in which labor is already realized, it would appear that the capitalist is purchasing not labor-power, but a finished commodity. This appearance is reinforced by the fact that the income of the individual producer depends upon his output--as productivity increases, his income increases correspondingly. Nevertheless, Marx concludes that wages by the piece are "nothing else than a converted form of wages by time."[25] Piece-wages are always, in the end, fixed by the capitalist at prices which are based on time-wages, prices which reflect the laborer's wages embedded in the product. If productivity sharply increases, piece-wages are soon cut.[26] Thus the price that the piece-worker receives for his product is not the full value of the commodity, but the "cost" of the labor embodied within it. The difference between the piece-wage paid to the producer and the product's full value is the surplus value, produced by the laborer and appropriated by the capitalist.

Piece-wages are, therefore, a special variation of the capitalist labor process where the product produced becomes the "vehicle" by which surplus value is transferred from the piece-worker to the capitalist. Piece-wages are a special form of time-wages. However, in the eyes of the capitalist, piece-wages have important advantages over time-wages. First, the "quality of the labor is controlled by the work itself, which must be of average perfection if the piece-price is to be paid in full." Second, given the nature of piece-work, it is in the personal interest of the laborer to see that the intensity of production is increased, as well as the length of the production period. Third, "since the quality and intensity of work are here controlled by the form of the wage itself, superintendence of labor becomes in great part superfluous."[27] Piece-wages thus enable the capitalist to enforce strict quality control, to increase both relative and absolute surplus value, and to control the entire production process with only minimum cost, risk, or effect on his part. With these "advantages," piece-wages may be considered the epitome of the capitalist labor process, maximizing both productivity and exploitation.

Given this reading of Marx, what can be said in summary about the capitalist exploitation of the propertied laborer? Capitalist development is generally impeded by modes of production and appropriation based

upon the independent labor of the propertied producer. Capitalism therefore tends to annihilate individual private property, separating laborers from the means of production and eliminating petty commodity production. However, even where individual private property persists,
autonomous production is not necessarily assured. As capitalism develops, the independence of the propertied producer may be gradually
eroded. The propertied laborer may continue to function as an individual
commodity producer, and yet become so entangled in exploitative relations
with capital that he no longer retains full title to the surplus product
of his labor. At a later stage, as capitalism establishes full hegemony, the propertied laborer may find that he is able to earn a
livelihood only by producing as a piece-worker for capital. Where the
labor of the propertied producer is employed by the capitalist payment
of piece-wages, the propertied laborer is made part of a capitalist labor
process. Individual private property is made to support a mode of
production based upon capitalist relations, and the effective property
held by the "independent" producer becomes a <u>basis</u> for capitalist
development, instead of a <u>barrier</u> against it.

CAPITALIST DEVELOPMENT IN AMERICAN AGRICULTURE: THE EXPLOITATION OF THE FAMILY FARMER

The preceding analysis provides a novel frame of reference from
which to reconsider the "problem" of the family farm. This problem has
been traditionally couched in terms of the curious failure of capitalist
relations to penetrate the agricultural sector as evidenced by the
persistence of family farming. However, in light of the preceding discussion, such evidence of stunted capitalist development becomes ques-
tionable and open to challenge. What now becomes <u>reasonable</u> is the notion
that the opposite may be true--that family farming is not incompatible
with capitalist development and that the family farm is less of a barrier
to capitalist relations than has been commonly supposed. Obviously, this
represents a fundamental shift in analytic perspective. One is led to
consider the family farm not in terms of its pre-capitalist heritage,
but in terms of its current capitalistic potential--a consequence of
its increasing integration into a system of exploitative capitalist
relations. Having examined the circumstances under which the exploitation of the propertied laborer is possible, we are now in a position to
examine the circumstances under which the exploitation of the family
farmer has become not only possible, but real.

Contract Farming as a Capitalist Labor Process

The agricultural equivalent of industrial piece-wages is found in
<u>contract farming</u>. Contract farming is agricultural piece-work, founded
upon relations of production that are contractually established between
non-farm capitalist firms and "independent" agricultural producers. It

is one of the two general types of vertical integration that are occurring
with increasing frequency between farm and non-farm enterprises in the
United States. When a non-farm firm owns all of the on-farm resources
and controls all of the on-farm decision-making, this type of vertical
integration is referred to as "ownership integration," or corporate
farming. In contrast, when a non-farm firm has title to only a portion
of the on-farm resources and shares decision-making power with the farm
owner, this type of vertical integration is referred to as "contractual
integration," or contract farming.

More specifically, contract farming denotes agricultural production
that is conducted under agreements (either written or oral) between farmers and processors, suppliers, or other firms that are at the first stage
before or after the farm. These agreements are called "production contracts" or "forward contracts" because they are made in advance of the
time of undertaking agricultural production; that is, agreement is
reached before the farmer has committed many of his variable resources
to the production of the specified commodity.[28] Under this form of agricultural piece-work, the farmer is paid to produce agricultural goods
at a unit price set by the capitalist--either so much per pound, per ton,
or per acre of product. The contract farmer lends to the production
process both his labor-power and the effective property within his possession. The contracting firm provides many of the production inputs
(seed, fertilizer, chicks, feed, etc.) while participating in many production decisions and holding full title to the contracted product of the
farmer's labor. Contract farming thus grants to the capitalist firm a
degree of control over both the on-farm production process and the off-
farm exchange process. At its most extreme, it may reduce the farmer to
a wage earner on his own land--a piece-worker who provides his own
tools and works under supervision to produce commodities which he does
not own. He sells his labor-power instead of chickens, apples, beans,
or beets.[29]

Capitalist control over the on-farm production process occurs as
contracting removes from the farmer's exclusive control the decisions,
resources, and tasks that have traditionally been part of his role as
an independent entrepreneur.[30] The capitalist contractor may make
many of the input, production, and marketing decisions concerning the
production of the contracted commodity. The contractor may provide
inputs, equipment, and custom services, and he may perform a number of
essential production tasks. The degree to which entrepreneurship is
transferred from the farmer to the contractor varies greatly from
commodity to commodity, from one contractor to the next, and from one
region of the country to another. But nearly all forms of contract
farming have this in common: they each allow the non-farm firm to
exercise some degree of direct control over the agricultural production
process.

The purpose behind such direct control is increased productivity as the capitalist firm attempts to assure that the contract farmer's potential for productive labor is realized as completely and intensely as possible. Contracting is therefore used by the capitalist firm to guarantee that: (1) production is tightly scheduled to facilitate processing, to extend the production season, and to increase the number of production cycles completed within each season; (2) production is highly organized and mechanized to maximize product output per man-hour of on-farm labor; and (3) new hybrids, chemicals, and techniques are rapidly incorporated into the production process to improve product quality, to increase yields, and to make maximum productive use of the equipment, facilities, and land provided by the farmer.[31] In short, direct control is exercised by the capitalist firm to bring about an intensification of the on-farm production process.

Equally significant, however, is what might be called "indirect control"--the control which contracting forces the farmer to exercise over himself. The contract farmer is paid to produce agricultural goods at a unit price set by the contractor. Further, he is paid according to the quality of the product and, sometimes, according to the time of delivery. Producing under such conditions, the family farmer will force himself and the members of his family to do what the capitalist contractor cannot force his own time-wage employees to do: he will work harder and longer with little increase in pay to increase productivity and to cheapen the unit cost of his product. He will plant earlier in the spring and attempt to bring in a harvest later in the fall. He will lengthen his working day whenever necessary. He will invest in new equipment and adopt new techniques in a constant attempt to intensify production. He will closely monitor and control the quality of his product. The capitalist contractor, in dealing with his time-wage employees, faces serious constraints in his efforts to increase the production of surplus value. He faces few such constraints in dealing with his piece-wage employees--"independent" family farmers producing under contract, a propertied labor force that is non-unionized, self-directed, and willing to work without the guarantees of minimum wage, job security, insurance, and other benefits commonly demanded by time-wage employees.

Capitalist control over the off-farm exchange process occurs as contracting permits the non-farm capitalist to determine the market price for products which the farmers produce. Because farmers are seldom able to match the market power of the contractors with countervailing power of their own, the contract price is seldom high enough to cover the farmer's production costs and the value of his labor embedded in the product. Consequently, the contractor is generally able, through the use of the production contract, to acquire the farmer's product at far less than its full value.

The contracted commodity thus becomes a "vehicle" for the transfer
of value from the farmer to the capitalist firm.

The production contract functions as an instrument for the capitalist extraction of surplus value. But the effectiveness of that
instrument--i.e., contract farming's effectiveness as a means of ex-
ploitation--is dependent upon two conditions: (1) the degree to
which the contractor is unilaterally able to determine the contract
price; and (2) the degree to which farmers' access to product markets
is limited or restricted. These might be called the coercive preconditions for contract farming.[32] Significantly, these conditions
are neither entirely independent of contract farming, nor completely
external to it. Contractual integration generally increases the
market power of contracting firms.[33] Likewise, contract farming
tends to eliminate all competing forms of production and marketing
within its sphere of influence.[34] Hence, while it is correct to
say that market power and market access are intervening variables
affecting the degree of exploitation associated with contract farming, it is important to recognize that contracting itself tends to
generate the conditions for its own effectiveness as a means of exploitation.

The essence, then, of contract farming is control. Through
contracting, the capitalist firm is able to control both the on-
farm production process, maximizing productivity, and the off-farm
exchange process, maximizing exploitation. Contract farming is a
self-reinforcing capitalist labor process, promoted by the non-farm
capitalist firm to assure the production and appropriation of surplus
value.

Capitalist Development in American Agriculture

Contract farming provides for the production of surplus value
by a class of "independent" agricultural producers and the appropriation of that value by a class of non-farm corporate capitalists.
These exploitative capitalist relations between those who "freely"
sell their labor-power (embodied in the contracted commodity) and
those who purchase it constitute a social basis for capitalist production and capitalist development in the agricultural sector.

The extent of such development, however, is difficult to assess,
for relatively little information is available on contract farming
in the United States. Nevertheless, it has been estimated that
over 17 percent of the total U.S. farm output was produced under
contract in 1970. In that same year, contract farming accounted
for 90 percent of the broilers produced, 85 percent of the processing vegetables, 95 percent of the fluid-grade milk, 98 percent of
the sugar beets, and nearly half of the sugarcane, turkeys, citrus,
and potatoes.[35] In more recent years, periodic surges in demand

have resulted in increased forward contracting for soybeans, corn, and cotton. In 1973, for example, 75 percent of the U.S. cotton crop was produced under contract.[36]

Such facts provide some indication of the increasing importance of contract farming in American agriculture. They say little, however, about the social relations that lie behind this form of production. It is accurate in most situations to assume that contractual integration involves the propertied producer in capitalist relations of production. Indeed, our analysis of contract farming as a capitalist labor process was based on precisely this assumption. But there are exceptions. Forward contracting may occur between farmers and agricultural cooperatives. It may occur under conditions where farmers face few coercive incentives to contract. It may occur under agreements that specify only the market in which the farmer must trade, leaving intact the farmer's other entrepreneurial prerogatives. Under circumstances such as these, contract farming may do little to entangle family farmers in capitalist relations of production. Consequently, contractual integration may be a somewhat inflated measure of the extent of capitalist development among the propertied producers of the agricultural sector.

On the other hand, capitalist development may exceed the incidence of contractual integration. Contract farming is not the only means that may be used by capitalist firms to extract surplus value from the family farm. Exploitation, for example, may occur through indebtedness as agricultural producers become increasingly dependent upon off-farm sources of production credit.[37] Further, since many financial institutions now insist upon sharing in farm management decisions as a condition of credit, indebtedness may be accompanied not only by transfers of value from the family farm to the corporate lender, but by incremental transfers of entrepreneurial control as well. The family farmer may also be drawn into relations of exploitation and control when purchasing equipment and supplies in markets dominated by monopolistic (or oligopolistic) corporate capitalists. Value is transferred from the farmer to the capitalist firm through both the credit arrangements established by the firm and the "monopoly overcharge" embedded in the commodity that changes hands. Thus, under conditions of monopoly capitalism, commercial relations between family farmers and corporate capitalists may remove from the agricultural sector much of the value created in agricultural production.[38]

Through each of these means--contracting, indebtedness, and monopoly control--the independence of the propertied producer is eroded, and the probability of his exploitation is increased.[39] This is not to imply that all trade with capitalist firms enmeshes the farmer in capitalist relations of production, nor that all exploitative relations are capitalist relations. An unfavorable "balance of trade" between agriculture and other economic sectors is not in itself evidence of capitalist agricultural development. Yet the relations that are established between "independent" agricultural producers and non-farm capitalist firms are increasingly character- ized by coercion, contract, and control; they increasingly resemble capitalist relations of production. Through contract farming and related means, family farming tends to become a capitalist labor process. The family farmer is made an object of capitalist exploita- tion, and the family farm becomes fertile ground for the growth and development of capitalist relations. Thus does the family farm become an integral part of capitalist agricultural development-- instead of a barrier against it.

SUMMARY AND IMPLICATIONS

Agricultural production in the United States has remained largely in the hands of family farmers, "independent" producers who own the farms on which they live and labor. A capitalist agriculture based on the wage-labor of persons who do not themselves possess the means of production has, for the most part, failed to develop. It has been common, therefore, to regard American agriculture as a non-capitalist sector of the economy and to see in the family farm an institutional impediment to the intrusion of capitalist relations. In short, the continued presence of family farming has been seen as proof of the relative absence of capitalist development in the agricultural sector.

We have proposed an alternate "theory" of the family farm, one that affirms the universality of capitalism and denies the a priori incompatibility of family farming and capitalist development. Draw- ing upon Marx, we have elaborated a theoretical perspective that re- gards individual private property as neither a shield against capital- ist exploitation nor an absolute barrier to the generalization of capitalist relations. Given this perspective, our analysis of Ameri- can agriculture has focused upon the exploitative capitalist relations that are currently evolving between family farmers and corporate capitalists. We have argued that capitalist development is occurring throughout the agricultural sector despite the presence of the family farm; indeed, the family farm has itself become a basis for such development.

What this implies is that the domination of capital has become so complete--so "universal"--that a laborer is seldom able to produce independently his own livelihood even if he does possess the means of production. Even the propertied laborer may be unable to avoid participating in a process of production where capital controls his productive activity and claims the surplus product of his labor. Under such conditions, the survival of certain forms of individual private property may actually be in the interest of capital. This has a number of important implications for the analysis of class and class conflict in the agricultural sector. We shall mention three.

First, the class status of agricultural producers must be defined with reference to more than just their possession (or non-possession) of effective property. While the ownership of the means of production remains critical, it is the producers' total relation to the means of production, their actual position in the production process, that finally determines their class position and class interests.

Second, reduced to an agricultural piece-worker and subjected to capitalist exploitation and control, the family farmer may come to direct towards the corporate capitalist an antagonism similar to that which is (periodically) displayed by the industrial worker. Moreover, the farmer may increasingly express such antagonism organizationally, joining with other farmers in the collective demand for better terms of contract, credit, and trade.

Finally, given the potential for social conflict that is inherent in the evolving structure of American agriculture, the persistence of a petit-bourgeois class consciousness among agricultural producers and the relative lack of conflict in the agricultural sector become important analytical problems. In attempting to deal with them, serious attention must be directed to the ideology of family farming as a means of agrarian social control. Ideology, as used here, is akin to Gramsci's notion of "cultural hegemony"-- a conception of reality, diffused throughout the institutions of a given society, that shapes and masks social relations, that conceals and legitimates the coercive power of the dominant class while securing the consent of subordinant classes.[40] Family farming may thus cease to be a mode of production based on the independent labor of the agricultural producer; yet, because of the ideology of family farming, agricultural producers may take little account of their growing subordination to capital. Likewise, politicians may act to subsidize the family farm, college researchers may continue to "support" the family farm, liberal activists may oppose corporate farming to "save" the family farm, and all the while they may scarcely notice that, even as the family farm remains, family farming as an independent mode of production is gradually ceasing to be.

NOTES

1. Marx, Karl and Frederick Engles, The Communist Manifesto, in The Marx-Engels Reader, Robert Tucker, ed. (New York: Norton & Company, 1972).

2. Frank, Andre Gunder, Latin America: Underdevelopment or Revolution (New York: Monthly Review Press, 1970), p. 239.

3. Amin, Samir, Unequal Development (New York: Monthly Review Press, 1976), p. 294.

4. Simon, Richard M., "The Labor Process and Uneven Development in the Appalachian Coalfields," paper presented before the Conference Group on Political Economy of Advanced Industrial Societies, New York, September 2, 1978. See also: Helen Lewis et al., eds., The Colony of Appalachia: Selected Readings (Boonesboro, North Carolina: Appalachian Consortium Press, 1978).

5. A notable exception is James O'Connor's analysis of the "competitive sector" of the American capitalist economy in his The Fiscal Crisis of the State (New York: St. Martin's Press, 1973).

6. Marx, Karl, Capital, Volume II (New York: International Publishers, 1967), p. 34.

7. The definition of the family farm and the prevalence of family farming are subjects of continuous controversy. Nevertheless, there is general agreement that family farming is characterized by (1) family ownership of land and other capital items, and (2) a dependence on family labor. On the basis of these criteria, it is fair to say that agricultural production in the United States is still characterized by a predominance of family-type farms. In 1974, 88 percent of the operators of farms and farmland in the U.S. were either full owners or part owners of these means of production (U.S. Census of Agriculture, 1974); moreover, the farm family provided nearly three-quarters of the labor in the agricultural sector--only in California, Arizona, Florida, and New Jersey did hired workers constitute more than 50 percent of the total agricultural labor force (USDA, Farm Labor, January 14, 1975).

8. See, for example: Radoje Nikolitch, "Family-Operated Farms: Their Compatibility with Technological Advance," American Journal of Agricultural Economics 51 (August 1969); Lauren Soth, An Embarrassment of Plenty (New York: Thomas Y. Cromwell Company, 1965); B. Delworth Gardner and Rulon D. Pope, "How is Scale and Structure Determined in Agriculture?", American Journal of Agricultural Economics 60 (May 1978). Also see Mann and Dickinson's critique of technological and "subjectivist" theories of the family farm in their "Obstacles to the Development of a Capitalist Agriculture," The Journal of Peasant Studies 5 (July 1978).

9. See, for example: K. Goss, F. Buttel, and R. Rodefeld, "The Political Economy of Class Structure in U.S. Agriculture: A Theoretical Outline," paper presented at the annual meeting of the Rural Sociological Society, San Francisco, California, September 1978; V.I. Lenin, "Capitalism and Agriculture in the United States," Capitalism and Agriculture (New York: International Publishers, 1946); Anna Rochester, Why Farmers Are Poor (New York: International Publishers, 1940).

10. Mann and Dickinson, op. cit.

11. Ibid.

12. It should be noted that none of the theorists that we have characterized as "Marxian" disregards entirely the increasing intrusion of capitalist relations into the agricultural sector. In particular, Goss et al. (op. cit. p. 23) call attention to the exploitation of the farmer by monopolistic non-farm segments of agriculture, and Rochester (op. cit. pp. 17-37) argues at length that the agricultural sector is an integral part of the American capitalist economy. However, because their primary concern has been either to prove that capitalism is eliminating the family farm or to explain why capitalism has been slow in penetrating the agricultural sector, they have devoted little attention to the ways in which capitalism has actually incorporated the family farm into its sphere of control--making of it a basis for the elaboration of capitalist relations.

13. Marx, Karl, Value, Price, and Profit (New York: International Publishers, 1967), p. 46.

14. Marx, Karl, Capital, Volume I (New York: International Publishers, 1967), Chapters VIII and IX. There is another essential function that should at least be mentioned--the simple reproduction of the relations between capitalists and wage-laborers. The capitalist labor process produces not only surplus value, but "it also produces and reproduces the capitalist relation" (Ibid., p. 578).

15. Ibid., p. 761. Individual private property is not merely an entity, but a "relation," the embodiment of the social relations that constitute the mode of production of independent propertied laborers. In contrast, "bourgeois (or capitalist) private property," property that is based on the labor of typically propertyless wage-laborers, is the locus of those relations that constitute the capitalist mode of production.

16. Ibid., p. 767.

17. Ibid., p. 765. Individual private property is "annihilated" both
     through capitalist expropriation (Ibid., pp. 761-763) and, in
     a later period, through the "disintegrating, resolvent effect"
     that capitalism has on forms of petty commodity production founded
     upon individual private property (Marx, Capital, Volume II, op.
     cit., p. 34).

18. The independent laborer is a self-sufficient, self-directed, and
     self-accumulating producer. That is to say, he is able to pro-
     duce his means of subsistence using his own resources, he is
     able to control the production process in which he expends his
     labor, and he owns the surplus that is the product of his labor.

19. Marx, Karl, The Eighteenth Brumaire of Louis Bonaparte, in
     Tucker, op. cit., p. 518.

20. Ibid., p. 515.

21. Ibid., p. 520.

22. Our ultimate concern is the extent to which capitalist relations
     have penetrated the American agricultural sector. It is there-
     fore important to distinguish between exploitative relations,
     which may plausibly be construed as merely unfavorable rela-
     tions of trade between economic sectors, and capitalist relations,
     which fundamentally affect the purposes, process, and relations
     of production within a given sector. This distinction between
     exploitation and capitalist exploitation becomes particularly
     significant in light of Michael Lipton's discussion of "urban
     bias" (Why Poor People Stay Poor, Cambridge: Harvard University
     Press, 1976). Lipton suggests that the transfer of value out
     of the agricultural sector and the exploitation of independent
     agricultural producers are not phenomena unique to capitalism.
     He argues that a rural-to-urban transfer of value will occur
     (and has occurred) under any type of economic system, whenever
     there exists an "urban bias" at the heart of that system.

23. Braverman, Harry, Labor and Monopoly Capital (New York: Monthly
     Review Press, 1975), p. 61.

24. Ibid., p. 60.

25. Marx, Karl, Capital, Volume I, op. cit., p. 551.

26. Eaton, John, Political Economy (New York: International Publish-
     ers, 1966), p. 89.

27. Marx, Karl, Capital, Volume I, op. cit., pp. 553-554.

28. Mighell, Ronald L. and William S. Hoofnagle, Contract Production and Vertical Integration in Farming, 1960 and 1970, USDA, ERS-479 (April 1972), p. 3.

29. As we shall later indicate, contract farming does not always conform to the "ideal type" that is here the object of our analysis. Not all contracting is between family farms and capitalist firms. Not all contracts permit the degree of control suggested here. Contract farming is conducted in many different ways and under a wide variety of contract types and terms. See: E.P. Roy, Contract Farming and Economic Integration (Danville, Illinois: Interstate Printers and Publishers, 1972).

30. See: Marshall Harris, Entrepreneurial Control in Farming, USDA, ERS No. 542 (February 1974); and Marshall Harris and Dean T. Massey, Vertical Integration Via Contract Farming, USDA, ERS Misc. Publ. No. 1073 (March 1978).

31. It is important to note that under most contract arrangements it is the farmer who provides most of the capital investment and assumes most of the capital risk associated with agricultural production. Such an arrangement holds special advantages for the capitalist corporation--advantages that make contract farming a particularly attractive alternative to corporate farming. (1) Contract farming does not tie up corporate capital in agricultural production where return on investment is generally quite low. The corporate contractor is therefore able to invest his capital in more profitable sectors of the economy (including, of course, his own industrial facilities). (2) In agriculture, the risk of production failure is always present. Under most forms of contracting, production losses are borne by the farmer, not by the corporate contractor. (3) Where the possibility exists that corporate assets may be nationalized--as in some Third World Countries--contracting permits the extraction of value with minimal corporate investment in fixed assets (such as farmland, irrigation systems, farm buildings, etc.).

32. There are, as well, other conditions that induce farmers to contract. Some of the most important of these are price instability, high variable costs, high product perishability, and the advice--or insistence--of creditors. We should also point out that since contracting may provide farmers with a number of benefits, farmers are not always coerced into contracting. On occasion, they may even promote it. For a discussion of various causes, consequences, advantages, and disadvantages of contract farming, see: John E. Davis, Property Without Power: A Study of the Development of Contract Farming in the United States, with Cases from New York and Tennessee, M.S. Thesis, Department of Rural Sociology, Cornell University, 1979.

33.   Hightower, Jim, Eat Your Heart Out (New York: Random House,
      1975), pp. 189-217; Harrison Wellford, "Poultry Peonate" in
      Sowing the Wind (New York: Grossman Publishers, 1972), p. 102;
      Harold F. Breimyer, Individual Freedom and the Economic Organ-
      ization of Agriculture (Urbana: University of Illinois Press,
      1965), pp. 104-107.

34.   Ibid., pp. 107, 217-218, 221-224; Earl L. Butz, "Social and
      Political Implications of Integration," Feedstuffs 31 (April
      25, 1959), pp. 50-58; W.G. Tomek and K.L. Robinson,
      Agricultural Product Prices (Ithaca, NY: Cornell University
      Press, 1972), pp. 221-224; and John E. Davis, op. cit.,
      Chapters 2 and 3.

35.   Mighell and Hoofnagle, op. cit.

36.   Paul, Allen B. et al., Farmers' Use of Forward Contracts and
      Futures Markets, USDA, ERS Agricultural Economic Report 320
      (arch 1976).

37.   Nonreal estate indebtedness per U.S. farm increased by 237
      percent between 1966 and 1976. Approximately half of the U.S.
      nonreal estate farm debt is owed to commercial banks. (Sources:
      USDA, Handbook of Agricultural Charts, Agricultural Handbook
      No. 504, 1976, p. 19; USDA, Balance Sheet of the Farming Sector,
      Agricultural Information Bulletin No. 416, 1978, p. 8).

38.   For example, in 1972 the U.S. Federal Trade Commission (FTC)
      published a study which estimated that the lack of competition
      among farm machinery manufacturers had cost farmers, in that
      year alone, an extra $251 million; in that same year, oligo-
      polistic animal-feed manufacturers extracted from farmers an
      extra $200 million (Hightower, op. cit., p. 173). The FTC's
      term for this practice is "monopoly overcharge." See also:
      Anna Rochester, op. cit.,pp. 17-37. Rochester speaks of a
      "complex apparatus" developed by industrialists and bankers
      for appropriating much of the value produced in agriculture"
      (p. 28).

39.   Significantly, once the farmer becomes involved in one set of
      exploitative relations, he often becomes involved in others as
      well. Creditors may insist that farmers produce under contract;
      contracting may lead to the increased purchase of equipment
      and supplies from monopolistic manufacturers; and so on.
      Interrelated as they are, these "means of exploitation" pro-
      mote not only the production and appropriation of surplus
      value, but the reproduction and proliferation of capitalist
      relations as well (Cf. Footnote 14).

40. Gramsci, Antonio, Selections from the Prison Notebooks (New York: International Publishers, 1971).

5. Social Differentiation in Agriculture and the Ideology of Neopopulism

ALAIN DE JANVRY

While the social and economic structure of societies transforms rapidly by evolutionary or revolutionary bounds, old controversies have a strong resilience and tend to reappear in their same content even if under new forms. This is the case for the debate on the nature and future of peasants and the family farm. In the late 1800s, the Russian populists argued that capitalism could not develop in their country for lack of an internal market and the impossibility of breaking into the international market against the competition of advanced capitalist economies. They defended, instead, the viability of a noncapitalist organization of agricultural production based on the economic viability of the old patriarchal peasantry and its organization in the communal mir[1]. Lenin and the Bolsheviks opposed this vision by arguing that (1) capitalism had already deeply penetrated into the countryside since the formal abolition of serfdom in 1861; (2) the majority of peasants were, in fact, on their way to proletarianization while an economically powerful kulak class was emerging; and (3) both proletarianization and a growing demand for manufactured inputs in agriculture were creating a rapidly expanding domestic market for Russian industry. It is this process of differentiation of the peasantry into social classes and elimination of the family farm that Lenin called "depeasantization."[2]

The same controversy emerged in 1895 within the ranks of the German Social Democratic Party. The revisionist wing was arguing that small farmers were increasing in numbers and economically viable. Their political support consequently had to be enlisted by satisfying their specific petty bourgeois demands. Kautsky, by contrast, pointed at the superiority of large capitalist farms, the rapid elimination of peasant producers, and their transformation into a labor reserve. This implied that the rural proletariat had to be the principal basis of political support. It had to be explained to the small farmers that their future was inevitably that of the proletarist and that, as such, their demands had to be oriented toward endorsing the demands of the proletariat.[3]

Starting in the late 1960s, the populist position had been actively revived in both the more and less-developed countries. In the United States, neopopulism has assumed the form of the defense of the family farm and of traditional rural communities.[4] This has been done by denouncing technological and institutional biases[5] and promoting such defensive measures as the 160-acre law on federal irrigation projects, the development of "intermediate" technologies, and the elimination of subsidies for larger-than-family farms and tax incentive programs that discriminate in favor of large farms and absentee investors.

In Europe, neopopulism has attempted to justify the performance of large masses of peasants--in particular, in France, Italy, Greece, and Spain--on the basis of the noncapitalist rationality of their economic calculus.[6] This has been used to explain why peasants, in producing for survival instead of profit, can outcompete capitalist farmers in many branches of production. For Eurocommunism, the presumed noncapitalist character of peasant farming implied the need to enlist peasant support by satisfying their own economic demands since they are not part of the mode of production to be opposed.

The revival of neopopulism has also been very strong in Third World countries and in international agencies. In Mexico, for example, it has been used by the ruling Institutionalized Revolutionary Party to claim potential economic viability for a large peasantry and engage into programs of expansion of the land base of the peasantry in the ejido sector.[7] Programs to create a commercial family farm sector and a "farmer road" to capitalist development have been at the core of the Organization of American States' support for systematic programs of land reform in the 1960s. Today, this "campesinist" ideology is at the basis of the programs of integrated rural development organized and financed by the World Bank, the United States Agency for International Development, and international agencies in most Third World countries.[8]

The question I want to answer in this paper is: why the rebirth of neopopulism and the fundamentalist ideology of the family farm? To do this, we need to look at the arguments advocated by neopopulists and scrutinize their validity. These arguments rest on three types of foundations--theoretical, empirical, and political. I will, consequently, successively address the questions of the theoretical, empirical, and political validity of the arguments presented in defense of the performance of the family farm under advanced capitalism and of peasants under Third World capitalism. The conclusion I will reach is that these arguments have no valid positive basis and that, in a normative sense, neopopulism is a fundamentally highly reactionary strategy which serves the function of disguising the real production and class structure in today's agriculture and the associated economic and political contradictions.

I. THEORETICAL BASES FOR THE PERMANENCE
OF PEASANTRY/FAMILY FARMS

At this level of the debate, the argument is not whether the
agrarian structure should be composed of family farms but whether
family farms do have the capacity of outcompeting other forms of
production and of maintaining themselves as family farms over time.
In other words, the theoretical debate is not in terms of normative
but of positive analysis.

The peasant or family farm is defined by the typical representatives of neopopulism, such as Servolin and Vergopoulos, in terms of
two fundamental assumptions: (1) the operator is the owner of the
means of production and the labor power involved in the production
process is only his and that of his family, and (2) the objective
of production is not to value financial capital and derive a profit
but to insure the subsistence of the family and the reproduction
over time of the means of production necessary for that purpose.

The essence of the neopopulist argument then rests on two propositions: (1) the family farm is economically superior to capitalist
farming--which makes use of hired labor and where the purpose of
production is profit seeking--at least in a number of well-identified
branches of production, and (2) family farmers do not differentiate
into a bourgeoisie and a proletariat but reproduce themselves over
time as family farmers.

The behavioral postulate that peasants produce to live and not
for profit-making is the key rationalization of these two propositions. If they do not produce for profit-making, then they will
remain in production even if market prices do not allow for a profit;
capitalist producers will not. Peasants will also generally accept
lower levels of imputed wages than offered on the labor market as
cost of preserving their independence and a life-style that allows
them direct appropriation of nature. As a result, there exists a
cost gap between peasant and capitalist farming that originates in
the differences in accounting concepts (profits and wages) among
the two types of enterprises.

Capitalist farms tend, however, to be more efficient, not so
much because of internal economies of scale which, to be captured,
often require relying on hired labor, but because of "pecuniary
economies" external to the farm. Due to its superior location in
the political economy, capitalist farming has privileged access to
technology, credit, markets, information, and infrastructure and is
able to influence the state into providing it with a set of subsidies (price support programs and tax advantages).[9] This institutional rent allows capitalist farms to increase the productivity

of labor to levels that tend to surpass those of family farms.

Whether it is capitalists who will outcompete family farms in
particular branches of production or the other way around then depends
on the relative magnitudes of the productivity and of the cost gaps
between the two forms of production. If the productivity gap exceeds
the cost gap, capitalist farming will rule. If it is the cost gap
that exceeds the productivity gap, then it is peasant farming that will
dominate in that branch of production and block the entry of profit-
seeking and wage-paying capital.

Thus, in a number of branches of production, peasants outcompete
capitalists. By internalizing into land values a rent that is defined
on the basis of noncapitalist production prices, they drive up the
price of land to levels that prevent capitalist penetration. And
they deliver to the economy commodities at a price lower than that
which would have to be paid to capitalist entrepreneurs. The conclusion is that the ultimate logic for capitalism as an economic
system is to let peasants assume the responsibility of producing
those particular commodities. Specifically, which commodities are
involved depends upon local conditions but tends to include activities
that are labor-intensive, relatively insensitive to economies of scale,
and have a low turnover rate of capital.[10]

The postulate of nonprofit maximization is also essential to
explain why family farmers reproduce themselves as such over time
instead of differentiating into social classes. The only possibility
for this to happen, given the fact that the means of production
are commodities and hence alienable from producers, is if farmers do
not control a surplus which they can use to gain access to land,
concentrate it into larger farms, and start using hired labor while
others would, in the process, become dispossessed and proletarianized.

Presumably, this can happen for either one of two reasons. One
is if peasants operate under economic and social conditions that
dispossess them from any surplus. Servolin and Vergopoulos indeed
advocate the role of the state in setting such unfavorable terms
of trade for food products (cheap food policies) that capitalists
are eliminated and peasants left with returns only allowing for
simple reproduction. This argument is, however, insufficient since
there necessarily exists a distribution of productivities among
family farms such that the impersonal mechanism of surplus extraction
through the terms of trade cannot eliminate all of the surplus of
every peasant, even if it does so on the average. Surplus extraction
may slow down differentiation but in no way cancels it. Hence, even
simple reproduction on the average would not insure the reproduction
of the family farm over time.

Thus, the argument that family farmers do not differentiate requires another explanation. This is sought, again, in the behavioral postulate of nonprofit seeking since, then, even differential productivity levels would not lead to social differentiation but mainly to different levels of consumption.

The theoretical bases for the permanence of a peasantry/family farm are highly suspicious. While it is indeed tenable to postulate that peasants under feudalism or as members of a primitive community are not profit-seekers, this is clearly untenable under the structural conditions of capitalism where labor and all the means of production are commodities. Under these conditions, the neopopulist behavioral postulate is based on a confusion between fact and essence. While the fact is that the family farm receives low returns on its resources-- an implicit rate of profit on capital well below average and low imputed wages[11]--the essence of this fact is not behavioral but structural: the family farm both (1) generates a small surplus because the structural conditions in which it is placed stifle its productivity, and (2) surrenders most of this surplus through unfavorable terms of trade as a consequence of its dominated position in the political economy.

If low, and even zero average, surplus retention is not behaviorally determined but is the consequence of the structural position of the family farmer and peasants, then differentiation will inevitably occur in spite of this. There is no theoretical possibility for peasants to remain in their contradictory class location.[12] However lengthy and painful the process may be, their future is full incorporation into one or the other of the two essential classes of capitalism-- the bourgeoisie and the proletariat.

II. EMPIRICAL BASES FOR THE PERMANENCE OF A PEASANTRY/FAMILY FARM

As always, data can be looked at one way or the other; and it is said, for that reason, that economists have never met a statistic they did not like. This is the case when looking at empirical evidence on the survival of the family farm.

The data do show the continued numerical importance of family farms and peasants. In the United States, while the total number of farms has decreased by 49 percent between 1950 and 1969, the share of family farms in the total number of farms has remained at a near constant 94 percent over the same period.[13] Family labor accounted for 76 percent of total farm employment in 1930-1939 and still 75 percent in 1969.[14] In France, farms between 10 and 50 hectares accounted for 43 percent

of the total number of farms in 1955 and for 51 percent in 1970.[15]
And in Latin America, the number of peasant farms (less than 5 hectares) has increased between 1950 and 1970 in 9 out of 11 countries.[16]
During this same period, 76 percent of the growth in total labor absorption in agriculture occurred in the peasant sector while wage
employment in capitalist agriculture only accounted for the complementary 24 percent.[17] In several countries the conjunction of high
demographic growth and a sharp absolute decline in wage employment has
led to a veritable explosion of peasant numbers. Thus, the annual
rate of growth of "employment" in peasant agriculture between 1960
and 1970 has been as high as 10.7 percent in Northeast Brazil, 8.3
percent in Guatemala, 3.3 percent in Peru and Chile, and 2.9 percent
in Bolivia.[18]

These data, which have been used by neopopulists as supportive
evidence of the resistance and viability of the family farm, assume
a whole different meaning when looked at in terms of social relations.
Thus, in the United States, the percentage constancy in the number of
family farms results from the simultaneity of rapid elimination of
family farms and rapid concentration of the land and of production in
capitalist farming. While family farms have been eliminated at the
staggering rate of 2,690 per week over the last 30 years, the largest
six percent of the farms (in terms of sales) captured 47 percent of
the cash receipts of all farms in 1969 and 53 percent in 1977.[19]
Tweeten has calculated that the Gini concentration index of cash
receipts from farming increased from .50 in 1960 to .61 in 1977.[20]
In California, the concentration of production is even higher as the
six percent largest farms produce 61 percent of the total crop production.[21]

Within the family farm sector itself, there is an enormous heterogeneity and a rapid process of differentiation. The upper group
accounted in 1977 for 24 percent of all farms and received 36 percent
of all cash receipts, while the lower group constituted 74 percent of
all farms and only accounted for 11 percent of total cash receipts.
The upper group has shared in the trend toward concentration of
production while the lower group is being decomposed and proletarianized. In these latter farms, the importance of off-farm employment
as a source of income is increasing rapidly. In 1977, 65 percent of
the households in that category reported off-farm employment; and
nonfarm income (wages and salaries, nonfarm business income, rents and
royalties on nonfarm assets, and transfer payments) accounted for 78
percent of their total net income. By contrast, in the upper family
farm group, the share of nonfarm income in total net income was only
31 percent, while it dropped to 20 percent in the six percent large
capitalist farms.[22] This increase in "semiproletarianization" of
family farms has been made possible by the decentralization of industry
toward rural areas that started in the late 1960s in response to the

growing squeeze on profits in industry and the consequent search for
new sources of cheap and docile labor.

As production becomes increasingly concentrated in large capitalist farms, the social relations of production in agriculture also change
toward the development of a rural proletariat. Thus, for the United
States as a whole, while the proportion of hired labor in total labor
use had remained constant for 20 years, it doubled between 1972 and
1977.[23] In California the hired labor force has grown over the past
10 years by 10 percent while the family labor force has fallen by over
30 percent.[24]

In France, the number of farms under 10 hectares has declined by
49 percent between 1955 and 1970, while the number of farms above 50
hectares has increased by 25 percent.[25] There is a clear tendency for
a polarization of rural society into two differentiated groups: on
the one hand, a rural bourgeoisie that accounts for some 10 percent
of the rural population produces more than one-third of the agricultural product, increasingly concentrates the land, and uses hired
labor; on the other hand, a peasantry is relegated to an accelerating
process of elimination, outmigration, and proletarianization. In
spite of these changing social relations, laborsaving technological
change in capitalist agriculture has actually led to a decline in
agricultural wage workers of 29 percent between 1963 and 1970, while the
number of farm households decreased by 16 percent.

In Latin America, the growing number of peasants hides the changing nature of the underlying social relations of production within
which they are imbedded. There has been a rapid elimination of semi-
feudal forms of land tenure since the mid 1950s, and this has been
accelerated in the 1960s by the program of land reforms promoted by
the Organization of American States. This has led to the expropriation of bonded and semiservile peasants from within the large estates
and their transformation into free-holding subsistence peasants, landless farm workers, or urban migrants. The status of peasants had
rapidly deteriorated toward smaller farm sizes and increasing levels
of proletarianization and hidden unemployment. In the 11 countries
previously mentioned, the average size of peasant farms declined on
the average at an annual rate of 0.5 percent during the 1950-1970
period, and these lands are generally being rapidly eroded. As farm
size becomes insufficient to insure the subsistence needs of the household in a majority of cases, off-farm sources of income are needed,
and semiproletarianization increases. Thus, the peasantry gradually
loses its status as producer of commodities and becomes transformed
into a labor reserve for employment in capitalist farms, factories,
and mines. The wages paid to this labor can be extremely low since
part of the subsistence needs of the household remains insured by the
production of food in the home plot where female, child, and underemployed labor is used.[26] In fact, there is some evidence that the

income of the poorest in the rural area has actually dropped in recent years.[27] The peasant sector thus becomes a residual which provides employment at decreasing levels of income for people who have no other alternative.[28] However, over time--in particular, under competition for land and water with capitalist farming--this growing "peasantry" is drawn closer and closer to absorption in one of the essential classes of capitalism--the proletariat.

III.   POLITICAL BASES FOR THE PERMANENCE OF A PEASANTRY/FAMILY FARMS

While the forces of economic growth thus tend to negate the reproduction of a rural petty bourgeoisie in its contradictory class location, the state can eventually play an active role in controlling this process of differentiation and attempt, for political purposes, to recreate a petty bourgeoisie. It is, consequently, important to analyze what the political role of the petty bourgeoisie is in legitimizing capitalist development.

Historically, the petty bourgeoisie has provided the objective basis upon which the ideology of liberal capitalism has been constructed. The ideals of liberty and equality; the pluralist tradition in political science with the concepts of majority rule and citizen sovereignty; as well as the neoclassical tradition in economics with the concepts of perfect competition, consumer sovereignty, and Pareto optimality, are based on a petty bourgeois, Jeffersonian vision of society which is not differentiated into irremediably antagonistic social classes and where the state is merely a noninterventionistic guardian of private property. The very development of capitalism, however, creates economic and social transformations that negate the reproduction over time of this objective basis: monopoly power increasingly replaces perfect competition, the petty bourgeoisie differentiates into a bourgeoisie and a proletariat, and the state assumes increasingly interventionistic economic and political roles. Economic base and ideological superstructure are no longer in correspondence, and a new ideological basis must be developed to legitimize the established economic and social structure.

In the advanced western capitalist countries, the dominant form this new ideology has assumed is that of social democracy which gives to the state an explicit role both as an economic coordinator and a welfare agent. The state thus acquires a new legitimacy as a mediator between capital and labor. This role is particularly effective in periods of sustained economic expansion even though it always remains contradictory since the fundamental exploitative condition of labor by capital has, of course, not been eliminated. This leads to a restructuring of the state which maintains the form of liberal democracy but gives much greater power to the executive branch and the presidency which becomes significantly immune from popular control.

Because several social groups are excluded from the "social democratic" contract, even in periods of economic expansion, other mechanisms of control are needed: this includes segmentation of the labor force and the associated ideologies of sexism and racism;[29] separation among social classes via recreation of a petty bourgeoisie; and, when these prove insufficient, repression.

The petty bourgeoisie can thus acquire a new function of legitimation under monopoly capitalism. Because of its contradictory location, it serves as a buffer between antagonistic social classes. In the case of the rural petty bourgeoisie, its ideological identification is with the mass of rural inhabitants, yet its economic interests are tied to those of the bourgeoisie. In the case of the black petty bourgeoisie, its ideological identification is with the ghetto dwellers for whom it tends to act as political representative while its economic viability is tied to the stability of the ghetto and favorable conditions in the economy at large.[30] Its recreation and protection by the state--from rural development to black enterprise programs--recreate expectations of vertical mobility and fluidity among social classes. And it also serves, for as long as it exists, the economic function of delivering cheap products and services to the rest of the economy for the reasons discussed in Part I.

While, as we have seen above, the petty bourgeoisie has been rapidly eliminated and transformed in U.S. agriculture, the myth of the family farm remains as strong as ever both as a presumed reality and as the norm of farm fundamentalism. In U.S. universities, neopopulist denouncements of the elimination of the family farm and the associated dismantling of traditional rural communities have led to strong claims for the need to protect and revive the family farm.[31] These claims, while sincerely motivated by the defense of farmers' welfare and traditional agrarian values, serve the purpose of prolonging the myth of the family farm and of providing the ideological backdrop to legitimize an attempted return at highly inequitable and inflationary farm income support policies based on the production costs of an average (and, hence, family) farm. The result is the possibility for the larger farmers with production costs below average to capture substantial excess profits at the expense of consumers and taxpayers.

A brief look at U.S. agricultural policy is necessary to place this statement in perspective.[32] The New Deal farm programs initiated by Roosevelt with the 1933 Agricultural Adjustment Act introduced a scheme of farm-price support and production controls for the purpose of protecting agricultural incomes. The defense of the family farm, then a powerful political entity, was put forward as the criterion to

establish the level of price support. As the structural situation
was rapidly transforming, it became increasingly clear that the benefits of those programs were concentrated among a small minority of
large farms and that the public was bearing the high fiscal cost of
these growing subsidies. This led in 1966 to the definition of a
"market-oriented" strategy--spelled out in what is known as the Berg
report--that stressed increasing commercial exports to reduce costly
stocks of grains and reducing domestic price support programs to
world market levels.

It is, however, only with the advent of the world food crisis
under the Nixon administration that these policies were implemented.
The rise in world market prices together with devaluations of the
dollar permitted, in 1973, doing away with government support of agricultural incomes. Grain stocks were liquidated on the world market
(e.g., the Russian wheat deal), and set-aside land diversion programs
were cancelled in 1974. Massive food exports created domestic inflationary pressures but increased farm incomes dramatically and improved
the deficit in the balance of payments.

However, this solution proved temporary as the world food situation improved after 1975; and the United States entered into a period
of stepped-up inflationary pressures and deficits in the balance of
payments. The resulting squeeze on farm incomes (as manufactured input prices and land values rose more rapidly than food prices) led to
the reestablishment in 1977 of the traditional commodity programs
including direct farm subsidies, acreage controls, and government-
supported stockpiling and this, again, principally to the benefit of
a minority of large commercial farmers. This time, however, the
economic and political justifications are much more tenuous. Fiscal
costs (in a post-Keynesian era) and agricultural exports have become
serious sources of inflation, while the petty bourgeois rationale for
farm income support has essentially vanished with the undermining of
the family farm. And nutritional and environmental advocates have
created strong countering demands on agricultural policy. Today, this
dilemma is a key contradiction in U.S. agricultural policy. And the
neopopulist myth of the family farm only serves to direct attention
away from the current structural reality of U.S. agriculture.

In Latin America, increased polarization into antagonistic social
classes that can hardly be reconciled in the context of social democratic contracts has led to the systematic implementation of two
mechanisms of control: sheer repression, on the one hand, managed
under the ideology of bureaucratic-authoritarian regimes;[33] and
separation by creation, under the aegis of the state, of a minimal
pampered petty bourgeoisie from among the ranks of the upper peasants.
It is in this context that extension of the _ejido_ program in Mexico
and promotion of integrated rural development programs in most countries

must be understood, both of which represent the advanced thinking of neopopulism. In Mexico, while freeholding peasants (farms under 5 hectares) have been rapidly eliminated--declining in numbers by 43 percent between 1960 and 1970--the state, under the administration of Echeverria, has attempted to "repeasantize" Mexican rural society by expanding the ejido sector. During this period, arable ejido land increased by 23 percent, and rural population in the ejido sector increased by 44 percent. As Bartra has observed, these data show "the bankruptcy and proletarianization of the peasantry and the extension of state protectionism in an attempt to compensate for the disequilibria and conflicts inherent in the process."[34]

Efforts at shoring the decomposition of the peasantry and creating a small family farm sector are also a purpose of integrated rural development projects. Here the mechanism is, however, highly contradictory since it uses an economic instrument--the diffusion of green revolution technology and credit among upper peasants--to achieve the political end of stabilization. Yet, this very instrument tends to accelerate differentiation and further decomposes peasants, thus negating its political end in the longer run. In both cases the state attempts to partially control the process of differentiation and elimination of a rural petty bourgeoisie for the sake of political stabilization. And the explicit ideological justification for this endeavor is found in the neopopulist advocacy of the superiority of the family farm and the economic viability of a peasantry.

IV.   CONCLUSION

As an ideology, neopopulism has the appeal of the traditional values of independence, egalitarianism, agrarianism, entrepreneurship, and puritanism. These values have been at the basis of the subversion of feudal society and of the homesteading of America and the rapid development of the forces of production. As such, it is still a vivid ideology today with tremendous emotional appeal. And it is, for this reason, so difficult to condemn. Yet, any ideology has to be assessed in terms of its significance in a particular social and economic context. The same ideology can thus appear highly progressive in one context and highly reactionary in another.

Today, the world capitalist system is highly integrated, the two essential classes of capitalism are the dominant--although certainly not exclusive--forms of social organization, and the monopolization of production has created economies of large scale. Individual economic entrepreneurship and self-employment have become cliches more than realities. Yet, the neopopulists suggest rolling back the clock to a Jeffersonian agrarian petty-bourgeois society: "... the

166   Social Differentiation in Agriculture

past is one indicator of a possible desired future state.   ...turning
back is not impossible, nor is it necessarily undesirable."[35] In the
current global economic and social structure, this proposal can only
be utopian or anarchistic. But, worse, the mythical reproduction of
the ideeology of the family farm serves the apology of hiding the real
economic and social class structure with its deeply antagonistic
economic and political contradictions. The defense of rural welfare
can no longer obtain via the petty bourgeoisie that has, today, out-
lived its capacity for social change. Progressive forces lie else-
where--in the formation of a growing rural and urban proletariat with
an ultimate communality of interests.

REFERENCES

1. A.V. Chayanov, Theory of Peasant Economy, ed. D. Thorner, B.
    Kerblay, and R. Smith (Homewood, Illinois: Richard D. Irwin, Inc.,
    1966).

2. V.I. Lenin, The Development of Capitalism in Russia (Moscow:
    Progress Publishers, 1974).

3. Karl Kautsky, The Agrarian Question, translated and summary of
    selected parts by J. Banaji, Economy and Society, Vol. 5, No. 1
    (1976), pp. 1-49.

4. R. Rodefeld, J. Flora, D. Voth, I. Fujimoto, and J. Converse,
    eds., Change in Rural America (St. Louis: The C.V. Mosby Company,
    1978).

5. Jim Hightower, Hard Tomatoes, Hard Times (Cambridge, Mass.:
    Schenkman Publishing Co., 1973).

6. C. Servolin, "L'Absorption de l'Agriculture dans le Mode de
    Production Capitaliste," in L'Univers Politique des Paysans dans
    la France Contemporaine (Paris: Colin, 1972); S. Amin and K.
    Vergopoulos, La Question Paysanne et le Capitalisme (Paris:
    Anthropos, 1974).

7. Roger Bartra, "Campesinado y Capitalismo en Mexico," Paper pre-
    sented at the Meeting of the Latin American Studies Association,
    Pittsburg, April, 1979; R. Stavenhagen, Social Classes in
    Agrarian Societies (New York: Anchor Books, 1975).

8. World Bank, The Assault on Poverty (Baltimore: The Johns Hopkins
    University Press, 1975); S. Wortman and R. Cummings, To Feed This
    World (Baltimore: The Johns Hopkins University Press, 1978).

9. E.P. LeVeen, "Public Policy and the Future of the Family Farm," Paper presented at the First National Conference on Land Reform, 1973; R. Rodefeld, "Trends in U.S. Farm Organizational Structure and Type," in Rodefeld, op. cit.

10. Amin and Vergopoulos, op. cit., pp. 52-54; S. Mann and J. Dickinson, "Obstacles to the Development of a Capitalist Agriculture," Journal of Peasant Studies, Vol. 5, No. 4 (July, 1978), pp. 466-481.

11. V. Fuller and W. Van Vuuren, "Farm Labor and Labor Markets," in Size, Structure, and Future of Farms, G. Ball and E.O. Heady, eds. (Ames: Iowa State Press, 1972).

12. On the concept of contradictory class location, see E.O. Wright, "Class Boundaries in Advanced Capitalist Societies," New Left Review, No. 98 (July-August, 1976), pp. 3-39.

13. R. Nikolitch, Family-Size Farms in U.S. Agriculture, U.S. Economic Research Service, Agricultural Economics Report No. 499, February, 1972, p. 4. Family farms are defined here as farms where not more than one-half of the labor needs are provided by hired labor.

14. Ibid., p. 18.

15. Herve Ossard, "L'Agriculture et le Developpement du Capitalisme," Critiques de L'Economie Politique, Nos. 24 and 25 (April-September, 1976), p. 144.

16. These countries are Brazil, Chile, Colombia, Costa Rica, Ecuador, El Salvador, Guatemala, Mexico, Nicaragua, and Peru.

17. Peter Peek, "Agrarian Change and Rural Emigration in Latin America," International Labor Office, Working Paper 10-6 (Geneva, August, 1978).

18. Emilio Klein, "Employment in Peasant Economies," International Labor Office, Regional Employment Program for Latin America and the Caribbean, Monograph No. 10, Santiago, Chile, March, 1978.

19. U.S. Economic Research Service, "Farm Income Statistics," Statistical Bulletin No. 609, July, 1978.

20. L. Tweeten, "Farm Commodity Price and Income Policy," Paper presented at the National Farm Summit, Texas A&M University (College Station, 1978).

21. P. LeVeen, "Survival of the Fittest? The Relationship of Size and Viability in California Agriculture," Department of Agricultural and Resource Economics, University of California, Berkeley, February, 1978, 47 pp.

22. U.S. Economic Research Service, op. cit.

23. Rodefeld, "Trends in U.S. Farm ...," p. 158.

24. E.P. LeVeen and D. McLeod, "American Agriculture in an Infla-
     tionary Era," Department of Agricultural and Resource Economics,
     University of California, Berkeley, 1978.

25. Ossard, op. cit., p. 144.

26. A. de Janvry and C. Garramon, "The Dynamics of Rural Poverty in
     Latin America," Journal of Peasant Studies, Vol. 4, No. 3 (April,
     1977), pp. 206-216.

27. K. Griffin, "Increasing Poverty and Changing Ideas About Develop-
     ment Strategies," Development and Change, Vol. 8, No. 4 (October,
     1977).

28. Klein, op. cit., p. 9.

29. R. Edwards, M. Reich, and D. Gordon, Labor Market Segmentation
     (Lexington, Mass.: D.C. Heath, 1975).

30. A. Blaustein and G. Faux, The Star-Spangled Hustle (New York:
     Anchor Press, 1972); and W.J. Wilson, The Declining Significance
     of Race (Chicago: University of Chicago Press, 1978).

31. Hightower, op. cit.; Rodefeld et al., op. cit.; W. Berry, The
     Unsettling of America: Culture and Agriculture (New York: Avon
     Books, 1977).

32. LeVeen and McLeod, op. cit.; A.D. O'Rourke, The Changing Dimensions
     of U.S. Agricultural Policy (Englewood Cliffs, N.J.: Prentice
     Hall, 1978).

33. G. O'Donnell, Modernization and Bureaucratic-Authoritarianism:
     Studies in South American Politics, Institute of International
     Studies, University of California (Berkeley, 1973).

34. A. Bartra, "Colectivizacion o Proletarizacion: El Caso del Plan
     Chontalpa," Cuadenos Agrarios, Vol. 1, No. 4 (October-December,
     1976).

35. Rodefeld et al., op. cit., p. 437.

Part **II**

AGRICULTURAL TRANSFORMATION IN THE ADVANCED SOCIETIES

6. Capitalism in Agriculture and Capitalistic Agriculture: The Italian Case

GIOVANNI MOTTURA and ENRICO PUGLIESE

The processes of restructuring already in motion for more than a decade in agriculture as well as in the other sectors of production have contributed to a new awareness of the interdependencies between the problems of agricultural producers and those of producers in other sectors. The interpretive scheme we will employ here is based on the concept of structural dualism in agriculture which has recently emerged as a dramatic and central issue at the heart of the agrarian problem. Structural dualism[1] describes, as is largely accepted in Italian literature on the topic, a situation in agriculture in which there are two distinct sectors involving different forms of the organization of production, different levels of productivity, different perspectives on consolidation, and finally different roles in relation to the overall process of capitalist development. One sector consists of what is commonly referred to in Italy as "capitalistic farms," that is, those large farms whose labor is entirely or mainly hired, and the other consists of "peasant"--that is, small family--farms whose labor is entirely or mainly drawn from family sources.

Without straying too far, it should be stated that such an approach does not merely involve the persistence in agriculture of two qualitatively different types of enterprises. Nor is it only a question of determining adequate methods of analysis for each of these realities so as to avoid reductionistic or distorted analyses. Nor is it only a matter of documenting how each factor relevent to the determination of a sector's evolution in such a context inevitably enters into a profoundly differentiated and differentiating process. Such factors range from the mechanization of cultivation to the mechanisms of the market, the orientation of public spending and, paradoxical as it may seem, to the politics of public protection of agricultural products, etc.

The fundamental problem is broader. To use the terminology of the Marxist tradition, the basic issue is that of understanding the "function performed by non-capitalistic forms of agriculture within capitalistic society"--that is, within a context characterized by the "evolution of agriculture into science" that led Kautsky to write during the last years of the past century that "in a matter of a few decades, agriculture, previously the most conservative of all forms of production, ... has become one of the most revolutionary, if not the most revolutionary, of modern forms." In other words, the problem seems to be that of understanding why the dualistic nature of agriculture continues to be a state of affairs capable not only of resisting, but of reproducing, itself at increasingly sophisticated and complex levels even within systems in which the logic of capitalistic accumulation has pervaded every aspect of social and economic life.

1.   The Issue of Backwardness

In the bulk of the current literature on the agricultural question one finds a recurrence of the basic notion of the backwardness of agriculture, in both economic and social terms. Such a notion is in our opinion at the root of many conspicuous misunderstandings and distortions, as much in bourgeois economics and sociology as in the analyses and political actions of the working class movement. In general, it is possible to demonstrate that anyone who adopts--implicitly or explicitly--this point of view, in whatever form it may be expressed, is inevitably forced to place on a secondary plane the study of the relationships between classes, whether in rural areas or in the system at large. We think it is useful to begin by expounding a few of the principal theoretical, historical, and conceptual reasons which would point to a class analysis (an analysis of the relationships among the classes) as the road leading to the most satisfactory explanation and understanding of the phenomena that apply to agricultural development in capitalistic societies.

There is a definite historical and political motivation at the root of this concept of backwardness. As Kautsky notes, the fact that capitalism develops initially in cities leads to an identification of agriculture--and more generally of rural areas as economic and cultural environments--with the past, and of industry and cities on the other hand with progress.

The essentially urban culture that characterizes modern capitalistic social systems contributes little to an understanding of the complexity and articulation of the phenomena which take place in agriculture. One of the firmest and most widespread convictions is that the numerical prominence of peasant farmers among the total number of those employed in agriculture--in other words the persistence of peasant farm organization--may be assumed to be a symptom of backwardness or of the modest degree of development of agriculture itself.[2] The idea implicit in this conviction is that the more accentuated the capitalistic character of a national social system, the more each of its productive sectors should mirror its character in their own state of affairs and internal mechanisms. Therefore every divergence from

this norm at the level of individual sectors will immediately appear
to be backwardness, or <u>historical lag</u>. The example of Italian agriculture allows us to raise some significant questions with respect to
such an interpretation.

2.   What is Meant by Capitalistic Agriculture

In order to clarify in what sense the perception of agriculture
as a "backward" sector in capitalistic society seems to us to be
erroneous and a source of error, we would like to briefly reconsider
a number of well-known concepts.[3] What we mean today by "agriculture"
may be defined in general as the ensemble of operations connected with
cultivation of the soil and livestock breeding geared toward the production of a particular kind of goods which are called "agricultural
products." What must be kept in mind in contrast to this definition
is that it does not deal with agriculture in general, historically
speaking, but rather with <u>this</u> agriculture, namely that of capitalistic society.

It is in fact only with the birth and establishment of this
society that the gradual separation of agricultural and industrial
activities comes about through the "dissolution of the farmer-artisan
class by manufacture (prevalently urban) and business." As a result
of this separation, the products of the soil become commodities.
There ensues the need to buy a growing quantity of manufactured items
and to pay taxes to a transformed state power which no longer accepts
payment "in kind." The farmer's need for money steadily increases,
and therefore so does the quantity of products he must sell to survive. Furthermore, once this process is set in motion, it continues
to reinforce itself. In fact, due to the existence of industry, the
products that a rural resident can readily sell are not those of his
winter artisan activities but those of his cultivation and animal
breeding which urban manufacture cannot produce. Thus, as Kautsky
writes, "the farmer had to in the end become what is meant today by
'farmer,' but which originally he was not at all: a pure and simple
cultivator."

One of the effects of this process at a societal scale is the
gradual narrowing of the farm family sphere. This occurs as a result
of the joint decline in extra-agricultural work (family craftsman-
ship) in agricultural work itself (in various operations--although
quite slowly for some time--there is the tendency for machines to
replace human labor), and in the decline in the quantity of farm
products destined for family consumption. There results therefore
an increase in the number of farm family members obliged to look
elsewhere for a source of support, selling their own labor power
(the only commodity at their disposal). Moreover, farm work is not
homogeneously distributed throughout the year. Consequently, the
farm family, obliged on the one hand to reduce its numbers is, on

the other hand, obliged to replace them with hired labor. The advantage of the latter is that however well they may be paid (and this is certainly not so in the majority of cases), they need only be employed for a period of time which coincides almost exactly with that in which they are productive. Thus, Kautsky concludes, "the same developments which on the one hand created the need for paid workers, on the other hand creates these very workers."

In the final analysis, therefore, one may say that the origin of what we today call "agriculture" constitutes one of the fundamental moments in which one finds the birth, diffusion, and affirmation of capitalistic division of labor. The question which emerges at this point is the following: is it possible, and if so in what sense, that non-capitalistic or indeed pre-capitalistic elements persist in this agriculture?

3.   The Role of Agriculture in Capitalistic Society

This is not an abstract or academic question. In fact, from the general scheme we have outlined, an anything but linear and homogeneous line of development would appear to emerge. Historical, geographical, and political differences, along with differences in overall developmental levels between the various capitalistic countries (not to mention between the latter and their colonies or spheres of influence), seem to so influence the development of agriculture that most observers are convinced of the impossibility of elaborating a universally valid theory.

In the domain of the working class movement, this has generated a radical opposition between two propositions which--although proven to be false by Kautsky and Lenin, have still managed to survive, and only partially transformed--reemerge today in the political and theoretical debate, socialist or not. On the one hand, there is the thesis in which the fundamental law of capitalistic development (growing proletarianization and growing concentration) is applied without major modifications to agriculture as well--"agriculture" being understood to be a combined grouping of business enterprises. On the other hand, there is the thesis generally founded on a reading of the available statistics by which--to use Kautsky's choice of words--"the future of agriculture would not be tied to capitalistic enterprise but to peasant farming enterprise."[4]

We think it useful and quite illuminating to report verbatim Kautsky's conclusions on this basic problem:

> I have carried out research to see which of the
> two opinions might be true, and contrary to all
> expectations, I reached the conclusion that neither
> one was universally true and that we must not ex-
> pect to find in agriculture either the end of the
> big enterprise or that of the small. We do find at

one pole the universal tendency towards proletarianization, but we also find at the other pole a
constant oscillation between the progress of the
small enterprise and that of the large. In conformity with this I have likewise reached the conclusion that agriculture does not by itself produce
the elements it needs to reach socialism. But
agriculture independent of industry, be it peasant
or capitalistic farming, increasingly ceases to have
a function in society. Industry dominates agriculture to the extent that industrial development increasingly determines the laws of agricultural
development. It is in this, in having brought to
light the industrialization of agriculture, that I
see the main point of my book.

This theme--which is richly supported with data and argumentation
in the first eleven chapters of Kautsky's book and which was creatively
elaborated on a theoretical and political plane by Lenin--allows us
to set forth some important points. In the first place, it precisely
delineates the domain of the discussion. The problem does not consist
in conceiving of agriculture as an entity distinct from or in opposition to industry, but rather conceiving of both as moments,
tightly bound to each other from the very start, in the articulation
and development of the overall capitalistic system.

Expressed in different terms, this means among other things that:
(a) it is not the percentage of capitalistic enterprises of the total
of agricultural enterprises at a given moment that characterizes the
agriculture of a country as more or less capitalistic at that moment;
(b) therefore the main theoretical problem is instead that of understanding the function or functions of agriculture within the range of
that particular system at that moment; and (c) such research must be
carried out concretely so as to single out, in light of general tendencies, contradictions potentially open to magnification in a general
revolutionary sense.

Furthermore, the proposed scheme offers the elements needed to
single out the two principal functions that agriculture performs within the capitalistic social system, i.e., those elements needed to
understand more precisely what is meant when we speak of "agriculture."
These functions are, namely: (a) the productive function for which
(as we will try to show in the following pages) capitalistic enterprise
clearly holds the advantage over all other types of presently existing enterprises; (b) the industrial reserve function whose survival
must be assured with the least possible risk to the sociopolitical
stability of the system.[5]

4.   The Functions of Agriculture and its "Backwardness"

Both functions of agriculture are always present in capitalistic
societies, albeit with varying intensity in the various phases of
development of societies. With this in mind, if we consider the
existing types of agricultural enterprises, it can be verified that
often, even in periods of notable capitalistic expansion in the
system as a whole, agriculture appears to be "backwards" and "un-
explainably out of step with the times." Attitudes such as these
arise from neglect of the second function of agriculture itself--
that which makes it the vital organ of the system. We believe
instead that only by taking into account both of these aspects is
it possible to go beyond schematism--capitalistic development equals
numerical growth of big enterprises to the point of total extinction
of all others--and beyond ruralistic or populist outlines--agriculture
as a sector with its own special characteristics which make it qualitatively different from other sectors. As we will try to demonstrate
later for the case of Italian agriculture, different weights are
assigned to the two faces of agriculture according to the different
stages of development of society as a whole and in relation to the
demands coming from outside the "agricultural sector," but which
ultimately managed to consolidate with demands and interests internal
to it.

The possible alternatives are of three types as outlined below:
(a) situations in which the main objective is that of capitalistic
development and which are thus characterized, among other features,
by the concentration of investments in capitalistic or peasant-
capitalistic enterprises and more recently of public financing in
agriculture as well. They are further characterized by the corresponding increase of wage earners relative to the total employed,
and by an increase in the productivity of the sector. Excluding
peasant-capitalistic enterprises (which will be discussed later),
the peasant enterprise in such periods emerges as a structure of
survival for a large portion of those "employed in agriculture" who
lack the possibility of finding on a short-term basis more, or at
least equally, profitable employment in other sectors; (b) situations
in which, on the contrary, the main objective is "to conform to the
peasant farmer's aspirations." In such situations there is an
appreciable decrease in private investment (including existing
capitalistic enterprises) and a directing of public funds for agriculture toward the creation of new direct-cultivation enterprises,
greater stability of farm families residing on the farm, the encouragement of new agrarian contracts, etc. At the same time, in such
periods one sees a decrease in the percentage of wage earners and
a decrease in labor productivity; (c) situations in which the two
faces of agriculture seem to strike a balance in an apparent "equi-
distribution" of investments and financing (showing an overall
increase) between capitalistic and peasant sectors.

The specific contexts and timing in which these three types of situations concretely manifest themselves will become clearer in subsequent pages. What should perhaps be added is that in some cases the "backwardness of agriculture" thesis rests not so much on the persistence of a peasant farming sector generally assumed to be non-capitalistic as on the types of contractual arrangements that are to be found in it. These arrangements, considered paleo-capitalistic-- that is, transitional forms to capitalistic agriculture--include sharecropping and especially the survival of enterprises characterized in essence by pre-capitalistic features such as the extensive Southern landed estate which persisted in Italy up to the 1950's, for example.[6]

Along the lines of what has been said, it should be clear how an interpretative scheme that emphasizes an argument such as the backwardness of agriculture can induce, in our opinion, rather serious theoretical errors. In general, such a scheme seems in fact not to take into account the fact that agriculture as we know it today is the result of the complex dynamics that have widened into the capitalistic division of labor. In this sense, this agriculture is entirely capitalistic, i.e., it reflects in its composition at any given moment the demands and contradictions of the overall social system to which it belongs.[7]

This reasoning in particular holds even for those whose discussion of backwardness focuses on the persistent influence exercised by the land revenue system. With the available data and Gramsci's fundamental observations, it is in fact possible to see how in Italy the taxes on land revenue in agriculture have actually marked a particular moment in national development--that of the extraction of capital needed to spark and feed capitalistic industrial and agricultural development in designated areas.

In this sense, the apparent persistence of pre-capitalistic production and social relationships throughout the national territory long after Unification can and must be correctly interpreted to be an aspect of the country's capitalistic development and not a lag or absence of it. Evidence for this is given by the fact that in Italy, once a certain level of overall development was reached, the alliance between capitalists and financiers that such accumulation requires was overcome without serious imbalances for the system. This also occurred without overcoming the underdevelopment of the South and the internal imbalances of the country which seemed to be connected to that alliance. The Southern question--the question of North-South dualism, of the underdevelopment of the South--continues to be the biggest problem of Italian development, notwithstanding that its connotations have partly changed. It is not difficult to see a series of functions which show connections between the demands of capitalistic development (according to the model presented) and the "backwardness" of

the South. In particular, one can see how the South has historically
functioned as the location of the principal share of relative overpopulation.

To return to the specific theme of these remarks, it is perhaps
necessary to emphasize that the function of agriculture as the seat
of relative overpopulation developed predominantly from the agriculture of the South and mountain areas. In conclusion, in a given
national social system, even within the same historical stage, the
two functions of agriculture can exercise a different influence in
different territorial areas of the system.

We should add somewhat to what has been said thus far. In the,
first place, it must be noted that the dynamic balances established
in various periods between the two principal functions of agriculture
are dictated by demands which transcend the "agricultural sector" and
so cannot be viewed as a spontaneous result of the relationships purely
internal to it. It is for this reason that in the analysis of such
cases, it is important to take into account the function of state
action, particularly the shape its agrarian politics takes. In the
second place, an observation particularly relevant today is the
possibility that in the presence of a particularly intense surge of
capitalistic development in agriculture, the creation of an industrial
reserve may exceed the actual needs and capacity for labor absorption
of other sectors and of the agricultural sector itself within reasonable time spans. In such a situation, which seems to be that of Italy
today, it is likely that the term "industrial reserve" in a narrow
sense can only be applied to a marginal part of the work force, be
it wage-earning or other (poor peasant farmers). The rest can be
analyzed much better in terms of pauperization, a concept which,
however, still needs to be adequately expounded on a theoretical
plane, given the tendency to incorrectly equate it with the concept
of lumpenproletariat.[8]

Concluding up to this point, one may say that the causes of the
apparent backwardness of agriculture in capitalistic society consist
in essence of institutional remnants of the past that remain functional
with respect to the primary objectives of the present. These objectives in turn may be socioeconomic--capitalistic agricultural development, creation of an industrial reserve--and/or ideological--diffusion
of peasant farmer-owned ideology, negation of proletarianization.

5. The Origins of the Prevalently Peasant Farming Nature of Italian
    Agriculture

A useful indicator for singling out the specific functions of
agriculture in the various phases of the national capitalistic
development, as well as the variations in the power relationships

between the classes involved, may be represented by statistics on the evolution of the agricultural labor structure.

Table 1.   Evolution of Agricultural Labor Structure, 1871-1970 (percentages).

Year	Independent Workers	(Part-Profit-sharers)	Dependent Workers (Farm Laborers)	Others
1871	42.7	(17.0)	56.9	0.4
1881	38.4	(13.7)	61.2	0.4
1901	53.2	(19.8)	46.4	0.4
1911	46.3	(18.7)	53.3	0.4
1921	55.0	(15.4)	44.7	0.3
1936	51.3	(20.0)	28.4	0.3
1959	75.7	(-)	24.3	-
1977	62.0	(-)	38.0	-

Sources: A Serpieri, La struttura sociale dell'agricoltura italiana, Roma, INEA, p. 123; and (for 1959 and 1977), ISTAT, Rilevazione nazionale delle forze di lavoro. The statistics on profit-sharers were not available from ISTAT.

With the achievement of national unification in Italy came a notable phase of capitalistic expansion in agriculture and a marked increase in the proletarianization of poor peasant farmers, evidenced by the increase of wage earners relative to the total employed in agriculture and by the subsequent great wave of migration.   Due to the dualistic nature that the national economy was taking on, however, this development had different effects in the various regions of the country.

In the South, in fact, although the appropriation of Manomorta property (church or institution-owned land appropriated by the state and then sold), often through violence, dishonest auctions, and similar methods, contributed to the impoverishment of peasant farmers and the growth of a new agrarian middle class, the situation in terms of prospectives did not seem to change very much.   Pressure on the situation came from the persistent presence and influence of large-scale absentee landowners and "rentiers," diminishing the potential dynamism of the new middle class stratum and rapidly forcing it as well to assume a parasitic or semi-parasitic role.   These landowners found themselves solidly reinstated as the "ruling class" of the South (after a year or two of uncertainty) by virtue of the close

correspondence of their objectives to those of Northern capitalists--
for the former, the basing of Southern economy on the demands of
the land revenue system with the possibility of investing profits
elsewhere, and for the latter, the utilization of capital drained
from the South to be directed toward certain "poles of development"
in the North.

In the northern regions, on the other hand, one of the most
rapidly visible processes during those years was the laying down of
the foundations of a modern capitalistic agriculture. The appearance
of industries linked to this kind of development (furnishers of technical means for the production and/or transformation of products),
important land reclamation projects (which employed labor that would
subsequently remain in the agricultural labor pool), and the first
developments of mechanization all contributed to creating in the
agricultural regions of the North and of part of the Central areas
an increasingly different physiognomy from that of the great majority
of Southern rural zones. In conclusion, during this period, notwithstanding the presence of pre-capitalistic remnants (essentially in
the Southern landed-estate structures which nonetheless remained
functional in terms of the demands of accumulation of the national
economy) and paleo-capitalistic residues such as the sharecropping
arrangements dominant in certain parts of Central Italy, the overall
capitalistic development of Italian agriculture proceeded rather
rapidly.

It would be quite difficult, however, to understand the phenomena
through which such a process is articulated without considering the
role of emigration. While capitalistic development transferred a
substantial number of poor peasant farmers to the ranks of more or
less "pure" farm hands (since many maintained the "administration"
of bare postage stamp plots of land for self-support), farm laborers
invested their savings accumulated in America in the land so as to
become farmers.

At any rate, as can be seen in Table 1, the prevalence of the
farm laborer within total agricultural employment remains significant
during the entire period from Unification to Fascism. Farm laborers
were most numerous (in relative terms) in 1881, before the emigration
phenomenon was to assume the massive proportions of the following
decades, and in 1911, after capitalistic development had reached its
highest point in the 20-year period at the turn of the century.

Notwithstanding the efforts of emigres to acquire land during
the period from Unification to WWI, the number of landowning farmers
remained nearly constant, as does its percentage of the total employed
in agriculture.[9] This means that the process of proletarianization
in this period is essentially unimpeded in spite of organizational
efforts on the part of small farmers. It is in this phase moreover
that the most pure form of capitalistic production--capitalistic
leasing--more fully develops.

On the eve of World War I, capitalistic tenancy covered almost 70 percent of the entire area farmed by lease, and at the end of the 1920's, this figure hovered around 67 percent. Accompanying this were processes of proletarianization of varying form and force that cut into the structure of the agricultural sector. This is evident from statistics pertaining to the incidence of dependent workers over the total employed in the sector: up until the first decade of the century, the percentage of dependent workers held at around 50 percent (53.5 percent in 1911), and in 1921, it was still about the same at around 45 percent. With the coming to power of Fascism, the entire arrangement of the Italian agricultural sector appears to have been profoundly modified within just a few years. Considering once more the structure of the agricultural labor force (which employed around 50 percent of the total active population until the eve of WWII), certain tendencies emerge as significant as of the late 1920's: (1) a reduction in the area farmed directly by the owner--capitalist or peasant farmer as the case may be--from 67.7 percent to 50.8 percent of the total between 1927 and 1936; (2) heavy expansion of peasant farming tenancy and contraction of capitalistic tenancy; between 1930 and 1945 the former increases from approximately 33 to 75 percent of the area open to lease; and (3) significant expansion of the area farmed through sharecropping.

Through this process of modification, then, for those who refer to a simplistic linear developmental model of the type previously mentioned, an apparently anachronistic process is establishing itself. This process--which has been called the peasantization of Italian agriculture--will constantly characterize Italian agricultural development well beyond the end of Fascism, even if in the 1950's it will be realized in other ways. As can be seen from Table 1, between 1921 and 1936, the percentage of independent workers farming their own or others' land goes from 55 to 71 percent of the employed. To understand what this means in reality, one must keep in mind the tendencies indicated above--especially the increase in the number of non-owning peasant farmers, heavily subjected to the land revenue system thanks to the operation called "Fascist contractual restoration." To the extent that such restoration made possible the application of cut-throat contracts allowing landowners to set the revenue considered satisfactory, it provided an incentive to abandon or relax entrepreneurial activity. This, among other things, translated into a contraction of demand for wage-earning labor, which in turn prompted an increasing number of wage earners to "become (peasant) farmers," tying themselves to an individual contract if only to have at hand a piece of land to cultivate.

But the diminished demand for dependent workers was also making its effect felt in wage levels; in 1933, wage levels were 20 to 25 percent less than 10 years earlier. To evaluate the effects of these

circumstances on the condition of the agricultural sector, it must be
kept in mind that they occurred in a "closed" environment, so to speak;
the regime had in fact gradually obstructed the traditional safety
valve of emigration that had been such an influencing factor during
the previous decades, and subsequently legislation against urbanism
had also placed a new imprint on the few channels left open. Thus
one can speak of the intensification of _forced_ demographic pressure
on the rural sector, a process whose inevitable outlet was in fact
the push toward a peasantization that would permit agriculture to
meet its function of being a _sponge sector_ for excess labor supply
without cutting into--rather, actually swelling--landowners' revenues.
This therefore resulted in a peasantization tied not to transfer of
owned land but to agrarian contracts.

The fundamental question all of this raises is why Fascism should
have chosen such a road to direct its agrarian politics. It seems
possible to us to very briefly sketch an answer, recalling two categories of questions. The years during which the process in question
was set off were those of the great world economic crisis, the agrarian
crisis being one of its most persistent effects. In those years the
phenomenon of return to the soil involved millions of people in all
capitalistic countries, even the most advanced. In this sense, then,
what happened in Italy between the end of the War and 1933 cannot be
considered an event unto itself, although it contains some special
elements which merit study. What seems instead to characterize the
Italian situation is the decisive modifications in agricultural
arrangements that ensured from the crisis.

The reason for this seems to be found in the second category of
questions relative to the more general structuring of the national
economic system during those years. This is the period in which Italy
became a predominantly industrial country. But while that occurred
through restructuring and oligopolistic concentration, and while it
profoundly altered the relationships between sectors and the degree
to which each of them contributed to the formation of revenue, it did
not have equal effects throughout the employment structure. It is
possible to grasp this fact if one considers levels of industrial
employment; in 1921, those employed by industry numbered 5,156,000;
by 1931, 5,776,000; and finally by 1936, 5,822,000--rather meager
increases if one remembers that those were the years in which the
share from agricultural production of the gross national product
decreased from about 40 percent to 26 percent (even with the primary
sector retaining 48.5 percent of all assets against industry's 30
percent and the 21.5 percent by the tertiary sector).

Under these conditions, peasantization was essentially an in-
voluntary choice. However, by putting at the disposal of landowners
a mass of labor prevented from going elsewhere, the political course

deriving from this choice inevitably widened into a removal of incentive for the technical and organizational development of average
and large farming enterprises (which had been intense during the
fifty years prior) and became a real obstacle to capitalistic development of the majority of rural areas. For the majority of the
Italian rural population, this meant expansion of the poverty of
peasantization, loss of contractual power, and an increase in self-
consumption.

These are the major lines of the Italian agrarian arrangements
at the close of World War II--a backwards arrangement in a technical,
productive and social sense, but not for internal reasons, i.e., the
presumed "structural peculiarities" of agriculture. This backwardness is something quite different. It is the specific role assigned
to agriculture in a determinate phase of capitalistic development of
the economic system of which agriculture itself is an integral part.

6. The Post-War Period and the 1950's: Continuity in a Turning Point

The tendency toward a growing peasantization of Italian agriculture
did not end with the fall of the regime that had favored it. Along
with an increase in absolute numbers of those employed in agriculture
in 1948 compared to 1936, there was a concomitant and very strong
domination of peasant farming. Such farmers represented more than
70 percent of agricultural labor and cultivated 66.9 percent of the
agricultural land. Of these farmers, moreover, an extremely high
percentage farmed on others' land as tenants, profit-sharers, share-
croppers, etc.

There is furthermore an ensemble of contraindications caused by
choices in economic policy made by Fascism which had been further
aggravated by the War. And, it must be remembered that these are the
years during which unemployment in agriculture reached its highest
levels (484,124 during peak months in 1947, 276,741 minimum at other
times) as well as within industry and the tertiary sector where,
given the greater territorial concentration, this unemployment was
more visible and threatening.

In this framework during the late 1940's, the relaunching of
"peasant farmer" objectives in agrarian politics matured. As is known,
the developmental model elaborated and applied by the Italian ruling
class from that point in time on hinged on the selection of industry--
certain of its sectors--as the dynamic element capable of bringing the
country out of the post-war depression by means of an overall renewal
of the process of accumulation. The pursuit of such a goal moreover
implied not only the directing of the majority of available resources
toward the industrial sectors judged to be particularly important, but

also the rapid implementation of mechanisms of control in the labor
market as well, since industry itself did not expect a substantial
increase in its demand for labor during short or average-duration
periods of time. The situation thus induced a reconfirmation of the
function of excess labor absorption assumed by agriculture for more
than two decades.

The times, however, had changed. The existence of an extensive
unionization movement in rural areas, in addition to the new political
framework, made the old instrument of contractual restoration (i.e.,
the further multiplication of peasant farmers subject to the land
revenue system) obsolete. In this manner, a new strategy began taking
root--a strategy whose roots ran deep in the Catholic political tradition, that of the diffusion of the small holding and the support of
family farms. As is known, such a political line was realized between
1948 and 1950 in the form of two legislative measures, the Land Reform
and legislation for the formation of small holdings. These two measures
(the second especially) were to have equally wide-spread effects on
the structure of the agricultural sector and on the larger political
economy during the following two decades.

Due to these measures, approximately 1,700,000 hectares of land
were transferred into the hands of peasant farmers through allotment
(around 600,000) or assisted purchase (around 1,000,000), during the
mid-1960's, according to INEA (National Institute for Agricultural
Economics) estimates. But these facts only minimally represent the
real situation of transferral achieved for the most part through
private negotiations and without benefit of assistance. It must be
remembered that between 1948 and 1961, the area subject to extraction
of revenue from peasant farming (farmer tenancy, partial cultivation
profit-sharing) amounted to a full 3,021,000 hectares. As to support
measures for direct-farming enterprises, these were realized in
privileged access to public finance channels of various types: subsidies, capital shares, assisted loans and credit in various forms.

Overall, the principal effects of this assistance policy during
the 1950's appear to fall into four tightly interconnected categories:
(a) The first and most immediate is the breakdown in the unit of the
labor front created in rural areas during the post-war period, which
meant the isolation not only of farm laborers but of the industrial
labor class as well. (b) The second, which serves as a grounding
point for the entire phenomenon, is the recrystallization of the
principal share of relative surplus population in the form of those
agriculturally employed in enterprises dependent in large measure
on the supply of public financing. (c) The third is the possibility
for moderate forces in the government to make a solid base of political
consensus out of such strata of farmers by means of the spreading of
capillary organizational structures modelled along corporate lines,

tinged with technical efficiency and given the power to regulate
the supply of public funds (e.g., Federconsorzi, C.N.C.D. "bononmiana,"
etc.). (d) The fourth is the expansion of the entire internal market
of agricultural means of production produced by industry (mechanical
and chemical especially), an expansion realized through the afore-
mentioned organizational structures. These organizational structures,
on one hand, functioned as vendors of those agricultural inputs,
while, on the other, functioned as professional associations equipped
to handle the procedures necessary to obtain state funds to purchase
these commodities. Thus a good deal of public financing of agriculture
could be redirected toward financing precisely those industrial sectors
deemed particularly important.

Alongside these processes one must consider the events which led
to the conversion of large portions of agrarian revenue into urban
revenue. The large-scale transfers of land to peasant farmers from
the beginning of the late 1940's served to stimulate land values.
But if the large and average absentee landowners affected by the new
political line were "compensated" through this process, the very nature
of the new policy tended to prevent this capital from reentering the
agricultural sector in the form of investments. (In stimulating spurts
of development in a capitalistic sense, this would have inevitably
caused the expulsion of labor from agriculture.) These funds were
therefore to a large extent directed outside the primary sector toward
that particular sector of industry which during the 1950's was undergoing a phase of general, heavy expansion (including employment levels),
namely the construction sector.

The years between 1950 and 1957-58 thus saw the unfolding in
agriculture of those processes which in the subsequent five-year
period--that of the "economic miracle"--would have their greatest
acceleration. The employment level in agriculture went from 48.8 percent to 35 percent of the national total, while at the same time the
value of the gross agricultural product increased significantly--at
current rates, around +1000 billion lire--even though agricultural
share of GNP does now a decline with respect to the total gross
national product (from around 22.8 percent to 18 percent). What does
not seem to change much for the entire decade of the 1950's is the
proportion of dependent and independent workers. Even in 1961, the
latter represented 73 percent of those employed in agriculture compared
to 74 percent in 1951 (while during the same period, with the intensification of migration after 1957, the portion of labor employed in
agriculture accounts for 13 percent of the total Italian employment).

The constant growth of migration revealed the true identity of
the ranks of relative overpopulation which had been "masked" by peasant
farmers. Industry became the leading source of employment, pushing
agriculture into last place in a matter of five years. This growth,

furthermore, put an end to peasantization as a tendency and a political
line. It must at any rate be made clear that what happened during the
years of the "economic miracle" was not (however much it may have
seemed to some at the time) "the end of the peasant farmer," but
rather the end of an artificial increase of the peasant sector and
its social consequences. And it is above all not the end of dualism
in agriculture, but simply the end of the forms and meanings it
acquired during a lengthy period dominated by the demands of labor
market control and of the launching of industry.

7. Capitalistic Development in the 1960's

In terms of public assistance, the years 1960-1970 are characterized
by two five-year plans for agricultural development: the so-called Green
Plans I and II. Plan I (1960-65) was ratified by the Parliament in a
political stage characterized by the end of the Christian-Democratic
monopoly of government power and by an economic phase of heavy expansion.
One of the two major Marxist parties, the Italian Socialist Party, was
about to reenter the government arena after 15 years of opposition, and
for the first time in the country's history, industry was becoming the
principal sector in terms of employment.

Notwithstanding the highly innovative phenomena that characterized
this period at both the economic and institutional levels, one receives
instead the impression of being face-to-face with a more systematic, revised edition of the policy lines that had motivated the agrarian politics of the preceding period. On the one hand, there is a series of
propositions, a clear example of which is given by Article 27 of the
Plan, which among other things furnished loans and grants for the
formation of small farm holdings. These loans and grants resulted in
the tying of many poor peasant farmers to the land and in the stimulation
of a land price increase to the advantage of capitalist farmers. Moreover, funding for a whole series of sunk investments was anticipated,
such as for land improvements for family farms. A large part of this
went to the construction of unneeded houses for farmers, many of which
have already been abandoned. An indication of the purpose of that
funding can be found in the regulations dictating the preferential
employment of family labor.

As for poor and average farmers, the effects of the investments
launched by the first Plan were: (a) a maintenance of bondage to the
soil for several more years of a sizeable number of farmers whose already precarious position had been increasingly unstable in general
and also in relation to the inevitable failure of the investments
made in farming enterprises, and (b) the perpetuation among a significant number of farmers of identification with the role of independent cultivators and of the belief in their future in agriculture.

It would become clear to them only later on that there was room for them neither in the agricultural sector nor in the other sectors of production.

The effect of the Plan on capitalistic farming enterprises was quite different. For them the investments were notably successful. The specifically capitalistic transformation of these enterprises-- increases in the organic composition of capital and in productivity-- was paid for by the proletariat and the agricultural semi-proletariat in two ways: (1) on the part of poor and average poor peasant farmers, through the increasing dualism in enterprise structure, and (2) on the part of farm laborers, through increased productivity and even increasing instability in employment levels. One of the major sources of aid to capitalistic development during this period can be seen in investments in mechanization. The national stock of machines went from 56,941 tractors and the like in 1950, to approximately 600,000 (plus an even greater number of other motorized farming tools) in 1970. It is especially important to keep in mind the different function of machines in capitalistic farming versus peasant farming enterprises. In the former case, they represent a rationalization of productive processes and therefore translate in effect into reduc- tions in costs and employment levels. In the latter case, they repre- sent instead an unsound investment and a cost burden which very often forces the poor or average-poor farmer to be underemployed in his own enterprise.

In many ways the second Plan represented a continuation of the first, but to the advantage of capitalistic farming enterprises and with a reduction in "assistance"-type funding, i.e., assistance for the purpose of social control in peasant farming enterprises. In other words, through greater selectivity with the second Plan, there was once again the tendency to decisively favor the productive function of agriculture, relegating to a secondary level the demands of socio-political regulation connected to the national labor market situation, which had previously dominated agrarian politics.

But capitalistic development cannot help but advance the expulsion of labor and proletarianization. The most striking phenomenon faced in this period is without a doubt the constant decline in agricultural employment, in both absolute and relative terms. Between 1963 and 1968, more than a million workers left agriculture, adding to the approximately one million workers that left between 1959 and 1962. (A third of a million would disappear between 1969 and 1976.) This primarily involved peasant farmers. Consequently, parallel to the drop in the number of agriculturally employed, there was a growing percentage of wage earning labor--from 27 percent in 1961 to 34 percent in 1971, and almost 38 percent in 1977--with expansion of

the area farmed by capitalistic means--from 25 percent of the utilizable
land surface SAU in 1948 to 42 percent in 1970.

It must be emphasized, however, that although the exodus proceeded
for about 15 years at a nearly constant rate, 1963 constitutes a break-
point between two profoundly different periods. In fact, during the
years of the "economic miracle," the exit of labor from agriculture
was the fruit of an increased capacity on the part of other sectors,
especially industry, to generate an additional demand for labor.
After 1963, the exodus continued its course despite the general fall
in the demand for extra-agricultural labor. The exodus thus emerged
instead as the consequence of the growing capacity of the agricultural
sector itself, modified in its structures and the direction of its
evolution, to autonomously expel labor. This last tendency seems
to be connected to the fact that the reduction in agricultural employment led to the involvement not only of the most unstable strata, made
paupers or already semi-proletariat, but also of a growing number of
cultivators who could under no circumstances be considered part of
the relative overpopulation which we have discussed. Proletarianization
does not only manifest itself in the "statistical" condition of passage
from independent worker to dependent worker. The increase of part-time
work is also, at least to a large extent, an expression of the proletarianization process. There are those who go from peasant farmer to
pure laborer, and those instead who, perhaps deceiving themselves into
thinking they can survive as peasant farmers, get by on many odd jobs.
Despite all the measures set into motion to conceal its effects, the
capitalistic development of agriculture thus had as a natural consequence the proletarianization of a considerable group of peasant farmers,
which manifested itself in a variety of ways--expulsion from rural areas,
passage to part-timer status, passage to farm laborer status, and finally,
relative impoverishment of those poor farmers for whom not even the
possibility of exerting pressure on the labor market existed. The
strong pressure for migration did not so much result from the attrac-
tion of industry, which during that time was not drawing labor, as
from mechanisms internal to agriculture, particularly the way in which
public funds were distributed to farming enterprises and the type of
investments made with such funds.

Between 1960 and 1973, there occurred a rather modest increase
in fixed gross investments in agriculture, especially when compared
to those of the 1950's. But more more significant than the absolute
statistics on the accumulation of investments are those pertaining
to their composition. During that period, investments in works of
land reclamation, improvements and transformations, i.e., labor-
increasing investments, went from 66.2 percent to 41.7 percent of
total investments, while those in agricultural machines, transport
and equipment, i.e., labor-saving investments, went from 33.8 percent to 58.3 percent.

These dynamics may be generally understood in light of the following statistics drawn from the last two general censuses (1961 and 1970). During this period, we find a large decrease in the number of agricultural enterprises (-686,000) and contraction of the cultivated land area (-1,507,500 hectares, of which 40,000 were lost due to expansion of urban areas or services). Such phenomena are principally attributable to the large decrease in the number of enterprises less than 10 hectares in area. Enterprises more than 50 hectares in area farmed according to capitalistic criteria show instead an increase in number, both in terms of average area, and as regards the livestock sector, an increase in the number of head of cattle.

We therefore have, in the first place, a restructuring that witnesses the expansion of capitalistic enterprises to cover an area equal to the overall area distributed during the 1950's by the Land Reform. This was a restructuring which furthermore found a supportive prop in the reformulation of Italian agrarian policies, once the bonds that had for the preceding decades caused the sector's specifically capitalistic development to lag were broken. However, this restructuring had strongly negative sides as well, and not only in the area of employment. One need only look at the difficulties with the balance of trade and payments resulting from the serious Italian agricultural deficit, and its origins, where one finds among other things the decreased production of the peasant farming sector.

8. Peasant Farming Enterprises and Capitalistic Enterprises: Observations on Structural Dualism in Agriculture

At this point it would be worthwhile to analyze the results of this historical evolution with reference to the present state of class relationships in agriculture. With regard to this, it is necessary to briefly refer to some political statistics that made possible and accompanied the type of state assistance which was referred to in the preceding paragraphs. These statistics are essentially: (a) the inability of the Left to overcome a sector line of interpretation of the agrarian question. More emphasis was placed on the overall problems of the sector (and precisely on its presumed backwardness) than on its class problems, namely the different interests of the various social groups present in agriculture (farm laborers and peasant farmers versus capitalists and landowners), and (b) the identification of an effective corporate line on the part of moderate bodies. This corporate line was capable for an extended period of time of exerting strong socio-political control on peasant farmers, managing to represent their immediate needs and to simultaneously mobilize them for economic policy choices which departed from their actual class interests.

Without entering into the merits of an analysis of the political policies of these bodies,[10] a suitable reference to the policies and the effects of "agricultural support" carried out by the <u>Federazione Nazionale di Coltivatori Diretti</u> as well as by the <u>Confagricoltura</u> is that of price supports. One of the stock phrases of this agrarian block has always been, "The price of agricultural products is the farmer's pay." There is nothing more blatantly false than this phrase. The high price of agricultural products is not only to the advantage of the capitalistic farmer but in the long run aggravates the condition of the poor and average-poor peasant farmer.

In actuality, price boosting stimulates the production of the products whose price is raised. If, for example, the production cost of whatever product in the capitalist farmer's enterprise is 10,000 lire per quintal and the middle or poor peasant farmer's 15.000 lire, when the price is boosted to 20,000 lire per quintal, the capitalist farmer makes a 10,000 lire profit while the peasant farmer only 5,000. These differences in profitability are magnified by the differential sizes of capitalist and peasant enterprises. But what counts is differences in the destination of profit. While the peasant farmer needs that money to survive, the capitalist farmer makes use of it in new investments which will allow subsequent rationalization of productive processes and consequent further lowering of production costs. Therefore, through price boosting, new capital with increased productivity is continually being pumped into the enterprises of capitalist farmers. In peasant farming enterprices, on the contrary, without the possibility of reaslizing equal transformations, costs must always remain high.

The fact that price boosting of products found staunch supporters among the moderate forces at work in Italian agriculture does not imply that it arose solely from their initiatives. An understanding of the alternatives in agrarian politics throughout the 1960's in our country, and of the same general transformations that occurred in agriculture, requires mention of the processes of European economic integration that were taking place with great force, particularly in agriculture during the 1960's. During this period, the administration of the Common Agricultural Policy (CAP) was essentially limited to the boosting of farm product prices through the FEAOG (The European Fund for Agricultural Policy and Price Support). However, this limited activity of the CAP had major effects on European agriculture. The non-neutrality of this policy is evident not only in the differential effects among the various types of enterprises mentioned above. It actually favored certain types of cultivation--grain and dairy--over others, thus favoring certain groups of cultivators (especially the big French grain growers). And, finally, it had differential effects on the various member countries of the CEE, putting some, like Italy, to a disadvantage, and others, like France and Holland, at a great

advantage with respect to financing.[11]   But the greatest contradiction
in this policy was determined by the increasing investments of the
FEAOG which created burdens for the overall economic system and its
productive sectors--especially for industry.

At the end of the 1960's, a critical evaluation of the effects
of European agricultural integration expressed by former CEE Commission president Mansholt[12] led to the proposal of direct payments
to enterprises as an alternative to price supports in order to restore equilibrium in agriculture. With ten years hindsight it can
be stated that in reality there were no serious modifications in the
nature of price support policy. The overall result of the "European
NEP" (new economic policy) was a diminution of autonomy in national
agrarian policies and a more intensive selectivity in assistance (also
with respect to Green Plan II). In other words, neither "price" nor
"structural" policy yielded different results, at least as far as
Italian agriculture was concerned. What we have in essence is a
consolidation of the capitalistic sector and the creation of a band
of "European" type enterprices, i.e., meeting the demands of capitalistic restructuring indicated by the CEE. One observes an increase
in fixed capital in the organic composition of capital (especially
favored by the significant State funding for mechanization), an
incremental gain in productive potential (favored by works of land
improvement for enterprises and reclained areas), a rationalization
of productive processes (favored by the possibility of utilizing new
technologies), and a progressive increase in differential profits
(favored by price supports).

The discrepancy between large and small enterprises is evident
if we consider, for example, the different ways in which they utilize
human labor. The non-capitalistic enterprise--the small peasant farming enterprise--has at its disposal in sufficient quantity only one
productive factor: labor. Its proletarianization is also expressed
as a progressive increase in abundance of family labor. Excess labor
can be either employed by capitalistic enterprises or utilized
"irrationally" within the peasant enterprise itself, as occurs in
phases of capitalistic development accompanied by "peasantization"
policies. This is what has happened in Italy during the last 20
years.

As can be seen from an analysis of Table 2, small peasant farming enterprises have a labor employment rate 10 times greater than
that of capitalistic enterprises. And this cannot be attributed
to different levels of farming intensity between the two types of
enterprises. The differences in labor employment levels between
capitalistic and non-capitalistic enterprises, between large and
small enterprises, persist even when the effects of altitude zones
are controlled. This excess labor employed in the enterprises of

average and poor peasant farmers therefore expresses the extremely
low productivity of the labor that characterizes them.

Table 2.   Average Labor Employment in Agricultural Enterprises by
Size and Altitude Zone.

| Size Classes | Employment of Labor Days/Hectare | | | |
	Total	Mountains	Hills	Plains
Up to 1	237	228	239	241
1.01 - 2.0	164	160	161	175
2.01 - 3.0	136	129	134	148
3.01 - 5.0	113	105	112	125
5.01 - 10.0	86	75	85	95
10.01 - 20.0	60	50	57	70
20.01 - 30.0	41	32	35	52
30.01 - 50.0	31	22	25	44
50.01 - 100.0	23	13	18	36
Over 100	11	3	11	27
Total	73	62	73	83

Source: E. Pugliese, "Politica del lavoro e occupazione in agricolture,"
in Riv. di Economia Agraria, 1971, no. 3.   The statistics were
drawn from ISTAT, Indagine sulla struttura delle aziende
agricole, Rome, 1970.

As further confirmation of the effect of excessive availability
of labor on the economic output of peasant farming enterprises, we
can present the results of a study connected by E. Pugliese and M.
Rossi of a sample of enterprises from the INEA-CEE pool.[13]   This
study involves data for a two-year (1969-70) period, and consequently
its economic output data are relevant only to that period.   What is
important, is the relative differences.[14]

Looking at Table 3, which refers to this group of enterprises,
one sees that the net product per work hour goes from 610 lire for
enterprises which use less than 400 hours per hectare of farmed land,
to 461 lire for those using over 800.   It must be noted that these
results tannot be attributed to "bad management."   In our opinion,
there are structural reasons which compel these "choices."   For the
peasant farming sector, labor is a limiting factor in the sense that
it is not possible to substitute variable capital with fixed capital,
for at least two basic reasons: (1) the peasant farmer does not have
access to the capital needed to acquire technical instruments to
rationalize the employment of labor, and (2) very often this process
of substituting variable capital with fixed capital is not convenient.

Lacking alternative occupational outlets, especially in the short-run, the employment of family labor on the enterprises is the only possible solution other than movement to a less "labor intensive" form of production. The enterprises in which the percentage of family labor of total

Table 3.   Economic Output in Relation to Work Loads and the Incidence of Family Labor.

Hours Per Hectare SAU	Net Product Per Work Hour (in lire)	Percentage of family Labor Over the Total	Net Product Per Work Hour (in lire)
0 - 400	610	0 - 75	710
400 - 800	525	75 - 95	511
800 - 1000	461	95 - 100	348

Source: E. Pugliese - M. Rossi, "Dualismo strutturale in agricoltura e mercato di lavoro," in Crisi e ristrutturazione dell'economia italiana, edited by A. Graziani, Einaudi, 1975; elaboration of the INEA statistics, Le azienda agrarie italiane. Dati strutturali ed economici, 1969 and 1970, 2-year averages for 1960 and 1970.

employed labor is under 75 take in a net product per work hour of 710 lire, while those enterprises in which all the labor is familial (when it exceeds 95 percent) take in a net product of 348 lire.

The capitalistic character of an enterprise is also defined in terms of its assets (Table 4). Enterprises with over 70 million lire of capital can rightfully be considered capitalistic. In such enterprises, the average value of the net product per work hour is 1,041 lire. At the opposite end, enterprises of this sample having a capital value less than 30 million lire average 437 lire for their net product per work hour (well below the average). At an intermediate level, i.e., that of enterprises with capital value between 30 and 70 million lire, work productivity also assumes an intermediate value.

One possible objection to the relation illustrated by this table is that it involves a spurious relation--that productivity may be a function of other variables, not necessarily that of capital value and thus not of a capitalistic nature of the enterprise. In anticipation of such an objection, data were computed according to categories of cultivation. Whether we are dealing with categories like horticulture (which has high labor requirements) or extensive categories, Table 4 still shows that the peasant farming enterprise is at a disadvantage.

This fact is rich in implication for the debate on the role of
the peasant farming sector. It is widely believed in Italy that the
peasant farming enterprise is the most suitable form of production
organization for certain forms of specialized production, namely
those requiring higher labor intensity. Therefore within the realm

Table 4.   Economic Output in Relation to Capital Value of Enterprise.

	Capital Value (in millions of lire)	Net Product Per Work Hour (in thousands of lire)	Net Product Per Work Hour For Individual Categories of Culti- vation (thousands of lire)				
			Herba- ceous	Horti- culture	Arbori- culture	Live- stock	Mixed
overall	0-30	437	373	339	491	337	302
	30-70	617	515	665	648	565	634
	70-1000	1041	745	1131	1082	725	---
land	0-20	415	358	399	492	337	302
	20-40	611	461	652	573	513	537
	40-1000	866	690	---	---	---	---
agrarian	0-10	480	398	470	539	374	381
	10-30	718	561	851	684	580	599
	30-100	1142	838	1221	---	761	---

Source: See Table 3.

of capitalistic development, peasant farming should have possibilities
for development, in addition to a precise function in the process of
accumulation.   These possibilities would result from technical-economic
reasons.   For such specialized production, the availability of family
labor would not pose an obstacle, but rather an element of advantage.
It is undeniable that more labor-intensive categories of cultivation
are more advantageous to enterprises which have a great deal of labor
at their disposal than are extensive categories.   At least family labor
remains unemployed or under-employed for a shorter period of time during
the year.   But the fact that the peasant farming enterprise has better
chances for survival--and therefore the capacity to bear higher family
labor loads--when it can specialize in more labor-intensive forms of
production does not mean that the discrepancies in production between
it and the capitalistic farming enterprise are significantly reduced.
It means only that, even if under-compensated, overall labor employment is greater and therefore so is absolute family income.

9. Structural Dualism and Social Stratification

The discussion thus far has essentially contained an implicit assumption concerning the identity between peasant farming enterprise and peasant farming family, between the position of enterprises within a context of economic stratification and the condition of peasant farmers within this stratification system. And to be sure, the existence of elements of structural dualism such as those previously cited reveals a condition of general weakness in the overall conglomeration we can define as the peasant farming sector.

However, another problem poses itself. It is true that the push toward proletarianization has indeed caused the exocus of farmers from agriculture and their passage from the state of independent workers to that of dependent workers. But then why does such a large number of peasant farming enterprises persist? Why does such a large number of peasant farmers remain in the sector?

The model of the two functions of agriculture that we expounded in the initial paragraphs of this paper represents to us a general explanatory framework. In order to enter into the more specific merits of this analysis of social stratification and of class relationships in Italian agriculture today, we would like to make some additional points.

A new phenomenon that must increasingly be taken into consideration is the change in relationship between the peasant farmer and the land, between the "agriculturally employed" and "agricultural occupations." A strange "backward-moving process" is taking place in agriculture. For Kautsky, the beginning of capitalistic agriculture corresponds to the moment in which the farmer becomes a "pure and simple cultivator." And yet today, with an ever increasing aggressiveness on the part of the capitalistic sector in agriculture and especially with the extension of industry throughout various rural areas of the country-- in short, with the "diffused factory" phenomenon--the ranks of the pure and simple cultivator are continually diminishing, be it (obviously) in absolute numbers, or in relative terms.

A new relationship is forming between the peasant farming enterprise and the peasant farming family. Not only is the number of family members that work on the farm steadily going down, but to a disproportionate extent there is a decrease in the proportion of total family income from agricultural sources for rural and specifically peasant farming families.[15] Even in areas where the labor market does not provide off-farm employment opportunities, the income deriving from extra-agricultural activity is substituted, albeit most modestly, by income from relief sources. This last point is especially true for the hill and mountain regions of the South in particular. Often here

the image of the poor _farmer_, formerly a partisan in struggles for
land, then in the migratory experience, is replaced by the image of
the _poor man_ who survives by doing, among other things, farm work.

But be it in those areas where developed agriculture flourishes
or in those where agriculture even assumes a marginal character, the
study of the social structure of agriculture implies the study of the
social structure of rural areas. In terms of methodological implications, this means that it is absolutely meaningless to base the
analysis of the structure and social stratification of the agricultural population from the analysis of the stratification of the enterprises, as do Barberis and Siesto, and G. Bolaffi and A. Varotti.[16]
The class position of the rural family is determined by the ensemble
of income produced by the various members of the family nucleus, and
above all by the source of income and the ways in which it is produced,
i.e., the position and social relationships of production of the
various income-producing members of the family. Only by not taking
into account these aspects is it possible to deny the existence of
the processes of proletarianization. This leads to an overestimation
of the developmental tendencies of certain limited strata in a capitalistic sense, e.g., the "molecular tendency," as Daneo has aptly defined
it, from the condition of "peasant farmer" to that of "family farmer."[17]

In Italy, in agriculture as in other sectors of production, the
small enterprise does not seem doomed to disappear. Its presence can
be functionally adapted to capitalistic development. The example of
decentralization of production in industry is not, however, indicative
of the vitality of the small enterprise. This plays a role only to
the extent in which it is situated as a moment in an overall cycle of
production in relation to the large enterprise, which represents the
initial phase in the processes of decentralization.

The survival of the peasant farming enterprise is not a sign of
its vitality. That applies for both its role in the labor market and
its subordination in adaptation to the process of capitalistic development. In one as in the other, the process of proletarianization is
expressed. Such a process is in fact the dominant tendency. And this
process is to be understood, as is obvious, in the sense of a progressive separation from the means of production--or at least in terms of
an increasingly untenable or marginal situation. This tendency is
correctly and very usefully identified by the Kautskian model of the
agrarian question. The results of the process or proletarianization
are multiple. In the various aspects of Italian agricultural reality,
we see the expression of the many and varied manifestations of the
process of proletarianization.[18]

FOOTNOTES

1. For a more detailed analysis of structural dualism of Italian agriculture, see E. Pugliese, M. Rossi, "Dualismo strutturale in agricoltura e mercato del lavoro" in Crise e ristrutturazione dell'economia italiana, edited by A. Graziani, Einaudi, 1975. On the topic of structural dualism see also the contributions of G. Bolaffi and A. Varotti, of Calzabini, of V. Cosentino and M. De Benedictis, and of M. Gorgoni in the anthology edited by P. Bartolini and B. Meloni, L'azienda contadina, Rosemberg and Sellier, 1978.

2. We are referring here to peasant farming and not family farming. By peasant farming, agricoltura contadina, we mean agriculture characterized by the group of persons who carry out manual work on a small agricultural enterprise run by them, be it owned or rented or administered through other arrangements (sharecropping, profit-sharing, etc.). For the ideological use of the concept of family farming see C. Daneo, L'azienda familiare in agricoltura, Critica Marxista, 1964.

3. The principal reference for these first paragraphs is K. Kautsky, La questione agraria, Milano, Faltrinelli, 1959. This book is still one of the fundamental points of departure for an understanding of the agrarian problem in capitalistic society (see Part I, Chap. 1-10 and Part II, Chap. 1 in particular). It is moreover essential in order to understand the use and development of these concepts by Lenin (Cf. V. Lenin, Scritti sulla questione agraria, Roma, Rinascita, 1958).

4. For a discussion of this important issue, Kautsky's preface to the French edition of The Agrarian Question is useful (see pp. 8-11 of the cited Italian edition). The introduction to the latter by G. Procacci is also useful.

5. It must be remembered that as explicitly noted by Marx, the term "industrial reserve" does not only refer to labor at the disposal of industry but also to labor at the disposal of capitalists (K. Marx, Il Capitale, 1st Book, Section 7, Chaper 23).

6. This last argument, for example, has exercised considerable influence on the agrarian policy of the Italian Left, especially since the end of World War II. The most fully developed formulation of such a thesis can in fact be found in the works of Emilio Sereni. Our ideas on the issue are that in this case one is dealing with a restrictive interpretation of the Gramscian plan, made possible by the necessarily fragmentary character of Gramsci's observations on this point.

7. Along these lines it must be emphasized--so as not to be accused
    of excessive schematism--that the contradictions mentioned may fall
    into three categories: those internal to the class in power, those
    between the ruling class and its allies, thsoe between the ruling
    class and the proletariat. Every opportunistic policy line is
    characterized by the confusion between these three levels.

8. The fact that the capitalistic function of agriculture (in a
    narrow sense) can never totally prevail over its other function
    is nothing more than a specific case of the fundamental law of
    capitalistic development, i.e., that the contradiction between
    capital and labor can never be eliminated because labor cannot
    be, and the latter's behavior moreover is not entirely determin-
    able from the movement of capital.

9. Farmers owning land, numbering 1,009,134 in 1871, remained relatively
    constant, 1,108,728 in 1911. During the same time span, farm laborers
    went from 3,196,750 to 3,277,715. The only increment of significance
    is in the number of tenants and sharecroppers which go, respectively,
    from 453,294 to 561,210, and 955,435 to 1,129,155. Cf. A. Serpieri,
    La struttura Sociale dell'Agricoltura Italiana, Roma, INEA, 1947.

10. On this issue we refer the reader to our Questione agraria e
    movimento operaio and the more recent essay by G. Mottura, "La
    strategia corporativa nelle campagne italiane" in the anthology
    edited by A. Caruso, L'ideologia corporativa, Faltrinelli, forth-
    coming.

11. On this topic see A. Zeller, L'imbroglio agricolo del mercato
    commune, as well as the articles in Rivista di Economia Agraria,
    1976, no. 3, by R. Fanfani, "L'agricoltura nei paesi della CEE
    nel periodo '63-'74: evoluzione strutturale e produttiva,"
    pp. 489-521, and by E. Ponzo, "Il finanziamento della politica
    agricola comune nel periodo '62-'74," pp. 523-546.

12. Cf. Commissione delle Comunita Europee. Memorandum sulla riforma
    della strutture dell'agricoltura italiana (Mansholt Plan). This
    memorandum served as a basis for the agricultural legislation of
    Common Market countries.

13. Cf. E. Pugliese, M. Rossi. "Dualismo strutturale in agricoltura
    e mercato del lavoro," op. cit.

14. These statistics, like those of the preceding table, are from the
    late sixties. There are now more recent statistics available from
    the 1970 census and subsequent CEE inquiries. We chose not to
    include them because upon summary analysis we discovered that there
    would not have been many differences.

15. The dispersion of industrial activity, especially in the rural
     areas of Northeast Italy, occurred by both the dispersion of
     small and medium-sized enterprise in small centers and the exten-
     sion of take-home work within peasant farming families. This
     type of territorial reality has new and peculiar aspects which
     are beginning to attract study. Cf. A. Bagnasco, Le Tre Italie,
     Il Mulino, 1977; A. Cavazzani, L'agricoltura a tempo parziale
     nelle Marche, Ente di Sviluppo della Marche, Ancona, 1978; also
     the article by M. Paci et al. in Inchiesta, no. 20, on "Ristrut-
     turazione industriale, piccola impresa e lavoro a domicilio."

16. C. Barberis and V. Siesto, Produzione agricola e Strati sociale,
     Angeli, 1975, and G. Bolaffi and A. Varotti, Agricoltura
     capitalistica e classi sociali in Italia, De Donato, 1973.

17. C. Daneo, Agricoltura e sviluppo capitalistico in Italia, Chap. II.

18. The authors greatly appreciate the assistance of Elenora Ber-
     tacchi in translating this manuscript into English. We are also
     endebted to the Western Societies Program of the Cornell Univer-
     sity Center for International Studies for their financial sup-
     port of the translation. This paper was originally presented
     at the X European Congress for Rural Sociology, Cordoba, Spain,
     April 1979.

7. Technology in Agriculture: Labor and the Rate of Accumulation

WILLIAM H. FRIEDLAND

This paper is primarily concerned with examination of the effects of labor on the innovational process. As a secondary but related issue, the paper examines some of the differences between technological development in industry and in agriculture.

The first argument that will be developed is that labor plays a three-fold role in the elaboration of technology. Invention, innovation and technological development unfold, therefore, under one or more of the following conditions:

1. To save labor costs.

2. As a substitute for a labor supply.

3. As a control factor when labor becomes "recalcitrant," e.g., strikes, slows down, or refuses in various ways to fulfill the expectations of upper echelons in the productive system.

Only the first of the factors above is concerned most directly with economics and economic rationality. In fact, a major point of the empirical cases discussed below is that the argument of economic rationality--that capital substitutes for labor--is often experienced more clearly after the fact than before. That is, technologicsal change is introduced for other reasons and, in the process, economies are realized. This is not to argue that innovation is never undertaken to realize direct economic benefits in saving labor costs; rather the contention is that while such savings often accrue, the motives for technological innovation originate because of the other reasons cited above.

With respect to these other two reasons, a more generic element underlies the search for technological development. This is the

*Paper presented at the 1978 annual meeting of the American Sociological Association, San Francisco, California, September, 1978

quest for the reduction of uncertainty. Rosenberg (1976) deals with
the issue of uncertainty with respect to the recalcitrance of labor
(1). Thus, he cites Marx, Samuel Smiles, Andrew Ure, James Nasmyth, Sir
William Fairbairn, Charles Babbage and others to demonstrate the
high level of consciousness that existed during the industrial revolution and the application of power to production. Early manufacturers and inventors became acutely conscious of their vulnerability
to strikes and other labor disturbances and stimulated the inventive
and innovative processes in attempts to reduce their vulnerability.
Rosenberg concludes:

> The preoccupation with substituting capital for
> labor (especially skilled labor) was more than
> just a matter of wage rates. Perhaps even more
> important was the great nuisance value of strikes.
> In part at least, entrepreneurial behavior must
> be understood in terms of an aversion to the
> uncertainties presented by strike possibilities
> whose disruptive effects were regarded as intol-
> erable intrusions into the domain of managerial
> decision making and responsibility (Rosenberg
> 1976:120).

Rosenberg emphasizes in a footnote the general character of
manufacturers' attempts to reduce uncertainties. Labor constituted
only one unceratin factor but was, at the time as well as later, a
crucial factor that employers sought to control. The way in which
employers in agriculture have responded to labor as an uncertain
factor of production, but particularly with respect to technological
development, is the subject of this paper (2). We, therefore, will
not consider two major strategies that agricultural employers have
traditionally utilized, labor over-supply and union-busting (3),
as means to control the uncertainties of labor. With this focus on
technological development and its usual concomitant, capital substitution, a somewhat clearer picture can be developed as to 1) how the
labor factor contributes to technological development in agriculture,
and 2) how the research and development process occurs in agriculture.
We will treat the first topic in some detail before turning to a
briefer, suggestive examination of the second.

AGRICULTURAL TECHNOLOGY AND THE LABOR FACTOR

Historically it can be argued that agricultural employers in the
west turned more deliberately to technology as a form of social control
only after 1964. Before that time, the two prime strategies used to
control labor were over-supply and anti-unionism. There were, however,
long-standing and notable developments in large-scale, mechanized

agriculture beginning in the 1880s in grain production (Paul, 1973).
Technological applications in this early phase were primarily focused
on the continuing labor shortage that western agriculture experienced
and on the typical search to reduce production costs. Since grower
interests were, on the whole, well taken care of through over-supply
of labor and successes with anti-unionism, it can be argued that
interest in technological development up to the 1960s was primarily
focused on cost cutting.

Capital substitution for labor was not always desirable during
this period since labor was, itself, relatively cheap. In one documented case, the development of vacuum cooling of lettuce, technology
permitted a return to greater labor intensivity and a decline in capital investment. Vacuum cooling is a process in which lettuce is cooled
by placing it in a large cylinder from which the air is then evacuated.
This not only reduces the temperature of the lettuce but maintains better
quality since lettuce is not brought in contact with ice. The consequence of the introduction of vacuum cooling in the early 1950s was to
eliminate shed packing of lettuce. At one and the same time, it undercut
the (relatively) well-paid, unionized, Anglo shed packers and replaced
them by poorly-paid Mexican bracero field hands. Although more labor
was used with vacuum cooling, its total cost as a factor of production
was lower (Glass, 1966). This example not only demonstrates the cost-
effectiveness and the improvement of the quality of the product through
new technology but also had the utilitarian effect (from the viewpoint
of employers) of eliminating unionism from the lettuce fields.

The end of the bracero program in 1964 produced the major shift
toward technological development, initially because of concern with
labor supply problems and, as time passed, with control over an increasingly recalcitrant labor force. The program, begun during the second
world war, continued over a 20 year period. During this time agricultural employers in the west were able to resolve the problem of labor
supply through inter-governmental arrangements between the United
States and Mexico. Despite contentions that bracero labor should not
have adverse effects on U.S. labor, a sober assessment of this program
can only conclude that it provided workers in the numbers required
by employers at relatively low rates of remuneration. Ending the
program meant disruption of the labor supply. The first reaction
of agricultural employers, when they finally gave up attempting to
resuscitate the program and to find ways to circumvent its ending,
was to turn to agricultural mechanization as a solution.

Agricultural mechanization, of course, has a long history throughout the world but especially in the United States (Partridge, 1973;
Holbrook, 1955), because with the enclosure of the bracero program,
the development of instant interest in agricultural mechanization
could be seen as the California State Legislature allocated $150,000
to stimulate mechanization research in the University of California

(Kelly, 1966). Thus, the end of the unlimited labor supply put underway a program in technological development through mechanization
research.

Two efforts at such application are particularly notable--in
processing tomatoes and in iceberg lettuce. In tomatoes, research
toward mechanization had been initiated in the 1940s by a maverick
plant scientist (4). Before long, as criticism of the bracero program
grew, an agricultural engineer began working on this project. Together, the plant scientist sought to breed a mechanically-harvestable
tomato for a machine that did not exist while the engineer was building a machine for a tomato which had not yet been bred. By the end of
the 1950s, research was sufficiently advanced so that commercial
production of the harvester could be licensed.

As long as the bracero program continued, tomato growers had
little interest in the machine. Although economic analysis indicated
potential cost savings through harvest mechanization, growers preferred to rely upon the tested and tried bracero program rather than
a complicated and expensive new machine. The effects of the end of
the bracero program can be seen in the rate of adoption of the new
technology illustrated in Table 1.

TABLE 1

Number of Tomato Harvesters and Percentage of Crop
Harvested, by Year, 1962-1970

Year	Number of Machines	Percentage of Crop Machine Harvested
1962	NA	1.0
1963	66	1.5
1964	NA	3.8
1965	224	24.7
1966	736	65.8
1967	1065	81.8
1968	1461	95.1
1969	1510	99.5
1970	1521	99.9

Source: Friedland and Barton (1975, 1976).

The table shows the disinterest until 1965 when bracero labor ceased to be available.

Forced to adopt the harvesting machine because of the disruption in labor supply, growers quickly began to realize economies of which they had never dreamed. Indeed, the new technology was so effective that California production, which had grown and then dropped as a percentage of total U.S. production, began to grow again. The effectiveness of the new machine is shown in Table 2, illustrating California's share of total U.S. production between 1946 and 1972. It might be noted that the machine has proven to be, at least up to present, useful for harvesting processing tomatoes largely only in California because of the relatively predictable growing conditions.

TABLE 2

California Tomato Production
as a Percentage of U.S. Production

Year	California Tonnage as Percentage of U.S.	Year	California Tonnage as Percentage of U.S.
1946	39.2%	1961	54.6%
1947	44.1	1962	59.8
1948	32.8	1963	60.5
1949	39.8	1964	65.8
1950	35.1	1965	55.1
1951	51.8	1966	67.3
1952	51.6	1967	61.5
1953	43.6	1968	70.4
1954	49.8	1969	68.9
1955	60.9	1970	66.5
1956	59.8	1971	69.9
1957	61.0	1972	78.0
1958	61.3		
1959	56.9		
1960	55.6		

Source: Friedland and Barton (1975:2).

The threat to the labor supply in lettuce was felt at the same time although the technological capacity was not ready-to-hand as was the case in tomatoes (5). Lettuce, like tomatoes, was a labor intensive crop depending almost entirely on bracero labor for harvesting. However, the productivity of labor in lettuce harvesting had increased enormously between 1960 and 1973 (6). Growers were therefore interested in a harvest machine, and one was quickly developed in 1964 by an agricultural engineer at U.C. Davis. This early harvester was crude in its conception but could have served as a labor substitute had it become necessary. Instead a transition occurred in the legal status of the harvest labor force in which the former bracero harvesters were admitted to legal immigrant status as "green-carders." This was feasible because the numbers involved were considerably smaller than the number of braceros harvesting tomatoes, and lettuce harvesting is a year-round activity in contrast to the relatively short tomato season. Lettuce growers quickly lost interest in harvest mechanization, and the Davis prototype was shelved although its developer continued to work on its refinement. There were no clear indications at the time about economies that might be effected by the machine, and this first prototype had a great many technical uncertainties. As long as the labor supply could be maintained, therefore, lettuce growers preferred labor over the machine.

After 1964 the rebirth of agricultural unionism in California became feasible (Friedland and Nelkin, 1972). Although Cesar Chavez had begun organizing the National Farm Workers Association in 1962, the end of bracero movement was necessary before agricultural unionism could become significant. Between 1964 and 1968, the NFWA, soon to become the United Farm Workers Organizing Committee and later the United Farm-Workers Union, grew and began to constitute a significant threat to agricultural employers.

Although originally organizing in table grapes, a commodity that is labor intensive and cannot be mechanized, it is, however, with our two previous cases--iceberg lettuce and processing tomatoes-- that the effects of unionism can best be understood in relation to technological development and adoption. In the case of lettuce, sudden interest became manifested by growers early in the 1970s. This was because the UFW finally "cracked" the table grape growers and won a number of contracts in 1970. In Salinas, the signing of the grape contracts threw lettuce growers into a paroxysm of panic. Despite exhortations from the California Farm Bureau not to move towards alternative unionism, lettuce growers began to sign contracts covering field workers with the Teamsters Union. Although the UFW had maintained some interest in organizing lettuce harvesters, up to this time their energies had been concentrated on table grape workers. As the growers began to sign contracts with the Teamsters, the UFW organizers rushed to Salinas, quickly organized the lettuce harvesters, and began a strike (Friedland and Thomas, 1974). Although Teamster unionism offered a preferred alternative to UFW unionism, growers remained uncertain about the future. They, therefore, turned once again to harvest mechanization research.

Two efforts at such research accelerated so that within a few years, two basic prototype systems became available. (7). One, developing from the original 1964 research at Davis, used a gamma ray emitter to selectively harvest lettuce, elevating the lettuce through a series of "fingers" that caught the lettuce as it was cut. The second, developed by the U.S. Department of Agriculture at its Salinas field station, used an X-ray emitter and rubber-conveyer belts to elevate the lettuce. By the summer of 1977, a field prototype of the Salinas machine was successfully tested, but growers manifested no interest in it.

What happened between the initial panic of growers in 1971, their remewed interest in mechanization, and their disinterest in 1977? Basically two things: first, a prototype machine was available and could be moved into production with considerable rapidity; second, growers had begun, in the interim, to live with the idea of the UFW and its permanent presence in the industry. This is not to say that growers were particularly delighted to see the UFW develop; if they had their "druthers," they would rather function without any unionism, let alone Chavez unionism. However, lettuce growers increasingly came to see the UFW as a "fact of life," as a condition of continuing existence in the industry. Further, lettuce growers began to view the union the way in which many sophisticated employers do--as an institution which can reduce uncertainty.

Between 1971 and 1977, lettuce growers had experienced considerable uncertainties with respect to labor. Originally believing their problems might be solved by signing with the Teamsters, they still had to deal with the UFW which organized a painful boycott against them. Then the Teamsters, for whom field worker organizing is at best peripheral, responded to a variety of pressures and moved out of organizing field workers. On top of this, the first labor legislation on agricultural unionism in the continental U.S. was adopted in California in 1975. Growers, in other words, had to live with unionism and to begin the process of stabilization. Since the UFW showed no indication of disappearing and began to show seriousness about contracts and their implementation, lettuce growers developed different attitudes toward the union.

By 1977, when the mechanical harvester prototype was tested, growers felt that they had a sufficiently predictable and manageable labor system; the harvest machine technology, on the other hand, represented uncertainties in costs and savings, soil compaction, quality of the harvest, and in how to handle the lettuce after it was harvested. Under these circumstances, growers became cool about continuing research, and at present no research in harvest mechani-

zation is taking place. But the point should not be lost: the stimulus to renewed interest in mechanization research followed from the
threat of unionism.

   If lettuce harvest mechanization was aborted a second time, the
situation in tomatoes was notably different as this crop moved toward
a second generation of technology through optical or electronic sorting. Electronic sorting represents adaptation of a technology developed for other purposes since the basic research on the process had been
accomplished years before by a U.C. Davis agricultural engineer for
citrus production. The process involves a light reflection principle
in which fruit is run through a series of channels beneath a light
source. The sorting device is constructed to accept light rays reflected back to a reception source within specified limits dependent
on the color of the fruit. If the color reflected is not within an
appropriate range, a device is triggered which discards the fruit.

   The transition to electronic sorting was stimulated in the summer of 1975 as a result of a union organizing drive of the UFW.
The immediate reaction of many tomato growers was to fit their machines
with the new devices. Here we might note that tomato growing had
undergone significant concentration as a result of the first generation of machine technology. The numbers of growers had dropped from
approximately 4000 to under 600 between 1962 and 1973 while output
in tonnage had increased by 51% (Friedland and Barton, 1975, 1976).
Despite this growing specialization in tomato production, growers
had not developed a concomitant sophistication in labor relations.
Because tomato harvesting continues to require a large number of tomato
sorters for relatively short periods, growers continue to be oriented
toward resolving the supply problem rather than other elements of the
industrial relations process. Wages and working conditions were
therefore less than optimal, and growers paid relatively little attention to the on-the-job conditions, supervision, and management.
As soon as the UFW made its appearance, grower reaction was to supplant
their labor requirements by capital substitution. And despite some
technical difficulties in the first year and the withdrawal of the
UFW after their one foray into organizing tomato harvest workers,
adoption of the new application has moved rapidly. It is estimated
that by 1982 the rate of displacement of sorters will be 60 percent.

   The reaction to union organization in processing tomatoes and
iceberg lettuce is thus very different in this recent period. Because
lettuce growing is a year-round activity, employers' attempts to
reduce uncertainty have concentrated on a management approach to the
labor force. Because tomatoes require heavy influxes of workers for
short periods of time, tomato growers have shifted toward capital
substitution to replace labor. In the lettuce case, technology
"stands in the wings," so to speak, potentially adoptable if lettuce
employers continue to experience difficulties with the labor force;

in tomatoes, as soon as the threat of unionization arose, growers moved to adopt. In both cases, however, distinct orientations exist toward developing and adopting technology as a means of reducing uncertainties.

These two cases emphasize that technology as a form of social control continues to be an important factor leading to technological development in agriculture. While the analysis as summarized by Rosenberg has proven correct, its application takes different form under varying conditions in agriculture. All growers look with greater interest to technological development whenever the labor factor ob- trudes or threatens to become uncontrollable, i.e., the quest for certainty remains a major contributor to technological development in agriculture with labor continuing to be the prime pressure point.

RESEARCH, TECHNOLOGY, AND ACCUMULATION IN AGRICULTURE

Rosenberg (1976:110-117) argues that one of the elements leading to inducement of innovation (or what we have referred here to as accumulation) has been sequencing. This concept has to do with the imbalances that develop in industrial processes where interdependence between different segments of the overall process is important. The classic case illustrating sequencing is drawn from English tex- tiles in the 18th century: "Kay's flying shuttle led to the need for speeding up spinning operations...(this) in turn created the shortage of weaving capacity which finally culminated in Cartwright's intro- duction of the power loom" (Rosenberg 1976:112). Rosenberg points out that sequencing, as an inducement to technological development, has been most important in industry and asks:

> Why have they (sequencing problems) not been
> equally important...in agriculture? ...Part
> of the answer, I would suggest is that the per-
> son receiving such signals (of imbalances between
> sequences) in agriculture--the farmer--is not,
> himself, competent by training or occupational
> experience to evaluate them in a creative way.
> In the industrial sector there has been a con-
> tinuous and direct confrontation between tech-
> nical problems and personnel with competence to
> solve them, whereas many of the problems of
> agriculture have had to await the development of
> specialized institutions (e.g., land-grant
> colleges) and specialized professions with re-
> quisite skills--genetics, soil chemistry, and,
> of course, mechanical technology as well (Rosen-
> berg 1976:307, note 24).

While the differences between agriculture and industry are notable, I would like to suggest that.the lesser significance of sequencing is a function of the different structure of production in agriculture as compared to industry, as well as to the discontinuities in production processes when the two production systems are compared.

Historically, research and development in industry is conjoined strongly to entrepreneurship; early scientists and technologists during the industrial revolution sought to financially exploit their discoveries. As industrialism developed, however, entrepreneurial activity moved towards financial management and away from R&D. Since R&D activities had to be continued, they became an internal function within many firms. With production processes highly integrated, it is not surprising that an orientation to bottlenecks and consequent sequencing as an inducement to innovation developed so clearly in industry.

In agriculture, in contrast, production is discontinuous. If a farmer grows wheat, once it has been grown and sold, the products' problems move elsewhere. The farmer is not interested in storage, transportation, processing, etc., except as it impinges on that part of the production process over which the farmer maintains control. Thus, discontinuities in production produce weaker signals, to use Rosenberg's term, about imbalances in the sequence.

Second, as Rosenberg has noted, agricultural R&D had to await the development of the land-grant complex to get most of its research done. This complex was a long time in construction, beginning with the Morrell Act of 1862 and not having its basic legal structure completed until the Smith-Lever Act of 1914. But the land-grant R&D complex, despite its considerable power as a research mechanism, is structurally incapable of being as responsive to sequential imbalances as industrial R&D organizations. This is not only because the agricultural R&D organization consists of three distinct, integrated-yet-semiautonomous structures, but because the very nature of those structures emphasize the production discontinuities in agriculture. Thus, the functions of the Agricultural Extension Service not only include the diffusion of discoveries made by scientists of the Agricultural Experiment Stations but also to serve as a "feeding device," defining as research problems for the Experiment Station scientists, the problems experienced by farmers. Yet, as has been noted even from early foundations (Rosenberg, 1977), Experiment Station scientists often prefer to work on problems delineated by their professional disciplines rather than "simple" applied problems with little theoretical consequences.

Research in the agricultural sector is consequently formally autonomous of agricultural production and therefore less responsive than industry. Yet even research conducted by commercial industrial firms for agriculture will experience a similar lack of responsiveness to sequencing pressures. Commercial firms producing inputs for agricultural production are not geared to deal with bottleneck problems as much as they are to deal with problems in their own sphere of production on which a profit can be realized. Thus, a petroleum firm is not fundamentally interested in research on fertilizers unless they can be made from petroleium and can produce profit. Thus, the discontinuities in agriculture reduce the importance of sequencing in agricultural technological innovation.

One process which appears increasingly significant may produce change in sequencing; this is the tendency toward vertical integration from processing, distribution, and marketing toward basic production that is occurring in some agricultural commodities. As such integration occurs, firms will become involved in the totality of production through distribution and the agricultural R&D process can be expected to come closer to the process found in industry.

CONCLUSION

This paper, through the use of two contemporary case studies in agriculture, has demonstrated that many of the conditions giving rise to technological development in the early phases of the industrial revolution continue in modern agriculture. The search for technological applications is concerned with cost-cutting, maintenance of the labor supply, and with control of the labor force, but in all cases is focused on the reduction of uncertainty for agricultural employers.

The research and development process in agriculture is, however, distinctly different from industry. This is not simply because of the institutional elements (e.g., the existence of the land-grant complex) but because of the discontinuities existing in agricultural production and the institutional autonomy of the land-grant system. Research and development in agriculture is, therefore, less notable than industry for developing sequential research and will continue to be so except as vertical integration occurs within agriculture.

FOOTNOTES

1. Rosenberg's essay is not limited to the role of labor in stimulating technological development. He also deals with a variety
   of other factors including technical imbalances (e.g., when one
   phase of production moves ahead of others creating disturbances
   in supply systems). In this paper our focus will be concentrated on the labor factor.
2. This paper, therefore, does not deal with the segment of U.S.
   agriculture in which family farming with no or few employees
   exists. Technological change in this sector of agriculture is
   extremely important but will be excluded from consideration
   here.
3. Labor over-supply has been the main strategy of large agricultural producers ever since agriculture developed in the west.
   On the general features of this strategy, see Fisher (1953),
   and McWilliams (1971). On a specific program geared at labor
   supply, see Galarza (1964) on the bracero program. An extensive
   literature exists on union busting. See, for example, London
   and Anderson (1970) and Chambers (1952) for California and
   Jamieson (1945) for the U.S.
4. On the history of tomato mechanization, see Rasmussen (1968).
   Schmitz and Seckler (1970) have provided an economic argument
   for the benefits of mechanized harvesting of tomatoes. For a
   critical assessment of the social consequences of mechanized
   harvesting, see Friedland and Barton (1975, 1976).
5. On early technological developments in lettuce production, see
   Smith (1961) and Glass (1966). For a more recent analysis of
   lettuce technology see Friedland, Barton, and Thomas (1978:
   Chapters 2 and 3).
6. Between 1960-1973, the average time in minutes per carton dropped from 12.67 to 3.57 or a decrease to 28.2% (Zahara, Johnson,
   and Garrett, 1974:536).
7. For more details on the two systems, see Friedland, Barton,
   and Thomas (1978:68-70). This study of lettuce as a system sets
   out the conditions under which the transition to mechanized
   harvesting will occur and projects the social consequences that
   can be expected to follow.

REFERENCES

Chambers, Clarke A.
    1952 California Farm Organizations. Berkeley: University of
    California Press.
Fisher, Lloyd H.
    1953 The Harvest Labor Market in California. Cambridge: Har-
    vard University Press.

Friedland, William H. and Barton, Amy E.
    1975   Destalking the Wily Tomato: A Case Study in Social Con-
    sequences in California Agricultural Research. Davis, Califor-
    nia: College of Agriculture and Environmental Sciences, Univer-
    sity of California, Davis. Research Monograph No. 15.
Friedland, William H. and Barton, Amy E.
    1976   "Tomato technology." Society 13 (September-October).
Friedland, William H. and Nelkin, Dorothy
    1972   "Technological trends and the organization of migrant farm
    workers." Social Problems 19 (Spring).
Friedland, William H. and Thomas, Robert J.
    1974   "Paradoxes of agricultural unionism in California."
    Society 11 (May/June):54-62.
Galarza, Ernesto
    1964   Merchants of Labor: The Mexican Bracero Story.   Charlotte:
    McNally and Loftin.
Glass, Judith Chanin
    1966   Conditions which Facilitate Unionization of Agricultural
    Workers: A Case Study of the Salinas Valley Lettuce Industry.
    Ph.D. dissertation, University fo California, Los Angeles,
    Department of Economics.
Holbrook, Stewart H.
    1955   Machines of Plenty: Pioneering in American Agriculture.
    New York: MacMillan.
Jamieson, Stuart
    1945   Labor Unionism in American Agriculture. Washington, D.C.:
    U.S. Government Printing Office.
Kelly, C.F.
    1966   "Preface" in Research on Agricultural Mechanization.
    Agricultural Experiment Station, University of California.
London, Joan and Anderson, Henry
    1970   So Shall Ye Reap. New York: Thomas J. Crowell
McWilliams, Carey
    1971   Factories in the Field. Santa Barbara: Peregrine.
Partridge, Michael
    1973   Farm Tools Through the Ages. Reading: Osprey.
Paul, Rodman W.
    1973   "The beginnings of agriculture in California: innovation
    vs. continuity." California Historical Quarterly 52 (Spring):
    16-27.
Rasmussen, Wayne D.
    1968   "Advances in American agriculture: the mechanical tomato
    harvester as a case study." Technology and Culture 9 (October):
    531-543.
Rosenberg, Charles E.
    1977   "Rationalization and reality in the shaping of American
    agricultural research, 1875-1914." Social Studies of Science
    7:401-422.

Rosenberg, Nathan
    1976 "The directions of technological change: inducement
    mechanisms and focusing devices." In Perspectives in Techno-
    logy, N. Rosenberg (ed.). Cambridge: Cambridge University
    Press. Pp. 108-125.
Schmitz, Andrew and Seckler, David
    1970 "Mechanized agriculture and social welfare: the case of
    the tomato harvester." American Journal of Agricultural
    Economics 52 (November):569-577.
Smith, Francis James
    1961 The Impact of Technological Change in the Marketing of
    Salinas Lettuce. Ph.D. dissertation, University of California,
    Berkeley, Department of Agricultural Economics

8. Betwixt and Between: Farmers and the Marketing of Agricultural Inputs and Outputs

OSCAR B. MARTINSON and GERALD R. CAMPBELL

INTRODUCTION

The marketing systems for America's agricultural inputs and outputs have seldom been examined by sociologists despite their significance for both rural and urban Americans. When the changing structure of agriculture has been the focal point of sociological research, the inquiry has considered primarily the demise of family farming and the rise of corporate forms of farm organization (Rodefeld, 1974; Goldschmidt, 1947). The farm input and output industries largely have been ignored, even by those who asserted they were writing about the rural sociology of advanced capitalist societies. Yet agribusiness, or agribusinesses to be more precise, clearly are at least part of rural society, if not its dominant actors, in several advanced capitalist nations. For this reason as well as others, the phenomenon of agribusiness deserves the attention of rural sociologists.[1]

The importance of understanding agribusiness is heightened when issues of control of the food and fiber sector of the economy are addressed. Journalists (Hightower, 1975; Robbins, 1974; Hamilton, 1972) have raised the spectre of large food merchandisers and processors extracting monopoly profits from consumers without alternative sources of sustenance. More soberly, economists have begun to examine the effects of economic concentration, advertising of differentiated products, and other market structure characteristics on the economic conduct of food merchandisers and processors (Imel et al., 1972; Marion et al., 1977).

The goal of these economists has been to evaluate the performance of the food industries in terms of the efficient allocation of resources and the maximization of consumer welfare. The results of their efforts are both important and interesting. There work is, however, often missing a sociological understanding of agribusiness and its impact on social life in nonmetropolitan America.

In light of its importance for rural society, the present chapter argues that rural sociologists ought to consider agribusiness as a topic

215

worthy of scholarly attention. While the term is often used loosely, and
perhaps perjoratively, the phenomenon to which it refers is a system of
social entities whose structural features and social relations are not
widely understood. Their influence, moreover, on the emerging structure
and control of agriculture and on the food and fiber sector of the economy
has not been examined by sociologists. The sociological analysis of
agribusiness thus needs to be undertaken.

The term agribusiness was first used by Goldberg (1968) in his
research on coordination of agricultural marketing. For Goldberg, agribusinesses were the firms involved in merchandising and processing agricultural products. While some agribusiness firms might be involved in
retailing or in farming, the firms' crucial characteristic apparently was
that they were basically intermediaries between the primary food producer and those from whom he purchased production inputs and to whom he
sold his food products. The sociology of agribusiness essentially attempts to understand the structure, function, and roles of middlemen
in the food and fiber sector of the economy.

Recently the term agribusiness has been expanded in meaning to
refer not only to corporate middlemen in the food and fiber sector but
also to firms whose scale of farming is best characterized as industrial.
In many of these cases, however, the same firms which formerly confined
their scope of business to buying from and/or selling to farmers have
begun to operate farms as well. Agribusiness thus has come to mean corporations involved in agricultural production as well as in the production
of farm inputs or processing and selling of farm outputs.

The possibility of agribusiness becoming the dominant form of food
production and distribution has been called to the attention of Americans
in recent years. Hightower (1975) and others have pointed out that
conglomerate corporations such as Tenneco, Boeing, Purex and several
additional firms currently are involved in major specialty crop farming
operations. Welford's congressional testimony graphically illustrated
the effects of vertically integrated poultry production by food conglomerates on small farmers throughout the South. The trade literature
for the grain industry reports that large merchandisers and processors
such as Cargill are becoming livestock feedlot owners and operators as
well. This diversification provides an outlet for grain and feed sup-
plements, allowing the diversified firm to take or defer profits to
maximize tax advantages. Other grain merchandising firms such as International Multifoods have vertically integrated themselves from grain
procurement to manufacturing of grain based food products. Whether
their next step is to become poultry or livestock feeders in order to
further rationalize their firms is yet to be determined. The spread
of agribusiness into agricultural production is a topic of importance,
but one about which little systematic (as opposed to anecdotal)
empirical knowledge exists.

Recently Zald (1978) has called to the attention of sociologists the need to understand better the social control of industries. Although large, differentiated industrial complexes have emerged and grown to prominence in modern American society, sociological theories of social control have not focused on industry, but on the individual. "Sociologists and social psychologists have developed concepts and research related to norms and interpersonal control--for instance, deviance and conformity, normative and comparative reference groups, exchange and power-dependence relations, and internalization and socialization of norms" (Zald, 1978:80). However, these concepts generally have not been applied to macro questions of societal control over large organizations and industries despite the need to do so (Zald, 1978:80). His suggestions regarding the social control of industries ought to stimulate sociologists interested in the sociology of agribusiness.

The present chapter examines extant substantive theories and recent empirical research that bear on the sociology of agribusiness. Its purpose is to inventory, both theoretically and empirically, what is known (and by implication what is not) about the phenomena called agribusiness and to suggest directions for future inquiry. Initially we consider several theoretical orientations toward agribusiness. Included are dependency, ownership vs. management control of industry, financial control, environmental control, and economic models of industrial organization. Next, recent empirical research on agribusiness is presented, and gaps in the available information are noted. In a final section, directions for future research are discussed, and implications of the changing structures of agribusiness for rural and urban America are considered.

PERSPECTIVES ON AGRIBUSINESS

The first theoretical framework which may be helpful for understanding the agribusiness phenomenon is the dependency perspective.[2] This orientation grew from a collective attempt by Latin American scholars to understand the developmental experiences of Latin America during the twentieth century. The perspective rejects the idea that the level of development experienced by a whole society or societal subsector can be explained by its endogenous conditions. Instead the relationships tying one subsector to another or one society to another must be examined. The level of development (or perhaps quality of life) experienced by societies and persons within them is derived from the evolving network of socioeconomic relations within societies and among societies. In particular the perspective maintains that national and regional development are most fruitfully understood in terms of the growth of capitalism and the market forces it unleases.

The dependency perspective argues that as capitalist economies develop, they produce both "spread" and "backwash" effects. The existence of the former suggests that economic growth in one part of an economic system generates development elsewhere in the system. The latter asserts that resources are drawn from peripheral parts of an economic system to be concentrated in its center, or core. The result is often uneven development and/or underdevelopment, especially in an economic system's periphery.

To define dependency with any degree of precision, however, is difficult, for reasons elaborated by Caporaso (1978). His discussion of conceptual issues surrounding the term asserts that it has two predominant usages: "dependency as the absence of actor autonomy and dependence as a highly asymmetric form of interdependence" (Caporaso, 1978:18). The dependency perspective, thus, is based on autonomy-- dependency and dependence-interdependence dimensions, each having its own intellectual heritage and implications for theory and research. The relevance of the dependency perspective for understanding agribusiness stems from the dependence-interdependence dimension.

Breimyer (1965) has suggested that the market relationships linking American agriculture with the rest of the economy have undergone change during the post World War II era. Organized markets and their institutionalized economic relationships, he asserts, are becoming a new autocrat over agriculture. The reason institutionalized markets are gaining autocracy over the institutions of farming is a striking feature of agricultural market structure--interdependence. The interdependence between the successive stages in the production and marketing sequence, Breimyer (1965:96) notes, "is the crux of the significance of marketing to agriculture." This significance stems from the drive to gain advantage in the successive exchanges making up the marketing process. Breimyer (1965:90) continues by telling us the following: "Wherever two or more economic processes are interlocked, there is an open invitation for one to gain some degree of control over one or more of the others. This is the heart of the reason for the great struggles for power that are taking place at various stages in the marketing and distribution of farm products today." The dependency literature, using the dependence-interdependence distinction, thus may be helpful for understanding the role of agribusiness firms vis-a-vis control of the food and fiber sector of the American economy.[3]

Use of the dependence-interdependence continuum draws our attention to the extent to which mutual control over exchange relationships exists throughout agricultural product and factor markets. For example, in a given exchange, one party to the transaction may need nothing from the other, but supply all the other's needs. The converse absolute exchange asymmetry may exist as well, although some degree of mutuality within the transaction is more likely. "Dependence as asymmetric interdependence is immediately a dyadic concept and a 'net' concept, i.e.

it is measured by looking at the differential between A's reliance on
B, and B's reliance on A" (Caporaso, 1978:18). In other words, dependency theory allows us to address questions regarding control of
the food and fiber sector by examining who is forced to rely on whom at
various points in agriculture's factor and product markets.

Essentially, a sociological assessment of agribusiness from a dependency perspective would focus on the exploitation of the farmer by
agribusiness firms through what Taylor (1977) has called contrived dependence. He asserts that two necessary conditions must be present in
order for exploitation through contrived dependence to occur. First
the power for one party in a market transaction to constrain the other's
alternative opportunities and to profit as a consequence must exist.
Second, the party in the stronger position must be willing to exploit
the weaker party in the exchange. Thus research derived from the
dependency perspective presumably would consider whether agribusinesses
are able and willing to constrain the opportunities of the farmer to
buy factor inputs at the lowest possible price and sell products at the
highest possible price. Such research would attempt to show that farmers
are reliant on those whom they encounter in their factor or product
markets and that exploitation results as a consequence. Subordination
of the farmer to agribusiness would be expected because of asymmetric
exchange in agriculture's product and factor markets. In this way
giant agribusiness firms located in the urban core, or center, of the
economy use their power to exploit the rural, agricultural hinterland
in America, according to dependency theory.

A second theoretical orientation which may be useful for understanding agribusiness considers the ownership and control of the large
agribusiness firm. Following Zeitlin (1974), the basic question raised
by this perspective asks how the ascendance of corporate agribusiness
as the predominant actor in agriculture's factor and product markets
has affected the political economy of farming and the rural stratification system. The perspective focuses on the extent to which agribusiness
ownership is separate from control of the agribusiness firm, and on the
meaning of alternative agribusiness ownership-control patterns for
control of the food and fiber sector of the economy.

As Reeder (1975) among others has indicated, concern over ownership versus control of the large business corporation has roots in the
classical economics of Adam Smith. Yet, until Berle and Means (1933)
raised the issue, the meaning of separating corporate ownership from
control had lain dormant. With the publication of their work, a body
of literature began to grow contending that diffusion of stock ownership had led to de facto corporate control by professional managers.

The sociological importance of the separation of ownership from
control, to the extent that separation had actually occurred, could be
that a stratification system based on classes had been replaced by an

occupational system grounded in the functional importance of one's job and in individual achievement. The locus of corporate control, moreover, would be in the hands of industrial bureaucrats rather than in those with ownership interests. These managers presumably would be motivated by non-profit goals and conduct, and would use low-risk, high growth management strategies. The result presumably would be a technocratic industrial society governed by benign bureaucratic elites from both the public and private sectors of the political economy.

Whether ownership and control have actually separated, is an open question (Zeitlin, 1974, 1976; Pedersen and Tabb, 1976). In an extensive review of the literature, Zeitlin argues it is unwarranted to assume that ownership and management have separated. Likewise it is inappropriate to make sociological inferences based on such an assumption. Zeitlin's (1974:1107) assessment is this:

> Our review of discrepant findings on the alleged
> separation of ownership and control in the large
> corporation in the United States, and of the problems
> entailed in obtaining reliable and valid evidence on
> the actual ownership involved in a given corporation,
> should make it clear that the absence of control by
> proprietary interests in the largest corporations is
> by no means an 'unquestionable,' 'incontrovertible,'
> 'singular,' or 'critical' social 'fact' ... On the
> contrary, I believe that the 'separation of owner-
> ship and control' may well be one of those rather
> critical, widely accepted, pseudofacts with which
> all sciences occasionally have found themselves
> bedeviled.

Thus class theories of social inequality, domination and change may still retain analytic value. Moreover, the fusion of the institutions of family and private property may still serve as the basis of America's stratification system. The main issues, he contends, are whether ownership interests still control the large corporation, despite corporate management by possibly propertyless functionaries; and whether the ascendance of managerial functions throughout the corporate work signifies the ascendance of corporate functionaries as well. "Do [the functionaries] constitute a separate and cohesive stratum, with identifiable interests, ideas, and policies, which are opposed to those of the extant owning families? Are the consequences of their actions, whatever their intentions, to bring into being social relationships which undermine capitalism?" (1974:1078). These are the kinds of issues sociologists might address with specific reference to agribusinesses were they to use an ownership versus control perspective. In so doing, sociologists also might assess the consequences of stability and change in the class structure of urban, industrial America for the nation's rural, agricultural sector.

Allen (1976, 1978), however, argues that the issue is whether geographically-based economic elites rather than social classes represent centers of common control. The question for sociologists of agribusiness thus should be (following Allen) whether ownership and control are derived from family or financial interests, or merely reflect the presence of geographical interest groups. His research on the evolution of corporate control suggests that "the corporate elite structure is organized in a large part about a series of more or less distinct and cohesive interlocking groups in which several corporations share a number of directors" (1978:612). Despite a decline in control by families and financial interests, he tells us, family and financial control still exist. Yet, "the emergence of management control among the large corporations is entirely consistent with the integration of these corporations into geographical interest groups" (1978:613). The extent to which corporate managers collectively constitute interest groups necessarily must be the subject of further empirical research. Whether such economic elites are present and active in agriculture's product and factor markets is thus an additional aspect of the sociology of agribusiness.

Research on the ownership and control of agribusiness corporations has to consider an important added dimension about which the previous literature on the ownership versus control debates has been silent. That dimension involves the presence of large cooperatives doing businesses in both agriculture's product and factor markets. The cooperative is, at least nominally, much different from the family held and/or controlled corporation designed to make profits. Local cooperatives are presumably created to provide goods and services to farmer patrons, with any surplus earnings to be returned to the patrons on a pro-rated basis. These cooperatives are organized and governed by their patrons on a democratic basis. Local cooperatives in turn may join together to create federated cooperatives, whose patrons are other cooperatives. Again, the boards of directors of the federated cooperatives are elected from among the members of the local cooperatives. Thus, control by member-patrons, or owners, ought to exist for a local cooperative and for any federated cooperative. But whether member-patron (i.e., owner) control of cooperatives in fact is the case remains to be demonstrated empirically.

The sociological literature on voluntary associations suggests by implication that democratic member-patron control of cooperatives may well be a myth. This circumstance stems from the tendency for oligarchic control to develop in most voluntary associations (Michels, 1949). Insofar as oligarchy has developed within America's agricultural cooperatives, they no longer can lay claim to an important justification for their existence.[4] To the extent that farmer owners are not part of any emerging oligarchy, having been replaced by cooperative managers, management control of the cooperatives could be said to exist. Whether these related circumstances have come to pass is unclear (Kravitz, 1974). The questions warrant additional attention, we feel, by sociologists of agribusiness.

A third orientation which may be applicable to agribusiness is derived from a further aspect of the debate over ownership versus management control of the large corporation. This orientation suggests that sociological attention be given to the role that banks play vis-a-vis control of the food and fiber sector of the economy. The financial control proponents assert that in order to do business in the modern capitalist economies, the large corporation remains dependent on the financial system for operating capital. Hence, despite the appearance of management control (or direct owner control, for that matter), a firm may be under the effective control of one or more banks or insurance companies.[5] Thus, analyses derived from such a perspective might seek evidence of bank control over firms doing business in agriculture's product and factor markets. Case studies might be performed, for example, to determine why banking system personnel are chosen to take over the management of grain milling or meat-packing firms. Who are the beneficial interests of such actions? What are the implications, if any, for the farmer or for rural communities? Likewise, the implications of rural credit shortages for agriculture and the rural communities need further consideration. Asymmetric interdependence in rural capital markets may explain emerging patterns of agricultural structure and rural community decline.

An additional aspect of the financial control perspective with direct implications for agribusiness involves cooperatives and their perhaps unique access to credit through the Farm Credit Administration. Some of the largest agribusinesses are cooperatives and thus are usually qualified to borrow from a branch of the Farm Credit Administration. To the extent that the capital needs of agribusiness cooperatives are fulfilled through the Farm Credit Administration, the Farm Credit Administration may hold the potential for controlling an important part of the food and fiber sector. While cooperatives were once seen as mechanisms farmers could use to gain control of their product and factor markets from private agribusinesses, inadequate access to capital may have limited the cooperative thrust. Under such circumstances, understanding the financial role of the Farm Credit Administration vis-a-vis agribusiness cooperatives might be a fruitful undertaking for the sociologist examining agribusiness.

A fourth perspective with potential for understanding the agribusiness phenomenon focuses on the relationships linking agribusiness firms to one another and to other organizations of consequence throughout the political economy. Dealing with the social environment of agribusinesses, the environmental control approach calls our attention to the importance of organizational environments for explaining the structural stability and change, as well as the behavior, of agribusiness firms and industries.

Aldrich and Pfeffer (1976) maintain that basically two models of organizations and their environments currently exist.[6] The first, a natural selection model, asserts that organizational characteristics develop as a response to the socioeconomic environment in which an organization must exist. Organizational forms survive and flourish to the extent that they fit their environment; they wither away to the extent that they do not. Their second model is characterized as a resource-dependency model. It asserts that organizations attempt to control their social environments instead of being controlled by them. The resource dependency model also pays greater attention to organizational decision-making processes. The natural selection model, Aldrich and Pfeffer argue, is applied most appropriately at the population level rather than at the individual organization level of analysis. For this reason as well as others which should become apparent shortly, we will elaborate only the resource dependency model of organizational environments.

The resource dependency model of organizations and their environments is derived from the idea that "organizatins are not able to internally generate either all the resources or functions required to maintain themselves, and therefore organizations must enter into transactions and relations with elements in the environment that can supply the required resources and services" (Aldrich and Pfeffer, 1976: 83). The results of entering into such relationships are several types of interdependencies based on differentiation, interorganizational division of labor, and control possibilities growing out of situations of dependence (Blau, 1964). These interdependencies are created as means for organizations to respond to contingencies in their environments, to more adequately deal with environmental uncertainty, and to manage their environments to the extent that managing can be done.[7]

Several efforts can be and have been used by organizations seeking to control their environment. In the economic arena these include informal interfirm arrangements to share markets (Phillips, 1960), mergers (Pfeffer, 1972a), joint ventures (Aiken and Hage, 1968; Pfeffer and Nowak, 1976), interorganizational co-optation via interlocking directors (Allen, 1974; Pfeffer, 1972b), contracts (Macaulay, 1964), ties to federal agencies (Bernstein, 1955; Hall, 1969; Kohlmeier, 1967; Stigler, 1971). "Another strategy works indirectly to influence or regulate interdependence using third parties such as trade associations, coordinating groups, or government agencies" (Miles et al., 1974). A major function of the interorganizational linkages resulting from efforts such as these has been the extra-

market control of economic activity. For this reason the organization-
environment relations of agribusiness firms may be of interest to
sociologists interested in understanding the maintenance of farmer subordination to agribusiness.

A final perspective comes from the discipline of economics. The
Industrial Organization paradigm as developed in economics views the
activity and performance in industries as being mainly due to the structure of the industry.[8] Joe Bain (1968) was chiefly responsible for
taking the theoretical work of Robinson (1933) and Chamberlain (1949)
on imperfect competition and developing the industrial organization
model. This model basically argues that structure causes conduct which
results in particular performance outcomes. The chief determinants of
market structure are the number and size distribution of buyers and
sellers, the degree of product homogeneity, and barriers to entry.
When markets depart from the perfectly competitive model characterized
by large numbers of buyers and sellers, homogeneous products and no
entry barriers, the firms in those markets are no longer forced to
choose the most efficient production pattern, are no longer forced to
set prices equal to marginal cost, are no longer forced to treat all
customers equally, and are no longer forced to adopt the latest cost-
reducing technology. Thus, economic performance, in terms of efficient
resource allocation and pricing, equitable treatment of customers, full
employment of resources and progressiveness, is hindered when industries
depart from a competitive structure.

The Industrial Organization model leads us to conclude that where
industries are imperfectly competitive, economic performance will be
less than could be expected from a competitive economy. The empirical
application of the Industrial Organization model has chiefly focused
on the relationship between economic concentration as measured by the
share of sales, assets, or employment accounted for by the four largest
firms in an industry and the profit rates of the industry measured by
returns on sales or assets. The empirical work to date appears to
support the theoretically predicted positive relationship between
industrial concentration and profit rates (Weiss, 1974).

The Industrial Organization model is chiefly oriented toward behavior among firms at the same horizontal level of activity (Clevenger
and Campbell, 1977). In fact, much of the empirical application of
the Industrial Organization model has focused on the interaction among
manufacturing firms. Thus, vertical integration and vertical competition
do not fit as neatly into the model as does horizontal competition.
But vertical integration is incorporated into the model in two ways.
First, vertical integration can be considered an element of market
structure in that vertically integrated firms may behave differently
than their non-integrated counterparts. The act of vertically integrating from one industry level into another (say manufacturing into

wholesaling) can also be seen as an element of firm conduct. The chief concerns surrounding vertical integration are the potential market fore-closure consequences for non-integrated firms and the potential that the integrated firm with market power may have for extending its power at one level to a second level of a production and distribution system.

The industrial organization paradigm also tends to concentrate its attention on single-product, single-market firms. Several economists (Mueller, 1977; Connor, 1978; Edwards, 1953) have attempted to expand the model to deal with the contemporary reality of the conglomerate (multi-market multi-product) enterprise. This expansion of the model has concerned itself chiefly with the strategies open to multi-market or multi-product firms, especially those who possess market power in one product or market which may influence their activities in other areas. Cross-subsidization of activities in one market with profits gained through market power in another market is a major concern in explaining market restructuring. This cross-subsidization often takes the form of massive levels of advertising as the conglomerate firm attempts to restructure a market which it has recently entered. The conglomerate firm may also be characterized by its attempts to differ-entiate products through advertising and produce a segmented group of products which permit an emphasis on product competition and reduce the need to compete on the basis of price.

Two more macro-concerns with conglomerate behavior are the possi-bility of mutual forebearance and reciprocity. In mutual forebearance, firms which meet in many markets are potentially subject to a pattern of less aggressive competition, especially price competition in any one market for fear of competition in other markets where they meet. Reciprocity involves the development of trade among conglomerate firms based on the ability of the firms to reciprocate. Firm 1 buys Product A from Firm 2 because Firm 2 will buy Product B from Firm A. As the extent of conglomerate firms spreads, the opportunities for reciprocity expand greatly because of the increasing spectrum of products where firms may have reciprocity potential.

The agricultural economics literature on marketing of agricultural inputs and outputs has had two main thrusts. The first of these has sometimes been referred to as the economic engineering approach or the production efficiency approach. This literature has been chiefly concerned with methods for improving the production efficiency of marketing activities such as processing, transportation, grading, sorting, and other physical handling and distribution functions. This literature has recently been reviewed by Breimyer (1973) and exhaust-ively examined by French (1977). Its chief contribution to under-standing the organization of agricultural markets lies in its examina-tion of technical factors such as scale economies, transfer cost, and acquisition costs which influence industry structure. Suffice it to

say that sociologists would find this literature most helpful in trying to examine the material forces which influence social organization.

The second major thrust in the agricultural marketing literature
has been devoted to a concern with market structure, conduct and performance. This literature also is the subject of Breimyer's (1973)
review and has recently been examined in depth by Helmberger, Campbell
and Dobson (forthcoming). While much of this literature does not pursue the Industrial Organization model to the extent of empirical
testing of structure-conduct-performance linkages, it can all be viewed
as evidencing a concern among agricultural economists for the impact
which economic organization has on economic conduct and ultimately
economic performance.

It is impossible to encapsulate all this literature in the brief
space allotted here. However, we will attempt to draw a few major
conclusions from it.

First, while agriculture is considered by many to be the last
extant example of a competitively organized sector, there is much in
the input and output markets for agricultural products which is more
closely akin to oligopoly than to competition. This is especially
true in farmer first handler markets. There is adequate evidence to
conclude that where markets for inputs and outputs are highly concentrated, contain substantial barriers to entry, or exhibit extensive
product differentiation, the agricultural marketing system performs
below its potential. Further, in many cases farmers are often unable
to develop countervailing economic power to prevent exploitation by
powerful input sellers or output buyers. Farmers have, however, been
able to implement countervailing activities through two main vehicles.
First, farmers may exercise political power to implement a series of
programs which reduce the potential exercise of market power such as
grades and standards and market news and programs, providing a
degree of publicly-protected market power to farmers such as market
orders and agreements. Secondly, through cooperative purchasing and
selling, farmers have developed some added power relative to sellers
and buyers and have collectively provided goods and services where
private sector firms found those activities unprofitable.

The marketing system for agricultural products has some unusual
coordination problems among vertical stages. This has led to the
development of several coordinating institutions such as direct vertical integration, contract production, cooperative integration,
and contract marketing, which serve to improve vertical coordination.
These mechanisms may improve coordination at the expense of equity and
may shift the focus of control away from the farm sector toward processing and input industries. In the next section we attempt to
provide some empirical examples which bear on issues surrounding
farmers and marketing systems.[9]

EMPIRICAL EVIDENCE

Empirical sociological research of the kind mentioned earlier that examines farm input and output markets is virtually non-existent. Work by agricultural economists, then, must serve as the social scientific basis for developing a sociological understanding of agribusiness. The subsequent section of this chapter consequently provides a broad description of the production and distribution system for America's food and fiber. Basic dimensions of size, economic organization, and performance of this sector are outlined and major trends are noted. Focusing necessarily on economic data, the discussion deals with the farm input industries, farming itself, and the farm output industries. It attempts to show selected aspects of the structure of agribusiness that affect, in turn, agribusiness conduct, and, ultimately, the performance of the United States food and fiber system. From the economic data, implications for sociological research are drawn.

It is useful initially to overview briefly the American food and fiber system. The term itself refers to all the people, businesses, public agencies, and institutions involved in producing and distributing the nation's food and fiber products. The annual food and fiber output currently exceeds $300 billion (1976), while the food and fiber system itself accounts for about 19 percent of the gross business activity in the United States and about 20 percent of total employment (Table 1). Farmers purchased nearly $82 billion worth of production inputs, and produced raw food and fiber worth $96 billion. In other words, 85 percent of farmers' total cash receipts were spent on inputs, services, interest, and taxes. The markets for farm products added $212 billion in costs to America's raw food and fiber by processing and distributing it, while consumers bought $285 billion worth of food and fiber products and exports claimed $23 billion.

Farm Input Industries

The farm input industries supply the technology without which America's modern agriculture would be impossible. The most important inputs in terms of expenditures are feed; fertilizer, chemicals, and seed; and farm machinery. Because of their importance, it is appropriate to consider the market structure of these industries (Table 2).

The farm machinery industry can be divided into two major segments. Full-line machinery makers produce tractors and equipment powered by tractors. Short-line manufacturers tend to specialize in feeding, barn cleaning, storage, or other equipment for specific farm tasks. Full-line machinery manufacture is concentrated in the hands of seven firms. The largest four of these firms accounted for 47 percent of farm machinery shipments in 1972. National market

TABLE 1

Contributions by Food and Fiber Sector
to Total U.S. Economy, 1976

Subsector	Sector Contributions to Gross National Product	Intermediate Inputs	Total	Civilian Employment
	---------Billion Dollars---------			Million persons
Farm	45.0	76.6	121.6	2.8
Food processing	38.7	105.1	143.8	1.7
Textiles and apparel manufacturing	25.8	50.0	75.8	1.9
Other manufacturing	37.7	55.3	93.0	1.6
Resource based industries and services	60.2	46.8	107.1	2.1
Wholesale, retail and transportation	121.0	50.6	171.6	8.8
Imports	---	25.2	25.2	---
Total, food and fiber	328.4	409.6	738.0	18.9
U.S. economy	1,706.5[1]	---	---	94.8[1]

[1] Survey of Current Business, U.S. Department of Commerce, Vol. 57, No. 7, pp. 20 and S-13, July 1977.

Prepared by Gerald E. Schluter, NEAD, ESS, USDA, October 1977.

concentration was considerably lower for specialized farm machinery, taken as a whole. Market concentration for key pieces of equipment, such as large tractors and combines, is substantially higher. Farm machinery is distributed through a network of franchised dealers. The number of farm machinery dealers declined by about 25 percent from 1958 to 1972, leaving farmers more dependent on those dealers who remained.

TABLE 2. Descriptive Statistics of Selected Food System Input Industries, 1972.

SIC[1]	Industry Title	Number of[2] Companies	Number of[3] Establish-ments	Number of Employees 1,000	Value of Shipments Millions	Value Added Millions	CR[4] 4	CR[5] 20
2873	Nitrogenous fertilizer	47	73	9.4	799.4	447.6	35	84
2874	Phosphatic fertilizers	66	145	14.9	1,178.9	426.4	29	83
2875	Fertilizer mixing	442	627	11.4	800.0	263.6	24	57
2911	Petroleum refining	152	323	100.8	25,921.1	4,594.7	31	84
2992	Lubricating oils and greases	386	443	8.1	703.1	295.8	31	58
3221	Glass containers	27	117	72.9	2,126.5	1,399.7	55	98
3274	Lime	68	103	5.7	238.1	129.3	37	79
3411	Metal cans	134	396	68.5	4,510.8	1,815.8	66	92
3523	Farm machinery and equipment	1,465	1,547	104.6	4,529.7	2,247.5	47	69
3551	Farm products machinery	636	688	31.9	1,000.1	605.2	18	42
3552	Textile machinery	535	578	32.7	822.8	487.6	31	61

[1] Standard Industrial Classification Code.
[2] Companies refers to ownership units; a company may operate more than one establishment.
[3] Establishments refers to operating units or plants.
[4] Percentage Share of Value of Shipments accounted for by the 4 largest companies.
[5] Percentage Share of Value of Shipments accounted for by the 20 largest companies.
Source: Census of Manufactures, 1972.

229

The importance of economic concentration in the farm machinery industry is twofold. On one hand, manufacturers are able to charge more for their equipment than competitive markets would allow. Canadian research (Schwartzman, 1970) on their farm machinery industry discloses, for example, that oligopoly has increased the prices Canadian farmers must pay for machinery over and above what competitive markets would bear.[10] That the same firms produce for the American market suggests that similar circumstances currently exist in the U.S.

On the other hand, economic concentration in the farm machinery industries may be leading to what Leonard and Weber (1970) have called criminogenic markets like those argued to exist for the major domestic automobile manufacturers. Dependency of the franchised farm implement dealer on the full-line machinery manufacturer may allow the manufacturer to squeeze the dealer in terms of floor-planning new equipment, making new products available, or requiring expensive retail facilities not warranted by the size of the prospective machinery market. The result may be the illegal padding of equipment purchase contracts, overvaluing trade-in equipment in order to make a sale, overbilling for repair work, and requiring financing plans that provide kick-backs to the dealer from a bank or finance company. The extent to which any of these white-collar crimes are committed is unknown, despite the possible adverse consequences for the economic and moral life of rural communities.

The feed manufacturing industry is primarily a regional industry with low national concentration. The four largest feed manufacturing companies accounted for 23 percent of the industries' shipments in 1972. In order to help stabilize sales and attract customers, some feed manufacturers and dealers have become involved in contract production of broilers, eggs, and other livestock species. These contracts provide a form of risk sharing between farmers and their feed suppliers. There has been a substantial increase in direct manufacturer-to-farmer sales of feed, bypassing local dealers. As average farm size grows this trend will likely continue. Yet the impact of such a trend on local rural communities has not been assessed.

Farmer cooperatives are an important part of the feed supply system, especially at the local dealer level. Farmer cooperatives account for about 20 percent of the manufacture and distribution of feed. As with most other feed dealers, cooperatives often combine grain marketing and feed supply as complementary activities.

Although national concentration in feed manufacturing is low, regional concentration is higher (Shepherd, 1970). Moreover, a basic ingredient in most feeds is soybean meal, which is produced as a by-product by a highly concentrated soybean oil milling industry. Hence, the feed manufacturers are necessarily dependent on an economically concentrated industry.

An additional consideration is that the level of economic concentration increases as the manufactured feed product becomes more specialized. Coupled with existing regional concentration, this circumstance may mean that farmer-consumers are indirectly facing oligopoly. Although cooperatives are important locally, they too may be dependent on oligopolist soybean meal manufacturers.

Since cooperatives are not among the leading firms producing soybean meal, the question of "why not?" immediately comes to mind. Sociologists studying agribusiness could begin to answer such a question but as yet have not done so. Agribusiness theories dealing with interorganizational ties among feed manufacturers, and with management versus farmer-owner control, are suggestive of where sociologists might begin to look.

There are many commonalities in the distribution of fertilizer, petroleum, and pesticide products from manufacturers to farmers. All of these inputs are dependent to a degree on petroleum and related products. Major manufacturers of these products are generally diversified petroleum or chemical companies with farm product sales a small portion of their product mix. Nitrogen fertilizer was manufactured by 47 companies in 73 manufacturing establishments in 1972. For the same period, 66 companies operated 145 phosphate fertilizer manufacturing establishments. Concentration in fertilizer manufacturing is generally moderate, with four-firm concentration ratios generally below 45.[11] Farmer cooperatives have played an increasing role in the manufacturing and distribution of fertilizers. Cooperatives accounted for 32 percent of farm expenditures for fertilizer in 1970.

The manufacture of insecticides is more highly concentrated than for fertilizers. The four largest manufacturers of insecticides accounted for 48 percent of shipments in 1972. Herbicide manufacture is even more concentrated with the four largest companies accounting for 77 percent of shipments in 1972. In both of these industries, product differentiation is relatively high with entry relatively difficult due in major part to high costs of research and development. Cooperatives have mainly served as distributors of pesticides, although they have entered manufacture of some basic products where patents have expired. In 1970 cooperatives accounted for an estimated 22 percent of farm expenditures on pesticides.

Petroleum refining contained 152 companies operating 323 refining establishments in 1972. The four largest companies accounted for 31 percent of the shipments while the 20 largest companies accounted for 84 percent of the shipments. Entry into this industry has been difficult due both to the high capital cost of refining facilities and the difficulty of obtaining crude oil supplies. The distribution of petroleum products contains elements of vertically integrated distri- butors owned or licensed by refining companies and independent whole- salers and retailers. Farmer cooperatives are important in distribu- tion of petroleum products, especially in the upper midwest. In recent years cooperatives have also expanded their role in petroleum refining. In 1970 cooperatives accounted for approximately 26 percent of the fuel oil purchased by farmers.

The changing role of farmer cooperatives can be seen more clearly in Table 3. The number of cooperatives handling feed, seed, ferti- lizer and lime, and petroleum declined from 1960-61 to 1974-75. Only the number of coops handling farm chemicals increased. The market shares for these farm inputs that coops handled changed as well. Coops increased their share of fertilizer and lime, petroleum, and farm chemical sales, lost part of their share of seed sales, and re- tained their share of feed sales.

TABLE 3

Farm Level Share of the Market Handled by Farmer Cooperatives
Major Farm Inputs, 1960-61 and 1974-75

Farm Supply Category	1960-61		1974-75	
	Number of Cooperatives No.	Market[1] Share %	Number of Cooperatives No.	Market[1] Share %
Feed	4,412	18	3,744	18
Seed	3,912	19	3,553	16
Fertilizer & Lime	4,276	24	3,865	30
Petroleum	2,798	24	2,624	35
Farm Chemicals	3,014	18	3,328	29

[1] Computed as the share of all farm expenditures for a particular input category handled by farm cooperatives.

Source: Farm Cooperative Service, United States Department of Agriculture, News for Farmer Cooperatives, February 1977, p. 4, Table 1.

The extent to which farm inputs are being manufactured by coop- eratives varies by type of input. Farm cooperatives manufacture substantial amounts of fertilizer, refine some of their petroleum

products, and are increasing their manufacturing activity of herbi-
cides.[12] These data suggest that collectively, cooperatives may be
increasing their share of farm input sales. The reasons for the gain
in market shares stem from the departure from the market of small
private farm input firms who cannot successfully compete with larger,
better financed, farmer-owned businesses. Moreover, in some cases,
such as petroleum supply, rural markets are being abandoned by even
the larger firms, allowing, and in some cases, forcing cooperatives
to fill the void. Whether the benefits of any increase in market
share are received ultimately by the farmer-owners of these cooperatives is unknown.[13]

Farming

There are roughly 2.8 million farms in the U.S. at the present
time, less than one-half the number of 30 years ago. However, the
rate of decline in farm numbers has slowed substantially in recent
years because of higher net farm incomes and the fact that many people
with favorable nonfarm opportunities have already left farming. The
number of farms with annual gross sales of $40,000 and over increased
above fivefold between 1960 and 1975, reflecting firm growth and risky
commodity prices. Today, 155,000 farms with annual gross sales of
$100,000 and over account for 60 percent of all farm sales, in
contrast to 23,000 farms and 17 percent of sales for 1960.

Ownership of farm businesses remains largely in the hands of
individuals, partnerships, and closely-held family corporations.
According to the 1974 Census of Agriculture, 98.7 percent of U.S.
farms are sole proprietorships, 8.4 percent are partnerships, 1.7 percent are corporations, and 0.2 percent are institutions and other
organizations. Large-scale corporate enterprises have entered farming on a selective basis and are prominent in commodities such as
eggs, broilers, sugar cane, sugar beets, fruits, tree nuts, certain
crops for canning, and nursery products. Cattle feeding is also
experiencing large-scale corporate inroads as well.

One of the most important changes occurring on family farms has
been the rising importance of nonfarm employment. In 1930, less than
one in six farms was part-time. However, modern transportation and
communication systems now make it relatively easy to combine the
advantages of farm living with working a 40-hour week in a nearby
community. Today, at least two out of three farm families receive
more than one-half of their income from nonfarm sources, and for
the nearly 2 million farmers with annual gross sales of less than
$20,000, nonfarm income accounts for more than 80 percent of total
family income.

A rising trend in gross farm receipts has been paralleled by a

steady rise in production expenses. Over the 1966-76 decade, farm
production expenses have more than doubled--rising from around $37
billion to almost $82 billion. Prices paid by farmers for production
inputs have about doubled in the past 10 years, accounting for most
of the increase. The input mix used to produce food and fiber has
shifted toward purchased items. More capital, machinery, fertilizer,
and pesticides are now used in farming, while the use of labor has
declined. Land used for crops decreased until the early 1960's, then
held steady, and increased by about 40 million acres from 1972-77.
Net farm income is now higher than in the 1960's and early 1960's,
but after shooting up to over $33 billion, it dropped to around $20
billion in 1976.

This sketch of farming in contemporary America highlights the
changes that have occurred. For the commercial farmers still earning
most of their living from farming, the dependence on factors and product markets has increased. American agriculture has become more
capital intensive, increasing interdependence between the farmer
and his markets. To the extent the farmer is subordinate to the
institutions and actors in the marketplace, he is open to exploitation. And to the extent that farmers are exploited, the rural
economy based on a healthy farm sector suffers as well.

Agricultural Product Markets

The diversity of products raised on America's farms makes it
difficult to characterize in summary fashion the product markets
for the agricultural commodities. It is useful, however, to divide
the marketing system for food and fiber products into four levels:
farmer/first handler, food processing and manufacturing, food
wholesaling, and food retailing. The present discussion deals with
the first two levels.

Farmers sell their products through a wide variety of firsthandler
outlets. There has been a general decline in the use of terminal and
auction market for most farm products. Farmers increasingly are selling directly to processor or distributor firms through private
negotiations. Most individual farmers have relatively few local outlets for their commodities. As scale economies have increased the
minimum efficient size of processing and distributing firms, the
degree of concentration in procurement of farm products has also
increased, often leaving farmers with few local outlets for their
crops and livestock. These changes in agricultural marketing are
increasing the dependency of the farmer on the remaining country
elevators, dairy plants, livestock buying stations, packing sheds,
and the like. The following, more detailed discussion summarizes
the recent literature dealing with the first-handler marketing of
lifestock, dairy products, grain, and fruits and vegetables.

The National Commission on Food Manufacturing (1966), in studying the organization of and competition in the livestock and meat industry, disclosed a post-World War II decline in meat packing concentration, but noted the appearance of livestock pricing and exchange arrangements which bypassed established markets. The outcome for farmers was unclear in their report.

Love and Shuffet (1965), however, documented the changes in hog prices paid to farmers which occurred with the emergence of a single dominant buyer at the Louisville (KY) terminal market. Prior to the decrease in competition, Louisville's weekly prices averaged higher than comparable ones in Indianapolis and Chicago terminal markets. After emergence of a dominant hog-buying firm, Louisville prices averaged substantially lower than the Chicago or Indianapolis ones used for comparison.

Research by Aspelin and Engelman (1966) on prices and supplies at a terminal market disclosed that cattle marketings by a larger packer-feeder depressed prices substantially at the market compared to other prices at other terminal markets. They also discovered that increases in cattle fed by the packer, which were transferred to the packer's own plant, had ten times the effect on the local choice steer prices as comparable increases in overall market supplies of choice slaughter steers. Their research illustrates the outcome of asymmetric inter-dependencies in the livestock marketplace.

Farmer to first handler markets for milk have been affected by mergers and consolidation of milk processors, which stem in turn from increased bargaining power from chain stores (Gruebele, Williams and Fullert, 1970). Research in competition in the marketing channels for fluid milk (Moore, 1966; Moore and Clodius, 1962) suggests that local economic concentration levels are high relative to other industries, little product differentiation apparently exists, and price-fixing and price leadership are present. These findings vis-a-vis farmer/first handler milk marketing are corroborated by the work of Williams et al. (1970). Whether the farmer is being exploited depends on whether he is selling to a cooperative and whether the cooperative's patronage divident offsets prices determined by a relative absence of competition.

In its study, the National Commission on Food Marketing (1966) concluded that competition at the first handler level in fruits and vegetables was non-aggressive and differentiated according to service to the grower. These circumstances stemmed from a market composed of a core of buyer-shippers and a fringe of grower-shippers. According to the study, the core followed a non-aggressive price policy toward growers, but themselves competed highly for sales to destination whole-salers and retailers. The presence of direct purchasing by retailers of fruits and vegetables has led to the decline of terminal markets for produce and removed some pricing and commodity movement information from public scrutiny.

Procurement of fruits and vegetables for processing (i.e., canning, freezing, or drying) is generally quite concentrated at the first handler level (NCFM, 1966). Whether the high levels of concentration adversely affect competitiveness is debatable. Research by Helmberger and Hoos (1965) concluded that locally, competition was vigorous because of high supply elasticities, fresh market alternatives, and/or the increasing importance of farm cooperatives.

The extent to which farmer/first handler marketing of grain leaves the farmer dependent on the grain marketing system is unclear. Locally, competition for grain is limited (Farris, 1966), although cooperatives may compensate for the relative absence of grain marketing alternatives.[14] Moreover, Farris (1958) found inaccuracies in price discounting and grading that work to the detriment of grain farmers. Given the role of commodity futures contracts and concentration in the grain processing industries, the farmer/first handler interdependency may be less interesting than those elsewhere in the grain marketing system.

The locus of asymmetric interdependence is illustrated by the phenomenon of vertical coordination, or vertical integration. Increasing producer risk resulting from larger, more specialized farms and growing consumer demand for highly processed products requiring specific raw products has resulted in pressure for vertical coordination of the food and fiber sector. Vertical coordination (Mighell and Jones, 1963) refers to the techniques and methods of bringing order to the series of successive exchanges found throughout vertical stages of production and marketing.[15] Alternative means of vertical coordination include some combination of market pricing, vertical integration, contracting and cooperation. The incentives for vertical coordination are essentially four--technological changes or complementarities, imperfect markets in adjacent stages, risk reduction, and reduction of exchange costs. About one-fourth of U.S. farm output is produced under production contracts and vertical integration. Farmer cooperatives and producer bargaining associations have a major coordinating role in marketing sugar beets, fluid milk, citrus fruits, and tree nuts. Individual producer contracts are important in broilers, processing vegetables, and turkeys.

A substantial amount of research on vertical coordination in poultry and hogs has examined alternative arrangements and consequences of vertical coordination in agricultural product markets. The National Commission on Food Marketing (1966) indicates that poultry integration stemmed from feed supply contracts, which were essentially a feed financing device. Feed manufacturers proceeded to gain control of hatcheries and broiler processing, thereby controlling the basic components needed for raising broilers--feed, birds and processing facilities. The availability of underemployed farmers willing to raise broilers under tight contracts with feed manufacturer-broiler processor firms kept these agribusinesses from growing the broilers. The agribusinesses also avoided costs associated with hiring labor by not growing their own broilers. Asymmetric interdependence thus afforded the agribusiness firms the opportunity to exploit farmers willing to raise broilers.

Attempts have reoccurred by agribusiness firms to develop contract production in the hog-pork sector similar to that which developed for poultry. Yet, disease problems (Newcome et al., 1971) and insufficiently motivated management (Campbell and Hayenga, 1973) appear to be barriers to change in the production and marketing of hogs. Holtman et al. (1974) concluded that complete control of hog supplies could reduce a packing plant's costs by ten percent, illustrating the potential benefits to agribusinesses derived from control of marketing processes.

Despite the increased use of direct selling and vertical coordination techniques, pricing of farm commodities at the farm level continues to be dependent on terminal market activities. While the volume of farm products flowing through these markets continues to decline, they remain the most prominent points of price making.[16] The increasing use of direct marketing has been accompanied by greater use of production and marketing contracts which facilitates the coordination of quantity, quality, and timing of farm product deliveries. The expansion of marketing and production contracts, moreover, has been facilitated by the availability of commodity futures markets. As the number of commodities traded on futures markets has expanded, buyers wishing to make forward commitments for delivery were able to hedge their price commitments more easily. Futures markets are also available for participants in the marketing system to hedge price risks. The increasing volume of trading on futures markets has also made them the focus of price-making forces and a source of pricing information. For these reasons futures trading needs to be examined with attention being given to the asymmetric interdependencies and interorganizational networks tying the futures trade to the livestock, grain, and other marketing systems for agricultural commodities.[17] Whether alleged domination of the commodity exchanges by merchandisers and processors bodes well for farmers is unclear. Little empirical research on the social environment of futures trading, however, speaks to such a question.[18]

The role of cooperatives ought not to be neglected in sociological analysis of agribusiness, since farmer-owned marketing cooperatives serve their farmer members by providing distribution and processing services. In 1974-75 farmer cooperatives accounted for approximately 30 percent of farm level marketings. Farmer cooperatives are most important in the marketing of dairy products, grain and soybeans, as

data in Table 4 indicate. Their increase in market shares for cotton
and cotton products, dairy products, fruits and vegetables, and grain
and soybeans suggest they are an element of agribusiness not to be
neglected. Whether cooperatives will gain market shares from corporate
agribusiness or vice versa remains to be seen, as do the consequences
for farmers and America's rural periphery. Yet an understanding of
the interdependencies and networks that constitute the organizational
environment of markets for these agricultural commodities might shed
light on future changes in American agriculture's product markets.

TABLE 4

Farm Level Share of the Market Handled by
Farmer Cooperatives. Major Farm Products
Marketed, 1960-61 and 1974-75

Product Marketed	1960-61		1974-75	
	Number of Cooperatives	Market[1] Share	Number of Cooperatives	Market[1] Share
Cotton & Cotton Products	561	22	494	26
Dairy Products	1,609	61	631	75
Fruits & Vegetables	697	21	436	25
Grain & Soybeans	2,661	38	2,540	40
Livestock & Livestock Products	532	14	572	10
Poultry Products	567	10	167	9

[1] Computed as the share of total cash farm receipts for a particular
commodity handled by farmer cooperatives.

Source: Farmer Cooperative Service, United States Department of Agriculture, News for Farmer Cooperatives, February 1977, p. 4,
Table 1.

Processing and Manufacturing

Nearly all food and fiber products are processed in some way
after they leave the farm. The degree of processing extends from
changing product form only slightly to increase its storability to
the manufacture of foods which have little resemblance to raw farm
products. The U.S.D.A. estimated in 1975 that there were over 23,000
food processing plants employing over 1.3 million workers. In nearly
every line of food processing activity, firms have become larger
and fewer in number.

Food processors rely heavily on other parts of the economy for needed inputs. In 1967, processors purchased 59 percent of the output of metal container manufacturers, 28 percent of the production of paperboard containers and boxes, and 26 percent of the output of glass container manufacturers.

In most food processing industries, companies operating multiple plants account for the greatest share of output. Food processing industries can be divided into those products which are primarily consumed by the producer of other goods (producer goods) and those products primarily consumed by households (consumer goods). The producer goods industries produce standardized commodities with little product differentiation. While these industries tend to be highly concentrated, in general they sell to relatively powerful buyers who often have expert purchasing departments to evaluate alternate suppliers products. In consumer goods industries the degree of product differentiation is an important determinant of the type of competition and price making. In general, as the degree of product differentiation increases, competition tends to move away from the price competition toward the use of couponing, special deals, and heavy advertising. In many cases manufacturers have invested heavily in new product development as a way of developing differentiated products. In general, product differentiation allows manufacturers increasing discretion over price levels.

Small manufacturers who were not capable of differentiating their products have increasingly relied on sale to retailers under retailer brands. Retailer-controlled brands have become especially important in bread, fluid milk, and fruits and vegetables.

There has been a general tendency for large food manufacturers to diversity their activities. This has included the expansion of product lines, contract production and integration into agriculture, and integration into food service and restaurants.

The relevance of the food processing and manufacturing industries for present purposes is that the conduct within these industries affects the primary market in which farmers sell their production. To the extent that relatively few processors or food manufacturers are bidding for farm production, prices received by farmers may be lower than if several were competing for the same production. In other words, with fewer and fewer buyers for his production, the farmer becomes more dependent on those who make his market. For this reason it is useful to look at levels of economic concentration within key food processing and manufacturing industries.

Data in Table 5 describe selected U.S. food and fiber industries. They indicate that, nationally, several industries are highly

TABLE 5. Descriptive Statistics for Selected Food and Fiber Manufacturing Industries, 1972.

SIC	Industry Title	Number of [1] Companies	Number of [2] Establish-ments	Number of Employees 1,000	Value of Shipments Millions	Value Added Millions	CR[3] 4	CR[4] 20	
2041	Flour & Other Grain Mill	340	457	16.1	2,380.0	509.8	33	75	
2046	Wet Corn Milling	26	41	12.1	832.2	331.2	63	99+	
2062	Cane Sugar Refining	22	33	10.9	1,742.7	383.9	59	99+	
2063	Beet Sugar	16	61	11.5	880.2	310.5	66	100	Producer Goods
2074	Cottonseed Oil Mills	74	115	5.5	458.7	88.2	43	99	
2075	Soybean Oil Mills	54	94	9.1	3,357.2	350.0	54	92	
2083	Malt	30	40	1.7	226.3	44.0	48	98	
2211	Cotton Weaving Mills	190	307	121.3	2,660.6	1,256.3	31	72	
2011	Meat Packing Plants	2,293	2,474	157.5	23,003.4[5]/	2,968.1	22	51	
2016	Poultry Dressing Plants	406	522	77.6	3,254.1	724.4	17	35	Low Differenti-ation Consumer Goods
2021	Creamery Butter	201	231	14.6	588.1	168.5	45	78	
2026	Fluid Milk	2,024	2,507	126.1	9,395.7	2,552.4	18	42	
2033	Canned Fruits & Vegetables	766	1,038	89.8	4,043.8[6]/	1,625.1[6]/	20	53	
2037	Frozen Fruits & Vegetables	136	208	42.8	1,848.8[6]/	694.6[6]/	29	69	
2044	Rice Milling	48	57	4.0	680.6	148.3	43	92	Moderate Differ-entiation Con-sumer Goods
2051	Bread, Cake & Relat. Prods.	2,800	3,318	193.5	6,132.0	3,518.1	29	50	
2079	Shortening & Cooking Oils	64	109	12.9	2,068.1	512.6	44	93	
2098	Macaroni	179	194	7.3	348.3	155.7	38	76	
2043	Cereal Breakfast Foods	34	47	12.9	1,125.5	688.4	90	99+	
2066	Chocolate & Cocoa Products	39	48	10.0	735.5	282.6	74	99	
2082	Malt Beverages	108	167	51.5	4,054.4	1,993.6	52	91	
2084	Wine, Brandy & Brandy Spirits	183	213	9.4	865.0[5]/	407.9	50	83	High Differen-tiation Con-sumer Goods
2085	Distilled Liquor	76	121	18.4	1,797.9[6]/	1,024.0[6]/	47	91	
2086	Soft Drinks: Bottled & Canned	2,271	2,683	121.1	5,453.8	2,336.7	14	32	
2095	Roasted Coffee	162	213	12.9	2,328.7	825.8	65	92	
2013	Sausage & Prepared Meats	1,207	1,311	58.1	4,632.4[6]/	1,099.0	19	38	
2022	Cheese, Natural & Processed	739	872	25.2	3,195.0	492.3	42	65	Not Classified
2045	Blended and Prepared Flour	115	137	7.9	704.6	306.8	68	92	

[1]/ Companies refers to ownership units, a company may operate more than one establishment.

[2]/ Establishments refer to operating units or plants.

[3]/ Percentage Share of Value of Shipments accounted for by the 4 largest companies.

[4]/ Percentage Share of Value of Shipments accounted for by the 20 largest companies.

[5]/ The value of shipments figures for this industry include extensive duplication arising from shipments in the same industry.

[6]/ Establishments in this industry reported value of production rather than value of shipments. Consequently formula for computing adjusted value added by manufacture was modified to include only changes in work in process inventories between the beginning and the end of the year.

Source: U.S. Bureau of Census, Census of Manufactures, 1972, Special Report Series: Concentration Ratios in Manufacturing, MC 72(SR)-2, U.S. Government Printing Office, Washington, D.C., 1975.

240

concentrated, i.e., four-firm concentration ratios exceeding 50 percent.[19]
These concentrated industries include cane sugar refining, beet sugar,
soybean oil, milk, wet corn milling, blended and prepared flour, cereal,
and breakfast foods, chocolate and cocoa products, roasted coffee, malt
beverages, and wine, brandy, and brandy spirits. Other industries
exhibiting substantial concentration (CR4 > 40 percent) are flour and
grain mills, malt, cottonseed oil mills, rice milling, butter, shorten-
ing and cooking oils, cheese and distilled liquor. To the extent that
this economic concentration is even higher at regional levels, it
could increase farmer dependency on those who process his production.
Likewise, higher levels of concentration which exist for several more
specialized food products manufactured by these industries may exacerbate the marketing situation faced by America's farmers.

Additional aspects of the factor and product markets for farm
products are transportation and market regulation. The transportation
system serves as the vital link between farmers, marketers and consumers. The transportation system is a mixed system of private enterprise, government regulations, and government ownership. The nation's
highway system is owned and maintained by federal, state, and local
governments as are ports and waterways. Transportation rates for rail,
air, truck, and barge systems are regulated by a variety of agencies,
with coordination of regulations a significant problem. Availability
of freight cars, deterioration of rural highway and rail systems, and
fuel shortages have all presented problems in moving the nation's food
and fiber.

To discuss the thicket of transportation issues affecting the
farmer goes far beyond the scope of the present discussion. That
farmers are dependent on transportation, however, is quite clear. The
regulation of transportation and determination of transportation rates
affect the farmer and the rural community. Yet the nature of the
organizational environment of the railroads, trucking firms and barge
lines is unclear. Whether director interlocks between banks, railroads, and grain processors, for example, affect proposed rate increases
is also unknown. In fact, if a fusion of industrial and financial
capital has occurred among all three of these economic actors, it may
reflect upper class control of an important component of the food and
fiber sector of the economy. The sociologist of agribusiness of necessity may need to examine the transportation industries as well as
the industries for farm inputs and outputs to clarify the market relations binding agriculture to the rest of the economy.

In order to insure that markets operate fairly it is often necessary to limit the range of behavior by market participants. In this
context, federal, state, and local governments have passed laws to
regulate markets. The food and fiber system is subject to many forms
of market regulation including: antitrust laws, trade regulations,
health standards, safety standards, labor rules, packaging rules,

product grades and standards and other dimensions of market behavior.

In some cases permissive legislation allows market participants a degree of self-regulation. Cooperatives and marketing orders are examples where farmers are allowed to make rules affecting prices and terms of trade. Patents, licenses, and trademarks are also examples where regulation protects the action of some market participants.

In general market regulations are designed to eliminate unfair or deceptive practices. In this sense market regulations attempt to give market participants the range of individual action which is consistent with maintaining market credibility. Of particular concern to the evolution of the food and fiber system is the growing number of regulatory agencies. In our industrialized food and fiber system the regulatory environment has become increasingly complex. While the need for regulation is accepted by most market participants, in some cases jurisdictional conflicts, regulatory delays, and corresponding costs and risks may be counterproductive.

The role of agribusiness in formulating and administering market regulation programs for agriculture is important to consider. Industry access to the Grains Division of the Agricultural Marketing Service by the large exporters has been documented, and problems associated with lax commodity exchange regulation by an agency of the U.S.D.A. led to creation of an independent regulatory agency for the trade in commodity futures contracts. Interorganizational ties between the federal government and agribusinesses may be stabilizing agriculture's product and factor markets to the detriment of farmers and Americans' rural hinterland. Inquiry of the kind noted earlier thus seems appropriate.

A SUMMING UP

While the empirical evidence is indirect, it seems consistent with a dependency perspective. The levels of economic concentration present in America's farm input and output markets suggest that structurally originating market power potentially exists. Agribusiness thus may be able to constrain the opportunities of farmers to buy factor inputs at the lowest possible price and sell production outputs at the highest possible price. But the extent to which exploitation by agribusiness occurs is unknown. Likewise, the extent to which farmer-owned cooperatives compensate for subordination of the farmer to agribusiness is unknown. Under these circumstances one task for the sociologist of agribusiness is to determine the extent to which the marketing relationships linking agriculture to the rest of the economy are exploitive, and whether marketing institutions exist which mitigate or perpetuate exploitation.

Economic models of industrial organization assert that competitive market systems rely generally on competition between economic enterprises to keep costs at a minimum. Such competitive systems rely on large numbers of competitors with limited market power to insure that the focus of competition is on price rather than excessive product differentiation. The production sector of agriculture tends to fit this model very well in most commodities. Yet, even in production agriculture we have continued to see increasing concentration. Some are concerned that even in some farm commodities, organizations of farmers have greater market power than is consistent with price competition.

In the input and product market sectors, market concentration appears to be a more common concern. The size of firms and the share of markets accounted for by the largest firms has been increasing for many farm input and product markets. Further, this trend appears to be prevailing in food distribution as well as manufacturing.

A question still under debate is the extent to which increasing concentration (often encouraged by scale economies) results in a tendency for decreasing price competition and increasing emphasis on product differentiation and other cost enhancing practices. A second question concerns the way in which changes in concentration, which result in different degrees of market power for different participants in the system, are consistent with equitable returns to all participants.

As the extent of owner control of agribusiness is largely unclear, the sociologist of agribusiness could turn his or her attention to such a question. Moreover, if a social upper class in fact exists, as has been alleged (Domhoff, 1967), how is it related to the food and fiber sector of the economy? If owners still exercise control in some or all of the agribusiness industries, is this a vestige of the past, waiting to be supplanted by one or more management controlled conglomerates? Or is activity in the food and fiber sector central to upper class interests? Answers to these questions, we contend, are clearly necessary if sociologists are to understand the underlying forces which account for change and stability in the structure of American agriculture.

Given the changing role of cooperatives in the farm input industries, issues regarding cooperative ownership and control also seem appropriate to raise. Are cooperative managers merely benign functionaries, or are they part of a separate stratum of rural America's managerial elite? Likewise, are the managers of the giant, federated cooperatives indirectly interlocked with their non-cooperative counterparts via directorships or memberships in other organizations? Finally, to what extent do cooperatives mitigate the asymmetric interdependence stemming from economic concentration in

America's farm input industries? These are additional questions that might be addressed by sociologists of agribusiness.

The organizational environments of agribusiness are also important to consider.[20] Were sociologists to use a resource dependency model of organizational environments, they might, for example, be able to explain the patterns of director interlocks among agribusiness, financial and other industrial firms. In this regard, reasons for any existing ties among cooperative enterprises nominally controlled by their members and private firms allegedly competing with the cooperatives might be understood more clearly. Ties among railroads, trucking firms, and the processors of agricultural products might also be examined with an eye toward environmental control. Likewise, the circulation of personnel from agribusiness firms to federal regulatory agencies and vice versa could be considered. The social reality of trading in commodity futures contracts perhaps could have additional light shed on it, if sociologists considered the trade in futures from a resource dependency model of organizational environments. These suggestions just begin to illustrate the range of topics sociologists might pursue using an organization-environment approach to agribusiness.

Whether American farmers are entering a period of feudalism, as some have argued (Perelman, 1977), cannot be determined from existing knowledge of the structure of American agriculture. To understand the structure, function, and conduct of agribusiness using the perspectives mentioned earlier, however, should broaden the knowledge base used for evaluating such an argument. It may also lay the groundwork for developing adequate public social control of industry.

FOOTNOTES

1. The authors appreciate the comments of the editors on an earlier draft of this chapter.

2. A recent issue of International Organization was devoted to the topic of dependency and provides an excellent point of entry into the literature. See also Valenzuela and Valenzuela (1978).

3. That control of the food and fiber sector is an important economic issue reiterated by R.J. Hildreth, K.R. Krause, and P.E. Nelson, Jr. (1973), and the North Central Public Policy Education Committee (1972).

4. That oligarchy may come about by chance alone is shown in Mayhew and Levinger's (1976) analysis of the effects of group size on the form its power structure will take.

5. Zeitlin (1964) argues that large commercial banks controlled by wealthy families are centers of economic interest which facilitate economic control by America's major capitalist families.

6. Recent work by Karpik (1978) may reflect a third orientation to organizational environments.

7. Cook (1977) presents an extension of the exchange model for analyzing interorganizational relations, which views organizational interactions as networks of exchange relations. Her discussion of interorganizational linkages, power and dependence, and the relationship between exchange networks and market structure is very useful to consider in the present context.

8. Extensive discussions of market power and economic concentration appear in the industrial organization literature. Besides Shephard's (1970) text, works by Bain (1967), Scherer (1970), and Blair (1972) are of particular interest for their theoretical and empirical content.

9. The subsequent section draws heavily on Campbell and Emerson (1978) and Helmberger, Campbell and Dobson (forthcoming).

10. Barber (1973) charges the farm machinery industry with following high price policies that foster inefficiency and high costs. He argues, however, that economies of scale might entail even greater concentration in the industry.

11. In his case study of the fertilizer industry, however, Markham (1958) concluded that many of the raw materials used in manufacturing fertilizer are purchased in highly oligopolistic markets.

12. Research by Youde (1966), Berry et al. (1965), and Walsh and Rothjen (1962) suggests the presence of cooperatives may enhance competition in markets where monopoly power would otherwise be exercised.

13. Evidence reported by Youde and Helmberger (1966) suggests that centralized cooperatives with market power may restrict their membership. See also Marion (1977) for an extensive discussion of agricultural cooperatives and the public interest.

14. Recent research by Campbell and Schmiesing (1970) however, indicates that local cooperatives affiliated with regional cooperatives do not perform any better in terms of turnover and gross margin than local elevators selling to other sales outlets.

15. See also Roy (1973) and Mighell and Hoofnagle (1972).

16. A series of papers which considered pricing problems in the food industry with special reference to thin markets is helpful to consider in the present context (Hayenga, 1979).

17. Schwantes et al. (1973) provide a useful starting point in terms of empirical research.

18. Research by Martinson (1978) suggests the presence of grain marketing system interorganizational networks derived from trade association committee memberships.

19. Data reported in this section came from the U.S. Bureau of the Census, Census of Manufacturers (1972).

20. For an approach to the study of extra-market sources of economic control using an interorganizational perspective, see Martinson and Campbell (1979).

REFERENCES

Aiken, Michael T., and Jerald Hage
1978 "Organizational interdependence and intraorganizational structure." American Sociological Review 33 (December):912-930.

Aldrich, Howard E., and Jeffrey Pfeffer
1976 "Environments of organizations," pp. 79-105 in Annual Review of Sociology, volume 2. Alex Inkeles, James Coleman, and Neil Smelser (Eds.). Palo Alto California: Annual Reviews, Inc.

Allen, Michael Patrick
1978 "Economic interest groups and the corporate elite structure." Social Science Quarterly 58 (March):597-615.

Allen, Michael Patrick
1976 "Management control in the large corporation: comment on Zeitlin." American Journal of Sociology 81 (January):855-894.

Allen, Michael Patrick
1974 "The structure of interorganizational elite co-optation: interlocking corporate directorates." American Sociological Review 39 (June):393-406.

Aspelin, A.L., and G. Engelman
1966 Packer Feeding of Cattle: Its Volume and Significance. USDA, AMS, Marketing Research Report 776.

Bain, Joe S.
1968 Industrial Organization (2nd ed.). New York: John Wiley.

Barber, Clarence
1973 "The farm machinery industry: Reconciling the interests of the farmer, the industry, and the general public," American Journal of Agricultural Economics 55 (December):820-878.

Berle, A.A., Jr., and G.C. Means
1933 The Modern Corporation and Private Property. New York: Macmillan.

Bernstein, Marver
1955 Regulating Business by Independent Regulatory Commission. Princeton, New Jersey: Princeton University Press.

Blair, John M.
1972 Economic Concentration. New York: Harcourt, Brace, Jovanovich.

Blau, Peter M.
1964 Exchange and Power in Social Life. New York: John Wiley.

Breimyer, Harold F.
1973 "The economics of agricultural marketing: A survey." Review of Marketing and Agricultural Economics 41: 115-166.

Breimyer, Harold F.
1965 Individual Freedom and the Economic Organization of Agriculture. Urbana, Illinois: University of Illinois Press.

Campbell, Gerald R., and Brian H. Schmiesing
1979 "Impact of buyer relationships on the performance of local grain elevators," North Central Journal of Agricultural Economics (January):39-45.

Campbell, Gerald R., and Peter Emersen
1978 "The United States food and fiber system: Selected aspects of structure and performance," University of Wisconsin-Madison: Department of Agricultural Economics Staff Paper 139 (February).

Campbell, Gerald R., and Marvin Hayenga
1973 "Vertical coordination shifts in the hog-pork subsector," University of Wisconsin-Madison: Department of Agricultural Economics Staff Paper 69.

Caporaso, James A.
1978 "Independence, dependency and power in the global system: A structural and behavioral analysis," International Organization 32 (Winter):13-43.

Chamberlain, E.H.
    1949   Theory of Monopolistic Competition (6th ed.).   Cambridge,
    Massachusetts: Harvard University Press.

Clevenger, Thomas S., and G.R. Campbell
    1977   "Vertical organization: A neglected element in market
    structure - profit models," Industrial Organization Review 5:
    60-66.

Cook, Karen S.
    1977   "Exchange and power in networks of interorganizational rela-
    tions," Sociological Quarterly 18 (Winter):62-82.

Domhoff, G. William
    1967   Who Rules America?   Englewood Cliffs, New Jersey: Prentice-
    Hall.

Farris, Paul L.
    1966   "The grain procurement industry," in J.R. Moore and R.G.
    Walsh (eds.), Market Structure of the Agricultural Industries,
    Chapter 10, pp. 249-265.   Ames, Iowa: Iowa State University Press.

Farris, Paul L.
    1958   "The pricing structure for wheat at the country elevator
    level," Journal of Farm Economics 40:607-624.

French, B.C.
    1977   "The analysis of productive efficiency in agricultural
    marketing: Models, methods, and progress," A Survey of Agricul-
    tural Economics Literature vol. 1.   L.R. Martin (ed.).   Minneapo-
    lis, Minnesota: University of Minnesota Press.

Goldberg, Ray A.
    1968   Agribusiness Co-ordination.   Boston: Harvard Business School.

Goldschmidt, Walter
    1947   As You Sow.   New York: Harcourt, Brace.

Gruebele, J.W., S.W. Williams, and R.F. Fallert
    1970   "Impact of food chain procurement policies on the fluid milk
    industry," American Journal of Agricultural Economics 52 (August):
    395-402.

Hall, Donald R.
    1969   Cooperative Lobbying: The Power of Pressure.   Tucson,
    Arizona: University of Arizona Press.

Hamilton, Martha M.
    1972   The Great Grain Robbery and Other Stories.   Washington,
    D.C.: Agribusiness Accountability Project.

Hayenga, Marvin L. (ed.)
   1979   "Pricing problems in the food industry." Madison, Wisconsin: University of Wisconsin College of Agricultural and Life Sciences Research Division, North Central Regional Publication 261 (February).

Helmberger, Peter, Gerald R. Campbell, and William D. Dobson
   (forthcoming)   "Organization and performance of agricultural markets." A chapter in Lee Martin (ed.), A Survey of Agricultural Economics Literature: Volume 3 -- Economics of Welfare Development and Natural Resources. Minneapolis, Minnesota: University of Minnesota Press.

Hightower, James
   1975   Eat Your Heart Out. New York: Crown.

Hildreth, R.J., K.R. Krause, and P.E. Nelson, Jr.
   1973   "Organization and control of the U.S. food and fiber sector," American Journal of Agricultural Economics 55 (December): 851-859.

Holtman, J.B., J.D. Sullivan, and H.F. Barreto
   1974   "Supply-control savings for hog slaughtering-processing plants," Agricultural Economics Report 258. Washington, D.C.: United States Department of Agricultural Economic Research Service.

Imel, Blake, et al.
   1972   Market Structure and Performance: The U.S. Food Processing Industries. Lexington, Massachusetts: D.C. Heath.

Karpik, Lucien
   1978   "Organizations, institutions, and history," in Organization and Environment. Lucien Karpik (ed.). Beverly Hills, California: Sage Publications.

Kohlmeier, Louis
   1967   The Regulators. New York: Harper and Row.

Kravitz, Linda
   1974   "Who's Minding the Co-op?" Washington, D.C.: Agribusiness Accountability Project.

Leonard, William N., and Marvin G. Weber
   1907   "Automakers and dealers: A study of criminogenic market structures," Law and Society Review 4 (February):407-424.

Love, H.G., and D.M. Shuffett
   1965   "Short-run price effects of a structural change in a terminal market for hogs," Journal of Farm Economics 47:803-812.

Macaulay, Stewart
   1963 "Non-contractual relations in business," American Sociological Review 28 (February):55-67.

Marion, Bruce (ed.)
   1977 "Agricultural cooperatives and the public interest."
   Madison, Wisconsin: University of Wisconsin College of Agricultural and Life Sciences, North Central Regional Publication
   256.

Marion, Bruce, W.F. Mueller, R.W. Cotterill, F.E. Geithman, and J.R.
   Schmelzer
   1977 The Profit and Performance of Leading Food Chains, 1970-
   1974. Joint Economic Committee, 95th Congress, 1st Session.

Markham, Jesse W.
   1958 The Fertilizer Industry: Study of the Imperfect Market.
   Nashville, Tennessee: Vanderbilt University Press.

Martinson, Oscar B.
   1978 "The American Grain Marketing System: An Organizational
   Analysis." University of Wisconsin-Madison unpublished dissertation.

Martinson, Oscar B., and Gerald R. Campbell
   1979 "Social network analysis: Suggested applications to economic control," Journal of Economic Issues (forthcoming in June).

Mayhew, Bruce H., and Roger L. Levinger
   1976 "On the emergence of oligarchy in human interaction,"
   American Journal of Sociology 81 (March):1017-1049.

Mighell, R., and W. Hoofnagle
   1972 "Contract production and vertical coordination in farming:
   1960 and 1970." Washington, D.C.: United States Department of
   Agriculture, Economic Research Service Agricultural Report 497.

Mighell, R., and L. Jones
   1963 "Vertical coordination in agriculture." Washington,
   D.C.: United States Department of Agriculture, Economic
   Research Service Agricultural Report 19.

Miles, Raymond E., Charles C. Snow, and Jeffrey Pfeffer
   1974 "Organization -- environment: Concepts and issues,"
   Industrial Relations 13 (October):244-264.

Moore, J.R.
   1966 "The fluid milk industry." In Market Structure of the
   Agricultural Industries. J.R. Moore and R.G. Walsh (eds.).
   Ames, Iowa: Iowa State University Press.

Moore, J.R., and R.L. Clodius
    1962 Market Structure and Competition in the Dairy Industry,
    Wisconsin Agricultural Experiment Station Research Bulletin 233.

National Commission on Food Marketing
    1966 Organization and Competition in the Livestock and Meat
    Industry. Washington, D.C.: United States Government Printing
    Office.

Newcome, S., G. Grimes, V.J. Rhodes, and C. Cramer
    1971 "Producing and marketing hogs under contract." Columbia,
    Missouri: University of Missouri Special Report 135.

North Central Public Policy Education Committee
    1972 Who Will Control Agriculture? University of Illinois
    College of Agriculture Cooperative Extension Service Special
    Publication 27 (August).

Pedersen, Lawrence, and William K. Tabb
    1976 "Ownership and control of large corporations, revisited,"
    Antitrust Bulletin 21 (Spring):53-66.

Perelman, Michael
    1977 Farming for Profit in a Hungry World. Montclair, New
    Jersey: Allanheld, Osman.

Pfeffer, Jeffrey, and Phillip Nowak
    1976 "Patterns of joint venture activity: Implications for anti-
    trust policy," Antitrust Bulletin 21 (Summer):315-339.

Pfeffer, Jeffrey
    1972 "Merger as a response to organizational interdependence,"
    Administrative Science Quarterly 17 (September):382-394.

Pfeffer, Jeffrey
    1972 "Size and composition of corporate boards of directors,"
    Administrative Science Quarterly 17 (June):382-394.

Phillips, Almarin
    1960 "A theory of interfirm organization," Quarterly Journal
    of Economics 74 (November):602-613.

Preston, Lee E.
    1975 "Corporation and society: The search for a paradigm,"
    Journal of Economic Literature 13 (June):434-453.

Reeder, John A.
    1975 "Corporate ownership and control: A synthesis of recent
    findings," Industrial Organization Review 3:18-27.

Robbins, William
1974 The American Food Scandal. New York: William Morrow.

Robinson, Joan
1933 The Economics of Imperfect Competition. London: Macmillan.

Rodefeld, Richard
1974 "The Changing Organizational and Occupational Structure of
Farming and the Implications for Farm Work Force Individuals,
Families, and Communities." University of Wisconsin-Madison
unpublished Ph.D. dissertation.

Roy, E.P.
1972 Contract Farming and Economic Integration. Danville,
Illinois: Interstate Printers.

Scherer, Frederick M.
1970 Industrial Market Structure and Economic Performance.
Chicago: Rand McNally.

Schwartz, Alexander, et al.
1973 Trading in Commodity Futures Contracts on the Chicago
Board of Trade. Washington, D.C.: United States Department of
Agriculture, Commodity Exchange Authority Marketing Research
Report 999 (July).

Schwartzmann, David
1970 "Oligopoly in the farm machinery industry," Ottawa, Canada:
Royal Commission on Farm Machinery Study 12.

Selznick, Phillip
1949 TVA and the Grassroots. Berkeley and Los Angeles, California: University of California Press.

Schepherd, William G.
1970 Market Power and Economic Welfare. New York: Random House.

Stigler, George J.
1971 "The theory of economic regulation," Bell Journal of
Economics and Management Science 2 (Spring):3-21.

Taylor, James R.
1977 "Exploitation through contrived dependence," Journal of
Economic Issues 11 (March):51-59.

Thurston, Stanley K., et al.
1976 Improving the Export Capability of Grain Cooperatives.
Washington, D.C.: United States Department of Agriculture, Farm
Cooperative Service, Research Report 34 (June).

United States Bureau of the Census, Census of Manufacturers
    1975 Special Report Series: Concentration Ratios in Manufacturing
    MC72 (SR)-2. Washington, D.C.: United States Government Print-
    ing Office.

Valenzuela, J. Samuel and Arturo Valenzuela
    1978 "Modernization and dependency," Comparative Politics
    (July):535-557.

Weiss, Leonard
    1974 "The concentration profits relationship and anti-trust,"
    in Industrial Concentration: The New Learnings. H.T. Goldschmid,
    H.M. Mann, and T.F. Weston (eds.). Boston: Little, Brown.

Williams, S.W., D.A. Vose, C.E. French, H.L. Cook, and A.C. Manchester
    1970 Organization and Competition in the Midwest Dairy Industries.
    Ames, Iowa: Iowa State University Press.

Zald, Mayer N.
    1978 "On the social control of industries," Social Forces 57
    (September):79-102.

Zeitlin, Maurice
    1976 "On class theory of the large corporation: Response to
    Allen," American Journal of Sociology 81 (January):894-903.

Zeitlin, Maurice
    1974 "Corporate ownership and control: The large corporation
    and the capitalist class," American Journal of Sociology 79
    (March):1073-1119.

9. Urbanization and the Rural Class Structure: Reflections on a Case Study

HOWARD NEWBY

INTRODUCTION

Since 1970 I have been involved in investigating social change in rural England, first through a study of farm workers (Newby, 1977), then later by way of research into the changing situation of farmers and landowners (Newby et al., 1978). In this paper I want to reflect upon some of the results of this research, thereby allowing myself to draw together a number of issues which have hitherto been considered separately. The thematic focus of this paper will be the impact of "urbanisation" on the rural social structure. By "urbanisation," I do not, of course, mean the physical development of towns and factories where only farms and fields once stood, but the movement into the countryside of an urban population--commuters, second-home owners, retired couples--whose present or past employment is located in towns and cities rather than locally in rural areas. Their arrival in the countryside, particularly since the Second World War, has ensured that English rural society is no longer entirely, nor even predominantly, an agrarian society. Indeed it is arguable that the single most important social change to have occurred in the countryside in recent years has concerned this changing social and occupational composition of its population. This change has not been entirely ignored by sociologists (see, for example, Pahl, 1965, 1970; Crichton, 1964; Thorns, 1968; Harris, 1974; Ambrose, 1974; an excellent survey of the literature is Connell, 1974). However, there has been no attempt to analyse systematically the consequences of these changes in so far as they affect the life-chances of the local, predominantly agricultural, population.

---

*This paper is based on research financed by the SSRC.

This paper represents, in a very schematic and discursive way, a modest beginning to this task. But first it is necessary to enter a word of caution. The account presented here is based upon research in a part of the country, East Anglia, which is in no sense representative of rural England as a whole. How far it is possible to draw generalised conclusions from this analysis is therefore a moot point. Indeed it is possible to argue that the situation in East Anglia exhibits the effects of urbanisation in the most <u>exaggerated</u> form, paradoxically because the region remains so predominantly agricultural, but also because East Anglian agriculture is so capital-intensive and so prosperous. As we shall see, this may well have contributed to the relative deprivation of the poorer sections of the local rural population--a factor which, it will be argued, is one of the major consequences of urbanisation-- to an extent which is not, or not yet, apparent elsewhere. On the other hand it should be realised that no single area or region of rural England can be regarded as "typical" such as its variability. Thus, rather than engage in a pointless search for typicality, it is more important to locate the area of study in the context of English rural society and its agricultural economy as a whole.

East Anglia is one of the most prosperous agricultural regions in the country, an area which is, without doubt, one of the most "capitalist organised business farming areas of Britain" (Frankenberg, 1966: 252). It is dominated by a type of agricultural production--cereals growing-- which is highly capital-intensive and which has been the vanguard of scientific, technological and entrepreneurial change. Farming in East Anglia is a serious business of making money and bears little resemblance, in either its visual aspects or as a way of life, to the bucolic world depicted in many popular books on English rural life and to which the urban population seems peculiarly susceptible. In general, farms in East Anglia are larger, more specialised, employ more labour and are more mechanised than in England and Wales as a whole. Even crop yields per acre tend to be significantly higher in the region, indicating not simply better physical and climatic conditions, but also the fruits of higher investment in machinery and other technological innovations which accrue to the larger holdings. Moreover, in common with other areas of England, the tendency is towards increasing scale of production, increasing specialisation and concentration, further capital investment and a consequent diminution in the number of holdings and the number of farm workers. (For details see Newby et al., 1978: 48-58). All of these trends are continuing and show no sign of ending in the near future--indeed entry into the EEC has accelerated some of them.

This economic base is reflected in the social structure of the region's agricultural population. Unlike some other areas of rural England, the larger and more labour-intensive system of arable agriculture in East Anglia has produced a clearly-defined and widely-recognised class structure of predominantly landowning farmers on the

one hand and hired farm workers on the other. Unlike other areas of
England, East Anglia has no tradition of small peasant holdings, farmed
by owner or tenant, except in the Fens. In general the predominant relationship on the land has always been one of employer and employee.
In the east of the region, for example, enclosure has existed since
Saxon times. Even the tenant farmers have traditionally been of a sufficient size to require a large amount of hired labour, while landlords
were never solely landlords, or even absentees, preferring instead to
farm some of their own land "at hand." There is, therefore, no history
of landlord-tenant conflict in East Anglia, but there is a tradition of
employer-employee conflict (see Hobsbawm and Rude, 1973; Groves, 1949;
Newby, 1977: Ch. 1, 4). Today, despite the recent involvement of the
City institutions in landownership, owner-occupation is well above the
national average (see Newby et al., 1978: Ch. 3) while the presence of
cross-cutting ties between landowners, owner-occupiers and tenant farmers
is considerable, nor can these groups easily, or very meaningfully, be
ordered hierarchically. As far as the agricultural workers is concerned,
tenurial status comes a long way down the list of attributes which he regards as being significant in the evaluation of local farmers; indeed
their tenurial status is often unknown--except to tax accountants.

In East Anglia, then, rural society has traditionally been a class-
divided society. Farmers and landowners formed an easily identifiable
rural ruling class which held a near-monopoly over employment opportunities, housing, the magistracy and local politics. Against their
extensive domination of rural institutions farm workers and other members
of the rural working class were relatively powerless. This domination
was, and to a large extent still is, reflected in the distribution of
wealth and income in the region's agriculture. There is a marked contrast between the prosperity of the region's farmers and the poverty of
its farm workers (Newby, 1972). While the capital value of land approached
2,000 pounds per acre, few farm workers own even their own homes. For a
farm worker to purchase and stock a viable farm in the area he would
need to find upwards of 1 million pounds, so it is not surprising that
social mobility between the two classes remains minimal. It is this
rigid and hierarchical class structure which appears to have been complicated by the arrival of ex-urban newcomers. Overwhelmingly professional
and managerial by occupation, they represent a new "middle class" (as
they are described by both farmers and farm workers) which has been
inserted into this dichotomous class structure. Their presence, as
most farmers have not been slow to realise, threatens the former political domination of the area's ruling class. They have also rendered the
rural class structure less coherent and less easily definable. As we
shall see, they have therefore created a certain amount of "status panic"
among the agricultural population and it has been on this aspect of their
impact that sociologists, including myself, have fastened. However,
while the cleavages between "locals" and "newcomers" which have been
introduced are real enough, there are other, more material, consequences
which require equal consideration.

It is the interplay between these objective changes and the perceptions which those affected have of them which forms a major theme of this
paper. Because the subjective responses of the agricultural population
are, perhaps, more familiar, I shall summarise my findings on this aspect
of contemporary rural social change very briefly before considering the
nature and extent of the more material changes induced by the urbanisation of the countryside.

The Changing Village Community

Perceptions of change among the rural population have often been
focussed on the issue of the English village "community." The influx of
newcomers into most villages has almost inevitably raised the question of
how far they have been responsible for destroying a "sense of community"
which, it is often assumed, had hitherto existed there. Yet the consequences of urbanisation on "community" need to be handled with care.
When the rural village was almost entirely an agricultural community then
there is a case to be made, as we shall see, that the close-knit and over-
lapping social ties produced a local social system in which everyone
more or less knew everyone else, but we should be wary of sanctifying
this with a misplaced nostalgia. The village inhabitants formed a "community" because they had to: they were imprisoned by constraints of
various kinds, including poverty, so that reciprocal aid became a necessity. The village "community" was, therefore, a "mutuality of the
oppressed" (Williams, 1973: 182). Whether gossip, bickering and family
feuds were or were not a more prevalent feature than a wholesome sense
of togetherness could vary from village to village and is ultimately a
matter of subjective judgement. Nevertheless the recent severe and rapid
dislocation of the village social structure has led to an ideology of
"community" being conferred upon its former qualities, a genuine sense
of loss having produced a harking back to a "golden age" of village life
which can be contrasted with an apparently less palatable present. Since
this is, in effect, as much an oblique comment on the present as a literal
interpretation of the past, what such accounts tell us about the quality
of village life in the past must be handled with considerable scepticism.
Moreover, because assessments of the "spirit" of community depend so
much on highly variable subjective preferences and values, it is virtually
impossible to generalise about whether there has or has not been a per-
ceptible "decline of community" in the English village.

Changes in the social structure of the village are, however, somewhat more amenable to generalisation, and I have typologically set out
these changes elsewhere (Newby, 1977: Ch. 6) as follows:

1) The Occupational Community

Before the arrival of ex-urban newcomers, the population of the
majority of rural villages were dependent upon agriculture for a living.
It therefore makes sense to call the village under these conditions an

"occupational community." In East Anglia, because the majority of farmers lived not in the nucleated core of the village but on the farms around
its periphery, the village itself consisted almost entirely of the dwellings of agricultural workers. This composition gave the village many
of the characteristics that have been noted of working-class occupational
communities elsewhere: a strong sense of shared occpuational experience,
a distinctive occupational sub-culture, an overlap between work and non-
work roles and loyalties, a prevalence of closely-knit cliques of friends,
workmates, neighbours and kin, and generally a strong sense of group
identity which marked off the village from the other which surrounded it.
On the basis of the limited historical evidence available, it also seems
reasonable to conclude that the distance in wealth, income, life-style
and, most importantly, authority decisively marked off the occupational
community of the agricultural worker from the more geographically widespread network of local farmers and landowners, creating the kind of
"oppositional" sub-culture and social imagry characteristic of similar
urban working-class communities with a nascent class conflict never far
from the surface of day-to-day relationships. Not only was the farm
worker highly integrated into this occupational community, but his
status was not attributed to him on the basis of income or conspicuous
consumption but largely on the basis of skill at work. By this means
the agricultural worker could accrue to himself much of the esteem and
self-respect which was often denied to him by the rest of society beyond
the village boundary.

2)   The Encapsulated Community

It is this interactional status system which the urbanisation of
the countryside has threatened to undermine. For many newcomers the village is not the focus of their social life, for both their work and their
leisure activities take them outside the immediate locality. The influx
of "strangers" can quite rapidly affect the nature of village society:
suddenly (so it seems) everyone does not know everyone else. The newcomer, moreover, does not, as in the past, enter the village as a lone
individual who must ingratiate himself locally in order to make life
tolerable. Instead the newcomer is one of a large group of recently-
arrived immigrants, whose values, behaviour and life-styles, being commonly based upon an urban, middle-class pattern, are very similar, while
being noticeably different from those of the locals. Quite quickly, then,
a new social division may arise--between on the one hand the close-knit
"locals," who form the rump of the old occupational community, and, on the
other, the newcomers. The former occupational community then tends to retreat in upon itself and become what might be called an "encapsulated community," since the locals now form a community within a community--a
separate and dense network encapsulated within the total local social
system.

When farm workers refer to the "loss of community" in their village
it is usually to this kind of change that they are implicitly referring,

for there are bound to be changing patterns of sociability developing in
the village to which they are unaccustomed and from which they feel excluded. This new element in the village population also tends to create
new dimensions of social conflict to replace the rural class antagonisers
of the occupational community. As the recent experience of many East
Anglian villages shows only too well, there are ample opportunities for
conflict to arise between locals and newcomers--most typically over issues
concerning housing and, broadly, "environmental" matters. The newcomers
also threaten the locals' status in their own village, since they lack
the ability or knowledge to judge the rural workers' skills. Instead the
newcomers tend to evaluate farm workers and other villagers on the basis
of urban, middle-class criteria of conspicuous consumption. The agricultural worker then reacts to this threat to his former status by changing
the basis of his own evaluations. Since non-acceptance on the basis of
length of residence is one of the few ways in which local workers can
retain any of their former status in the village, they re-define the
criteria of status allocation along these lines and restrict their social
contacts to those who share these judgements with them.

3) The Farm-Centred Community

    Changes in the nature of the rural housing market and the mor-
phology of the housing stock (to be considered in more detail below) have
resulted in a growing proportion of farm workers living in tied cottages.
These are located not in the village, for the most part, but on the farm,
so that the "community" for these workers tends to become the farm itself.
Such a situation may be called a "farm-centred community." Here the farm
tends to become the centre of the farm worker's world and, estranged both
geographically and socially from the village, contact with village society
becomes more perfunctory and more instrumental. Increasingly the village
is used merely for its amenities--schools, shops, etc.--rather than as a
social centre, while on the farm the agricultural worker lives in a somewhat privatised world, for the most part socially invisible to the rest
of society. The sense of isolation which might otherwise ensue is, however, mitigated by the close contact with neighbours and workmates in
other tied houses and by increasing contact with the employer. In
general, relationships between the farmer and his workers become more
informal, more personal and--because of their propinquity--more pervasive.
Although there is a risk that life can become too self-preoccupied and
claustrophobic, farmers nevertheless find it easier to inspire some degree
of personal loyalty among their workers and allow the class animosities
of the occupational community to be reduced.

    One of the conclusions which I emphasised in The Deferential Worker
was therefore that there had been a reduction in the social distance
between farmers and farm workers, partly brought about by the impact of
newcomers on the village. Because of the ways in which the changes wrought
by urbanisation have worked their way through the local social system,
the contrast between the more affluent life-styles of the newcomers and

the power living standards of local farm workers had not resulted in greater conflict between farmers and their employees. If anything, farm workers could not identify more with farmers than they had in the past. For example, farmers could find common cause with their workers in complaining about the "interference" of outsiders in their own farm's and village's affairs. Moreover, farmers, at least, continued to appreciate the skills of farm workers, so that the latter could obtain much higher esteem from their employers than they could expect from many newcomers. This did not mean that the objective differences in wealth and income have been in any way reduced, but relationships have become easier and more informal. This has been aided by two further factors. The continuing mechanisation of agriculture has, together with other labour-saving innovations, brought about a steady decline in the size of the average farm labour force which has attenuated the workplace oppositional sub-culture of farm workers while allowing more frequent and direct contact with employers. In addition, farmers have become dissociated from many of their former authority roles, partly because of the professionalisation and bureaucratisation of local government and partly because of displacement by newcomers. Consequently farmers and landowners no longer have an automatic passport to local political dominance (see Newby et al.: Ch. 6).

As far as the newcomers are concerned, they have generally wished no harm to anyone, so that any animosity which they have evoked has been entirely unintended and unanticipated. Indeed at times it has seemed difficult to see what the newcomers could do to alleviate the resentments they have occasionally caused. If they respectfully withdraw from village affairs they find themselves branded as "stand-offish" or "jumped-up"; but if they participate fully they are accused of "taking over" the village. The newcomers have often acted as easily identifiable scapegoats who can be blamed for many of the deprivations which the contemporary rural population suffers--poor amenities, remoteness from the centres of decision-making, and so on. This is not to suggest that the basis of local-newcomer conflict is entirely illusory--far from it. However, the social separation of the two groups and the consequent tendency of each to stereotype the other has magnified the conflict involved. The effect of the urban, middle-class exodus to the countryside has not been entirely a detrimental one, even for the locals. A comparison between a "commuter village" and one which has suffered the ravages of rural depopulation unhindered by the arrival of newcomers soon shows this. Changes in the village have not so much been caused by newcomers moving in, as by the fact that the underlying economic base can no longer support the old occupational community. The disruptions caused by newcomers have been merely a tangible symptom of this change.

Nevertheless at the ideological level the impact of the newcomers has been considerable. Over a wide variety of literally parochial conflicts they have created new social cleavages and prompted rural employers and employees to unite against a "common enemy." They have allowed the vertical ties between farmers and farm workers to become consolidated, drawn much of the class antagonism arising out of poor pay and conditions away from employers and towards themselves, and enabled a pervasive nostalgia for the "good old days' when the village was a "real community" to be substituted for a more realistic assessment of the causes of contemporary rural deprivation. (Compare farm workers' and farmers' images of society in Newby et al., 1978: 309-313.) Thus 92 per cent of the farm workers that I interviewed in Suffolk believed that they had more in common with farmers than with other members of the working class, even though a majority of farm workers were quite willing to identify themselves as "working class." The proportion of farmers who reciprocated in this view, though lower, was still a majority, varying between 53 and 74 per cent according to the sample from which they were drawn (see Ibid.: 314-315).

This, then, has been one major effect of the urbanisation of the countryside in East Anglia. Since I was centrally concerned with the problem of ideology it was on this aspect that I concentrated in The Deferential Worker, and for that reason only a cursory reminder of the main outlines of the analysis presented there has been given here. However, to concentrate attention upon the disruptive social effects of the newcomers alone does tend to divert attention from other agents of social change which have been responsible for the urbanisation of rural England. In addition it tends to obscure the workings of the various economic and political mechanisms which are responsible for the allocation of life-chances in the countryside and where the participants might be divided along altogether different lines to those of "locals" and "newcomers." It is to these more material factors, where the urbanisation of the countryside might be considered part cause but also part effect, that I want to devote the remainder of this paper. This requires almost beginning the analysis of social change in rural England again, but this time from a rather different perspective. In order to understand why the urbanisation of the countryside has taken place at all, it is necessary to begin with an examination of the rural, and particularly the agricultural, economy. This is not to argue that the many changes which have occurred in rural life in recent years can only be considered in economic terms, for this is patently not true. The urban, middle-class exodus to the countryside would not have occurred without certain culturally-induced assumptions about the wholesome authenticity of rural life. But equally the newcomers could not have been accommodated without an exodus of the rural working population in the opposite direction, an exodus provoked by the continuous substitution of capital for labour in the system of agricultural production. Therefore it is still necessary to regard the production of food (together with associated manufacturing, processing and service (activity) as being responsible, either directly or indirectly, for most of the observed changes in English rural society. Consequently it has been possible to discern a unity in the general direction of rural social change, even though there have been considerable variations in timing and extent from locality to locality. It is to be a consideration of these underlying economic trends that we can now turn.

The Reconstruction of Rural England: The Role of the State

The economic conditions of the agriculture industry today are in complete contrast to those which predominated in the 1920s and 1930s when thousands of acres of productive land lay unfarmed and degenerated into wasteland, when fences were pulled down to be used as firewood and when thousands of farm workers were either unemployed or suffering from falling wages. Since the Second World War, however, whatever the short-term fluctuations, the state has implemented the urban demand for cheap (by historical standards) and plentiful food, while simultaneously offering the farmer the guarantee of stability and, for the "efficient" (i.e., low-cost) producer, profitability. The state has also acted as midwife for what has become known as the second agricultural revolution--the transformation of the technology of food production and the many social changes which have flowed from this. Farmers have been granted the conditions under which they would embark upon a programme of increasing productivity and cost-efficiency which has been unmatched virtually anywhere in the world. The agricultural sector has plummeted to a mere 2.8 percent of the population, while farm productivity has increased fourfold since before the war. Farms have become fewer, larger and more specialized and farming has been transformed from a dignified and arcadian "way of life" to a highly rationalised business. (For some excellent descriptions of this process see Self and Storing, 1962; Donaldson and Donaldson, 1972; Edwards and Rogers, 1974; Beresford, 1975.)

Agricultural policy has been entirely single-minded in its aims: the production of more and cheaper food. It has not concerned itself with the social implications of the drive towards "agribusiness," except as a twinge of concern over the plight of the uplands. In general, however, there is a quite startling contrast between the undoubted success of this policy in terms of its stated goals in successive White Papers (the expansion of home production, the increase in cost-efficiency, the maintenance of a prosperous agriculture) and its mostly deleterious social effects on the countryside in either depopulating rural areas at an even faster rate than hitherto or polarising them socially between the expanding large producers and the marginalised smaller ones, between both of these and rural workers.suffering inadequate service provision and, indirectly, between the local poor and affluent newcomers. These social effects have rarely been monitored, let alone built into the policy calculations of the Ministry of Agriculture, where the assumption that what is good for farmers must be good for the rural population as a whole has been perpetuated by a mixture of "bureaucratic and commercial vested interest, self-justification and reluctant necessity," as Josling (1974: 231) has put it. In the face of a good deal of evidence to the contrary, it has taken three decades for this assumption to be questioned--and even now it remains a central tenet of faith. Thus, although the Ministry has recently appointed "socio-economic advisers" with a permit to consider the wider social implications of agricultural change, it has done so only as an obligation under EEC policy. Perhaps a charitable view of their

role would be to regard them as the "do-gooders" of ADAS, the Ministry's
advisory service--tolerated, but ignored when the tough decisions have
to be made. In the early days, at least, most were ex-ADAS advisers sent
out to grass, already steeped in the Ministry's conventional wisdom and
at something of a loss over what their function should be. They therefore tend to accept the view that the vitality of English rural society
can be measured by the prosperity of English farmers.

Since farmers comprise a varying but significant proportion of the
rural population there is, of course, a grain of truth in this proposition.
But by no means have all sections of the rural population benefitted
equally from post-war agricultural policy, and some have been relatively
disadvantaged. The small farmer might therefore beg to differ from the
conventional view--and so might the farm worker and his wife, the environmentalist, the unemployed rural school-leaver and even the young
couple on the waiting list for a rural council house. It is possible to
trace a chain of events from the political economy of modern agriculture
to the problems encountered by each of these groups, yet the formulation
of agricultural policy has mostly ignored the possible external consequences and at best been indifferent to them. To a large extent this has
been the result of a division of labour within the civil service which has
allowed the Ministry of Agriculture to respond to a clear and unambiguous
demand to reduce the cost of food production, while other departments, both
nationally and locally, have been left to mop up the social consequences.
Moreover, the urban majority of the population has shown little interest
in rural change except in its most visual aspects--tractors and combine
harvesters replacing horses, the disappearance of hedgerows, etc.--as
long as food has remained cheap. They, too, have remained largely indifferent to the social problems of rural areas, particularly as their
perception has often been clouded by misplaced sentiment. As long as
agricultural policy was, literally, delivering the goods, what was happening to the fabric of life in the countryside could be complacently overlooked.

As far as the formulation of agricultural policy in the immediate
post-war period was concerned, it is doubtful whether any serious consideration was ever given to its possible social implications in the
countryside, for all its encouragement of rapid technological change.
This was because of its essentially retrospective foundations, built upon
the contrasting experiences of agricultural depression during the interwar years and the need to maximise food production at almost any cost
during the Second World War. The invocation of one or the other could
always be relied upon to silence any critic, whether from within the
farming industry or outside. The affluence of succeeding decades also
ensured that the cost of agricultural support never intruded into the
consciousness of the taxpayer and was therefore not too closely examined.
Even when the result was chronic over-production or the "feather-bedding"
of "barley barons," the consumer generally benefitted from lower prices

and the proportion of public expenditure devoted to agriculture was so small that the extra revenue required was hardly noticed.   During the 1970s, however, the political climate surrounding agriculture has changed quite dramatically.   Entry into the EEC has switched the burden of agricultural support from the taxpayer to the consumer and this, together with the general inflation in the British economy during this decade, has ensured that the cost of food production has become once more a hot political issue. Now that the cost of over-production is borne directly by the consumer, resentment has grown over the support of "inefficient" farmers, whether at home, or, more often, in Europe.   The purely defensive aspects of agricultural policy have come under increasing political pressure with the main emphasis of recent debate having concerned the need to protect consumers rather than producers.   This has undoubtedly strengthened the political hand of the large-scale producers still further, even though they already benefit disproportionately of state support, for they can point to their greater cost-efficiency and potential for expansion by virtue of further hefty injections of capital investment.   Such a political reaction to inflation, however, continues to be discussed with little or no consideration of what the future of English rural society will look like as a result.

Within the rural population it is not too difficult to discern which groups have been the greatest beneficiaries of post-war agricultural policy.   The promotion of "efficiency" has been of enormous benefit to the large-scale producers, who have swallowed the lion's share of agricultural subsidies (see Donaldson and Donaldson, 1972).   The massive programme of capitalisation has also allowed a "knock-on" effect to benefit large sections of the agricultural engineering and agro-chemical industries and even the construction industry.   Farm workers, on the other hand, have received little relative improvement (see Newby, 1977: Ch. 3). It is also now accepted by agricultural economists that one of the major beneficiaries has been landowners (who now, of course, include a majority of farmers).   As Josling has pointed out in a review of agricultural policies in developed countries:

> The predominant conclusion is that land, as the input
> least elastic in supply, gains the most in per unit re-
> turns, and hence in the asset price of the stock from
> which land services are obtained. Though this may not
> hold for individual farm programmes, and may be modified
> over time by the availability of land-saving technology,
> the impact of these conclusions has now been incorporated
> into the conventional wisdom of farm politics (Josling,
> 1974: 247).

In other words, sustained intervention in agriculture has not only guaranteed the incomes of "efficient" producers, but has enhanced the investment value of agricultural land--precisely the factor which has recently prompted the renewed interest of the City institutions.   Certainly

the inflation in land prices, which has consistently outstripped the
general rate of inflation since the war, has enormously increased the
wealth of the agricultural landowner (see Newby et al., 1978: Ch. 3).
It is apparent that agricultural policy in this country has not been very
concerned with distributive justice.

While agricultural policy was helping to transform rural England
from within, a quite different set of land-use policies were, ironically,
derived to protect and preserve it from the external threat of urban encroachment. It was the aim of town and country planning to preserve
the quality of rural life in the post-war period, just as agricultural
policy was to provide it with a strong economic basis. In theory the
system created by the 1947 Town and Country Planning Act involved a
radical reform of the laissez-faire approach to land use in the countryside. The underlying political aims were liberal and progressive, containing a strong element of planning for the least fortunate, whereas in
practice the system created seems to have almost systematically had
the reverse effect. (See the assessment by Hall et al., 1973.) There
have been a number of reasons for this. The first concerns the essentially negative and protective nature of most rural planning. The traditional English reverence for the rural way of life has ensured that
precisely what it was that was being preserved has never been examined
too closely. There has been a fallacious belief that the "traditional
rural way of life" was beneficial to all rural inhabitants, an influential
but unexamined assumption that was a product of an unholy alliance between
the farmers and landowners who politically controlled rural England and
the radical middle-class reformers who formulated the post-war legislation.
Consequently agriculture was given a prior claim over both land use and
labour in rural areas and was exempted from most aspects of development
control. The aim of agricultural policy to promote an efficient agriculture became translated in land-use planning terms into the desire to
promote a ubiquitous agriculture, irrespective of the ensuing distribution
of costs and benefits. Restricting the location of industry in rural areas
in the wake of such policies would depress rural wage levels, increase the
outward migration of the agricultural population, and hinder the viability
of rural services.

By the late 1960s, many rural planners were becoming acutely aware
of these weaknesses. One leading County Planning Officer, Ray Green,
even went so far as to argue that "the ... years since the Town and Country
Planning Act of 1947 represent two decades of wasted opportunity for
positive rural planning (Green, 1971: 1)." Some attempt was made to
remedy this situation in the Town and Country Planning Act of 1968.
This Act introduced a system of structure plans which covered not only
land-use but population change, employment, transport, and housing.
In rural areas they were to aim at implementing positive resource development rather than reflect the former predominantly negative planning
policies. There was also less emphasis on the production of maps and a
move towards surveys of relevant social and economic inputs (until

curtailed by public expenditure in 1974). The structure plan system also offered a means of transcending the divide between urban and rural areas, although this did not become a possibility until after the re-organisation of local government in 1973/4. However, there has been a considerable gap between the evidence uncovered by the structure-plan surveys and the actual policies which have eventually emerged. In 1976, for example, the Countryside Commission was moved to comment in its Annual Report that "the content of structure plans in general does not convince us that the potential of the new development plans system for tackling rural problems has been realised." The reasons for this, as we shall see, have lain not so much in the outlook of the rural planners themselves, but in the balance of political forces which underlie the planning process on the county and district councils.

Since 1947, then, the presumption that the countryside should be preserved, almost exclusively, for agriculture has ensured that the major source of employment in rural areas should be the farming industry. Yet the number of employment opportunities in agriculture has, as we have seen, declined rapidly since the war--a fact which has been written in quite explicitly to state agricultural policy. By directing new industrial development away from rural areas, conventional strategic planning policy has had two important consequences: it has restricted the rate of economic growth in the countryside; and it has weakened the bargaining power of existing rural workers by reducing the number of competitors for local labour. Strategic planning has therefore contained a strong element of planning for the interests of the better-off. Rural employers have clearly gained from the preservation of a low-wage rural economy--indeed, in some areas it has been given indirect encouragement. The ex-urban newcomers, who have arrived to fill the gap left by departing rural workers looking for employment and higher wages in the towns, now fight hard to keep the countryside devoid of any taint of industrial development,thus preserving their "village in the mind" (Pahl, 1965) and as a by-product enjoying the opportunity of calling upon a pool of local cheap labour to perform the standard upper middle-class range of domestic services. On the other hand farm workers, for example, have been trapped in a low-paying industry with declining employment opportunities and with increasing dependence upon tied housing. A policy of preserving the rural status quo has thus turned out to be redistributive--and in a highly regressive manner. Occasionally rural planners have become aware of these tendencies, but the political will has been lacking to bring about a change in policy. For example, in 1975 the report of the East Anglian Regional Strategy Planning Team placed considerable emphasis on the need to attract more industry into the area so that local wage levels would be raised:

> Away from the major centres, poor job prospects cause
> considerable local concern. Opportunities are limited
> to agricultural employment and incomes tend to be low
> ... There should be opportunities for individuals to

to increase their incomes and widen their interests
through a better choice of jobs and training opportunities.

The report met with considerable opposition from the region's county
councils and was later quietly shelved by the Department of the Environment, which had publicly disagreed with many of its conclusions.

Agricultural policy and planning policy were intended to provide a
framework whereby rural England could be reconstructed from the ravages
visited upon it during the Depression. (They were not, of course, the
only such policies, but the ones which I have chosen to concentrate on
in this paper due to lack of space.) In many respects these policies
have been extraordinarily successful, as any comparison between the
situation now and that which prevailed in the 1930s will easily demonstrate.
However, this highly abbreviated and generalised account has attempted
to highlight some of the less obvious and less publicly discussed aspects
of these policies. First, it is apparent that agricultural policy and
planning policy have not only been institutionally separated, but have
worked against each other. While the MAFF has been promoting widespread
technological change and the consequent diminution of the agricultural
population, rural planning has been overwhelmingly preservationist in
sentiment. The inevitable collision between these policies is currently
being fought out over landscape and environmental issues. Secondly, both
sets of policies have tended to be socially regressive insofar as they
have affected the rural population. Thirdly they have enabled the
changing social composition of rural society to proceed virtually unhindered and without much thought for the consequences for the rump of
the old rural working population. They have become a residual population,
the flotsam of agricultural change, left stranded in the countryside and
finding their needs being consistently overlooked now that they are in
a minority. To appreciate fully the extent of these changes it is necessary to see how these policies have been implemented at the local level.
The state has provided a framework for guiding rural social change--but
only a framework. Many of the consequences of the urbanisation of
the countryside are a result of local political pressures and the routine
application of local political power.

The Local Response

The implementation of state agricultural policy has been left, for
the most part, in the hands of individual private landowners and farmers.
Planning policy at the local level has, however, been formally under the
aegis of elected councillors, advised by their professional officers.
Although apparently separated institutionally (as they still remain
nationally), these policies often come to coincide due to the traditional
domination of local government in rural areas by farmers (for data,
see Moss and Parker, 1967). Although the balance of political forces

has varied from place to place and is changing over time, in general the
political power in rural areas remains firmly in the hands of the most
prosperous residents. In a few countries this has involved the continuation of the old squirarchical rule of farmers and landowners, although
their omnipotence has clearly been declining. Elsewhere they have been
displaced in local government by professional and managerial middle-
class newcomers, who at least appear to threaten the old hegemony. However, the evidence from our study of local political power in Suffolk
(Newby et al., 1978: Ch. 6) suggests that appearances are deceptive. In
terms of policies if not personnel, there is a remarkable continuity.
The newcomers fully support the preservationist stance of strategic
planning policy with regard to the countryside. They have no desire to
admit industrial, or even housing, development which in some cases is
the very thing from which they have sought to escape by moving into a
rural area. Indeed their zealous advocacy of the status quo frequently
brings them into conflict with farmers over the environmental effects of
modern farming practice. Similarly, as major ratepayers (agricultural
land is exempt) they wholeheartedly endorse the extremely conservative
budgetary policies advocated by farmers and landowners which is the main
plank of the latter's political policy at the local level. Both groups
are therefore profoundly preservationist in their policies and have
maintained a strong accord over the desire to exclude as far as possible
virtually any significant industrial or residential development from the
countryside, whether for agricultural or environmental reasons. This
policy has therefore triumphed, despite the changes which have occurred
in the personnel of county council planning committees. It is not
therefore coincidental that many of the set-piece rural planning conflicts
have concerned the impact of nationally-taken decisions upon particular
rural localities (Stanstead, Cublington, Drumbuie, etc.), for this is
often the only occasion on which the routine of rural planning policy
is disturbed. On other occasions the alliance of landowners and affluent
newcomers on many county councils continues the everyday routine of
directing development proposals away from the countryside.

It would be possible to pursue the effects of these policies
across the whole range of resources called upon by the rural popula-
tion--employment, education, health services, welfare, and so on. However, because of restrictions on space in a paper of this kind I shall
concentrate on only one: housing. As an illustrative case of the impact
of newcomers on the local population, housing is an apposite example.
Not only is it an intrinsically crucial resource, but it is one for
which the entire rural population--locals and newcomers, farmers and
farm workers, agricultural and non-agricultural families--are competing.
(The same cannot be said of, for example, employment.) It therefore
vividly exemplifies the impact of the newcomers at the level of the
distribution of material resources. In addition, the system of housing
allocation acts as an intermediary between the economic changes in agriculture and the structure of rural society by its effect on influencing
who lives where. To this extent housing in the countryside has always
been used as a form of social control (see Newby, 1977: Ch. 3).

During the nineteenth century, housing in rural areas was kept in chronic short supply by the fear that their occupants might become a burden on the poor rate. In the twentieth century this shortage has remained while many of the principles which underlie the problem have merely reasserted themselves within a new institutional framework. Until the newcomers arrived in the countryside, for example, the domination of rural areas by farmers and landowners, both as employers and as local councillors, ensured that they were effectively the landlords of the housing stock within reach of most workers--council housing, privately-rented houses and tied cottages. Their desire to keep the rates down made them reluctant to build council houses. Farm workers could instead be housed in tied cottages, which had other advantages in addition to providing suitable accommodation, not least of which concerned the reinforcement of ties of dependency. Tied cottages also depressed farm wages, making farm workers unable to afford council house rents. Thus, the rents could not be lowered without raising the rates, while farmers were not going to voluntarily raise wages just so that their workers could afford to live in council houses. Consequently, whether as ratepayers or as employers, the farmers who ran the majority of rural councils found it expedient to construct as few council houses as possible. These tendencies have remained unaltered by the arrival of the newcomers--in fact, in other ways their impact upon rural housing has been little short of calamitous. By 1974, on the eve of local government reorganisation (and the disappearance of separate housing statistics for rural areas), rural district councils provided only 20 per cent of the rural housing stock, compared with 31 per cent provided by local authorities elsewhere. Farm workers were thus becoming increasingly dependent upon tied cottages (up from 32 per cent to 54 per cent since the war) while they and other rural workers were faced by a declining pool of privately-rented houses in rural areas, following the effects of successive Rent Acts and their lucrative sale to affluent newcomers. In view of the history of rural housing it was therefore somewhat ironic to find in 1976 that changes in tied cottage legislation were being opposed by the farmers' lobby on the grounds that there were insufficient safeguards against local authorities refusing to meet their housing responsibilities.

Since the Second World War, however, the political control of rural councils has not been the only factor influencing the rate of rural house-building. A salient feature of this period has also been the incorporation of a specifically rural housing problem into the general problem of the nation's housing, coupled with increasing central government intervention in, and control of, rural housing provision (see Rawson and Rogers, 1976). Rural councils have obviously found themselves hamstrung by expenditure cuts and the imposition of cost yardsticks which rarely take account of the peculiar difficulties of remote rural districts. This has also been accompanied by a change in emphasis in housing policy. Between the wars the aim of housing legislation was to stimulate the construction of as many houses as possible in rural areas;

but since 1947 the aim has been to control the number of houses in rural
areas as part of overall planning policies designed to contain the growth
of urban sprawl, prevent the loss of good agricultural land and protect
the visual quality of the countryside. Far from encouraging local
authorities and private developers to build more rural houses, as in the
1930s, there has been active discouragement, involving the imposition of
strict planning controls, particularly over housing in open countryside
and in other sensitive areas such as Green Belts and Areas of Outstanding
Natural Beauty. The increasing affluence of the rural population wrought
by the urban middle-class exodus has tended to mask the continuing and
severe pockets of poverty which exist in the countryside and have led the
"problem" of rural housing to be regarded less as a problem of social
welfare and more as an issue concerning land-use planning and countryside
preservation.

Thus since the 1947 Act, the granting of planning permission for
rural housing has arguably been concerned more with the visual quality
of the countryside than with alleviating problems of housing need among
the rural population. By placing strict control on rural housing development these policies have also brought about a planned scarcity of housing, which, in the face of increasing demand from newcomers, has made a
rural house a desirable good with a premium price. Until the early
1960s, the effects of rural depopulation, the delapidation of much rural
property and the cost of travel to urban centres all contributed to the
lower price of rural housing compared with urban areas. But as the
surplus rural housing was gradually soaked up by commuters and second-
home owners, and as housing which had once been a damning indictment
of years of neglect and deprivation was restored and renovated, so
relative scarcity began to increase prices about those prevailing for
comparable suburban and even urban housing. The pressure on rural development has thus become more intense. Between 1961 and 1971, the
population census recorded an increase of 1,700,000 in the rural population, and although some of this was accounted for by contiguous urban
development spilling over the boundaries of surrounding Rural Districts,
there is little doubt that the population pressures on most of rural
England are now those of increasing demand rather than those resulting
from rural depopulation. The preferred solution to this has not been
to build even more houses to relieve the upward pressure on rents and
prices, but to impose even more stringent controls--conservation areas,
village "envelopes," and so on. As prices inexorably rise, so the
population which actually achieves its goal of a house in the country
becomes more socially selective.

Planning controls on rural housing have therefore become--in
effect, if not in intent--instruments of social exclusivity, although
this often depends upon implementation as much as on the principles
cushioned in the legislation. For example, the insistence upon the
use of certain building materials, the standards of design and external finish and the density of housing development reflect the

traditional concern of planning authorities with how a house or a
village looks rather than who will actually live in it. Housing which
is not "detrimental to the character of the village" frequently means,
in effect, high-cost, low-density architect-designed houses for the
upper-middle class. As the environmental lobby has emerged as an influential force in the formulation of rural development control policies,
so the dilemma between the requirements of maintaining an attractive
village landscape and the provision of rural housing for those in need
becomes more acute. This dilemma has been sharpened by the fact that
many village newcomers are not only in the vanguard of the environmental
lobby but are quite explicitly socially exclusive in their preferences:
having made it to their restic redoubt, they wish to pull up the draw-
bridge behind them to keep out the madding crowd on the council house
waiting lists. They often oppose <u>any</u> new housing development, private
or public, and, given that snobbery is rarely far from the surface of
their judgements, are particularly opposed to the construction of new
local authority estates in the countryside. In this case the rhetoric
of environmentalism and the pursuit of social exclusivity coincide.

Although there has been some awareness on the part of rural planners
that these policies are exaggerating the scarcity of rural housing and
achieving comparatively little for those in greatest need, there is not
the political will in most areas to remedy the situation. Here the role
of the newcomers has been decisive. As the main representatives of the
environmental lobby in the countryside, they have pushed the implementation of development control more in the direction of increased restric-
tion rather than greater flexibility. Housing policies thus continue to
be concerned with visual quality rather than with the needs of the people
who inhabit rural areas. As Rawson and Rogers conclude in their review
of recent policies:

> The general restriction of planning methods for rural
> housing to development control and a concern with the
> fabric of the built countryside pervades the whole atti-
> tude of structure planning to rural housing, not just
> policies. Only rarely do plans consider more than the
> simple spatial attributes of the housing stock. Housing
> quality is examined usually by area rather than by
> social group and there is little information on different
> income groups in the countryside and their needs and de-
> mands for housing. This is surprising when one remembers
> the importance frequently given to local housing need
> which can only be satisfactorily defined in relation to
> an understanding of social groups and information on
> incomes.

> It follows that policies for rural housing do not con-
> sider the social implications which might result from
> their implementation. There is, for example, little or

no discussion on the possible distributional effects
on different social groups of conservation policies
regarding rural housing nor of the economic and
social implications for rural housing of key settlement strategies (Rawson and Rogers, 1976: 17).

Current housing policies seem to be producing a polarisation of the
rural population. While the demands of the rich and the affluent can be
met within the framework of current housing policies, the needs of the
poor increasingly cannot. During the 1970s the provision of rural housing for those who cannot partake in the inflated market sector has been
pitiful. Between 1967 and 1973, the number of council houses built
annually in rural areas was almost cut in half, from 35,000 to 18,000,
while private-sector housing held steady at just over 70,000. Since 1973,
with the switch of housing resources--and, equally significantly, rate-
support grants--to the inner-city areas, conditions have hardly improved.
The result is that once those who are unable to purchase, or eschew the
tied cottage, have negotiated their way through the labyrinthine and
highly variable eligibility rules to achieve a place on a council housing
waiting list, they join a queue which is currently growing at a faster
rate than additions to the council housing stock and which in some cases
even exceeds the total number of families housed by the District Council
(for East Anglian evidence, see Newby et al., 1978: Ch. 6).

The case of housing illustrates well one of the major processes
which has accompanied the urbanisation of the countryside--its social
polarisation. Hitherto this polarisation has been portrayed in terms of
"locals" and "newcomers" and at the level of ideology this is undoubtedly
accurace. However, at the level of access to material resources and the
distribution of life chances, the polarisation occurs between an affluent
majority (of both newcomers and local farmers and landowners) and a poorer
and relatively deprived minority. The cross-cutting nature of these
cleavages draws the resentment of the deprived minority towards the newcomers. While the newcomers have provoked a gut reaction to the sense of
having been taken over by affluent and alien strangers, focussing attention on them alone diverts attention from the fact that rural housing
is not only a matter of (increasing) demand, but of supply and need. Here
the antagonism towards newcomers as a tangible manifestation of the rural
housing problem (for example, over second-home ownership) allows the role
of local farmers and landowners in implementing these policies to go
almost unnoticed.

Polarisation and Democratic Dilemmas

The social polarisation of the countryside has been a slow but inexorable process since the end of the Second World War. Within agriculture the large-scale landowner and farmer have generally benefitted
at the expense of the small-marginal producer and the farm worker. At
the same time a stark contrast has arisen in most villages between a

comparatively affluent, immigrant, ex-urban middle class and the remnants of the former agricultural population tied to the locality by their (low-paid) employment, by old age and by lack of resources to undertake a move. The former group lives in the countryside mostly by conscious choice (and this includes the majority of farmers and landowners) and has the resources to overcome the problems of distance and access to essential services. The latter group, by contrast, has become increasingly trapped by lack of access to alternative employment, housing and the full range of amenities which the remainder of the population takes for granted. While there can be little doubt that the material conditions of the rural poor, the elderly, the disabled and other deprived groups have undergone a considerable improvement in absolute terms since the war (in the sense that they are better fed, better housed, better clothed, and better educated), in relative terms they have encountered little improvement and in many cases in recent years an alarming deterioration. Their poverty is often submerged--socially, and even literally, invisible--and there is a danger that, as rural England increasingly becomes middle-class England, their plight will be ignored and their needs overlooked.

This polarisation process can be observed not only in areas like housing and employment, but across the whole range of social services, especially health services, and even the provision of apparently mundane amenities from shop to sewerage. The affluent sections of the rural population can, of course, overcome any problems which may arise by stepping into their cars and driving to the nearest town, whereas the poor, the elderly and the disabled are particularly vulnerable to any decrease in the level of local public and private services in rural areas, and especially public transport. It therefore makes little sense any longer (if it ever did) to contrast the backwardness of rural amenities compared with those in the towns, for the major divisions lie within the rural population between those in need and suffering multiple social deprivation and those who have benefitted from living in the countryside in recent years and for whom access to a full range of services and amenities does not present a problem. Numerically it is the latter group which has consistently been in the ascendancy over the last thirty years and who have achieved a firm grasp on the levers of local political power. As a result, the deprived section has found it increasingly difficult to obtain recognition of its requirements, let alone feel capable of diverting a larger proportion of resources in its direction. The economics of public service provision have suffered from the self-reliance of the newcomers, who, as ratepayers, have demonstrated an understandable reluctance to foot the rapidly-rising bill on behalf of their less fortunate neighbours. All too often this is the political reality (and it seems unlikely to change) which underlies the neglect of housing, public transport and the whole range of social, health, and welfare services in rural areas.

During a period of general stringency in public expenditure, the pressure to preserve only those services which "pay"--that is, are

self-supporting--has become increasingly strong. Ayton has examined the
implications of these policies for the rural population in Norfolk:

> The opportunities for change in the rural situation
> are constrained and influenced by the existing physi-
> cal infractructure, in terms of settlement pattern,
> systems of public utilities and communications net-
> works, and the resources available for modifying it.
> While it is difficult to anticipate the level of
> financial resources that will be available, it is
> clear that they will, for some time, be limited, and
> planning policies must be framed within the content
> of what is feasible, or reasonably likely. Those
> services which are financed from the rates (e.g.,
> education, highways, sewerage, water) will be much
> more of a constraint than those which are "self-
> supporting" and budgetted nationally (e.g., elec-
> tricity, gas, telephones). Investment choices must
> be made in those sectors which can influence policy-
> making in a more restrictive and specific way than
> the general aim of minimising public expenditure
> (Ayton, 1976: 62).

This is an interesting comment, albeit presented with a public servant's
tact, on local decision-making in a county which is by no means atypical
(in its political complexion) for a rural area. What, one wonders, would
have happened to rural electrification had it been left in the hands of
local ratepayers? Be that as it may, Ayton goes on to discuss the policy
options within these constraints and their impact upon individuals and
local communities. For the relatively deprived section of the rural
population it provides a depressing, though instructive, glimpse of what
occurs when their needs are discounted in favour of lower rates. In
order to place Ayton's data in some perspective, it is important to
realise that 66 per cent of Norfolk villages are below 500 in population
and 44 per cent below 300, while at the other extreme only 11 per cent
are over 1,000. As Ayton points out:

> It is the small size of average village that is
> critical in terms of the services and facilities
> that can be expected in each one. Studies carried
> out by the Planning Department of Norfolk County
> Council have identified critical thresholds related
> to various services. For example, at the 300-500
> population level, it is estimated that the village
> can support a shop, a pub and a school with between
> 30 and 50 pupils. But a primary school with 100
> pupils, a fairly economic level, requires a support
> population of 1,000, while a "middle" school of
> 240 pupils requires a population of 4,000. Each

> doctor has to have at least 2,000 patients and so a
> practice of three doctors needs a support population
> of about 6,000. A regular surgery seems viable only
> where a village population exceeds 1,800. A district
> nurse is provided for 3,000 population and chemists
> are provided on the basis of a 4,000 to 4,500 popula-
> tion catchment (Ibid: 65).

In a rural county like Norfolk this places the location of many of
these services at some considerable distance, and therefore cost, from
many of those who need them. Although Ayton is simply bowing to economic
realities here, it is worth pointing out that, in the case of public
services, these "realities" are in principle (though, one suspects, increasingly rarely in practice) politically negotiable. Within the context
of existing rural politics, however, Ayton's conclusions are inevitable:
to concentrate service provision in the largest villages, "backed by
programmes to maintain reasonable social services in settlements not
selected (e.g., mobile libraries, health visitors, meals-on-wheels, and
public transport)" (Ibid.: 67). The individual must make an informed
choice between "a small village [and] direct access to services--he cannot get both together" (Ibid.).

To the affluent rural ratepayer, whose opinions carry considerable
weight in County Hall, this seems an entirely rational solution. Not
only is the cost of service provision held down or even reduced, but by
taking advantage of economies of scale it may even be possible to avoid
needless under-utilisation and improve the range of services offered.
The reality for the deprived is, however, rather different--the two-mile
trudge down the muddy lane for the farm worker's wife to catch the Monday
and Thursdays only (except Bank Holidays) under-threat-of-closure bus; the
elderly trapped in their isolated cottages; the Post Office two miles
away; the hospital twenty miles distant. The poor and the elderly have
not "chosen" to live in their villages in any meaningful sense; they
have been stranded there by three decades of rural social change and by
growing public indifference to their plight. They lack the resources to
convert their needs into demands, yet it is to demand rather than need
that most rural public services respond. While the level of rates remains
sacrosanct they have no voice in the decision-making process, form no
lobbies or pressure groups, but quietly grumble or complain and somehow
struggle on. Meanwhile the level of rural services has slowly but irreversibly declined.

It is easy to overlook these problems amidst the restored cottages
and the two-car homes which now pervade the English village. The other
face of rural England is more difficult to seek out since it is now less
openly admitted. At least in the past when rural poverty was the norm,
the experience of deprivation was one that could be shared by the majority
of the village population. But now poverty brings with it a sense of
exclusion rather than mutuality. The urbanisation of the countryside has

enabled a life-style that was once only distantly and fleetingly observed to be encountered at first hand among the new inhabitants. The
rural poor find, somewhat disconcertingly, that they and their needs are
increasingly regarded as residual--or even unacknowledged. Publicly-
debated issues have moved on to problems in which they are denied the
luxury of participating. They find that more attention seems to be given
to the visual appearance of the countryside than to the standard of living of those who are employed in maintaining it; that greater concern is
expressed over the effects of pesticides on butterflies than on farm
workers. Their new minority status hardly lends itself to making a fuss,
however, nor to the expectation that they can achieve any tangible change
if they attempted to do so. Consequently their inclination is to "make
do," while the general public is given little reason to alter its image
of a cosy and contented countryside.

Conclusion

The major effect of urbanisation in the countryside has therefore
been to transform rural England into a predominantly middle-class territory. The policies which systematically disadvantage the rural poor
can now, therefore, be assured of local democratic support. This suggests that any striking improvement in the relative living standard of
the rural poor will in the future--as in the past--be brought about by
changes initiated nationally rather than locally, through the trickling
down into rural areas of reforms and innovations introduced on a uni-
versalistic basis. While there is a paradox in the growing polarisation
of rural society being accompanied by the increasing identification between
farmers and farm workers, in many respects the newcomers have provided
the wherewithal for both of these processes. Estranged from the alien
newcomers, farm workers have increasingly recognised a common identity
with farmers as fellow "locals." However, the farm workers, together
with others among the deprived rural population, is often entirely unaware that, miles away in the council chamber, representatives of both
the farmers' and the newcomers' interests are busy agreeing upon
political policies which are to their detriment, Plus ça change ...

References

Ambrose, Peter
    1974 The Quiet Revolution (London: Chatto and Windus for Sussex
    University Press).

Ayton, John
    1976 "Rural settlement policy: problems and conflicts," in P.J.
    Drudy (ed.), Regional and Rural Development: Essays in Theory and
    Practice (Chalfont St. Giles: Alpha Academic), pp. 59-68.

Beresford, Tristram
  1975 We Plough the Fields (Harmondsworth: Penguin Books).

Connell, J.
  1974 "The metropolitan village: spatial and social processes in
  discontinuous suburbs," in J.H. Johnson (ed.), The Geography of
  Suburban Growth (London: Wiley).

Crichton, R.
  1964 Commuter Village (Newton Abbot: David and Charles).

Donaldson, J.G.S. and F. Donaldson
  1972 Farming in Britain Today (Harmondsworth: Penguin Books).

Edwards, A. and A. Rogers (eds.)
  1974 Agricultural Resources (London: Faber).

Frankenberg, Ronald
  1966 Communities in Britain (Harmondsworth: Penguin Books).

Green, R.J.
  1971 Country Planning (Manchester: Manchester University Press).

Groves, Reg
  1949 Sharpen the Sickle (Windsor: Porcupine Press).

Hall, Peter et al.
  1973 The Containment of Urban England (London: Allen and Unwin).

Harris, Clement
  1974 Hennage: A Social Structure in Miniature (New York: Holt,
  Rinehart and Winston).

Hobsbawm, E.J. and G. Rude
  1973 Captain Swing (London: Lawrence and Wishart).

Josling, T.E.
  1974 "Agricultural policies in developed countries: an overview,"
  Journal of Agricultural Economics 25 (1): 229-263.

Moss, L. and S. Parker

  1967 The Local Government Councillor (London: HMSO).

Newby, Howard
  1972 "The low earnings of agricultural workers: A sociological
  approach," Journal of Agricultural Economics 23 (1): 15-24.

Newby, Howard
    1977   The Deferential Worker (London: Allen Lane).

Newby, Howard, Colin Bell, David Rose, and Peter Saunders
    1978   Property, Paternalism and Power (London: Hutchinson).

Pahl, R.E.
    1965   Urbs in Rure (London: Weidenfeld and Nicholson).

Pahl, R.E.
    1970   Whose City? (London: Longman).

Rawson, Marilyn and Alan Rogers
    1976   Rural Housing and Structure Plans (London University: Wye
    College, CPU Occasional Paper).

Self, P. and H. Storing
    1962   The State and the Farmer (London: Allan and Unwin).

Thorns, D.
    1968   "The changing system of rural stratification," Sociologia
    Ruralis, Vol. VIII (2): 161-178.

Williams, Raymond
    1973   The Country and the City (London: Chatto and Windus).

Part III

THE STATE AND AGRICULTURE IN THE ADVANCED SOCIETIES

10. State and Agriculture in Two Eras of American Capitalism

SUSAN A. MANN and JAMES A. DICKINSON

I. INTRODUCTION

In this chapter, we consider historical and analytical aspects of the relationship between agriculture and the state with particular reference to the advanced capitalist countries. The discussion will primarily focus upon American agriculture and U.S. federal government policies. Our object is to cast an understanding of the state and agriculture, as well as the relationship between them, in terms of the determinate characteristics of capitalist production.

This paper has several parts. First, we examine some of the special characteristics of agricultural commodity production and the state as they appear under capitalism; the theoretical and analytical distinctions established here set the framework for the rest of our analysis. Then we move to an examination of the relationship between state and agriculture in two different eras of American history: the era of U.S. internal settler colonialism and the era of monopoly capitalism and imperialism. For the first era, we examine the part played by particular forms of agricultural production in the territorial consolidation of the U.S. nation state during the latter half of the 19th Century as well as the role of the state in the expansion of commercial agriculture. For the latter era, we outline some of the state agricultural programs designed to reproduce units of agricultural production under conditions of mature capitalism and point to the contradictions of such programs as they appear on the domestic and international levels. Our aim is these sections is not to provide a detailed history of the role of the state in American agricultural development, but rather to use concrete history to illuminate certain analytical aspects of this process, and conversely, to unravel the history of this development with the aid of theory.

283

II.   THE CAPITALIST STATE AND AGRICULTURAL
COMMODITY PRODUCTION

We begin our analysis of the interrelationship of state and agriculture in bourgeois society by first establishing the essential
character of the capitalist state and then by specifying special
features of agriculture as regards capitalist commodity production.

Generally, the state may be said to undertake the reproduction
of the social structure of a society to the extent that this reproduction is not achieved automatically by the economy.[1]   In this capacity, the state has three basic functions.   First there is the economic
function which consists of the provision of the general technical and
social conditions of production which are not assured by the private
economic activity of the dominant class.   Second, there is the
political function which consists of the repression by the police,
army and judiciary of any internal or external threats to the prevailing order.   And thirdly, there is the ideological or hegemonic
function in which the state attempts to integrate the dominated class
into society by transforming the ideology of the ruling class into the
ideology of society as a whole.   These latter two functions represent,
respectively, the exercise of force and authority, and as such constitute
the real and ideal moments of state power.   In the following discussion
we are primarily interested in the economic aspect of state functions in
general, and their relationship to agriculture in particular.

Now in bourgeois society the functions of the state are carried
out by agencies that are not only separate from the direct producers,
but also from the mass of individual capitalists, whose competitive
interactions constitute the core of the commodity economy.   At this
point we must make a distinction between two "levels" of the existence
of capital and specify the significance of this distinction for the
state.   On the one hand, there is the level of capital in general,
which consists of the average conditions of production that appear as
a result of the interaction of many individual capitals; it is at this
level that the tendential laws of capitalism operate.   On the other
hand, there is the level of the individual capitalist (the "firm")
whose subjective actions not only go into establishing the general
conditions of production but who, in turn, is required to operate within
objective constraints set by these general conditions.[2]   In this sense,
the interests or requirements of capital in general are qualitatively
different from those of any one capitalist, or indeed, of any one fraction of capital.   For example, the individual capitalist will be concerned about the reproduction of the portion of the labor force he
employs but not necessarily about the reproduction of the proletariat
as a class.

This distinction between capital in general and the individual capitalist has important implications for our understanding of the state under capitalism. First, it means that the representation of the interests of capital in general cannot be constituted on the basis of any one capitalist, as say compared to feudal society, where the largest landowner could without contradiction represent the interests of all landowners since the principle of competition was absent. Thus under capitalist production, the largest capitalist or indeed any particular fraction of capital cannot directly constitute the state, since state power would immediately be used to destroy all competition, hence precipitating the system to absolutism and monopoly. Second, the provisioning of the general conditions of production may require a level of generality that is beyond the necessarily limited purview of any one capitalist. And third, the scale of enterprise required to undertake the production and reproduction of these general conditions of production may exceed the resources of private enterprise. The significance of these latter two points is apparent in the state's role in the provision of such necessary services as the postal system, highway construction, a stable currency and so forth.

In addition to the above, there is another decisive feature of capitalist commodity production which has implications for the state and its functions. It is of considerable importance that not all aspects of production and reproduction in a commodity society can be carried out capitalistically, that is, on the basis of wage labor and the extraction of surplus value. An obvious example of this limitation would be the inability to produce the commodity labor power by capitalist methods; instead, the commodity which provides the basis for capitalist accumulation--value-creating labor power--continues to be produced noncapitalistically within the confines of the privatized household.[3] Thus, one of the fundamental limitations of capitalist production is that it only permits social relations to occur if they are profitable; a capitalist economy cannot, in and of itself, secure the inherent social nature of its existence simply through the competitive interaction of its many constituent parts. In this sense, capitalism not only generates uneven development, but also requires a special institution--the state--which is outside and alongside competition, and therefore is not subject to the limitations of capital since state activities are not governed by the necessity of profit maximization.[4]

In this respect, the "ruling class" is not synonymous with the "class that rules." Indeed, it is this very separation of administration from property which allows the state to act as mediator and protector of the fundamental aspects of property relations. Hence, we must understand the state not merely as a political instrument of repression, but also as an essential moment in the reproduction

process of capitalism whose prime function is to provide those imminent
conditions of production that capitalism neglects. It is in this
capacity as "ideal total capitalist"[5] that the state importantly inter-
faces with agriculture as a branch of production.

In addition to the household, the other major branch of production where non-capitalist units of production continue to exhibit a
remarkable vitality is agriculture. Indeed, it is precisely the persistence of family labor farms in the advanced capitalist countries
that marks agriculture out as a special case of uneven capitalist
development. We shall therefore preface our discussion of the relation of state and agriculture by examining some of those peculiar
features of agricultural commodity production which act to retard
the full extension of capitalist relations of production into the
countryside.[6] There are three major factors which interest us in
this respect.

First, certain spheres of agricultural production are characterized by a relatively fixed and lengthy total production time, as is
the case where the crop only matures annually. This lengthy production
time places important constraints on the rate of turnover of capital
and hence on the rate of profit for any capital invested in that sphere.
For example, in a capitalist enterprise, the rate of profit can be
increased simply by increasing the number of turnovers a capital
can complete in a given period of time, all other conditions being
constant; and indeed the industrial capitalist ever seeks ways to
enhance the velocity of turnover. However, in certain spheres of
agriculture, not only is total production time relatively lengthy, but
also the ability to significantly reduce this production time is
restricted by natural factors and cannot be easily socially modified
or manipulated as occurs in industry proper.

Second, some spheres of agricultural production are also characterized by a significant gap between total production time and labor time
such that for many agricultural commodities there are lengthy periods
when the application of labor is almost completely suspended as for
example when the seed is maturing in the earth. This divorce between
total production time and actual labor time has two effects of significance for capital. On the one hand, it leads to a highly
seasonal nature of labor requirements which in turn generates labor
supply, recruitment and management problems. On the other hand, the
intermittent employment of labor is also accompanied by an intermittent employment of constant capital or farm machinery, which results in the under-utilization of constant capital, such that machinery
lies "idle" during the "off season." This problem is generally
exacerbated given the high organic composition of capital that
characterizes many types of agricultural production. Together, then,
these factors make agriculture a relatively risky and hence comparatively unattractive area for profit maximization. Consequently,

it is not surprising that those spheres of agricultural production marked by these features tend to be left in the hands of petty producers.

Another special feature of agriculture is that it is generally more susceptible to violent fluctuations in price and hence income than other branches of production. This characteristic is partly attributable to the fact that agricultural production is more directly subject than is industry to uncontrollable natural factors, such as the weather, which can result in sharp variations in crop yields and hence in marketable produce. Moreover, the relatively lengthy production time required for numerous crops places limits upon the farmer's ability to respond quickly to changes in price. Put simply, in the short run, it is very difficult to increase or decrease production once a crop is planted. If the crop only matures annually, there is a substantial "lag" in the farmer's reaction to price changes.[7] The farmer can vary the proportion of the crop he chooses to sell at any one time; however, in the case of perishable crops this choice is very circumscribed, while with more durable agricultural commodities other costs are incurred. For example, livestock not slaughtered for market still have to be fed, unmarketed grain has to be stored, and fields lying fallow quickly become overgrown with weeds and bush and thus require extra effort if production is to be renewed.

In contrast, the industrial entrepreneur can respond more flexibly to the market by augmenting or curtailing production to an exact amount. Such precise and continuous adjustment of production is not possible for the farmer since he cannot be sure what yield per acre he will obtain, nor how many young animals will be born or survive. The range of error for crops is compounded by the fact that total output for many crops varies more with yield per acre which the farmer cannot control, than with acreage, which he can.[8]

In short, the inability of the farmer to react quickly to the market results in overproduction and underproduction which in turn perpetuates a vicious cycle of price fluctuations. Moreover, the resilience of certain agricultural commodities to production along capitalist lines means that these spheres are left in the hands of a multitude of petty producers; and a multitude of producers which is compelled by price changes to make decisions regarding the scale of production at certain set intervals only serves to intensify variations in the volume of total crop production from year to year. Indeed, the famous "hog cycle," everpresent in any introductory economics text, is itself testament to the price fluctuations which result from the uncoordinated economic activities of large numbers of small producers.[9]

In summary, then, these peculiar aspects of certain spheres of agricultural production implicate the state in the reproduction of these non-capitalistic spheres.[10]   In this sense, state subsidies to non-capitalist agricultural producers are not necessarily in conflict with the interests of capital as a whole, for if capital itself is unwilling to enter certain fields of food production due to low profitability, then these subsidies can be seen as functioning to assure adequate supplies of means of subsistence for variable capital. Consequently, as we shall discuss at greater length below, "agricultural welfare" which has become a significant feature of many advanced capitalist nations today, reflects just one of the numerous cases where the state functions to secure those very conditions of production which cannot be assured by private capital.   However, let us first turn to an analysis of the role of the state in the settlement and expansion of agriculture during 19th Century America.

III.   THE ERA OF INTERNAL COLONIZATION: STATE AND AGRICULTURE IN THE SETTLEMENT OF THE AMERICAN WEST

So far, we have discussed the capitalist state analytically and shown how its form is to be deduced from the nature of capitalist commodity production; we have also pointed to the peculiar nature of agriculture as regards capitalist production.   Now, the modern state is not only constituted abstractly, as a "necessary deduction" from the logic of capitalism, but is also constituted materially and hence historically.   In this sense, the capitalist state takes on an extensive moment such that it appears as a nation state.   By nation state in this context we mean an integrated territory over which the organs of the state exercise jurisdiction, continuous administration, as well as claiming the right to the legitimate use of force.   Moreover, under capitalism, the territory of the nation state becomes co-extensive with the home market.

We can distinguish two historical progressions as regards the consolidation of the territorial basis of the modern nation state in the advanced capitalist countries.   On the one hand, in the classic European context of the transition from feudalism to capitalism, a lengthy period of settlement has already established the territorial basis upon which the modern European capitalist states emerged. Thus, in this situation the prime task of the bourgeois revolutions was not to settle uninhabited areas as a precondition to the articulation of the home market, but rather to eliminate the residues that had accumulated as a result of previous history, i.e. the vestiges of feudalism.   In these situations, to constitute the nation state entailed primarily the elimination of internal customs and tarriffs, the breaking up of local autonomy and particularisms, the standardization of the monetary and credit systems, and the integration of the

citizen with the state by abolishing feudal rights and obligations.
Generally, then, nation building involved the transformation of the
social relations that prevailed among an already existing population
and did not require significant territorial expansion.

On the other hand, the development of nation states out of the
overseas European colonies demanded expansion over whole continents,
the subjugation and/or elimination of the indigenous peoples and the
settlement of frontier lands by members of the dominant "white"
population. This process of nation building via internal settler
colonialism has characterized the history of the U.S.A. as well as
all other "new European states" such as Australia, New Zealand, Canada
and South Africa. Moreover, we can distinguish two types of settler
colonialism in this respect: one which is based on the direct seizure
of land and the subjugation of the indigenous population as a source
of cheap labor; and another, which is similarly based on the seizure
of land but instead of enslaving the indigenous population entails
its liquidation. In the former case, settlement is established primarily on the basis of capitalist forms of production, or the semi-
capitalist plantation type economies. In the latter case, which
was characteristic of the U.S.A. particularly during the latter half
of the 19th Century, the preservation of the indigenous population
as labor is not a primary consideration since colonization is predicted primarily on the settlement of rural petty commodity producers.[11]

Now it is apparent that both historical patterns involve an
agrarian question, but in radically different forms. In the classic
European situation, the "agrarian question" centered upon the transformation of land into a commodity by such devices as the termination
of communal rights, curtailing access to common grazing land, enclos-
ures, etc., and thereby the separation of the peasant producer from
his means of production.[12] In internal settler colonial regimes,
the agrarian question also involved the commoditization of land by,
for example, the "disposal of the public domain" to private interests
and the appropriation of Indian lands previously held in common as
occurred in the U.S.A. However, in this situation, only the indigenous
population was displaced from the land, while the "colonists" were co-
joined with the land in the areas of new settlement. Consequently,
in contrast to the classic form where land is "seized" from some of
the "citizens of the state," settler colonialism requires that some
of the "citizens" directly seize the land. Needless to say, both
progressions are founded on violence, fraud and theft.

The historical resolution of the former question, which witnessed
the origins of the proletariat in the institutionalized violence of
the state, is well-known.[13] However the question of the relationship
between agriculture and the internal settler colonial state has received comparatively little attention. It is to this question that
we now turn.

We can characterize the U.S.A. as an internal settler colonial
state beginning with the colonial policies inaugurated by the Northwest Ordinance of 1787 until the end of the 19th Century when the
continental frontier was finally closed, capitalism had reached a
decisive level of articulation, and the Spanish-American War fore-
shadowed a new era of American imperialism.[14] This understanding of
the U.S. state in the 19th Century has been largely overlooked in
the standard histories of the era, perhaps because colonialism is too
often incorrectly associated merely with the possession of overseas
colonies. However, the history of U.S. overland expansion serves as
a reminder that possessions may be acquired by the simple process of
pushing into sparsely inhabited contiguous territories and by enslaving
the indigenous population or replacing it with settlers belonging to
the dominant people. Indeed, throughout the 19th Century white
settlers progressively expropriated, segregated and exterminated
the American Indians, occupied their lands, and under the direct administration of the U.S. federal government formed the "colonies"
which have euphemistically been referred to as "territories."
Ironically, the political relations between these territories and the
federal government were modelled on the old pre-independence British
colonial system with appointed officials directly administering the
territories and their inhabitants allowed little or no political
representation. In fact, in this respect, the U.S. internal colonial
system was, as Eblen says, "decidedly more authoritarian" than its
British antecedent.[15]

Whilst the U.S.A. has had a relatively long history of internal
settler colonialism, for the purposes of our analysis we shall focus
primarily on what has been referred to as America's "Second Empire,"
that period covering the last half of the 19th Century when the U.S.
federal government undertook the overland colonization of the vast
regions lying west of the Mississippi River. It was during this era
that non-capitalist producers of wheat became established in a region
which had previously been considered the "Uninhabitable American
Desert;" indeed, the centres of American wheat production continued
to shift westward during this period marking the beginnings of
the American wheat belt as we know it today.[16]

Moreover, this period is of particular interest because it also
saw the rise and decline of the much acclaimed bonanza wheat farms
and hence for a limited period during the 19th Century, capitalist
wheat farms existed alongside and in competition with rural petty
commodity producers of wheat. However, while the former proved to be
a relatively short-lived phenomenon, the family labor farms survived
the era and underwent unprecedented growth and expansion.[17]

Our focus is therefore initially on the relationship between U.S.
internal settler colonial policies and rural petty commodity production.

Our analysis has two sides. On the one hand, we will show how the
state acted to establish the necessary preconditions for the settlement of rural petty commodity in the Western regions. On the other
hand, we will also show how certain features of rural petty commodity
production made it the ideal form of production on which to secure
the rapid settlement of the American west. Thus we shall illuminate
the dialectic between state and agriculture in the territorial aspect of U.S. national building.

The first groups of significance to penetrate the area west of
the Mississippi were miners and free range cattlemen.[18] The early
miners were prospectors who spent years roaming the countryside and
only in the event of a successful strike did they "settle" and stake
their property claims. The free range cattlemen operated on the
basis of open grazing on public lands and hence must be distinguished
from the later ranch-cattle industry which operated on enclosed grazing and hence private property in land. Thus, these early pioneers
were essentially nomadic and increasingly came into competition with
the remaining Indian tribes who were themselves nomadic, and likewise
depended on free access to land and natural resources to sustain their
way of life. As the miners and cattlemen pushed westward, they reduced the area freely available to the Indians, thus precipitating
the latter's resistance which was to culminate in the Indian Wars.

Now both of these early forms of production in the West required
some commercial links with the more developed regions of the country.
On the one hand, the miners, who we can regard as petty commodity producers, were dependent upon the market both for the purchase of their
means of production (spades, mules, etc.) and for the realization of
the value of their product (gold and silver). On the other hand, free-
range cattle ranching--a capitalist form of production using wage-
earning cowboys--needed markets to dispose of mature cattle.

The lack of a developed transportation and communication system
on the frontier would ordinarily have presented obstacles to successful commodity production--be it capitalist or noncapitalist. However, the absence of infrastructural development was not fatal to
these particular forms of production because of the special characteristics of the commodities they produced. For example, cattle could
be driven to market on their own four legs, hence the famous cattle
drives across the plains to the nearest railhead. Also, mined gold
and silver by virtue of being the "universal equivalents" could
function with relative ease anywhere as a means of exchange. Moreover, the low bulk and high value of these "commodities" allowed
them to be easily transported by pack horse or mule and hence
precluded the necessity of a fully developed transportation system.

However, other commodity producers, particularly wheat producers,

could not operate on such an undeveloped frontier. Indeed, a pre-
condition to the extensive settlement of such producers was the
establishment of an adequate transportation network to facilitate
market transactions. In turn, in contrast to these early "pioneers,"
wheat production required fixed settlement at the very least for the
length of the production cycle. Consequently, wheat production required physically and legally defined boundaries and hence private
property in land. However, at the beginning of the period we are
examining, the vast majority of land in the American West was either
part of the government domain or recognized Indian land held in
common by tribes. The transformation of this public and communal
property into private property was, then, a central feature of the
history of western agricultural settlement.

Successful colonization of the West by agricultural commodity
producers depended upon several factors: (1) the pacification of
the Indians; (2) the transformation of the public domain into private property; (3) the development of an adequate infrastructure to
link settlers economically and politically to the more developed
regions of the country; and (4) the availability of credit facilities.
These preconditions we argue could not be achieved by capital or the
petty-producer alone and hence required the active intervention of
the state.

The importance of these social and economic preconditions to the
successful settlement of agricultural producers is evidenced by the
fact that it was only two decades after the federal government
officially encouraged colonization of these regions with the Homestead Act of 1862 that settlement began to occur on any significant
scale. This "lingering" of the population frontier on the borders
of the Great Plains has been attributed correctly by several historians to the failure to realize these preconditions until the
mid-1880's.[19] We now turn to an examination of the role of the
state in the social preparation of the American West for agricultural
settlement.

The Indian Barrier: One of the most important and direct roles
of the U.S. government in preparing the frontier regions for settlement was the pacification of the Indians through a policy of segre-
gation and extermination. This policy mirrored the fact that since
U.S. overland expansion was predicated on the expansion of a particular
form of production--petty commodity production--it did not require
that the indigenous population be kept intact to provide a labor
force.[20]

By the end of the Civil War, only a few tribes retained sufficient strength to effectively contest Western expansion. Initially,
the major opponent of the Indians was the U.S. frontier army. This
army was ideally suited for the brutal task of subduing the Indians

since it was composed largely of "brutes, misfits and ruffians."[21]
The enlisted corps drew heavily from "undesirable" lumpenproletariat
elements--drunkards, perverts and criminals, as well as from the
social wreckage of the Civil War.[22]   In turn, as in contemporary
settler colonial regimes, foreign mercenaries formed a conspicuous
part of the frontier army.[23] Yet despite these manpower problems,
this motley crew was equipped with some of the most significant
advances in weapons technology. With the advantage of breech-loading
rifles and the famed Colt 45 repeating revolvers (ironically known
as the "peacemakers"), the bluecoats were initially able to inflict
heavy losses upon the Indians. However, the Indian warriors gradually came into possession of these weapons themselves (largely through
traders) and to some extent the combatants were equalized.[24]

Behind the gun came the missionary. The federal government
established many of the Christian Indian missions which became
"totalitarian institutions" regulating every phase of Indian life.
The barbarism of these institutions is reflected in the fact that
while missions differed somewhat from region to region their death
rates were uniformly high; indeed, in some cases, losses by death
even exceeded new recruits by birth and "conversion."[25] In short,
brute force and ideology were used hand in hand to suppress native
religions, languages and social organization.

While the U.S. government provided the essential moment of force
required to subjugate the Indians, it is important to note that a
number of features of the Indian tribal organization made them particularly vulnerable to conquest. On the one hand, the tribes were
culturally different one from another; they spoke different languages
and worshipped different deities. Moreover, allegiance was traditionally accorded to family, band or tribe rather than race. Consequently intertribal warfare and traditional rivalries reduced the
possibility of a united Indian resistance to westward expansion.[26]
On the other hand, the highly democratic political and decision-
making structures of these "pre-state," communal societies hampered
the ability to reach the kind of quick decisions required for successful military opposition.[27]

Finally, a number of "latent consequences" of westward expansion
such as the extermination of the buffalo by professional hunters and
a lack of resistance by Indians to white man's diseases (smallpox,
cholera, syphillis, etc.) further undermined the capacity and will
of the Indians to resist the final solution of "reservations."[28]

As early as the mid-1880's most of the tribes had been corralled
onto reservations,[29] and the surrender of Geronimo in 1886 marked
the collapse of the last powerful Indian tribe ranging free from
reservation constraints. Almost no area remained to which the

Indians could flee. Stockmen and longhorns occupied the former Chey-
enne and Sioux hunting grounds. Mining communities were established
all over Oregon and Idaho where the Nez Perce, Pauite and Bannock had
sought refuge. In a short two decades, the western Indians were
effectively subdued or exterminated, their land appropriated and the
remaining tribes forced onto reservations and government dole.[30]

The Homestead Act and Western Settlement: Traditionally, the
Homestead Act of 1862 has been regarded as the decisive legal factor
in the growth of commercial agriculture in the West: not only did the
act officially sanction the transformation of the public domain into
private property, but also its "avowed" intention was to provide free
land for small producers. However, as several historians have pointed
out, the petty producer was not the major beneficiary of the government's "free land" policy. Indeed, it has been estimated that homesteaders, including those who were mere pawns of land speculators,
received only one out of every six or seven acres of the land that
came as a "free gift" from the government.[31]

The divorce between the formal intent and real outcome of the
Homestead Act is attributable to a number of factors. On the one hand,
there were clear inadequacies in the legislation itself. For instance,
no provision was made to cover the transportation expenses that might
be incurred by a potential settler moving to the frontier, nor was
any provision made for any training in agriculture.[32] Moreover, the
initial 160 acre allotments were inadequate for the semi-arid conditions of the U.S. prairies being too large for successful irrigated
farming and too small for dry farming.[33]

On the one hand, a more serious factor which undermined the intent
of the Homestead legislation was the government's own practice of
granting huge tracts of the most fertile land to railroads, state
governments and other "vested interests." This process not only
robbed the Indians, but also meant that none of these lands became
available for "free" homesteading.[34] Generally, the settler had the
choice of either buying his land at exhorbitant prices from "vested
interests" or settling far from transportation routes where facilities
for social and economic intercourse were limited.[35]

It is not surprising that land monopolization in fact increased
at a faster rate after the Homestead legislation.[36] Indeed, with
large expanses of railroad lands, state lands, and Indian lands open
for private purchase, there were few obstacles to land monopolization and speculation. However, whilst non-agricultural mercantile
and capitalist interests were the major beneficiaries of the "free
land" policy of the U.S. government, the frauds and evasions perpetuated under the Homestead Act nevertheless functioned to transform
the public domain into private property.

Infrastructural Development: The major impact of the government's free land policy on commercial agriculture was twofold. First, as we have already pointed out, the act officially sanctioned the transformation of the public domain into private property. Second, the government land grants to private enterprise were vital for the development of a transportation infrastructure, in particular the construction of the transcontinental railroads. For in fact not only did these enormous undertakings require immense social organization and huge quantities of capital, but, as has been persuasively argued, only government financing and guarantees made these projects possible at all.[37]

The importance of government financing for western railroad construction is attributable in part to the substantial differences between these lines and the earlier eastern or midwestern lines. Most importantly, since the western railroads were not built to connect already established markets and population centres, their construction preceeded settlement on any significant scale. Consequently, private railroad companies could not rely on the prospect of immediate profits to finance their ventures, but instead anticipated returns as markets and population grew.[38] Therefore, while the government financing of the transcontinental railroads was a precondition for the expansion of agricultural commodity production, conversely the ultimate success of the railroads was predicated on the freight and passenger revenues from future settlement. Moreover, since the Homestead Act did not effectively promote spontaneous settlement, the railroads and land speculation companies had to resort to the direct recruitment of settlers from eastern cities and abroad. Indeed, these companies spent thousands of dollars advertising abroad, advancing expenses for land, travel and supplies to "interested" settlers, and in some cases donated land for the construction of entire towns so as to attract new recruits.[39]

In summary then, whilst government practices on the one hand served to undermine the formal intent of Homestead Act, on the other, they facilitated the development of an adequate infrastructure to link potential commodity producers with the more developed regions of the country. In this way, the settler colonial state, while acting in the direct interests of nonagricultural mercantile and capitalist interests, indirectly fostered the expansion of commercial agriculture in the regions west of the Mississippi.

State Banks and Credit: State-level government also stimulated agricultural expansion by the licensing of state banks which extended credit facilities to the petty producer. In this respect, the importance of credit for small producers has an historical as well as analytical determination. On the one hand, as a direct consequence of the land monopolization which followed the Homestead Act, many settlers had no option but to buy land at high prices from the

railroad and land speculation companies as well as borrow their transport and initial outlay expenses from these vested interests. Thus,
from the very beginning, indebtedness was inevitable and a condition
of existence for many settlers.

On the other hand, even settlers who might have started out
"independently" were later compelled to borrow either to tide themselves over from one harvest to the next or in order to expand and
scale of their production. As regards this latter point, it is
important to note that since petty commodity production operates only
at the level of simple circulation, it cannot, unlike the capitalist
firm, accumulate or expand via the reinvestment of surplus value
extracted in production. Expanded reproduction for the petty producer therefore requires access to an additional source of capital
which is usually borrowed and hence acquired through credit. Thus,
unless the petty producer can generate sufficient savings from
the advantages of differential rent, an increase in the scale of production requires increased indebtedness.

On the western frontier adequate credit facilities were initially
underdeveloped. National banks, although they assured a uniform
currency throughout the Union, were limited in their capacity to
extend credit to western farmers by a number of legal restrictions.
For instance, national banks could not lend on mortgages and were
restricted to a minimum capitalization of $50,000 which effectively
prevented their establishment in areas with a small population.[40]
In particular, prairie and plains farmers usually lived a long way
from centers where sufficient money could be raised to organize a
national bank. These restrictions and conditions, then, in addition
to the absence of any federal farm-loan agency, meant that farmers
were compelled to rely for credit on local merchants or implement
dealers, who, because of their monopoly situation could charge
exhorbitant interest rates.[41]

To alleviate this situation, western states such as Wisconsin,
Nebraska, Kansas, Oklahoma and the Dakotas authorized the establishment of state banks to service the credit needs of farmers and small
businessmen. In contrast to the national banks, these state banks
could lend on mortgages and be created with as little as $5,000
capital. The development of these new credit facilities resulted in
an impressive growth of the country's money supply as more and more
money took the form of deposits as opposed to currency in circulation.
So rapidly did these state banks grow in fact that by 1876 their
deposits already exceeded those of the national banks.[42]

As such, whilst credit facilities provided under the auspicies
of state banks to a large extent broke the hold of local merchant or
userer's capital, the small producer in no way was able to escape

the enmeshing effects of credit and instead found himself under the
more rational domination of finance capital.

Rural Petty Commodity Production and State Expansion: We now
examine how certain features of agricultural commodity production
served to facilitate the rapid settlement of these frontier regions
and thus indicate how agricultural expansion dovetailed with the
objective interests of finance capital and colonizing aims of the
U.S. state.

Now any state that is engaged in colonization, either to complete
the territorial basis of the home market, and/or to foster the
interests of various fractions of the bourgeoisie (i.e. railroads,
finance capitalists, etcl), has itself an interest in both increasing
the speed of settlement and keeping the costs of necessary infrastructural development within the frontier to a minimum. Moreover,
since U.S. internal settler colonialism was part of a process of
nationbuilding, there was also an interest in maintaining integral
relations between the frontier and the more developed regions of the
country. Several features of agricultural commodity production facilitated these concerns.

Firstly, and perhaps most obviously, since the settlers.were
producers of agricultural commodities, they were able to produce
directly the most basic element of their means of subsistence--food.
This fact served to simplify immensely the required level of infrastructural development since food supplies for settlers did not have
to be shipped or supplied from other regions. Consequently, the
social division of labor could remain relatively rudimentary within
the frontier itself. Indeed, historians have documented that the
farmer-settlers generally produced enough food for their own sustinence
in addition to their cash crop;[43] and even under prairie conditions,
which as a rule discouraged diversified commercial farming, settlers
were seldom exclusively mono-crop producers. Thus, simply because
they were engaged in agricultural production, these settlers were
able to undertake a significant part of their own reproduction.

Second, any form of production for exchange, whether capitalist
or non-capitalist, of necessity requires external relations with the
larger economy since the commodity producer is dependent upon markets
both for the purchase of means of production and for the realization
of the value of the produced commodity. Thus, in contrast to the
peasant producer who is engaged primarily in production for use and
hence has to be induced by non-economic factors (i.e. feudal bonds)
to yield up his surplus product or labor and, who, in the absence or
reduction of these extra-economic factors always has a tendency to
sink into autarky, the commodity producer cannot reproduce the
conditions of his existence in total isolation from the larger
economy. Rather, because both his product and means of production

take the commodity form, he is compelled to maintain external ties.

The political significance of these economic links between the settlers on the frontier and the more developed regions of the country is
reflected in the opposition of the colonizing state to the establishment of entirely independent and self-sufficient communities which sought
to avoid or reduce the constraints of ties to the larger capitalist
economy. This was evident, for instance, in the U.S. government's pre-
judicial treatment of the Mormons in Utah.[44]

In turn, the expansion of agricultural commodity production in
frontier regions necessarily fosters the development and articulation
of the home market in three important ways. First such expansion extends
the market within the frontier itself. Second, to the extent that agricultural produce is directed towards other than strictly local markets,
it supplies centers of industrial capitalism, both nationally and inter-
nationally, with cheap means of subsistence for variable capital, thus
stimulating industrial capitalist development as a whole. Finally, the
expansion of agricultural commodity production increases the demand for
manufactured farm implements and other inputs, thus enhancing the development of those specific industrial capitalist enterprises which
specialize in the production of agricultural means of production.

Now whilst it is clear that agricultural commodity production in
general served to speed up settlement, reduce infrastructural costs and
develop integral links between the frontier and the metropole, it was
a particular form of commodity production that proved most efficient in
these respects. Indeed, it was rural petty commodity production, as
opposed to capitalist forms of agricultural production, which finally
predominated and so left its mark on American Western development.

The superiority of petty commodity production over capitalist
forms of production in the rapid settlement of new lands lies in the
familial nature of this form of production. First, the identity of
household and enterprise which is the hallmark of petty commodity production means that the production unit contains within it the possibility
of reproducing or supplementing its own labor force through procreation.
Moreover, the family also provides an adequate base for the intergenerational transmission of knowledge relevant to small scale farming, as
well as the acquisition of those basic skills such as reading, writing
and elementary arithmetic required for market transactions. Consequently, not only did petty commodity production preclude the necessity of a developed labor market on the frontier with all the problems
and expenses that such a market implies, but also it obviated the
necessity of developing secondary socializing institutions, e.g.,
schools, technical institutes, and so forth.

In turn, the familial nature of petty commodity production has
important implications for the expansion of this form of production.

It is apparent that not only does petty commodity production have the ability to reproduce its own labor force, but also, under certain conditions it can generate new units of production through the intergenerational transmission of property. Thus, in cases where there is more than one eligible offspring (usually sons), farm income can be used to establish new and competing units of production alongside the original unit. This characteristic of family labor enterprises which was noted by Hegel well over a century ago,[45] is referred to in the contemporary literature as the process of "fission."[46] This process means that the expansion of petty commodity production can take on an extensive or geographic moment through the multiplication of like units. However, it must be noted that this process of fission can only occur under certain historical conditions, such as when the acquisition of additional land is unproblematic (i.e. absolute ground rent is minimal or absent) or where there are no traditional or legal restrictions governing the intergenerational transmission of property (i.e. the absence of systems of impartible inheritance such as primogeniture or ultrimogeniture).[47] For a limited time during the late 19th Century, these conditions were present on the U.S. western frontier and facilitated the rapid settlement of petty producing units.

Here we must emphasize the different character of expanded reproduction under capitalist production. On the one hand, the expansion of capitalist production involves an inherent tendency towards the concentration and centralization of capital -- a process in which less successful firms are progressively driven out of business or absorbed through competition. Thus unlike fission, capitalist expanded reproduction tends to reduce rather than increase the number of competing units.[48] On the other hand, this tendency towards the concentration and centralization of production also entails an accumulation of property and hence an increase of the scale of production. Capitalist accumulation therefore tends towards vertical concentration, the crystalization of the class structure and the geographic as well as social concentration of labor.

In contrast, fission negates accumulation since it requires the division of property and the duplication of productive units on a similar scale. The expansion of petty commodity production can involve, therefore, a horizontal as opposed to a vertical moment, a provisioning of laborers with their means of production as opposed to a divorcing of laborers from their means of production, and hence a dispersion as opposed to a concentration of labor and property. This ability of petty commodity production to "multiply and divide" therefore implies a geographical moment which in turn establishes a link between this form of production and overland state expansion. Indeed, in the history of U.S. internal settler colonialism, this distinctly extensive moment to rural petty commodity production served to populate, consolidate and secure territorial boundaries both from encroachment by indigenous

elements such as the American Indians, as well as from the foreign
claims of neighboring Mexico and Canada.[49]

A final feature of petty commodity production which made it particularly amenable to settlement of the American West is the fact that
the petty producer can continue to produce as long as the costs of
production do not exceed the realized value of his commodities. That
is, petty commodity production can maintain itself merely at a level
of simple reproduction and is not compelled to achieve the average rate
of profit as is the capitalist enterprise.[50] This is not to say that
petty commodity production is immune to the objective determination of
the market. On the contrary, both the costs of production and the
value of the commodity produced are subject to market constraints.
Hence, if there are technical changes which effect the scale of production and thereby reduce the socially necessary labor time needed
to produce a marketable commodity, the petty producer is under pressure
to expand production in order to be competitive and sell his goods on
the market. As we noted above, this implicates petty commodity production in a subordinate, debt relation to finance capital. In contrast,
however, the capitalist enterprise must not only ensure that its
realized value covers the costs of production, but also profits must
tend towards the average rate of profit or capital will seek more
lucrative fields of investment. This difference is not generally
important or visible in many branches of production (e.g. textiles),
since many commodities are quite amenable to capitalist production and
hence through competition capitalist firms by their greater scale and
efficiency can usually undersell and thereby displace petty producers.

However, this difference is significant in the case of the particular
commodity which predominated on the western frontier. Under the semi-
arid conditions of the U.S. prairies, wheat proved to be the most viable
crop for commercial farming. In turn, as we mentioned earlier, cereal
grain production has a number of peculiarities which make it problematic
for profit maximalization under capitalism. The relatively lengthy
production time coupled with the large gaps between production time and
labor time make this crop an unattractive commodity for capitalist
pentration.[51] However, to the petty commodity producer, for whom the
average rate of profit is not a necessary condition for survival, wheat
production can be a viable type of commercial farming.

In summary, then, petty commodity production has a number of
features not present under capitalist forms of production which facilitate its expansion onto undeveloped frontiers. The familial nature of
this form reduced the necessary infrastructural developments which had
to be undertaken by the settler colonial state. The nature of expansion,
through fission provided an extensive and geographic moment which dovetailed with the territorial designs of the expansionist state. Finally,
the ability of petty commodity production to survive without receiving
the average rate of profit made this form more amenable to the type of

agricultural production most viable on the western prairies. Consequently, while U.S. settler colonialism was indeed a capitalist state form, its expansion onto the western frontier was more easily facilitated by the expansion of this non-capitalist form of commodity production.

IV. STATE AND AGRICULTURE UNDER MONOPOLY CAPITALISM

In the previous section we explored the dialectic between territorial consolidation, the development of capitalism and the expansion of commercial agriculture west of the Mississippi. From our analysis it is apparent that state agricultural policies during this period of internal settler colonialism were primarily extensive in character and scope; that is to say, state policy tended to promote directly and indirectly the settlement of agricultural producers and the general expansion of agriculture.

However, we have also pointed out that a fundamental economic function of the state under capitalism is to ensure the reproduction of those spheres of production which, whilst vital to the national economy, might not be assured of reproduction through the actions of private capital alone. Moreover, in this respect, we have established that agriculture is a branch of production marked by risks and uncertainties of a different order to those experienced by other sectors of the economy such that agriculture is, to a significant degree, resistant to capitalist penetration. Now, with the closing of the frontier and the development of the U.S. economy into a monopoly stage, these special features of agriculture necessarily become more pronounced; conversely, new kinds of state agricultural policies emerge in response to the changing problems facing agriculture. Such programs and policies which function to reproduce agriculture under conditions of monopoly capital we may designate as expressing the intensive side or aspect of the state-agriculture relation.

In this section, therefore, we review the origin and development of some of the most important of these "intensive" programs. First, we briefly review the role of the state in agricultural research and development. Then we show how price support/farm income maintenance programs have evolved into a full-blown system of agricultural "welfare" which, paradoxically, have functioned to perpetuate rather than resolve the problems of agriculture in an industrial-capitalist economy. Finally we shall show how domestic agricultural policy has had repercussions on the conduct of U.S. foreign policy and hence becomes implicated in American imperialism.

Research and Development: By the last half of the 19th Century
the fundamental peculiarities of agriculture in relation to capitalism
had already become sufficiently apparent to warrant direct state involvement in this sphere of the economy.   Indeed, the U.S. Department
of Agriculture was the first government agency established (in 1862)
to serve the interests of a special clientele.[52]   Moreover, it was
during this same period that the state became involved in agricultural
research and development.

The origins of such government sponsored research can be traced
back to the Morrill Land Act of 1862 which authorized federal land
grants for the establishment of agricultural colleges.   Formal recognition of the need for the state to support agricultural research came
25 years later when the Hatch Act (1887) secured federal matching payments for state experiment stations as well as authorizing expenditures
for the establishment of an in-government research organization, which
was later to become the Agricultural Research Service.   It is interesting to note in this respect that the original justification given for
federal involvement in agricultural research was that, on the one hand,
farmers were too small to undertake such research themselves, and on
the other, increases in farm productivity benefitted producers and
consumers alike and hence society at large.[53]   In the provision of
agricultural research the state is thus clearly acting in a capacity
of "ideal total capitalist."

It is also interesting that private funding for agricultural
research and development is located primarily in the capitalist sectors
of agricultural production (e.g. crop specialty industries) and in the
capitalist agricultural input industries.   Generally, this privately
funded research has a specific goal and purpose--namely profitability
--whereas government research, both at the state and federal levels,
lacks such a clearcut goal and consequently has been described as dis-
jointed, unco-ordinated and unplanned.[54]   Both private and public
funding of agricultural research have expanded rapidly over the last
century.   Indeed, it has been estimated that public appropriations
for these purposes have almost doubled in each decade from the initia-
tion of the programmes up to the present.   By 1976, spending on agricultural research amounted to some $1.9 billion dollars, with the
public and private sectors accounting for about 50 percent each.[55]

On the one hand, agricultural research, both public and private,
has served to mitigate or reduce some of the peculiar risks associated
with agricultural production and therefore has fostered greater capitalist penetration of this sector.   For instance, much research has been
given over to devising methods to reduce the preponderance of production
time over labor time in agricultural production.   This is exemplified
in the transformation of poultry and egg production into almost continuous production processes where labor is constantly applied and

absorbed, rendering these spheres amenable to capitalist forms of production. Similarly, other advances have served to reduce the risks and uncertainties associated with a production process based on natural and biological processes. Artificial insemination, fast fattening processes, and advances in disease and pest control have all served to remove some of the natural constraints on agricultural production. In turn, in some cases, agricultural research has succeeded in achieving fundamental breakthroughs which have the potentiality of ending the bifurcation of agriculture and industry proper. An important example here would be the development of hydroponics which effectively removes plant production from dependence on the land. In all of these cases, it is fair to say that research and development functions to remove objective barriers to the capitalist penetration of the countryside.

In addition, research and development, particularly by the farm input industries (fertilizers, pesticides, machinery, etc.), has dramatically increased the productivity of both capitalist and non-capitalist sectors of agriculture. For example, today from one-third to one-half of the crop production in the U.S. is attributed to fertilizer use--fertilizers which are supplied to the direct producer by one of the largest and most highly concentrated capitalist industries.[56] Companies like DeKalb and Pioneer have developed hybrid seed strains adapted to the particular climatic and soil conditions in various regions of the country and now control 50 percent of the market for seed grains.[57]

We must note, however, that whilst these developments have dramatically increased levels of agricultural production, the quality of what is produced has declined. Thus, the protein content of corn has steadily fallen over the past 50 years as new and more refined hybrids have been introduced. Oats and wheat show similar declines in quality and, indeed, according to the U.S.D.A., some wheat being harvested in the U.S. is so low in protein as to be unfit for milling.[58] This absurd situation is of course to be expected since the goal of any economic system based on profit maximization is not the production of use value, but rather the realization of exchange values.

Thus we can see that research and development has contradictory effects on the role of the state in agricultural production. On the one hand, research and development can, by reducing the obstacles to the capitalist penetration of agriculture, also reduce the need for state support and intervention. However, on the other hand, by functioning to increase productivity, research and development can also exacerbate the problems of agricultural overproduction therefore calling forth the need for increased state intervention. It is to this latter problem that we now turn.

Agricultural Welfare and the Welfare of Agriculture: The most important of the government's current agricultural programs has by and large emerged as a consequence of agricultural over-production and taken the form of mechanisms to manipulate and control this overproduction, rather than to abolish its root causes.

The origin of agricultural overproduction can be traced back to the colonization of the American hinterland when the expansion of commercial agriculture onto the western frontier was accompanied by a massive increase in total farm production. This period of geographical expansion was also coupled with significant increases in agricultural productivity nationwide and has led many observers to characterize the era from the end of the Civil War up until the First World War as the "Golden Age of American Agriculture."[59] And indeed, this period was marked by an unprecedented growth in the number of farms and a spectacular increase in farm production; both the number of farms as well as total farm output virtually tripled, whilst output per worker doubled.[60]

However, whilst American farmers today may be tempted to look back longingly on this era as the "heyday of family farming," their selective memories fail to recall that this great prosperity in American agriculture was neither distributed evenly across the country nor among farm households themselves. That is, American farmers, then as now, did not constitute a homogenous social class but rather included the beneficiaries as well as the victims of the massive changes which marked this era of agricultural expansion.[61]

Moreover, in this same era, American industrial capitalism reached a decisive level of articulation. As in other spheres of the industrial economy, suppliers of farm inputs and machinery underwent rapid concentration and centralization of production. By the late 19th Century, the monopolization of the farm machinery industry was evident. Indeed, during the 1880's alone, the number of manufacturing firms in this field fell from 1,943 to 910, while invested capital more than doubled.[62] Similarly, the large meat packing and food processing industries grew with astonishing speed. In short, while farm production itself increased dramatically, agriculture's position within the larger economy tended to decline relative to industry. These developments were to have significant repercussions for direct agricultural producers.

The domestic and foreign demands generated by the First World War only served to further stimulate agriculture. During the war years, the expansion of agriculture took place largely on the basis of investment in constant capital rather than labor, since the war itself competed with farming for man-power, and, between 1917 and 1919 the value of farm assets rose substantially.[63] However, in order to increase production to meet wartime demands a large number of farmers were forced to go into debt. After the Armistice, farmers were faced by a dramatic decrease in demand and plummetting farm prices. The farmer's situation was exacerbated by the fact that many of the resources

committed to agricultural production during the wartime boom were
economically fixed, hence leading to heavy capital losses. Thus
between 1919 and 1922 prices received by farmers declined by 40 percent, while the rate of bankruptcy, foreclosure and other signs of
economic distress reached record levels. As many observers have noted,
the Depression for agriculture really began in the early 1920's.[64]

Throughout the 1920's, the National Farmers' Union and the Granger
movement fought unsuccessfully for government subsidies to stabilize
farm incomes. However, it was not until 1929 that the government
officially admitted the problems of agricultural overproduction.
In response to continued stockpiling of surplus production the government passed the Hawley Smoot Tariff which imposed the highest tariff
on agricultural imports in U.S. history. But this move did not resolve the problem since foreign nations immediately retaliated to
keep out U.S. agricultural exports.[65] It soon became clear that
tariff-based protectionism was inadequate to the problem at hand.

Well into the Great Depression, agricultural surpluses continued
to pile up in record amounts. For example, on August 1, 1932, world
carry-over of American and foreign cotton was sufficient to provide
74 percent of the volume consumed over the next twelve months; in this
sense, the problems of overproduction were apparent both on a national
and a world scale.[66]

In the face of growing social unrest, the Roosevelt administration
eventually developed and implemented programs specifically designed
to stabilize farm incomes and curtail production. This was the beginning
of direct government funding of the agricultural sector which has continued up until the present day, and forms the core of U.S. agricultural
policy.[67] Perhaps the most important of the New Deal agricultural
policies was the Agricultural Adjustment Act (AAA), initially implemented in 1933 and later reformulated in 1938. Under the AAA, public
funds were provided to farmers who participated in acreage allotments
and marketing quotas. Payments were also made to farmers to make up
the difference between the prevailing market price for commodities
and a government "target" or support price. These parity payments were
designed to give farmers the same purchasing power which they had
enjoyed over a 1910-1914 base period. The AAA also set up the Commodity Credit Corporation (CCC) which was to become the government's
principal arm for the acquisition, handling, storage and sale of
surplus commodities. Farmers received payment in the form of non-
recourse loans for the surpluses taken off their hands by this
government agency.

During the 1930's, the government disposed of farm surpluses
through the Federal Surplus Relief Corporation which distributed the
surpluses as donations to needy families, charitable institutions,

victims of national emergencies, the national school lunch program and
the Food Stamp Program; this procedure established the first institutional link between agricultural "welfare" and non-agricultural welfare.
As welfare is an integral feature of any capitalist economy, and therefore would have to be provided in any case, the linking of these two
types of welfare gave farm legislation a twofold purpose and hence
greater legitimation and support.

Other New Deal agricultural policies included a conservation
program which provided public funds to farmers who diverted acreage
from soil depleting crops which were in surplus, to soil conserving
legumes and grasses, as well as the beginnings of a national crop
insurance program which insured farmers against natural disasters such
as droughts, floods, insect plagues and so forth--those "Acts of God"
which private insurance companies were unwilling to underwrite. However, despite the fact that premium rates were often so high as to
deter farmers in high risk areas from taking advantage of this latter
program, national crop insurance has remained available to farmers ever
since, even though there is as yet no national health insurance program
for American citizens. In sum, we can say that all of the programs
initiated during the New Deal reflect the peculiarities and risks
associated with agricultural production as well as the increasing need
for direct state intervention in the reproduction of this sphere.

From 1938 to the present the particularities of the farm acts
have been modified many times to meet varying conditions such as war,
differential market conditions for various crops and so on. In general,
however, the current government programs incorporate many of the
fundamental principles embodied in the New Deal legislation. In particular, the government payments are made to those farmers who participate in marketing quotas, comply with acreage allotments and/or
participate in land diversion programs. In turn, while the exact
methods of calculating parity payments have changed considerably over
the years, the aim of stabilizing farm incomes through government
supports has remained fundamentally the same. Now, rather than
providing a detailed history of the changes in American farm legislation over the last few decades--details which are available from a
variety of other sources--we shall instead make some general observations regarding both the impact and consequences of farm legislation
as well as the contradictions which it embodies.

First, it should be noted that parity payments and nonrecourse
loans do not technically constitute "welfare" since these support
mechanisms require the production of commodities and hence some activity
by the recipient as a prerequisite to government aid. Nevertheless,
we argue that these subsidies reflect a sensitivity on the part of the
government to the peculiarities of agricultural production such that
the farmer, as contrasted to other commodity producers, is differentially protected from the vicissitudes of the market. Indeed, as many

observers have noted, since acreage allotments and marketing quotas
are voluntary and not mandatory, the farmer cannot lose.[68] If the
farmer chooses to participate because the prevailing market price is
low he can place his commodities in government storage and receive a
loan equivalent to the current "support" price. If the market price
does not rise, the farmer can take the support price by defaulting on
his loan and yield up his production to the government. However, if
the market price rises above the "support price" he can sell his commodity, pay off the loan and keep the difference. How many other types
of small businessmen have such regal treatment! As one observer has
noted, ".....farming probably has received more special government
solicitude over the last fifty years than any other sector of the
economy."[69]

In contrast, the non-farm population bears a double burden.
As taxpayers, on the one hand, they pay the costs of government support
programs which are now estimated at over four billion dollars
annually.[70] On the other hand, they pay higher prices for food than
would otherwise be the case under a competitive market. Indeed,
whilst farmers claim to be adverse to the payment of welfare independent of labor, they cannot simultaneously pretend to be self-
reliant.

This contradiction between the ideology and reality of welfare
becomes apparent if we look at debates over farm bills in Congress.
With a steady decline in the farm population over the last century,
rural interests have been forced to align themselves with urban
interests in order to secure the passage of farm legislation. The
Food Stamp Program, which we have already noted is linked to the disposal of farm surpluses, provided an important basis for this rural-
urban coalition. Nevertheless, a number of rural representatives
have consistently fought against the inclusion of urban welfare provisions in farm bills, thus ironically jeopardising welfare for
agriculture.[71]

Of course, we agree that urban welfare is clearly different from
the system of agricultural "welfare"; however, this difference does
not hinge merely on the technical definition of what constitutes welfare. Rather an important distinction between urban and rural types
of government support lies in the question of "who gets what."
Agricultural welfare, in contrast to urban welfare, is clearly welfare
for the well-to-do. Historically, government agriculture support
programs have tended to disproportionately benefit the wealthier
farmers. Indeed, from 1933 to the present, government price support
programs have been distributed amongst farms almost exactly in proportion to the share of total production each farmer has controlled.
Consequently, the largest farms have historically received and continue
to receive the lion's share of government largesse.[72] Moreover, as
agriculture itself has become more concentrated, so too have farm

benefits. The extent of this inequality is evidenced in recent empirical studies of the distribution of government benefits amont the farm population. For example, in 1969, the wealthiest 5 percent of all farmers received 42.4 percent of government benefits; in contrast, the poorest 20 percent of farmers received a mere 1.1 percent.[73] This stratification in the countryside, we argue, is encouraged and perpetuated by the government farm programs.

The consistent inequalities in the distribution of farm benefits indicate a growing divorce between the formal claim of the government to be supporting and protecting the family farm as the backbone of rural America and the impact of its actual farm programs which disproportionately benefit large enterprises and hence further the ruination of small holders. A product of this contradiction between ideology and policy is the rise of the American Agriculture Movement and other disenchanted rural lobbies which threaten to undermine the cohesion of the rural coalition and explode the myth of American agriculture being composed of like-sized, like-minded family farmers.[74]   In 1977, for instance, reform advocates tried unsuccessfully to prohibit federal farm subsidies to corporations in which those holding majority interests were not solely engaged in farming. In the absence of any fundamental reform of the farm programs, we can anticipate continued unrest among the less privileged ranks of American farmers.

Now some commentators have argued that direct government payments in the form of income supports as opposed to price supports would correct some of the inequities which exist among farm producers. According to this view, direct payments could be specifically directed towards the poorer farmers, since they would no longer be "tied" to the proportion of marketable produce. In turn, this would allow for a greater play of market forces in determining the price of agricultural commodities, thus reducing food prices for the non-farm population. Whilst no doubt direct payments could achieve these objectives, they would not resolve the root cause of the farm problem--agricultural overproduction. On the one hand, such measures would serve to encourage the smaller, less efficient farmer to stay in production; and on the other hand, they would serve to insulate the largest producers from government intervention. In the long run, it is quite possible that direct payments alone would only exacerbate the problems of overproduction and hence precipitate the need for still greater and more expensive government support.[75]

Indeed, we should note that in many ways current farm programs encourage overproduction. Acreage allotments and marketing quotas have been easily undermined by the intensification of production resulting from the increased use of fertilizers. Consequently, controls on acreage have been largely offset by increasing yields per acre. For example, when the AAA in 1938 provided government

payments for farmers who participated in acreage allotments or marketing quotas for corn, wheat, rice and cotton, yield per acre began to
show an upward trend for all four crops.[76] In recent years, it has been
estimated that intensification of land use has reduced the overall
impact of production controls by one-half.[77]

Again, land retirement programs contain similar loopholes such as
the ability to divert only the least fertile land from production.
Here farmers generally "rent" their land to the government who then
holds it out of production. This program has drawn much criticism
from farm program adversaries since essentially the farmer is being paid
not to produce. In this case the obvious question arises as to why
the government does not simply buy the land rather than making annual
rental payments which in the long run not only exceed the market price
of the land, but also can never resolve the problem. For instance,
it has been estimated that if the costs of government assistance
programs had been used to purchase land over the 30 year period preceeding 1967, the problems of overproduction would have been resolved
several times over.[78] However, government policy is not informed by
a cost/benefit analysis which would clearly demonstrate the greater
viability of a land purchase program, but rather by the exigencies of
a system based on private property where serious nationalization
policies are not, and indeed cannot, be considered.

In fact, the U.S. government has not even seriously considered
the less radical solution of placing effective "voluntary" controls
on farm inputs.[79] As we have suggested, advances in farm productivity
which have exacerbated the problems of over-production are in part
attributable to farm capitalization and hence increased expenditures
on constant capital (farm inputs and machinery). However, controls on
capitalization such as high sales taxes on fertilizers, farm machinery
and so forth would not only effect the efficiency of the direct producer, but would also significantly interfere with the profits of
American agribusiness corporations.

The most that can be said for the U.S. farm programs is that
they to some extent stabilize farm incomes and thereby reduce some
of the economic risks associated with agriculture. However, such
programs have failed to achieve the formally stated goals of reducing
inequalities in the countryside and controlling agricultural overproduction. Indeed, government support programs tend to both promote
rural stratification and perpetuate overproduction, hence generating
a constantly renewed demand for government support. Moreover, since
these programs have been developed within the context and realities
of a system based on "free" enterprise and private property, the government is unable to replace voluntary programs which do not work with
mandatory programs that do. Indeed, for a capitalist economy, we can
agree with Paarlberg when he writes, "Controls that actually control
are not wanted."[80]

Perhaps the most telling comment on the U.S. economic system is that over the last six decades the problems of domestic agriculture have been only resolved or at least temporarily obscured by war. As we have already noted, World War I temporarily delayed the appearance of substantial domestic overproduction in agriculture. The disruption of world agricultural production coupled with the Lend-Lease Program to the Allies at the outbreak of World War II once again provided ready channels for the disposal of American agricultural surpluses. Moreover, the entry of the U.S. itself into the war further stimulated domestic production and government policies shifted from payments designed to curtail production to incentives to increase production. After the war, the Marshall Plan postponed the appearance of substantial overproduction; however, as agricultural production recovered in Europe and Japan, domestic U.S. surpluses again became evident. The Korean War in its turn generated new demand for agricultural production delaying once more the unfolding of the real contradictions in the U.S. farm economy. However, a year after the end of the Korean War the U.S. had stockpiled 934 million bushels of wheat, 920 million bushels of corn and 11 million bales of cotton.[81] It is not surprising, then, that in this same year the U.S. government introduced a novel way of disposing of domestic farm surpluses. That is, with the passage of P.L. 480 in 1954 it became apparent that agricultural surpluses accumulated by the government were in the future to become an integral part of the U.S. foreign aid program hence implicating agriculture in the practice of U.S. imperialism. It is to this aspect of the manipulation of agricultural overproduction that we now turn.

Food as a Weapon: A major vehicle by which the government disposes of surplus agricultural production under its control is the so-called "food aid" program conducted on the basis of the Agricultural Trade and Assistance Act, better known as P.L. 480 (1954) and the Food for Peace Act (1966). Such "aid" programs by the U.S. have often been presented as munificent and benign endeavors to reduce world hunger by supplying the poorer countries with much needed food resources through outright gifts or low prices and easy credit terms. Indeed, the stated intent of the Food for Peace Act was "to use the abundant agricultural productivity of the United States to combat hunger and malnutrition."[82] However, as many critical observers have pointed out, in fact only a small fraction of "food aid" is distributed in the form of outright gifts or sales on easy credit terms.[83] Instead these programs actually serve both the domestic and international interests of the U.S. imperialist state and function to maintain recipient countries in an almost perpetual state of dependency and underdevelopment.

Indeed, foreign food "aid" programs have served a number of domestic economic interests. First, food aid programs have helped to reduce the problems of agricultural overproduction by providing an effective means of disposing of massive farm surpluses which since they could neither be sold at home or abroad accumulated in the silos and

warehouses of the Commodity Credit Corporation (CCC).[84] The disposal
by the government of these surpluses as part of foreign aid, then, not
only reduced the costs of storing and servicing these accumulated surpluses,[85] but also gave a twofold purpose to the government's farm
subsidy program. On the one hand, agricultural "welfare" or subsidy
payments which in any case would have to be made to quell farmer discontent and stabilize farm incomes and prices became part of the
general expenses of foreign aid.[86] On the other hand, the giveaway
of these surpluses could be manipulated in such a manner as to secure
the "loyalty" and dependency of the recipient country. Indeed, the
link between domestic farm surpluses and imperialist interests is
evidenced by the numerous instances where recipient countries have been
prevented from undertaking their own development programs which might
interfere with the disposal of U.S. farm surpluses. In Formosa, for
example, rice production was intentionally "de-emphasized" despite
the fact that rice exports could have provided a major mechanism for
increasing Formosa's ability to become self-supporting.[87] Thus,
government crop disposal programs have two sides: they are an integral
part of promoting economic and political stability at home whilst
at the same time they serve imperialist interests abroad.

Second, the U.S. food "aid" programs have also functioned to
foster and safeguard private U.S. capital both at home and abroad.
This aspect of foreign aid has both direct and indirect dimensions.
In the first instance, recipients of food "aid" are often contractually
obligated to purchase an additional volume of U.S. goods as a condition
for the continuation of such aid. Indeed, under the Kennedy and Johnson
administrations the tying of aid to the purchase of other U.S. commodities became a central feature of the aid program generally, such that
by 1968 some 95 percent of new aid was directly tied to an agreement to
purchase additional U.S. goods and services.[88] Such agreements led to
increased markets for U.S. produced goods and hence benefit industrial
and agribusiness sectors of the U.S. economy while simultaneously making
it more difficult to producers in recipient countries to compete.[89]

Indirectly, agricultural aid and development programs (such as
the Green Revolution) frequently require recipient countries to
purchase other U.S. goods in order to carry out and sustain changes
in production methods. For example, the widespread adoption of new
hybrid "miracle" strains of wheat, rice and other crops not only
depend on the importation of seed grain but also of expensive farm
machinery, fertilizer and so forth.[90] In a similarly indirect manner,
food "aid" programs often last just long enough to establish Western
agricultural commodities as an integral part of the recipient country's
diet. In Guatemala, for example, CARE introduced a high protein milk
(CSM) which was too expensive to produce locally, and because this
milk was initially distributed free, it became a popular alternative
to the locally prepared milk. Thus, when CARE ceased distribution, U.S.
companies were able to move in to produce and market CSM to the marked

disadvantage of local producers.[91]

Moreover, many conditions attached to "aid" programs often amount to nothing more than safeguards for U.S. capital abroad. Indeed, up until 1968, under the Hickenlooper Amendment to P.L. 480, any foreign country which nationalized U.S. investments without adequate or satis-factory compensation stood to have its food "aid" withheld. In this respect, it is interesting to note that when the World Bank refused to continue these sanctions, under the Nixon regime, support for the food aid program among government conservatives began to wain.[92]

The safeguarding of U.S. interests abroad includes more than the protection of U.S. capital and often involves the direct military and political concerns of the U.S. imperialist state. Increasingly, aid has become conditional on the recipient country's willingness to provide leases for U.S. military bases, signatures on diplomatic agree-ments or the purchase of armaments and weapon systems so that the recipient country develops a military capacity which saves the U.S. the cost and embarrassment of establishing its own military presence on foreign soil. In this way, select countries are promoted as the "policement" of potentially volatile regions of the world. Recent events in Iran suggest the frailty of such arrangements. However, the "aid" packages offered to Spain (long denied access to the E.E.C. partly at least because of its anti-democratic government) in exchange for U.S. air base rights are a good case in point.[93] As Secretary of Defense McNamara remarked in 1964, "In my considered judgement...the foreign aid program generally, has now become the most critical element of our overall national security effort..."[94] Given these global military considerations, it is scarcely surprising that P.L. 480 was transferred from the U.S. Department of Agriculture to the State Department.

For the recipient countries, foreign aid has on the whole functioned to maintain them in a position of greater dependency. While the "dumping" of U.S. agricultural surpluses has indeed in some cases lowered the domestic price of food and raw material, it has also stunted the growth of indigenous agriculture and hence retarded agricultural capital formation. As Andre Gunder Frank writes of the case of Brazil, "...loans under P.L. 480, euphemistically called "Food for Peace," do not supply a single dollar but consist rather of cruzeiros derived from the sale in Brazil of American surplus wheat which, like all other "dumping," competes unfairly with and inhibits the development of Brazilian wheat production."[95] Some countries have even been forced to take commodities under P.L. 480 which they them-selves had a domestic surplus. For instance, Pakistan as a condition of receiving P.L. 480 wheat, was also forced to take cotton at a time when there was already a surplus of domestic cotton on the market. This condition was not only disasterous for indigenous cotton growers,

but also reduced Pakistan's foreign exchange earnings by further forcing down the price of cotton.[96] Other repercussions to indigenous
agriculture from P.L. 480 include the delaying of much-needed agrarian
reforms as well as the increasing ruination of peasantry who can no
longer subsist in the face of the lowered food prices caused by
"dumping."[97]

In addition, not only has food "aid" functioned to stunt agricultural development, but it has also had a similar effect on the recipient
country's industrial development. For example, when India tried to
develop its own fertilizer industry in the mid-1960's, the U.S. government gave notice that henceforth food shipments would be on a month-
to-month basis.[98] In turn, through its military linkages, food "aid"
has had insidious implications for all of the laboring population in
these countries--both industrial and agricultural--since the manipulation of food supplies has been used to contain incipient revolutionary
movements led by progressive forces. Indeed, the U.S. has a long
history of manipulating food supplies to contain anti-imperialist
and/or socialist revolutions. After the Russian Revolution of 1917,
these efforts took the form of armed intervention as well as support
of anti-Bolshevik forces with food and economic supplies. In Hungary,
the manipulation of food supplies was a critical factor which helped
to defeat the Bela Kun government in 1918.[99] More recently, this
manipulation appears to have become a staple of U.S. foreign policy.

Whilst food "aid" in the form of concessional sales is supposed
to provide food to underdeveloped countries on easy credit terms,
ironically, the price paid by the recipient country is often higher
than those prevailing on the world market. This is, in part, a consequence of the fact that the U.S. law stipulates that "aid" commodities
be shipped on American bottoms which consequently substantially
increases overall costs. For example, in 1953, shipping wheat to
Pakistan on American ships cost $26 per ton as against $12 to $14
per ton on foreign ships.[100]

In turn, the fact that most "aid" is in the form of concessional
sales or loans as opposed to outright grants, or tied to obligatory
future purchases of U.S. goods, serves to increase the foreign debts
of the recipient country. In the long run, this international system
of "debt peonage" means essentially that the recipient country is
bankrolling its own dependency.[101]

There have been substantial changes in the U.S. aid program in
recent years which reflect to some extent at least a growing awareness
among the American public as well as the recipient countries that
food as "aid" is but a guise for food as "weapon" in the maintenance of
U.S. imperialist hegemony. Between the late 1950's and 1960's, U.S.
aid primarily took the form of bilateral concessional sales which

involved obligatory political, economic and military agreements of the kind we have discussed above. However, by the time the Republican administration took office in 1969, several factors made these bilateral aid programs less tenable; criticism of U.S. foreign intervention was generally on the rise as a consequence of the Viet Nam War and both liberals as well as radicals were calling into question the real design and purposes of the aid programs. Consequently, the Nixon administration made a number of important changes in the way aid programs were managed.

First, bilateral agreements were replaced by multilateral disbursements of aid by such bodies as the World Bank and the International Monetary Fund. Second, the power to grant aid was transferred from the legislative to the executive branch of government with the effect that the military and paramilitary aspects of aid were removed from the control of Congress. Third, congressional funding was replaced by borrowing on international capital markets, which further removed aid from "democratic" control and a modicum of public scrutiny. Finally, pressure was placed on America's allies in the advanced capitalist nations to share the costs of maintaining "democracy" in the world. It was hoped that not only would other nations start to share the costs of maintaining U.S. hegemony, but also that a lowered profile of the U.S. in foreign countries would further obscure its actual role and quell some of the rising anti-American and anti-imperialist criticism and unrest.[102]

Above, we have pointed to some of the ways in which food "aid" serves to promote stability of domestic politics, foster certain vested American economic interests and function as a weapon in the arsenal of U.S. foreign policy. Indeed, the ability, let alone the willingness, to use food as a weapon is itself a reflection of the gross inequalities which exist between the advanced capitalist and the underdeveloped countries. The "affluence" and overproduction of countries like the U.S. stand out in sharp contrast to the poverty, starvation and malnutrition which afflict the vast proportion of the population of the Third World. Indeed, the fact that 210 million Americans consume in grain equivalent as much as 1.5 billion people in the Third World, or that the 1-1/2 million tons of fertilizer used on the lawns, cemeteries and golf courses of North America could produce enough additional food to feed some 80 million people captures with particular vividness such inequalities.[103] In the face of such statistics, it is difficult for the social scientist to resist the temptation to identify the major contradiction in the world today as no longer a question of class, but rather a question of nations plundering other nations.[104]

However, inequalities of food distribution are not restricted to the underdeveloped countries. America is itself characterized by a massive incidence of malnutrition among sectors of its population

as well as an increasing disparity of diet standards between rich and
poor. That inner city children exhibit the physical and mental effects
of malnutrition and that some senior citizens are reduced to eating dog
food is a stark reminder in our own backyard as to the class nature of
the problem.[105] On the other hand, China's success in feeding a
population of 800 million only <u>after</u> the 1949 revolution further suggests
that inequalities in the distribution of food is related to more fundamental inequalities in the distribution of property than any technical
factor. In this respect, the ultimate resolution of the contradictions which generate poverty and starvation in the midst of plenty both
in America and abroad clearly depends upon profound changes in the
social, economic and political relations that currently prevail.

V. CONCLUSION

In our review of the role of the state in American agricultural
development we have stressed the contradictory nature of agriculture
as a branch of production as well as the contradictory nature of state
agricultural policies. On the one hand, certain features of agriculture
have served to limit direct capitalist penetration of this sphere, and
in turn, this has resulted in a situation where a significant part of
agricultural production is left in the hands of the petty producer.
On the other hand, we have noted how state agricultural policies have by
and large emerged as a response to this uneven capitalist development
and how these policies are implemented in such a way that the contradictions embodied in this uneven development are never transcended.

Historically, we have argued that the expansion of American agriculture onto the western frontier could not have proceeded autonomously,
but instead depended upon direct and indirect state intervention at
both the federal and local levels. Conversely, we have also pointed
out how the expansion of commercial agriculture during this era of
internal settler colonialism played an important role in developing
the coherence of the U.S. nation state and fostering the articulation
of the home market. However, in this process direct agricultural
production was importantly subordinated to financial and industrial
capital as we have noted in the case of the railroads, banks and farm
input industries.

By the turn of the 20th Century, the contradictions which marked
the agricultural sector had become heightened and hence more visible.
This was in part a consequence of the fact that the geographical spread
of American agriculture was accompanied by significant increases in
farm productivity nationwide. Thus in the era of U.S. monopoly capitalism we find that the problem of overproduction becomes a constant
feature of the agricultural sector. First, despite the fact that

large and important spheres of agriculture remain in the hands of petty
producers, this has not committed these sectors to a low productivity.
Indeed, quite the reverse: technological advances derived from agricultural research and development and supplied by capitalist input
industries have allowed for dramatic increases in productivity over
the past century. In turn, however, this general increase in productivity has resulted in perennial overproduction and hence violent
price fluctuations and general economic instability. Indeed, even with
today's massive state support for agriculture, farm incomes show the
greatest degree of variation.

Second, increased productivity has not led to a decline in the
need for state support, but on the contrary, as agriculture has become
more productive, so state intervention has become more imperative,
more extensive and more expensive. In turn, as we have noted, many
of these state agricultural policies accentuate and perpetuate overproduction and inequalities in the countryside and hence function to
reproduce those very conditions which called forth the need for state
support in the first place. Generally, the state has become the displaced
locus of the contradictions of agriculture, and war in its turn the
great obscurer of these contradictions.

Finally, unable to resolve the problems of domestic agriculture
in any rational way because of the dictates and constraints of private
property and private accumulation, the state has increasingly looked
upon the productivity of agriculture and its surpluses as a convenient
resource to be employed in the exercise of imperialist hegemony. That
agricultural overproduction exists alongside a steady decline in the
quality of agricultural products and a deepening crisis of malnutrition
and hunger at home and abroad is not surprising; capitalism is the
production of exchange values and only incidentally satisfies human
needs.

In the last analysis, it is the fundamental peculiarities of
agriculture which determine the nature, extent and scope of state
intervention in this sector, yet not only does the state reproduce
agriculture through these policies, but also it reproduces the very
contradictions which mark this branch of production as well.

*   *   *

Susan Mann received her B.A. from the University of Maryland and
an M.A. from the American University, Washington, D.C. Currently she is
a doctoral candidate in the Department of Sociology, University of
Toronto. She is co-author of the article "Obstacles to the Development
of a Capitalist Agriculture" which appeared recently in the Journal of

Peasant Studies and has written several articles on women and domestic labor under capitalism.

James M. Dickinson received his B.A. from the University of Kent, England and his M.A. from the American University, Washington, D.C. He is co-author with Susan Mann of "Obstacles to the Development of a Capitalist Agriculture." Currently he is a doctoral candidate in the Department of Sociology, University of Toronto where he is undertaking an analysis of state social policies in the reproduction of the working class.

REFERENCES

1. E. Mandel, Late Capitalism (London: New Left Books, 1975), p. 474. The following discussion of state functions relies heavily on Mandel's Chapter 15.

2. Elmar Altvater, "Some Problems of State Intervention," in J. Holloway and S. Picciotto (eds.), State and Capital (London: Edward Arnold, 1978), pp. 40-43.

3. For an important discussion of this in particular and of the externality of the state as regards capitalist production in general, see A.T. Aumeeruddy, "Labour Power and the State," Capital and Class, No. 6, 1978, pp. 42-66.

4. Altvater, op. cit., summarizes: "Not all social functions can be carried out capitalistically whether because the production of certain material conditions of production yields no profit or because the level of generality of many regulations under prevailing concrete conditions is too great for them to be performed by individual capitals with their different particular interests."

5. F. Engels, Anti-Durhing (Moscow: Progress Publishers, 1969), p. 330.

6. For a more detailed discussion of this problem, see S.A. Mann and J.M. Dickinson, "Obstacles to the Development of a Capitalist Agriculture," Journal of Peasant Studies V (4), pp. 466-481.

7. K. Marx, Capital Vol. III (Moscow: Progress Publishers, 1967): "It is in the nature of things that vegetable and animal substances whose growth and production are subject to certain organic laws and bound up with natural time periods, cannot be suddenly augmented in the same degree as, for instance, machines and other fixed capital..." (p. 118). See also R.L. Cohen, The Economics of Agriculture (Cambridge: Cambridge U.P., 1965), pp. 100-101.

8. Cohen, op. cit., p. 103.

9. See for example Paul A. Samuelson, Economics (New York: McGraw-Hill, 1961), pp. 485-486. Note that for Samuelson price fluctuations in agriculture are alleviated by the activities of speculators thereby giving a social role to this essentially parasitic stratum.

10. K. Marx, Capital Vol. II (Moscow: Progress Publishers, 1967), p. 237; see also pp. 114-115.

11. This is not to ignore that agriculture in certain regions of the U.S., particularly the Old South, was based on slave plantations. However, it was not the indigenous population that was enslaved; rather labour was imported from Africa. Thus agricultural expansion in the U.S. whether on the basis of plantations or petty commodity production units was not predicated on the preservation of the indigenous American Indians.

12. There are of course important national variations here. For example, the French peasant was much more successful in retaining communal rights and institutions than his English equivalent. See A. Soboul, The French Revolution (New York: Vintage, 1975).

13. See for example K. Marx, Capital Vol. I (Moscow: Progress, 1967), pp. 667-701; and M. Dobb, Studies in the Development of Capitalism (new York: International Publishers, 1970), pp. 221-254.

14. Jack Eblen, The First and Second United States Empires (Pittsburgh: University of Pittsburgh Press, 1968), pp. 1-8.

15. Eblen, op. cit., p. 42.

16. Fred. A. Shannon, The Farmers Last Frontier (New York: Farrar & Rinehart, 1945), p. 162.

17. Shannon, op. cit., p. 154; see also H. Briggs, "Early Bonanza Farming in the Red River Valley of the North," Agricultural History VI (1), pp. 26-27.

18. For a discussion of these early colonists see Shannon, op. cit., pp. 28-30 and 197-201.

19. See Walter P. Webb, The Great Plains (New York: Ginn and Co., 1931); and Harriet Friedmann, The Transformation of Wheat Production in the Era of the World Market 1873-1935: A Global Analysis of Production and Exchange. Unpublished Ph.D. dissertation, Harvard University 1976, pp. 152, 171-172. We must also note here the possible effects of the Civil War in retarding Western infrastructural development.

20. Hence the case of the U.S.A. is more akin to forms of settler colonialism which characterized New Zealand or some of the Carribean Islands where the extermination and isolation of the indigenous population was the rule. The historical experience of the U.S.A. in this regard is reflected in an almost natural affinity for contemporary settler-colonial regimes.

21. John Tebbel and Keith Jennison, The American Indian Wars (New York: Harper, 1960), p. 260.

22. Robert M. Utley, Frontier Regulars: The United States Army and the Indian 1866-1891 (New York: Macmillan, 1973), p. 22.

23. Tebbel and Jennison, op. cit., p. 260; see also Utley, op. cit., p. 22.

24. Utley, op. cit., pp. 71-72.

25. For a detailed discussion of the Indian missions see Jack D. Forbes (ed.), The Indian in America's Past (Englewood Cliffs, N.J.: Prentice-Hall, 1964), pp. 75-76.

26. Utley, op. cit., p. 5; and Fred A. Shannon, An Appraisal of Walter Prescott Webb's "The Great Plains" (New York: Social Science Research Council, 19), pp. 64-66.

27. Utley, op. cit., pp. 5-6.

28. Clark C. Spence (ed.), The American West: A Sourcebook (New York: Crowell, 1966), pp. 351-352; and Shannon, op. cit., p. 64.

29. Spence, op. cit., p. 342.

30. Utley, op. cit. The consolidation of the U.S. Government's reservation policy did not signal the final chapter in the pacification of the American Indians. In the late 1880's after this consolidation was complete, the government changed its policy. Henceforth, the Indian was not merely to be isolated, but rather he was to be absorbed, assimilated into the "American way of life." This policy was most fully expressed in the Dawes Allotment Act which sought to sever the community of the tribe by breaking up the reservation holdings and dividing them among Indian families. This transformation of the reservation into private allotments served both to individuate the Indian and to open the remaining reservation land to possible purchase by white settlers.

31. Shannon, Farmers Lost Frontier, op. cit., p. 51; see also Henry George, Our Land and Land Policy (New York: Doubleday and McClure, 1901), pp. 89-90.

32. Indeed the costs of moving 500-1,000 miles and acquiring the basic farm implements were an expense few could afford. See Shannon, op. cit., p. 54.

33. Wayne D. Rasmussen (ed.), Readings in the History of American Agriculture (Urbana, Ill.: Univ. of Illinois, 1960), p. 113.

34. For a discussion of the disposal of the public domain see Paul Wallace Gates, "The Homestead Law in an Incongruous Land System," American Historical Review XLI (4), pp. 652-681.

35. For example, over 183,000,000 acres of the public domain were given to or reserved for railroad companies, an area equal to almost 1/10 of the entire land area of the U.S.A. By a conservative estimate this amounted to a free gift of over $500 million net value. Moreover, the railroads later sold much of this land to settlers at almost triple the government's pre-Homestead Act price. See Shannon, The Farmers Last Frontier, op. cit., pp. 64-66; and George, op. cit., p. 4.

36. Shannon, op. cit., p. 52.

37. Friedmann, op. cit., p. 165; Webb, op. cit., p. 276. However, as Shannon suggests, government construction and operation as opposed to private ventures would have been less costly to the public "had not such a solution been unthinkable to the rulers of that generation." Shannon, op. cit., p. 67. See also K. Marx, Grundrisse (Harmondsworth, Middlesex: Penquin Books, 1973), pp. 524-537, for an important discussion of the relationship between the development of the means of communication and transport and capitalist development.

38. Friedmann, op. cit., p. 164-165. Hence an immediate source of revenue for the railroads was land speculation through sale of the huge tracts of fertile land largely donated by the federal government.

39. Shannon, op. cit., p. 41-44.

40. Louis M. Hacker, The Course of American Economic Growth (New York: Wiley, 1970), p. 222. Shannon, op. cit., p. 185.

41. Shannon, op. cit., p. 188.

42. Hacker, op. cit.

43. Briggs, op. cit., p. 32; Shannon, op. cit., p. 162. This was not the case for capitalist wheat farms; the "bonanza" wheat farms were highly specialized producers and imported large quantities

of foodstuffs to provide for their wage labourers.

44. Eblen, op. cit., pp. 6-7.

45. G.W.F. Hegel, Philosophy of Right, trans. T.M. Knox (New York: Oxford U.P., 1971), p. 122.

46. Max Hedley, "The Transformation of the Domestic Mode of Production," paper presented to Canadian Sociology and Anthropology Association Annual Meeting. Fredericton, New Brunswick; Harriet Friedmann, "Simple Commodity Production and Wage Labour in the American Plains," Journal of Peasant Studies VI (1).

47. For a discussion of other conditions that may preclude the possibility of fission, see Hedley, op. cit.

48. Friedmann, op. cit.

49. Eblen, op. cit., p. 5.

50. A.V. Chayanov, The Theory of Peasant Economy, D. Thorner et al. (eds.) (Homewood, Ill..: Richard Irwin and Co., 1966), pp. 4-5; and Friedmann, op. cit.

51. Indeed the bonanza farms could only exist as long as they were able to acquire cheap and fertile lands. Here the temporary "super profits" from differential rent offset the problems of profit maximization. However, with the increased settlement of the region not only did land prices begin to soar, but also the increased volume of wheat production coupled with the general economic crises of the 1880's and 1890's sent wheat prices plumeting downwards. Under these conditions the bonanza farms were incapable of making the average rate of profit and these capitalist enterprises disintegrated leaving wheat production in the hands of petty producers. For a discussion of the initial advantages held by these capitalist farms and their later demise, see Briggs, op. cit.

52. James O'Connor, The Fiscal Crisis of the State (New York: St. Martin's Press, 1973), p. 67.

53. Alex F. McCalla, "Politics of the Agricultural Research Establishment," in The New Politics of Food, Don F. Hadinger and William P. Browne (eds.), Toronto: Lexington Books, 1978), pp. 77-78.

54. Ibid, p. 81, p. 90.

55. Ibid, p. 78.

56. Michael Perelman, Farming for Profit in a Hungry World (Montclair, NJ: Allanheld, Osmun & Co., 1977), p. 169.

57. H.J. Frundt, American Agribusiness and U.S. Foreign Agricultural Policy. Unpublished Ph.D. dissertation, Rutgers University, New Brunswick, NJ, 1975.

58. Perelman, op. cit., p. 46.

59. Wayne D. Rasmussen, Readings in the History of American Agriculture (Urbana, Ill.: Univ. of Illinois Press, 1960), p. 104.

60. Vernon Carstensen, Farmer Discontent 1865-1900 (New York: Wiley, 1974), p. 2.

61. V.I. Lenin, "Capitalism and Agriculture in the United States of America," in Collected Works Vol. 22 (Moscow: Progress Publishers, 1974); and Carstensen, op. cit., p. 5.

62. Shannon, op. cit., p. 139.

63. Francis Van Gigch, "Historical and Economic Summary of U.S. Agriculture," in The Overproduction Trap in U.S. Agriculture, Glenn L. Johnson and C. Leroy Quame (eds.), (Baltimore: John Hopkins University Press, 1972), p. 160.

64. Ibid; Frundt, op. cit., pp. 44-46.

65. Frundt, op. cit., pp. 73-74.

66. Anna Rochester, Why Farmers are Poor: The Agricultural Crisis in the United States (New York: International Publishers, 1940), p. 218.

67. For a discussion of New Deal agricultural policies see Wayne D. Rasmussen and Gladys Baker, "Programs for Agriculture 1933-1965," in Agricultural Policy in an Affluent Society, Vernon W. Rattan et al. (eds.)(New York: W.W. Norton, 1969), pp. 69-88; and Walter W. Wilcox and Willard W. Cochrane, Economics of American Agriculture (Englewood Cliffs, NJ: Prentice-Hall, 1960), chapters 25-27.

68. Stephen Chapman, "Welfare Tractors," The New Republic, March 3, 1979, pp. 16-17.

69. Ibid.

70. G.E. Brandow, "Cost of Farm Programs," in Benefits and Burdens of Rural Development, Iowa State University Center for Agricultural and Economic Development (Ames, Iowa: Iowa State University, 1970), p. 82.

71. John Peters, "The 1977 Farm Bill: Coalitions in Congress," in The New Politics of Food, op. cit., p. 25.

72. John A. Schnittker, "Distribution of Benefits from Existing and Prospective Farm Programs," in Benefits and Burdens of Rural Development, op. cit., p. 90. See also Frundt, op. cit., pp. 55-56.

73. Schnittker, op. cit., p. 96.

74. Peters, op. cit., pp. 26-27.

75. Don Paarlberg, American Farm Policy (New York: Wiley, 1964), pp. 306-314. See also Luther G. Tweeten, "Commodity Programs for Agriculture," in Agricultural Policy in an Affluent Society, op. cit., pp. 110-111.

76. Rasmussen and Baker, op. cit., p. 76.

77. Paarlberg, op. cit., p. 297.

78. E.O. Heady, "Trends and Policies of Agriculture in the U.S.A." in Economic Change and Agriculture, J. Ashton and S.J. Rogers (eds.), (Edinburgh: Oliver and Boyd, 1976), p. 227.

79. Paarlberg, op. cit., p. 303.

80. Paarlberg, op. cit., p. 298.

81. Van Gigch, op. cit., p. 168. Van Gigch also provides a detailed discussion of how wars have obscured the problems in U.S. agriculture.

82. Quoted in D. Gale Johnson, "Potential Role of Humanitarian Efforts," in World Agricultural Trade: The Potential for Growth, Proceedings of a Symposium sponsored by the Federal Reserve Bank of Kansas City, May 1978, p. 97.

83. Food for Peace "distributes" surplus agricultural commodities in a number of ways: sales for foreign currencies, barter for strategic materials, sales on long term credit, and direct donations. Sales for foreign currencies forms by far the largest. For data see Paarlberg, op. cit., pp. 288-289.

84. Michael Hudson, Super Imperialism: The Economic Strategy of American Empire (New York: Holt, Rinehart, Winston, 1972), pp. 129 and 144. As Paarlberg notes, op. cit., p. 290, without foreign aid, U.S. surplus stocks in 1963 would have been double what they actually were.

85. H. Alavi and A. Khusro, "Pakistan: The Burden of U.S. Aid," in Imperialism and Underdevelopment: A Reader, R. Rhodes (Ed.), (New York: Monthly Review Press, 1970), p. 69. Alavi and Khusro estimate the cost to the U.S. government of storing farm surpluses to be more than a billion dollars a year.

86. Hudson, op. cit., p. 129.

87. Alavi and Khusro, op. cit., p. 69.

88. Hudson, op. cit., p. 153.

89. David Tobis, "Foreign Aid: The Case of Guatemala," in Readings in U.S. Imperialism, K.T. Fann and Donald Hodges (eds.), (Boston: Porter Sargent Publisher, 1971), p. 252.

90. Hudson, op. cit., p. 147; see also Mitchell, op. cit., p. 203. For a full discussion of the "Green Revolution," see Perelman, op. cit., chap. 14. Perelman reports that in the case of Indonesia, the Green Revolution not only led to massive corruption, social differentiation, etc., but actually precipitated a major famine as pesticides killed off the fish upon which the people depended as a major source of protein.

91. Frundt, op. cit., pp. 111-112.

92. Hudson, op. cit., p. 164.

93. Ibid., p. 156.

94. Ibid. President Johnson is also quoted as describing the U.S. foreign aid program as "The best weapon we have to insure that our own men in uniform need not go into combat.", p. 157.

95. Andre Gunder Frank, "On the Mechanisms of Imperialism: The Case of Brazil," in Readings in U.S. Imperialism, Fann and Hodges (eds.), op. cit., p. 244.

96. Alavi and Khusro, op. cit., p. 70.

97. Hudson, op. cit., p. 133.

98. Perelman, op. cit., p. 115.

99. Harry Magdoff, "Militarism and Imperialism," in The Capitalist System, R. Edwards, M. Reich, and T. Weisskopf (eds.), (Englewood Cliffs, NJ: Prentice-Hall, 1972), p. 424.

100. Alavi and Khusro, op. cit., p. 69.

101. Hudson, op. cit., p. 153.

102. For a detailed discussion of these changes see Hudson, op. cit., pp. 157-163.

103. Don Mitchell, The Politics of Food (Toronto: James Lorimer & Co., 1975), pp. 198 and 200.

104. For examples of theorists who have succumbed to this temptation, see A. Emmanuel, Unequal Exchange: A Study of the Imperialism of Trade (New York: Monthly Review Press, 1972) and S. Amin, Accumulation on a World Scale (New York: Monthly Review Press, 1974). Conversely, for a critique of this view, see C. Bettel-heim, in A. Emmanuel, op. cit., Appendix I, or E. Mandel, Late Capitalism (London: New Left Books, 1975), Chapter 11.

105. Mitchell, op. cit , p. 198. For details on malnutrition in the U.S.A., see Herbert G. Birch and Joan Dye Gussow, Disadvantaged Children: Health, Nutrition and School Failure (New York: Harcourt, Brace, 1970), esp. chapter 9; and Hunger USA: Report by the Citizens Board of Inquiry into Hunger and Malnutrition in the USA (Washington, D.C.: New Community Press, 1968).

11. Agricultural Policy and the Decline of Commercial Family Farming: A Comparative Analysis of the U.S., Sweden, and the Netherlands

PETER R. SINCLAIR

The social organization of farming in Europe, North America and Oceania has presented a major anomoly during the nineteenth and twentieth centuries. Petty commodity production on commercial family farms persisted as the most common type of agriculture, while other sectors of the economy were being organized on the basis of capitalist wage labour. Today, despite the defensive efforts of farmers' movements, commercial family farming is in a state of decline. My purpose in this paper is to examine the relationship between agricultural policies and this development. For too long rural sociologists have left analysis of the impact of the state on agriculture to economists and a few political scientists.[1] Here I shall try to redress the situation to some extent by arguing that the long-run effects of state policy are contrary to the goals of most agrarian movements and inconsistent with the state's ideology of protecting commercial family farmers. The reason for this is that agricultural policy does not counteract tendencies towards the proletarianization of farming and its greater articulation with organized capitalism.

After clarifying my use of the term "commercial family farming," the main features of agricultural policy in advanced capitalist societies will be presented with special attention to the United States, Sweden and the Netherlands. This is followed by a critical analysis in which recent changes in the social structure of agriculture ar interpreted as evidence of transition to capitalist farming. Finally, the ideological conservatism of policy is discussed in relation to neo-Marxist theory of the state.

COMMERCIAL FAMILY FARMING IN CRISIS

Initially, it is worthwhile to clarify how the category "commercial family farm" is to be understood in this paper. The commercial family farm is a petty commodity enterprise, i.e., a small-scale production unit which is oriented to the market. Thus, it is distinct from the peasant farm in which production is mainly

327

for household consumption. Furthermore, the scale of the family farm
is such that it can be operated using family labour with only occasion-
al hired help. If more than 50 percent of labour on a farm is hired,
it is reasonable to call such a unit "capitalist." The family farmer,
while participating in a system dominated by the capitalist mode of
production is not him/herself a capitalist and the family farm is not
a capitalist enterprise. With regard to land tenure, the family farmer
does not necessarily fall into the class of petite bourgeoisie, whose
members own the means of production. This is often the case, but the
term also encompasses petty commodity producers who are tenants or
partly tenants. While having different class interests in some respects,
commercial owner-operators and tenants share sufficient common problems
to justify their incorporation within the single category of family
farmers.

Commercial family farmers have been faced with a set of endemic
problems which are now well known: fluctuating and low incomes (in
many cases) relative to wage and salary earners. As Hallett (1968:14)
shows, there is considerable variation among countries in the relative
position of farm incomes. Also, the variation within agriculture is
greater than between average farm income and the average in other
sectors. In addition to the uncertainties which derive from the biological nature of farming, there is a persistent economic pressure on
farmers in developed economies. This is a result of the relatively
low increase in the demand for food compared with increases in per
capita income. Given that technical innovation also stimulates agricultural productivity, the consequence will be lower prices for farm
products and lower farm incomes unless the number of farmers is reduced
to compensate for greater productivity. Since the factors of production
in agriculture cannot be moved quickly from one commodity which is over-
supplied to another which is in demand, and since the skills of farmers
are not easily transferable to other economic sectors, there have been
periods of severe distress for commercial family farmers as a result of
low incomes. The depression of the 1930's stands out as the most
disastrous period, but the general problem persists. This conclusion
is weakened somewhat by the combination of rapid economic growth and
declining food production at the world level in 1972, which produced
a temporary spurt in farm incomes relative to others. Since then,
however, the terms of trade have moved once again against farmers
(OECD, 1977a).

In response to the recurrent crises of overproduction, commercial
family farmers have ventured along several paths. Many have abandoned
agriculture, although not in sufficient numbers to eliminate the
problem. Others have simply kept on producing as before, resigned
to existing conditions, hoping for improvement. Some have expanded
their holdings, reduced unit costs of production and tried to establish
profitable enterprises in the existing market structure. Yet another
alternative has been the support of political and economic social

movements to defend their enterprises. Particularly in the latter
case, it has been impossible for the state to ignore the crisis of
commercial family farming.

AGRICULTURAL POLICIES

The survival of petty commodity production in a subordinate
position within contemporary capitalism has posed particular problems
for state officials. In the first place, as I have noted, commercial
family farmers have organized to pressure the state into programmes
to defend their interests. At the same time, agribusiness corporations
involved in processing and marketing have an interest in low cost
inputs, i.e., low farm gate prices. Conversely, they have an interest
in the maximum price of food at the retail level consistent with
profitable operation. Consumers, on the contrary, favour a low cost,
high quality food product. Furthermore, state officials, as overlords
of the general health of the economy, must consider the effect of
agriculture on the balance of trade as well as the protection of the
national food supply if there should be a curtailment of external
supplies for any reason. From this social environment a set of
policies of considerable complexity and doubtful consistency has emerged
in each of the advanced capitalist societies. Before providing a
theoretical interpretation and critique, some of the main features
of these policies will be outlined. Basically, we may divide them
into two categories--income support and structural reform policies.

Income support is most commonly provided by some form of state
regulation of prices. Specific techniques include import levies and
state purchasing of "surpluses." Some countries pay producers direct
subsidies out of general tax revenues when market prices are below
negotiated levels. Others, e.g., the United States for several
decades, try to maintain prices by establishing quota limits for
producers and by subsidizing farmers who withdraw resources from
production or divert them to other commodities. Finland introduced
a licencing system for egg and pork production in 1975, and Australia
operates a similar system in dairy production. State marketing boards
have been widely used in some places, particularly Britain and the
Commonwealth.

In many respects the income support measures are only short term
solutions to the low income problem. The real need is to reduce the
number of farms and rationalize structures where they are inefficient
so that the level of production in normal times will not outstrip
demand. At least, this is the desired aim within the contest of a
capitalist market economy and has long been advocated by agricultural
economists. Beginning in most countries after the Second World War
and expanding rapidly in the mid-sixties, many states accepted this

advice and instituted structural reform programmes. Since these
programmes aim to create an agriculture with a smaller number of more
efficient producers they are in some respects in contradiction with
the income support measures which discourage off farm migration by
boosting farm incomes. Of course, such measures are necessary for
political reasons and, also, to make the transition smoother and less
dislocating for the farmers involved. Once again there are many different structural reform programmes. Grants, loans and advice may be
offered to assist the creation of viable holdings. The state may
supervise and intervene in land transfers to ensure that they lead to
a better structure. In those countries, generally central European
ones, with problems of fragmentation, state financed consolidation
programmes exist. Finally, discontinuation payments and special
pensions or retraining allowances may be introduced to persuide some
farmers to give up the land. In regions where it is felt advisable
to retain a minimal level of population, part-time farming may be
encouraged and articulated with general regional development programmes
as in northern Norway. Given this variety of programmes and the
varying conditions found in the advanced capitalist countries, it is
advisable to examine several specific societies in more detail.

The first of our "thumbnail" sketches will deal with the United
States, selected for its position as the world's most powerful capitalist society. Although there are many farms in the U.S. too small
to provide adequate incomes, there has never been a problem of fragmentation thanks to the settlement patterns and an absence of inheritance
norms encouraging subdivision of property. Furthermore, the movement
of people out of farming has been so substantial that the U.S. does
not have a well developed programme of structural reform. Only the
Conservation Reserve of the 1956 Agricultural Act withdrew land from
production on a long term basis. In other cases farmers have been
paid to divert part of their farms from particular commodities, but only
for a year at a time and with no consideration of reducing the number
of farms. State assistance has been available (since 1916) under the
Farm Home Administration Act to provide direct loans, loan insurance,
and grants for various farm improvement schemes, including enlargement.
The grant programme now includes assistance to public bodies to prepare
and carry out general rural social and environmental protection projects.

The main thrust of U.S. policy from the nineteen-thirties to
the sixties has been a set of specific commodity programmes to maintain
the general level of farm incomes. In the depressed agricultural
conditions after the First World War, terms of trade moved strongly
against farmers with the result that farm organizations pushed for
"parity" prices based on the pre-war ratios. One of the first tangible
results was the establishment of the Federal Farm Board in 1929.
With a capital of $500 million, its aims were to sustain farm income
and reduce market fluctuations by helping co-operatives to store
excess products. This measure was inadequate to cope with the disaster

of the thirties and was followed in 1933 by the Agricultural Adjustment
Act which included a policy of supply management with the aim of restoring
farm prices to the level of 1909-14. Support came from the American
Farm Bureau Federation, but the programme was declared inadequate by
the National Farmers Union, the Grange, and the Farm Holiday Association.
Under the 1933 Act, the state was empowered to enter into voluntary
acreage reduction agreements, to provide advance payments to producers
which did not have to be repayed if selling prices did not cover them
(nonrecourse loans), to negotiate marketing agreements, and to license
marketers and processers. Other sections allowed major expansion of farm
credit and advocated an inflationary monetary policy. Under the new
law acreage quotas were established for cotton, wheat, corn, rice,
tobacco, hogs, milk, sugar, and peanuts. By 1934, market or volume
quotas were also introduced in cotton and tobacco after receiving
approval in referenda of producers. In addition, farmers were compensated for taking land out of production. Marketing agreements established minimum prices for producers of certain products (especially
milk, fruit and vegetables) and provided more stability in their
distribution. In these cases, prices rather than production were
controlled, with the result that the government had to store or dispose
of any excess.

A new comprehensive Act in 1938 incorporated the goals of certain
earlier legislation (such as soil conservation) and set out more
detailed commodity programmes. "New Features included (a) non-recourse
loans for producers of corn, wheat, and cotton under specified supply
and price conditions if marketing quotas were approved in referendum,
(b) crop insurance for wheat, and (c) payments, if funds were available to producers of corn, cotton, rice, tobacco, and wheat in amounts
which would provide a return as nearly equal to parity as the available
funds could permit" (Tweeten, 1970:304). Also promoted was scientific
research to extend the potential uses of farm products and thus expand
their markets. Before these policies had been long in effect, the war
economy pushed up the demand for most products and output was further
stimulated by price guarantees well above prewar levels. These guarantees were not reduced significantly until the 1950's. But support
prices still continued through the sixties. Without adequate production control at a time of rapidly improving technology, the consequence was that large surpluses accumulated bringing pressure on the
state budget, while not solving the farm income problem.

As voluntary supply control programmes were extremely expensive,
considerable pressure for mandatory controls developed in the early
sixties. Comprehensive legislation was prepared along these lines and
supported by all general farm organizations except the Farm Bureau,
but it was narrowly voted down in the House. Another attempt to
introduce mandatory controls was defeated in the wheat referendum of
1963. Attacking the loss of individual freedom through excessive
bureaucratic control, the Farm Bureau was once again a significant

force in the outcome.   Thus, the supply control programmes continued until 1973 with only minor modifications, although there were signs that U.S. agricultural policy was becoming more market oriented.

This market orientation was accentuated in the 1973 Agricultural and Consumer Protection Act.   Under the new system, target prices are established for wheat, feed grains and cotton, and when market prices fall below them, the state makes compensatory payments to producers. The level of the target price is therefore critical.   Since for 1974, "Total costs exceeded the target price" (OECD, 1976:12), we can see that the income maintenance approach of previous decades has been substantially relaxed.   Furthermore, deficiency payments are not based on actual cultivated areas, but on the farmer's share of a national acreage allocation, which is an estimate of the number of acres required to produce a crop to meet the anticipated demand.   Provision is made to provide financial support in case of natural disaster. Whereas the 1970 Act had introduced a maximum payment of $55,000 in any one commodity programme, this amount was reduced in 1973 to $20,000 in all programmes combined.   Also, since February, 1976 rice has been moved out of the quota control commodities in which only peanuts, extra long staple cotton and tobacco remain.   Given the low level of target prices the federal government had in effect moved away from price support payments and accumulation of food reserves.

With regard to trade, the U.S., as a powerful net exporting country, has often pushed for reduced barriers.   The Common Market has been a special target in this regard.   Yet the U.S. itself uses import quotas to protect the dairy industry and, during 1974-6, took measures against the import of Canadian cattle and beef.   A major bilateral agreement on wheat sales to the Soviet Union was also negotiated.   In the early seventies, conditions of food shortage led to the elimination of export payments; conversely, the monitoring of export commitments in order to safeguard domestic supplies became more important.

This short review allows us to see that U.S. agricultural policy has moved in this century from a free market strategy to supply management-income maintenance and back to a reliance on the market (with some exceptions as noted).   Target prices are "well below production costs at present, having the object of insuring minimum returns in exceptional years of over supply" (OECD, 1976:40).   It is doubtful if this policy can be maintained against the economic, political, and social consequences of long term oversupply should these market conditions occur again.

Agricultural policy in Sweden is worthy of particular attention because of the structural reform programme which dates from 1947. Specific programmes should be seen within the framework of the overall policy objectives.   The primary goal of the 1947 Agricultural Act

was to provide income parity between farmers and other occupational
groups. This involved both a price support policy and structural reforms.
Although Sweden did not suffer from the problem of fragmentation, thanks
to reforms dating from the eighteenth century, many farmers had too
little land. In these circumstances, the 1947 Act promoted the
establishment and support of "basic farms" of some 10 to 20 hectares
of arable land. Tendencies towards surplus production in the 1950's
led the government to stress a more vigorous rationalization programme
and the withdrawal of marginal land from production. Income parity
was explicitly defined in 1955 as a net income to farm operators
equivalent to the average industrial worker's income in low cost areas.
This was considered achieved, but proved impossible to sustain by
existing methods. By the time the next major Act was proclaimed in
1967, there was no specific income target, only a general commitment
to provide adequate incomes for those involved in primary industry.
Continued reform was promoted and a national production target of
80 percent self-sufficiency was established instead of the higher level
then obtaining. This level was judged sufficient to provide adequate
food supply in emergency situations. The rapidly changing economic
conditions of the early seventies led to the setting up of a new
commission to consider the state of agriculture. Reporting in 1977,
this commission does not recommend increased acreage in active farms
but promotes continued rationalization of these farms.

Until 1967, the rationalization programme had as its target the
establishment of viable family farms. While this goal has not been
abandoned, assistance is now given to larger farms in order that
maximum use may be made of technical advances which require larger
scale operation. Also, since 1972 farm policy has been integrated
in a model of regional and national physical planning.

In order to promote rationalization the Swedish government
offers the usual research, advisory, and educational services. It
also regulates land transfers, purchases and disposes of real estate,
and assists farmers with investments. Responsibility for administering the government programmes rests with the County Agricultural
Boards (CAB) which work under the National Board of Agriculture and
in collaboration with the National Board of Forestry as well as the
National Board of Education which is responsible for vocational
training. Individual programmes of the ministries are integrated at
the local level in the CABs.

Formed in 1948, the CABs were the vehicle to provide state
assistance for the enlargement of small farms (under 10 hectares)
into "basic" family farms. In these early years, purchases of additional farms were generally refused if the two units were separately
viable. We have noted that this policy was gradually relaxed until,
in the sixties, demands of industrialists for more labour led to a
more radical policy in order to shift factors of production out of

agriculture (OECD, 1972:255). The present powers of the CAB in real
estate are based on the Land Acquisition Act of 1965, the purpose of
which is to promote economically efficient holdings. CAB permission is
required for all sales except those between family members. This
permission may be refused on the basis of land use criteria, in
which case the Board must purchase the land at the agreed price.
Most land, however, is acquired though farmers offering it directly
to the Board, sometimes after an active search by the Board to procure
resources for expansion of other farmers. The importance of CAB activity in real estate may be appreciated when we realize that about
40 percent of land purchased by farmers for expansion comes from
CAB holdings. Generally arable land is held for about two years,
forest for three. While allowing some farms to expand, CABs may also
withdraw marginal land from farming and reallocate it to forest or
recreation use. In 1973, 7,200 hectares of arable land and 37,900
of forest land were purchased by the Boards, while sales were slightly
higher. Thus, we can see that the real estate activities are largely
self financing, and, as Table 1 shows, have expanded considerably
since 1952. Stagnation in recent years is largely the result of rising
land prices in the central and southern plains.

Financial assistance to farmers is also channelled through the
CABs. In general, to be eligible for support farms must be capable of
development into full-time, efficient units; part-time farmers can
not be assisted. Furthermore, only farms which could not otherwise
be improved ar eligible. Where assistance is provided it normally
takes the form of state guarantees on loans granted by normal commercial institutions. Interest rates and repayment periods are more favour-
albe to farmers with this form of support. Activities that may be
assisted are purchasing of land, acquiring new stock and equipment during
a reorganization process, and improving farm infrastructure. In the
latter case rather small grants to a maximum of 25 percent of the
cost or 50,000 Kr. per farm are also available. In a few cases special
grants related to purchase of new land may be awarded.

With regard to northern development, the Swedish government has
a more generous policy of assistance under its special rationalization programme. The intent here is to counteract excessive depopulation and economic stagnation. In consultation with a local village
population, government specialists develop a plan for the creation
of viable holdings of some 60-70 hectares of arable land combined
with 400-500 hectares of forest. In these special projects 40 percent
of investment costs are paid by the state. Also, it is only in the north
that part-time farms are eligible for assistance, although this is on
condition that farming is the main occupation, that the land is not
needed for the expansion of other holdings, and that combined income
from farming and other sources should provide adequate living standards.

Table 1

Purchasing and Selling of Farm Real Estate by Country Agricultural
Boards, 1952-73 (thousands of hectares)

	1952	1957	1962	1968	1973
Arable Land					
Purchases	2.5	2.7	6.6	8.0	7.2
Sales	1.5	2.4	5.3	9.0	9.9
Land held at end of year	3.7	6.8	10.0	19.0	16.3
Forest Land					
Purchases	8.7	15.1	31.5	34.0	37.9
Sales	5.5	8.3	26.2	30.0	44.3
Land held at end of year	39.0	60.7	70.6	128.0	98.8

Sources: James (1971:260); OECD (1974a:46)

In addition to the above programmes, farmers wishing to abandon
their holdings may receive special retirement compensation payments.
They are also able to participate in the retraining programmes and
receive the readjustment allowances which are provided as part of the
general labour market policy.

Despite the significant long term involvement of CABs in farm
structure, by 1975 only 21 percent of holdings had more than 20 hectares of arable land, although the number of farms fell from 262,000
in 1955 to 132,000 in 1975. In 1972, the average income of primary
industry employers was 80 percent of the overall average income.
Furthermore, in the farm sector, even large operators tend to have
substantial income from non-farm occupations. On farms below 10 ha.
this tends to be the main source of income.

Farm income is strongly influenced by price policy. In Sweden,
national prices are negotiated by the National Agricultural Marketing
Board, farmers' organizations and representatives of consumers'

interests, then submitted to parliament for approval. Responsibility
for administration rests with the Marketing Board. The reviews are
generally for three year periods with provision for biannual adjustments related to changes in production costs. greed prices were
maintained until 1973 by selective, variable import levies combined with
schemes to store domestic surpluses. Internal production fees have also
been assessed. Since 1973, however, Swedish policy has shown signs of
major change in response to rapid inflation. A general price freeze
on basic foods in 1973 resulted in government subsidies in order to
maintain farm income while keeping down consumer prices. Such a policy
tends to help low income families who pay lower taxes and thus contribute
less to the subsidization of farm income. This divorce of producer
costs from consumer food prices was a radical departure for Swedish
agricultural policy. Furthermore, in 1974, special support was introduced for small milk producers by paying higher prices for low volume
deliveries. A similar scheme for pig farmers came into effect in
1975. In the long run, such measures are inconsistent with rationalization policy because they support low income, "non-viable" holdings.
Whether this represents a temporary departure to deal with a special
short term problem or a major policy reversal remains to be seen.

The Netherlands, like Sweden, has a comprehensive structural
programme. It has, however, been selected for special consideration
here because it operates within the European Economic Community's
(EEC) marketing framework, and, unlike Sweden, must include land
consolidation as a major part of the structural programme.

As a member of the EEC, Dutch market policy is based on the Common
Agricultural Policy which is administered in the Netherlands through
commodity boards on which employers and employees from various stages
of the food industry are represented. The Common Agricultural Policy
involves internal free trade in a market protected by variable import
levies. Within the EEC common price levels are promoted and retained
at a high level by intervention in the market. Target prices are
set at the level obtaining in the main deficit area within the community. An intervention price is then set 5 to 10 percent below the
target price. When market prices drop to this level, support buying
occurs. Dairy produce, fat cattle, veal calves, sugar, rice, wheat
barley, rye, maize, olive oil, fruit and vegetables are supported
in this way. Pig meat, egg and poultry producers are excluded but are
protected from outside competition by the import levy. Ad valorem
tariffs, licences, quotas and minimum quality standards may also be
applied in some cases. Conversely, producers are encouraged to market
outside the EC by receiving support in the form of an export subsidy
when prices in the world market are lower (James, 1971:215-7).

Dutch agriculture operates within this protectionist framework.
Several special supply control schemes exist to control milk and fruit
production. The programme for up-rooting fruit trees was so success-

ful that the area in orchards had been reduced by one-third in 1973.
Also, minimum vegetable and fruit prices are established below which
produce is removed from the market and producers are reimbursed from
a levy fund assessed against all deliveries.

The major goal of Dutch policy has been structural change.
This is true despite the reputation of the Netherlands for efficient
modern agriculture. Until the mid-fifties, farm incomes were relatively satisfactory, but then oversupply and small-scale production
created a social problem. In 1959, farm size averaged 10.5 hectares,
and only 12 percent of farms had more than 20 hectares. Fragmentation
into small plots was also a troublesome issue. In response to this
situation the Dutch have evolved a comprehensive set of planning measures.

A general land and water development policy incorporates rural
and farm problems in a national context. Thus, around 1970 about
8,000 hectares per annum was being transferred from agricultural to
urban use and another 1,000 into recreation or nature conservancy
areas. At the same time about 3,000 hectares were being reclaimed
for agriculture in the polders. At each level of government land use
is controlled to take into account agricultural, environmental and
recreational needs. "The schemes aim at a complete overhaul of outdated structures through the re-arrangement of plots, water management,
access roads, landscaping and facilities for recreation" (OECD,
1972:183).

With regard to physical planning in agriculture, land consolidation
is of prime importance. In many areas farms have been excessively
sub-divided through inheritance rules, mechanization is difficult and
supporting infrastructure inadequate. Once such an area has been re-
commended for consolidation by some recognized group (a municipal
authority, farm organization, or one-third of local landholders),
a plan is prepared. If a majority of landholders or owners of over
one-half the land approve the plan by vote, it is then implemented.
The preparation stage may last up to five years, followed by five to
ten years of actual consolidation work. The land itself is valued
by independent assessors and then reallocated so that each individual
ends up with the same value of land he had prior to the reform.
Appeals against the valuatioon are allowed. After this stage, necessary
physical improvements are made, final deeds registered and landowners
charged for their share of the costs, which they can repay at low interest over thirty years. The state's share is about 65 percent. This
process is obviously very slow. Yet it is of major significance to
Dutch farmers given that, in 1959, 1.5 of the country's 2.3 million
hectares of farm land were considered in need of consolidation.
By 1972, 435,000 hectares had been restructured, and another 560,000
had passed the preparatory stage. Consolidation does not itself add
to the size of farms, but is a vital first step and does improve

productivity on existing farms.

Structural policy is implemented by the Foundation for Land
Administration which purchases agricultural land and redistributes
it at a later date. Land may be acquired from farmers in a consolidation
area, on the open market, or from those giving up farming under a
discontinuation scheme. In addition to the market price for their
land, farmers, in consolidation areas, whether owners or tenants, have
been eligible for substantial liquidation grants since 1970, i.e.,
payments conditional on giving up farming. As a supplement to the
sale of its land, the Foundation has been able to operate a Land Bank
since 1972 from which land may be leased back to farmers for up to
26 years. Recipient farms have to be at least medium size operations.

Established in 1962, the Foundation for Agricultural Development
and Rationalization (0 and S Fund) encourages some farmers to leave
agriculture and assists others to improve their holdings. The termination scheme changed several times from its introduction in 1964 to
the 1972 form described here. A lump sum payment is made depending on
the size and use of the farmland. Furthermore, an additional amount,
based on their average productive capacity in the previous three years,
is paid to farmers less than 50 years old while those between 50 and
65 years receive a monthly payment. Qualifying clauses restrict
eligibility for the first payment to low income owners under 65 years
old, and for the second payment to those with farming as a main occupation. In the early seventies this progarmme was attracting several
thousand farmers a year.

The state also offers vocational training schemes in which the
regular financial allowance is supplemented (from the 0 and S Fund)
in the case of farmers and dependent workers in order to bring their
incomes up to the level of the average male industrial worker. Yet
only about 200 per year take part.

The other main component of 0 and S activity is to promote expansion and technical innovation in a relatively small number of farms.
In accordance with EEC structural policy, interest subsidies are
paid on loans for certain approved investments. Outside the EEC regulations, the 0 and S Fund also defrays the cost of supplying relief
labour services. Most long term credidt is supplied by the Co-operative
Bank and investment loans have been guaranteed since 1951 by the
Agricultural Loan Guarantee Fund. Finally, through the promotion
of agricultural research and wide ranging extension services the
state contributes still further to rationalization.

In the Netherlands, the state's policies have no doubt contributed
to the transformation in agriculture. In 1970, there were 126,015
farms compared with 210,625 in 1950. In 1950, 62 percent of farms were
less than 10 hectares in size; in 1970, the comparative figure was

38 percent. Herds of more than 30 dairy cows increased by 75 percent in the period 1968-72. While these changes are important, the continuation of small-scale, fragmented enterprises means that further change is desired by the government.

CRITIQUE

Although most farmers' organizations show a strong ideological commitment to the preservation of the family farm (agrarian fundamentalism or Bauerntum), and although politicians usually claim that such a goal underlies or is consistent with their agricultural policy, the objective developments in class relations suggest a quite different contribution of the state in most advanced capitalist societies. By easing and legitimizing the absorption of commercial family farmers into industrial capitalist society, agricultural policies such as I have described contribute to the growth of a capitalist food and fibre industry. Whether intentional or not the state's policies are often an ideological cloak around the proletarianization of agricultural labour.

One indicator of the decline of family farmers is simply the reduction in their numbers, only halted or reversed in a few countries during the 1972-4 boom in farm prices. From Table 2 we observe large annual declines during 1964-74 in all OECD countries on which data is available (with the single exception of New Zealand). Many who leave farming retire from the labour force and do not join the working class; others become urban wage labourers. If we consider the retiral of farms rather than farmers, this is also an indicator of proletarialization since many are sold or abandoned due to the absence of heirs who have found urban wage incomes more attractive.

In many countries it is also apparent that the decline in farmers' numbers is accompanied by a growth of part-time farming. For example, the percentage of U.S. farm operators reporting at least 100 days per year of non-farm work rose from 11 percent in 1934 to 30 percent in 1959 to 40 percent in 1969 (Buse and Bromley, 1975:37). In West Germany, Norway, and Japan, there has been a marked increase since 1950 (OECD, 1977b). The change in Japan has been dramatic for those farms in which off-farm income exceeds net farm income as this category increased from 21.6 percent of all farms in 1950, to 63.2 percent in 1974.

The term "part-time farming" covers a variety of circumstances in which farmers spend part of their time in and derive part of their incomes from non-farm occupations which generally involve wage labour. It is useful to distinguish among part-time farmers according to the relative importance of off-farm work with regard to both labour time

Table 2. Annual Percentage Change in Agricultural Labour,* by Class Position.

	1964-74			1972-73			1973-74		
	Salaried Workers[1]	Operators[2]	Family[3]	Salaried Workers	Operators	Family	Salaried Workers	Operators	Family
Canada	0.1	-3.5	-2.8	4.1	..	-8.1	1.1	1.0	2.0
United States	-0.8	-2.9	-5.6	3.1	-0.7	-9.6	7.6	-1.4	-7.3
Japan[4]	-6.7	-2.7	-7.4	11.5	-3.7	-11.6	3.4	-1.0	-8.0
Australia	..	..	..	-6.9	-2.7	-26.7	-6.8	1.2	..
New Zealand	..	0.3	-4.8	5.9	-3.8	1.4	8.2	2.7	-2.3
Austria	-7.0	..	-9.4	-5.1	..	-4.4	-6.5	..	..
Belgium[5]	-4.5	-4.2	..	..	4.7	3.8	..	-3.9	-5.5
Denmark	..	..	..	-8.0	..	..	8.7	..	..
Finland	..	..	..	7.7	..	-10.5	-4.5	..	-2.0
France	..	..	..	-4.3	-4.2	-4.4	-4.3	..	-4.0
Germany	-4.5	-3.9	-5.0	-3.4	-4.0	..	-6.1	-3.1	-3.9
Ireland	..	..	..	..	..	-2.1	-1.5	..	-1.8
Italy	-2.4	-3.9	-8.3	-1.2	-2.9	-7.2	..	-2.8	-4.0
Luxembourg	-5.4	-3.4	-8.0	..	..	..	..	-3.8	-4.9
Netherlands	-3.1	-2.8	..	..	..	-2.5	-4.8	-4.3	-2.1
Norway	..	..	..	..	..	..	-7.0	-4.3	-18.9
Portugal	..	..	..	-6.1	..	-3.1	-7.2	-0.9	-1.1
Spain	..	..	..	..	-1.6	..	-9.7	..	-8.3
Sweden	..	..	..	-3.7	..	-9.1	-3.9	..	-6.0
United Kingdom	-4.4	-2.2	..	1.2	-1.0	..	..	..	..

Notes.

* Includes hunting, forestry and fishing.
1. Wage earners and salaried employees.
2. Employers and persons working on own account.
3. Unpaid family workers.
4. From 1973 data include Okinawa Prefecture. Figures exclude fishing.
5. Data included under 1964-74 are for 1963-73.
.. Negligible.
... Not available.

Source: OECD (1977a: 42).

and income. Fuller (1975) also provides a classification based on "adjustment time" so that part-time farmers may be considered as leavers, new entrants, and persistent or stable in their dual occupations. Both Fuller (1975:45) in his study of Hasting's County, Ontario, and Coughenour and Gabbard (1977) in their research on rural Kentucky report a considerable number of part-time farmers who aspire to become full-time ones, but who do not have sufficient capital resources to achieve that goal. They are usually younger than those who wish to give up farming. Some evidence on this is available from a German study of supplementary income farmers which showed that only 12.4 percent wished to abandon the farms, but this percentage rose to 33.8 for the over 65 group (OECD, 1977b:12).

Apart from hobby farmers, a significant category close to large urban centres, part-time farming may be interpreted as an adaptation arising from the need either to avoid the large capital outlay which is now required for the successful operation of commercial farms or to improve, by non-farm employment, the income situation of families with properties which they do not wish to or are unable to expand. In either case, most operators are interested in keeping the farm going for such reasons as its contribution to a cheap food supply, security in economic crisis, as a hobby, to provide supplementary income, or simply to maintain a tradition (OECD, 1977b:12). Kentucky part-time commercial farmers value highly the ideal of independent decision-making on the farm, although fewer believe that they actually are free (Coughenour and Gabbard, 1977:13). With the exception of new entrants to commercial farming, we are dealing in most cases with the transformation of family farmers into worker-entrepreneurs or worker-peasants (distinguished according to the relative importance of domestic and market oriented production). In some cases this is a transitional status between farmer and worker, but in others we can expect part-time farming to be a more permanent adaptation. I am referring in particular to those regions in which off-farm employment is limited by low industrial investment and in which part-time farming is also encouraged through state assistance. In recent years both West Germany and Norway have recognized the importance of small, part-time farms for maintaining the quality of the environment, minimally acceptable population densities and adequate living standards in their more disadvantaged regions. Therefore, they are supported as part of regional development programmes, rather than eradicated in the pursuit of "rational" farm structures (OECD, 1977b).

Although farm numbers have declined it is sometimes claimed that commercial family farms are still the principal basis for agricultural production since increases in labour productivity mean that there is less need for hired labour. Therefore, hired labourers "disappear" at a faster rate than farmers. This view may be challenged from data in Table 2 which show that, in the United States, Canada, Japan, and Italy, wage labourers became more important relative to farmers

in the decade 1964-74. For 1973-4, Denmark and New Zealand may be
added to the list. It is also significant that the absolute number of
wage labourers in all these countries except Italy actually <u>increased</u>
in that year. What is implied by this data is the rising importance
of capitalist and corporate farms. This can be backed up from other
sources. In Canada, for example, the number of non-family incorporated
farms, while still a small percentage of the total, increased from
911 to 1,864 in the years 1971-6 (Statistics Canada, 1973:13-1; 1978:
13-1). For the United States, Rodefeld (n.d.:Table 8) reports that
capitalist farms (a combination of Rodefeld's larger-than-family type
and industrial type) amounted to 4.9 percent of all farms in 1964,
but accounted for 35.4 percent of all sales. It is possible that,
if European rationalization programmes succeed, their long term impact
will be rather like the North American pattern in those commodities
not dominated by cooperatives.

In advanced capitalist societies, the structural position of
farmers also changes as a result of vertical integration in cooperatives. Producers' co-operatives are found throughout these societies,
especially in Scandinavia and parts of western Europe. From the
perspective of the farmer the co-operative may appear to be a
successful adaptation to advanced capitalism, but it also has the
effect of turning a group of petty commodity producers into
capitalist entrepreneurs.

Basically, co-operatives are non-profit organizations in which
producers combine to become more effective entrepreneurs. The cooperative's members are responsible for general policy decisions
and hire managers to achieve their objectives. These farmer "corporations" may manufacture and purchase inputs, supply credit, provide
research and technical assistance to members, as well as process and
market what they produce. Any surplus beyond what is reinvested is
distributed to members according to the volume of business which they
contribute to the co-operative. Co-operatives cut out non-farmers
from the production process but they do not redistribute income or
involve collective ownership at the farm level. (Co-operative
machinery pools would be an exception to this.) Furthermore, although
farmer members may use very little hired labour <u>on the farm</u>, collectively they are major capitalist employers. For example, the Swedish
co-operatives employed a total labour fource of 55,000 persons in
1975. Since co-operatives have also become highly centralized and
bureaucratic structures, it is possible that the farmer owners are
dominated by their managers who control expertise. The extent to
which this is true requires further research. In any case, when we
see the food and fibre industry as a whole rather than focus on the
farm component, co-operative systems then appear as a form of capitalist enterprise, specially adapted to the conditions of agriculture,
rather than a defence of petty commodity production.

Even where they do not expand into capitalist enterprises, the structural position of commercial family farmers is being changed as they become integrated with agribusiness corporations through various forms of contract farming. (To a lesser extent co-operatives also engage in contracting.) In the United States contracting is widespread especially in broilers, vegetables and turkey production. In Britain, Canada, Belgium, Switzerland, France and the Netherlands, this form of vertical integration has made considerable gains. A British survey disclosed that 17 percent of farms had "some form of written contract" (OECD, 1974b), while in Belgium 98 percent of green peas and 75 percent of green beans are produced in this way (OECD, 1973b).

Through vertical integration the corporation avoids investing in farm land, yet is assured of a market for the farm supplies produced by it and/or receives produce of guaranteed volume and quality for subsequent processing. The contracts usually leave the farmer with no more than routine day-to-day decision-making as the integrating firm contributes supplies, sets prices, determines key aspects of production schedules, provides technical supervision, etc. (see sample contracts in Roy, 1963:467-555). "The result is to leave under the control of the farmers only those operations most suited to the size of their farms, for example certain cultural operations such as plough-ing and sowing" (Le Bihan, 1969:332).

This situation, however, is not without advantage to the producer who always has a guaranteed buyer and often a guaranteed price. Also, the supplies, credit and technical input of the integrating firm may lead to more efficient production and higher income for the farmer than if he operated independently. The price, neverthelss, is a loss of control so substantial that we would do better to describe the farmer as a piece-work wage labourer than a petty commodity producer. In these circumstances, there are advantages for farmers in forming col-lective bargaining unions which can build or rebuild an alliance with the labour movement as a whole. This conclusion must be modified to the extent that the farmer retains part of his time and resources for "independent" commodity production.

From the above analysis, it may be concluded that, allowing for important regional differences, state policies either promote or do nothing to hinder the decline of commercial family farming. Small farmers understand this very well and have expressed their displeasure with state policy on many occasions. Withholding produce by the National Farmers' Organization in the United States, demonstrations against the powerful McCain's corporation by National Farmers' Union potato growers in New Brunswick and a cattle "strike" by the Canadian Agriculture Movement in Alberta and Saskatchewan are only a few recent examples of action by producers who understand the precarious position of commercial family farmers.

To this point I have criticized agricultural policies for being insensitive to the actual structural developments in farming. Another and more fundamental criticism is that very few politicians, farm organization leaders, or agricultural economists even consider a non-capitalist alternative to present trends in social organization. The growth of capitalist farm units demonstrates that in some commodities there are technical developments which themselves suggest the viability of some form of collective ownership. Some spontaneous developments of this nature have occurred in Saskatchewan wheat farming, but there has been inadequate support from the state. Even where family size operation is most advisable from a technical standpoint, this could be accompanied by a socialization of agribusiness components of production. Furthermore, even small enterprises might benefit from social ownership of the land if long-term leases were made available as in the Netherlands. Consumer food costs might also be held down without adverse effects on farm income (see Mitchell, 1975, for a description of land banking in Saskatchewan). Such changes would require an ideological re-education which is extremely unlikely because of the capitalist hegemony over the state.

This brings us to the need for a theory of the state to explain the agricultural policies we have observed in this paper. Recent neo-Marxist scholarship takes us some way towards an answer.[3] The functional theories of O'Connor (1973), Habermas (1975), and Offe (1976) all see the state as a set of institutions which pursue the general interests of capitalism by attempting to redress "unresolved steering problems" (Habermas, 1975:4). Principal among these are problems of legitimation and of rationality/accumulation. Habermas (1976:375) states the general point clearly as follows:

> We may think of the state as a system which employs legitimate force. Its output consists of autocratically-executed administrative decisions; for these it requires an input of mass loyalty, as little attached to specific objects as possible. Both directions may lead to critical disturbances. Output crises take the form of crises in rationality: the administrative system does not succeed in fulfilling the imperatives of control which it has taken over from the economic system. This results in the disorganization of various areas of social life. Input crises take the form of crises in legitimation: the legitimation system does not succeed in maintaining the necessary level of mass loyalty.

Often the resolution of one of these problems increases the other since actions to promote accumulation or economic "rationality" may produce a withdrawal of legitimacy by groups who experience depriva-

tion, while solutions to crises of legitimation may hinder accumulation
(see especially O'Connor, 1973:6).

From this perspective agricultural policies dealing with structural reform may be interpreted primarily in terms of the accumulation
function. The historical problems of economic viability in farming
"force" state intervention in order to smooth out the work of the market.
Also, as Goss, Buttel, and Rodefeld suggest elsewhere in this volume,
policies which favour or do not counteract the activities of agribusiness
corporations promote capital accumulation within food and fibre industries
taken as a whole.

Policies to support farm income, especially the use of compulsory marketing boards, are against corporate interests in that they
raise the price of raw materials. (Subsidies do not have this effect.)
They are necessary, however, especially in societies with large farm
populations, to counter a damaging crisis of legitimation. It is
surely no accident that such measures were instituted in most countries
during the depression of the thirties. Income support schemes are in
contradiction with the state's involvement in accumulation in so far
as they discourage it from occurring. In fact, our evidence shows that
capitalist expansion and strength in so far as they provide a reservoir
of cheap labour for industry, protect the balance of payments position,
and provide some measure of national security against a contraction
in external supplies.

Despite the insights of this kind of analysis, it suffers from
a teleological bias. The consequences of policies are invoked as their
explanation. Neo-Marxist theory of the state in general requires a
renewed sensitivity towards causal, historical analysis of policy
formation. Such an analysis will emphasize the ideologies and class
interests of those who are influential in creating policies and of those
whose attitudes and behavior are taken into account. If the state is
relatively autonomous, as many Marxists argue, we must ask why it
nevertheless behaves in such a way as to promote the general interests
of capital, even against the demands of specific capitals. Therefore,
such traditional concerns as the recruitment of state officials and their
cultural orientations continue to be important. The interdependence
between officials and corporate actors is central, but so too is the
politician's own need for popular legitimation. It is this latter
problem which may be responsible for so much short-term and ad hoc
policy formation.

CONCLUSION

With regard to agriculture and the state, I would like to end
with some speculation regarding future developments. Tendencies
towards liberal corporatism[4] which have become apparent in many
advanced capitalist societies in general will continue and become more
important in agriculture. Already, corporations, farm organizations,
consumers, and the state agencies combine to work out prices and other
policies in some societies.

The family farmers that survive will continue to be difficult
to mobilize for change because their dependent class position is
countered by a work situation which allows illusions of entrepreneurial
independence to survive. Of course, this ideology is strongly promoted by capitalists and the state because of its conservative effect.
As Offe (1976:397) states:

> In advanced systems of state-regulated capitalism,
> political stability can more reliably be ensured
> through the systematic exclusion and suppression
> of needs which if articulated would endanger the
> system, than through the granting of a politically
> privileged status to a minority that already enjoys
> economic dominance...

But it is also possible that the artificial harmony of corporatist
decision-making will break down (Panitch (1977) reports recent evidence of this) and spawn more radical farmers' union movements to
press for fundamental change. The alternative evolution would be
the continuation of present capitalist developments under a more
repressive state apparatus.

FOOTNOTES

1. A review of Rural Sociology from 1966 to 1977 revealed no article
    with a focus in this area, while Sociologia Ruralis has published
    three.
2. In this section I have drawn heavily on the Organization for
    Economic Co-operation and Development's (OECD) reports on agricul-
    tural policy (OECD, 1972, 1973a, 1974a, 1976, 1977a). They have
    been supplemented by Brandow (1977), Friedman (1974), Gulbrandsen
    (1969), Halcrow (1977), Hallett (1968), James (1971), Linden and
    Swedborg (1968), Mitchell (1975), Peper (1969) and Tweeten (1970).
3. I find, however, that the well known work of Nicos Poulantzas is
    based on a definition of the state so encompassing that it is
    useless in practice. For Poulantzas (1969, 1973, 1976) that which

maintains the cohesion and class relations of a social formation is part of the state system. Hence the cultural and ideological institutions, as well as the repressive apparatus, are part of the state. Indeed, only the revolutionary working class parties and the productive system itself seem to escape the boundaries of the state. Such a definition seems altogether too broad.

4.   To me the clearest definition of liberal corporatism is that of Gerhard Lehmbruch (1977:94) to whom it is:

> an institutionalized pattern of policy-formation in which large interest organizations cooperate with each other and with public authorities not only in the artic- ulation (or even "intermediation") of interests, but... in the "authoritative allocation of values" and in the implementation of such policies.

This is a useful working definition in which corporatism appears as a distinct political structure and in which it is not assumed, with the "pluralists," that the state is a neutral forum in which an unbounded number of groups meet to negotiate their respective interests.

REFERENCES

Brandow, G.E.
  1977 "Policy for commercial agriculture, 1945-71." In Agricul- tural Economics Literature, Volume One, L.R. Martin (ed.). Minneapolis: University of Minnesota Press. Pp. 209-92.
Buse, R.C. and Bromley, D.W.
  1975 Applied Economics. Ames, Iowa: Iowa State University Press.
Coughenour, C. Milton and Gabbard, Anne V.
  1977 "Part-time farmers in Kentucky in the early 1970's: the development of dual careers." Report RS-54. Lexington: Univer- sity of Kentucky.
Friedman, Karen J.
  1974 "Danish agricultural policy, 1870-1970: the flowering and decline of a liberal policy." Food Research Institute Studies 13:225-38.
Fuller, Anthony M.
  1975 "The problems of part-time farming conceptualised." In Part-time Farming. Problem or Resource in Rural Development, A.M. Fuller and J.A. Mage (eds.). Norwich: GEO Abstracts. Pp. 38-56.
Gulbrandsen, Odd
  1969 "Swedish experience in agricultural policy." In Economic Problems of Agriculture in Industrial Society, U. Papi and C. Nunn (eds.). London: MacMillan. Pp. 409-19.

348 Agricultural Policy

Habermas, Jurgen
    1975 Legitimation Crisis. Boston: Beacon.
Habermas, Jurgen
    1976 "Problems of legitimation in late capitalism." In Critical
    Sociology, P. Connerton (ed.), translated by Thomas Hall.
    Harmondsworth: Pengiun. Pp. 363-87.
Halcrow, Harold B.
    1977 Food Policy for America. New York: McGraw-Hill.
Hallett, Graham
    1968 The Economics of Agricultural Policy. Oxford: Blackwell.
James, Gwyn
    1971 Agricultural Policy in Wealthy Countries. Sydney: Angus
    and Robertson.
Lehmbruch, Gerhard
    1977 "Liberal corporatism and party government." Comparative
    Political Studies 10 (April):91-126.
Le Bihan, Joseph
    1969 "Vertical integration and development of farms: the per-
    fecting and diffusion of innovations in integrated systems."
    In Economic Problems of Agriculture in Industrial Societies,
    U. Papi and C. Nunn (eds.). London: MacMillan. Pp. 325-43.
Linden, Hands and Sweborg, Erik
    1968 Policy for Swedish Agriculture in the 1970's. Stockholm:
    LT's forlag.
Mitchell, Don
    1975 The politics of Food. Toronto: Lorimer.
O'Connor, James
    1973 The Fiscal Crisis of the State. New York: St. Martin's.
OECD
    1972 Structural Reform Measures in Agriculture. Paris: OECD.
OECD
    1973a Agricultural Policy in the Netherlands. Paris: OECD.
OECD
    1973b Agricultural Policy in Belgium. Paris: OECD
OECD
    1974a Agricultural Policy in Sweden. Paris: OECD.
OECD
    1974b Agricultural Policy in the United Kingdom. Paris: OECD.
OECD
    1976 Recent Developments in United States Agricultural Policies.
    Paris: OECD.
OECD
    1977a Review of Agricultural Policies in OECD Member Countries.
    Paris: OECD.
OECD
    1977b Part-time Farming. Germany, Japan, Norway, United States.
    Paris: OECD
Offe, Claus
    1976 "Political authority and class structure." In Critical
    Sociology, P. onnerton (ed.). Harmondsworth: Pengiun. Pp. 388-
    421.

Panitch, Leo
    1977 "The development of corporatism in liberal democracies."
    Comparative Political Studies 10 (April:61-90.
Peper, Bram
    1969 "Agricultural policy and social policy. The future of the
    family farm." Sociologia Ruralis 9:221-34.
Poulantzas, Nicos
    1969 "The problem of the capitalist state." New Left Review
    58:67-78.
Poulantzas, Nicos
    1973 Political Power and Social Classes. Lond: New Left Books
Poulantzas, Nicos
    1976 "The capitalist state: a reply to Miliband and Laclau."
    New Left Review 95:63-83.
Rodefeld, Richard D.
    n.d. "Trends in U.S. farm organizational structure and type."
    Unpublished paper and revised version of paper presented to the
    Rural Sociological Society, San Francisco, August, 1975.
Roy, E.P.
    1963 Contract Farming U.S.A. Danville, Illinois: Interstate.
Statistics Canada
    1973 1971 Census of Canada. Agriculture Canada. Catalogue
    96-701. Ottawa.
Statistics Canada
    1978 1976 Census of Canada. Agriculture Canada. Catalogue
    96-800. Ottawa.
Tweeten, Luther
    1970 Foundations for Farm Policy. Lincoln: University of
    Nebraska Press.

Part IV

RURAL UNDERDEVELOPMENT
AND RURAL POVERTY

12. The Highlands of Scotland as an Underdeveloped Region

IAN CARTER

Scotland is <u>terra incognita</u> for British sociology. Little work has been done by sociologists on Scotland, rather than in Scotland. This situation is to be explained by a number of factors. The first is that departments of sociology are of relatively recent growth in Scottish universities.[1] Consequently, the vast majority of sociologists working in Scotland today were neither born nor trained in the country. A second factor is the marked centripetal tendency among British sociologists; English conurbations, and above all London, draw them inexorably, for this, after all is where the action is (and the consultancies to government departments). A third factor leading to the small amount of sociological work on Scotland is an assumption of British homogeneity;[2] if all parts of Britain exhibit similar social structural features (even if some parts are lower down the evolutionary scale than others), then there is no point in going to distant parts to do research that could be done more quickly and comfortably within a fifteen-mile radius of Hampstead.

Two consequences typically have followed from the operation of these factors; sociologists have either ignored Scotland or they have misunderstood Scotland. An example of the strategy of ignorance is Johns's textbook on the social structure of modern Britain; the book contains no index reference to Scotland, and the sole reference that I can find in the text is a footnote in which we learn that the average Scotsman gets one-half as many official holidays as the average citizen of the USA (Hohns, 1965: 123). Examples of the strategy of misapprehension are legion; the most usual kind is the assumption that Scotland is an antediluvian province of England, demonsrating social structural features once present in more "advanced" parts of England but long since superseded by rationality and modernity. This assumption, which can lead to effigy-burning in Princes Street, is not unknown--sad to say--among British sociologists of development (Dore, 1965: 379).

Such errors of omission and commission would not matter if it were true that Scotland may adequately be described as a province of England explicable solely in terms of English history and social structure.   But this is not in fact the case.   The Union settlement of 1707 contained explicit safeguards against English assimilationist tendencies for the Roman Law based Scots Law, for the Presbyterian Kirk, and for the relatively egalitarian (and European-influenced)Scottish educational system. Some degree of assimilation to English forms has occurred.[3]   But the dearth of work on the sociology of Scots Law and, perhaps even more importantly, on religion in Scotland, makes it difficult to see just how significant are these institutional differences which still divide Scotland from England and how these institutions work themselves out in the social life of Scotland (Kellas, 1968: 230-231).

But we are not only concerned here with the fact that generalizations about Britain, which are really based on England, may be invalid if they fail to take into account significant and on-going differences between England and Scotland.   Scotland presents some sociological problems that are not to be found in England.   Chief among these, for my purposes, is the matter of the Highlands.   Hobsbawm notes (1969: 98) that one of the casualties of the Agricultural Revolution in England was the peasantry:

> By 1790 landlords owned perhaps three-quarters of the
> cultivated land, occupying free-holders perhaps fifteen
> to twenty per cent, and a peasantry in the usual sense
> of the word no longer existed.

As so often happens with empirical statements about the historical course of social and economic change in the later eighteenth century in England, this statement is mirrored by generalizations about the consequences of change in agrarian societies:

> In the modern world peasants are anachronisms, and it is
> inevitable that they disappear.   Peasants themselves have
> demonstrated time and time again that they prefer a dif-
> ferent, and what they believe to be a better life (Potter,
> 1967: 378).

The crofters of the west Highlands and Islands form a peasant group that obdurately refuses to die, to the discomfort and annoyance of planners and economic geographers.   Darling says of Lewis, in the Outer Hebrides, that it "is almost unique in the modern Western world in its being a society still separable from its peasant agriculture" (1955: 142). Collier noted the extremely low division of labour characteristic of the crofter's life and of crofting communities, and the way in which economic functions are highly integrated with the family (1953: 35). How did these peasants survive in Britain, arguably the nation in which the most complete of all destructions of the peasant sector took place (Hobsbawn, 1969: 15-16)?   No sociologist has thought it worth his while to ask the question.

My concern in this paper is with a different question, although crofting will reappear in the argument. I am principally concerned with the Highlands and Islands Development Board and its strategies for the economic development of the Highlands.

THE HIGHLANDS BOARD: REMIT AND INTERPRETATION

The Highlands and Islands Development (Scotland) Act of 1965 gives very wide powers indeed to the Board constituted under its terms "for the purpose of assisting the people of the Highlands and Islands to improve their economic and social conditions and of enabling the Highlands and Islands to play a more effective part in the economic and social development of the nation." The Board is to prepare, concert, assist, and undertake measures for the economic and social development of the crofting counties.[4] It may acquire land, by compulsory purchase if necessary, and it may hold, manage, and dispose of land. It may erect buildings, provide equipment and services, and hold or dispose of these buildings and services. It may establish businesses and then, if it pleases, dispose of them. It may train people, produce publicity about the Highlands and the activities of the Board itself, and use a wide range of methods to bring jobs to the crofting counties. It may give grants or loans, or unspecified criteria, to anybody carrying on commercial or industrial operations that would promote the economic and social development of the area. It may also charge for its services, accept gifts, commission or undertake research, and borrow money. The finance for the Board's activities comes from the Secretary of State for Scotland, and it is to him alone that the Board is answerable.

This is a formidable list. No other agency engaged in regional development in Britain has been presented with such an armoury. But the breadth of its powers merely reflects the breadth of its remit. Two features of this remit deserve notice. First, pace Lugard's dual mandate, the Board is to promote both the development of the crofting counties and of the nation as a whole. This is common to all British regional development policies. Second, the Board is to promote both economic and social development simultaneously. Apthorpe has noted the hegemony that one university discipline--economics--enjoys in development planning. Any interdisciplinary approach in this field is, he suggests, more of a horse and rider relationship, with economics in the saddle, rather than a relationship of equals (Apthorpe, 1970: 4-7). So it is with the HIDB (Carter, 1972, 1973). The Board has an implicit definition of social development as "non-economic development,"[5] and identified non-economic objectives in the first annual report as the prevention of outmigration from the crofting counties as a whole, the maintenance of population levels in peripheral areas, and "adding another perfectly possible way of life to that in the great cities"

(HIDB, 1967: Foreword). But it is clear that economic criteria have primacy over non-economic, and when a conflict occurs--as between the need to maintain population levels in "remote" areas and the pull migration implicit in a growth centre policy--it is the economic policy that wins out.

The Board's economic orientation is shown in the way in which "the Highland Problem" is conceptualized. Just before the Board was established, D.I. MacKay published an analysis of the economic prospects of the Highlands. He saw no solution to the economic problems of the area in any development of the staple primary industries; both agriculture and fishing would continue to decline absolutely in importance. Forestry offered some long-run employment opportunities, but these would be relatively few in number. The only safe long-term bet for the regeneration of the Highland economy would be a large-scale development of manufacturing industry. But the high cost of such industrial development would involve the sacrifice of economic opportunities in more favoured locations elsewhere in Britain and hence would not be justified on purely economic grounds (MacKay, 1965: 79-81).

The first annual report of the HIDB outlines the agency's strategy for the Highlands. It shows a high level of agreement with MacKay's gloomy prognosis. There are some differences of detail--tourism is seen to have important short-run possibilities, for example, and fishing is seen to have development potential in those few areas of the crofting counties where it retains some vitality--but by and large, the Board, like MacKay, plumped for manufacturing industry as the salvation of the Highland economy (HIDB, 1967: 3-4). This industry was to be concentrated in growth centres, where inter-industry linkages and the most effective use of infrastructure would minimize the effect of the disadvantageous situation of the Highlands, far from major British markets.

The Board's policy commitments derive from an assumption about the category of economic region into which the Highlands fall. McCrone puts the Highlands in a class of poorly developed rural regions (1969: 14):

> Agricultural regions, untouched by industrialization,
> which, as national income rises, cannot provide their
> population with living standards comparable to the
> rest of the country.

The HIDB brackets the Highlands with the Mezzogiorno in Italy, North Norway and parts of Holland and Eire, as a problem region of this kind (1967: Foreword):

> ...Areas of their countries that the various revolutions
> in agriculture, industry and technology have passed by.

The basic problem of the Highlands on this definition is not geographic remoteness, compounded by bad communications and a convoluted terrain, but isolation from those market forces that govern the rest of Britain and that would transform the Highlands if once they came to operate there. Thus, the economic development strategy for the Highlands is to bring the area into the "modern" economy. The creation of strong nexi of manu- facturing industry is intended not only to alter the sectoral distribu- tion of economic activity in the Highlands, but also to produce spread effects of economic growth and growth-mindedness throughout the crofting counties. The HIDB's view of the nature of "the Highland Problem" and its strategy for the solution of that problem, assumes that the Highlands are an "archaic," "lagging" economic sector isolated from the cold winds of market forces. Thus the Highlands are seen to be an "archaic" sector of a dual economy.[6] It is this that we will be questioning.

HIGHLANDS AND LOWLANDS BEFORE THE
EIGHTEENTH CENTURY

From the time of the rise of clanship as the organizing principle of Highland social structure between the twelfth and fourteenth centuries (Grant, 1961: 23) until the destruction of clanship in the eighteenth century, a clear division existed between the Highlands, the Lowlands, and the North (Mitchison, 1962: 4). The exact geographical position of the division depends to some extent on whether one uses economic or cultural criteria in distinguishing Highlands from Lowlands--as Figure 1 shows-- but historians are unanimous in telling us that such a division existed and was perceived to be important by Highlanders and Lowlanders. The Highlands formed a relatively autonomous social and political sector within Scotland; a point which may be demonstrated through an analysis of elite marriage patterns. Marriages of the heads of the main line and septs of Highland clans and Lowland families were political actions, in that they forged and maintained alliances, until the decentralization of political power in Scotland was brought to an end by the triumph of Royal authority in Lowland areas and the military conquest of the Highlands by the Hanovarian government after the '45. An analysis of elite marriage patterns should thus demonstrate the area within which Highland clan chiefs and Lowland lairds thought it worth while to make political alliances through marriage.

Tables 1 and 2 show that in the case of the MacDonalds and MacKenzies, two important west Highland clans, elite marriages were contracted almost exclusively within the Highland area[7] before 1700.

Table 3 shows that the elite of the Lowland family of Burnett of Leys, living close to the Highland Line in Aberdeenshire, contracted no marriages with Highland partners before 1700. After 1700, however, while the Burnetts retained their firm resolve not to marry across the Highland Line, a greatly increased proportion of MacDonald and MacKenzie clan

FIGURE 1
Definitions of the Highlands

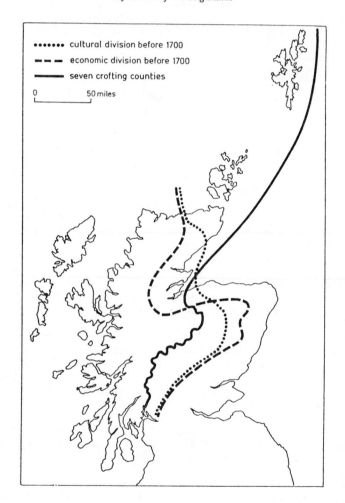

TABLE 1.   Marriage Patterns of Clan MacDonald, 1500-1880.

| | Origin of Wife (per cent) | | | |
	Highland	Lowland	Total (per cent)	N
1500-1699	93	7	100	46
1700-1880	66	34	100	80

Source: Calculated from data in Mackenzie, 1881.

TABLE 2.   Marriage Patterns of Clan MacKenzie, 1500-1900.

| | Origin of Wife (per cent) | | | |
	Highland	Lowland	Total (per cent)	N
1500-1699	92	8	100	59
1700-1900	62	38	100	69

Source: Calculated from data in Warrand, 1965.

Table 3.   Marriage Patterns of Family of Burnett of Leys, 1500-1900.

| | Origin of Wife (per cent) | | | |
	Highland	Lowland	Total (per cent)	N
1500-1699	0	100	100	16
1700-1900	0	100	100	18

Source: Calculated from data in G. Burnett, 1901, C. Burnett, 1950.

gentry contracted marriage with Lowland partners.[8] This one-way flow of
influences across the Highland Line reflects the increasing hegemony
of the Lowland aristocracy, and through them the English aristocracy,
throughout Scotland in the eighteenth and nineteenth centuries and was
one of the more subtle forms of the institutional incorproation (Pearse,

1971: 75) of the Highland social sector.

The data presented above suggest that the Highlands formed an autonomous social and political sector before the eighteenth century. This conclusion is supported by other evidence. The central authorities, the Scottish kings, were unable to control the Highlands on a continuing basis as late as the reign of James VI and I in the early seventeenth century (Grant, 1930: 528-542; Smout, 1969: 106-107). The customary strategy applied to the Highlands by the central authorities--divide and rule--increased division in the area without promoting centralized rule.[9] Contemporary accounts emphasize the narrow and hostile stereotypes held by Lowlanders of Highlanders and vice versa. James VI and I held the characteristic Lowland attitude to the Highlanders, albeit in a strong form:

> As for the Hie-lands, I shortly comprehend them al into
> two sorts of people: the one, that dwelleth in our maine
> land, that are barbarous for the most part yet mixed
> with some shew of civilitie: the other that dwelleth in
> the Iles and are alluterlie barbares ... reform and civi-
> lize the best inclined among them, rooting out or trans-
> porting the barbarous and stubborne sort and planting
> civilitie in their roomes (James VI and I, Basilikon Doron,
> quoted in Smout, 1969: III).

Samuel Johnson noted the unfavourable attitudes towards Lowlanders held by Highlanders as late as 1770:

> By their Lowland neighbours they would not willingly be
> taught; for they have long considered them a mean and
> degenerate race. These prejudices are wearing fast
> away; but so much of them still remains, that when I
> asked a very learned minister in the islands, which they
> considered as their most savage clans: 'Those,' said
> he, 'that live next the Lowland.' (Johnson 1775: 31--
> original emphasis).

We are dealing here with a case of two ethnic groups, in Barth's sense of the phrase: groups formed through self-ascription or ascription by others, based on a perception of shared meanings (Barth, 1969: 10). Economic exchanges across the Highland Line (which we will consider below) need not represent on this argument an attenuation of differences between the ethnic groups of Highlanders and Lowlanders: rather, by demonstrating the lack of shared meanings between Highland and Lowland actors, such exchanges could reinforce the differentiation (Barth, 1969: 15-16). Barth notes that the persistence of a poly-ethnic system--such as the Scotland of Lowland, Highland, and North sectors which we are considering--depends on relatively high stability in the cultural features associated with ethnic groups; although this does not mean that there is no crossing of the cultural and ethnic group boundary on an individual level (1969: 21).[10] This high stability existed between Highlands and Lowlands,[11] re-inforced not only by cultural differences but by economic, religious, and social differences.

Gaelic was the language of the Highlands and the Lordship of the Isles gave rise to a Gaelic high culture. The destruction of the Lordship in the fifteenth and sixteenth centuries began "the degradation of the old Gaelic civilization to a folk culture" (Grant, 1961: 27). In the Lowlands, however, Scots was the language and the Great Tradition (in Redfield's phrase) which Lowland peasants copied was the culture of pre-industrial Scottish cities such as Edinburgh and Glasgow.

The economic structure of both Highlands and Lowlands was based on the runrig joint farm. A number of tenants, with their sub-tenants, if they had any, worked on a single farm with a high degree of co-operation in tasks such as ploughing. The arable land was divided into "infield," which was intensively manured and intensively cropped, and "outfield," which was manured less (if at all) and bore infrequent crops. Each tenant was allocated a number of "rigs" of infield and outfield, on which he grew his subsistence crops--oats to eat and barley to drink, and was allocated a "souming," the right to graze a specified number of beasts on the common grazings. The land was periodically reallocated. Rents, amounting to a third or a half of total produce, were paid to domain-holders in a mixture of cash, kind, and labour services.

In Lowland areas joint tenants paid rent directly to the laird. In the Highlands, however, tenants usually paid rent to a tacksman who lived on the difference between rents aggregated from a number of joint farms and rents paid to the chief. The differences between Lowland and Highland social structure are elusive. Smout summarizes the differences thus: "Highland society was based on kinship modified by feudalism, Lowland society on feudalism modified by kinship (1969: 44)."

This raises some conceptual problems. A feudal society marked by strong vertical kinship relations is a contradiction in terms for Coulborn (1956: 196-197). What Smout seems to mean is that the land tenure sys-tem in the Highlands and Lowlands was feudal in a sense that most authorities would accept. Under wardholding, the chief or laird held his lands of the king and leased the land either directly to joint ten-ants or to tacksmen who then leased to tenants. Rents were paid in cash, kind, or labour, as we saw above, but the main objective of an inferior to a superior under wardholding was not economic but military-- the obligation to follow the superior if called "out." Thus the clan system was capable of being transformed at a moment's notice from an economic to a military institution. The chief was transformed from a landlord to the leader of the clan in battle. The rentier tacksmen became the duine uaisle, the lieutenants of the clan, fulfilling a crucial role in organizing and controlling the clan host. The tenants and sub-tenants became the clansmen, the foot soldiers of clan warfare.[12]

Runrig was an essential part of this military agreement, for the
periodic reallocation of land allowed an increasing population, and therefore more fighting men, to occupy a given amount of land up to the limit
set by subsistence. It thus represented a finely tuned adaptation to a
situation, common to both Highlands or Lowlands before the centralization
of political power, where a paper title to land was worthless without the
military force to support it.

When one considers the nature of the relationship within this system,
however, the idea of feudalism seems rather less appropriate. Perceived
kinship links between a superior and an inferior seem to have had some
importance in Lowland "families;" among Highland clans they were of crucial
importance. "Clan" is a translation of "children." The chief was not only
a landlord; he was a kinsman. This provided an affective element in the
vertical, multi-stranded relationship between chief, tacksman, and clans-
man, which is far removed from the contractual relationship of classic
feudalism. It was the reneging of chiefs on their kinship obligations
to tenants, as the tenants saw it, that gave such bitterness to the reaction to the Highland Clearances. Furthermore, the "feudal" rule of
primogeniture was, on occasion, supplanted in the Highlands by tanistry,
whereby any chosen male heir could become chief (Grant, 1930: 477).

Although the runrig joint farm was common to both Highlands and
Lowlands, in one respect the economic structure of the one differed from
the other. The Highlands were a pastoral area--producing a cash crop of
black cattle as well as a subsistence crop of oats and bere, while Lowland agriculture was basically arable.[13] Exchanges took place between
the two areas, with Highland exports of black cattle paying for needed
imports--grain in dearth years, timber, and manufactured goods (Gray,
1957: 42-43). The sale of black cattle was crucially important for
the Highland economy, since the cash product of such sales provided the
bulk of rent payments. This, and a cultural preference in the Lowlands,
for wages in kind rather than money, produced a paradoxical situation
in the early stages of agricultural improvement, when rents were paid
in money more frequently in the "archaic" Highlands than the "modern"
Lowlands.

The passage of time accentuated the differences between Highlands
and Lowlands. From the sixteenth century wardholding gave way to feuferme land tenure. Under this form of feudalism, if we can call it
feudal, an inferior's obligations to his superior were (and are) economic rather than military. "Feuing was primarily undertaken as a method
of increasing revenue. The cash nexus was predominant (Grant, 1930:
279-280)." The spread of feuferme thus represents an attempt at the
commercialization of agriculture, since feu duties were originally set
at the level of economic rents. But wardholding remained as the land-
tenure arrangement of the Highlands, giving rise in Lowland breasts to
fears about the implications of the continued existence of such a

"martial society." These fears were reinforced by further fears about the religious and political adherence of Highlanders. The triumph of Presbyterianism in the Lowlands following the Reformation and the Convenanting Wars, and the subsequent development of parish schools throughout the Lowlands, threw into high relief the continuing Catholicism of some Highland areas, the (to Presbyterian Lowlanders) heathenism of the rest, and the lack of formal educational facilities throughout the Highlands. The willingness of at least some Highland chiefs to come "out" in support of Jacobitism--or in opposition to Whig royal agents in the Highlands--made the Highlands politically suspect.

This, then, is the background to the market incorporation of the Highlands. I have argued elsewhere that one should take the institutional incorporation of the Highlands to be anterior to market incorporation (Carter, 1971), but what I wish to consider here is the account of the nature and process of market incorporation given by economic historians of the Highlands.

LIBERAL ECONOMICS AND THE MARKET INCORPORATION OF THE HIGHLANDS

In 1776 Adam Smith published his The Wealth of Nations. In the course of his discussion of the influence of towns in the improvement of agriculture he provided a potted economic history of the highlands. He noted the essentially "feudal" nature of Highland society before the eighteenth century:

> The occupiers of land were in every respect as dependent upon the great proprietor as his retainers. Even such of them as were not in a state of villanage, were tenants at will, who paid a rent in no respect equivalent to the subsistence which the land afforded them. A crown, half a crown, a sheep, a lamb, was some years ago in the highlands of Scotland a common rent for lands which maintained a family. In some places it is so at this day; nor will money at present purchase a greater quantity of commodities there than in other places. In a country where the surplus produce of a large estate must be consumed upon the estate itself, it will frequently be more convenient for the proprietor, that part of it be consumed at a distance from his own house, provided they who consume it are as dependent upon him as either his retainers or his menial servants (Smith, 1776: II, 199).

Smith is arguing that the Highland economy was only weakly influenced by trade, if at all, since the surplus economic produce must be consumed on the estate itself. Further, the estate owner (clan chief or, if the two offices were not held by a single individual, feudal superior) used the economic surplus from his estate to maintain his economic, social, and political control of the local area. This situation was not changed, Smith argues, by the imposition of the feudal law by central authorities. The local autonomy of chiefs remained very high.

> But what all the violence of the feudal institutions
> could never have effected, the silent and insensible
> operation of foreign commerce and manufactures brought
> about. These gradually furnished the great proprietors
> with something for which they could exchange the whole
> surplus produce of their lands, and which they could
> consume themselves without sharing it either with ten-
> ants and retainers ... For a pair of diamond buckles
> perhaps, or for something as frivolous and useless,
> they exchanged the maintenance, or what is the same
> thing, the price of the maintenance of a thousand men
> for a year, and, with it the whole weight of authority
> which it could give them (Smith, 1776: II, 203).

Two hundred years of political economy and, latterly, economic his-
tory have not added greatly to this basic story. The clan system is still seen to have been oriented to social needs rather than economic needs until the abolition of wardholding land tenure in 1747 knocked away the prop to this martial society.[14] Smout argues that the clan system inhibited the market incorporation of the Highlands:

> Undoubtedly social factors impeded the penetration into
> the Highlands of the economic forces that could have
> changed them. The surplus the Highlanders tried to sell
> outside was black cattle, but the widespread social insti-
> tution of stealing cattle from a neighbouring clan was so
> prevalent that it seriously reduced the profitability of
> ranching within the hills, and thus limited the impact
> that market forces could have upon the Highlands until
> they were completely reduced to law and order (Smout,
> 1969: 341).

Thus the Highlands were only weakly linked to trade until the quaintly named "pacification of the Highlands" by Hanoverian troops after the '45.[15]

Smith's description of an effete elite selling its patrimony for a diamond buckle is mirrored by more recent accounts of the rising debts loaded on Highland estates as chiefs adopted increasingly expensive consumption habits, shifting their reference group from other chiefs and clansmen to the Lowland and English aristocracy (Gray, 1957: 149).

But more recent writers rest their analysis of the economic transformation of the Highlands on much firmer evidence than was available to Smith and recognize more factors in this transformation than just impersonal economic forces. The institutional incorporation of the Highlands, particularly the legal changes tha followed the '45, are seen to have some importance (Smout, 1969: 343-344); but impersonal economic forces are still, as with Smith, the major explanatory variable. The commercialization of Highland agriculture through extensive sheep-farming, and the consequent eviction of tenants to make way for sheep, and the Highland Clearances of the late eighteenth and nineteenth centuries, are seen to have been the result not of human action but of the Invisible Hand:

> But, although it was a situation in which the rich
> and the ruthless had the best chance of survival,
> it would be mistaken to put the blame for the re-
> sulting clearances simply upon greedy or malign
> landlords, for they were really the results of im-
> personal forces beyond the control of either land-
> lords or tenants of 'the total impact of the power-
> ful individualism and economic rationalism of
> industrial civilisation on the weaker, semi-communal
> traditionalism of the recalcitrant fringe' (Gaskell,
> 1968: 26, quoting Gray, 1957: 246).

Furthermore, the definition of what constitutes agricultural improvement in the Highlands is very specific. The model is improved agriculture in the Lowlands, where runrig joint farms were abolished and replaced by consolidated farms. Subsistence production was replaced by production for the market and efficiency was raised through new cropping arrangements--the rotation of arable crops with turnips and leys, for example--and technical innovations such as drainage and the steel plough. The vertically articulated social structure of laird and joint tenants was replaced by a polarized structure of capitalist farmers and industrialists on the one hand, and landless labourers on the other (Smout, 1969: 347). Smout notes that some marginally Highland areas--parts of Perthshire, Angus, Aberdeenshire, Banffshire, and Cromarty, that is, the eastern fringe of the Highlands--did see an evolution towards such a "modern" agrarian system. By contrast, in the north and west Highlands, peasant society was not destroyed (a necessary condition for "modernity"), but merely changed to a different kind of peasant society. Runrig joint farms were abolished, to be sure, but crofts took their place. Crofts were (and are) small, consolidated arable units, individually tenanted, and carrying the right to a souming on common grazings. The crofting system allowed population levels to increase up to the level set by subsistence through subdivision of crofts. This system is seen as "the one instance in Scotland of the improvers' failure to improve (Smout, 1969: 347). It was only with the mortality crisis of the potato famine of 1846-7 that the crunch came for many west Highland estates and they were cleared, or sold, and then cleared, for the creation of "modern" capitalist sheep-farms.[16]

Opposition to clearance for sheep-farms and later for deer forests, strangely muted in the early nineteenth century, eventually resulted, partly as a result of contemporaneous land reform agitation in Ireland and Wales, in the establishment of the Napier Commission to examine the conditions of Highland crofters and, in 1886, in the Crofters Holdings Act. This Act gave a high degree of security and heritability of tenure to crofters within the seven crofting counties[17] who could satisfy a number of conditions. Current economic thinking suggests that this was a mistake in that it froze the economic structure of west Highland and Island areas; the HIDB described crofting as a "stultifying form of land tenure (HIDB, 1967: 4)." Farquhar Gillanders goes further. He regards the Crofters Holding Act as a disaster:

> It is my belief, however, that the 1886 legislation heralded the death of crofting as a way of life, insulating it almost completely from normal economic trends and legally ensuring that crofting land could not now be developed into viable economic units (Gillanders, 1968: 96-97--original emphasis).

The solution for the ills of the Highland economy follows from this premise:

> The real hope for the Highlands today...cannot be in tourism but in the simple courage to implement proved economic principles. The Highlander must cease to regard himself as a member of a chosen race to whom normal economic laws do not apply (Gillanders, 1968: 148).

Thus whether one believes that the agricultural revolution never touched the Highlands (HIDB, 1967; Foreward; McCrone, 1969; 14) or merely that it was rendered incomplete by the 1886 legislation (Turnock, 1970: 108, 114), the policy conclusion derived from this analysis of the Highlands as an "archaic," "feudal," "subsistence-based" economic sector is similar--open the subsistence sector to the market forces of the "modern" economy.

LIBERAL ECONOMICS AND LATIN AMERICA

The consensual view of Latin American agrarian history is that, like the history of the Highlands reviewed above, it represents an incomplete transition from a "traditional," "archaic," "feudal" structure to a "modern," "capitalist" structure. I will illustrate this argument with material from the highly regarded introductory text by Jacques Lambert.

Lambert argues that the encomienda, which delegated part of the sovereign's rights to individuals and gave rise to mutual personal duties on the part of masters and dependents, became associated with land ownership and produced the feudal latifundio, "the fundamental institution of Iberian colonialism" (Lambert, 1967: 59). Latifundios are defined as "large estates operated under archaic methods and only partly put to use (Lambert, 1967: 59)." Such estates are multifunctional institutions, providing economic, social, and political functions for a local region. The latifundio proved to be an admirably adapted institution for the solution of the basic problem of Iberian colonization: how to control large tracts of land with a relatively small number of Iberian colonists. But as the market forces of the "modern" economy began to impinge on the Latin American economy, the latifundio became dysfunctional. The political genesis of the latifundio as a means of controlling a given area of territory is reflected in the owner's interest in upholding his political position; this means maintaining the isolation of his estate, as far as possible, from the market forces of the modern economy.

The latifundio is feudal, for Lambert, in that the relationships on the estate are based on reciprocal rights and duties and not on the cash nexus.[18] But not all estates in Latin America are latifundios. Estates exceeding 2,500 acres occupied 73 per cent of the agriculture and cattle-raising lands in "modern" Argentina in 1945 (Lambert, 1967: 61-62) and earned a large part of the foreign exchange of that country. But these were, in the main, "modern" plantations, highly efficient and highly capitalized, employing wage labour rather than tenant labour (Morner, 1970), and not "feudal" latifundios.[19] The total involvement of plantations in cash crop production for the market means that motives of economic maximization predominate in plantations. In latifundios, by contrast, agricultural production is set at a level that provides a barely sufficient subsistence for the "feudal" dependents, plus a surplus which the owner can use to satisfy his consumption demands and dominate the local political structure (Chonchol, 1965: 84). Social needs have precedence over economic needs. Lambert's prescription for economic (and socio-political) development in Latin America thus includes, as a major element, the full involvement of "feudal" latifundios in the money economy and their consequent and inevitable transformation into "modern" plantations. The dual economy in Latin America, created as in Boecke's classic formulation by the introduction of mature capitalism into a pre-capitalist system (Lambert, 1967: 60), must give way to economic modernity in a final triumph of capitalism.

THE FRANK THESIS AND THE "LATIFUNDIO"

This dual economy account of the nature of the Latin American agrarian sector has recently been challenged by a number of Marxist economists and sociologists, notably Frank (1967, 1970); Vitale (1968); and

Stavenhagen (1968). The members of this school have their differences.
But they all tell the same story about the origins of Latin American
underdevelopment, if not about solutions.

The basis of the argument is that the Iberian conquest was impelled
by commercial motives. Vitale goes further in claiming that late fif-
teenth-century Iberia was in the process of transition from feudalism to
capitalism, and that the conquest stemmed from specifically capitalist
motives (1968: 36-37). Other authors take the conquest to have been
mercantilist rather than capitalist (Stavenhagen, 1968: 16; Frank, 1967:
242), but one of the problems of this school is that the difference between mercantilism and capitalism is never clearly specified--if, indeed,
they accept the existence of such a difference (Riddell, 1972: 93).
Regardless of the precise label which we attach to the motives for conquest, however, they were, it is argued, undeniably commercial, and the
development of large agricultural estates was similarly commercial. The
growth of the Mexican hacienda, as of estates in other mining areas, took
place in pursuit of profit, first by providing food for the "growth pole"
of the silver mines (Furtado, 1970: 13-16) and for export crops and then,
with the decline in profitability of mining in the seventeenth century,
as a more profitable economic enterprise than mining. The desire to
monopolize land and income which might be used by competitors or independent producers (Frank, 1970: 234-237) gave rise to the particular form
of the estate--occupying vast tracts of land but using very little of it
for productive purposes.

Furtado argues that latifundios were established in pursuit of profit,
but that later they became feudal institutions (Furtado, 1970: 53).
This, for Frank, is a nonsense. Both the dual economy account of the
movement from an "archaic" economy to the "modern" economy and the Marxist account of the transition from feudalism to capitalism are evolutionary
and cannot handle regressions. The view of latifundios as feudal institutions, when the genesis of such estates was mercantilist or capitalist,
is based on the illegitimate interference from the existence of non-cash
nexus relationships within the latifundio that the latifundio as a socioeconomic system is pre-capitalist (Frank, 1967: 239). The genesis of the
latifundio was commercial for Frank, so it remains commercial. There is
no analytical difference between a latifundio and a plantation; both exist to maximize profit for the owner, but in the latifundio this purpose
is concealed by the seemingly non-commercial relationship between owner
and peasants. But the very non-commercial nature of these relationships
is determined by market forces; payment oscillates between cash and non-
cash according to the economic interest of the owner (Frank, 1967: 234-
235, 266). Even the modes of production within the latifundio can be
altered in "feudal" directions if it is to the advantage of the owner
so to do. Increased demand for wheat led to free producers on Chilean
wheat latifundios being transformed into "feudal" peons (Frank, 1970:
244).

A corollary of Lambert's view of latifundios as large estates within the "archaic" sector is that the latifundio is, at best, weakly linked to national and international trade. For Frank, on the other hand, trade with national and European markets brought the latifundio into being. But this is an exploitative relationship; economic surplus is sucked out of the "remote" areas and consigned along chains of metropolitan-satellite relationships through the "modern" sector and then to an overseas metropolis. This process continues until the surplus arrives at a highest order world-capitalist metropolis.[20]

> Moreover, each national and local metropolis serves
> to impose and maintain the monopolistic structure and
> exploitative relationship of this system...as long
> as it serves the interests of the metropoles which
> take advantage of this global, national, and local
> structure to promote their own development and the en-
> richment of their ruling classes (Frank, 1970: 6-7).

Three consequences follow from this. First, the dual economy model, with its assumption of two dynamics in one society--an economic dynamic in the "modern" sector and a non-economic dynamic in the "archaic" sector-- is clearly inadequate (Frank, 1970: 221-230). The "archaic" sector, like the "modern" sector, is the result of a single historical process--the penetration of capitalist modes of production and motivations to the "remotest" areas of Latin America (and Asia and Africa).[21] Second, evolutionary accounts of economic development, which are based on extrapolations of the historical experience of now developed nations (usually Britain and the USA), will give misleading predictions in the context of underdeveloped countries, for the developed countries may once have been undeveloped--in a primal economic state--but they were never systematically underdeveloped through the establishment and maintenance of exploitative metropolitan-satellite relationships (Frank, 1970: 4). Finally, the policy prescription derived from dual economy premises--to open the "archaic" sector to the cold winds of the market economy--would, on the monopoly capitalism argument, increase underdevelopment rather than promote development, since present underdevelopment is itself the result of just those market forces that dual economy theorists see to be an economic panacea.

THE FRANK THESIS AND THE SCOTTISH HIGHLANDS

We have seen that the consensual view of Highland economic history before the growth of capitalist sheep-farming shares many features with Lambert's views on Latin America. In both cases one has an agrarian structure based on units engaged in extensive agriculture (runrig joint farms and latifundios) and the prevailing motivation underlying agricultural production is, in both cases, non-economic; enough wealth must be produced to satisfy the consumption demands of the owner, whether "latifundist" or clan chief, but beyond this the interest of the owner lies not in maximizing economic production and profit but in maintaining his social and political domination of the local area. The dual economy policy prescription in both cases is to open up this "feudal" sector to the play of market forces; to bring latifundios and Highland estates within the "modern" economy.

Do Frank's arguments about Latin America have relevance to the Scottish context?[22] How adequate is the view that, before the commercialization of Highland agriculture through sheep-farming, the Highlands formed a precapitalist economic sector?[23] R.H. Campbell asserts that high prices for black cattle and kelp during the Napoleonic Wars inhibited the penetration of market forces to Highland areas "by enabling an anachronistic economy to continue to exist still longer" (Campbell, 1965: 36). Thus Highland estates engaged in producing cattle and kelp were outside the "modern" economy; economic motivations were subsidiary to social and political motivations for owners of such estates. How adequate is this view?

The trade in black cattle, the staple cash crop of Highland agriculture, was of very great importance to the Scottish economy before the Union:

> By the middle of the seventeenth century the cattle
> trade to England had, despite all handicaps, grown
> to such proportions that Scotland was described as
> little more than a grazing field for England (Haldane,
> 1952: 18).

But this trading relationship was asymmetrical. With the reorientation of Scots trade from Europe to England after the Treaty of Edinburgh of 1560 and the Union of the Crowns in 1603 (Smout, 1965: 456-457), the Scottish economy became increasingly dependent on exporting cattle (and, to a lesser extent, linen) to England, while England, although dependent on imported supplies to satisfy the demand for beef, had alternative sources of supply in Wales (Bonser, 1970: 78) and Ireland. The closing of the Border to the cattle trade by the English in 1704 was thus a highly effective economic sanction (Hamilton, 1963: 88); it was followed three years later by the Act of Union which represented the end of Scottish pretensions of a political and economic policy independent of that of England.

The Union established free trade throughout Britain. One of the greatest immediate beneficiaries of this was the cattle trade, which increased in scale throughout the eighteenth century. It was calculated that in 1794, 60,000 beasts were sold at the central tryst in Falkirk, at an average price of ₤4 sterling (Hamilton, 1963: 96). As the trade grew in volume, so the links with England were strengthened. The central tryst was moved from Crieff to Falkirk in the eighteenth century, partly to ease access from south-west Highland areas, but also because of the greater accessibility of Falkirk for English buyers (Hamilton, 1963: 91). The cattle trade had an important influence on the economic development of the Lowlands, since the need for credit on the part of cattle drovers was one spur to the development of the Scottish banking system, which Campbell sees to have been one of the necessary preconditions for the growth of manufacturing industry in the Lowlands (Campbell, 1965: 68-73). The Highlands derived some profit from the sale of cattle, but most profit was made by drovers and graziers outwith the Highlands. The price for cattle in the Highlands rose as high as £5 or £6 per head during the Napoleonic Wars (Hamilton, 1963: 96): in 1812 the Navy victualling yards paid an average price of £15 per head (Haldane, 1952: 175). The lucrative trade of salting beef was entirely confined to England (Hamilton, 1963: 96). Thus the Highlands produced relatively low-value primary products; the profits from converting these products went into other hands.

But, of course, some profit did accrue to the Highlands, and it was extremely important in the Highland economy. Cash derived from the sale of cattle formed the major part of rent payments from tenant to landlord. Hamilton argues that:

> In the Highlands the livelihood of laird and peasant depended on the sale of cattle at remunerative prices ...This industry thus lifted the economy from mere subsistence to farming for profit (Hamilton, 1963: 89).

Note the assertion that the rearing of black cattle was a commercial operation. Nor were chiefs adverse to taking a part in the risky business of financing the droving trade.

> The cattle dealers of the eighteenth century found it necessary to 'engage a co-adventurer in an intended speculation.' The names of Highland chieftains and Lowland lairds appear little less frequently than those of graziers, cattle dealers, merchants and businessmen of the cities in the story of this hazardous trade (Haldane, 1952: 61-62).

It is difficult, on these grounds, to see the Highland economy as non-commercial. The failure of landlords to innovate with new methods of agriculture and with improved breeding (Bonser, 1970: 78) could be seen not as an economically irrational decision based on the precedence of social needs before economic, but as a rational economic decision in a situation where landlords were already enjoying profits from the cattle trade and in which new methods would have involved heavy capital outlay for an uncertain economic return. The kelp industry presents a similar picture.

Kelp is an alkaline ash obtained by burning seaweed. In demand as a fertilizer and for soap-making and glass-making, the price of kelp rose from about ₹2 per ton in 1750 to over ₹20 in 1810 (Gray, 1951: 197-198). This astronomical rise was due in part to the cutting-off of supplies of Spanish barilla during the Napoleonic Wars. The rise in price led owners of kelp estates, the Clanranald estates on the west coast and in the Hebrides, for example, to become increasingly dependent on kelp manufacture for their income; in 1823 the Clanranald factor wrote that "it is entirely a kelp estate (Gray, 1951: 206)." This growing dependence of the landlords' income on the process of gathering and burning kelp had two major effects. First, since kelping was a labour-intensive industry, it was in the interest of the landlord to have a large population on his estate. Emigration was discouraged, and it has been suggested that landlords encouraged immigration to the kelping areas (Prebble, 1963: 248). Land tenure was reorganized: the old runrig joint farms gave way to a system of small, consolidated, individually tenanted crofts, which provided work for the crofter and his family for only two or three days a week, leaving them the rest of the time for kelping. The subdivision of crofts was allowed, to enable the largest possible population to live at subsistence level. The change from the joint farm to crofting reduced the differentiation among tenants, consigning all to a similar position (Caird and Moisley, 1961: 89). Clanranald introduced the potato to South Uist in 1743--the potato gave a higher subsistence crop yield than oats[24]--and coerced his tenants into accepting it (Graham, 1899: 1, 172).

The second major effect had to do with profit. Since the costs of producing kelp rose less steeply than the selling price, kelp production became increasingly profitable. At the peak price of ₹20 per ton in 1810 the landlord's profit was ₹16 (Gray, 1951: 202). As the profit rose, so did the landlord's involvement in the productive process. From letting out kelp rights to entrepreneurs, landlords moved on to contracting directly with kelpers (tenants) for the disposal of their product. Monopolistic control was established by making tacksmen market their tenants' kelp through the landlord. Tenants became wage labourers, standing in a dual relationship to the landlord: tenant to landlord and employee to employer.[25] Rents were set at a level where they creamed off the whole cash product from kelping, leaving the tenant the occupancy of his croft as the reward for his labours (Gray, 1951: 200-201). When the price for kelp crashed at the end of the Napoleonic Wars with the renewed importation of barilla, tenants could not pay their money rents. The landlord therefore took the whole cash product from kelping, taking rent from tenants in the form of wage labour. Landlord-tenant relationships settled down into a form of demonitized tenant labour, with tenants subsisting on produce from their crofts and on relief from the landlord. This relationship lasted on the Clanranald estate until 1838, when the estate was sold to Gordon of Cluny, "one of the most ruthless removers in the Isles (Prebble, 1963: 250)."

The view that it was only with the clearance of kelping estates for
extensive sheep-farming that these areas were incorporated in the capitalist economy is surely wrong. The driving force of the kelp industry
had been the desire of landlords to maximize profit. The emphason on
production of a single cash crop for markets outwith the Highlands, with
the greatest possible profit to the landlord, makes the kelp-estate just
as capitalist an operation as the monocrop sheep-estates which followed
it.[26] The seemingly "feudal" nature of kelp-estates after the price
fall is the result, as in Frank's interpretation of the latifundio, of
a process whereby a capitalist operation, once closely integrated into
the capitalist economy, has been left beached by the receding of those
market forces that brought it into being. To regard kelp-estates as
"anachronistic" and, by implication, pre-capitalist (Campbell, 1965:
36); to regard the crofting system as "the one instance in Scotland
of the improvers' failure to improve (Smout, 1969: 347)" because it
meant merely a change from one kind of peasant society to another kind,
instead of a total destruction of the peasantry, is to do two things.
First, as we have seen, it means misinterpreting the nature of the cattle
trade and the kelp industry, and therefore the nature of the Highland
economy in the eighteenth and early nineteenth centuries. Second, such
arguments demonstrate the tyranny of Lowland, and through them of
English, models in Highland economic history. Only those changes which
produce a polarized social structure of capitalist farmers and landless
wage labourers are to count as "improvement." Yet if one takes the
critical feature of improvement to be not particular social structural
outcomes but the turn to commercial agriculture, then the English and
Lowland experience becomes only one of several possible ways of "modern-
izing" agriculture (Moore, 1967: 413-483). The kelp industry is a
paradigm case of what Moore calls conservative modernization:

> ...The landed upper class will use a variety of
> political and social levers to hold down a labour
> force on the land and make its transition to com-
> mercial farming in this fashion (Moore, 1967: 420).

The particular form which this took in the case of the kelp estates is
similar to Moore's description of Japan, where:

> A landed aristocracy may maintain intact the pre-
> existing peasant society, introducing just enough
> changes in rural society to ensure that the peasants
> generate a sufficient surplus that it can appropriate
> and market at a profit (Moore, 1967: 433).

The fact that the attempts of kelp landlords to develop their estates
took a different form from the attempts of Lowland landlords, and had
different consequences, does not disguise the similarity in the underlying intention in both situations--to maximize profit.

Where does this leave the policy of the Highlands and Islands Development Board? First, it is clear that the Highlands may be underdeveloped, but they are not undeveloped. The "ecological devastation" of large parts of the Highlands (Darling, 1968: 37-38) is the result of the removal of indigenous woodland cover, and subsequent overgrazing by sheep, which removed the residual fertility formerly locked in the land by the tree cover. This overgrazing is clearly the result of the search for maximum profit in sheep-farming, but the destruction of the woodland stemmed in large part from similar causes. Some cutting took place in order to remove refuges for wolves, footpads, and rebels before the eighteenth century, but thereafter the major reasons were, to produce charcoal for the smelting of iron by English ironmasters who had largely exhausted wood stocks farther south, to improve grazing for sheep and, in the nineteenth century, to make birch bobbins for Lowland and Lancashire cotton mills (Hamilton, 1963: 189-192; Darling and Boyd, 1969: 70-74).

Second, any view of the Highlands as an area "that the various revolutions in agriculture, industry and technology have passed by" (HIDB, 1967: Foreword) is patently mistaken. The Highlands today are not independent of such processes--they are the result of them. A number of consequences follow from this on Frank's assumptions. Any attempt to strengthen the links between the Highlands and the "modern" economy through a large-scale exploitation of indigenous Highland raw materials (pace the HIDB's determined efforts to promote the development of the mineral resources of the crofting counties) will increase the underdevelopment of the area by reinforcing the satellization of the Highlands. Alternatively, the growth of industry based on imported raw materials--British Aluminium's Invergordon smelter is an obvious example --would result in a metropolitan rather than a satellite industry. But the smelter is unlikely to have a great positive impact on the economic life of the Highlands for three reasons. First, it is highly capital-intensive, and despite its high capital cost, around £37 million, will create relatively few jobs. Second, it is unlikely to act as the propulsive industry in a growth pole spatially located in the Highlands, since metal fabrication industries are typically sited close to markets. Third, to return to the monopoly capitalism argument, since the smelter is owned outside the Highlands (and, indeed, outside Scotland) the profits from its operation will leave the area. This contrasts with the growth of Lowland industry in the late eighteenth and nineteenth centuries, which was very largely Scottish owned.[27] It is quite possible, however, that the smelter (and the most recent panacea for the Highlands--the oil boom--which has important locations in the Inner Moray Firth area) could have serious negative consequences for the Highlands. In the time when the British navy was a force to be reckoned with, two of its major bases were at Scapa Flow in Orkney and Invergordon in the Moray Firth. The closing of these two bases caused severe economic and social dislocation in the areas concerned. There is no evidence that, after the exploration and development phases of the oil boom are completed, which seems likely, at present, to be a fairly short period, the same fate will not overcome those areas which believed that oil would bring permanent prosperity.

Finally, one might see metropolitan-satellite processes at work within the crofting counties. We noted above the contradiction between a growth centre policy and an attempt to maintain given population levels in areas outside the growth area. The HIDB is committed to both these policies, but the Economist, that objectification of economic rationality, noted in 1970 that it was arguable whether any economic purpose was served by having remote parts of the Highlands inhabited all year round, since the profitable enterprises--tourism, forestry--could be worked by seasonal labour (Economist, 21 February 1970, XXXI). Even discounting such radical suggestions as this, which lies in the same tradition of hard-headed liberal economic thinking about the Highlands as the Sutherland Clearances, a centralist economic development policy is likely to have a devastating effect on the crofting areas,[28] which are the last toehold of the Gaelic language and culture in Scotland. It all depends on what you mean by development.

NOTES

1. This does not mean that sociological, or at least proto-sociological, concerns did not occupy Scottish academics in the past. But the Scottish Moralists--Smith, Hume, Reid, Hutcheson, Stewart, Ferguson, Millar, Lords Kames and Monboddo among them (Schneider, 1967)--did not call themselves sociologists. Their speculations in this field grew out of their professional concerns as lawyers and--the Scottish academic catch-all--moral philosophers (Davie, 1964).

2. One of the most striking assertions of British homogeneity of recent years is Alford's thesis that class membership is now the only social factor exercising a significant effect on British voting behaviour. Nationality, regional loyalties, and religious affiliations used to be significant but are no longer: Britain is psephologically homogeneous (Alford, 1963: 108-109, 144-145). No better example could be adduced of the way in which social science is discomfited by events; the upsurge of Welsh and Scottish nationalism and the events in Ulster make Alford's thesis seem, at best, quaint. Even before these events, however, it had been demonstrated that Scottish political behaviour was not consistent with Alford's thesis (Budge and Urwin, 1966: 132).

3. For Scots Law see T.B. Smith (1963, 1970); for university education see Davie (1964: 7-8). The problem in considering assimilationist tendencies is to distinguish between changes that are the result of a conscious (or taken for granted) application of English patterns and changes coming from a simultaneous adaptation to new circumstances in

in both Scotland and England. For the latter see MacCormick (1966: 201-204) and Withrington (1970).

4. For the definition of the crofting counties see Figure 1.

5. The Board's annual statistics include a category labelled "non-economic." When challenged to say what they are doing to promote social development, Board spokesmen invariably point to this category. Between 1965 and 1970 non-economic grants constituted 2 per cent of the amount of money disbursed by the Board in grants and loans (HIDB, 1971: Appendix X).

6. I take Belshaw's summary as my definition of a dual economy:

> The notion of dual economy implies that, within one political framework, there is one sector which operates according to the principles of modern capitalism. This sector is commercially sophisticated, linked with international trade, dominated by motives of maximization, and in the colonial context, almost entirely in the hands of aliens or residents of alien extraction...Opposed to this sector and separated from it is the traditional peasant economy, which according to the puristic form of the theory, is conservatively oriented, interested in security and continuity rather than change, not concerned with maximisation of profit or of resource use, oriented towards the satisfaction of social needs rather than reacting to international forces, and incapable of engaging dynamically in trade and commerce. Except for a very small minority of Westernised natives who have left traditional society, the indigenous population lies in this sector (Belshaw, 1965: 96).

7. Defined as in the cultural definition in Figure 1.

8. In this analysis "Lowland" is a residual category, embracing all areas outside the Highlands and the North.

9. Cregeen argues that one of the main factors leading to the decision of clan chiefs in the south-west Highlands to support the Jacobite Rebellion in 1745 was their opposition to the expansionism of the Dukes of Argyll, who were the chiefs of Clan Campbell and Royal agents in the south-west Highlands (Cregeen, 1965: 159-160).

10. A celebrated example of such crossing was Alexander Stewart, "the Wolf of Badenoch." A younger son of King Robert II, the Wolf "went native" and descended on Elgin in 1390 with his "wild Wykked Heland-men" and burned the burgh and Cathedral (Kermack, 1957: 62).

11. "The pendulum has swung back, and once more it is not easy to realise how utter and how clear-cut was the dividing line between the Highlands and the Lowlands during the four hundred years between the fourteenth century and the eighteenth century (Grant, 1930: 149)."

12. It is possible to make an analytical distinction between these economic and military aspects of land tenure, but this distinction did not exist for the actors themselves, as the prevalence of cattle-reiving in the Highlands demonstrates.

13. This pastoral-arable division explains the divergence between the economic and cultural divisions in Figure 1. The Aird--the district around Inverness--and the east coastal strip to Caithness were arable areas within the Gaelic sector. Cattle stocks were held in some Lowland areas, notably Aberdeenshir and Galloway.

14. In at least one area, the Argyll estates, important economic changes preceded the '45. Leases were being offered by competitive bidding in 1710, and hereditary tacks were abolished in 1737 (Cregeen, 1965: 169-170).

15. Disarming Acts were imposed on Highlanders after both the '15 and the '45. On both occasions cattle drovers were specifically excepted from the provisions of the Acts.

16. For a very concise statement of this view, and the derived conclusion that the Highland elite was dancing to a social tune and disregarded economic opportunities, see Hobsbawm (1969: 301-303).

17. The crofting counties were identified in 1886 as the most convenient administrative area for handling the problems of crofting. Their subsequent reification as "the Highlands and Islands" makes little sense on economic, cultural, historical, or development policy grounds.

18. "Thus, in different ways, a large proportion of the rural population came to be scattered in small structural units, self-sufficient from the viewpoint of the organisation of production, subject to tutelege, whether direct or indirect...of a ruling class that extracted from it a surplus in a manner resembling the pattern generally known as feudalism (Furtado, 1970: 16--original emphasis)."

19. Part of the confusion over latifundios and plantations is the result of conflicting definitions of the difference between the two. Furtado does not make this distinction. He defines a latifundio as an estate employing more than twelve workers in a permanent capacity, whether in the "modern" or the "archaic" sector (Furtado, 1970: 54-58). Chonchol distinguishes between traditional estates and modern plantations, but argues that both make very inefficient use of land and labour (Chonchol, 1965: 83). Stein and Stein echo Lambert's distinction between the "feudal"

latifundio and the "modern" plantation. The hacienda is seen as a patriarchal social nucleus as well as a unit of agricultural production, while the plantation is defined historically as "an independent economic unit, created to produce staples for external, that is, European consumption (Stein and Stein, 1970: 39, 40)."

20. Laclau criticizes Frank for making the presence or absence of a link with the market the criterion for the existence of capitalism (1971: 20). This leads, he asserts, to Frank having an excessively wide conception of capitalism which does not allow him to distinguish between capitalism, in the Marxist sense, and other modes of production. Indeed, Laclau sees the crucial failure of Frank to be his unwillingness to define capitalism, with Marx, as a mode of production (1971: 25). These criticisms of Frank, although well founded, are not central to my argument, since Laclau accepts Frank's demolition of the dual economy thesis (1971: 24), and it is with this that we are here concerned.

21. "The regions which are the most underdeveloped and feudal-seeming today are the ones which had the closest ties to the metropolis in the past (Frank, 1970: 13)."

22. Buchanan has attempted to explain the upsurge in support for Welsh and Scottish nationalism in the mid-1960s as a response to economic satellization, using Frank's terms. Unfortunately, however, he assumes that the Highlands and Scotland are co-extensive (Buchanan, 1968: 38-39) --an interesting form of the strategy of misapprehension. His argument depends on the Lowlands standing in the same satellized situation to the English metropolis that I am here arguing for the Highlands; and the argument will not hold. Lowland industrialization was the result of the English allowing a place in the metropolitan sun for certain specialized heavy industries, provided that they were complementary with the English economy and not competitive, and Scottish capital was invested abroad--three-quarters of the foreign investment in ranching in the United States in the 1870s and 1880s was Scottish (Campbell, 1965: 79). See also Nairn, 1968: 45.

23. Marx certainly believed that the Highlands were pre-capitalist. Indeed, in one of his swingeing attacks on the Sutherland Clearances he categorizes the clan system as not just pre-capitalist but pre-feudal ("The Dutchess of Sutherland and Slavery" in Bottomore and Rubel, 1963: 131-132). Once again one sees the categorical problems that the Highlands present to sociological typologies; the clan system contained feudal elements such as wardholding land tenure and elements drawn from the kin-based social structure of pre-feudal Scotland and Ireland, such as tanistry.

24. On the influence of the potato in Highland and Lowland Scotland see that monument of comparative sociology (Salaman, 1949: 344-408).

25. Thus the kelp industry counts as a capitalist enterprise on Laclau's criteria: the labourer's sale of his wage labour (Laclau, 1971: 24).

26. Although the price of kelp fell after 1815, production on the Clan-ranald estate did not fall. In 1815 the estate handled rather more than 1,100 tons, in 1838 it handled 1,300 tons (Gray, 1951: 201, 202).

27. But no longer. American-controlled businesses alone accounted for over 10 per cent of total employment in Scottish manufacturing industry, for 12 per cent of total output, and for an estimated 27 per cent of Scotland's manufactured exports in 1968 (Johnston, Buxton and Mair, 1971: 88). Nor is the definition of what constitutes a "Scotish company" unambiguous. The largest company registered in Scotland is Burmah Oil. See the fund of data, from turnover and profits to chairman's salary, for the fifty largest Scottish-registered public companies in Hawthorn, 1971.

28. The population of the crofting counties rose by 6,443 between 1961 and 1971: a significant event, since the population previously had been falling continuously since 1841. But the population of the burgh of Inverness alone rose by 5,143 between 1961 and 1971. Population growth at the centre is accompanied by decline at the periphery.

REFERENCES

Alford, R.
    1963 Party and Society. Chicago: Rand McNally.

Apthorpe, R.
    1970 Development studies and social planning. In R. Apthorpe (ed.),
    People Planning and Development Studies: Some Reflections on Social
    Planning. London: Cass.

Barth, F.
    1969 Introduction. In Barth, F. (ed.), Ethnic Groups and Boundaries:
    the Social Organization of Culture Difference. Boston: Little Brown.

Belshaw, C.
    1965 Traditional Exchange and Modern Markets. Englewood Cliffs,
    NJ: Prentice-Hall.

Bonser, K.
    1970 The Drovers, Who They Were and How They Went. London:
    Macmillan.

Bottomore, T. and Rubel, M. (eds.)
    1963 Karl Marx: Selected Writings in Sociology and Social Philosophy.
    Harmondsworth: Penguin.

Buchanan, K.
      1968 The revolt against satellization in Scotland and Wales.
      Monthly Review 19 (10): 36-48.

Budge, I. and Urwin, D.
      1966 Scottish Political Behaviour: A Case Study in British
      Homogeneity. London: Longmans.

Burnett, C.
      1950 The Burnett Family, with Collateral Branches. Los Angeles.

Burnett, G.
      1901 The Family of Burnett of Leys, with Collateral Branches.
      Aberdeen: New Spalding Club.

Caird, J. and Moisley, H.
      1961 Leadership and innovation in the crofting communities of the
      Outer Hebrides. Sociological Review 9: 85-102.

Campbell, R.
      1965 Scotland Since 1707: the Rise of an Industrial Society.
      Oxford, Blackwell.

Carter, I.
      1971 Economic models and the recent history of the Highlands.
      Scottish Studies 15: 99-120.

      1972. The Highlands Board and Strath Kildonan. Catalyst 5: 21-22.

      1973. Six years on: an evaluative study of the Highlands and
      Islands Development Board. Aberdeen University Review 45: 55-78.

Chapman, R.W. (ed.)
      1924 A Journey to the Western Islands of Scotland. Oxford: Oxford
      University Press.

Chonchol, J.
      1965 Land Tenure and Development in Latin America. In Velez, C.
      (ed.), 1965.

Collier, A.
      1953 The Crofting Problem. Cambridge: Cambridge University Press.

Coulborn, R.
      1956 Feudalism in History. Hamdem, Connecticut: Archon Books.

Cregeen, E.
      1965 The Changing Role of the House of Argyll in the Scottish
      Highlands. In Lewis, I. (ed.), 1965.

Darling, F.
    1955 West Highland Survey. London: Oxford University Press.

    1968 Ecology of Land Use in the Highlands and Islands.   In
    Thomson, D. and Grimble, I. (eds.), 1968.

Darling, F. and Boyd, J.
    1969 The Highlands and Islands. (Revised edition) London: Collins.

Davie, G.
    1964 The Democratic Intellect (2nd edition). Edinburgh: Edin-
    burgh University Press.

Dore, R.P.
    1965 Land Reform and Japan's Economic Development: a Reactionary
    Thesis. In Shanin, T. (ed.), 1971.

Frank, A.
    1967 Capitalism and Underdevelopment in Latin America: Historical
    Studies of Chile and Brazil. New York: Monthly Review Press.

    1970 Latin America: Underdevelopment or Revolution. New York:
    Monthly Review Press.

Furtado, C.
    1970 Economic Development of Latin America: a Survey from
    Colonial Times to the Cuban Revolution. Cambridge: Cambridge
    University Press.

Gaskell, P.
    1965 Morvern Transformed: a Highland Parish in the Nineteenth
    Century. Cambridge: Cambridge University Press.

Gillanders, F.
    1968 The Economic Life of Gaelic Scotland Today. In Thompson,
    D. and Grimble, I. (eds.), 1968.

Graham, H.
    1899 The Social Life of Scotland in the Eighteenth Century. (Two
    volumes.) London: A. & C. Black.

Grant, I.
    1930 The Social and Economic Development of Scotland Before 1603.
    Edinburgh: Oliver & Boyd.

    1961 Highland Folkways. London: Routledge.

Gray, M.
    1951 The kelp industry in the Highlands and Islands. Economic
    History Review 4: 197-209.

    1957 The Highland Economy. Edinburgh: Oliver & Boyd.

Haldane, A.
    1952 The Drove Roads of Scotland. Edinburgh: Nelson.

Hamilton, H.
    1963 An Economic History of Scotland in the Eighteenth Century.
    Oxford: Clarendon Press.

Hawthorn, J.
    1971 Top Scots. Scotland (November): 17-27.

Higgins, B.
    1968 Economic Development (2nd edition). New York: Norton.

HIDB (Highlands and Islands Development Board)
    1967 First Annual Report. Inverness: HIDB.

    1971 Fifth Annual Report. Inverness: HIDB.

Hobsbawm, E.
    1969 Industry and Empire. Harmondsworth: Penguin.

Jenkins, R.
    1971 Exploitation. London: McGibbon & Kee.

Johns, F.
    1965 The Social Structure of Modern Britain. Oxford: Pergamon Press

Johnson, S.
    1775 A Journey to the Western Islands of Scotland. In Chapman,
    R.W. (ed.), 1924.

Johnston, T., Buxton, N. and Mair, D.
    1971 Structure and Growth of the Scottish Economy. London: Collins.

Kellas, J.
    1968 Modern Scotland: the Nation since 1870. London: Pall Mall.

Kermack, W.
    1957 The Scottish Highlands: a Short History. Edinburgh: Johnston
    & Bacon.

Laclau, E.
1971   Feudalism and Capitalism in Latin America. New Left Review
67: 19-38.

Lambert, J.
1967   Latin America: Social Structures and Political Institutions.
Berkeley: University of California Press.

Lewis, I. (ed.)
1965   History and Social Anthropology.   London: Tavistock Publications.

Lichtheim, G.
1971   Imperialism.   London: Allen Lane.

MacCormick, D.
1966   Can Stare Decisis be abolished?   Juridical Review: 197-213.

MacCormick, N. (ed.)
1970   The Scottish Debate: Essays on Scottish Nationalism.   London:
Oxford University Press.

McCrone, G.
1969   Regional Policy in Britain.   London: Allen and Unwin.

MacKay, D.
1965   Regional planning for the north of Scotland.   Aberdeen University Review 41: 75-83.

MacKenzie, A.
1881   History of the MacDonalds and Lords of the Isles.   Inverness:
A. & W. MacKenzie.

Magdoff, H.
1968   The Age of Imperialism.   New York: Monthly Review Press.

Miller, K. (ed.)
1970   Memoirs of a Modern Scotland.   London: Faber & Faber.

Mitchison, R.
1962   Agricultural Sir John: The Life of Sir John Sinclair of
Ulbster, 1754-1835.   London: Bles.

Moore, B.
1967   Social Origins of Dictatorship and Democracy.   Harmondsowth:
Penguin.

Morner, M.
1970   A Comparative Study of Tenant Labour in Parts of Europe,
Africa and Latin America, 1700-1900.   Latin American Research
Review 5: 3-15.

Nairn, T.
     1968   The Three Dreams of Scottish Nationalism.   New Left Review
     49: 3-18.   Reprinted in Miller, K. (ed.), 1970.

Pearse, A.
     1971   Metropolis and Peasant.   In Shanin, T. (ed.), 1971.

Petras, J. and Seitlin, M. (eds.)
     1968   Latin America: Reform or Revolution: Greenwich, Connecticut:
     Fawcett.

Phillipson, N. and Mitchison, R. (eds.)
     1970   Scotland in the Age of Improvement.   Edinburgh: Edinburgh
     University Press.

Potter, J.
     1967   Peasants in the Modern World.   In Potter, J., Diaz, M. and
     Foster, G. (eds.), 1967.

Potter, J., Diaz, M., and Foster, G. (eds.)
     1967   Peasant Society.   Boston: Little Brown.

Prebble, J.
     1963   The Highland Clearances.   Harmondsworth: Penguin.

Riddell, D.
     1972   Towards a Structuralist Sociology of Development?   Sociology
     6: 89-96.

Salaman, R.
     1949   History and Social Influence of the Potato.   Cambridge:
     Cambridge University Press.

Schneider, L. (ed.)
     1967   The Scottish Moralists on Human Nature and Society.   Chicago:
     University of Chicago Press.

Shanin, T. (ed.)
     1971   Peasants and Peasant Societies.   Harmondsworth: Penguin.

Smith, A.
     1776   The Wealth of Nations.   Three volumes (2nd edition).   Dublin:
     Whitestone.

Smith, T.
     1963   Legal Imperialism and Legal Parochialism.   Juridical Review:
     39-55.

Smith, T.
    1970   Scottish Nationalism, Law and Self-government.   In MacCormick,
    N. (ed.), 1970.

Smout, T.C.
    1965   The Anglo-Scottish Union of 1707: the Economic Background.
    Economic History Review 16: 455-467.

    1969   A History of the Scottish People, 1560-1830.   London: Collins.

Stavenhagen, R.
    1968   Seven Fallacies about Latin America.   In Petras, J. and
    Zeitlin, M. (eds.), 1968.

Stein, S. and Stein, B.
    1970   The Colonial Heritage of Latin America: Essays on Economic
    Dependence in Perspective.   New York: Oxford University Press.

Thomson, D. and Grimble, I. (eds.)
    1968   The Future of the Highlands.   London: Routledge.

Turnock, D.
    1970   Patterns of Highland Development.   London: Macmillan.

Veliz, C. (ed.)
    1965   Obstacles to Change in Latin America.   London: Oxford University
    Press.

Vitale, L.
    1968   Latin America: Feudal or Capitalist?   In Petras, J. and
    Zeitlin, M. (eds.), 1968.

Warrand, D.
    1965   Some MacKenzie Pedigrees.   Inverness: Carruthers.

Withrington, D.
    1970   Education and Society in the Eighteenth Century.   In Phillip-
    son, N. and Mitchison, R. (eds.), 1970.

13. Industrial Growth and Development Policies in the British Periphery

ROBERT MOORE

In the early stages of capitalist industrial development the resources
of the countryside and the colonies were appropriated for the benefit
of industry in towns and cities. The industrial provinces were also
expropriated themselves. For example, Durham County had its main resources exploited in the nineteenth and early twentieth centuries, and
the profits from this were invested elsewhere in banking, property, or
new industries, or invested overseas. Thus a county which generated
considerable industrial wealth was by virtue of its social relations
to capital deprived of benefits from that wealth.

At a later stage the peripheral areas may again become useful as
sources of labour. Industry seeking to reduce labour costs may replace
men with machines, import migrant labour, employ women, or relocate in
an area of plentiful and/or less expensive labour. Meanwhile the deprivation of the provinces becomes the "regional problem" and a focus of
ameliorative measures designed to encourage industries to relocate
away from the overcrowded and overemployed areas. The interests of the
state and industry may coincide in this. Thus one "solution" to the
problem of Liverpool or Glasgow may be to encourage foreign multinational companies who may make, assemble, tranship, market, or store
their goods in such "development" areas. The three largest employers
in Peterhead, a small town on the north east coast of Scotland, are:
a branch of General Motors, a canning factory for a Swiss-based transnational food corporation, and an engineering works belonging to an
English conglomerate based upon the electrical trade.

The reason for conducting research in Peterhead was that whilst
part of a development area (Scotland), it has recently become an asset
to multi-nationals and to the state by virtue of its proximity to the
North Sea oil and gas fields. In the course of research on the social
impact of oil it became clear that the actual effects were mediated by
the intervention of the state, both directly and by virtue of the evolution of a body of regional development and planning policies. But the
policy framework within which oil developments took place was not one
designed to cope with primary extractive industry but with conventional

"regional development" problems--unemployment, emigration and low rates of investment. The disjunction between needs and policy nicely highlighted the role of the state and its response to the problem of peripheral areas. This paper is intended as a description of this significant disjunction.

The north and north east of Scotland contains 14 percent of the population of Scotland and 1.4 percent of that of the U.K. In the small towns, heavy unemployment is measured in hundreds. This has to be contrasted with the chronic unemployment of many thousands and the industrial dereliction of the populous midlands. One altruistic Peterheadian suggested that in "the national interest," even a "St. Kilda solution" (evacuation of the whole population) was acceptable if it saved the British economy and brought benefits to the more populous regions thereby. Drastic as this may seem, and given that Peterheadians are neither a rare nor migratory species, such a policy could be seen as acceptable for the greater good in a programme either of accelerated capital accumulation or of socialist reconstruction. It is suggested later that it may be misleading to think in terms of an homogenous "national" interest in this way. But crucially it remains a fact that what happens in the north east is relatively unimportant to most Scots or to the U.K. population at large--and this is part of the problem we have to address in attempting to understand what was happening there.

In observing Peterhead the sociologist is not looking at a town that is as unique as it is to a Peterheadian nor at a location which simply has problems of planning and policy, as an administrator might see it. Theoretical issues are raised by events in Peterhead, and it is the questions raised by these to which the sociologist primarily applies himself, believing that whilst he may not immediately satisfy either the Peterheadian or the planner he will be able to offer them a wider and more general perspective upon the events that interest them and help them to a fuller understanding thereby.

Theoretical problems especially gather around the notions of industrialisation and development. Our image of industrialisation is rooted in a stereotype of the English industrial revolution; we think of the forced-movement of rural population into rapidly expanding towns and of the rise of mass employment in large-scale extractive and manufacturing industry. This primary industrialisation is then followed by growth in retailing and services, the rise of business and municipal administration, and the expansion of banking, insurance, "the city," and the state.[1] This growth of industry is accompanied by the rise of new classes--a property-owning entrepreneurial middle class and an industrial working class. The latter, starting from a condition of economic and political dependency, organises its interests in the trade union and the Labour party, and through them begins to transform the relationships between the classes.

When we say that large scale industry comes to the north and north east of Scotland as a result of oil, we must not imply a repetition of this history. Nonetheless politicians and some policy-makers seem to adhere to the stereotype and equate industrialisation with the development of manufacturing and the creation of large numbers of jobs. Is this just a simple mistake or does the historical model serve an ideological purpose in concealing the interests served by the development policies adopted?

II

The discovery of North Sea oil and the decision to exploit it commercially were greeted euphorically in the region:

> ...[F]or generations we watched our youngsters pack up
> and drift south looking for work ... if we can build up
> a proper industrial base ... all the rest will follow.
> And that means jobs; more important it means careers,
> some kind of fulfilment in the north. It may even mean
> colleges and teacher training schools. Let the London
> newspapers, the gentry and the southerners bleat all
> they like. North Sea oil represents a way out of genera-
> tions of neglect, decay, demoralisation and exploitation
> (Rosie 1974: 56).

But the euphoria was not universal; sociologists responded more cautiously because of their knowledge of the social process of economic development, both historically and in other parts of the world today. We had theories about developments which enabled us to connect events and make sense of the course of events. These are discussed briefly in the book I have written about Peterhead and in a paper (Moore, 1978). Importantly, we had theories which disconnected ideas of industrialisation from development and suggested outcomes to the current course of events that were unlikely to reinforce the euphoria.

Industrial enterprise is not new to the north and north east of Scotland, and the current changes are not rooted in a primal industrialisation process. The optimistic view of oil appeared to be based on an idea that the north and north east of Scotland were non-industrial or pre-industrial regions needing capital and a change in traditional attitudes for industrialisation to take place. Oil would provide the economic base, foreign capital the opportunities, and the oil men an injection of new ideas; a hitherto backward part of Britain would take off with high employment into affluence and modernity. Even social problems were foreseen in terms of urban industrial society--strained social resources, family disruption, and the collapse of traditional social controls.

The theory implicit in this outlook and elaborated in much of the classic economic and sociological literature explains very litt.e   Ian Carter (1974) has argued that the Highlands are not backward in relation to industrial areas. They have developed (or become underdeveloped) in response to the needs of the wider society. The crofting system, itself a response to the economic opportunities created by industrialisation in the 18th and 19th Centuries, and the incorporation thereby of the Highlands and Islands into capitalist society comprise a system highly deleterious to agriculture, resulting in decreased agricultural productivity. Like many contemporary underdeveloped societies, the Highlands and Islands had to import food, having previously been self-sufficient. Similarly, the area around Aberdeen could be seen not as pre-industrial but post-industrial--a previous base in textiles, quarrying and (more debatably) paper, having largely collapsed. According to the critics of the classic theories, the north of Scotland has always been an integral part of the British economic and social structure, but its position in that structure has been dependent and subordinate (Carter, 1974). In spite of some quite large "development" schemes, there has been no autonomous self-sustained growth in the north so that it therefore remained economically dependent.

The main weakness of traditional theories was the division of the world into sectors at different stages of development. Critics of these theories stress the one-ness of the world economic system and the inter-dependence of the parts. The most productive theoretical developments that take account of this have surrounded the idea of "dependent development." Dos Santos has described dependent development in the following way: "When some countries can expand through self-impulsion while others being in a dependent position, can only expand as a reflection of the expansion of the dominant countries" (quoted in O'Brien, 1975: 12). The word "dominant" is significant because Dos Santos is not discussing the functional dependence of equal members of a social structure all on the same path to development, but rather relations of domination and subordination among these members.

One problem with the notion of dependent development has been its generality. We can, after all, readily agree that the world is one system of interaction but this tells us nothing at all about the structure of social relations between and within particular societies or the consequences of particular social arrangements for specific populations. We are now more precisely specifying the institutional characteristics of dependent development. Possible approaches can be illustrated in borrowing a formulation from Galtung by examining dependent development in terms of an international vertical division of processing, of capital and of labor (Galtung, 1971).

The division of processing involves the dependent region in low levels of processing and the dominant in higher levels of processing. Autonomous industrialisation in the dependent region is usually precluded because dependent development is geared to the production and export of relatively raw materials, so that the maximum value may be added to them in existing industrial areas near large markets. This was a fact of life in many colonies, and is still a fact of life in many ex-colonies. Opportunities for local entrepreneurs are found mainly in servicing this kind of production. Peterhead would be industrialising on the basis of oil if it was moving into, say, plastics manufacture and pharmaceuticals. But it is a long way from the market for plastic goods or highly processed petro-chemical products. Most of the region's oil products will be feedstock for industries elsewhere. The only exception we might expect to find is that processes that are dangerous, polluting, or otherwise unacceptable in industrial areas might be sited there.

The division of capital needs no comment. The U.K. itself could not provide the finance needed for North Sea oil exploitation, and the north east and Peterhead certainly could not provide any. Normally, profits accrue to capital. Will, then, all the profits migrate, perhaps to where the maximum value is being added to oil, in manufacture? We cannot answer decisively because state intervention is an important factor and furthermore the government can not be changed by the direct intervention of foreign companies as is the case in some Third World nations. It is to be expected, however, that neither a Westminster nor an Edinburgh government will give Peterhead priority when large-scale social and economic problems of a politically damaging nature press elsewhere.

Under a dependent division of labour, the research, planning, and control of production comes from outside, and the region provides un-skilled, semiskilled and service workers only. Key questions we have to ask include: how long does it take local men and women to move into more skilled and managerial posts; how long does it take for educational institutions to provide training for advanced and specialised scientific and engineering skills--and how long does it take young men and women to motivate themselves to acquire these skills? Will it all take longer than the profitable life of the oil fields? The life of the oil fields is dependent on economic and polit-ical forces outside local control.

This last set of problems is crucial because if what proves to be the relatively transient demands of the oil industry draws men and women out of existing industries, this may have the effect of perman-ently disabling industries that would otherwise be main sources of future employment. If this was to happen we could say that the region had been actively underdeveloped, because its latter state would be worse than its former. This could be aggravated by accelerating emigration if young people and educational institutions adapted themselves to conditions that no longer held; indeed the region might once again provide skills for other parts of the world on a large scale, as it is the last resource to be exported from underdeveloped countries that always seem to be its potentially most valuable, namely its manpower and womanpower.

Dependency theories do not suggest a simple division of the world into exploiters and exploited. There are opportunities for local entrepreneurs to start or expand businesses. And these may come to constitute a politically important class as native supporters of intruding economic and political interests. A significant part of the local working class enjoys high wages for a portion of many working lives. We referred to the "transient" demands of the oil industry; if the demand is for labour for 25 years, then it clearly does not seem transient if you are 20 years old and unemployed. Average wages in the north east are now around 95 percent of the Scottish average, having been about 75 percent for many years. But two features of this local prosperity have to be noted. Firstly, new inequalities overlay or replace old ones--not the unequal relations of master and employee or differences of class but inequality between those who are in the progressive sector of the international economy of oil, enjoying relatively high income and perhaps high prestige and those who are in the now stagnant or declining sector with lower incomes and prestige and perhaps employed in businesses made precarious by oil. Thus while wages go up, differences between the highest and lowest widen and consumption patterns, and styles of life may become conspicuously differentiated. It was changes like these, but perhaps not so clearly perceived, which underpinned fears of irreversible and undesirable changes in a "traditional" way of life in Peterhead.

Secondly, benefits enjoyed are not based on any indigenous and autonomous economic activity but on activities outside local control. The traditional economy of the north east has been based primarily on local industries, largely locally-owned and connected to the rest of the British economy mainly by markets only. This is changing at strategic points. Work by Hunt (1978) has shown that whereas in 1969 the majority of companies in industrial manufacture and the servicing of manufacture were locally controlled in Aberdeen City, majority control passed out of the area by 1974. It seems that in Peterhead, too, major new employers are not local, and in some cases not even British. New kinds of economic enterprise are locating themselves in the region in order to exploit offshore oil. The techniques and organisation of the extraction, processing, and marketing of oil are the province of multi-million dollar transnational corporations which are in the most technically advanced sector of capitalism. The relation of these corporations to the governments of nation-states and the enormous economic and political power they wield have given rise to a set of problems, "the power of the multi-nationals." Part of the basis of this power lies in the relationship between the corporation and the states of the advanced industrial societies, notably the U.S.A.

Theories of industrialisation and theories of development help us to understand much of what is happening in northern Scotland, and this would be the case if the region was neither industrialising nor developing. However, these theories have been used in a way that stresses the uneven economic development of regions and highlight the spatial or geographical distribution of costs and benefits of economic change. Capital has been extracted from both the British regions and colonies overseas without being invested locally or replaced. Northern Ireland and the Scottish midlands developed textiles, shipbuilding, coal, iron, and steel at particular phases of the British imperial economy. Now both experience major industrial decline whilst southeast England and the European industrial triangle flourish. The state has, meanwhile, evolved policies to redress the uneven spatial distribution of industrial changes. But has the whole population of the south east England, or Birmingham, so enriched itself at the expense of Scotland, Northern Ireland, and the English regions that there is now no poverty, no poor housing, no deprivation of any kind in the south east? The suggestion is absurd.

The decline of one region may be the necessary condition of the development of another, but the costs and benefits are unevenly distributed socially within the regions. There are people unemployed, lacking adequate housing, and with poor educational opportunities in Ballymena, Stonehaven, Spennymoor and Stepney. Fortunes are made in the city of London at the expense of people in all these locations, just as there is a local class in each place which benefits from local deprivation. The unemployed, the poor, and the affluent each have common interests that cut across region or locality and have more in common with people like themselves elsewhere than they have with those in better or worse social and economic positions in their own neighbourhood. The extent to which they actually recognise these common interests is highly problematic as is the concept of the "national interest" looked at in this way.

It is certain classes who are the beneficiaries of the relative deprivation of the declining areas or the growth of the growth areas. The state intervenes here too to effect a degree of redistribution between classes, but it does not act in a neutral way. The crucial point is that an analysis centred upon the causes and effects of events upon a region or locality misses the class aspect, which may be much more significant. Thus parts of our analysis of Peterhead focused upon possible transformations of local classes and the ways in which they articulate with the wider class structure. Of special interest was the possibility of the emergence of a new intermediary fraction of the old local middle class of small businessmen and professionals who will stand between incoming interests and the local community. Equally important would be the development of a more organised working class, augmented and mobilised through the introduction of large scale "industrial" construction and service activities, national trade

unions, and more agressive non-local employers. In other words, we
tried to understand Peterhead not as a location with different interests
from Edinburgh or London but as the focus of particular facet of class
conflict: this helped shape the line of sociological enquiry into oil-
related developments in Peterhead.

Economic change is social change. It is in considering the
political impact of oil that we see the sharpest contrasts between
theories based on the idea of industrialisation and dependent development. A discussion of power and control in the town formed a major
part of the study of Peterhead. In this part of the analysis, as in
all others, the role of the state was again of major significance. In
common with every other town in Britain, Peterhead is subject to the
authority of "the state" in its various manifestations. The policies
adopted by the state are usually orientated to national considerations,
and how these impinge upon any one locality as a matter for empirical
enquiry. Three aspects of state policy--those policies concerned with
the economy at large, with planning, and with regional development--
have been especially influential upon Peterhead. This would be true
whether Peterhead was an "oil town" or not. But the State also intervened quite directly in the affairs of the town. What is the state's
interest in oil that makes Peterhead so much more significant in its
plans than it was four years ago? The answer lies in Peterhead's
strategic location in the recovery of oil. North Sea oil will enable
the U.K. to become a net exporter rather than importer of oil, and
natural gas will be a substitute for other imported fuels. Gaskin
et al. reckon that this will entail a balance of payments benefit of
between 5,000M pounds a year by the early 1980's (Gaskin et al., 1978: 28).
Secondly, oil and gas are sources of taxation revenue to the state
worth between 3 billion and 4 billion pounds per annum in the early
1980's (ibid.). The revenues accruing to central government are
described by the authors as "the major benefits from North Sea oil
and gas production" (1978: 16).

Thus although the taxation regime brings enormous benefits to the
oil industry itself, the major beneficiary in the U.K. is the state.
How then does the state relate to a small town caught up in oil developments? Part of our analysis concerned economic policy and the
effects of wage restraint upon local firms trying to compete with
incomers accustomed to paying high wages. Local authority expenditure
cuts also prevented the provision of certain infrastructural items
(like adequate sewage treatment) and, quite importantly, prevented
the growth of the research activity that was necessary for local
and regional social policy development. Another part of our analysis
focused upon planning where state intervention took one crucial planning
decision out of local control because it was a matter of "national"
importance. We also explored the implications of the lack of power
to prevent speculation in land (prior to the Community Land Act) and

the problems of planning in situations of almost total uncertainty.
We might also have looked at the dependence of the state upon the oil
industry for technical advice in planning (an even more acute problem
for BNOC).

How do existing policies engage with present changes? The state
has a range of policies quite specifically geared to the perennial
problems of the peripheral areas. Regional policies are designed to
help identifiable areas, but there are other policies concerned with
counteracting the uneven distribution of wealth, income and social
capital. Rating policy is a case in point; the Exchequer operates a
scheme for balancing the rates between richer and poorer authorities.
One of the major claims of those locals who sought to encourage
development in Peterhead was that projects such as the Scanitro Ammonia
Plant, the Natural Gas Liquids plant to be built by Shell/Esso,
and the offshore bases generated high rateable values and therefore
high rate incomes which would benefit the locality. It is true that
higher rate income would be generated, but the argument is spurious
because a pro rata loss of rate support grant would keep the net income
the same. In this case, therefore, arrangements to help poorer areas
also prevent them from benefiting from economic development by redistributing away the increased rate income.

When we turn to regional policy as such we find that Peterhead
is part of the Grampian Region which is part of the Scottish Development area. Incoming companies may, therefore, qualify for any of a
range of grants, tax allowances or loans. The grant and loans are as
follows:

Regional Development Grants: This covers 20 percent of the building
costs and 20 percent of the cost of new plant and machinery. It is
available for enterprises in manufacturing and processing.

Removal Grants: Projects moving into a development area may
qualify for up to 80 percent of the cost of removing plant and materials
and the employer's net statutory redundancy payments at the previous
location.

Selective Investment Schemes and Interest Relief Grants: The
former is confined to projects of at least 500,000 pounds, but both
contribute to the cost of interest charges, at a level to be negotiated.

Transferred Workers Removal Assistance: Under this scheme grants
are made either for moving key workers in, or for sending local unemployed for training at a parent plant. The grants cover travel,
removal, disturbance, etc.

Industry Schemes: Certain industries (including machine tools,
wool textiles, red meat slaughter) qualify for grants and loans for
building and machinery needed to modernise or rationalise production.

Service Industry Grants: These cover a grant of 1.5 thousand pounds for each new job created, and a grant to cover rent for five years. To qualify, the firm must create at least ten new jobs, and it must have a genuine choice of location.

Tax Allowances: In the first year in a development area an enter- prise may claim 100 percent of capital expenditure on machinery and equipment and may write off 54 percent of the construction cost of buildings (and then 4 percent per year).

Incoming industry therefore seems to attract very considerable state subsidies in a development area. Because the whole of Scotland has been a development area, wherever Scanitro or Shell/Esso located themselves they would at least have received 20 percent of their capital costs from the state, 54 percent of these costs allowed against tax, and the whole of their equipment costs in the first year. The most that local employers could have hoped for was a cash grant or loan towards modernisation. This seemed unfair when local employers had weathered economic difficulties in the local community, were "loyal" to Peterhead and then had to watch a newcomer--only after rich pickings and already forcing wage rates up--gain state aid on a big scale. At least this was how locals expressed it during planning enquiries.

A sociologically significant point about the array of grants and loans is that there is a theory underlying it. It is a very simplistic theory of economic development based upon the classic development of industrial capitalism. The development areas are either "backward" and therefore need modernisation (through Industry Schemes), or in need of "development," and this is equated with the growth of manufacturing or processing. Why else exclude service industries unless they have a genuine choice of location? Obviously oil-related service industries do not have this choice; they are where the oil industry needs them. So perhaps the logic is: if an industry will come anyhow, why subsidise it? The same logic could be applied to Scanitro and Shell; they will be sited in a technically and commercially suitable location in order to carry on a highly profitable activity. Should they therefore benefit from the inducements offered to encourage other manufacturing and processing companies who might otherwise not choose to come to a development area?

The policies described not only rest upon certain theories, they support particular interests. Capital-intensive industry stands to gain the most, even though the policies are ostensibly designed to create employment. A recent report made a similar point with reference to the SDA. The Agency is charged with the pursuit of social objectives, including the generation of employment, for example, but has to do so according to the normal commercial criteria of profitability, effi- ciency, and modernity. None of these factors favours the generation

of employment as such, and they may discriminate against small, new
and indigenous firms (Fraser of Allender 1978: 34-46).[2]

The logic of regional policy no longer fits Peterhead because it
was not a policy devised to cope with the situation now found in the
oil-affected areas. Processing provides few jobs, and most of the
locally-recruited personnel would work in unskilled occupations. The
servicing and maintenance of off-shore installations will be a long-
term undertaking outlasting the development and construction phases
of work offshore and onshore. It is an activity which uses considerable
labour and which has to upgrade the skills of locally-recruited
employees; it therefore provides jobs and training. If offshore servicing attracted state aid, Aberdeen's loss of full development area
status might have favoured Peterhead and offset some of the disadvantages of distance from the railhead and poor roads. Furthermore,
existing bases might have taken on additional employees and made
innovations in anticipation of developments in the future if they
could have raised funds or tax relief from the state.

It is certainly anomalous that the sector most likely to sustain
economic growth, long-term employment, and the stimulation of small-
scale engineering and electronic works does not qualify for development
aid. If the provision of jobs and skills has been a major objective
in the north east, then the equation of development with manufacturing
with jobs in the present circumstances is likely to subvert that objective because manufacturing and processing in petro-chemicals are
capital-intensive, not labour-intensive, whilst "service" activities
create jobs, skills, and spin-off developments. Service activities
will perhaps have a stronger multiplier effect than processing in
pulling more money into the local economy through wages, and in the
creation of extra demand for consumer goods and services. If it is
agreed that private economic enterprise should receive state aid in
development areas, it seems illogical to exclude the kinds of firms
that are likely to operate in Peterhead. Meanwhile planners and
councillors think in terms of finding factories for industrial estates
or encouraging petro-chemical processing.

In the north east context the notion of "service sector" is itself
anomalous and confusing. Service enterprise is seen as following
industrial activity; it is a tertiary activity dependent upon primary
or secondary production. But the term "service" has more than one
meaning; the "service sector" includes retailing, banking, insurance,
hotels, catering, and so on. These are services to industry and consumers, but not producers of goods in themselves, and therefore "non-
productive." Servicing activities in Peterhead do not produce goods
either, but neither are they services in the sense of being non-
productive. If oil production is primary production, then off-shore
supplies and servicing are part of it. They might even be defined as
a pre-primary sector. It could be argued that banking is a similar

service, but the location and type of bank (or indeed the source of capital and "banking" facilities) is unimportant from the point of view of facilitating production. To make oil production possible, bases can only be situated in certain locations, and onshore bases are an integral part of offshore work. If oil companies were also base operators it seems probable that the costs of running a base would be tax allowable as a cost of production. That they are operated by servicing companies as such puts them in a non-manufacturing, non-processing sector and therefore outside the category of enterprises qualifying for state aid--even though, paradoxically, the state had to go into business to promote offshore servicing itself. The use of categories like "servicing industries" or "tertiary sector" is rela-tively meaningless where one company may encompass a wide range of production and (traditionally) service activities or another may provide provide only a service without which production is not possible. Each enterprise is treated separately for aid purposes and not seen as part of an "industry" in which in this case subcontracting is normal.[3]

In choosing examples of the way in which national policies fail to match the situation in Peterhead, we are not suggesting a con-spiracy against Peterhead. The state develops policies to cope with what is defined as a regional problem, and it is within the limits of such policies that regional and local governments have to deal with particular local contingencies. The problems of Peterhead would not make the state alter national policies, and in this sense Peterhead is a peripheral location subject to policies devised to cope with problems elsewhere. The wry observation was made by a number of in-formants in Peterhead that had oil been struck in the English Channel, there would have been no wage restraint. In other words, the interests who would have experienced "unfair competition" for labour in the south east would have had sufficient political influence to change the course of incomes policies. As a corollary to this observa-tion, Peterhead would have fallen even further behind in wage levels.

The incoming multi-nationals have therefore stood to gain much from regional policies, especially financial incentives. Yet they are companies which could afford their North Sea developments without resource to state aid and which were forced by geography and geology, not by financial incentives, to come to a development area. In recog-nising this the state has compounded the problem. Aberdeen has been removed from development area status. This penalises all the non-oil firms who have to compete with oil, and further it makes it more diffi-cult for them to modernise or expand. And yet these local non-oil industries will be increasingly important as the significance of oil declines in the 1980's. Once oil is excluded from the calculations, manufacturing is declining in Aberdeen, as in the U.K. as a whole (Gaskin et al., 1978). It would have made more sense according to the logic of development aid to impose a "choice of location" condition upon manufacturing and processing rather than making a wholesale change

to the area's status. The way in which the state intervenes also under-
lines the whole problem of the notion of "region." Regions are just
lines on maps dividing the country up for management purposes. Administrators, planners, and policy-makers deal with problems on a locational
basis, but this does not mean that they are dealing with an entity
(called a region) which has its own problems; they treat aspects of
wider problems that may seem to have geographical locations. In the
case of Aberdeen, the problems have been confused with the location so
that when oil does well it is assumed that Aberdeen is doing well.
The extent to which the location of problems makes the problems different or peculiar is an empirical problem. Similarly the extent to
which social, economic, and political relations in particular locations
have a discrete and significant autonomy which enables us to use a
notion like "region" for analytical purposes has to be established and
not simply assumed.

III

We have dealt for some time upon "the state" in stressing the
dependence of a town like Peterhead. It would be a mistake to see
the state as monolithic and omnicompetent. The planning enquiry to
consider the building of the Shell/Esso NGL plant showed the corporations and the state to be inefficient and unable to make sense even
of the data they had (Moore; forthcoming). There are also examples of
conflicts within and between state agencies and between levels of
government which have consequences for Peterhead. This is clearly seen
in the failure of the Secretary of State to develop "an oil and gas
strategy for Scotland ... and to indicate the role of the Buchan area
in that strategy" (Contingency Plan for Petro-Chemical Industries in
Buchan, para 1.1). The Secretary of State for Scotland, for example,
is in a similar position to a local authority. He needs to develop
resources and technical skills for research and the evaluation of
policy, working from the same poor data base in the same conditions
of uncertainty. There is uncertainty about the technical means of
recovering oil resources, disagreement over the magnitude of profitably exploitable resources, and arguments over the effects of taxation
on profitability. The oil industry does not profer neutral technical
advice on these questions, and yet the Secretary of State is largely
dependent on the oil industry for information. The industry is therefore in a strong bargaining position and especially so given that they
are the main agents for realising the government's economic goals.
Thus, for example, "...recent predictions of delay or even a rundown
in North Sea developments, resulting from the tax and participation
proposals, amount largely to a negotiating posture by the oil companies"
(J. Francis, 1974: 22). The establishment of BNOC may reduce this
dependency of the state upon the companies while tying its financial
interests more closely to theirs.[4]

Policy decisions by the Scottish Office directly concerned with Peterhead, and relating to the management and use of the harbour and provision of a site for a supply base upon land reclaimed by the Crown, were a direct intervention by the state in the town. Both were to be developed in the national interest and with little reference to local interests or even local knowledge. It was assumed that the locality would be able to adapt advantageously to these projects. Had the Shell/ Esso proposal for loading NGL in Peterhead Bay Harbour gone ahead, however, there would have been substantial physical and operational changes in the harbours which may have had an adverse effect upon fishing. This potential conflict of interests was not fought out to any conclusion because the applicants withdrew in confusion. But it could arise again either with the natural gas pipeline which must be provided or in the event of Shell/Esso deciding to use Peterhead Bay Harbour for the export of NGL after all, if the Mossmorran project fails to materialise.

Peterhead has moved therefore from being a town based on small local firms and branches of national firms in a politically remote location, to being a centre of activities for multi-national firms in a world economy and a town where the state has intervened over and above the normal provision of welfare state benefits, taxation, law and order, etc. to aid the activities of the multi-nationals. The implications of this are worth spelling out in a little more detail and in terms of the interests of local capitalists, the "new" capitalists, and the government. The old capitalists in Peterhead historically benefited from low wages and low rates. For the in-coming oil-related companies operating in Peterhead in a world-wide range of locations and dealing in vastly expensive construction, or capital-intensive production, wages are not the most important factor. They are prepared to pay to get a job done on time, and they are relatively uninterested in their influence upon local wage rates. The government, however, wished to encourage development whilst controlling wages. This discriminated against local employers who could only raise wages to compete with incomers during the brief relaxation of wage restraint. Incomers could set their wage levels on arrival and then improve them through the offer of bonuses and overtime or by subterfuge. The government seems to have turned a blind eye to this. Plainly there are exceptions to this rather simple "rule." Incoming firms like British Oxygen Company and Aberdeen Service Company who intend to operate offshore supply and service bases in Peterhead for some years have an interest in reducing wage inflation, both to limit their own costs and to reduce the hostility of the local employers alongside whom they have to work. The local capitalists were accustomed to a dependent work force--grateful for jobs, unorganised, and willing to accept relatively low wages. The local myth of sturdy independence helped sustain their interests. They were anti-trades unions. The incoming firms were accustomed, in Europe and the USA at least, to dealing with organised workers, and the unionisation of workers offered a further means of control, or at least rational communication with their employees.[5] This is very much the view of both major political parties--namely that the unions should control the work force, and their senior officials should police the pay policy currently in force. The "incorporation" of the working class into the institutions of capitalism so that they accept market relations and the logic of capitalism--rather than having them independent and in opposition--would seem to be the desirable outcome for the state. The local capitalists wanted low rates and taxes and were anti-welfare state as evidenced by low rates, high council rents, and poor urban facilities in the days when Peterhead was an "independent" burgh. The big corporations also prefer low taxes, but by and large accept the logic of taxation; by spending taxes,the state is able to support the families that will raise new workers, the schools that will train them, and the medical service that will keep them in good health. The welfare state and the nationalised industries provide good services to the most advanced sectors of capitalism. The state taxes as a matter of course, and depending upon its political complexion and the pressures to which it is subject, shifts the costs of producing and sustaining labour either towards labour itself or towards capital. With the decline of political consensus and the faltering of the world economy from the late 1960's onwards, Labour governments have, in fact, cut the "social wage," namely that part of total household income which comprises the spending or consumption of welfare state benefits or services. But they also needed to maintain the electoral support of organised labour. It is in this kind of policy conflict that one sees the class conflicts within which governments are locked. Mrs. Thatcher's variant of conservatism is very much in tune with that of the Peterhead petty bourgeoisie, and Mr. Callaghan's corporatism is in tune with that of the large corporations--except insofar as even they now feel the wages policies to be unduly restrictive upon them.

Peterhead is not simply a new locus for developments in the national and international economy. It is a location in which national class conflicts can be seen to be fought out in a way that was not possible with labour dependent and unorganised. If the working class had been organised in Peterhead, they would have redefined the housing issue from one of keeping rates down to one of the distribution of resources. However, questions of the distribution of resources are no longer decided at the burgh level. Thus Peterhead's incorporation into larger political and administrative units has coincided with the raising of wider political issues of power and the distribution of social resources. Alongside such questions the local problems of a small town and the misalignment between policy and needs is of very minor interest to the state. The state's avowed policy has been to favour the periphery, but when the periphery offers such potential benefits to the state and the corporations, absolute priority is given to extracting the benefits to the centre.

FOOTNOTES

[1] A number of these features might also be preconditions for industrial-isation, rather than the effect.

[2] The fact that commercial criteria do not dictate high employment may be the reason why we are expected to become accustomed to our one million unemployed and the fact that full employment is no longer an objective of policy.

[3] By not integrating servicing into their own activities, off-shore operators subcontract financial risks and fluctuating employment to other companies. They also subcontract some "non-progressive" industrial relations.

[4] And will BNOC be staffed by "oil men?" Certainly many will be trained by the oil industry under agreements with BNOC (Wybrow, 1968).

[5] See Shapiro (forthcoming) for a discussion of the role of the state and national trade union leaderships in aiding the large construction companies by undermining the power of locally-organised labour.

REFERENCES

Carter, I.
    1974 "The Highlands of Scotland as an underdeveloped region", in
    E. de Kadt and G. Williams (eds.), Sociology and Development,
    London: Tavistock.

Francis, J.
    1974 Scotland's Pipedream, Edinburgh: Church of Scotland.

Fraser of Allender Institute
    1978 Quarterly Economic Commentary, Vol. 4, No. 2 (October).

Galtung, J.
    1971 "The European Community and the Developing Countries."
    Makere University, duplicated.

Gaskin, M. and MacKay, D.I.
    1978 The Economic Impact of North Sea Oil on Scotland (HMSO).

Hunt, D.
    1978 The Engineering Industry in the Grampian Region (NESDA).

Moore R.
   1978 "Northern notes towards a sociology of oil," in Scottish
   Journal of Sociology (September).

Moore, R.
   Forthcoming "A Study of the Social Impact of Oil on Peterhead."

O'Brien, P.
   1975 "A critique of Latin American theories of dependency," in
   I. Oxaal et al. (eds.), Beyond the Sociology of Development.
   London: Routledge & Keegan Paul.

Rosie, G.
   1974 Cromarty: The Scramble for Oil, Canongate Publishing Co.

Shapiro, D.
   Forthcoming A Study of Labour Relations at Nigg and Kishorn,
   London: Penguin.

Wybrow, P.
   1978 "Marxist Theories of the State: North Sea Oil - A case
   Study." Unpublished B.Sc. thesis, Bath University.

14. The Political Economy of Rural Development: The Case of Western U.S. Boomtowns

ANN R. MARKUSEN

INTRODUCTION

Both economics and sociology, by studying rural development in isolation and by applying dominant paradigms, have failed to produce a coherent analysis of capitalist dynamics in rural areas. I begin by critiquing these approaches. In their place I propose a Marxist approach which emphasizes the dynamics of the capitalist mode of production. To understand the particular case of the rural area, however, it is necessary to distinguish between the micro-dialectical and macro-dialectical levels. While much good work and debate characterizes contemporary Marxist work on the latter front, micro-dialectical analyses of communities and places have not been well developed. To do so requires an elaboration of the Marxist model to take into account the presence of prior modes of production, of uncharacteristic sectoral concentrations (especially agriculture and resource-based production), and of unusual rent and profitability circumstances. While capitalism may relentlessly expand and accumulate across the globe, particular areas experience the pace of capitalist development as uneven and unpredictable because of these local peculiarities.

I then use the remarkable case of the Western U.S. energy boomtown to illuminate the particularity of contemporary rural experience with capitalist expansion. A study of three counties in Northwestern

---

*A prior version of this paper appeared in the Review for Radical Political Economics, 10:3, 1978. I owe a great deal to the helpful criticisms of my Bay Area and Washington, D.C. Kapitalistate collectives, and to Matt and Kim Edel, Marsh Feldman, Kenny Fox, Martha Gimenez, Heidi Hartmann, Peter Marcuse, Lee Reynis, Rick Simon, Bill Tabb, and Dwayne Ward. My thanks also to the people of Meeker, Craig, and Steamboat Springs, Colorado, for the chance to try out these ideas on a speaking tour and in many a boomtown bar.

Colorado illustrates the importance of local class structure, sectoral
composition, rent conditions, and State sector policies. This analysis results in several hypotheses about the strength of local opposition to energy development and the possibilities for interregional
coalitions to stop it. In the spirit of self-criticism, I end the
paper with several caveats about radical political economy and radical
sociology approaches to rural development.

ECONOMIC, SOCIOLOGICAL, AND MARXIST APPROACHES TO RURAL DEVELOPMENT

The development literature has been dominated by economists.
Without reiterating their arguments, I will briefly address the problems with their approach. First of all, economists limit the definition
of development to monolithic indicators of economic growth such as
gross regional or national income. Pollution, epidemics, mental
illness, cultural destruction, and mortality rates could (and do)
escalate without interfering with an optimistic evaluation of regional
development if per capita output is going up (Giminez, et al., 1977).
Secondly, efforts to increase output are aimed at "inputs" into the
process--land, labor, and capital. Each is disembodied from its relationship to the other and accorded a moral right to a return (rent,
wages, and profit). Despite the Cambridge controversy and its demon-
stration of the impossibility of treating capital as an operational
category separate from labor, economists continue to talk about physical capital as the key to development and counsel incentives as a way
to woo capital construction (e.g., the Carter urban policy). As a
companion policy, communities and regions are urged to provide at public
expense the infrastructure that will make capitalist production possible.

At a deeper level, the employment by economists of concepts such
as the individual and the firm obscure the real exploitative connection
between corporations and labor. Economists do not recognize the
concept of class. This prevents any analysis of class struggle as a
shaper of the rural development process. And while so-called growth
theory pretends to supply a dynamic analysis, it only speculates (in
an unsatisfactorily nonoperational way) about marginal changes and
adjustment, not about the essence of capitalist evolution. All of
these constitute ideological, not logical, problems with economic
theory.

Sociological approaches suffer from a different set of problems.
They begin by admitting class as a conceptual category that is important, but proceed to trivialize the concept by eliminating the interrelationships among classes as the basis for class definition and
analysis. For instance, a recent book on one industry in rural areas
(Lucas, 1971) posits stages of development (construction, settlement,

transition, maturity), and a detailed set of worker categories (e.g., seven types of construction workers), but the stages and typologies are labelling devices without any coherent theory of dynamics or of class conflict and formation.

To understand what is occurring in rural areas as a whole, or in a particular place, we need a more coherent analysis that can merge concerns with capitalist dynamics with the experience of people in specific places. Marxist methods of analysis offer us a way of constructing such an analysis. The general model laid out in Capital by Marx and the many elaborations of it to deal with imperialism and development problems, from Luxembourg and Lenin through Amin and Brenner, offer us a basis to work from (Editorial Collective, RRPE). Without reiterating its general dynamics, I argue in this paper that an elaboration of the Marxist model is necessary to deal with rural development in advanced capitalist countries.

In order to handle analytically the experience of a particular region or rural area, I have had to make a distinction between the macro-dialectical level and the micro-dialectical level in Marxist theory. At the macro-dialectical level, geographical space can be analyzed as patterned by the dynamics of capitalist expansion across the globe, in search of wage labor and raw materials. This process historically has been accompanied by cultural opposition and destruction, and by State partnership that creates political entities which ossify, impede further development, or permit manipulation by other States and corporations (Markusen, 1979). But the relentless accumulation process continues much as Brenner (1977) argues, attempting to homogenize across all places and peoples.

At the micro-dialectical level, particular places and peoples frequently experience capitalist expansion as a much rougher and uncertain process. Thus, while we can use certain models to describe capitalist expansion overall, we must derive from them submodels of particular areas which can explain the conjection of one or more peculairities which give a region its distinct characteristics. For the most part, analysis at this level cannot be carried out without an historical account of the regions or areas under study. The particular ethnic composition, prior modes of production, State structure, and even physical features of a place, as well as the particular moment in history when capitalist incorporation occurred, are essential to understanding their experience. Given the historically evolved local economic structure, we can then look at current class structure, sectoral structure, State structure, and the short-run returns to capitalist production which provide the framework for an analysis of conflict over energy development.

This paper develops such a micro-dialectical analysis for Western U.S. boomtowns. The Western energy boomtown makes a remarkable case study because it contains remnants of prior modes of production and culture, because it hosts the challenge to local agriculture from an industrial sector which competes for the same resources, and because the nature of energy development at the moment is accompanied with both high profit levels and intense government involvement. Thus it contains many aspects which occur in isolation in other rural development cases. The analysis here is not exhaustive of micro-dialectical analysis, which would have to address issues such as ethnicity, race, and religion more directly for other types of areas. But it should serve as a model for pursuing Marxist analyses of particular rural places.

CLASS STRUCTURE IN THE ENERGY BOOMTOWN

The class structure of Western boomtowns can be delineated using Marxist categories. In order to demonstrate adequacy of the Marxist class framework, I apply it to a study area composed of several typical boomtowns in Colorado, using 1970 data. Anticipating the complexities introduced in the next section on sectoral competition, I also develop the distribution of these classes by sectors in the study area.

For an analytical framework for examining class position of groups involved in Western energy development, I use the definitions suggested by Poulantzas (1975), with one modification. The Poulantzian schema posits four main classes: the primary two--capitalist and working class--and two intermediate groups whose class situations are a function of an overlap with the former mode of production and of the current stage of capitalist development--the traditional and the new petty bourgeoisie. The new petty bourgeoisie is distinguished from the traditional by wage labor and lack of control over the physical means of production, but from the working class through their control over ideology, self-policing of their own ranks, and possession of human capital used in mental as opposed to physical labor. These definitions, particularly the distinction between traditional and new petty bourgeoisie, allow me to illuminate the contradictory situation that various groups occupy when confronted with energy development. I include "unproductive" but nonprofessional wage labor (sales, clerical, and service workers) in the working class, following Wright (1976). However, I retain health workers, teachers, and other technicians in the petty bourgeois category for the purposes of this analysis. In rural areas, the absence of unionism among such groups and their placement in petty bourgeois-dominated sectors argues for this assignment, at least currently.

One caveat about the framework. While the class categories
may be useful to us for a general analytical investigation, they
are not particularly useful for organizing work. In regional responses to an earlier draft of this paper, the one consistent angry response
came from ranchers and farmers who object to being <u>called</u> petty
bourgeoisie. To them, it represents the pretentiousness of academic
theorizing. They cannot identify with words they cannot pronounce.
They prefer to define themselves by occupation. Since data do exist
for occupational categories and since they are a close proxy for
class position, I proceed in later sections of this paper to use
commonly understood occupational categories as proxies for class.

The study areas consist of three Northwestern Colorado towns,
each in a different county and approximately 35 to 100 miles apart.
Little distinction exists between a town--in each case the only one
of significant size in the county--and its rural surroundings (see
Figure 1). The population of each town and county is given in
Table 1. The small population for the extensive land area attests

FIGURE 1:
*UPPER COLORADO RIVER BASIN AND
NORTHWESTERN COLORADO COUNTRIES*

Southwestern U.S.
River Basins

SOURCE: Morris, 1975.

to the meager ability of the land to support people under current
production and transportation conditions.

Table 1

Population for Northwestern Colorado Towns and Counties, 1970

Town	Population	County	Population
Craig	4290	Moffat	6341
Meeker	1579	Rio Blanco	4842
Steamboat Springs	2340	Routt	6592

Source: U.S. Census of Population, 1970.

The area confronts multiple potential energy developments.
It already produces some oil and hydroelectric power, has a new
underground coal mine, is hosting the construction of several coal-
fired electricity-generating plants, and may be the site of extensive
oil shale development. The major difference among the communities
(besides variations in local energy production) is the degree to
which tourism presently provides jobs. In the town of Steamboat
Springs, the ski industry and summer tourism are important employers,
although the former--developed by LTV Corporation--is comparable to
the corporate intruder in the energy case.

The significance of the Western energy boomtown is belied by
the small numbers of people involved in each case. There are
literally thousands of communities in the West (and in offshore oil
areas and the Appalachia) that are undergoing rapid, disruptive
development. One estimate of the magnitude of this change can be
calculated from figures in an Argonne National Labs study (Stenehjam
and Metzger, 1977:13:32-33). They estimate that 220 counties in the
United States will host significant increases in coal production in the
next seven years, and that 145 of these will experience medium to
severe disruption because of their current rural structure. These
145 counties will involve 2.4 million people in coal development
alone. An alternative estimate in the Western case is that 450,000
to 600,000 new residents will be moving into sparsely settled areas
in mining operations in the Rocky Mountain region by 1985 (Federation
of Rocky Mountain States, 1975:34-41). Add to these figures the numbers of migrants to nonextractive energy jobs, to nonenergy activities
in the private sector, and to public sector activities of all sorts,
for every region. In addition, count the numbers of people who are
already in the communities entered. A safe estimate would be 5 to 15

million Americans involved in rapid growth boomtowns.

A few sociological facts about the study area are in order. The population turnover in these counties is ususually large, due to the marginality of local production. The 1970 census recorded that more new people moved into the area percentage-wise than was true for the nation as a whole. Each community also has a substantial number of people who have lived there all their lives and whose community memory dates back several generations. This creates a cultural cleavage between oldtimer and newcomer groups that generally corresponds to different sectoral, but not class, positions.

The age structure of the population is approximately similar to that of the United States as a whole, although people locally believe that young people 18 to 30 years of age are underrepresented. The latter impression stems from the common outmigration of young people who have grown up in the area to working-class jobs in larger western cities, while immigration in this age group includes young professionals who work in health, education, local government and social services, young jocks and entrepreneurs who attempt to live off the ski industry, and some gilded hippies who want to mime John Denver's lifestyle. Age is therefore an issue and tends to complicate the community's attitude toward an issue like welfare, since welfare recipients include impoverished local people but large numbers of ski bums as well.

Ethnically, the area is almost completely homogeneous. Despite large numbers of Chicano and Black people in Colorado, the energy-rich northwest counties are predominantly white. Local residents in Steamboat, when asked, identified one Asian American family and two Vietnamese orphans. No native Americans live in the area. Meeker is named after the general who massacred the last of the local Utes near the present town site. Since ranching is the primary agricultural activity, there is virtually no migrant labor. Women's labor-force participation rates are the same or slightly less than the United States average and understate the work of women in farm and household production. As in other places, very few occupations are integrated by sex. Women hold low-paying sales, service, and clerical jobs. In cases of tourist development, many work as domestics cleaning motel rooms, waiting tables, and doing laundry.

While the study area is not typical, in that there are many variations in community history, ethnicity and current production conditions across the set of boomtowns, it is representative. Its major problems can be deciphered using the axes of class, sectoral change, location in state structure, and rent conditions.

Table 2 proposes the class designations for the employed members of the labor force in the Tri-County area. Since they are derived from census occupational data, they do not correspond strictly to

Table 3. Sectoral Position of Classes and Occupations in Colorado, 1970:*
Percent Workers in Class/Occupation in Industry

Class/Occupation	Agri-culture	Mining	Sector Construc-tion	Mfg.	Transp. Comm/Util.	Whole-sale/Retail	Finance, Insur., Real est.	Ser-vice	Govern-ment
K									
TPB Mgt/Admin	-	-	14.8	-	-	50.0	5.3	17.4	-
Farmers	99.1								
NPB Sal'd M/A			6.0	11.1	7.4	27.3	12.2	13.5	14.4
Professionals				12.1			18.2	37.6	33.8
W Sales				8.1		66.6			
Clerical				10.7	10.2	20.3	20.1	20.4	19.9
Service						27.5		59.9	8.4
Industrial		3.3	17.6	29.5	13.1				
% Work Force in Sector, Tri-county	14	9	10	3	8	20	3	17	16
% U.S. Work Force in Sector	4	1	5	27	6	21	5	16	18

Source: U.S. Department of Commerce, Bureau of the Census (1970); Colorado and U.S. Occupation by Industry figures are not available for small places in published data. Colorado figures are suggestive of distribution by sector, although from the distribution of workers by industry in the Tri-County area, it is clear that the Colorado figures overstate the % local workers in manufacturing and understate the percentages in mining and construction for industrial workers. Blanks indicate less than 5 percent.

412

the above class definitions. The occupational distribution illuminates the ways in which local class composition differs strikingly from U.S. and Colorado class composition as a whole. The most important difference is the large representation of the traditional petty bourgeois groups in the local economy. Since these groups frequently dominate the local political structure, their interests and ideological perspectives are an important force in the struggle over development. The other significant feature is the proportionately smaller size of the working class.

Class situation is not enough to determine the stake that various class members have in energy development. Since the entire production complexion of the community may change, the vulnerability of the particular sectors that class members work for is also significant. Table 3 shows the distribution of class membership across the various industrial sectors (note following the table.) The table shows that the livelihood of present day northwestern Colorado is based predominantly on agriculture, mining, and construction employment, unlike the manufacturing-led structure of U.S. production as a whole. Furthermore, classes are concentrated differentially across a limited number of sectors. In addition to the obvious case of farmers, the other traditional petty bourgeois are concentrated in construction, trade, finance/insurance/real estate, and services. The concentrations of new petty bourgeois are similarly high in secondary and tertiary sectors. These sectoral distributions, as I will suggest below, are critical for conditioning class unity and stance toward development.

SECTORAL CHANGE AND THE COMPETITION FOR LAND AND LABOR

Sectoral composition of production is an important modifier of class stakes in boomtown development. In his rather meager writing on uneven development, Marx identifies uneven spatial distribution of production as a byproduct of sectoral concentration. Capitalist division of labor introduces concentrations of workers in specialized production activities at certain sites:

> Just as a certain number of simultaneously
> employed laborers are the material pre-
> requisites for division of labor in manufac-
> ture, so are the number and density of the
> population, which here correspond to the
> agglomeration in one workshop, a necessary
> condition for the division of labor in
> society (Quoted in Holland, 1977:39).

In boomtowns, past sectoral concentration produced a population with stakes in certain sectors, demonstrated by the inclination of area workers to think of themselves in sectoral terms as well as by occupation ("I'm a farmer, a miner, a construction worker.") Rapid change in these sectors elaborates conflict over development.

In the Western boomtown, the local economy is relatively small compared to the size of most incoming energy operations. The particular production structure of the new sector and its consequences for other local sectors shape the character of boomtown struggles. Energy production as a new sector introduces large numbers of migrants, some permanent, some temporary, and because of its capital-intensive nature, induces a boom/bust cycle over time. Furthermore, since it requires tremendous amounts of land, particularly for water resources, it tends to replace existing sectors like agriculture and tourism that are dependent on extensive and particular land uses. Since many people see their immediate or long-run situations dramatically improved or worsened because of change in a particular sector, these sectoral consequences intermediate the class struggle.

Sectoral change and volatility is not a new phenomenon in many western areas. The decimation of the Native American populations, whose economy was based on extensive land use for hunting, fishing, farming, and food gathering by white settlers and military forces, began a modern history of frequently violent change under capitalism, fluctuating with the prices of commodities, both agricultural and mineral, on the world market, and with the availability of labor power. The current population descends from various settler immigrations connected with past booms and false employment promises.

The tri-county area described above has experienced dramatic population and sectoral change since World War II. This volatility has resulted over a 30 year period in the replacement of agriculture and mining as the major employing sectors by services and trade, although this is in part a reflection of more rapid increases in productivity in the former. Table 5 shows the ranking by industry for 1940 and 1970 for the Green River Basin, of which the Tri-county area is a part (see Figure 1). The major components of the economic base remain agriculture, mining, and tourism, the latter accounting for high service and trade figures.

Theories of dependency cast little light on the Western boomtown situation. Western boomtowns do resemble many Third World countries in their specialization in primary sector production. Because of uneven degrees of competition characterizing local primary producing sectors, and monopoly sector production of "imported" commodities (cars, processed food, gasoline, consumer durables), they suffer from unequal terms of exchange and differential degrees of price volatility (Emmanuel, 1972). However, political domination is the central feature of work on imperialism and dependency. While state

Table 4

Percentage Change in Population and Employment,
1950-70, for Tri-County Area

County		Routt	Rio Blanco	Moffat
Population	1950-60	-34.0%	-6.0%	-7.6%
	1960-70	+11.7%	+9.1%	+18.8%
Agriculture	1950-60	-33.2%	-50.2%	-48.3%
	1960-70	+ 3.4%	-6.5%	+2.1%
Other Sectors	1950-60	Coal -50%	Oil & Gas: stable	Mining: up
	1960-70	Tourism/Con-struction up	Oil & Gas: down	Mining: -150%

Source: Gilmore and Duff (1973).

Table 5

Ranking of Industries by Percentage of Total
Employment, Green River Basin

	1940 Rank	%	1970 Rank	%
Agriculture	1	31.3	4	11.0
Mining	2	22.7	3	12.9
Services	3	15.3	1	28.1
Trade	4	12.4	2	19.3
Transportation	5	7.5	8	5.3
Construction	6	3.8	5	7.8
Government	7	3.3	6	6.3
Manufacturing	8	5.5	7	5.5
Comm/Utilities	9	3.8	9	1.3

Source: Udis and Kraynick (1974).

power affects boomtown development, its character differs from a
Third World country. The greater vulnerability of U.S. local communities to events in the capitalist structure of production makes
it even less necessary than in other parts of the world for capital
to develop a local elite. Personnel can be transported in and out
with little regard for the local population. Only to the extent
that local communities have any legal powers to obstruct development
(zoning, public service provision) do energy empires attempt to develop alliances with community political and business leaders. On
the other hand, local communities possess some political rights and
representation at state and federal levels, which produce state sector
struggles documented below.

    In place of a theory of imperialism or internal colonization,
we need a detailed look at the requirements of different sectors and
the ways in which they change locally with capitalist energy development. In the boomtown case, the introduction of a new energy sector
has multiple consequences. First of all, it competes for the existing
labor force and frequently induces immigration. The new jobs have
different short-run and long-run futures and a heightened degree of
volatility of uncertainty. Secondly, it competes for land used in
other sectors. Because of water, mineral, and space needs, or through
degradation of the environment, it renders some land unavailable
or unfit for use in agriculture or tourism. Livelihoods in these
sectors may be wiped out and some outmigration may be induced. Third,
secondary sectors dependent on local incomes generated in the primary
sectors may experience differential impacts from the change in sectors,
changing jobs and income prospects. Finally, the sectoral change
may disrupt the social and physical environment and public services,
so that degradation of use values may contribute to development struggle. Each of these deserves a brief consideration.

    Labor requirements of energy development vary tremendously across
energy development activities. Underground coal mining is quite
labor intensive; strip mining requires very few operators. Labor
intensive activities generally employ relatively unskilled labor and
therefore promise jobs to local people. These jobs are usually filled
by people previously unemployed or underemployed, drawn from the
surrounding rural areas. In some cases, the new sector may affect the
labor supply available to other sectors, wiping out marginal operations,
and may exert an upward pressure on wage rates. Since these jobs
are generally unskilled and competitive, and high levels of local
unemployment exist, this is not common.

    However, energy development in the West more frequently intro-
duces capital intensive activities: surface mining, large conversion
and power plants, and energy transportation systems (e.g., pipelines).
For example, consider the organic composition of a coal gassification
plant, presented in Table 6. Here direct labor inputs account for

only 10 percent of the value of output. Most of the other inputs are imported or carried out in urban areas, so few related jobs are created locally.

Table 6

Organic Composition of Capital for
Lurgi Coal Gassification Plant

Input/Cost Category	Percent of Total Value
Coal	30
Chemicals	5
Power	10
Machinery	20
Labor	10
Administration	5
Finance	20

Source: Federal Power Commission, cited in Morris (1975).

In such production activities, initial construction requires many workers for a short-run period, but operation employs only small numbers of workers. Benchmark construction and operating employment for a number of energy activities is presented in Figure 2 and Table 7. The construction activities require skilled labor that is frequently imported; immigrant or roving construction crews are hired before local workers. In many cases, energy development thus introduces a dual labor force in which highly skilled immigrants, sometimes unionized, work at higher wages than longer-term local people.

A final characteristic introduced by energy development is a heightened degree of volatility and job insecurity, not only because of the boom/bust cycle associated with construction, but also because of the extractive nature of some energy operations, which unlike agriculture and tourism, consume nonrenewable resources. Vulnerability to commodity price changes because of new discovery or technological change is more severe than in agriculture or tourism. Furthermore, the exhaustion of material inputs inevitably closes down an operation which can produce a ghost town instantly. Two recent examples (both at Christmastime, 1977) in Lark, Utah, Kennecott Copper Corporation evicted 650 people from company-owned houses because the

Table 7
Typical Energy Projects

Project	Size	Construction Time	Peak Force Construction	Operating Force
Coal Export Mine	9M tons/yr.	2-3 years	175-200	325,475
Electric Generating Plant (including coal mine)	700 MW 2,250 MW	4-6 years 6-8 years	750-950 2,000-3,000	75-100 350-400
Oil Shale Processing Facility (includes mining)	50,000 bbl/day	3-4 years	3,000-3,500	1,050-1,250
Nuclear Power Plant	1.600 MW	5-9 years	2,500	150
Offshore Oil and Gas Support	Per Rig	3-4 years	175	90
Platform Fabrication Facility	2 platforms/yr.	5 years	400	1,000-1,500
Deepwater Port	2 mooring spaces	3-4 years	1,250	75-90
Liquid Natural Gas (LNG)-Conversion Plant	1,000 mcf/day	2-3 years	300-400	50-100
Oil Refinery	250,000 bbl/day	2 1/2-3 years	3,500-4,500	450-900

Source: Meeker (1976:3).

418

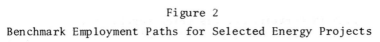

Figure 2

Benchmark Employment Paths for Selected Energy Projects

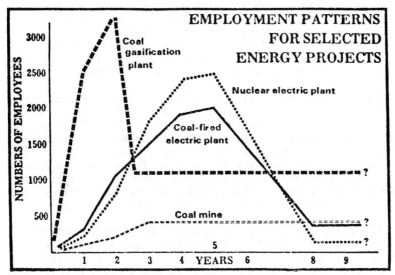

SOURCE: Meeker (1976:4).

ground under them will become part of its "world's largest" Bingham Mine; in Yerington, Nevada, Anaconda Copper Company closed its Weed Heights Mine, wiping out 450 jobs, which support at least one-third of the local economy (Associated Press, Colorado Springs, Gazette/ Telegraph, 1977; Denver Post, 1977).

Competition for land may also result in direct displacement of agricultural and tourist sector jobs. In some cases, land is bid away from these sectors for space, mineral rights or water rights. In others, the negative effect on alternative sectors works through externalities imposed on production through lowering the water table, increasing water salinity levels, air and water pollution, and removal of natural environments such as wild rivers or forests with recreational and wildlife values. Little work has been done to date estimating the precise interrelationships between sectors via competition for land and resources (Leistritz, 1977). However, ranchers groups in Montana claim that reclamation claims are false and that the threat to agriculture and ranching is severe and uncharted (Northern Great Plains Resource Council, 1976). How many jobs are lost in more traditional sectors through energy development will vary with each location. Fears of adverse effects mobilize groups with the greatest stakes in those sectors.

Jobs and income in tertiary sectors which service the local population (retailing, restaurants, gas stations) will also be affected by sectoral change. While small enterpreneurs, who generally have a precarious livelihood to begin with, view increased population favorably, some are finding that new populations frequently attract MacDonald's and other franchise operations which win the patronage of newcomers (Gold, 1974). Local chambers of commerce frequently battle internally over the development issue for just these reasons.

Direct results for the quality of life in a community constitute a final source of conflict over development induced by sectoral change. The despoilation of the environment, the loss of political control at the town hall, the breakdown of the tightly-knit community tradition, problems with public service provision, and growth induced local inflation frequently constitute severe problems for a boomtown population. If their livelihood is not tied to or potentially improved by the new sector, or if they are highly mobile incoming professionals, people may oppose development on one or more of these grounds.

Each of these sets of problems introduced by sectoral change may serve as a basis for opposition or political coalition pro or con development. If development were simply a case of expansion of existing sectors, none of these conditions would color the class consciousness of people involved. However, their presence complicates attitudes toward development and fuels conflict over capitalist expansion in energy sectors. In the next section of this paper, I map out how these features of sectoral change affect the politics of energy development.

LAND VALUE AND RENT

The power to appropriate rent introduces a second source of complexity to boomtown energy development. One or more features of the dynamics of capitalist accumulation in the energy sector can produce a short- to intermediate-run excess profit which can be the subject of local struggle. This excess profit can be appropriated by different local groups through land ownership and land use regulation, converting it into rent. The three types of rent (differential, monopoly, and absolute) distinguished in Marxist theory may all exist; their relative importance and their absolute levels are critical to the formation of boomtown politics.

The Marxist theory of rent has been developed considerably in other sources (Marx, 1967, 1974; Mandel, 1968; Harvey, 1973; Edel, 1976; and Walker, 1975). A brief summary here should suffice. The Marxist theory of production contends that the exchange value of commodities produced under capitalist modes of production will be

determined by the average labor time embodied in them. However, because capital advanced requires an average rate of profit across all
sectors and because different organic compositions of capital characterize various sectors, the transformation of values into prices
involves an adjustment for profit equalization. Monopoly power in
ceratin markets or over a necessary input, such as land and its
accompanying resources, may in addition push prices of certain commodities above value. Profit realized from the sale of commodities may
be diverted into rent.

Marx identified three types of rent that accompany rent-generating
circumstances under capitalism: differential, monopoly, and absolute
rent. Differential rent can accrue to land because of differences
in quality enhancing labor productivity. Monopoly rent can be captured by owners of land because commodities produced with that land
as an input are monopolized and their market price is thus higher than
the cost of production plus average rate of profit. Absolute rent
can be approximated by landowners if land is monopolized by a class
separate from the capitalist class as a whole and is withheld from
production unless it receives a rent which drives the price of the
product above the cost plus average profit level. The three types
of rent deserve separate attention, since each has different implications for class consciousness and unity and development strategies.

Rent exists in boom towns only when land ownership and control
patterns separate local groups from the corporation that organizes
production and realizes the revenues from sale of the product. If
no group appropriates excess profit from the energy corporation, it
remains profit and not rent. In Marx's view, rent was appropriated
by a separate class, landlords, remnants of the previous feudal mode
of production. In using the concept of rent in the current analysis,
the delineation of classes is less precise, for the forms in which
rent is appropriated involve various class fractions, and in some
cases workers themselves, because of their ability to affect the
availability of land for production in one form or another. For
instance, state intervention to require that energy corporations clean
up the environment or pay for some of the local socioeconomic costs
of development, or worker threats to strike and sabotage at particular sites, may force a transfer of excess profits to community and
worker groups because of their ability to affect the use of land in
production. These forms compliment or conflict with more traditional forms of rent appropriation, involving direct land ownership.
Thus the struggle to appropriate rent includes groups who own land
and groups who can prevent the employment of land through militance
or state intervention.

Differential rent occurs when the productivity of labor at a
particular site exceeds that at the marginal production site with
the same organic composition of capital and is appropriated by some

group. The high productivity may be a result of features internal to
the land, such as high grade ores or thin overburden, or it may be
a result of external features, such as location advantages given
the existing transportation network and location of consuming industries. There is good reason to believe that differential rent is
a prominent feature of Western coal-based development. Coal deposits
are close to the surface and easy to exploit with stripping technology. They are also low in sulphur, thus favored by new environmental regulations. Growth in Western energy-using industries and the
improvements in Western transportation systems further favor Western
coal. Corporations stripping it appear to be realizing excess profits, a function of the current world energy situation, the decline
of industrial production in the Northeast, and UMW militance, all
of which affect the short-run price of energy and the profitability of
other sources, especially Appalachian coal. Coal in the northern-
most of these states--North Dakota, Montana, and Wyoming--appears
to be appropriating the greatest excess profits, due mainly to differences in quality and accessibility of coal. While the following
discussion focuses on coal, similar circumstances attend most forms
of land-based boomtown development.

Several groups potentially contend for this excess profit:
the corporation realizing it, local landowners, workers in the corporation, suppliers, consumers, and groups organized through the
state sector, such as consumers in the regulatory process, communities in the land-use process, and all citizens in cases of public
ownership. It is unlikely that either suppliers or consumers will
be able to capture the differential rent, unless they constitute a
monopoly or monopsony. State sector regulation could capture it by
using a cost-plus calculus for rate-making. But since the rate regulation is imposed on the coal users (utilities) and not the coal
producers, this strategy works only when a utility produces its own
coal and accurate cost figures are obtainable. When it purchases
from other corporations, the market price, including differential rent,
must be paid. The flurry over natural gas pricing demonstrates that
regulation is not an easy means for preventing differential rent
from being appropriated.

Landowners, to the extent that they are separate from the capitalists owning the production apparatus, have a good opportunity
to extract all of the differential rent. If they have perfect
information, and are willing to withdraw land from production if
they do not receive the full rent (a land strike), they hold a powerful position in bargaining. Three groups operate as landowners:
farmers and ranchers, who hold extensive lands whose minerals or water
may be profitably exploited for energy development, and financial
groups (not necessarily local) who may be able to speculate through
real estate deals. However, the vast holding of the federal and
state governments in the West make the State the biggest landlord.

To date, the State has not used land policy to appropriate differential rent, but has leased its land at very low rates to private
energy corporations (Council on Economic Priorities, 1974). This
process essentially endows capitalist interests with private property rights to public land, including the right to speculate and sell the
leases. An exception is the use of the severance tax by several
states (Montana, Wyoming, North Dakota). The tax attempts to recoup
losses from nonexisting property taxes on public land and to capture
part of the differential rent. In the future the two levels of government (federal and state) may clash over appropriation of differential
rent via mineral leasing procedures vs. the severence tax. This
situation raises questions about political ownership of land and its
fruits; are they regional or national?

Workers, if they are organized, can potentially capture a substantial portion of differential rent. They may be able to force wages
up by threatening not to work or by threatening sabotage of land use.
In those processes where the organic composition of capital is high,
the differential rent can be viewed as a potential fund for buying off
workers. For instance, strip mining employs relatively few highly
skilled machine operators to dig and move many tons of coal, compared
to deep mining. Corporations can be forced to pay high wage rates
to discourage unionization, especially since the UMW, if it represented their workers, would tax every ton of coal for the pension
fund. The better organized and more militant workers are, and the more
difficult it is to find other workers, the more likely workers are to
wrest away part of differential rent.

Communities and states have also been able to appropriate some of
the differential rent through land use regulations, such as facility siting or ability to withhold public services. In a few cases in
Wyoming and Montana, energy corporations have paid for roads, prepaid
taxes, or adjusted production patterns to diminish the boom impact
on local communities because of a threat to charge corporations for
the local fiscal and social costs. Ironically, the most exemplary of
these cases involves a huge consumer coop, Missouri Power Basin
Corporation, which agreed that local people affected by production
(their consumers) had legitimate claims on the development process
(Markusen, 1977:75).

Monopoly and absolute rent differ dramatically from differential
rent because their origins are not tied to the characteristics of
local land. Monopoly rent occurs when landowners or land use controls
appropriate part of the monopoly profits of the production sector using
its land, where the profit derives not from differential productivity
of land but from market power, superexploitation or workers, or higher
productivity levels from short-run technological superiority. For
instance, if the coal industry controls a substantial portion of coal
lands, it can act as a landlord to oligopolized auto or steel sectors,

appropriating excess profits passed backward in the form of higher
prices for coal, a hidden form of rent. This rent can then be battled
for within the community in which the coal is produced.

Absolute rent arises when landowners conspire to withhold land
from production unless they receive a return higher than the price
of production would cover, forcing up the price of the commodity.
While absolute rent is not likely to occur in a situation where a
separate, landed class does not exist, international cartels do control some land-based production. Like OPEC, they may operate as a
land monopoly and drive up the price. This allows all producers of
oil to charge that price, and producers of substitutes like natural
gas and coal to do likewise, so that absolute rent accrues to U.S.
multinationals in all energy sectors as well as to OPEC producers.
Such rent can also be the subject of class struggle.

Monopoly and absolute rent cannot be captured by a local group
unless they are linked with similar demands across regions. Unlike
the case of differential rent, which is tied to the specific characteristics of local land, monopoly and absolute rent arise from the
appropriation of profits across the entire production sector, so
that an effort to wrest them away at any one location may produce
relocation of the production sector.

The existence of different types of rent will shape the struggle
at the local level. Significant differential rent can permit gains
by organized groups locally and in the extreme may result in regional chauvinism and cleavages between workers in the same industry in
different regions. The funds accruing to Montana from its 30 percent severance tax and the high wages for unorganized strip mine
operators in that state demonstrate that differential rent can be
captured in part. Monopoly and absolute rent cannot be captured by
local or regional groups, but only across regions through class
coalitions. The possibility of appropriating this form of rent encourages corporations to conspire (and to bust unions) to set energy
prices and unions to organize all unorganized groups in their sector.
In the case of monopoly rent, it may produce alliances of labor and
capital within a sector against another, which may be manifested in
battles for protective tarrifs or subsidies (merchant marine vs.
oil industry) and correspond to regional cleavages (North East manufacturing vs South West oil and natural gas).

Rent in all three cases is a product of property claims and class
struggles. It is not a function of inherent qualities in land.
Therefore, its existence is generally tenuous and short run, for
capitalist dynamics continually seek cheaper forms of material
inputs, accelerating the search when rent appropriation raises the
cost of constant capital. Therefore, the belief by local workers or
local government that energy development will bring windfall gains and

prosperity may be a costly short run illusion, since new mineral finds, new technology and fluctuation in substitute commodity prices may reverse profitability. Furthermore, once the initial bribe, or promise of a bribe, has secured development rights, the local community may find itself completely dependent on one employer and forced to roll back its demands. The history of the Mesabi Range begins with a marble town hall in Hibbing, but the region limps along today with very high rates of unemployment and outmigration, despite two sets of tax forgivenesses by the state of Minnesota.

Within boomtowns, class composition and the sectoral rent and state sector conditions of energy development produce different degrees of opposition to or enthusiasm for development. For reasons outlined above, local class stakes in development are not unambiguously agreed on. For each group, there may be a difference between expectations and the realities of development, and between short and long run consequences. Only the capitalist class, whose absentee members own the corporation, have a clear stake in favor of development. Workers, many of whom are currently in low-paying seasonal jobs, may hope for more stable, higher-paying jobs; others may lose jobs they now have and be forced to move out. Farmers and small entrepreneurs may gain through land appreciation or enhanced sales, but may lose productive capacity without compensation or suffer accelerated competition from new, externally financed businesses. All older residents suffer a degree of dislocation and community disruption. New professionals individually respond to their own material base and to environmental considerations.

Class alliances within the region and outside the region depend on the conjuncture of the forces documented above. Several hypotheses arise from the previous analysis.

Sectoral Conditions:

1. The more risky the energy development, the more severe its disruptive dynamics, and the more pronounced its boom/bust path, the greater the local opposition to it.

2. The stronger the traditional sectors, such as agriculture, ranching, and tourism the greater the local opposition to energy development.

3. The greater the degree of competition for land, water, and derivitive political power from energy development, the greater the local opposition.

4. The higher the rate of local unemployment and the greater the probability that incoming activity will hire local people, the less the local opposition.

Rent Conditions:

1. The greater the differential rent appropriated by the energy
    sector, the greater the possibilities for a local coalition
    of classes to appropriate some of it as the price of develop-
    ment, or for energy corporations to buy off local opposition
    from this rent fund.

2. The greater the rent in any form currently appropriated locally
    through alternative land uses, the greater the opposition to
    energy development.

3. The greater the monopoly or absolute rent appropriated by the
    energy sector, the greater the possibilities for local appropri-
    ation through alliances across regions, through devices such as
    collusion on severance tax levels or unionization.

State Sector Conditions:

1. The refusal by state or federal government to appropriate rent
    on land they own results in the possibility of its appropria-
    tion by other groups through land regulation or taxation.

2. The stronger the local or state level opposition to development,
    or assertions of right to control development, the greater the
    corporate pressure at higher levels to overrride or buy off
    opposition.

I have explored these hypotheses at greater length elsewhere
(Markusen, 1978). The best evidence is provided by the contrasts
between the several Western states currently experiencing massive
energy development, especially Montana and Texas. Much more empirical
work can be done to document these suppositions and to flesh out their
implications for organizing. And, as I noted above, I have limited
the case here to a relatively ethnically homogenous region; other
rural areas might require an additional axis to properly develop
a Marxist analysis. For instance, an understanding of Appalachian
energy development or of coal production on the Navajo reservation
would require the introduction of ethnicity and culture.

PROBLEMS WITH MARXIST APPROACHES

The above analysis could be termed "structuralist" in its attempt
to derive a set of hypotheses about the current state of conflict
over development from a set of socioeconomic conditions. It leaves
no room for consciousness and the human will in the process of change.
Thus it violates the Marxist precept of the unity of theory and practice,

a not unusual feature of academic work pursued by someone like myself outside the community under study. Thus, before closing, I would like to raise some issues regarding the usefulness of this type of analysis and the dangers of pursuing Marxist work solely in the academy and in the separate disciplines.

The first problem arises from the prescriptive expectations of hypothesis generation in the social sciences. Marxist methodology shuns predictive statements because it champions the importance of consciousness and struggle as the source of change. So, while it attempts to describe theoretically the nature of conflict under capitalism, it does not specify the precise form of dismantling of the contradictory structure not the recipe for a new socialist society. These are both expected to arise democratically from people's practice and opposition to capitalism. Theoretical attempts to derive or prescribe action from statements about people's positions at a certain moment preempt the process by which practice re-works the very reality being analyzed. In concrete terms, this means that workers or ranchers may very well act differently from the hypotheses derived above. Marx said it best: "The philosophers have only interpreted the world in various ways; the point, however is to change it" (Marx, 1972). And, in fact, our analysis ought to be aimed at enabling them to do so, rather than second guessing their posture. And for that purpose, perhaps supportive propaganda would be better than the analysis presented in this paper.

This reflection raises a whole series of questions about the object and content of our analysis. The use of characterizations such as "petty bourgeois" for ranchers is not a very tactful means of propagandizing a potentially quite progressive group. It may be that the demands of the academy on our theoretical work lead to distortions that make it less accessible and useful for people involved in actual struggles. This may happen in two ways.

First, there is the premium placed by the academy on "rigor." This usually translates into the use of quantitative data, however messy, and the use, even creation, or technical language particular to the discipline. "Rigor" does not refer to a concern with the most significant questions; indeed it tends to encourage the discussion of trivial ones. In the process it prevents the engagement of people whose lives are under study and are affected by the deployment of social science because they do not have access to the elements of the analysis.

Second, the separation of radicals across the disciplines, requiring that each group of Marxists practice and submit to judgment in a particular social science, has resulted in a cleavage within the ranks of Marxist social scientists. Marxist sociologists tend to use methods such as typologies and survey research techniques

characteristic of their discipline. Marxist political economists
tend to use production models and econometric techniques characteristic of their discipline. Marxist geographers emphasize space as
an analytical category, subsuming everything else under it. Marxist political scientists lable eras the "Age of ..." just like their
academic counterparts. As a whole, we have not succeeded in replacing conventional social science methodology with Marxist methods.
Our work is more frequently oriented toward our nonradical colleagues
than it is to a progressive constituency, a characteristic which
Perry Anderson (1976) notes is true of Western Marxism as a whole
since World War II. In the process, we risk evolving our own internal differences. A holistic analysis that comprehends the entire
dynamic of capitalism can only be built by pooling our work and
unifying our method.

With respect to rural development, for instance, the political
economists need enrichment with modes of analysis from sociology,
political science, and psychology on the nature of culture, class
formation, and the role of the State. Liekwise, incomplete analyses by rural sociologists on class position arising from land ownership, the existence of rent and profit, and location within a
simple core-periphery dimension could be enriched by a fuller understanding of capitalist production dynamics. It is my hope that my
contributions as political economist to this volume on radical alternatives in sociology will illustrate the strengths and weaknesses
of an approach informed by training as an economist and contribute
toward building the interdisciplinary Marxist approach. Our own
struggle is to free ourselves from facing inward to our separate
disciplines and to work toward providing an alternative vision for
rural people.

REFERENCES

Anderson, Perry
     1976 Considerations on Western Marxism. London: New Left Books.
Associated Press
     1977 (December 26) "Card portrays firm as uncaring Santa."
     Colorado Springs Gazette/Telegraph.
Associated Press
     1977 (December 27) "Mine closing hits town hard at Christmas-
     time." Denver Post.
Brenner, R.
     1977 "The origins of capitalist development." New Left Review
     4 (July-August).
Council on Economic Priorities
     1974 Leased and Lost. New York: Author.

Edel, M.
    1976 "Marx's theory of rent: Urban applications." Kapital-
    istate 4(5):100-124.
Editorial Collective
    1978 "Introduction to the special issue on uneven regional
    development." Review of Radical Political Economics 10(3).
Emmanuel, A.
    1972 Unequal Exchange. New York: Monthly Review Press.
Federation of Rocky Mountain States
    1975 Energy Development in the Rocky Mountain Region. Denver,
    Colorado: Author
Gimenez, M., Greenberg, E., Markusen, A., Mayer, T., and Newton, J.
    1977 "Uneven development and capitalist inequality: A Marxist
    approach." In Economic Development, Poverty and Income Distri-
    bution, W. Loehr and J. Powelson (eds.). Boulder, Colorado:
    Westview Press.
Gilmore, J. and Duff, M.
    1973 Policy Analysis for Rural Development and Growth Manage-
    ment in Colorado. Denver, Colorado: Denver Research Institute
Gold, R.
    1974 A Comparative Study of the Impact of Coal Development
    on the Way of Life of People in the Coal Areas of Eastern
    Montana and Northeastern Wyoming. Missoula, Montana: Insti-
    tute for Social Science Research.
Harvey, D.
    1973 Social Justice and the City. (Chapter 5). Baltimore:
    John Hopkins University Press.
Holland, S.
    1976 Capital Versus the Regions. London: MacMillan.
Leistritz, F.L. and Murdock, S.
    1977 "Research methodology applicable to community adjustment
    to public land use alternatives." (Discussion paper). Fargo,
    North Dakota: Department of Agricultural Economics and Depart-
    ment of Sociology, North Dakota State University.
Lucas, R.
    1971 Minetown, Milltown, Railtown. Toronto: University of
    Toronto Press.
Mandel, E.
    1968 Marxist Economic Theory (Vol. 2). New York: Monthly
    Review Press
Markusen, A.
    1978 "Class, rent and sectoral conflict: Uneven development
    in Western U.S. boomtown." Review of Radical Political Econo-
    mics 10(3).
Marx, K.
    1967 Capital (Vol. 3). New York: International Publishers.
Marx, K.
    1974 Theories of Surplus Value (Vol. 2). New York: Interna-
    tional Publishers.

Marx, K.
    1972 "Theses on Feuerbach." In The Marx-Engels Reader.
    New York: W.N. Norton
Meeker, D.
    1976 Rapid Growth from Energy Projects: Ideas for State and
    Local Action. Washington, D.C.: Department of Housing and
    Urban Development, Office of Community Planning and Development.
Morris, G.
    1975 An Interregional Trade and Input-Output Model of the
    Colorado River Basin with Special Reference to Resource Con-
    straints. Unpublished doctoral dissertation, University of
    Colorado.
Northern Plains Resource Council
    1976 (May-June). "Stripping Montana." The Plains Truth
    5(4).
Northern Plains Resource Council
    1977 (November). The Plains Truth 6(9).
Northern Plains Resource Council
    1978 (January). The Plains Truth 6(11).
Poulantzas, N.
    1975 Classes in Contemporary Capitalism. London: New Left
    Books.
Stenehjam, E. and Metzger, J.
    1977 Socioeconomic Implications of the National Energy Plan:
    Comparative Social Costs of Increased Coal Production to 1985.
    (Draft). Argonne, Illinois: Regional Studies Program, Argonne
    National Laboratory.
Udis, B. (ed.)
    1967 An Analysis of the Economy of the Upper Main Stem Sub-
    Basin of the Colorado River Drainage Basin in 1969 with Empha-
    sis on Heavy Water using Industries. Boulder: Bureau of
    Economic Research.
Udis, B. and Kraynick, R.
    1974 A Comparative Analysis of Employment Change by Industry
    in the Colorado River Basin and in the United States. Boulder:
    Bureau of Economic Research.
U.S. Department of Commerce, Bureau of the Census
    1970 U.S. Census of Population and Housing. Washington, D.C.:
    Author.
U.S. Federal Power Commission
    1973 Second Supplement to Application of El Paso Natural Gas
    Company for a Certificate of Convenience and Necessity. (Docket
    No. CP73-131). Washington, D.C.: Author.
Walker, R.
            "Contentious issues in Marxian value and rent theory:
    A second and longer look." Antipode 7(1).
Wright, E.O.
    1976 (July-August). "Class boundaries in advanced capitalist
    societies." New Left Review 98.

Part **V**

RURAL ECOLOGY

15. Ecology and Ideology

PHILIP D. LOWE and MICHAEL W. WORBOYS

INTRODUCTION

In the late 1960s and early 1970s public interest in changes in the natural and physical environment showed a dramatic increase. Apart from the expressed concern for the preservation of landscape and wildlife, the protection of amenity, and the abatement of pollution, there have been those who have suggested that the future of modern industrial society is threatened by environmental disaster. A perceived crisis of such dimensions has led to many proposals, even blueprints, for radical social changes most of which involve a complete rejection of the structures and goals of modern industrial capitalism.

Since the mid 1970s, environmental concern, and with it the apparent immediacy of the environmental crisis, has somewhat receded. The environmentalists' warnings of natural decay have been superseded by apocryphal warnings of the decline of Western capitalist democracies, as a sharp downturn in the business cycle has set its own limits to growth. It is now appropriate to ask what constituted the environmental crisis. The biologist, Lord Ashby, whilst chairman of the standing Royal Commission on Environmental Pollution--itself a response by the British government to mounting environmental concern in the late 1960s--suggested that we face not a single crisis, but a critical period, or climacteric, as a series of natural systems threatened collapse under a tide of industrial pollutants, and with the successive exhaustion of key resources. Yet others, such as John Maddox (1972), then editor of Nature, questioned the very

*Philip Lowe would like to acknowledge the financial support of the British Social Science Research Council.

existence of a crisis, other than in the minds of the "prophets of doom." Interestingly, Ashby (1975) himself has subsequently declared that "The danger is political, not ecological, collapse."

If perceptions of the problem have varied widely, so have individual responses. Reactions to various publicized environmental dangers have encompassed the whole gamut from sublimely optimistic beliefs in the ability of the market and of human ingenuity, especially the development and application of science and technology, to respond with rational and non-disruptive solutions; through to very bleak and deeply pessimistic views of the "human predicament" and despondency over the possibilities for survival of the human species (e.g. Beckerman, 1974, and Heilbroner, 1974). Furthermore, whilst public concern over the environment grew, certain very prominent and immediate aspects of environmental pollution--such as smoke in many British and American cities, and effluent in the Thames and Hudson rivers--showed distinct signs of improvement. These and many other environmental problems are not new, some having reached serious proportions during the nineteenth century, and yet the social response, usually in terms of public alarm, has been episodic and specific. Examples of previous periods when public anxiety over environmental change was intense, widespread, and organized include, in Britain, the Victorian public health movement and the turn-of-the-century "Back to Nature" movement; and, in America, the conservation movements of the Progressive Era and of the New Deal.

Such observations naturally focus attention on the specific social mechanisms underlying the generation, diffusion, mobilization and coordination of contemporary environmental concern in order to explain both why this arose when it did, and variations in the meanings people attach to the environment and environmental change. One particularly fruitful source of insights has been the literature of social movements--a term taken to mean forms of collective behavior which are relatively unstructured, self-conscious attempts to introduce innovations into a social system (Banks, 1972). Cotgrove (1976) has identified a single coherent movement comprising those groups and individuals who "openly challenge what is in many ways the central or master-value in industrial society--the primacy of economic goals--and set against these welfare-values which are incompatible with or in conflict with purely economic ends." Cotgrove draws particular attention to their use of environmental dangers as levers to promote particular recipes for social change.

One prominent and enduring feature of many environmental problems is their implication of modern science, both as cause and as solution. From the anxiety over radioactive fall-out and pesticides, through to current worries about fluorocarbons, nuclear power, and hazards of the work-place, science has been cast as the villain of the piece. Yet scientists have also been in the forefront in alerting society about these problems and campaigning for action. Moreover, a leading role for science has been proposed in assessing risks from pollution, in developing new resources, and in the general formulation of solutions and strategies in response to environmental problems.

This ambivalence with regard to science--which is, incidentally, very common where science impinges upon social issues--creates many difficulties. For example, different scientists may regard the same problem very differently. Whose assessment or warning should the public believe? To solve environmental problems, do we need more science, less science, or different science?   To which group of scientists, if any, do we turn for solutions? One common response to questions of this sort has been to look to ecology and ecologists as sources of "wisdom." The received notion that ecology is about wholeness and the natural has left it seemingly untainted by the reductionist and industrial associations of most modern science.

Indeed, its marginality to mainstream science, of which ecologists have long complained, now proves to be an asset in a period when science generally is being questioned and attacked. Many environmentalists and environmental pressure groups have fallen in behind the banner of Ecology. They have used ecological information vicariously and promoted the adoption of ecological values, giving rise to a whole new genre of social polemic best described as popular ecology. In short, ecology has become a social movement as well as a branch of biology and it is the connection between these two aspects of ecology that needs to be explored.[1]

In this paper, we intend to suspend judgement on the nature and impact of changes in the natural environment. Moreover, we are unable to provide an analysis of the political economy of the environmental crisis. What we do examine, however, is the role of ecological information and beliefs in the perception of an "environmental crisis." Following the definition of ideological determination as "knowledge...created, accepted or sustained by concealed, unacknowledged (or) illegitimate interests" (Barnes, 1977: 33), we wish to argue that the place of science in the environmental crisis is best understood by regarding ecology as ideology.

POPULAR ECOLOGY AND THE "END OF IDEOLOGY"

What is clear in the literature of contemporary environmentalism and popular ecology is a general rejection of conflict, especially political conflict (indeed, politics and conflict are frequently treated as synonymous evils): the lesson of ecology in its broadest sense is supposedly harmony, balance, and symbiosis, and conflict is felt to be dysfunctional to the working of natural and social systems. In this respect, popular ecology is the natural successor to other post-war movements and debates involving scientists and concerning science and technology. For example, both the Atomic Scientists' Movement and the Campaign for Nuclear Disarmament were motivated in part by the belief that nuclear weaponry introduced a new and radical logic into international relations that demanded an end to national and ideological conflicts. Similarly, in the "end of ideology" writings of the 1950s and early 1960s, politics were deemed redundant, as societies with diverse ideologies apparently converged through the overriding and deterministic effects of science-based, technological development (Waxman, 1968). In the literature of popular ecology, political differences are declared equally redundant, but this is because of the imperatives of man's ecological situation. Compelling physical and natural constraints supersede diverse moral and political values--the new social order being of necessity subject to "ecological determinism" (McHarg, 1966).

Thus, social cohesion, national unity, and internationalism are common prescriptions in popular ecology and here recall the holistic social and scientific philosophies, also based on ecology, of the interwar years, of which Jan Smuts, the South African Statesman and architect of the League of Nations, was a leading exponent (1926). These stressed the organic bonds within--and holistic character of--plant, animal, and human communities. The lesson of ecology was then, as now, functional interdependence and order within complex groupings and associations of natural organisms. As the British biologist, J. Arthur Thomas (1931), commented addressing an audience of public school boys in the year of the Great Depression: "We suggest, then, that the external linkages which Natural History reveals have an evolutionary importance, making, on the whole, for stability and balance. The analogy in human society is not far to seek." Similarly, ecologists in New Deal America stressed the relationship between man and environment and the evidence of coexistence and mutual dependence in natural communities in response to political concern over the dangers of regional and class conflicts (Clements, 1935; Adams, 1935; Hanson, 1939). In South Africa in the 1930s, ecology was used to justify white supremacy (i.e., ecological dominance) as well as the separate development of the different races to avoid inter-racial strife (i.e., competitive exclusion) (Bews, 1931).

Within contemporary environmentalist literature, antipathy towards political conflict has a number of dimensions. Firstly, environmental problems appear ubiquitous. Pollution and natural resource scarcities are seen not to respect national frontiers-- the slogan of the 1972 United Nations Conference on the Human Environment was "Only One Earth." Also it seems that different economic and political systems are not immune from environmental degradation. Thus, according to the late Margaret Mead (1976), speaking as President of the American Association for the Advancement of Science, "Capitalism, Communism and Socialism are all bad in protecting the environment."

Secondly, political differences are seen as an impediment to solving the environmental crisis. It was Aldous Huxley (1970) who claimed that only by "shifting our collective attention from the merely political to the basic biological aspects of the human situation" could we hope to solve environmental problems. According to the ecologist, Frank Fraser Darling (1963), "In a world where the only hope for man is internationalism, nationalism is the political ecological factor which prevents any constructive action to curb population increases." Similarly, other commentators have argued that present political preoccupations and divisions make effective action impossible and must be abandoned as an essential prerequisite to tackling environmental problems. "The confrontation of America and Russia of Communism and a 'Free Economy'," one writer declares to be "a distraction, an evasion of the main issue which now confronts the human race and ought to reduce our political and economic squabbles to a domestic level" (Allsopp, 1972: 33). In Britain, the establishment of an Ecology Party indicates the presumption that environmental issues transcend orthodox political alignments: the party "views conventional political rivalries as dangerously irrelevant, in that they obscure the nature and urgency of the problems we have to face up to" (1979).

A related point often made is that "ecological truths," objective and dispassionate, present people with certain clear and unavoidable choices and courses of action that should eclipse dogmatic political assertion. A view frequently re-echoed is that "almost all theories, Liberal or Marxist, about the future development of capitalism, imperialism, or the 'third world' will become of strictly academic interest when ecological considerations intervene and so action derived from them becomes irrelevant" (Stoneham, 1972).

Finally, it is thought that the stark reality of the situation supposedly facing all mankind and powerfully conjured up with such metaphors as "spaceship earth" and the "biosphere," might enable, even induce, men to mend some of the many social divisions and conflicts between them. "When the enemy is nature...rather than another social class," observes Robert Heilbroner (1970: 283), "adjustments [by capitalists and managerial classes] could be made that would be impossible in ordinary circumstances." It is in this sense that ecology is seen as a "subversive science" (Shepard and McKinley, 1969), and why environmentalism has been described as "the only truly radical movement of today" (E. Goldsmith, 1975). In the words of Max Nicholson (1976), "Naive as they look, and indeed are,

the ecologists and their fellow travellers bid fair in history to
relegate Karl Marx to the status of a smalltime bungling amateur at
the task of triggering world revolution."

However, the apolitical stance of popular ecology has rightly
attracted charges of neglecting, even masking, major social divisions and conflicts. There are huge differences in the human environment and in the power of classes, groups and nations to command
scarce resources, and thereby to ensure that their own environments
are relatively clean, secure and comfortable--the distinction between
first class and steerage, and the bridge and the engine room on
spaceship earth (Enzensberger, 1974). Not only is the diagnosis
of popular ecologists seriously flawed but their prognoses appear
hopelessly naive and utopian because of their lack of recognition
and understanding of the realities of power and inequality that
must confront any action. They have no theory of how we get from
here to there. In addition, popular ecologists often show a strong
distrust of practical politics, whether they be conventional party
politics or class struggle. They have been more concerned to
dramatize the choice--if we go on as we are then the world will
be overtaken by disaster, to survive we must change radically both
our attitudes to nature and our social order--than to detail the
steps by which the necessary changes might be effected. As Cotgrove (1976) comments, "There is a strong millenial flavour to the
rhetoric of many environmental activists, especially those who derive their message from ecology: the blueprint for survival is
holistic, requiring the total transformation of society."

Yet, insistence on the immediate and complete transformation of
society defies its inception. Thus, there is a strong disparity
between the radical ecological prognosis and the few, rather mild,
remedial and reformist measures either sought or achieved in various
countries. Indeed, the practical achievements of environmentalism,
especially compared with the intensity of its crisis rhetoric, have
been slight (Albrecht, 1976; Sills, 1975). Furthermore, its political naivete has made it particularly prone to incorporation and
manipulation by powerful state and economic interests--on the look-
out for speedy technological fixes to pressing problems (Weinberg,
1973; Hemingway and Newman, 1978). Meanwhile, it has been mainly
the established environmental groups that have reaped the extra
public interest in environmental protection--groups like the British
National Trust whose membership went from 158,000 to 613,000 between
1965 and 1977, and the American Sierra Club which grew from 30,000
to 174,000 over the same period. Such organizations, dating from the
1890s, are well integrated into the framework of government. They
do not conflict with widely held social goals and values. Indeed,
in tending to be supportive of the dominant political and value
system, they are essentially conservative (Lowe, 1975a; Clifford
and Lowe, 1979).

THE ENVIRONMENTAL CRISIS AND THE SCIENTIFIC COMMUNITY

Most popular ecologists would not completely abolish politics.
Some view politics as the refined tool of environmental management,
enabling fine and delicate control of human well-being within the
greater and larger purposes of the biosphere. In the words of Frank
Fraser Darling (1970), the ultimate concern of politics is "to
develop some yardstick for human content; to be able to measure
the lesser degree of discontent and psychosomatic disease in re-
habilitated environments." The implication is that, as well as
transcending political differences, environmental problems are
also non-political in the sense that their solutions are management
or technical issues. Hence, no longer should politics be about
power, its use and distribution, but, instead, about the forms and
techniques of government most appropriate to cope with urgent environmental problems. This identification of environmental problems
as technical issues has many implications. It can be argued that
such a response is fundamentally conservative, the problems being
fragmented and so narrowly defined that the solutions sought would
in no way overtly disturb the prevailing social order. Furthermore,
it raises interesting questions about the political role of science
and technology, in that technical problems are commonly diagnosed
by scientists and engineers and require their expertise for devising solutions.

That science has been implicated both as cause and solution of
many environmental problems is just one aspect of the rather ambi-
valent, even schizophrenic, social response to modern science. The
choice open to society is frequently cast as being between a complete
rejection of science and technology, on the one hand, and even more
resources for science and its application to ever more facets of
social and economic life, on the other. The further option of a
change in the nature of science and technology, through a change in
their political control and in their social relations, is not open
through such a politically denatured formulation of the problem.

The conventional response of the British scientific establishment to environmental problems was expressed in 1972 by the Council
for Scientific Policy when it urged that "more science will be needed,
not less, to provide remedies and to enable society to take pre-
cautions against pollution" and called for the "closer integration
of science into social policies." Thus more "scientific" planning,
monitoring, and management are advocated in such forms as technology
assessment, policy science, environmental impact analysis, quantitative environmental forecasting, and ecological evaluation--activi-
ties viewed by their practitioners as so many exercises in applied
rationality, but open to criticism for clothing implicit political
assumptions and implications in a pseudo-scientific mystique of

"objective" knowledge and "rational" techniques. What is clear is
that their practice seems to be based on the assumption of the availability of consensually-defined social goals which, if absent, can be
summonsed by the persuasive presentation of the facts of the matter.
In this process, science is used to legitimate the authority and
policies of government and powerful elites (Wynne, 1975).

Conservation, when treated in these terms, appears to be an un-
adulterated good thing. Defined as the wise or rational use of
natural resources, equated with applied ecology, and underpinned
with its own battery of quantitative techniques, conservation seems
beyond the realm of politics. The chief justification for conservation has been that it rests on consensually-agreed ends. However,
the supposed political consensus surrounding the practice of conservation has in fact been a coalition of powerful vested interests,
largely those who control and own land and natural resources. Their
use of ecological rhetoric has enjoyed the active support or acqui-
escence of professional ecologists. And it is at this point that
environmentalism is directly related to the professional concerns
and ambitions of ecologists over status and rewards. The plausibility of ecologists is of crucial importance and is directly involved in the popularization of the environmental crisis, just as
their professional concerns are deeply enmeshed in "technical" solutions to the crisis. Indeed, conservation exhibits the characteristics associated with other policy areas where the influence of
experts is in the ascendancy, and where expertise is employed to
enhance their own status and to protect those interests on which
they depend.

The institutionalization of a scientific discipline such as
ecology is generally accompanied by the competitive development of
a disciplinary ideology which publicizes the putative social utility
and world-view of the discipline and plays an essential role in the
establishment of cohesion and a sense of collective identity amongst
its practitioners (Hagstrom, 1965). The emergence of ecology as a
distinct discipline dates from the turn of the century, but only
belatedly has it made the transition from "little science" to "big
science."

In Britain, government recognition of its potential utility
came in 1949 with the creation of the Nature Conservancy as both a
research council for ecology and an agency for the formation and
management of nature reserves (Duff and Lowe, 1979). Initially,
the Nature Conservancy commanded a very much smaller share of resources than the other research councils, and ecology, with its
amateur connotations of natural history, had a low status in the
scientific community. But the Conservancy proved very successful
in lobbying government and promoting ecology, and took the lead
role in forging various pressure groups into an effective and
dynamic environmental lobby.

In America, government promotion of ecology had begun earlier, in connection with the emergency federal conservation programs of the New Deal. These programs, though, were terminated with the onset of the Second World War, and ecology suffered badly through the 1940s and 1950s with the massive switch of resources to military and industrial science. However, by the late 1950s, the National Science Foundation was giving modest support to ecological work and training, and a keen interest in the subject of ecology was being shown by the Atomic Energy Commission (now the Energy Research and Development Administration), which has since become one of the foremost sponsors of ecological research (McIntosh, 1976).

Like their British counterparts, American ecologists played a crucial part in the 1960s in popularizing the existence of an environmental crisis and figured prominently in the institutional developments that were the outcome of the resulting public and governmental concern. The funding of ecology was stepped up, and senior ecologists were drawn into the higher levels of government. Increasingly, ecological expertise has been used to legitimize major technological and planning decisions (Lowe, 1975b; Nelkin, 1977).

The interests of ecologists have been promoted in the development of education and research policy, but also in proposals for an ecological input into many other aspects of public policy, especially in relation to the planning and management of land and natural resources. Such advocacy has been reciprocated by various emergent, land-oriented, professional groups who have found in ecology a certain scientific basis and justification for their practice, as well as a rich source for elements in the construction of their own professional self-images. For example, recreation managers, landscape architects, and some sections of the planning profession have hitched their wagons to the rising star of ecology (McHarg, 1969; Woodbury, 1975).

AN ECOLOGICAL WORLD ORDER

The appeal to ecology, as we have shown, has gone beyond the search for tactical responses and technical solutions to particular environmental problems, towards the claim that ecology can contribute to a radical reordering of human purposes and a re-orientating of society away from environmental disaster. Thus Max Nicholson who for many years (1952-1966) was Director-General of the British Nature conservancy, has given the following definition of the scope of ecology (quoted by Mellanby, 1973):

> Ecology is the study of plants and animals in
> relation to their environment and to one another.
> But it is also more than that: it is the main
> intellectual discipline and tool which enables
> us to hope that human evolution can be mutated,
> can be shifted on to a new course, so that man
> will cease to knock hell out of the environment
> on which his own future depends.

The findings, concepts, and approach of ecology have indeed
proved a rich source of ideas and analogies in the construction of
environmentally sound social programs--niche theory, the ecosystem
concept, energy flow, materials recycling, limits of tolerance, and
succession have been deployed in many and varied contexts. The
emergence in the 1970s of the Ecology Party in Britain and of "Green
Parties" elsewhere in Western Europe and North America is one manifestation of this particular form of scientism. Beyond this have
come calls for ecological ideals, an ecological ethic, an ecological
morality, ecological values, and ecological determinism.

Certainly, the synthetic nature of ecology and its claims to
transcend the narrowness of other disciplines have always been a
source of its popular support (Lowe, 1976). But, in this case,
science appears to be seeking and adopting a leading role in
society as an authoritative value-affirming and consensus-generating
institution. John McHale (1971), for example, observes that the
operation of science as "a 'value-free' institution" avoiding the
evaluation of the effects of its discoveries upon society, and the
attitude of social detachment and insularity amongst scientists,
may no longer be tenable in "a world society increasingly dependent
upon science and in which large-scale science is also dependent
upon public support." He proposes that "one solution for this
dilemma of science may well be the assumption of leadership in
framing a new ecological ethic that would outline the ground rules
that are now required for adequate control of our massive technological capabilities."

According to McHale, this initiative would be aided considerably by a scientific community that is "globally ubiquitous" and
by the role of science as "a 'value-affirming' and goal-setting
agency [whose] status is now equal to and, in many areas, greater
than the older social institutions (for example, church, government, family, education), upon which this function traditionally
devolved." Here the role of an "ecological ethic" in enhancing
the status and authority of science is seen as integral to the
function of science as an institution, perhaps the institution,
for integrating society, affirming its central values, and generating social cohesion. The powerful American business chief, Cabot
Lodge (1970), has agreed that "ecology and unified sciences (general

systems analysis) form a morally sanctioned force of consensus in society."

Thus, at a time of change and dissent from established values, when it is generally agreed that traditional institutions have lost much of their authority, science, albeit reunified and chastened by the example of ecology, is turned to by those who value order and stability as the one authoritative voice. However, such appeals to science come at a time when its own moral influence has also been assailed by the attacks of what many identify as an anti-science movement (Ravetz, 1971). The response of critics like Roszak to the social problems of modern science has been to reject science-- the objective, rational and calculating consciousness--in favor of a more subjective, intuitive, and feeling type of knowledge. For Roszak (1973: 401), the discipline of ecology, and not high energy physics, should be the model science--a view shared by influential and respected proponents of ecology such as Max Nicholson and Barry Commoner.

The separate debate over social responsibility in science has raised other questions about the direction and control of science (M. Goldsmith, 1975). The self-doubt that has been generated has prompted some leading scientists to demand greater solidarity and less dissent within the scientific community so as to render it less vulnerable to external attack and to preserve its authority in society. Indeed, external fragmentation has been identified as one cause of the inability of science to respond effectively to environ-mental problems, and calls for a "functional scientific community" and a "unified science," based on ecology and the related general systems theory predict the consequent restoration of the weakened position of science in society (Hancock, 1971; Bohm, 1971; Goldsmith, 1970; and Haskell, 1972). The integrative image of ecology, its promise of making whole that which was fragmented, and its widespread popular support, might help revive the moral influence of science, and regenerate consensus both within and outside of science. In the words of Eugene Odum (1977), the leading American systems ecologist, "going beyond reductionism to holism is now mandated if science and society are to mesh for mutual benefit."

As we have seen, a number of people have suggested that only ecology can be a secure source of values: that "human values are founded in objectively determinable ecological relations within Nature" (Colwell, 1970). In particular, it is thought that sci-entists alone might specify the absolute physical constraints to existence which increasingly are seen as determinative of life. For example, in recent years there has been a number of well publicized exercises in which scientists have sought to specify, on scientific criteria, the human "carrying capacity" of areas, regions, and nations, including the optimum population for Britain,

as well as the absolute global limits of population growth and industrial development (House, 1974; House and Williams, 1976; Taylor, 1970;
Meadows et al., 1972).

This point of view which sees Nature, interpreted by science, as
a source of absolute values, and therefore of authority, finds particular expression in the Ecologist--the magazine which, in 1972
issued the Blueprint for Survival whose appeal for a "Movement for
Survival" resulted in the formation of the British Ecology Party.
Edward Goldsmith (1970b), the editor of the Ecologist, has gone
so far as to claim that:

> Assuming that all parts of the system can be quanti-
> fied, we can then formulate the essential principle
> of all systems, which we can refer to as the law of
> optimum value. There must be an optimum value for
> every part of the system, which is determined by that
> of the other parts. To allow one of these values to
> increase without reference to the others is to destroy
> the essential structure of the system, and bring about
> its breakdown. So if we regard the United Kingdom as
> a system, there is an optimum population at any given
> moment. There is an optimum number of houses, an
> optimum number of cars; there is also an optimum
> standard of living, an optimum differential between
> the wages paid to different people; there is an op-
> timum longevity and even an optimum amount of social
> deviation. It must follow that there is no conceiv-
> able variable whose value can be increased or de-
> creased indefinitely without bringing about the
> breakdown of the system. Nothing is good or bad
> per se.

Goldsmith's belief in the certainty and ubiquity of a "cybernetic
approach to the study of society and ecosystems" is staggering, but
represents a strong reaffirmation of faith in science as a social and
moral regulator. He has called for the establishment of "a unified
science, in terms of which it will be possible to understand the
interrelationship between such diverse things as societies, plants
and minerals, in their specific contributions to the working of the
biosphere... Once this is done it is but another step for our educational apparatus to imbue people with that sense of values and to
supply them with that information which will enable them to fulfill
their correct functions as members of their families, communities
and ecosystem" (1970a).

Others, in a similar manner, have based appeals to order in
society on an appeal to ecology, emphasizing either its holistic,
unified character or its revelation of the amalogical order of
Nature. Many of the articles in the Ecologist, for example, express

alarm at the loss of stability and authority in society and are addressed to the question of what mechanisms of control exist to turn
chaos into order. The Ecology Party is particularly concerned with
the disorder and pathological condition of modern industrial society--
its social disintegration, anonymity, alienation and instability--
arising from its scale and mobility. The party has campaigned, in
Britain and in local, national, and European elections for a move
towards decentralized, self-regulating communities to achieve social
and ecological balance.

Edward Goldsmith bases his prescription for a new social order
on the example of traditional and primitive societies. If we are to
avoid "social and ecological upheavals," Goldsmith insists that our
society must be reorganized on lines such as these (1970c):

> they are organised in families and small communi-
> ties, which are held together by a closely inter-
> woven set of associations that assures that every-
> one is linked, in some way, to everyone else. They
> are self-regulating.... Their members have a strong
> sense of responsibility towards their family and
> their community. Their numbers are small and they
> are imbued with a deep respect for the natural world
> surrounding them, of which they know they are an
> integral part.... Their members are happy in the
> fulfilment of their natural roles as differentiated
> members of their families, communities and ecosystems,
> and it is this happiness above all else that creates
> the stability that still eludes us.

Similar prescriptions have appeared in a number of ecological mani-
festoes, of which the most celebrated have been the Blueprint for
Survival and the ecological utopia of the Scots-born, American regional
planner, Ian McHarg (1969), who has envisaged an orderly, harmonious
world of the future manned entirely by "Naturalists," fully conscious
of their interdependent duties to society and to the biosphere. The
picture painted in each of these is that of a Gemeinschaft-type society
with its organic social bonds (Cotgrove, 1976). Though visions of the
future, they hark back to a once stable and harmonious past shattered
by industrial growth.

The social order to be recreated is presented as natural in being derived from an a priori unity, based on a community which ante-
dates the individual and on the common sentiments which grow out of
a shared physical life and locality. Authority is derived from the
general will of the community and overrides individual freedoms--
"mutual coercion, mutually agreed upon," in the words of the American
human ecologist, Garret Hardin (1968), or the ideal of the "self-
policing" community envisaged by the Ecology Party (1979).

The sense of the unity in an ordered social organization is also seen to generate a hierarchical structure as a natural law of group life. Indeed, to many ecologists, struggle, hierarchy, and inequalities are inevitable, even acceptable, as the outcome of men fulfilling their natural functions socially and ecologically. Only in small, self-regulating communities, it is argued, can the conditions emerge to control aggression and legitimate hierarchy and inequality through the exercise of traditional authority.

CONCLUSIONS

Much environmentalism thus reflects customary anxieties about the impact of technology on society and disenchantment with de-humanizing and impersonal routine and bureaucracy. Recurring images of disintegration and decay are enhanced by an overriding sense of crisis. There is concern over conflict and fragmentation in society and a loss of traditional order and authority, particularly within the scientific community, and a deep-seated wish for the reimposition of control and authority through renewed consensus and social cohesion. The appeal to ecology is an appeal to solidarity and haromony-- in Fraser Darling's term, "The Unity of Ecology" (1963). In particular, ecology is seen to emphasize stability and balance.

The environmental crisis thus highlights a crisis of confidence within science and a crisis of science's authority in society. Mary Douglas (1972), the anthropologist, supports this view in drawing attention to the problems of credibility that scientists face in warning society of possible environmental dangers. Problems of plausibility do not arise in small, integrated societies, and only arise "if the society falls apart, and separate voices claim to know about different environmental constraints." Indeed, environmentalism has been interpreted as a bid by certain scientists to relocate and extend the basis of scientific authority (King, 1973). Science as a mere source of useful knowledge confers upon scientists the very limited and fragile power of technicians, but the ecologists' claim to appreciate the wisdom of Nature, as well as the orthodox scientists' knowledge of natural laws, might legitimate a more continuous and central involvement in the formulation of political purposes and values. Max Nicholson, who has envisaged the application of ecology "to the management of the earth with computer aid," dedicated his book, The Environmental Revolution, to the "New Masters of the World" (1970).

The constant appeal to ecology represents a reinstatement of the prestige of science and a reaffirmation of its role as an authoritative and integrating social institution. The appeal to ecology is an appeal to what is natural, defined for us by science as a source of moral and social control. Above all, the holistic

character of ecology is seen to transcend conflict, to mend fragmentation, to instil reverence for the "whole system" with its complex,
irreducible, systemic properties, and to invoke respect and quies-
cence--Commoner's third law of ecology is "nature knows best" (1971).
Seen in these terms, popular ecology represents a deeply conservative
response to a perceived crisis of authority in Western society.

NOTES

[1]Below, we intend to use the following terms in the following senses:

Environmentalism is a broad and diverse social movement including
many groups and individuals (environmentalists) who are actively
concerned over the changing state of the environment.

Ecology is a scientific discipline--a branch of the natural sciences
whose practitioners, ecologists, study the relationship between
organisms and their environment.

Popular ecology is that brand of environmentalism which bases its
stance on the findings and concepts of ecology, and which is pro-
pounded by popular ecologists, an amorphous group of scientists,
writers, journalists and other environmentalists.

REFERENCES

Adams, C.C.
     1935   "The relation of general ecology to human ecology."
     Ecology 16: 316-335.

Albrecht, S.L.
     1976   "Legacy of the environmental movement." Environment
     and Behaviour 8: 147-168.

Allsopp, B.
     1972   Ecological Mortality. London: Muller.

Ashby, E.
     1975   "The danger is political, not ecological, collapse."
     Times Higher Education Supplement No. 217 (19 Dec.): 13.

Banks, J.
     1972   The Sociology of Social Movements. London: Macmillan.

Barnes, B.
     1977   Interests and the Growth of Knowledge. London: Routledge
     and Kegan Paul.

Beckerman, W.
    1974   In Defence of Economic Growth.   London: Cape.

Bews, J.W.
    1931   "The ecological viewpoint."   Nature 128 (15 Aug.): 245-
    248.

Bohm, D.
    1971   "Fragmentation in science and society."   In W. Fuller
    (ed.), The Social Impact of Modern Biology.   London: Routledge
    and Kegan Paul.

Cabot Lodge, J.
    1970   "Changes in corporations: needed a new consensus."
    Harvard Today (March): 6-10.

Clements, F.E.
    1935   "Experimental ecology in the public service."   Ecology 16:
    342-363.

Clifford, J.M. and Lowe, P.D.
    1979. "Environmentalists under the microscope."   ENDS No. 18:
    19-21.

Colwell, T.B.
    1970   "Some implications of the ecological revolution for the
    construction of value."   In E. Lazlo and J.B. Wilbur (eds.),
    Human Values and Natural Science.   New York: Gordon and Breach.

Commoner, B.
    1971   The Closing Circle: Confronting the Environmental Crisis.
    London: Cape.

Cotgrove, S.
    1976   "Environmentalism and utopia."   Sociological Review 24
    (new series): 23-42.

Council for Scientific Policy
    1972   Third Report, Cmnd. 5117.   London: H.M.S.O.

Darling, F.F.
    1963   "The unity of ecology."   The Advancement of Science
    (Nov.): 297-306.

Darling, F.F.
    1970   Wilderness and Plenty.   London: BBC.

Douglas, M.
    1972   "Environments at risk."   In J. Benthall (ed.), Ecology,
    the Shaping Enquiry.   London: Longman.

Duff, A. and Lowe, P.D.
    1979   "Britain." In E.J. Kormondy (ed.), Handbook of Contemporary
    Developments in World Ecology. Westport, Connecticut: Greenwood
    Press.

Ecology Party
    1979   The Real Alternative: Election Manifesto. Birmingham: The
    Ecology Party.

Enzensberger, H.M.
    1974   "A critique of political ecology." New Left Review No. 84
    (March/April): 3-31.

Goldsmith, E.
    1970a   Ecologist 1 (July): 5.

Goldsmith, E.
    1970b   "Bringing order to chaos: a cybernetic approach to the
    study of society and ecosystems." Ecologist 1 (July): 20-22.

Goldsmith, E.
    1970c   in Ecologist 1 (Dec.): 10.

Goldsmith, E.
    1975   "The two ecologies." Ecologist 5: 367.

Goldsmith, M. (ed.)
    1975   Science and Social Responsibility. London: Macmillan.

Hagstrom, W.O.
    1965   The Scientific Community. New York: Basic Books.

Hancock, J.
    1971   "Environmental problems and the reunification of the sci-
    entific community." In W. Fuller (ed.), The Social Impact of
    Modern Biology. London: Routledge and Kegan Paul.

Hanson, H.C.
    1939   "Ecology in agriculture." Ecology 20: 111-117.

Hardin, G.
    1968   "The tragedy of the commons." Science 162: 1243-1248.

Haskell, E. (ed.)
    1972   Full Circle: The Moral Force of Unified Science. New York:
    Gordon and Breach.

Heilbroner, R.
    1970   Capitalism and Socialism. New York: Random House.

Heilbroner, R.
    1974   An Inquiry into the Human Prospect. New York: Norton.

Hemingway, R.J. and Newman, J.F.
    1978   "Environmental studies." In F.C. Peacock (ed.), Jealott's
    Hill: Fifty Years of Agricultural Research 1928-1978. Bracknell,
    Berkshire: Imperial Chemical Industries.

House, P.W.
    1974. "The carrying capacity of a region: a planning model."
    Omega 2: 667-676.

House, P.W. and Williams, E.R.
    1976   The Carrying Capacity of a Nation. Lexington, Mass.:
    Lexington Books.

Huxley, A.
    1970   "The politics of population." In G.A. and R.M. Love (eds.),
    Ecological Crisis. New York: Harcourt Brace Jovanovich.

King, M.D.
    1973   "Scientists as moralists." Technology and Society S:
    15-18.

Lowe, P.D.
    1975a   "The environmental lobby." Built Environment Quarterly 1:
    73-76, 158-161, 235-238.

Lowe, P.D.
    1975b   "Science and government: the case of pollution."
    Public Administration 54: 287-298.

Lowe, P.D.
    1976   "Amateurs and professionals: the institutional emergence
    of British plant ecology." Journal of the Society for the Biblio-
    graphy of Natural History 7: 517-535.

McHale, J.
    1971   The Ecological Context. London: Studio Vista.

McHarg, I.L.
    1966   "Ecological determinism." In F.F. Darling and J.P. Milton
    (eds.), Future Environments of North America. Garden City, N.Y.:
    Natural History Press.

McHarg, I.L.
    1969   Design with Nature. Garden City, N.Y.: Natural History
    Press.

McIntosh, R.P.
    1976   "Ecology, since 1900." In B.J. Taylor and T.J. White
    (eds.), Issues and Ideas in America. Norman, Oklahoma: Univer-
    sity of Oklahoma Press.

Maddox, J.
    1972   The Doomsday Syndrome. London: Macmillan.

Mead, M.
    1976   in New Scientist 69: 566.

Meadows, D.H. et al.
    1972   The Limits to Growth. New York: Universe Books.

Mellanby, K.
    1973   "What ecology definitely is not." Times Higher Education
    Supplement No. 100 (14 Sept.): 1.

Nelkin, D.
    1977   "Scientists and professional responsibility: the experience
    of American ecologists." Social Studies of Science 7: 75-95.

Nicholson, M.
    1970   The Environmental Revolution. London: Hodder and Stoughton.

Nicholson, M.
    1976   "The ecological breakthrough." New Scientist 72: 460-
    463.

Odum, E.P.
    1977   "The emergence of ecology as a new integrative discipline."
    Science 195: 1289-1293.

Ravetz, J.R.
    1971   Scientific Knowledge and Its Social Problems. Oxford:
    Clarendon Press.

Roszak, T.
    1973   Where the Wastland Ends. London: Faber.

Shepard, P. and McKinley, D. (eds.)
    1969   The Subversive Science: Essays Towards an Ecology of Man.
    Boston: Houghton Mifflin.

Sills, D.L.
    1975   "The environmental movement and its critics." Human Ecology
    3: 1-41.

Smuts, J.C.
    1926   Holism and Evolution. London: Macmillan.

Stoneham, C.
    1972   "The unviability of capitalism." The Spokesman 23: 61.

Taylor, L.R. (ed.)
    1970   The Optimum Population for Britain. London: Academic Press.

Thomson, J.A.
    1931   "The new natural history." The Scientist: A Public Schools
    Journal of Popular Science I (part 1): 3-6.

Waxman, C.I. (ed.)
    1968   The End of Ideology Debate. New York: Simon and Schuster.

Weinberg, A.M.
    1973   "Technology and ecology--is there a need for confronta-
    tion?" Bioscience 23: 41-45.

Woodbury, S.R.
    1975   The Application of Ecological Concepts to Planning: An
    Initial Annotated Bibliography. Monticello, Illinois: Council
    of Planning Librarians.

Wynne, B.
    1975   "The rhetoric of consensus politics: a critical review
    of technology assessment." Research Policy 4: 108-158.

16. Agriculture, Environment, and Social Change: Some Emergent Issues

FREDERICK H. BUTTEL

INTRODUCTION: CRISIS IN U.S. AGRICULTURE?

It is truly remarkable to consider that the almost universal confidence in and optimism concerning agriculture in the 1950's and 1960's have been supplanted by such a widespread feeling of crisis in the 1970's. This of course is not to suggest that American agriculture is under attack from all quarters; most agricultural researchers and groups we may loosely characterize as the "agricultural establishment" do tenaciously hold to the desirability of the present structure of the agricultural/food system (Buttel and Schwarzweller, 1979). However, it is fair to say that a broad range of groups--ranging from critically-oriented social and biological scientists to middle class reform/"public interest" groups--has raised many pointed questions about the ability of the agricultural system to provide food at reasonable prices, to meet the material needs of the majority of farmers, or to be ecologically sustainable, given the massive resource requirements of food raising and distribution in the U.S.

Two new social forces have led to this rising tide of criticism. The first is the emergence of the domestic "land reform" movement, with the Agribusiness Accountability Project, Rural America, and National Land for People having been the most visible organizations in this movement. Other prominent groups such as the Ralph Nader organization, the Conference on Alternative State and Local Public Policies, and the Exploratory Project for Economic Alternatives, while not devoting their efforts exclusively to agriculture, have placed high priority on change in agriculture in order to meet their overall goals. These groups have a common understanding that the trajectory of social change in U.S. agriculture and its food system over recent decades has had a variety of undesirable impacts on rural people (including, but not limited to, farmers), rural communities, and, in some cases, the urban/consumer population (see, for example, Barnes, 1972). They generally see that "land reform"--that is, increasing access to land--is necessary to improve the rural condition, and some of these groups further advocate control over (if not a dismantling of) the corporate food marketing/processing/distribution/retailing system in order for the agricultural system to better meet the needs of consumers.

The second principal social force that has led to criticism of the American agricultural system is the environmental movement (Buttel and Flinn, 1977; Stockdale, 1977; Buttel and Larson, 1979a). While the early years of environmental movement activity were largely oriented toward issues of concern to the urban population (e.g., air and water pollution, preservation of recreational habitats), considerable attention was directed to the agricultural environment by the early 1970's. A series of studies in the early 1970's demonstrating the high level of resource subsidies in the agricultural system, the prevalence of irreversible deterioration of agroecosystems, the vulnerability of the system to resource shortfalls, and the possible threats to human health from pesticides and food preservatives (see, for example, Pimentel et al., 1973, 1975, 1976; Perelman, 1972; Perelman and Shea, 1972; Steinhart and Steinhart, 1974) were in substantial measure responsible for this increased attention to the environmental problems of agriculture.

The American agricultural system has thus become subject to widespread criticism for its tendencies to marginalize the rural population and degrade the ecosystems on which it is based. The final years of the 1970's have witnessed the publication of tens of books (see, for example, Berry, 1977; Shover, 1977; Lerza and Jacobson, 1975) which see the American agricultural system in the midst of a potentially crippling social, economic, and ecological crisis. Their underlying diagnoses of the malaise or crisis in U.S. agriculture are quite similar, and most have argued that protection of the family farm, curbing of corporate agriculture, and the adoption of organic farming and/or alternative agricultural techniques are important steps in addressing the problems of the food system.

The present paper has three interrelated objectives. The first is to assess the nature and extent of "crisis" in U.S. agriculture. Secondly, I provide a sociological analysis of the diagnoses that critics have set forth concerning the social and ecological problems of the food system. Finally, I make some general observations on the possible roles that agriculture might play in strategies to enhance environmental quality and better meet human needs in the American political economy.

Before discussing the socioeconomic and ecological problems of U.S. agriculture, I wish to make some comments on the issue of whether the agricultural system is in a state of "crisis." In the sense that the notion of "crisis" is typically used--that is, a state of imminent breakdown or collapse, which will lead to social change--I believe it is fair to say that the American system of food raising and distribution is not in a state of crisis. While farmers of all sizes are presently experiencing economic problems, these problems do not appear to be sufficiently severe to either arrest the trend toward concentration and centralization of capital, on one hand, or annihilate small-scale producers, on the other (see, for example, Gardner and Pope, 1978). In other words, the agricultural system continues to reproduce itself, resulting essentially in continued quantitative change toward concentration of assets and sales and a decelerating trend towards demise of the small farmer. The ecological version of the thesis of crisis in agriculture is usually based on the notion that agriculture is resource-intensive (especially energy-intensive) and that energy scarcity will undermine the viability of the system. However, it now seems apparent that even if massive energy supply shortfalls should appear in the future, the agricultural sector will receive priority in energy allocation because of the threat of agricultural disruption setting off food price inflation (as well as a crippling balance of payments situation). Thus it would appear that characterizing the agricultural system as being in a state of imminent crisis or breakdown is exaggerated.

This is not to dismiss the fact that small farmers are continuing to be forced out of agriculture; that the majority of farmers must seek off-farm work in order to remain on the land; that farmers are burdened by high levels of debt, high land prices, and overchanges on purchases of agricultural inputs; or that food prices have rapidly inflated (far in excess of the overall level of inflation) and have been an increasing burden on the budgets of the urban poor. While the agricultural system itself may not be in a state of crisis, this masks the individual crises that afflict its victims each day. In terms of C. Wright Mills" (1959) distinction between "private troubles" and "public issues," the social costs attendant to the course of agricultural change and development remain private troubles rather than public issues.

There is, however, one sense in which U.S. agriculture can be said to be in crisis, in addition to the personal crises attributable to the present structure of agriculture. American agriculture is part of a larger crisis of resource scarcity and redundancy of labor that afflicts the whole of the society. This crisis of the larger society is likely not imminent in the next five to ten years, but it indeed is beginning to prompt many social conflicts and threatening to undermine the energetic basis of the trajectory of development set forth during this century (Buttel and Larson, 1979b). The necessity for allocating scarce energy resources to agriculture in order to curb food inflation and maintain social harmony can only exacerbate the resource problems in other sectors of the economy. The fact that there are now less than 2.8 million farms and less than 4.2 million persons engaged in agriculture (Bratton and Voorheis, 1978), with the number of persons engaged in agriculture progressively declining, implies that agriculture is a modest part of a much larger problem of labor redundancy. The private troubles of agriculture, then, while not threatening the immediate demise of this sector, are contributing to a much larger crisis in the society as a whole.

THE U.S. AGRICULTURAL/FOOD SYSTEM: MAIN FEATURES AND A
SOCIOECONOMIC AND ECOLOGICAL CRITIQUE[1]

It was noted earlier that the U.S. agricultural/food system has been
subjected to a wide range of criticism for what are claimed to be excessive or intolerable socioeconomic and ecological "costs" that have been
paid for apparent increases in labor and land efficiency. This section
parallels those critiques by examining the major structural features of
U.S. agriculture and the food system and the social and environmental
problems that result from each. The analysis will be organized into five
major arenas of agricultural activity: (1) labor and scale of production,
(2) the food delivery system, (3) the relationships of rural people to
the state, (4) provision of agricultural inputs to replenish soil and
control pests, and (5) energy and resource use. Each of these structural
dimensions pertains either to the internal organization of agriculture
or its relations with the larger society. A summary of this discussion
is presented in Table 1. These comments are not meant to be a total, un-
compromising indictment of the U.S. agricultural sector. Rather, the
purpose of this discussion is to point out the many limitations of U.S.
agriculture and to provide an alternative perspective from that of agricultural social scientists who see nothing but perfection and success
in the U.S. food raising and distribution sectors (see, for example,
Pasour and Bullock, 1977).

Labor and Scale of Production

Table 1 summarizes the major structural features and their limitations with respect to the first dimension of agricultural organization.
These interdependent structural features include:

1. substitution of capital for labor (Frundt, 1975).

2. high levels of mechanization (Perelman, 1973a, 1977; Oelhaf,
    1978; Goss, 1976, 1977).

3. an increasing predominance of large-scale, specialized farm
    production units (Rodefeld, 1978; Buttel, 1979a; Belden with
    Forte, 1976).

4. tendencies toward corporate or absentee ownership, vertical
    integration, and the emergence of a full-time hired labor
    force (Rodefeld, 1974, 1978; Buse and Bromley, 1976).

5. persistent (and increasing) levels of inequality (Shover, 1977).

It is useful to emphasize, as alluded to above, that these five aspects of labor and scale of production are interdependent and mutually
reinforcing (see especially, Oelhaf, 1978). For example, the progressive

Table 1. Structural Features of U.S. Agriculture and Socio-Ecological Critiques from the Perspectives of Sustainability and Equity.

Structural Dimensions	Structural Features	Critique of the Structural Features
I. Labor and Scale of Production	1. Substitution of capital for labor 2. High level of mechanization (60% of farm energy use is to power machines) 3. Increasingly large-scale production units 4. Tendencies toward corporate and absentee ownership, and the emergence of a full-time hired agricultural labor force 5. Persistent (and increasing levels of inequality	1. Increase energy intensity 2. Decrease ability of young persons to enter and remain in farming 3. Foster monoculturing and excessive specialization 4. Reduce ability of agriculture to absorb redundant labor 5. Result in rural community decline and polarization among agricultural regions 6. Create tendencies among overproduction and low agricultural returns 7. Result in forced exodus of rural people to urban regions 8. Monoculturing and specialization increase the risk of system failure 9. Result in genetic loss from homogeneous crop breeding
II. Food Delivery System	1. Large amount of processing of food after it leaves the farm 2. Most food consumed outside the region it was produced in 3. Most food delivered to consumer through a series of large, oligopolistic firms	1. Increase energy intensity 2. Reduce food quality 3. Requires high transportation costs (and energy subsidies) 4. Result in high consumer prices 5. Result in hunger in a milieu of abundance and overproduction 6. Farmers and consumers subject to the control of food marketers and retailers 7. Farmer has no direct link to the consumer (results in mutual hostility)

457

Table 1 (continued).

Structural Dimensions	Structural Features	Critique of the Structural Features
III. Relationship of Rural People to the State (Including the Land Grant College Complex)	1. Government agricultural policies favor large farmers through R&D, Extension, and farm programs 2. Rural interests subordinated to urban interests 3. Systematic favoritism toward the interests of agribusiness	1. Increase energy intensity 2. Have hastened the exodus of rural and farm people to the cities (see above, section on labor and scale of production) 3. Contribute to the underdevelopment of rural areas
IV. Agricultural Inputs to Replenish Soil and Control Pests	1. Displacement of organic inputs by inorganic and synthetic inputs 2. Provision of inputs by large, oligopolistic firms	1. Increase energy intensity 2. Cause decline in soil structure, organic matter content, and microbiotic soil life 3. Increase erosion 4. Manures and other biological residues tend to be wasted 5. Facilitate monoculturing and regional specialization 6. Increase pollution from run-off 7. Result in poisoning of food, soil, and people 8. Reduce food quality (especially with respect to vitamin content) 9. Monocultures aggravate pest problems 10. Increase risk of carcinogenic effects 11. Make farmers dependent upon extra-community elites for agricultural inputs 12. Subject farmers to the exploitation of high administered prices from input providers

458

Table 1 (continued).

Structural Dimensions	Structural Features	Critique of the Structural Features
V. Energy and Resource Use	1. High reliance on fossil fuels for inputs to food production and to deliver processed food and fiber 2. Dependence on "cheap" inanimate energy 3. High energy intensity and sharp negative net energy (avg. energy ratio of 0.1) 4. Destruction of agro-ecosystems	1. Present trajectories of energy and resource use limit the ability of agriculture to be an energy-producing sector 2. Present trajectories may irreversibly depreciate the level of agricultural resources available to future generations 3. System is vulnerable to resource shortfalls 4. Present trajectories lead to avoidance of questions of distribution and equity

substitution of capital for labor in U.S. agriculture has been in large part concerned with farmers' acquisition of instruments of mechanization, which in turn facilitate large production units, foster inequality, and make farm property attractive for corporate investment. From another vantage point, an alternation in one or more of the five aspects of labor and scale of production will essentially entail a drastic modification of the other related structural elements.

Table 1 lists nine major "social costs" or "externalities" that may be attributed to the present condition of U.S. agriculture with respect to labor and scale of production. The first consequence, and the one most central to the thrust of this paper, is that of increased energy intensity (see, for example, Perelman, 1972, 1973a, 1976, 1977; Perelman and Shea, 1972; Belden with Forte, 1976; Oelhaf, 1976). Mechanization is central to the character of both labor and scale of production in U.S. agriculture (Buttel, 1979a) and the energy intensity of agriculture (Goss, 1976; Oelhaf, 1978). Over 60 percent of all energy utilized on farms is for powering machinery (Oelhaf, 1978).

Nevertheless, mechanization and the other related aspects of labor and scale of production have a variety of other undesirable social consequences. Substitution of capital for labor, mechanization, and the emergence of large--often corporate--farms decrease the ability of young persons to enter and remain in farming, reduce the ability of agriculture to absorb redundant labor, result in forced exodus of rural people to urban regions, and cause rural community decline and polarization of agricultural regions (Belden with Forte, 1976; Buttel, 1979b; Rodefeld, 1974; Goss, 1976; Shover, 1977; Goldschmidt, 1978; Flora et al., 1977). In addition to these impacts on the careers and livelihoods of rural people, other social and ecological effects may be noted. The first is that of fostering monoculturing and high levels of specialization (Hill and Ramsay, 1977; Perelman, 1973b). Monoculturing and specialization in turn increase the risk of system failure--that is, the possibility that a given farm or agricultural region will be adversely affected by some exogenous perturbation such as a drought or downturn in the price of a commodity (Oelhaf, 1978). Monoculturing has further resulted in what many observers see as a dangerous genetic loss from homogeneous plant breeding (Clark, 1975: 64).

Last, but not least, we may identify the chronic tendency toward overproduction (and resultant unstable agricultural returns) as another important consequence of the character of labor and scale of production in present-day agriculture (Frundt, 1975). Although we may regard this tendency toward overproduction as being endemic in Western agricultural systems organized under the rubric of capitalism (Newby, 1978), this overproduction tendency is particularly strong in the U.S. In part, overproduction has resulted from the rapid technological advance in U.S. agriculture (Johnson, 1972) which of course parallels the progressive mechanization and increases in farm sizes discussed above. Unlike most agricultural systems in Western Europe that retain a substantial component of small-scale, diversified "peasant" farming, most U.S. farmers have only one possible option for adapting to rising costs and unstable commodity prices--produce more (Frundt, 1975; Newby, 1978; Belden with Forte, 1976). Thus the highly mechanized, large-scale farming system of the U.S. (with associated high capital costs and indebtedness) aggravates tendencies toward overproduction in agriculture, resulting in low returns and incomes among farmers.

The Food Delivery System

The following are the major characteristics of the U.S. food delivery system (again, see Table 1):

1. there is a large amount of processing of food after it leaves the farm (Hightower, 1975; Belden with Forte, 1976; Hall, 1974).

2. most food is consumed outside the region it was produced in (Oelhaf, 1978).

3. most food is delivered to the consumer through a series of large, oligopolistic firms (Hightower, 1975; Shover, 1977; Frundt, 1975).

An initial consequence of the structure of the food delivery system is again that of increased energy intensity. High levels of food processing and widespread transportation of processed foods both add to the level of energy subsidy required for the agricultural/food system (Steinhart and Steinhart, 1974a, 1974b). In fact, the energy subsidies in the food delivery system clearly overshadow those of the food raising sector itself (Steinhart and Steinhart, 1974a). These high levels of food processing and transportation also lead to higher prices than would be the case if food were processed less and consumed within the region it was produced in (McLeod, 1976; Belden with Forte, 1976).

Many physical and biological scientists have become concerned that the U.S. food delivery system has resulted in lower food quality (Hall, 1974). Overprocessing, excessive use of preservatives, and diminution of nutritional quality have all been argued to be results of the marketing strategies of large, oligopolistic food corporations (Hightower, 1975; Robbins, 1974). Perhaps the ultimate deleterious consequence of the present structuring of the food delivery system is that of substantial hunger in the milieu of abundance and overproduction. The tendencies toward high food prices (along with overprocessing, high transportation costs, and nutritional declines) contribute most to this paradox of abundance with deprivation (George, 1977; Kotz, 1971).

Critics of the U.S. food delivery system have tended to place most emphasis on the control that food marketers, processors and retailers have over the consumer (see especially Hightower, 1975; Robbins, 1974; Hall, 1974). However, it is important to note that the control of food firms extends to the farmer as well. Farmers characteristically are "price-takers," and the centralization of corporate control over the acquisition of food commodities may be seen to have equally undesirable consequences for the farmer and the consumer. A final impact of the food delivery system on the farmer and consumer is that the direct link-ages between food producers and food consumers have been largely severed. Farmers market their food to corporate food firms--not the consumer. As a result, there continues to be much mutual hostility between farmers and consumers (Merrill, 1976). We will note below some ways in which certain fractions of farmers and consumers might well have some common interests in agriculture's role in the emergence of a sustainable society.

Relationships of Rural People to the State

Most aspects of agricultural organization discussed above are re-lated in some way to politics and policy determination--that is, to the state. A critical aspect of agricultural structure, then, is the nature of the role that the state plays in subsidizing or penalizing the interests of various groups associated with the agricultural/food system. Three major aspects of the relationships of rural people to the state are:

1. government agricultural policies (e.g., R & D, Extension, and Farm Programs) favor large farmers over smaller farmers (Bonnen, 1968; Ford, 1973; Hightower, 1973; Marshall and Thompson, 1976).[2]

2. state policy toward agriculture has systematically favored the interests of agribusiness over those of the farmer and consumer (Frundt, 1975).

3. state policy has generally subordinated the interests of rural people to those of urban people (Shover, 1977).

Again, a fundamental adverse consequence of these relationships of rural people to the state is that of state policies encouraging and, in effect, subsidizing large-scale, energy-intensive farm units. As Marshall and Thompson (1976: 2-4) note, large farms use proportionately more energy-intensive inputs (large machinery, chemical fertilizers, and pesticides) than do small farmers (see also Oelhaf, 1978: Ch. 4; Buttel, 1979a; Buttel and Larson, 1979a). State policy has thus encouraged a type of agricultural structure that increases the dependence of farmers on nonrenewable energy resources.

State policy has also contributed to the types of inequalities in rural areas discussed above under the rubric of labor and scale of pro-duction. These policies have both hastened the exodus of farm and rural people to cities, and contributed to the underdevelopment of many rural areas. In sum, the present structure of U.S. agriculture should not be regarded as "natural" or the necessary result of the social organization of an advanced industrial society such as that of the U.S. Indeed, this agricultural structure has been molded by purposive decisions made by state officials, in conjunction with their interest group clienteles. The differences in agricultural structures among the Western societies attest to the extent to which they may be influenced by state policies (Newby, 1978; Buttel, 1979a).

Agricultural Inputs to Replenish Soil and Control Pests

Two major aspects of the provision of agricultural inputs to re-plenish soil and control pests are of concern in this paper:

1. displacement of organic inputs by inorganic and synthetic in-puts (Belanger, 1976; Oelhaf, 1978; Commoner, 1976).

2. provision of inputs by large, oligopolistic firms (Hightower, 1975; Frundt, 1975).

As alluded to above, inorganic and synthetic inputs are more energy intensive than those which farmers at one time provided from their own land (e.g., animal manures, green manures). Thus, these new modes of replenishing soil and controlling pests add to the other tendencies dis-cussed above for increased energy intensity of agricultural production.

Lastly, farmers are subject to the same types of oligopolistic control noted above with respect to food marketers when they purchase agricul-tural inputs. These inputs are manufactured and marketed in a fashion not unlike that of their food industry counterparts, and many observers have pointed out that input providers extract high profits from their farmer clients (Hightower, 1975; Frundt, 1975).

Energy and Resource Use

Many of our comments thus far have touched on the energetic and en-vironmental character of present-day U.S. agriculture. Energy and re-source use are here considered to be a separate identifiable parameter of agricultural organization in light of the fact that agriculture essen-tially is a socio-ecological system for converting solar energy and the earth's nutrients into food and fiber. Therefore, the manner in which agriculture relates to the natural environment is quite important. Four major features of energy and resource use in U.S. agriculture are:

1. high reliance on fossil fuels for inputs to food production and to deliver processed food and fiber (Clark, 1974; Steinhart and Steinhart, 1974a, 1974b).

2. dependence on inexpensive inanimate energy (Clark, 1974; Merrill, 1976: 320).

3. high energy intensity and sharply negative net energy of agricultural production (Steinhart and Steinhart, 1974a, 1974b; Pimentel et al., 1973; Slesser, 1976; Oelhaf, 1978).[3]

4. destruction of agro-ecosystems (Perelman, 1977; Watt et al., 1977; Oelhaf, 1978; Brink et al., 1977; Carter, 1977; van Bavel, 1977), especially through soil erosion, salinization, loss of organic matter, soil sterility, and diminution of water tables.

Each of these aspects of energy and resource use in U.S. agriculture has been discussed above--particularly with respect to energy utilization. As the Steinharts (1974a) have estimated, the energy ratio of the U.S. food system (the ratio of calories of food energy produced per calorie of inanimate energy input) has declined from about 1.0 in 1900 to about 0.1 in the 1970's. The fact that approximately 10 calories of inanimate energy subsidy are required to produce, process, distribute, and prepare one calorie of food should temper the enthusiasm expressed by boosters of the U.S. food system. However, it is, of course, dangerous to look only at the energy efficiency of agriculture and ignore the social and economic parameters of the food system. It is interesting to note that after the pioneering energy input-output analyses of American agriculture in the early 1970's (especially those of Pimentel et al., 1973; Steinhart and Steinhart, 1974a; Perelman, 1973a), there emerged a literature quite critical of such "energy analyses" (see especially Pasour and Bullock, 1977; and Connor, 1977, for a summary). The major criticism of the energy approach has been that food has far more value than its energy content, otherwise humans would be better off to eat petroleum or stand in the sun. It is emphasized that agriculture accounts for only three to four percent of total societal energy consumption and that substantial reductions in energy use in this sector will have only minimal impacts on total energy consumption in the U.S. We will return to this issue in greater depth below.

The fourth aspect of resource use in agriculture--destruction of agroecosystems--was also touched on briefly above. Soil erosion is certainly the most urgent of these trends (see especially van Bavel, 1977). Nevertheless, soil sterility, salinization, diminution of water tables, and loss of organic matter are also pressing concerns for the sustainability of agricultural systems in the future (Watt et al., 1977). Present trajectories of energy and resource use thus may irreversibly depreciate the level of agricultural resources available to future generations. As Perelman (1977) points out, present agricultural practices resemble more the mining of a nonrenewable resource than they do the sustained yield of a renewable resource. Further, as Lockeretz et al. (1975) have argued, the present structure of energy and resource use in agriculture make that agriculture vulnerable to resource shortfalls--

particularly with respect to inanimate energy. Current projections for
the availability of inanimate energy resources by 1985-1990 (see Lovins,
1977, for a summary of these studies) may well portend a difficult crisis
of agricultural adjustment within the next two decades.

Lastly, it may be argued that current trajectories of energy and
resource use in agriculture lead to avoidance of the questions of distribution and equity. Schnaiberg (1975) and Morrison (1976) have pointed
out, when the economy is growing--or when there is widespread confidence
in growth in the future--subordinate strata tend to be content with
getting their constant share of an increasing "pie." The same phenomenon,
I would argue, holds in agriculture as well. The trajectory of agricultural expansion--witnessed over the past several decades along with
its underlying basis in the mining of oil and soil--tends to lead both
farmers and consumers to be complacent with the present distributional
character of agricultural production and exchange relations. Farmers
continue to see their key adaptive strategy as enlarging their operations
and increasing their productivity on an individual basis (i.e., more
mechanization and use of inanimate energy). Consumers, on the other
hand, tend to view accelerated agricultural productivity as holding down
food prices. As a result, subordinate rural strata and consumers tend
not to see any compelling need for redistribution of agricultural resources or redirection of the food delivery system. In sum, progressive
expansion of agricultural production and energy/resource consumption
deflect attention away from the distributional parameters which must be
a cornerstone of future social change if it is to yield a more progressive, ecologically sustainable society.

NEOPOPULIST STRATEGIES FOR SOCIAL CHANGE IN AGRICULTURE:
A FRIENDLY CRITIQUE

The social and ecological criticisms of the U.S. agricultural and
food systems which we have summarized above have led to a series of over-
lapping proposals or rallying points for new directions in agricultural
and food policy. These images of or directions for change may be considered neopopulist, in both the best and worst senses of the term. By neopopulist, we mean that these proposals for change assume the persistence
of a system of private property in agriculture and seek to perfect that
system, in continuity with American populism of the late 19th century
(Rogin, 1966). The ideological focus of these neopopulist arguments for
change is essentially "reform leftist"--that is, critical of the status
quo and of dominant economic interests that profit most from the system,
but (for pragmatic or other reasons) not overtly radical or socialist
in character. Neopopulism thus tends to reflect deeply felt dissatisfactions with the present system of agriculture and food distribution,
but may tend to lack a comprehensive analysis of the economic system so
as to accurately estimate the viability of its proposals (either in terms

of possibilities for implementation or their consequences, if implemented).

There have been six interrelated cornerstones of the neopopulist agenda for change in American agriculture. These include:

1. curbing or eliminating corporate ownership of farms
2. protecting and encouraging small, family-sized farms
3. demechanization and appropriate technology
4. organic agriculture
5. localism in food production and consumption
6. agricultural self-sufficiency

The purpose of this portion of the paper will be to present a friendly critique of each of these directions for change. Before proceeding, I wish to emphasize that each of these neopopulist proposals reflects a potentially progressive strategy for addressing the many problems of the agricultural sector. However, as I will expand upon below, each tends to be presented in a highly utopian manner which may obscure difficulties in implementation, overestimate potential benefits, or ignore the range of other associated social changes necessary for the strategy to bear fruit. Typically, advocacy of one of these neopopulist strategies will be based on an analysis of only the superficial appearances of a problem, rather than the root causes of the problem. The ultimate goal of this critique is to demonstrate how each strategy may be seen as part of a larger agenda for change, rather than each strategy being pursued in isolation from the others with self-defeating, utopian single-mindedness.

Curbing or eliminating (nonfarm, nonclosely-held) corporate operation of farms was the issue on which original domestic land reform movement organizations first cut their teeth. The underlying assumption behind arresting the spread of corporate agriculture was that corporate farms were receiving unfair advantages (especially tax breaks due to their incorporated legal organization) relative to "family farmers" and were outcompeting and displacing family-sized farming operations (Ray, 1969). Movement proponents have made extensive efforts to induce the federal and state governments to restrict corporate ownership of farms. Limited successes in state legislation have been registered during the 1970's (Belden et al., 1979).

Several dubious or incomplete assumptions underlie efforts aimed at curbing corporate operation of farms. The first is that operation of farms by large, nonfamily corporations is widespread. The second assumption is that farms owned by large, nonfarm corporations exhibit profit rates substantially in excess of family-sized or large farms operated as unincorporated sole proprietorships. A third assumption is that if competition from corporate farms were eliminated, the viability of the family-sized farm would increase. Fourthly, corporate farms were seen to be wasteful of energy and resources (Bible, 1978). A final, usually implicit, assumption has been that the most pernicious form of nonfarm corporate penetration in the food system is in agriculture itself, rather than in marketing, processing or retailing of agricultural commodities.

Each of these assumptions in support of curbing corporate farms is either inaccurate or a partial oversimplification. While definitive data are lacking, it is apparent that large, nonfarm corporations likely account for less than ten percent of agricultural land ownership or sales (Rodefeld, 1979). While it should be acknowledged that the proportion of land controlled by such corporations is increasing (Rodefeld, 1978), the prevalence of nonfarm corporate-owned operations would appear to be sufficiently small so that the difficulties of the small- or family-type (i.e., petty bourgeois) farm cannot be attributed solely to corporate agriculture. Secondly, the persistent economic difficulties of farmers, along with the problems of routinizing agricultural operations in order to effectively utilize a full-time hired labor force (Mann and Dickinson, 1978), have tended to serve as limitations on the profitability of nonfarm corporations engaging in farming: Cordtz (1978) in fact reports that many corporate farming operations have encountered severe economic difficulties and eventually ceased farming operations.

The most important issue in the debate over nonfarm corporate operation of farms is whether such farms are outcompeting and squeezing out smaller, "family-type" farms, or, on the other hand, whether the major problems of survival of family-type farms lie in areas other than "unfair" competition from corporations. While not to dismiss the fact that there may be some localized tendencies (especially in California, Florida, and irrigated agricultural regions) for better-financed corporation farms to supplant smaller operations, the major economic difficulties of family-sized farms derive more from chronic overproduction and price instability in agriculture and the exploitation of farms by nonfarm, nonagricultural corporations (input suppliers and output marketers) in the sphere of exchange than from direct corporate competition (Frundt, 1975). Further, while corporate farms do appear to be more energy- and resource-intensive than smaller farms (Buttel and Larson, 1979a), these farms are likely no more energy wasteful than other large-scale industrial farms operated as sole proprietorships. Finally, the corporate farming issue may serve to deflect attention from the fact that nonfarm corporations need not own and operate agricultural land in order to exercise control over agriculture (see, for example, Davis, 1979). The most important issue, I would argue, is the impact of corporation control of the entire food sector, including factors such as exploitation of farmers through contractual integration; the elimination of marketing options as a result of the ascendancy of a centralized, integrated food processing and distribution system; and the vulnerability of farmers to exploitation in the administered price systems of input providers and output marketers (Frundt, 1975). Essentially the corporate farming issue can be summarized by asking: Will the survival of family-type farms be greatly enhanced if the operation of farms by nonfarm corporations is eliminated? The answer to this question is likely, "no."

Protecting or bringing about a renaissance of the "family" farm is often considered to be the opposite side of the same coin of curbing corporate agriculture, i.e. broadening access to land and reducing resource extravagance. Family farms are often taken to be synonymous with non-corporate farms, which conceals an immense amount of variability in farm types (Rodefeld, 1978). However, most neopopulist intellectuals and reform advocates see the family farm as being a small-scale farm in which the owner and his or her family provides the vast majority of management and operational labor. Granting this provisional definition of a family farm, there are two limitations to this idealized conceptualization. The first is that such family-type organization is compatible with technological systems that enable the family to operate an extremely large-- and very resource- and energy-intensive--operation. Secondly, the majority of "small" farms is highly dependent on off-farm income (Marshall and Thompson, 1976; Cavazzani, 1977). Thus a significant fraction of ostensibly family farms are likely as resource-extravagant as nonfarm corporate-operated farms, while the majority of family farms is insufficiently viable to earn an adequate income for the farm family without off-farm work. Movement proponents, then, may be idealizing a somewhat dated image of the independent, small- or modest-scale family farmer who derives most the family income from agriculture.

Many proponents of social change in agriculture have recognized that merely banning corporate farms will do little to save the disappearing family-type farm and that to do so will require major alterations in governmental policy (see especially Belden with Forte, 1976). The major requirement will be to direct government policy away from price supports and commodity programs which concentrate government payments among larger farms (Ford, 1973) and toward federal "income supports" which limit payments to larger farms and encourage modest scale operations (Belden with Forte, 1976). Instead of price supports which add commodity payments to the price of foodstuffs and have regressive economic impacts on the low income household, income supports would be totally financed from the government treasury and place more of the burden on the high income taxpayer. Such a program, which historically was first proposed by Charles F. Brannan, Secretary of Agriculture in the Truman administration, has a number of desirable features. It has, however, two major interrelated limitations. The first is the fact that in order for the program to be successful, it must be sufficiently extensive to counteract the strong tendencies toward concentration and centralization of capital in a capitalist economy. Its cost would therefore be quite high. The second problem is that such a program would provoke massive opposition because it would undermine the economic position of the most powerful and well-organized farmers--namely, large farmers--and create anxiety on the part of corporations such as food processors who prefer to deal with large farmers (Goss et al., 1978). In addition, the high cost of the program in an era of a protected fiscal crisis of the state (O'Connor, 1973) would make such legislation quite difficult to pass. Because of the likely opposition to a form of a Brannon Plan among privileged farmers, the Farm Bureau, and most segments of agribusiness, the Plan would have to have strong support from the working class. Working class support for this program may eventually be forthcoming as food price inflation continues to outstrip the overall rate of inflation (and thus dramatically reduce the effective purchasing power of the poor; Nulty, 1977), but this is an unlikely prospect in the near future.

Demechanization and "appropriate technology" have become major proposals for change among critics of the U.S. agricultural system. Demechanization and appropriate technology are usually assumed to involve employing smaller-scale machinery (or, in some cases, returning to animal or human power) in order to more effectively utilize surplus labor and reduce energy consumption. In their most crude form, arguments for implementing appropriate technology in agriculture assume a reductionistic technological determinism; large-scale technology is viewed to be alienating, wasteful of resources, a cause of economic inequality among farmers, and the major factor behind the economic insecurity of migrant farm workers. Some observers even suggest that the rapid development of mechanization technology by the land grant colleges essentially forces all farmers to mechanize in order to remain competitive (Hightower, 1973).

The major difficulty with enthusiastic pronouncements about this resource-conserving, "liberatory," and "revolutionary" potential of "appropriate technology" is that it begs the questions of how we decide if a technology is appropriate or inappropriate or what kinds of social changes are necessary to implement a technology. If we ask those questions, it becomes clear that technology is profoundly embedded in a larger social structure, and that technical fixes are both unlikely to be implemented and need not imply evolutionary or revolutionary social change. We may identify at least three major reasons for the extensive mechanization of U.S. agriculture: (1) large-scale, mechanized farms have been encouraged by government policy (see above), (2) mechanization and increased scale of operations are rational responses for a farm operator facing a cost-price squeeze, and (3) mechanization will be implemented if farmers are threatened with an unreliable or rebellious labor force (Friedland et al., 1978). Merely introducing alternative technologies will do little to change the underlying forces--state agricultural policy, overproduction, and agricultural class conflict-- that have led to mechanization in the first place.

Organic agriculture is a technological phenomenon closely akin to the small-scale machinery we referred to under the rubric of "appropriate technology." In fact, organic agriculture is often taken to be an integral part of appropriate technology, since organic farming techniques tend to be most suitable for small-scale operations (Oelhaf, 1978; Powers et al., 1978). Organic farming is a system of agriculture which eschews manufactured fertilizers and pesticides for which it substitutes natural or organic sources of fertility (e.g., legumes, animal and green manures, crop rotations) and biological strategies of pest control.

Organic farming has been demonstrated to be remarkably successful in terms of economic viability and energy conservation (Lockeretz et al., 1978; Klepper et al., 1977). Organic farming would appear to be particularly useful for small-scale farmers who face chronic shortages of capital, since organic farming dramatically reduces input costs (Buttel et al., 1979).

However, it would appear quite unlikely that organic farming can revolutionize agriculture from below. Introduction and perfection of organic methods will not in and of themselves alter the fundamental forces leading to increased farm size and energy intensity in agriculture. These forces for increased farm size which were previously discussed will make widespread adoption of organic farming techniques increasingly infeasible, particularly because large-scale farms tend to be incompatible with diversified, mixed-crop and livestock operations necessary to make maximum use of the natural recycling properties of agroecosystems (Oelhaf, 1978). Similar to demechanization and appropriate technology, organic farming on a wide scale would appear to be possible only if the incentives for and forces leading to increased farm size can be attenuated. In other words, organic farming is unlikely to lead to major social change; rather, the opposite must prevail if organic farming and energy-conserving forms of agriculture are to appear.

A fifth suggested direction for change in agriculture is localism in food production and consumption (see especially Belden with Forte, 1976). The rationale for localism in the food system is that local production for local use will dramatically reduce energy and resource consumption in the processing and marketing sectors of the food system. Localism can come about in several forms. The most prevalent is direct marketing of agricultural produce from farmer to the consumer, typically through roadside stands or farmers' markets. A second, more comprehensive, mechanism is the emergence of community canneries or flour mills which enable essentially year-around consumption of locally-produced food commodities. A frequently unrecognized positive benefit of a potential move toward localism in the food system is that the jobs created in cooperatives or community canneries would provide badly needed employment in rural communities (Britt et al., 1978). Finally, localism in food production would imply greater regional crop diversity, be most consistent with the diverse enterprise mixes useful in organic farming, and would help reduce soil erosion and other forms of land degradation that result from monoculturing.

The focal point for decentralization of the food system is the consumer cooperative. Cooperative forms of social organization have a number of extremely attractive features. Coops have great potential for better meeting the needs of small farmers and the poor who have been marginalized by recent trends toward stagflation. Cooperatives facilitate democratization and local participation in and control of economic activities. Cooperatives can circumvent the centralized food distribution system, increasing farmers' incomes and reducing consumers' food costs (Belden with Forte, 1976; Schaaf, 1977). However, coops also have a number of limitations when they attempt to function in the interstices of a capitalist political economy. Sound business practices are essential to ensure survival. "Success" may get out of hand, causing large coops to function in a fashion not unlike comparable agribusiness firms. Working people tend to lack the self-confidence necessary to be an effective participant in a cooperative venture. Sustained commitment to the coop may be problematic, and a lack of voluntary commitment may force the coop to hire professional managers and full-time employees (Schaaf, 1977). Finally, the fact that a large portion of the U.S. population lives in large cities which have limited accessibility to sufficient local farm land to provide for local needs curtails the potential of localism or decentralization in the food delivery system.

The final aspect of neopopulist agendas for social change in agriculture is self-sufficiency or self-reliance. In part, localism can be considered a form of self-sufficiency at a community or regional level. However, it is often suggested that self-sufficiency should extend to the individual or household as well. By adopting self-sufficient lifestyles, farmers and rural residents can at least partially insulate themselves from the vagaries of the commercial economy and sharply reduce their energy and materials consumption. Self-reliance is usually seen to be closely linked with organic farming, since organic farming techniques allow subsistence food production with a minimum of off-farm inputs (including, but not limited, to energy and resource-related inputs; Youngberg, 1977).

Self-reliance has one progressive aspect as a strategy for meeting material needs. Self-sufficiency enables those marginalized by the political-economic system to assert some measure of control over their lives and adapt to poverty and unemployment. However, self-reliance has a number of major limitations as a long-term strategy for social change. For one, self-reliance tends to be an inherently individual strategy and makes no contribution to an overall organized movement for change. Secondly, self-reliance may inadvertently serve the interests of capital. Self-reliant members of the lumpenproletariat are not politically threatening and do not require welfare expenditures. Insofar as many of the rural poor for wages, self-reliance lowers their reproduction costs and enables employers to pay lower wages, and hence increases their exploitation.

Each of the neopopulist strategies for change in agriculture just discussed has a common underlying limitation--the lack of a comprehensive perspective on the functioning of agriculture and the food system in a capitalist economy. Each tends to be aimed at fighting social or technological "enemies"--corporate farms, large-scale technology, fertilizers and pesticides--that are the immediate appearances of problems, but are only partially the underlying roots of these

problems. These strategies all have a number of limitations owning to
their tendencies to ignore how changes in production relations are necessary to alter the trajectory of agricultural development that both fails
to meet human needs and unnessarily degrades the physical environment.

It should be mentioned once more that these comments should be
construed as a friendly critique. A more beneficient and resource-
conserving agricultural system indeed is incompatible with large-scale
corporate agriculture, and will certainly be a system of modest scale
farms, using organic techniques, and orienting the majority of production toward community or regional markets. The criticisms detailed
above are thus not meant to depreciate the wisdom of the goals sought by
neopopulist analysts of the agricultural system. Indeed, the purpose
of the section that follows is to specify how these insights may be
incorporated in a broader movement for social change in the U.S.

FORCES FOR CHANGE IN THE FOOD SYSTEM

It was noted that while it is premature to suggest that the U.S.
agricultural system is in a state of crisis, this system may be entering an era in which its material, political, and ideological bases of
support are tenuous. Understanding the social forces that are currently
affecting the food system is essential in order to anticipate the most
effective "levers" for change. This portion of the paper identifies
five major emergent forces in the food system and their implications for
social change.

Perhaps the most pervasive expression of the malaise of agriculture
is the progressive food inflation the U.S. has experienced throughout
the 1970's. Multy (1977) points out that food inflation has raced ahead
of the overall rate of inflation (along with disproportionately high
rates of inflation in other "necessities" of life--housing, medical
care, and consumer use of "basic energy," i.e. direct energy consumption
in the home). She points out that food inflation has averaged 7.8 percent per year while inflation in "non-necessity"--essentially luxury--
commodities has averaged 5.2 percent per annum during the decade. Food
inflation is important in several respects. For the poor, food is an
extremely high proportion of the budget. Nulty (1977: 607) demonstrates
that the second decile of income earners spends slightly over 44 percent
of their disposable incomes on food, on the average (while families in
the eighth decile spend an average of 19.1 percent of their disposable
incomes on food). Rapid inflation in food prices thus dramatically
lowers the purchasing power of low-income households relative to higher
income households. Therefore, food inflation undermines the ideological
position that the food system has evolved in a beneficent way--that the
structure of agricultural system can be justified because it produces
large quantities of inexpensive food. In other words, higher food prices

threaten to exacerbate the legitimation crisis (Habermas, 1975) of the state.

The second aspect of the changing milieu of agriculture and resource management is energy scarcity and energy price inflation. Energy scarcity is important for reasons that go bdyond its effects on energy price inflation. Energy scarcity makes the agricultural sector increasingly vulnerable to energy supply shortfalls. Research conducted by economists, for example, has demonstrated that energy demand in agriculture is highly price inelastic; because the sector has very inflexible demands for energy, existing quantities of energy are needed, almost regardless of price (Buttel et al., 1979). However, energy price inflation is also crucial. Energy price inflation contributes significantly to food price inflation (Belden with Forte, 1976), particularly because of the heavy use of energy in the food processing and marketing industries (especially due to long-haul transport in a regionally specialized agricultural system).

The environmental difficulties experienced by agriculture are a further aspect of the growing malaise of agriculture in the U.S. The ultimate implication of degradation of agroecosystems is decline in agricultural productivity. Perelman (1976) has noted that agricultural productivity in the U.S. has begun to level off during the 1970's. This plateau of productivity is apparently due in part to plant and animal physiology limits to production (Jensen, 1978). However, Pimentel et al. (1975, 1976) point out how land degradation and loss of agricultural land are irreversibly depreciating the productivity of the land resource. Environmental degradation and productivity plateaus contribute to the food inflation and energy scarcity dilemmas of modern agriculture. For example, Pimentel et al. (1976) have noted that productivity stagnation can be traced in substantial measure to soil erosion; soil erosion in return requires additional energy inputs (particularly in the form of fertilizer) in order to compensate for the fertility declines due to erosion. Inflation in food commodity prices therefore occurs because production increases cannot keep pace with increased production costs associated with energy inputs. In sum, environmental degradation and leveling off of productivity are nascent forces in the political economy of agriculture that may further erode the legitimacy of the agricultural system.

A further emergent force in the agricultural/food system may be a diminished--or at least the strong potential for a diminished--antinomy between the farmer and the working class. Historically farmers and the working class have been politically divided because policies that benefit farmers in general (especially higher "farm gate" prices through federal price supports) tend to disadvantage working class consumers by way of higher retail food prices (Belden with Forte, 1976). However, as the farmer's share of the retail food dollar decreases--the most recent figure being roughly 38 percent--policies that boost farm income have relatively less effect on the purchasing power of the working class.

The farmer's share of the retail food dollar has decreased primarily because of the expansion of the food processing industries and the progressively higher costs associated with transportation in a regionally
specialized agricultural production system. Many analysts have come to
suggest that both farmers and the working class will come to recognize
that the interests of neither group are served by the agribusiness sector
and that farmers and the working class may have some basis for uniting
around their common concerns (Belden with Forte, 1976; Berry, 1977).

Two final aspects of the changing political-economic milieu of
agriculture are themselves exogenous to the agricultural system itself,
but may have important relations to the determination of future agricultural policies.. These two forces are the interrelated phenomena of
economic stagnation and the fiscal crisis of the state (see, for example,
Sherman, 1976; O'Connor, 1973). These forces may become particularly
important in future agricultural politics because they imply that there
are limits to the traditional "solutions" to agriculture and food problems. Economic stagnation (along with persistent inflation and unemployment) threatens to usher in a situation in which rising food prices can
no longer be compensated for by rapid growth in disposable family income.
The fiscal difficulties of governments--especially the federal govern-
ment--portend an era in which the state apparatus is limited in its
ability to meliorate social problems related to the accumulation and
legitimation functions of the state. The state increasingly faces an
important contradiction: the preferred mode for addressing problems
of economic stagnation and balance of payments deficits is to increase
exports of agricultural goods. However, exports of agricultural commodities will tend to exacerbate food (and overall) inflation and thereby
present legitimation problems on the part of the working class. Thus the
state may increasingly face a situation of impasse and stalemate with
respect to agricultural and food problems. This impasse and stalemate
may then present opportunities for new policy initiatives, or encourage
farmers and workers to seek local and regional strategies to address
their common interests for change in the food system.

FARMERS: A PROGRESSIVE FORCE FOR SOCIAL CHANGE?

What most neopopulists take as an article of faith and what I look
upon as a hopeful possibility is that certain fractions of farmers and
the working class can unite in various ways to pursue common interests
in change in the food system. Most neopopulist observers see farmers
as the progressive force, since these persons can be most readily aroused
over issues such as curbing corporate farming or preserving the family
farm. Neopopulists hope to bring the subordinate working classes along,
making appeals along the lines that the family farm is most efficient and
can provide food at reasonable prices. Orthodox Marxists, on the other
hand, take the progressivity of the urban working class as an article of

faith while looking upon petty commodity producers as the anarchronistic remnants of a previous mode of production. Neither perspective can serve as a guide for change in the food system. The neopopulist dream of uniting two million petty bourgeois farmers with the peripheral support of urban people is unrealistic. Small farmers are an important political force because of their small numbers, difficulties in organization, and marginality to the political process. On the other hand, capitalist development has not annihilated petty commodity production ("propertied labor") in agriculture. While petty commodity producers occupy an ambiguous class position in advanced capitalism, petty commodity production will likely continue to be a predominant form of production in agriculture (Mann and Dickinson, 1978).

Except for neopopulist idealism, it is fair to say that the vast majority of social scientists has written off farmers and rural people as progressive agents of social change. The reason for discounting the change potential of farmers and rural people is their political-ideological conservatism. The prevailing liberal, pluralist assumption about the course of progressive social change is that such change is instituted, if not initiated, by the state. Conservative farmers and rural people are seen as resisting liberal initiatives at state regulation of private decision making or state support for deprived groups. Orthodox Marxists, on the other hand, see petty commodity producers as being tied to the interests of capital and casting their lot with interests of the dominant class.

Young and Newton (1979) have made some noteworthy observations that run counter to the presumption of a lack of progressivity on the part of farmers and rural people generally. They have noted that the apparent conservatism of rural people can be traced to their actual or preferred attachment to private property--either agricultural or small business property. Young and Newton suggest that the ideological predilections of rural people can be best decomposed in terms of two elements: (1) a strong belief in "free enterprise" (which is used incorrectly by large-scale capital to describe their actions), and (2) some amount of resentment of big business and big government. Their argument is that the principal ideological vacuum among rural people is their inability to identify who wins and who loses in an economy dominated by large-scale capital. However, Young and Newton indicate that it is a mistake to dismiss the ideological predispositions of rural people as being anachronistic and useless as a lever for bringing about change. These ideologies, in their view, are both deeply held and reflect realistic dissatisfactions with the political economy. Ideological support for free enterprise, for example, can be a powerful critique of an agricultural system which increasingly concentrates property in the hands of 100,000 large-scale farmers. Such an ideology also contrasts loudly with the marginalization of small businesses in rural communities or the dominance over rural communities by absentee-owned corporations. Essentially one can raise the question: if free enterprise is so valuable and appropriate for a society such as the U.S., why is it that our enterprise system is so unfree--that only a few persons hold productive property and the majority of the population has little or no access to and security with property? If one begins to take the ideologies of rural people seriously, it becomes possible to envision a disparate collection of progressive strategies and policies that are compatible with these ideologies. Several of these will be discussed below.

Before considering some potentially progressive strategies for rural social change, several issues remain with regard to the question of uniting certain fractions of farmers, rural people, and the working class. The first issue pertains to the observation made earlier that the maintenance of a traditional system of modest-scale "independent family farms" is unrealistic in an economy whose major law of motion is the concentration and centralization of capital. This neopopulist image for change neglects the necessity to alter agricultural production relations so that modest scale can be consonant with economic security and environmentally-progressive agricultural practices. The key implication here is that considering the impracticality (on both ideological and environmental grounds) of large-scale collectivized agriculture, attention must be paid to transitional forms of production relations that can meliorate the concentrating and centralizing tendencies in a capitalist agricultural system.

A second issue pertains to the role and commitment of the working class in a rather narrow issue such as the structure of agriculture. Food price inflation may wreck havoc with the budgets of low income workers, but because the food system itself lies outside of their daily activities, one cannot expect a high level of commitment from the working class to change in agriculture. Two circumstances, however, may facilitate broader working class involvement in a movement to alter the structure of agriculture. The first is that a substantial fraction of the traditional blue-collar working class lives in nonmetropolitan areas. While nonmetropolitan counties accounted for 27.2 percent of the nation's population in 1970, craftsmen and operatives were a higher proportion of the nonmetropolitan labor force than of the metropolitan labor force (33.0 and 27.9 percent, respectively; Hines et al., 1975). The working class is likely to become increasingly nonmetropolitan in character as population and industry continue to decentralize (Beale, 1975). Finally, the nonmetropolitan working class tends to earn low wages (Hines et al., 1975), heightening the impact of food inflation on their limited budgets and increasing the need for change in the food system.

A third issue pertains to whether it is possible for farmers and the working class to work together in sustained efforts for change in the agricultural system. Although Populism represented a significant coalition of farmers and the urban working class (Goodwyn, 1976), this type of coalition is frequently viewed as being more of an historical curiosity than a promising transitional strategy. However, Syzmanski (1979) has effectively argued that the conditions of advanced capitalism present only two middle-run historical options for change: socialism or monopoly capitalism. The "third-road" of restoring a competitive system of independent entrepreneurs ceases to be a viable option. Thus the petty bourgeoisie must necessarily be merged into movements led by either the dominant class or the working class. Syzmanski (1979: 60-61, 64) argues that:

> [i]n a time of decisive battle between the two greatest modern classes, the petty bourgeoisie, being forced to take sides, can go either way. Which way it goes is in good part determined by the effectiveness with which one or the other viable class reaches out to it and mobilizes it, and further, in good part determines the outcome of the test of strength between the two viable classes...[I]t is not wise to emphasize the elimination of the need for professionals or small businessmen. To do so is both foolish and unscientific. To stress such questions is to drive the petty bourgeoisie to fascism, and thus prevent socialist revolution.

Thus it is possible to argue that while farmers will not be the sole vanguard in a transition to a resource-conserving, equitable agricultural system, their concerns can be shaped in progressive directions. The recent flood of participation by farmers--especially small farmers--in cooperative strategies ranging from direct marketing to tax reform indeed suggests the growing acceptance on their part of the impracticality of returning to a traditional independent, small-holder utopia and growing recognition of the need for alternative strategies.

TOWARD COOPERATIVE STRATEGIES FOR CHANGE

In the foregoing analysis of neopopulist images of social change in agriculture, it was suggested that these images are not so much undesirable in a general sense as they are unrealistic in terms of the laws of motion in advanced capitalist societies. Restoring a system of independent, small-scale farmers is not only quite unlikely politically, but would only be a transitory phenomenon as the tendency toward concentration and centralization of capital re-creates the highly unequal land holding structure that presently characterizes the U.S. Therefore transitional strategies must recognize the need for simultaneous changes in production relations in agriculture and industry.

The focal point for change in agriculture and the food system is cooperation among farmers, among working class consumers, and eventually between both groups in producer-consumer cooperatives. Cooperatives among

small and moderate-scale farmers enable them to establish new markets
(e.g., direct marketing or sales to local institutions such as schools,
hospitals, etc.), purchase farm inputs at lower rates, and pool expensive
equipment. Consumer cooperatives allow purchasing of food commodities
at prices lower than those that prevail at large retail outlets. In addition, producer and consumer coops are valuable experience in demonstrating that cooperative organization can be extended to other realms of
production, including industrial production. Britt et al. (1978) point
out, for example, that community canneries and other worker-controlled
enterprises are often the logical extension of consumer food coops.

However, perhaps the greatest advantage of cooperative strategies
for social change in the food system (as well as other realms of production and consumption) is that locally-based cooperatives can be a meeting
ground for the interests of farmers, small rural businesses, and the
working class. Producer and consumer cooperatives (and their merging
into combined producer-consumer coops) are essentially vehicles of
community social and economic development. Cooperatives and their community development corporation/worker-controlled industry spin-offs are
mechanisms that enable rural communities to both retain employment
associated with meeting basic needs (e.g., food production) and to
curb dependence of rural communities on absentee-owned--potential "run-
away"--firms for employment. Cooperative forms of economic organization
thus provide a vehicle for bringing petty commodity producers along with
the working class in terms of their common interests in enhancing the
viability of their communities. At the same time, increased localism
in the food system would have many of the environmental benefits rightly
accorded to it by neopopulist observers.

Vail (1976) has pointed out a number of ways in which farmer cooperation can begin to alter the social relations of agricultural production in a beneficient way. He outlines three major areas of potential
cooperation: (1) political action, (2) farm support activities and (3)
farm production activities. Firstly, cooperatives, in Vail's view, can
be a mechanism of forging the interests of small- and moderate-scale
farmers into a common political voice, e.g., for progressive property
rate structures. Secondly, cooperatives confer some amount of countervailing power which can be pitted against the established market power
of food processors; supermarket chains; and machinery, petrochemical,
and feed suppliers. This enables farmers to bargain more effectively
over prices, delivery conditions, etc. Collective organization can also
allow farmers to take advantage of certain economies of scale normally
captured only by large producers, e.g., volume discounts on bulk orders
of inputs and premium prices for bulk deliveries of produce. Further,
farmer cooperation makes possible a degree of division of labor. Cooperative members can take advantage of the specialized skills or equipment of their fellow members. Thirdly, cooperation in the sphere of
production activities can take the form of pooling physical capital
(i.e., spreading the overhead costs of expensive capital equipment),

cooperation in the division of labor, and cooperation in crop storage and processing (to expand countervailing power or bargaining strength with middlemen by being able to store or partially process their products).

Farmer cooperatives and consumer cooperatives of course may potentially have some conflicting interests. Farmer cooperatives aim to increase returns to farmers, while the raison d'etre of the consumer food coop is to reduce food costs. However, as noted previously, the inherently local or community character of cooperatives should tend to mitigate against protracted struggles over commodity prices since the well-being of both groups is interdependent. Local consumer coops depend upon a viable local agriculture and vice versa. The local character of food system cooperatives, then, serves to further diminish the antinomy between petty commodity producers and the working class that has tended to be reinforced by the development of essentially nationwide markets for raw agricultural commodities and retail food products.

CONCLUSION

This paper has sought to provide an overview of the interrelations between what many observers feel are emerging socioeconomic and environmental crises in U.S. agriculture. While the "crisis" label may be exaggerated, it has been argued that the environmental problems of U.S. agriculture are inherent in the major structural features of that system (and not mere aberrations in an otherwise desirable system). More importantly, the socioeconomic and ecological problems of modern agriculture may be presenting the conditions--e.g., massive food inflation, productivity stagnation--that can enable coalitions of rural people and the working class to shape a more progressive food system in the coming decades.

The most visible academic and quasi-academic voices for change in the food system have been from those referred to here as "neopopulists." They have argued for such strategies as curbing or eliminating corporate farming, protection of the independent family farmer, appropriate technology, organic farming, localism in the food system, and agricultural self-sufficiency in order to form a more equitable and resource-conserving food system. Each of these strategies can be seen to have serious limitations, largely because each tends to be based on a relatively benign view of the dynamics of capitalist development. It should again be emphasized that these neopopulist strategies are by no means undesirable, but rather in the form in which they are usually articulated, they involve no basic change in production relations (other than a vague desire to return agriculture to an idealized state of a system of modest-scale independent family farms--which has never really existed in the U.S.; Perelman, 1977).

One of the articles of faith for neopopulists is that the consensus among farmers over the desirability of the family farm makes farmers the key progressive force in the food system. Many Marxists typically view farmers as being hopelessly tied to private property and reluctantly-- albeit firmly--allied with the interests of large-scale capital. The neopopulist position is unrealistic in the current political economy for reasons summarized earlier. The orthodox Marxist position has been sub- ject to some much warranted criticism by neo-Marxist observers who instead see the petty bourgeoisie as a "swing class" in the course of social change. The position advanced in this paper is that local co- operative organization--ranging from farmer coops to consumer coops, community development corporations, and worker-controlled firms--can be a useful lever for bringing together the interests of petty commodity producers and the working class in a broad movement for change in the food system and in other realms of production.

It is useful to mention in closing that a major implicit premise of this paper, i.e., that rural areas may be an important locus for change in an advanced society such as the U.S., is a decided departure from prevailing theories of social change (inlcuding those frequently accepted by rural sociologists!). Most social change theory written in this cen- tury has explicitly or implicitly assumed that the ultimate motor for change is to be found in the urban, metropolitan, or industrial sectors of an advanced society. While not discounting the importance of social relations in the metropolitan society for charting the course of social change, it is likely that the rural sector will assume increasing im- portance in future social conflicts and social movements. The malaise of agriculture discussed earlier undermines the assumptions of many social scientists that the agricultural sector is unimportant in the structure of the larger society. The energy and environmental "crises" have magnified the vulnerability of the advanced societies to interrup- tion of the processes of food raising and distribution. Uncertainties over energy raise the strong possibility that the advanced societies may become increasingly rural in character as the energy requirements of the centralized metropolitan production system become more difficult to sus- tain. In sum, the agricultural and rural sectors may become increasingly important as foci for conflict and change. The present paper hopefully is a first step in this reorientation.

FOOTNOTES

1. This section is taken from Buttel and Powers (1978).

2. These, of course, are general tendencies. Obviously, certain policies or programs may, in the aggregate, benefit small-scale producers, but the overall impact of the constellation of government agricultural policies is argued to have the opposite impact.

3. "Net energy" refers to the energy generated from a process (such as agriculture), minus the energy required to complete this process. Negative net energy implies that a given process uses more energy than it produces。

REFERENCES

Barnes, Peter
    1972 Who Owns the Land? A Primer on Land Reform in the U.S.A.
    Berkeley, CA: Center for Rural Studies.

Beale, Calvin L.
    1975 The Revival of Population Growth in Nonmetropolitan America.
    ERS-605. Washington, D.C.: Economic Research Service, U.S. Depart-
    ment of Agriculture.

Belden, Joe et al. (eds.)
    1979 New Directions in Farm, Land and Food Policies. Washington,
    D.C.: Conference on Alternative State and Local Public Polidies.

Belden, Joe, with Gregg Forte
    1976 Toward a National Food Policy. Washington, D.C.: Exploratory
    Project on Economic Alternatives.

Berry, Wendell
    1977 The Unsettling of America. San Francisco: Sierra Club Books.

Bible, Alan
    1978 "Impact of Corporate Farming on Small Business." In R.D. Rode-
    feld et al. (eds.), Change in Rural America. St. Louis: C.V. Mosby.

Bonnen, James T.
    1968 "Distribution of Benefits from Selected Farm Programs." In
    U.S. President's Advisory Commission on Rural Poverty, Rural Poverty
    in the United States. Washington, D.C.: U.S. Government Printing
    Office.

Bratton, C. Arthur, and Myrtle Voorheis
    1978 "Farm Income Data: New York and United States." A.E. Ext.
    78-23. Ithaca: Department of Agricultural Economics, Cornell Uni-
    versity.

Brink, R.A., J.W. Densmore, and G.A. Hill
    1977 "Soil Deterioration and the Growing World Demand for Food."
    Science 197 (12 August): 625-630.

Britt, Carolyn, and Tom Walker, with Michael Schaaf
     1978 "Jobs and Energy in New England: Food Production and Market-
     ing." Bath, Maine: Coastal Enterprises, Inc.

Buse, Reuben, and Daniel Bromley
     1976 Applied Economics. Ames: Iowa State University Press.

Buttel, Frederick H.
     1979a "Agricultural Structure and Rural Ecology: Toward a Political
     Economy of Rural Development." Paper presented at the X European
     Congress for Rural Sociology, Cordoba, Spain (April).

Buttel, Frederick H.
     1979b "Agricultural Structure and Energy Intensity: A Comprehen-
     sive Analysis of the Developed Capitalist Societies." Comparative
     Rural and Regional Studies 1: forthcoming.

Buttel, Frederick H., and William L. Flinn
     1977 "The Interdependence of Rural and Urban Environmental Problems
     in Advanced Capitalist Societies: Models of Linkage." Sociologia
     Ruralis 17: 255-280.

Buttel, Frederick H., and Oscar W. Larson III
     1979a "Farm Size, Structure, and Energy Intensity: An Ecological
     Analysis of U.S. Agriculture." Rural Sociology 44: 471-488.

     1979b "Whither Environmentalism? The Future Political Path of the
     Environmental Movement." Unpublished manuscript, Department of Rural
     Sociology, Cornell University.

Buttel, Frederick, H., William Lockeretz, Martin Strange, and Elinor C.
     Terhune
     1979 "Energy and Small Farms: A Review of Existing Literature and
     Suggestions Concerning Further Research." Report prepared for the
     Project on a Research Agenda for Small Farms, National Rural Center,
     Washington, D.C.

Buttel, Frederick H., and Sharon Powers
     1978 "Agriculture in the Transition to a Sustainable Society."
     Paper presented at a joint session of the annual meetings of the
     Rural Sociological Society and Society for the Study of Social
     Problems, San Francisco, California.

Buttel, Frederick H., and Harry K. Schwarzweller
     1979 "The Council for Agricultural Science and Technology: Some
     Field Notes and Recommendations for Action by the Rural Sociological
     Society." Rural Sociological Society Newsline 7: 10-22.

Carter, Luther J.
    1977 "Soil Erosion: The Problem Persists Despite the Billions Spent
    on It." Science 196 (22 April): 409-411.

Cavazzani, Ada
    1977 "Part-Time Farming: A Functional Form of Agricultural Organiza-
    tion in the United States." Unpublished manuscript, Department of
    Rural Sociology, Cornell University.

Clark, Wilson
    1975 "U.S. Agriculture is Growing Trouble as Well as Crops."
    Smithsonian 5: 59-65.

Commoner, Barry
    1976 The Poverty of Power: Energy and the Economic Crisis.   New
    York: Knopf.

Cordz, Dan
    1978 "Corporate Farming: A Tough Road to Hoe." In R.D. Rodefeld
    et al. (eds.), Change in Rural America. St. Louis: C.V. Mosby.

Connor, Larry J.
    1977 "Agricultural Policy Implications of Changing Energy Prices
    and Supplies." In W. Lockeretz (ed.), Agriculture and Energy.
    New York: Academic Press.

Davis, John E.
    1979 "Property Without Power." Unpublished M.S. Thesis, Department
    of Rural Sociology, Cornell University.

Flora, Jan L., Ivan Brown, and Judith Lee Conboy
    1977 "Impact of Type of Agriculture on Class Structure and Social
    Well-Being in the Great Plains." Paper presented at the annual
    meeting of the Rural Sociological Society, Madison, Wisconsin.

Ford, Arthur M.
    1973 The Political Economics of Rural Poverty in the South.
    Cambridge, MA: Ballinger.

Friedland, William H., Amy E. Barton, and Robert J. Thomas
    1978 Manufacturing Green Gold: The Conditions and Social Consequences
    of Lettuce Harvest Mechanization. Davis: California Agricultural
    Policy Survey, University of California, Davis.

Frundt, Henry John
    1975 "American Agribusiness and U.S. Foreign Agricultural Policy."
    Unpublished Ph.D. dissertation, Department of Sociology, Rutgers
    University.

Gardner, B. Delworth, and Rulon D. Pope
    1978 "How is Scale and Structure Determined in Agriculture."
    American Journal of Agricultural Economics 60: 295-302.

George, Susan
    1977 How the Other Half Dies: The Real Reasons for World Hunger.
    Montclair, NJ: Allanheld, Osmun and Co.

Goldschmidt, Walter
    1978 As You Sow. Montclair, NJ: Allanheld, Osmun and Co.

Goodwyn, Lawrence
    1976 Democratic Promise. New York: Oxford University Press.

Goss, Kevin F.
    1976 "Consequences of Diffusion of Innovations: The Case of Mechani-
    zation in U.S. Agriculture." Unpublished M.S. thesis, Department of
    Communication, Michigan State University.

Goss, Kevin F., and Richard D. Rodefeld
    1977 "Consequences of Mechanization in U.S. Agriculture." Paper
    presented at the annual meeting of the Rural Sociological Society,
    Madison, Wisconsin.

Goss, Kevin F., Frederick H. Buttel, and Richard D. Rodefeld
    1978 "The Political Economy of Class Structure in U.S. Agriculture:
    A Theoretical Outline." Paper presented at the annual meeting of
    the Rural Sociological Society, San Francisco, California.

Habermas, Jurgen
    1975 Legitimation Crisis. Boston: Beacon.

Hall, Ross Hume
    1974 Food For Nought: The Decline in Nutrition. Hagerstown, MD:
    Medical Department, Harper & Row.

Hightower, Jim
    1973 Hard Tomatoes, Hard Times. Cambridge, MA: Schenkman.

    1975 Eat Your Heart Out. New York: Crown.

Hill, Stuart B., and Jennifer A. Ramsay
    1977 "Limitations of the Energy Approach in Defining Priorities in
    Agriculture." In W. Lockertez (ed.), Agriculture and Energy. New
    York: Academic Press.

Hines, Fred K., David L. Brown, and John M. Zimmer
    1975 Social and Economic Characteristics of the Population in Metro
    and Nonmetro Counties, 1970. Agricultural Economic Report No. 272.
    Washington, D.C.: Economic Research Service, U.S. Department of
    Agriculture.

Jensen, Neal F.
     1978 "Limits to Growth in World Food Production." Science 201: 317-320.

Johnson, Glenn L.
     1972 "Theoretical Considerations." In G.L. Johnson and C.L. Quance
     (eds.), The Overproduction Trap in U.S. Agriculture. Baltimore:
     Johns Hopkins University Press.

Klepper, R. et al.
     1977 "Economic Performance and Energy Intensiveness on Organic
     and Conventional Farms in the Corn Belt: a Preliminary Comparison."
     American Journal of Agricultural Economics 59: 1-12.

Kotz, Nick
     1971 Let Them Eat Promises. Garden City, NY: Anchor Doubleday.

Lerza, Catherine, and Michael Jacobson (eds.)
     1975 Food for People, Not for Profit. New York: Ballantine.

Lockeretz, William et al.
     1975 The Vulnerability of Crop Production Systems to Energy Problems.
     Report CBNS-AE-2. St. Louis: Center for the Biology of Natural
     Systems, Washington University.

     1978 "Field Crop Production on Organic Farms in the Midwest."
     Journal of Soil and Water Conservation 33: 130-134.

Lovins, Amory B.
     1977 Soft Energy Paths. Cambridge, MA: Ballinger.

McLeod, Darryl
     1976 "Urban-Rural Food Alliances: a Perspective on Community Food
     Organizing." In R. Merrill (ed.), Radical Agriculture. New York:
     Harper Colophon.

Mann, Susan A., and James M. Cickinson
     1978 "Obstacles to the Development of a Capitalist Agriculture."
     Journal of Peasant Studies 5: 466-481.

Marshall, Ray, and Allan Thompson
     1976 Status and Prospects of Small Farmers in the South. Atlanta:
     Southern Regional Council.

Merrill, Richard
     1976 "Toward a Self-Sustaining Agriculture." In R. Merrill (ed.),
     Radical Agriculture. New York: Harper Colophon.

Mills, C. Wright
    1959   The Sociological Imagination.   New York: Oxford University Press.

Morrison, Denton E.
    1976   "Growth, Equity, Environment and Scarcity."   Social Science
    Quarterly 57: 292-306.

Newby, Howard
    1978   "The Rural Sociology of Advanced Capitalist Societies."   In
    H. Newby (ed.), International Perspectives on Rural Sociology.
    London: Wiley.

Nulty, L.E.
    1977   Understanding the New Inflation: The Importance of the Basic
    Necessities.   Washington, D.C.: exploratory Project for Economic
    Alternatives.

O'Connor, James
    1973   The Fiscal Crisis of the State.   New York: St. Martin's Press.

Oelhaf, Robert C.
    1978   Organic Agriculture.   Montclair, NJ: Allanheld, Osmun and Co.

Pssour, E.C., Jr., and J. Bruce Bullock
    1977   "Energy and Agriculture: Some Economic Issues."   In W.
    Lockeretz (ed.), Agriculture and Energy.   New York: Academic Press.

Perelman, Michael
    1972   "Farming With Petroleum."   Environment 14: 8-13.

    1973a "Mechanization and the Division of Labor in Agriculture."
    American Journal of Agricultural Economics 55: 523-526.

    1973b "A Minority Report on the Economics of Spatial Heterogeneity
    in Agricultural Enterprises."   In Monoculture in Agriculture.
    Washington, D.C.: U.S. Department of Agriculture.

    1976   "Efficiency in Agriculture: The Economics of Energy."   In R.
    Merrill (ed.), Radical Agriculture.   New York: Harper Colophon.

    1977   Farming for Profit in a Hungry World: Capital and the Crisis
    in Agriculture.   Montclair, NJ: Allanheld, Osmun and Co.

Perelman, Michael, and Kevin P. Shea
    1972   "The Big Farm."   Environment 14: 10-15.

Pimentel, David et al.
   1973 "Food Production and the Energy Crisis." Science 182 (2
   November): 443-449.

   1975 "Energy and Land Constraints in Food Protein Production."
   Science 190: 754-761.

   1976 "Land Degradation: Effects on Food and Energy Resources,"
   Science 194: 149-155.

Powers, Sharon, Jesse Gilbert, and Frederick H. Buttel
   1978 "Small Farm and Rural Development Policy in the U.S.:
   Rationale and Prospects." In Rural Research in U.S.D.A., Hearings
   before the Subcommittee on Agricultural Research and General Legislation of the Committee on Agriculture, Nutrition, and Forestry,
   U.S. Senate. Washington, D.C.: U.S. Government Printing Office.

Ray, Victor
   1969 The Corporate Invasion of American Agriculture. Denver:
   National Farmers Union.

Robbins, William
   1974 The American Food Scandal. New York: Morrow.

Rodefeld, Richard D.
   1974 "The Changing Organizational and Occupational Structure of
   Farming and the Implications for Farm Work Force Individuals,
   Families, and Communities." Unpublished Ph.D. Dissertation, Department of Sociology, University of Wisconsin.

   1978 "Trends in U.S. Farm Organizational Structure and Type." In
   R.D. Rodefeld et al. (eds.), Change in Rural America. St. Louis:
   C.V. Mosby.

   1979 "Farm Structural and Structural Type Characteristics: Recent
   Trends, Causes, Implications, and Research Needs." Paper prepared
   for the Project on a Research Agenda for Small Farms, National Rural
   Center, Washington, D.C.

Rogin, Michael
   1966 The Intellectuals and McCarthy. Berkeley: University of
   California Press.

Schaaf, Michael
   1977 Cooperatives at the Crossroads. Washington, D.C.: Exploratory
   Project for Economic Alternatives.

Schnaiberg, Allan
    1975   "Social Syntheses of the Societal-Environmental Dialectic:
    The Role of Distributional Impacts." Social Science Quarterly 56:
    5-20.

Sherman, Howard J.
    1976   Stagflation: A Radical Theory of Unemployment and Inflation.
    New York: Harper & Row.

Shover, John L.
    1977   First Majority--Last Minority. DeKalb, IL: Northern Illinois
    University Press.

Slesser, Malcolm
    1976   "Energy Requirements of Agriculture." In J. Lenihan and W.W.
    Fletcher (eds.), Food, Agriculture, and the Environment. New York:
    Academic Press.

Steinhart, John S., and Carol E. Steinhart
    1974a   "Energy Use in the U.S. Food System." Science 184 (19 April):
    307-315.

    1974b   Energy: Sources, Use, and Role in Human Affairs. North
    Scituate, MA: Duxbury.

Stockdale, Jerry D.
    1976   "Technology and Change in U.S. Agriculture: Model or Warning?"
    Sociologia Ruralis 17: 43-58.

Syzmanski, Al
    1979   "A Critique and Extension of the PMC." In P. Walker (ed.),
    Between Capital and Labor. Boston: South End Press.

Vail, David
    1976   "The Political-Economic Logic of Farmer Cooperation." Unpub-
    lished manuscript, Department of Economics, Bowdoin College.

van Bavel, C.H.M.
    1977   "Soil and Oil." Science 197 (15 July): 213.

Watt, K.E.F. et al.
    1977   The Unsteady State. Honolulu: University of Hawaii Press.

Young, John A., and Jan M. Newton
    1979   Capitalism and Human Obsolescence. Montclair, NJ: Allenheld,
    Osmun and Co.

Youngberg, Garth
    1977   "Alternative Agriculturalists: Ideology, Politics, and Prospects."
    Paper presented at the Agricultural Policy Symposium, Washington, D.C.
    (July).

17. The Quiet Revolution in Land Use Control Revisited

CHARLES C. GEISLER

> This country is in the midst of a revolution in the way
> we regulate the use of our land ... It is a quiet revo-
> lution, and its supporters include both conservatives
> and liberals ... The ancien regime being overthrown is
> the feudal system under which the entire pattern of land
> development has been controlled by thousands of indi-
> vidual local governments ... The tools of the revolution
> are new laws taking a wide variety of forms but each shar-
> ing a common theme--the need to provide some degree of
> state or regional participation in the major decisions
> that affect the use of our increasingly limited supply
> of land.
>
> Bosselman and Callies (1971: 1)

> From a sociological and economic perspective, it would
> be an interesting study by itself to attempt to 'tract'
> and explain the evolution and transition from all equity,
> to reasonable equity, to thin equity (even to no equity
> in some cases) that has taken place in our history ...
> Very few seem to own anything outright anymore.
>
> Montgomery (1977: 590)

Private property is widely regarded as inherent in western capitalism. This impression is in dire need of reappraisal, however, in view
of twentieth century trends in the concentration of capital. Nearly
forty years ago, for instance, Joseph Schumpeter observed that private
property under capitalism was "evaporating" (1942: 141). This observation readily encompasses private property rights in real property, land,
as well. The fact that the "evaporation" in land property rights is
neither well documented nor well understood motivates the present chapter.

Land use planners, resource managers and a long list of legal commentators commonly view the gradual disappearance of private property
rights among land owners as a necessary by-product of an expanding urban-
industrial society. Simply put, the public interest in such a society
increasingly "demands" that private interests such as those traditionally

honored in the fee simple ownership and decentralized control of land,
be abridged.[1] Indeed, this is the essence of the quiet revolution in
land use control. In what follows, I advance a somewhat different perspective. I argue that the quiet revolution is inseparable from basic
developments in capitalism itself, namely the corporate revolution in
production-property relationships. As such I contend that the quiet
revolution in land control is part of a larger alienation of property
rights between social classes.

There is a three-fold logic to this argument. First, I draw historical attention to the fact property institutions are continually
in flux rather than, as is often assumed, static. Of particular relevance and impetus to this flux in the American context is the growth of
a highly concentrated production system from the predominantly competitive, agrarian capitalism of previous centuries. Next, I inquire into
the legitimating role of government as erstwhile private property rights
in land become public. This amounts to a commentary on how land use
policies are integral to long-term economic policy and how public and
private agendas overlap in shaping the "public interest."

Finally, I will suggest that the quiet revolution in land use control
is in fact not a recent phenomenon. Rather, it is one manifestation of
the historic redistribution of property rights away from independent producers and small capitalists to larger units of capital for whom the
absolute ownership of land is secondary to its control. Again, active
government intervention is necessary to make this interclass alienation
of property possible. I offer evidence from both eminent domain and
land regulatory policy traditions, with special attention to modern
coastal zone management legislation.

Property in American "Antiquity"

Policies encouraging decentralized ownership and control of
America's seeming inexhaustible lands in the eighteenth and nineteenth
centuries has many intellectual moorings.[2] Some of these, as Thorstein
Veblen recounted in the American Journal of Sociology in 1898, arose
from the natural law theories of the French physiocrats and others
from the labor theory of value of the English classical economists.
Competitive, free-market capitalism of course had similar origins:

> The leaders of public thought in the new nation were
> heavily influenced by the property concepts of Black-
> stone, Locke, Smith, and Bentham. Stressing the views
> first of one, then another sometimes all four, property
> emerged as ordained of God, a natural, inalienable
> right, absolute, individualistic and central to the
> laissez faire economy of New Jeruselem (Cribbet, 1965:
> 251).

William Blackstone, who construed ownership as a natural right,[3] was widely read in the colonies by John Adams and others who would either hold office following Independence or who participated in the Constitutional Convention of 1787 (Bosselman et al., 1973). It was of course Blackstone who penned the famous statement that "so great, moreover, is the regard for the law of private property, that it will not authorize the least violation of it; no, not even for the general good of the whole community" (Thomas, 1972: 28). English common law on property, echoing Blackstone and implanted in North America, conferred upon property owners near absolute dominion over their lands and the tradition of self-regulation (Large, 1973).[4]

Even more than Blackstone, however, John Locke was summoned in America to invigorate notions of a laissez faire society. It was Locke who declared that "government has no other end but the preservation of property," an orientation reflected in the thinking of Adams and Hancock (Philbrick, 1938: 713). Jefferson, father to so much of the legal and political Weltanschauung of the nineteenth century, steeped himself in Locke's natural rights philosophy on property. Jefferson moreover established personal ties with such physiocrats as Dupont de Nemours and Destutt de Tracy, and resided in Paris from 1784 until the eve of the French Revolution in 1789.[5] The Declaration of the Rights of Man, written that same year, and the French constitutions which followed, both exalted private property rights (Philbrick, 1938).

The above intellectual strains tended to reinforce the "closed" or fee-simple ownership system of real property in the youthful United States. The consensus of these doctrines on the sanctity of private property almost certainly followed from a common revulsion to socage, primogeniture, conditional ownership, and other feudal property relationships which threatened to reinstate themselves in the new nation.[6] In what may prove from a longer historical perspective, to be an aberration peculiar to early capitalism, correlative or less-than-absolute property rights were effectively eclipsed for over a century.[7] One is hardly surprised, then, that the ideology surrounding property would come to emphasize owner rights over responsibilities (Davis, 1976) or that Toqueville, visiting the United States in the nineteenth century, would write:

> In no country in the world is the love of property more active and more anxious than in the United States; nowhere does the majority display less inclination for those principles which threaten to alter in whatever manner, the laws of property (Sakolski, 1957: 294).

The Nineteenth Century: The Disposition of Public Lands

Just as the doctrine of divided property rights or conditional ownership sprang from the material conditions of feudalism (Philbrick, 1938), so did the rejuvenation of exclusive property or absolute ownership find a nurturing economic setting in the agrarian capitalism of the United States. Hardly had the upheavals of the Independence movement subsided when land use policies were formulated to direct and encourage the economic growth of the nation (Tarbell, 1971). This contrasted sharply with land use policies to follow in the twentieth century, fashioned to control growth through the regulatory police powers of the state. The economic reality of the nineteenth century was territorial expansion and consolidation, a reality facilitated by three closely related land policies.

First among these was the rectangular survey method of bringing remarkably efficient order to land west of the original states (Johnson, 1976). Upon agreement by seaboard states to ceed their western land allotments, a congressional committee chaired by Jefferson proposed a uniform grid system to expedite further settlement (Marschner, 1959). The result, in 1785, was passage of a six-mile-square township system and immediate inception of surveying in the western territories. Without such a system, the second crucial policy of massive land disposition would have been chaotic indeed. Disposition and productive settlement were front line defenses against the territorial claims of Indians and foreign nations.

The continental expansion of the United States through the nineteenth century produced an extraordinary transfer of virgin land from public to private hands (Table 1)--a transfer probably accomplished through guarantees of fee-simple ownership and minimal government interference. By 1834, government records indicate that 104 million acres of public lands had been surveyed and listed for sale and that sixteen years later, in 1850, 167 million acres had attained similar status (Barlowe, 1965). Consecutive homestead acts followed, sustained productive use or prior military service being the formal conditions of entitlement.[8] As is well known, the easily acquired land patents for homesteading led to repeated land fraud, speculation and resource devastation.[9]

The conversion of an astonishingly vast public domain into a fee-simple empire of private property owners hastened the rise of independent producers, both farm and nonfarm, as well as small capitalists. No counterpart to the landless peasant of the old world existed, and popular dissent invariably was channeled into land-based, conservative alliances (Dowd, 1977). Prevailing religious outlooks fostered industriousness whereas the prevailing political ideology of Jefferson, Jackson and later populists was intricately wed to a broad-based closed property system. The most significant challenge to this system, the

TABLE 1.   Public Land Grants by United States to Aid in Construction of
           Railroads, Wagon Roads, Canals, etc.:   1823 to 1871 [in
           thousands of acres].

| Year | Total Grants | Purpose of Grant | | | |
		Railroads	Wagon roads	Canals	River improvements
1871	3,253	3,253	--	--	--
1870	129	129	--	--	--
1869	105	--	105	--	--
1867	25,173	23,535	1,538	100	--
1866	200	--	--	200	--
1865	42,794	41,452	941	401	--
1864	2,349	2,349	--	--	--
1863	31,401	30,877	524	--	--
1857	6,689	6,689	--	--	--
1856	14,085	14,085	--	--	--
1853	3,379	2,629	--	750	--
1852	1,773	1,773	--	--	--
1851	3,752	3,752	--	--	--
1847	1,845	840	--	--	1,005
1838	139	--	--	139	--
1828	1,338	--	--	938	400
1827	2,273	--	202	2,071	--
1823	49	--	49	--	--

Source: Bureau of the Census, U.S. Department of Commerce.   Washington,
          D.C.: Series J21-25, p. 430.

precapitalist property-production relations of the ante-bellum South,
was successfullly contained by the Civil War and by assorted legislation
forging east-west political and economic alliances (Cochran and Miller,
1961; Bogue, 1969).

A third policy in this era "monetized" the land--that is, land was
substituted for capital (Hurst, 1964).   The notion of "spending land in
place of money" for basic infrastructure originated with Hamilton and
permitted economic growth to proceed even in the face of chronic shortages of fluid capital.   From the "bank" of public lands, for example,
came nearly 100 million acres for expanding educational facilities
(Marschner, 1959).   Land grants were further used to induce railroads
to extend their lines west, right-of-way strips sometimes reaching 20
miles in width.   That railroads became the leading oligopoly of the

nineteenth century economy cannot be divorced from the fact that they
received a total of 128.6 million acres of public land grants, or almost
one-sixth of such lands available (CSG, 1974). Railroads and other
critical growth industries were also granted utility status, another
source of generous eminent domain powers (Hurst, 1964; Scheiber, 1973).

Thus, the nineteenth century witnessed a continent changing hands.
With the public interest expressed in terms of Manifest Destiny, the
public domain was consolidated, surveyed, and capitalized for private
ends. Government policy encouraged entrepreneurial activity, settlement
and land engrossment. Land stewardship, where present, was a matter of
individual discretion.[10] The lack of public intervention and regulation
assured the unity of ownership and control. Private landowners and
small entrepreneurs personified classical liberalism by pursuing the
fruits of their inalienable property rights. The undoing of this decentralized, privately-owned production system was at hand, however.
The passing of laissez-faire capitalism presaged by the appearance of
its noncompetitive offspring:

> The new industrial, urban way of life was constructed
> only by making the old commercial and rural way derelict;
> the new large-scale organizations were introduced only at
> the expense of the family firm and small partnership
> (Jones, 1968: v).

From Invisible to Visible Hand

In his work, America as a Civilization, Max Lerner wrote:

> Americans have been of twofold mind on the question of
> their natural resources. They've neglected and wasted
> them, and when they discovered the extent of their waste,
> they grew panicky and gave themselves an intense conser-
> vation movement (1957: 112).

Throughout the nineteenth century, land served as capital and as a
primary determinant of social standing in America's agrarian capitalism.
With urbanization and the maturing capitalism, however, primary ties to
the land languished. In such a setting, traditional property rights
and the ethic of privacy which accompanied them were subject to challenge and reinterpretation. These challenges, by and large, came neither
from agrarians nor proletarians.[11] Rather, middle and upper class reformers, sobered by profligate resource use (Buttel, 1975), became the
mouthpiece for alternative property arrangements.

First among these were the "new economists," such as Richard T.
Ely, and conservationists more generally, both having significant
intellectual roots in Germany.[12] When Ely and his collaborators met

in 1885 to found the American Economic Association, they broadly questioned the shibboleths of laissez-faire economics, and "favored the
adjustment of property rights to new social conditions" (Cribbet, 1965:
225). Frequently this adjustment meant public purchase of land, thus
removing it from the disorders of the market place. Presidents Harrison,
Cleveland, McKinley and Roosevelt, anxious to expand the public domain
while land was still affordable, purchased 192 million acres of forest
reserves (Barlowe, 1965), and established numerous federal agencies to
administer and manage land and other resources (Petulla, 1977).

It is tempting to view the conservation movement bridging the nineteenth and twentieth centuries as the triumph of public-interest planning.
It sought to overthrow the wanton resource exploitation of laissez-
faire capitalism and the unregulated property system that was its hallmark. So too did it mark a historic departure from policies seeking
to dispose of public domain and leave economic development to the invisible hand of the market. Yet, as historian Samuel P. Hays relates,
the conservation movement was less a check on capitalist growth per se
than on small-scale production which, by late in last century, impeded
the formation of ever-larger monopolistic units of production:

> The lack of direction in American development appalled
> Roosevelt and his advisors. They rebelled against a
> belief in the automatic beneficence of unrestricted eco-
> nomic competition, which, they believed, created only
> waste, exploitation, and unproductive economic rivalry.
> To replace competition with economic planning ... would
> not only arrest the damage of the past, but could also
> create new heights of prosperity and material abundance
> in the future. The conservation movement did not involve
> a reaction against large-scale corporate business, but
> ... shared its views in a mutual revulsion against unre-
> strained competition and undirected economic development
> (1971: 266).

Resource depletion which beset the United States late in the last
century accompanied the changing size and nature of production units
which followed from a conjuncture of post-Civil War events: protracted
one-party rule partial to business growth, protective tariffs, a national
currency and banking system, weak enforcement of both the Sherman Anti-
Trust and the Interstate Commerce Acts, and a gospel of Social Darwinism
legitimating fabulous accumulations of wealth (Hurst, 1964; Jones, 1968,
Tarbell, 1971). Industrialists in this milieu lost little time in establishing resource trusts (Kolko, 1963; McConnell, 1966) to monopolize
natural resources to the fullest:

> Minerals could be exploited, forests could be destroyed,
> streams could be polluted, water could be wasted, air

> could be contaminated, and buildings could be constructed
> in growing cities without regard to elementary principles
> of health (to say nothing of aesthetics), all in the
> sacred name of private property (Cribbett, 1965: 253).

In other words, nineteenth century land policies, premised on re-source abundance, hastened both rapid economic expansion and the concen-tration of basic growth sectors of the economy. The premier, but by no means solitary, example of monopolization springing from generous public land policies was the railroads.[13] Despite the emergence of the "visible hand" of government (Chandler, 1977) and the sustained efforts to reform land abuses by Grover Cleveland, Henry George, and numerous conservationists (Tarbell, 1971), the replacement of decentral-ized agrarian capitalism by large, centrally-owned and administered units of capital proved immune to most forms of public regulation.

Again, one must turn to land policies and to the public interest ideologies surrounding them to fully understand this phenomenon. Given the historic sanctity of private property in the early political economy of the United States, policies which condemned or confiscated private property were exceptional and required exceptional justification. The expropriation powers of eminent domain were (and are) an inherent attri-bute of sovereignty so long as they were employed for public "purpose" or "use" and property owners were granted just compensation. The government alone possesses such sovereignty. In what may have been the most significant land development policy of the nineteenth century, the power of eminent domain was delegated not only to state and eventually local government, but also was accorded to private corporations in vir-tually every state (Scheiber, 1973).

This practice had its heyday in the years between 1870 and 1910:

> No longer did judges or framers of state constitutions
> rely so much upon sophistries about "public use." In-
> stead, they now merely paused to assert prescriptively
> that one private interest or another--mining, irrigation,
> lumbering or manufacturing--was so vitally necessary to
> the commonwealth as to be a public use by inference. In
> some of the western states, they went beyond that; with-
> out verbal evasion, they simply declared certain types of
> private enterprises to be "public" in their constitutions
> (Scheiber, 1973: 243).

Mining, lumbering and grazing interests attained nearly unlimited access to remaining public lands and most resources therein.[14] Lawyers who viewed such developments as blatant attempts to turn the public purpose to private use faired poorly, as a rule, in courts of law. Moreover, compensation, whether public or private, was usually token. This was true even after the Supreme Court belatedly ruled in 1897 that, because of the Fourteenth Amendment, the Fifth Amendment's "just compensation" requirement applied to all state-level eminent domain proceedings.[15]

In other words, even as nationwide policies of land disposition to small freeholders received official endorsements at all levels of government, so too were policies of land dispossession given official sanction. The former transferred land from public to private domain; the latter from one private owner to another. Both policies wore richly embroidered public interest mantles, and were executed in praise of free enterprise growth and expansion. Both contributed, nonetheless, to the redistribution of property rights away from smaller owners and producers, who according to prevailing economic theory, best fit the free enterprise model (Caldwell, 1979). The time was ripe for a revolution in economic organization and ultimately in property rights themselves.

This revolution, aptly called the corporate revolution by Redford (1971), was self-evident to even the most casual observer by the turn of the century. Some industries witnessed firms controlling up to 80 percent of the market (Kolko, 1963). These were precedents for merger and monopolization of additional sectors prior to WWI. Between 1895 and 1910, some 300 firms disappeared annually through merger, a process which created many of the nation's most influential businesses via horizontal and vertical growth (Porter, 1973). Mergers were facilitated in this period by the appearance of general incorporation laws by the states (through which holding companies spread), by conservative court interpretations of the Sherman Anti-Trust Act (Redford, 1971), and by the rapid spread of a national capital market via the rise of industrial securities (Porter, 1973). The concentration of power through conclomerate mergers produced economic centralization (Dowd, 1977), thus paving the way for monopoly capitalism. Herein, relatively few large firms enjoyed control over particular product markets while expanding, through acquisition of other businesses, their production share of the total market.

The Rise of Police Power Regulations

At one level, land use policies of the nineteenth and twentieth centuries in the United States are markedly different. Regulation, under the police powers of government, leaves property titles intact. That ownership rights therein may be abridged to prevent public harm and compensation, at least in theory, is not an issue. Eminent domain, on the other hand, expropriates the full property fee and, again in theory, compensates the former owner for loss of title. The former can be likened unto medical therapy based on prohibited behaviors; the latter, by comparison, amounts to radical surgery.

At another level, however, such differences are academic. In practice, both policies originate in the sovereign powers of the state, are constrained by explicit public interest provisos, and have the net effect of redistributing property rights among social classes. That is, the two

policies may be viewed as variations of an overarching policy which, over
time, transfers ownership and/or control of land resources to larger and
larger units of production.[16] Eminent domain was most appropriate prior
to the build-up of dense urban areas. From a compensation viewpoint, the
price of land was low, reflecting its abundance. Land use regulation under
the police powers was better suited to the high land rent settings of cities
wherein land was scarce and its function as capital had passed.

American cities at the turn of the century, into which flooded rural
migrants and foreign immigrants, were largely unplanned. "We did not, for
the most part," writes Wilbur Thompson (1975: 189), "build great cities in
this country; manufacturing firms agglomerated in tight industrial complexes
and formed labor market pools of half a million workers." Social as well
as spatial disorder reigned (Harvey, 1973), the chaos of free market capitalism being mirrored in the built environment of the day. Incompatible
land uses and land speculation resulted. Vast quantities of real estate
on the outskirts of most American cities "were hewn up for development
with jerry-built homes and without proper roads, water, schools and other
city services" (Delafons, 1969: 27-8).

In the early decades of this century, a peculiarly American form of
land use regulation, zoning, emerged as the principal countermeasure to
such social-spatial incompatibility. Deriving from the nuisance doctrines
of common law (Bosselman et al., 1973), zoning rested its legal authority
on the police powers of the respective states. These powers, granted in
the Tenth Amendment to the states or their delegates, enabled state legis-
latures to enact laws prohibiting anything injurious to the "public order,
safety, health, morals or general welfare." The reach of the police powers was limited only by the official interpretation of this broad public
interest mandate.

Zoning first appeared in the heavily settled eastern states such as
New York, its initial use being a response to garment industry attempts
to encroach onto elegant Fifth Avenue. By 1926, 564 cities had adopted
zoning ordinances. This number grew to 800 in 1931. Over the next 40
years, almost 7,000 municipalities and 2,000 townships would follow this
example (Coke and Gargan, 1969). This swift acceptance was attributable
on the one hand to passage by Congress of the Standard State Zoning Enabling Act in 1922, drafted by then Secretary of Commerce, Herbert Hoover,
and the 1926 ruling by the Supreme Court in Euclid v. Ambler Realty Co.
upholding the constitutionality of such ordinances (hence the terminology,
"Euclidean Zoning"). But there was another reason for the popularity of
zoning, rooted in its ability to appeal simultaneously to liberals and
conservatives.

In reality zoning wore two faces, one turned to the future and to
an amplified public interest in land, the latter to the status quo. The
Euclid case, for instance, was argued before an eminently conservative

Supreme Court, Mr. Justice Sutherland endorsing this use of the police powers to protect private property (Toll, 1969).[18] To be sure, the maintenance of racially pure, middle and upper class neighborhoods has been one of zoning's recurring motivations since its inception (Norton, 1979). Conversely, zoning signaled a historic separation of land ownership from land control through government intervention.[19] The more ominous implications of this latter face were tolerated because regulation was invariably delegated to local units of government (Nelson, 1977).

In sum, private property rights held inviolate under the Fifth Amendment of the Constitution continued to be relativized.[20] The redistributive consequences of police power regulation in the name of a vaguely defined public interest remained unappreciated. Yet Justice Holmes warned, in dicta prepared for his famed Mahon v. Pennsylvania Coal Co. decision (1922), of the petty larceny potential of the police power.[21] Had Holmes lived 50 years later, when the quiet revolution had moved from local units of government to the state and federal levels, perhaps he would have used the term grand larceny.

From Micro to Macro Planning

The Jeffersonian notions that strong government was evil, that planning one's economic livelihood was a personal matter, and that poverty was a right of the individual, lost support in the twentieth century. As Arthur Schlesinger, Jr. (1959: 52) states:

> Slowly the liberal tradition was overhauled ... The Hamiltonian progressivism of Theodore Roosevelt ushered in a period of energetic government. Woodrow Wilson understood even more plainly the need for executive vigor and government action. Franklin D. Roosevelt carried out these tendencies more decisively than Wilson, and the New Deal achieved the emancipation of liberalism from this aspect of the Jeffersonian myth.

Public planning of land and related resources advanced dramatically during and after the Depression. As this occurred, the institution of private property convulsed, as did the small capitalists and independent commodity producers, both urban and rural, whose livelihood depended on it.

Aggregate rural occupational figures of the New Deal years would seem to belie much change in the closed property system. Some 6.8 million Americans, the nation's peak agricultural population, inhabited more than half the land in the 48 continental states suggesting, if anything a renaissance in Jeffersonian ideals. As shown in Table 2, however, one in three farms in this period was less than 50 acres, implying their temporary nature. Between 1935 and 1974, the number of farms plummeted by four million, while the average farm size more than doubled.

TABLE 2.   Number and Percentage of Farms and Percent Distribution of
Farms and Land in Farms by Size Classes, 1935.

Size of Farm	Number of Farms	Distribution by Percent	
	(Thousands)	Farms	Acres
Under 10	571	8.4	0.3
10-49	2,128	31.2	5.3
50-99	1,444	21.1	9.9
100-179	1,428	21.2	18.4
180-259	506	7.4	10.3
260-499	640	9.4	26.4
1,000 and over	88	1.3	29.4
TOTAL	6,812	100.0	100.0

Source: Our Land and Water Resources.   USDA Miscellaneous Publication
No. 1290, Economic Research Service (May, 1974).

With the proletarianization of the yeoman farmer and of many small
businessmen who had supplied such farmers in rural trade centers, the
competitive marketplace lost its oldest allies.   Increasingly, families
that wished to till the land had to relinquish full-ownership to do it.
In 1880, when free land was plentiful, three out of four farmers were
owners or part-owners of the land they worked.   From roughly that year
forward, full-ownership gave way to tenancy, so that only about half the
farmers owned their land when the actual number of farms in the 1930s
was peaking (Bennett, 1956).   As a USDA study on the matter concluded
in 1936, farmers were losing their ownership ties to land (Turner, 1936).

Finally, even those farmers who retained full title to their property
experienced socialization of their property rights due to new levels of
public planning and regulation under the New Deal.   Compared to the nineteenth century, government programs directed at farmers were monumental in
scope.   Today's farmers, as is well known, rely on federal programs in
every step of the production process from acquiring land to marketing and
pricing final products.[22]   Farming in America has evolved into an enterprise where legal ownership of land is subordinated to shorter-term
questions of credit extension, subsidy maintenance and tax shelters.

Public planning of course transcended agriculture.   Hardly had the
Euclid decision been handed down when, in 1927, the Committee on the Bases
of a Sound Land Policy produced its report, "What About the Year 2000?,"
stressing the need for a comprehensive national land policy.   This report
precipitated a national mapping inventory of farm-area types in conjunction with the 1930 census, a National Conference on Land Utilization held

in 1931, the National Advisory and Legislative Committee on Land Use, and the National Land Use Planning Committee (Tugwell and Banfield, 1951).

Out of this last committee issued studies and recommendations fostering the Tennessee Valley Authority, perhaps the nation's boldest assertion of public property rights. Forthwith, this committee merged with the National Planning Board to become the National Resources Committee, a leading example to the growing commitment by national leadership to conservation themes dating back to 1870. Also, in 1927, the American Law Institute began its monumental Restatement of the Law of Property which, published nearly a decade later, distinguished various interests in property which had evolved in common law as the United States accelerated on its course of urban-industrial development (Wunderlich, 1969).

One function of the National Resources Committee was to stimulate planning at the sub-federal level. While the planning tradition in America goes back to the contributions of Pierre L'Enfant, Olmstead and others in the nineteenth century,[22] such planning posed no serious problems for the institution of private property (Dunham, 1964). This situation altered as the Department of Commerce's Standard State Zoning Enabling Act (1923) and Standard City Planning Enabling Act (1928) spread from statehouse to statehouse. By 1935, the National Resources Committee reported to President Roosevelt that 46 State Planning Boards had been established, the first task of which was usually a state-wide land use study in conjunction with transportation and public works planning (Stitch, 1974).

The New Deal era was therefore a watershed period in the dismantling of private property and in advancing the quiet revolution in land use control. It was in this era that economists launched their defense of greater public regulation or "social control" of land use (e.g., Ely and Wehrwein, 1938; Sakolski, 1957; Clawson, 1975). As Ely and Wehrwein (1938: 470) argued:

> Insofar as land and resources are affected by public interest, no landowner holds title to land to the exclusion of the rights of the public including future as well as present generations. Our political philosophy must give meaning and content to the vague idea of "public vs. private rights" to land. The right to control land uses exists and lies in the sovereign power of the state and may be exercised through the police power, eminent domain and taxation.

The dismantling of private property in general, and of exclusive, fee simple land rights in particular, was profoundly influenced by private as well as public planning. It is useful if not imperative at this point to consider how these planning agendas overlapped due to the changing scale and organization of private sector production.

The Property "Fission"

There is a danger in tracing the rise of conditional property rights in the United States of ignoring the important contribution of the corporate revolution already referred to and, what is more, of putting the government cart before the corporate horse. Particularly during the New Deal, an entirely new relationship emerged between government and business, one of collaboration in pursuing shared economic objectives (Schlesinger, 1959) and in jointly planning the economy of the future (MacPherson, 1973; Galbraith, 1975). Of the eleven regulatory agencies born during the thirties, for example, all but two "were engineered by the industries or other affected interests themselves, often for the purpose of immunizing cartel practices from antitrust restraints" (Lazarus, 1973: 217).

The growing accord between business and government in this period, while not unprecedented, is important because of the centralization each entity was undergoing and the power into which this centralization was translated. Max Lerner, in a well-known essay entitled "The Property Revolution" comments on consequences of this centralization for smaller units of capital:

> Industrial property became centralized, family ownership
> waned, the corporate form pushed aside the others, the
> size of the property unit shifted--and America, which
> had once been a society mainly of small property owners,
> became a society not only of the Big Technology and the
> Big Corporation, but also of Big Property." (1957: 298)

But "Big Property" was not to be equated with private ownership as in the closed property system. The property agenda of large capital was changing, shifting from unalloyed support for private property to support for quazi-public property. Joseph Schumpeter, a student of changing capitalism and its property legacy, wrote the following:

> The capitalist process pushes into the background all
> those institutions, the institutions of property and
> free contracting in particular, that expressed the needs
> and ways of the truly "private" economic activity. Where
> it does not abolish them, ... it attains the same end
> of shifting the relative importance of existing legal
> form ... or by changing their contents and meanings
> (1942: 140-1).

One interpretation of this changing agenda, based on the dispersion of stock ownership among large scale "public" corporations, emerged in the early 1930s.

The Modern Corporation and Private Property by A.A. Berle and Gardner L. Means was for many the "bible" of the New Deal when it appeared in 1932.

Means, soon to become an influential advisor to the National Resources Planning Board, provided data for the work from his doctoral dissertation entitled The Corporate Revolution. An analysis and commentary on the 200 largest non-banking corporations in 1930 resulted. Berle and Means concluded that the dissolution of private property was a by-product of the corporate revolution. Ownership had proliferated, they reasoned, through growth in the securities market. This was accompanied by a corresponding reduction in control accorded to any individual share, however. Though underestimating the residuum of controlling shares retained by the capitalist class (Burch, 1972; Nichols, 1969; Zeitlin, 1974),[24] the authors pointed to the "fission" occurring in property owned by the average person:

> The translation of perhaps two-thirds of the industrial wealth of the country from individual ownership to ownership by the large, publically financed corporations vitally changes the lives of property owners, the lives of workers, and the methods of property tenure. The divorce of ownership from control consequent on that process almost necessarily involves a new form of economic organization of society (1932: vii-viii).

In differentiating between legal ownership and actual control, Berle and Means mention another significant datum. This was the fact that, prior to the differentiation between ownership and control, capital itself differentiated into small and large-scale (quasi-public) units of production. While noting that the latter had replaced the former, they left the reciprocal relationship unanalyzed. The overthrow of private property could ultimately only serve to overthrow small capital and independent producers for whom private property was essential. Whereas business could set the conditions for the overthrow of private property, only the government could make it official and do so with legitimacy.[25] Thus the component lacking in the work of Berle, Means and their interpreters was the complementary role of government in effecting the property revolution.

This role was a by-product of rather normal government growth policies in an era of monopoly capital production. Capitalist growth requires increasing the productivity of capital as a whole. This in turn means public policies designed to eliminate relatively unproductive sectors of the economy (small or medium capital and independent producers) on the one hand and a series of benefits for the monopoly sector (subsidies, socialization or production costs and permissive legislation) on the other (Wright, 1978). Perhaps the greatest challenge for the modern state lies in reconciling the growth needs of monopoly capitalism and the public interest which, both socially and environmentally, deteriorate from such growth. It is precisely here that land use policies, essentially mechanisms for directing growth in capitalist societies, become the central issue.

The Dilemma of Local Control

The ability of state and federal government bodies to rationalize
production in today's highly concentrated economy is severely impeded by
the institution of local control of land use. A highly decentralized
system of local government, well adapted to a free-market economy, proliferated and established roots in the last century. Such police powers
as zoning and property taxation were delegated to local municipalities
by the respective states. Zoning served as a crude but convenient planning devise in an era when capital was essentially local. It became, for
example, a chief means by which municipalities could expand their tax base
while protecting local property values (Babcock, 1965; Nelson, 1977).
Many local interests, elite and otherwise, thus became tied to zoning and
remain so today (Form, 1954).

As nonmonopoly forms of production waned in the present century, however, a dilemma arose from the standpoint of rationalizing production: a
vast array of 14,000 local governments were legally entrusted with discretion over land resources.[26] Many came to view local control as a
fragmented, parochial way to accomplish growth management, including
environmental advocates:

> Environmentally responsible land use planning and control
> demands some totally new approaches. A conventional wis-
> dom which protects "local land use prerogatives--a guarantee
> of inaction--and limits "interference" in local and state
> planning efforts to massive federal handouts must be stamped
> out like a plague. The old ways just aren't working any
> more (Hanson, 1974: 267).

But the heart of the matter was not environmental conservation, important
as this was. Rather, local control was dysfunctional to growth management in a transformed, highly centralized context. Its objective was the
viability of the local community, rather than an impersonal production
system whose units were loyal to regional or even international markets
(Coke and Gargan, 1969).

The quiet revolution may be viewed, therefore, not only as a rede-
finition of property rights but also as a gradual overthrow of the local
system of government wherein the closed property system thrived. Nonmonopoly production and the local governments with which it co-evolved
depended on private property. Monopoly production submitted to open or
public ownership so long as private control over capital accumulation
was not impaired. Such impairment was unlikely at higher, more centralized levels of government. Thus, as economic power has become centralized,[27] so have land use growth controls.

Social Control Versus Local Control

In the 1940s and 1950s, many states expanded their police powers in rural areas, particularly with the establishment of conservation districts (CSG, 1974). More omnibus land use planning got underway in the 1960s with Hawaii's 1961 statewide zoning program. In an article entitled "Hawaii's Quiet Revolution Hits the Mainland," James Nathan Miller summarizes that state's initiative:

> Very simply, what Hawaii's law does is to take a concept
> that has been sacred for 300 years of American history--
> the idea that privately owned land is a commodity--and
> superimpose on it a new concept: that privately owned
> land is also a public resource. It's an idea that could
> do more to save the face of the U.S. countryside than
> all the environmental laws yet passed (1975: 40).

In the early 1970s, at least seven more states enacted major forms of state land use management: California, Florida, Maine, Minnesota, New York, Oregon and Vermont. In reporting on the quiet revolution, Gladwin Hill of the New York Times suggested the extent of its impact on American life:

> This new "land ethic" has implications that reach far
> beyond land itself. It is already affecting millions
> of people--what they can do with their property, where
> they can build or buy new homes, how close they will be
> living to industry, power plants and shopping centers,
> where they spend vacations, and in countless other ways
> (1973: 1,4).

Though comprehensive land use planning proved abortive at the federal level, more than 60 federal laws and programs affecting land use have been implemented since WWII (Lamb, 1975).

Wresting control of land resources from local jurisdictions and property powers with constitutional rights has been an arduous process, however. It essentially began in the 1930s when courts first held that states were the ultimate proprietor of real property and that ownership of land was merely a variation of tenancy (Rhode Island, 1975). In the same period the American Law Institute (ALI) contributed to the legal reinterpretation of land in its Restatement of the Law of Property. More recently, in its Model Land Development Code, ALI has undertaken a basic overhaul of the Standard State Zoning Enabling Act of 1928 upon which most local zoning is founded. According to a report issued by the House of Representatives' Committee on Interior and Insular Affairs in 1974, "The central thesis of the Model Code is that land use decisions impacting the interest of more than one local government should be subject to a decision-making process which includes all interests affected,

whether they by statewide or regional in nature."[28]   In other words, acceptance of the Model Code, recently completed after more than a decade
of drafting, will augment the preemption of local land use prerogatives
by higher levels of government.

There are other sources of momentum in the drive to overhaul local
control. Among the Model Code's authors was Fred Bosselman, a co-author
of both the Quiet Revolution in Land Use Controls (1971) and the Taking
Issue (1973). Both works were commissioned by the President's Council
on Environmental Quality and both offer persuasive "public interest"
arguments for expanding social control over land in America. The former
expresses the intricate relationship between the environment and the
public interest, thus urging an expansion of police powers, whereas the
latter prods judges and lawyers to recognize the legitimacy of such policies.[29] While it is undeniably true that public ownership of land can
ameliorate certain social and environmental conditions,[30] the mutual concern for planned growth by large capital and key public agencies means
that public ownership, partial or otherwise, will lodge ultimate control
with large capital (Kehoe et al., 1975).

The Case of Coastal Zone Management

This essay will end with a contemporary illustration of how real
property rights are redistributed through inflating police powers. The
example provided is the Coastal Zone Management (CZM) Act of 1972, as
amended in 1976. This legislation is based on the commerce clause of
the Constitution, often called the "federal police power." Like its
police power equivalent at the state level, its use must conform to the
"public interest" (Finnell, 1978). It is by no means the only illustration available,[31] but serves the purpose of demonstrating how private
interests are confounded with those of the public in matters of strategic land policies.

When the 1972 CZM legislation (P.L. 92-583) was passed, more than
50 percent of the nation's population was crowded within those counties
designated as "coastal" by the Act. This figure was projected to climb
to 75 percent by 1990. Such densities promised devastation of tidelands,
bays, and fragile estuaries crucial to fisheries, wildlife, and the human
food chain more generally:

> Population growth in the coastal regions has been putting
> tremendous pressure on coastal ecosystems. Cities require
> energy, navigation channels, port facilities, transporta-
> tion corridors, recreation facilities, land for industrial
> and residential development, and means of waste disposal,
> all of which may harm or endanger coastal resources (NRDC,
> 1978: 9).

Unequivocably, the public interest would be served by restricting growth in the coastal zone. The CZM Act of 1972 called explicitly for such recognition of the "national interest" in the 30 selected coastal states (Mandelker, 1975).

Perhaps the most bitterly contested aspect of the original CZM legislation was the siting of power plants, reliant on vast quantities of water for cooling purposes, and allied energy facilities. When the energy crisis struck in 1973, the public interest as articulated in the 1972 Act was subjected to severe criticism by the energy industry. The argument was straightforward: the industry must have access to the coastal zone (including the outer continental shelf) for future extraction, production, and growth. As part of Project independence, initiated in 1973, the federal government announced plans to accelerate the Outer Continental Shelf Leasing Program to 10 million acres (slightly less than the total acreage leased in the previous 21 years) (Schneider, 1976). This goal went unmet, however, due to suits by environmental organizations and coastal states.

In his 1975 State of the Union Address, Gerald Ford urged public support for massive onshore energy installations and announced that the nation would need the equivalent of 200 new 1,000-megawatt nuclear electric generating plants, 150 new 800-megawatt coal-fired plants, 30 new major oil refineries, and 20 major synthetic fuel plants. Amendments to the CZM Act followed in 1976 (P.L. 94-370). Now energy self-sufficiency was included as a national goal, and permits for energy development were tied to national security.[32] So too was a generous 1.2 billion dollar appropriation included for state energy planning and development, as well as loans and bond guarantees to state and local governments incurring costs of public facilities and services. Outer continental shelf sales in 1976 amounted to 1.4 billion dollars (Schneider, 1976), or roughly the amount of taxpaper's money that went to coastal states and communities to minimize impacts.

Since 1976, the major oil companies, while not owning the coastal zone, have substantially (and legally) increased their control of it. They have been granted dredge and fill permits to construct refineries, discharged hydrocarbons and other contaminants into the air, strained regional water supplies and thermally polluted coastal waters, and disrupted previously established coastal industries (NRDC, 1978). In an unusual show of arrogance, the American Petroleum Institute (unsuccessfully) sued California, Massachusetts, and Wisconsin in early 1978 for not conforming to energy facility plans proposed by the industry. Among other claims, the Institute charged that the programs adopted by these states did not accommodate the national interest in siting energy facilities, something the industry argued was now a quid pro quo for having state CZM programs approved and funded (NRDC, 1978).

Here, then, is a case of manifestly public interest land use
legislation amended to serve selective and particularistic ends. That
private beneficiaries can invoke the "national interest" on their own
behalf is ominous, especially where national security becomes an issue. National security includes military preparedness, which in turn
requires resource stockpiles and energy reserves. Thus, President
Carter's view of legislation promoting energy self-sufficiency as a
"moral equivalent to war," for example, underscores how the energy
industry's growth agenda might easily override other national interests in the coastal zone. Such override in the name of energy exigencies would not be unprecedented.[32] In sum, the ultimately
political character of the public (or national) interest is perhaps
best stated in recent research prepared by the American Bar Association.

> Land use decisions are often difficult to character-
> ize as either legislative or adjudicative. Normally
> they are a blend of the two--almost always including
> an element of policy making. Rarely are standards
> specific enough to remove the element of ad hoc dec-
> laration of the "public interest" (Finnell, 1978, 225
> ff.).

Concluding Remarks

If one accepts that institutions of property and the public interest ideologies which surround them are tied to more global changes in the
production system, certain revisions in various long-standing notions
of property follow. These revisions affect liberal, conservative and
radical positions and policies which relate to property. Liberals, for
example, are highly visible in planning initiatives. A principal justification for land use planning among liberals is distributive justice.
The market, from this standpoint, no longer provides a satisfactory
mechanism for allocating resources equitably nor for protecting the
physical environment. Greater social control of land by government
would mean more socially redeeming uses of land and related resources.
But as Lowi (1972) warns generally and Godwin and Shepherd (1974) af-
firm in the domain of land use, distributive justice frequently benefits some classes in society more than others. The separation of
ownership from control and corporate attention to the latter bears
directly on and illuminates this occurrence. And it further calls
into question the bankrupt notion that centralized social control is
a priori more publically minded than local control (Popper, 1979).

Conservatives, on the other hand, view land use planning as an
encroachment by big government (McLaughry, 1975), if not a signal step
toward socialism (Dietze, 1963). This essay reconsiders the long-term
forces underlying land socialization in the United States. It is

capitalism itself which has transformed private property, including land, and hastened its emergence as a public good. Moreover, large capital has taken the forefront in such change, which explains why initiatives in decentralized, small-scale ownership (which conservatives might abide) are relatively rare and often ill-fated. The quiet revolution is in essence a conservative revolution, though one with which most conservatives cannot identify.

Property ownership is of course central to Marxist distinctions between proletarian and bourgeoisie class interests. From this perspective, a continental divide into property rights separates the owners of production from non-owning producers--the working class. The petty bourgeoisie are therefore "transitional," and incorporated within the class struggle only with difficulty. The preceding analysis suggests, however, that under monopoly capitalism the centrality of private property in class polarization is receding. Not only do class interests transcend property ownership, but limiting property relations to the industrial workplace tends to confine Marxist analysis to the political economy of a bygone capitalism. Likewise, inattention to land use policies by most Marxists perpetuates an important misconception. This is that primitive accumulation, of which such policies are an example (Geisler, 1979), is strictly a precapitalist occurrence.

To conclude, there are social impacts associated with the public ownership of land which escape most social impact analyses. Behind the everyday "windfalls and wipeouts" accompanying the quiet revolution and believed by some to balance each other, there is a more systematic shift in property rights which is not in balance. These wipeouts are disproportionately experienced by independent producers, indigenous people, and even small capitalists whose traditional property systems, each in their own way, are senescent in the face of monopoly capitalism.

FOOTNOTES

[1] An example of this viewpoint, widely held, is found in Wunderlick (1968): "The realities of a dense, interdependent population, State intervention in economic processes, and State concern for citizen welfare have called for revisions in our concepts of property." Economists typically stress the externalities of dense urban living which zoning or other controls would internalize and environmentalists have looked to land use planning as a sine qua non to greater environmental reform and containment of urban sprawl.

[2] For a systematic treatment of ownership theories, see Pound (1953). According to Anderson (1974: 66): "The real thrust of Republican jurisprudence was concerned with... civil law governing units between disputing

parties over property...The great, decisive accomplishment of the new Roman law was...its invention of the concept of 'absolute property'-- domunium ex jure quiritium. No prior legal system had ever known the notion of an unqualified private property: Ownership in Greece, Persia or Egypt had always been 'relative,' in other words conditional on superior or collateral rights of other authorities and parties. It was Roman jurisprudence that for the first time emancipated private owner- ship from any extrinsic qualifications or restraints, by developing the novel distinction between mere 'possession'--factual control of goods, and 'property'--full legal title to them..."

[3]Blackstone's thinking was heavily influenced by the Revolution of 1688. He chose to use the natural law basis of property ownership to refute the Divine Right of Kings and related property privileges assumed by the House of Stuart.

[4]For worthwhile treatments of property relationship in the colonial period, see Lockridge (1968) and Meek (1968).

[5]Griswald (1963) reminds us that Jefferson's intellectual comradery with the Physiocrats was not without a heavy dose of New World revisionism, as is apparent in Jefferson's "prospectus" to De Tracy's Political Economy, which he edited. For an earlier study on the natural law per- ceptions of the best and the brightest in Revolutionary America, see Becker (1922).

[6]The reappearance of less-than-absolute property rights in the twenti- eth century has been referred to as the "new feudalism" (Nelson, 1977). Not only does this oversimplify feudalism, but, more importantly, ab- solute property in the purist sense existed neither in antiquity nor in the infant United States (Hecht, 1964). Certain rights (e.g., taxa- tion, escheat) have always been retained by superior sovereignties. Quiritary rights were, however, largely abolished by Justinian in favor of bonitary ownership--the enjoyment of rights in property without owner- ship. Partial possession of land further evolved in the leasehold system of medieval Germanic law, and, as feudalism developed, the ab- solute dominium of Roman jurisprudence was further divided and relativ- ized.

[7]Correlative rights depend on the legal separability of property. This separability is best conceptualized in the "bundle-of-rights" concept taught in law schools. As Bertrand and Corty (1962: 8) state: "The bundle of rights idea is portrayed graphically by the fasces which was used as a symbol of authority in the Roman Empire. The fasces consist of a bundle of sticks tied around an ax. The sticks are symbolic of the varying rights in land, while the ax represents the supreme authority and superior rights of the state."

[8]While the basic condition of tenure harkened back to the classical labor theory of value cited above, conditions of ownership changed in time. "Cash sale policy for revenue purposes was modified in 1800 by the credit system. It was modified still further in 1841, by the preemption law that permitted settlers to obtain patents to the land by complying with the prescribed length of residence on it, the cultivation requirements, and payment of the statutory minimum price for the land. Paying for the land they had to improve, however, was not popular with the settlers, and the fee homestead law was enacted in 1862. Under this act, a settler could locate the claim 160 acres of public land and receive a patent to it by complying with the requirements, which included building a house, living on the land for 5 years, and cultivating a certain acreage" (Marschner, 1959: 22).

As has often been reiterated, Frederick Jackson Turner's claim that the American frontier had "closed" with the exhaustion of "free" land in 1890 was symbolically accurate but technically incorrect. Homesteading continued at a rate of 3 million acres or more between 1898 and 1926, and three-fourths of the 247 million acres patented to homesteaders between 1868 and 1946 occurred after 1900 (Barlowe, 1965).

[9]The notorious Yazoo land frauds are a case in point. Here, 30 million acres, consisting of nearly the entirety of Alabama and Mississippi today, were sold by the Georgia legislature for less than two cents an acre, and then resold in the form of scrip to thousands of gullible investors. Such swindles created fortunes for a few at public expense (Barnes, 1971). From 1860 to 1900, for every free farm entered and kept by a farmer under the Homestead Act of 1862, nine were bought from railroads, speculators or the government (Hofstadter, 1955: 54). Regarding speculation, Gates (1943) documents at length how Ezra Cornell used land script awarded to Cornell University under the Morill Act of 1862 to buy nearly 500,000 acres of virgin forest in north central Wisconsin-- a windfall for the Cornell endowment fund but not for the state's environment and later economy. Land bought for as low as a dollar an acre under the Homestead Act sold for upwards of $60 an acre when Cornell disposed of its extensive holdings.

[10]Occasional exceptions to the nonregulatory approach prevailing in common law occurred, such as weed control, irrigation and drainage districts (Clawson, 1975). Foresighted watershed-wide planning proposals for the arid west made by John Wesley Powell (1920) were disregarded by Congress.

[11]Socialism in this period failed to provide leadership in the transformation of private property. Lipset (1961) documents the spread of cooperativism and state ownership of grain elevators, mills, packing houses, and storage facilities in the central plains, initiatives disavowed by Socialists until the eve of WWI. Neither, in large measure,

did the impetus to transform private property come directly from the
working class, as early socialists might have wished. Despite over 500
strikes a year between 1880 and 1894 and the power to disrupt production
(Brecher, 1972; Taft, 1964), the Knights of Labor and the American
Federation of Labor demurred on questions of socialism (Ash, 1972) and
of fundamentally revised property relationships.

[12]Both Gifford Pinchot, the very embodyment of the conservation movement,
and Ely, among other young Americans of later influence, received higher
educations in Germany and were influenced by the German historical
school as well as the challenges to absolute property ownership emerging on the continent (Cribbet, 1965).

[13]Among the many accounts of nineteenth century rail empires, two of the
most useful are Baran and Sweezy (1964) and Chandler (1977).

[14]Lumber companies in the nineteenth century had unlimited free access to
national forests, as did ranchers to public rangelands. Hardrock mining
companies, under the Mining Law of 1872, could extract minerals with an
option to purchase deposit-bearing lands. This law, still in effect
today and covering 87 percent of all federal lands outside of Alaska,
requires neither permit nor royalty to the U.S. Treasury.

[15]In the famed slaughterhouse decisions of 1872 (reviewed at length in
Commons, 1968), the U.S. Supreme Court upheld a Louisiana statute per-
mitting monopoly operation of slaughterhouses in that state, thereby
causing property and market losses for smaller operations. In 1884,
however, this decision was reversed, one of many judicial indications
that legal support for eminent domain for private purposes was waning
(Philbrick, 1973).

[16]Even the apparent difference in compensation requirements fades in
importance when it is recalled that compensation was required as a negative check on the police powers until 1870 (Schelber, 1973: 242) and
that, as suggested, compensation under eminent domain was often minimal.

[17]In its original and simplist form, zoning consisted of dividing cities
and towns according to predefined and presumably incompatible types (e.g.,
commercial, residential, industrial) (Babcock, 1966). This classification of property according to "higher" and "lower" uses reflected the
mechanistic outlooks of Taylorism, in vogue in business at the time.

[18]According to Toll (1969: 244), an article in Harvard Law Review stated
in 1927 that "It is somewhat of a shock to discover that in the six years
since 1920 the Supreme Court has declared social and economic legislation
unconstitutional under the due process clauses of either the Fifth or the
Fourteenth Amendment in more cases than in the entire fifty-two previous
years during which the Fourteenth Amendment has been in effect."

[19]This point is elaborated by both Heyman (1968) and Ward (1969). According to the former:

> Property rights consist of powers of an owner to dispose
> of and use his land...They can and have been adjusted
> over time by both courts and legislatures as there have
> been changes in population, technology and social goals
> ...A good example of this is land-use regulation. At
> one time regulation was imposed only against nuisances.
> Later legislatures were permitted to prohibit nuisance-
> like activities. This increased the scope of justified
> objectives for the exercise of public power and concom-
> mitantly reduced the scope of property rights. Lately
> there has been a further progression so that positive
> enhancement of the general welfare is a permissible
> basis for regulating private use of land (Heyman, 1968:
> 31).

[20]The Fifth Amendment of the Constitution states: "No person shall...be deprived of...property, without due process of law; nor shall private property be taken for public use without just compensation." As is elaborated below, with passage of the Fourteenth Amendment, these protections were made applicable to the states (see Chicago, B.&Q.R.R. v. Chicago, 166 U.S. 226, 1897).

[21]Brandeis' alternative formulation, a minority position at the time, was: "Even relatively severe government restrictions on land use are not an unconstitutional taking of land, since the property would still remain in the hands of its owners. The government would merely be preventing the owner from conducting a land use which would interfere with the paramount rights of the public." (Pennsylvania Coal Company v. Mahon, 1922). A recent example of Brandeis being summoned to represent the environmental or new land ethic position appears in Brown and Coke (1977).

[22]The dependency of the farm community on the federal government in the present century became clearly delineated during the New Deal. A partial list of farm-related federal programs included soil banks and rural electrification, Agricultural Conservation Payments, Land Bank Loans as well as loans for disasters, seed and feed, Resettlement Administration loans and grants for rehabilitation, Farm Security Administration and later the Farmers' Home Administration, the Commodity Credit Corporation, the Reconstruction Finance Corporation, the Soil Conservation Service, the Agricultural Administration Act and the Tennessee Valley Authority (Barlowe, 1965).

[23]For a brief account of nineteenth century planning, see Reps (1972).

[24]The managerial extension drawn by Berle and Means is that the quest for profits accompanies ownership in traditional, small-scale capitalism. Without ownership incentives, however, managerial controllers of contemporary corporations operate under different motivations--namely, efficiency growth and good business for its own sake (1932: 9). These are the underlying traits which Galbraith (1967, 1973), among others, attributes to the technostructure. Presumably, such motivations distinguish managers from capitalists themselves who managerial theorists believe are fading in importance. Countering this, Zeitlin (1974: 1077) cites Max Weber's writing on bureaucratic ascendency: If "'the immediate appropriation of managerial functions' is no longer in the hands of owners, this does not mean the separation of control from ownership, but rather 'the separation of managerial function from ownership.' 'By virtue of their ownership,' Weber saw, 'control over managerial positions may rest in the hands of property interest outside the organization as such'" (Zeitlin emphasis). In other words, while there may be separation of ownership and control this separation is not universal, especially among upper class owners.

[25]Note, for example, the increasing legal interest in new property forms (e.g., Cohen, 1927; Philbrick, 1938; Cross, 1955; Reich, 1964; Hecht, 1964; Wunderlick, 1968; Large, 1973; Natural Resource Journal, 1975).

[26]There is some disagreement as to the actual number of local governments which have jurisdiction over land use controls. Estimates range from a low of 10,000 to 60,000, the latter representing virtually all or most government entities that could be considered "local" (for example, see Hill, 1974).

[27]The reader might wish to consult data in Paul Samuelson's (1976: 116) well known introductory economics text. These data which indicate that the four largest firms control in excess of 90 percent of the market in many industries are nonetheless treated as somewhat of an exception by Samuelson. In 1972, however, four firms (a common gauge of monopoly control) controlled over 50 percent of the business in 105 of 327 U.S. manufacturing industries. Moreover, where only two manufacturing corporations had assets exceeding $1 billion in 1929, by 1976 there were 159 billion-dollar corporations in the United States with 54 percent of total manufacturing assets (Mueller, 1978).

[28]The Model Code, over ten years in the drafting, is intended as an overhaul of the Standard State Zoning Enabling Act passed in the 1920s and, inadvertently, the source of much subsequent fragmentation in land use planning. The code reform was promoted by Chicago attorney, Richard Babcock, and Dennis O'Harrow, Executive Director of the American Society of Planning Officials in the early 1960s. The Ford Foundation supported Babcock's initial study of exclusionary zoning, resulting in the widely-read book, The Zoning Game. Herein, suburban zoning is shown to

disregard the more general residential interests of the metropolis (a broadening of the public interest which preceded environmental arguments in the making).

Still another influential book reflecting the ALI Code reforms was The Use of Land (1973), sponsored by the Rockefeller's Brother Fund. Among other recommendations, it proposed that landowners bear the costs of police powers restrictions without compensation unless land is physically taken. Various drafts of the ALI Code were furthermore in national land use planning legislation of the 1970s, and in state land use legislation in Florida, New Jersey, and elsewhere (Brown, 1975). See Mandelker (1976) for further comment on the new code.

[29]The theme of expanded public ownership usually at higher levels of government, repeats itself in most of Bosselman's writing and in that of other members of his Chicago law firm as well. For example, see Babcock and Feuer (1977).

[30]Many welcome examples of this trend are available, most notably in the writings of Aldo Leopold (1966), Carl Orton Sauer (1974), and other land ethnic proponents. To be sure, the authors of The Quiet Revolution in Land Control have been influenced by such writings, suggesting how the land ethic may be conveniently appropriated to justify greater social control as here discussed (e.g., Hill, 1974; Caldwell, 1974).

[31]There is considerable evidence that large private interests find largesse in a variety of public land use policies. For instance:

> Large developers tend to support centralized, state-
> level, land use control over decentralized control. A
> large developer with, perhaps, one central office
> supervising operations in several states can be influ-
> ential at the state level while there would be much larger
> total costs if he had to participate in decisions made in
> numerous localities (Erwin et al., 1977: 51).

New communities, a departure from traditional land use planning, have on occasion been built on public lands (Hait, 1977). Corporations with large land endowments periodically deed property to the government, seeking both tax write-offs and residual rights to resources (e.g., Union Bag Camp's 1978 donation in southern Georgia to the U.S. Fish and Wildlife Service). The U.S. Forest Service's Roadless Area Review and Evaluation (Rate II), in response to urgings by mining and other resource development companies, is recommending the opening of some 28 million acres of former wilderness to development, probably only the beginning of a roadless area reclassification effort for industrial use (Crowlie, 1979). The Bureau of Land Management (BLM), which with the

Forest Service manages 90 percent of Alaska's lands, is so blatantly pro-industry, Secretary of the Interior Cecil Andrus has re-Christened it the "Bureau of Livestock and Mining" (Schiefelbein, 1979).   Through-out the southeast, the nation's largest timber companies have yoked the federal government into draining thousands of acres of wetlands for conversion to tree plantations (NRDC, 1979).   The Department of Agri-culture's multiple subsidies to large agribusiness are by now legendary and the Department of Transportation's Highway Trust Fund is to the automotive and trucking industries what the railroad acts of the nine-teenth century were to rail monopolies.

[32] It is noteworthy that federally required environmental impact state-ments have been waived only once in the ten years since the passage of the National Environmental Policy Act (NEPA).   This Congress did to expedite the movement of oil from Alaska to the lower States in the Trans-Alaskan Pipeline in the wake of the energy crisis (Taylor, 1978).

REFERENCES

Anderson, Perry
     1974   Passages from Antiquity to Feudalism.   London: New Left Books.

Ash, Roberta
     1972   Social Movements in America.   Chicago: Markham.

Babcock, Richard F.
     1965   The Zoning Game.   Madison: University of Wisconsin Press.

Babcock, Richard F. and Duane A. Feurer
     1977   "Land as a commodity affected with the public interest."
     Washington Law Review 52 (November): 289-334.

Barlowe, Raleigh
     1965   "Federal programs for the direction of land use."   Iowa
     Law Review 50: 337-367.

Barnes, Peter
     1971   "The great American land grab."   New Republic (June 5).

Baron, Paul A. and Paul M. Sweezy
     1966   Monopoly Capital.   New York: Monthly Review Press.

Becker, Carl
     1922   The Declaration of Independence: A Study in the History
     of Political Ideas.   New York: Hartcourt, Brace & Co.

Bennett, Henry G.
1956 "Land and independence--America's experience" In Kenneth
Parsons, R.J. Penn and Philip Raup (eds.), Land Tenure. Madison:
University of Wisconsin Press.

Berle, Adolph A., Jr. and Gardiner C. Means
1932 The Modern Corporation and Private Property. New York:
Commerce Clearing House.

Bertrand, Alvin L. (ed.)
1962 Rural Land Tenure in the United States. Baton Rouge:
Louisiana State University Press.

Bogue, Allan G.
1969 "Senators, sectionalism and 'western' measures of the Republican
Party." In D.M. Ellis (ed.), The Frontier in American Development.
Ithaca: Cornell University Press.

Bosselman, Fred and David Callies
1971 The Quiet Revolution in Land Use Control. Washington, D.C.:
Council on Environmental Quality.

Bosselman, Fred, David Callies and John Banta
1973 The Taking Issue. Washington, D.C.: Council on Environmental
Quality.

Brown, Peter G.
1975 The American Law Institute Model Land Development Code, The
Taking Issue, and Private Property Rights. Washington, D.C.: The
Urban Institute.

Brown, Steven R. and James G. Coke
1977 Public Opinion on Land Use Regulation. Columbus, Ohio:
Academy for Contemporary Problems.

Brecher, Jeremy
1972 Strike! San Francisco: Straight Arrow Books.

Burch, Philip H., Jr.
1972 The Managerial Revolution Reassessed. Lexington, Massachusetts:
Lexington Books.

Buttel, Frederick H.
1975 Class Conflict, Environmental Conflict and the Environmental
Movement: The Social Bases of Mass Environmental Beliefs, 1968-
1974. Unpublished Ph.D. dissertation. University of Wisconsin,
Madison.

Caldwell, Lynton K.
    1972 "Environment: A new focus for public policy?" In Dennis L.
    Thompson, Politics, Policy and Natural Resources. New York: The
    Free Press.

Caldwell, Lynton
    1979 "Law and Land." In Richard N. Andrews (ed.), Land in America.
    Lexington, Mass.: Lexington Books.

Castle, Emery N.
    1978 "Property rights and the political economy of resource scarcity."
    American Journal of Agricultural Economics 30 (February): 2-9.

Chandler, Alfred
    1977 The Visible Hand. Cambridge Mass.: The Belknap Press of
    Harvard University Press.

Clawson, Marion
    1975 "Economic and social planning conflicts in land use planning."
    Natural Resources Journal 15 (July): 475-489.

Cochran, Thomas E. and William Miller
    1961 The Age of Enterprise. New York: Harper & Row (1942).

Cohen, M.R.
    1927 "Property and sovereignty." Cornell Law Quarterly 13: 8-30.

Coke, James G. and John J. Gargan
    1969 "Fragmentation in Land-Use Planning and Control." Research
    Report No. 18. National Commission on Urban Problems. Washington,
    D.C.

Commons, John R.
    1968 Legal Foundations of Capitalism. Madison: University of
    Wisconsin Press (1924).

Cross, Harry M.
    1955 "The diminishing fee." Law and Contemporary Problems 20:
    517-539.

Cribbet, John E.
    1965 "Changing concepts in the law of land use." Iowa Law Review
    50: 245-278.

Crowlie, David
    1979 "'RARE II': Is it boon or blight?" Rural Affairs 4: 8.

CSG
1974 The Land Use Puzzle. Lexington, Ky.: Council of State Governments.

Davis, Kenneth P.
1976 Land Use. New York: McGraw-Hill Book Co.

Delafons, John
1969 Land Use Controls in the United States. Cambridge, Mass.: MIT Press.

Dietze, Gottfried
1971 In Defense of Property. Baltimore: Johns Hopkins University Press (1963).

Dowd, Douglas F.
1976 The Twisted Dream. Cambridge, Mass.: Winthrop Publishers, Inc.

Dunham, Allison
1964 "Property, city planning and liberty." In Charles M. Haar (ed.), Anglo-American Planning Practice. Cambridge, Mass.: Harvard University Press.

Dunham, Allison
1976 A Model Land Development Code. Washington, D.C.: The American Law Institute.

Ely, Richard T. and George S. Wehrwein
1940 Land Economics. Madison: University of Wisconsin Press.

Erwin, David E., James B. Fitch, R. Kenneth Godwin, W. Bruce Shepard, and Herbert H. Stoevener
1977 Land Use Control. Cambridge, Mass.: Ballinger Publishing Co.

Faulkner, H.U.
1951 The Decline of Laissez Faire, 1897-1917. New York: Rinehart.

Finnell, Gilbert L., Jr.
1978 "The federal regulatory role in coastal land management." American Bar Foundation Research Journal 2 (Spring): 168-288.

Form, William H.
1954 "The place of social structure in the determination of land use: some implications for a theory of urban ecology." Social Forces 32 (May): 317-323.

Galbraith, John K.
1967 The New Industrial State. Boston: Houghton Mifflin Co.

Galbraith, John Kenneth
    1975 Economics and the Public Purpose. Boston: Houghton Mifflin
    Co.

Gates, Paul Wallace
    1943 The Wisconsin Pine Lands of Cornell University. Ithaca, New
    York: Cornell University Press.

Geisler, Charles C.
    1979 A Sociological Interpretation of Land Use Planning in
    Capitalist Society. Unpublished Ph.D. Dissertation, University
    of Wisconsin, Madison, Wisconsin.

Godwin, Kenneth R. and W. Bruce Shepard
    1974 State Land Use Policies: Winners and Losers. Report sponsored
    by Battelle Memorial Institute and Rockefeller Foundation. Oregon
    State University, Corvallis, Oregon.

Green, Philip P., Jr.
    1974 "The American Law Institute Model Land Development Code."
    In Proceedings of the Conference, Land Use Planning: Implications
    for Citizens and State and Local Governments. Columbus, Ohio:
    Battelle.

Griswold, A. Whitney
    1963 Farming and Democracy. New Haven, Connecticut: Yale Uni-
    versity Press (1948).

Hait, Pam
    1977 "Arizona's trust lands: A plum for developers?" Planning 43
    (December): 18-21.

Hanson, Roger P.
    1974 "A national land use policy - toward a new land ethic."
    In Proceedings of 24th Institute on Oil & Gas Taxation (February
    7-9) Dallas: Southwestern Legal Foundation.

Harvey, David
    1973 Social Justice and the City. Baltimore: Johns Hopkins Uni-
    versity Press.

Hays, Samuel P., Jr.
    1971 Conservation and the Gospel of Efficiency. New York:
    Vintage Books.

Hecht, Neil
    1964 "From seisin to sit-in: evolving property concepts." Boston
    Law Review 44: 435-466.

Heyman, Ira M.
  1968 "The great 'property rights' fallacy." Cry California
  (Summer): 29-34.

Hill, Gladwin
  1973 "Public control growing in a land use revolution." Land-
  Use Controls Quarterly 4 (Winter): 8-33.

Hill, Gladwin
  1974 "When 60,000 governments try to decide on land use." New
  York Times (December 8):News of the Week in Review, 4

Hofstader, Richard
  1955 The Age of Reform. New York: Vintage Books.

Horwitz, Morton J.
  1977 The Transformation of American Law, 1789-1860. Cambridge:
  Harvard University Press.

Hurst, Willard
  1964 Law and Economic Growth: The Legal History of the Lumber
  Industry in Wisconsin, 1836-1915. Cambridge, Mass: Belknap Press
  of Harvard University Press.

Johnson, Hildegard B.
  1976 Order Upon the Land. New York: Oxford University Press.

Jones, Peter d'A. (ed.)
  1968 The Robber Barons Revisited. Lexington, Mass.: D.C. Heath
  and Co.

Kehoe, Dalton, David Morley, Stuart B. Proudfood, and Neal A. Roberts
  1975 Public Land Ownership: Frameworks for Evaluation. Toronto:
  Lexington Books.

Kolko, Gabriel
  1963 The Triumph of Conservatism: A Reinterpretation of American
  History, 1900-1916. Chicago: Quadrangle.

Lamb, Richard
  1975 Metropolitan Impacts on Rural America. Chicago: University
  of Chicago Press.

Large, Donald W.
  1973 "This land is whose land? Changing concepts of land as
  property." Wisconsin in Law Review No. 4: 1041-1083.

Lazarus, Simon
1973 "Halfway up from liberalism: regulation and corporate power."
In Ralph Nader and Mark J. Green (eds.), Corporate Power in
America. New York: Grossman Publishers.

Lerner, Max
1957 America as a Civilization. New York: Simon and Schuster.

Leopold, Aldo
1966 Sand County Almanac. New York: Ballantine Books, Inc.
(1949)

Lipset, Seymor Martin
1961 Agrarian Socialism. Berkeley: University of California Press
(1950).

Linowes, R.R. and D.T. Allensworth
1973 The Politics of Land Use. New York: Praeger.

Lockridge, Kenneth
1968 "Land, population and the evolution of New England society."
Past and Present, 39: 62-80.

Lowi, Theodore
1972 "Population policies and the American political system."
In Richard Clinton, William Flash and Kenneth Godwin (eds.),
Political Science in Population Studies. Lexington, Mass: D.C.
Heath & Co.

Marschner, F.J.
1959 Land Use and Its Patterns in the United States. Agricultural
Handbook No. 153, Washington, D.C.: USDA.

McClaughry, John
1975 "The Land Use Act--an idea we can do without." Environmental Affairs (January): 595-626.

MacPherson, C.B.
1973 Democratic Theory: Essays in Retrieval. Oxford: Clarendon
Press.

Mandelker, Daniel R.
1976 "The national and state interest in land development controls."
In D.R. Mandelker (ed.), Environmental and Land Controls Legislation.

Meek, C.K.
1968 Land Law and Custom in the Colonies, London: Frank Cass and
Company Ltd.

Miller, James Nathan
    1975 "Hawaii's 'quiet revolution' hits the Mainland." Reprinted
    in Readings on Land Use Policy. Prepared by Environmental Policy
    Division Congressional Research Service for Committee on Interior
    and Insular Affairs, United States Senate (June). U.S. Washington,
    D.C. Government Printing Office.

Montgomery, J. Thomas
    1977 "Leverage," The Appraisal Journal 45 (October) : 590-600.

Mueller, Willard F.
    1977 "Industrial concentration and market power: sources, conse-
    quences, and social control." Economic Issues 10 (June): 1-4.

Natural Resources Journal
    1975 Symposium on Natural Resources Property Rights. Natural
    Resources Journal. Albuquerque, N.M.: University of New Mexico
    Law School.

Nelson, Robert H.
    1977 Zoning and Property Rights: An Analysis of the American
    System of Land-Use Regulation. Cambridge: MIT Press.

Nichols, Theodore
    1969 Ownership, Control and Ideology. London: Allen and Unwin.

Norton, Robert
    1979 City Life-Cycles and American Urban Policy. New York:
    Academic Press.

NRDC
    1978 "Treading the thin edge." NRDC Newsletter 7 (December/
    January).

NRDC
    1979 "How the Corps '404' Permit Program can help the small forest
    and woodlot operator." Washington, D.C.: Natural Resources
    Defense Council.

Petulla, Joseph M.
    1977 American Environmental History. San Francisco: Boyd &
    Fraser Publishing Company.

Philbrick, Francis S.
    1938 "Changing conceptions of property in law." University of
    Pennsylvania Law Review 86 (May): 691-732.

Plamenatz, J.
    1963 Man and Society. Vol. 1. London: Longmans.

Popper, Frank
     1979   The Politics of Land-Use Reform.   New York: Twentieth Century
     Fund.

Porter, Glenn
     1973   The Rise of Big Business, 1860-1910.   New York: Thomas Y.
     Crowell Co.

Pound, Roscoe
     1953   An Introduction to the Philosophy of Law.   New Haven: Yale
     University Press.

Powell, John Wesley
     1962   A Report on the Lands of the Arid Region of the United States.
     (2nd Edition).   Cambridge, Mass.: Belknap Press of Howard Univer-
     sity Press (1879).

Redford, Emmette
     1971   "Centralized and decentralized political impacts on a develop-
     ing economy: interpretations of American experiences."   In James J.
     Heaply (ed.), Spacial Dimensions of Developmental Administration.
     Durham, N.C.: Duke University Press.

Reich, Charles A.
     1964   "The new property."   Yale Law Journal 73 (April): 733-787.

Reilly, William K. (ed.)
     1973   The Use of Land: A Citizen's Policy Guide to Urban Growth.
     New York: Thomas Y. Crowell Company.

Reps, John W.
     1972   "Public land, urban development policy, and the American
     planning tradition."   In Marion Clawson (ed.), Modernizing Urban
     Land Policy.   Baltimore: Johns Hopkins University Press.

Rhode Island, State of
     1975   "Regulation of critical areas through a state land management
     program."   Statewide Planning Program Technical Paper No. 57
     (September).   Providence, R.I.

Sauer, Carl Orton
     1974   Land and Life.   Berkeley: University of California Press.
     (1963).

Sakolski, Aaron M.
     1957   Land Tenure and Land Taxation in America.   New York: Tobert
     Schalkenbach Foundation.

Samuelson, Paul M.
    1976 Economics. 10th Edition. New York: McGraw-Hill.

Scheiber, Harry N.
    1973 "Property law, expropriation, and resource allocation by
    government: the U.S. 1789-1910." Journal of Economic History 33
    (March): 232-251.

Schiefelbein, Susan
    1979 "Alaska: The great land war." Saturday Review (February):
    14-20.

Schlesinger, Arthur, Jr.
    1959 The Age of Roosevelt. Boston: Houghton-Mifflin.

Schneider, Devon M.
    1976 "Coastal states are buoyed by more government bucks."
    Planning 42 (October): 14-16.

Schumpeter, Joseph A.
    1975 Capitalism, Socialism and Democracy. New York: Harper
    Colophon Books (1942).

Stitch, Ronald K.
    1974 "The current status of state land use policy." Public Policy
    Study No. 8. Washington, D.C.: The Heritage Foundation, Inc.

Taft, Phillip
    1964 Organized Labor in American History. New York: Harper & Row.

Tarbell, Ida M.
    1971 The Nationalizing of Business. Chicago: Quadrangle Paperbacks.
    (1936)

Taylor, Randall L.
    1978 "NEPA pre-emption legislation decisionmaking alternative for
    crucial federal projects." Environmental Affairs 6: 373-389.

Thomas, Fran
    1972 Law Action: Legal Frontiers of Natural Resources Planning.
    Madison: Land Economics Monographs, University of Wisconsin.

Thompson, Wilbur
    1975 "Economic processes and employment problems in declining metro-
    politan areas." In George Steinlieb and James W. Hughes (eds.).
    Post-Industrial America: Metropolitan Decline and Inter-Regional Job
    Shifts. New Brunswick, N.J.: Center for Urban Policy Research.

Toll, Seymour I.
    1969 Zoned American. New York: Grossman Publishers.

Tugwell, R.G. and E.C. Banfield
    1951 "Government planning at mid-century." Journal of Politics 13:
    133-163.

Turner, H.A.
    1936 A Graphic Summary of Farm Tenure. Washington, D.C.: USDA
    MP-261 (December).

USDA
    1974 "Our land and water resources." Miscellaneous Publication
    No. 1290. Washington, D.C.: Economic Research Service, U.S.
    Department of Agriculture, Bureau Service (May).

Veblen, Thorsten
    1898 "The beginnings of ownership." American Journal of Sociology
    4 (July): 352-365.

Ward, Donald E.
    1969 "Decline of property rights through zoning." Surveying and
    Mapping 29: 97-100.

Wright, Eric Olin
    1978 Class, Crisis, and the State. London: New Left Books.

Wunderlich, Gene
    1969 "A concept of property." Agricultural Economics Research 21
    (January): 1-6.

Zeitlin, Maurice
    19   "Corporate ownership and control: The large corporation and
    the capitalist class." American Journal of Sociology 79 (March):
    1073-1119.

About the Contributors

FREDERICK H. BUTTEL is Assistant Professor of Rural Sociology at Cornell University. His primary research interests include structural change in western agricultures, environmental sociology, and political sociology. Buttel is co-author of a forthcoming book entitled Environment, Energy, and Society to be published by Wadsworth in 1980.

GERALD R. CAMPBELL is Associate Professor of Agricultural Economics at the University of Wisconsin-Madison. He holds a Ph.D. in agricultural economics from Michigan State University. His major research interests are in the control of agricultural marketing systems, with special emphasis on the impact of vertical integration and contract farming on economic concentration and market performance.

IAN CARTER is Senior Lecturer in Sociology at the University of Aberdeen. He has published widely on agrarian social history and literary history in Scotland. He is the author of Farm Life in Northeast Scotland, 1840-1914 (Edinburgh: John Donald, 1979) and Scottish Peasant Life (London: Frank Cass, forthcoming).

JOHN EMMEUS DAVIS is a doctoral candidate in Development Sociology at Cornell University. The paper included in this volume is based on research conducted for his Master's degree at Cornell which focused on comparative aspects of contract farming in New York and Tennessee.

ALAIN de JANVRY is Associate Professor of Agricultural and Resource Economics at the University of California, Berkeley. De Janvry is widely known for his work on the political economy of underdevelopment in Latin America and structural change in the world food economy. His work has appeared in the Journal of Peasant Studies, American Journal of Agricultural Economics, Latin American Perspectives, and the Quarterly Journal of Economics.

JAMES M. DICKINSON is a doctoral candidate in Sociology at the University of Toronto. He holds an M.A. degree from American University, Washington, D.C. He is co-author with Susan Mann of a seminal article, "Obstacles to the Development of a Capitalist Agriculture," which appeared in the Journal of Peasant Studies in 1978. His current research is devoted to the analysis of state policies in the reproduction of the working class.

WILLIAM H. FRIEDLAND is Professor of Community Studies and Sociology at the University of California, Santa Cruz. Prior to moving to the University of California in 1969, he was on the faculty of the New York State School of Industrial and Labor Relations at Cornell University where he began conducting research on agricultural labor in New York during the mid-1960's. He is currently researching the structural forces shaping the discipline of rural sociology and, with a team of co-workers, has been conducting a series of studies focused on the sociology of commodity production and the development of a comparative analysis of agricultural production system.

527

528

CHARLES C. GEISLER is Assistant Professor of Rural Sociology at Cornell University, having recently completed his Ph.D. in sociology at the University of Wisconsin-Madison. His current work centers on the political economics of community control over land use and on the political sociology of regional planning. Geisler's articles have appeared in journals such as Rural Sociology and the Western Sociological Review.

KEVIN F. GOSS is Research Officer, Regional Services Division, Western Australia Department of Agriculture in Perth. He recently received a Ph.D. in rural sociology from Pennsylvania State University. Goss' major research interests include agricultural and rural community change processes and comparative rural sociology. He is co-author of Corporate Farming in the United States: A Guide to Current Literature, 1967-77 (AE & RS Report No. 136, Pennsylvania Agricultural Experiment Station, 1978) and "Toward a Small Farm Policy for the United States" (in Rural Research in USDA, Hearing before the Subcommittee on Agricultural Research and General Legislation, Committee on Agriculture, Nutrition and Forestry, U.S. Senate, May 4-5, 1978

PHILIP LOWE lectures in countryside planning at University College, London. He is currently engaged in research into the role of environmental groups in British politics and the history of ecology in Britain and the U.S.

SUSAN A. MANN is a doctoral candidate in the Department of Sociology, University of Toronto, having previously received her M.A. from American University, Washington, D.C. She is co-author of the article, "Obstacles to the Development of a Capitalist Agriculture" which appeared in 1978 in the Journal of Peasant Studies. Mann has also written several articles on women and domestic labor under capitalism.

ANN R. MARKUSEN is Assistant Professor of City and Regional Planning at the University of California, Berkeley. She previously taught economics at the University of Colorado and served as a Brookings Public Policy Fellow. Her research covers regional political economy, theories of the state, urban public policy, and feminist theory. She is currently working on a book entitled Regional Political Economy.

OSCAR B. MARTINSON is Assistant Professor of Sociology at Luther College, Decorah, Iowa. He holds a Ph.D. in Sociology and an M.A. in Public Policy and Administration from the University of Wisconsin-Madison. Martinson's major research interests focus on extra-market sources of economic control and on public and private regulatory structures and processes affecting agriculture and natural resources.

ROBERT MOORE is Professor of Sociology at the University of Aberdeen. His work has primarily focused on race relations, the sociology of religion, and labor migration. He is the author of four books, including Race, Community and Conflict (1967) and Pitmen, Preachers and Politics (1974).

GIOVANNI MOTTURA is with the Institute of Economics, University of Modena, Italy.

HOWARD NEWBY is Senior Lecturer in the Department of Sociology, University of Essex, England. His research interests center around agricultural labor, landownership, and community politics in the advanced societies. He is the author of several books, including Community Studies (with Colin Bell), The Deferential Worker, and Property, Paternalism, and Power (with Colin Bell, David Rose, and Peter Saunders). He is also editor of International Perspectives on Rural Sociology (Wiley, 1978).

ENRICO PUGLIESE is a faculty member at the University of Naples, Italy. During the 1979-80 academic year he will be a Visiting Professor of Sociology at the University of California, Santa Cruz.

RICHARD D. RODEFELD is Assistant Professor of Rural Sociology at Pennsylvania State University. His major research interests include the trends in and causes and consequences of structural change in U.S. agriculture. His most recent publications include Change in Rural America: Causes, Consequences and Alternatives (senior editor; published by the C.V. Mosby Co.) and Changing Character and Structure of American Agriculture: An Overview (U.S. General Accounting Office, 1978).

PETER R. SINCLAIR is Associate Professor of Sociology at the University of Guelph. His publications have largely focused on Canadian agricultural movements, social change in a suburban village, political alienation in Canada, and East European agriculture. Sinclair's current research projects concern agrarian social structure and comparative political systems.

MICHAEL WORBOYS is a lecturer in history at Sheffield City Polytechnic. He is currently engaged in research into the history of British colonial science and the social history of biology.